LOGIC and RHETORIC

LOGIC and RHETORIC

James William Johnson

ASSOCIATE PROFESSOR OF ENGLISH
UNIVERSITY OF ROCHESTER

THE MACMILLAN COMPANY — NEW YORK
A DIVISION OF THE CROWELL-COLLIER PUBLISHING COMPANY

© JAMES W. JOHNSON 1962

First Printing

Library of Congress catalog card number: 62–10773

The Macmillan Company, New York
Brett-Macmillan Ltd., Galt, Ontario

Printed in the United States of America

DESIGNED BY HERMANN STROHBACH

FOR K.R.H.

It would be misleading for me to tell you that LOGIC AND RHET-ORIC is a completely new approach to the teaching of freshman English, and I certainly would not be rash enough to suggest that it solves all the problems that you and I encounter as we grapple in the classroom with students, the language, and ideas all at once. Yet I do offer it to you as one answer—and a workable one—to the recurrent question: "What should we teach the freshmen?" In spite of the endless discussion that follows the asking of that question, all of us *know* what we should teach our students: to think clearly, to write as effectively and accurately as they can, and to learn to deal with the ideas recorded in written language. LOGIC AND RHETORIC has been written for a course that aims to show freshmen how language is the agent of thought and how patterns of writing correspond to patterns of thinking. The readings have been chosen for their subject matter, their logical structure, and their qualities as prose. The result is a book that is not purely and simply a logic text, a rhetoric, or a reader, but a fusion of all three. In themselves the elements of this textbook do not differ radically from those in several other texts. But LOGIC AND RHETORIC is first and foremost a synthesis that tries to show the student the direct relationship between what he thinks, how he thinks it, and how he expresses it. From its first page to its last, this text emphasizes the fact that language *is* thought, and it shows the arbitrary forms of thinking basic to the student's future education.

Because of its synthetic premise, this book fell naturally into several expository chapters, each correlating the basic assumptions of logic with a basic type of rhetoric, and each illustrated by a variety of essays. The order of the chapters—with problems of the kinds of writing and thinking treated earlier than problems more purely those of language—is, of course, only one possible arrangement. If you wish to take up later chapters before earlier ones, the text readily permits this, though in logical development the book as a whole follows a consistent plan and can be studied in physical order with profit. The exercises at the close of every chapter were written to stimulate original thinking and writing by the student; I hope you will find that the questions pique the slow student as well as the quick one. Such mechanical matters as punctuation and the research paper are not treated in this book. We are fortunate these days to have a variety of single works dealing with such matters, and it is possible to use this book with whatever handbook, controlled research pamphlet, or selection of additional readings you choose. As a final word to those who may disagree with some of my stated assumptions, I might say that I offer this text in all diffidence, realizing full well that it is not the sole or final answer to That Question. It *is* a partial answer, however, and I hope that you too will find it a practicable one.

Rochester, N.Y.   J. W. J.
December, 1961

TABLE OF CONTENTS

PART II

SECTION I THOUGHT AND LANGUAGE

SECTION II EDUCATION

SECTION III PEOPLE, SINGLY AND COLLECTIVELY

SECTION IV THE ARTS, FINE AND OTHERWISE

SECTION V SCIENCE: SOCIAL AND NATURAL

SECTION VI RELIGION AND PHILOSOPHY

PART I

PART I

Have you ever stopped to consider the amazing act you are performing this instant? You are reading. You have deliberately placed this page, with its patterns of symbolic characters, before your face, and your eyes are moving in spasmodic jerks from left to right and in smooth sweeps from right to left. The movement of your eyes and the occasional turning of the pages are the only external actions which the observer can see of the vastly complicated process you are presently carrying on.

What happens when we read? The science of optics has told us of the way light rays are refracted from the surface of the page and focused by the pupil of the eye. The neurologist can trace in some detail the transmission of impulses from the retina of the eye through ganglia of nerves to the brain. Biochemistry, physiology, and psychology are fields which tangentially describe the way the brain functions to react to these impulses. But no one knows precisely what the final action—*understanding* what the words on the page *mean*—is, or how it takes place. The "click of comprehension" remains an unexplained mystery.

To wonder about the nature of understanding or to speculate about the causes of comprehension is to enter the province of psychology, and no textbook on English composition undertakes such a step without peril. Yet the act of reading written words, like the act of uttering words to be heard or writing words to be read, *is* the concern of any book that claims to deal with the uses of language to express thought. We must, then, at least acknowledge the existence of important, unsolved psychological questions that affect our suppositions about the uses of language. And if by doing this we only admit the vast extent of our ignorance of the how's and why's of the way thought and language are interrelated, we can console ourselves that the wisest man of ancient Greece was wisest only in that he claimed to recognize the extent of his ignorance.

What exactly is a thought? No one can say for certain. Not even men who have spent their lives in examining the workings of the mind are positive as to whether a thought is a physical sensation, a mental picture, an emotional impulse, or something else. Experts disagree about whether we think in pictures more than we think in words; and though the ability to convey thoughts through patterns of sound called language is an obvious

3

human talent, the causes of this talent are scientifically unknown. Why do human beings possess the "habit of words"? Is the ability to produce and use language the consequence of the shape of the human brain, or something else? Why do languages differ so widely—not only in vocabulary but in principles of structure? What causes the same language to alter through centuries of usage, the way English has changed from Anglo-Saxon into modern English? In the light of constant shifts in language, is it possible to identify any one usage as the "right" or "proper" one and other usages as "improper"?

These and other questions about language have plagued men for centuries. Man long ago felt that the commonplace phenomenon of language was somehow miraculous and tried to understand it. The account of the Tower of Babel in the Old Testament book of Genesis is one early effort to account for differences in language. Plato's theory of divine inspiration is another ancient attempt to explain man's way with words. And since the establishment of language academies in Europe in the seventeenth century—one of which, the *Academie Française,* still exists—systematic efforts have been made to understand and "regulate" the "human habit" of words. From the compiling of the first dictionaries in the eighteenth century down to the development of the fields of linguistics and semantics in the twentieth, men have tried to expand and formulate their knowledge of how and why language functions as the chief means of communication between human beings.

In the section entitled "Thought and Language" at the end of this book you will find essays by philosophers, linguists, semanticists, and grammarians, explaining their fields and setting forth their theories about the way we think and express thought through language. In some ways, John Dewey's essay on thinking, Susanne Langer's explanation of the symbolic nature of language, and Stuart Chase's discussion of how language shapes thought are all conjecture or "educated guessing." Even so, these hypotheses are sufficiently convincing to permit us to assert that there is a positive correspondence between the way a man thinks and the way he uses words, spoken or written. We may further assert that the greater a man's simultaneous control of his faculties of thinking and expression through words, the more perfectly developed is his intelligence.

You may think this is an exaggerated estimate of language as the test of intelligence, but you need only to think about so-called I.Q. tests to see that intelligence is measured largely through one's vocabulary, ability to make verbal analogies, and adeptness with words generally. Whatever the limitations of testing intelligence by a person's use of language, no other method quite as satisfactory has been devised. While the fundamental relationship between thinking and verbally expressing ideas may not be fully understood, in practical terms one is used to measure the other.

Similarly, though nobody can explain precisely why language is produced by the human brain or what causes language variations, certain psychologists have learned that patterns of thought reflected in the use of language may be statistically computed or counted. Combinations of words into a structured language admit only so many variations. The practical evidence of this relationship between thinking and linguistic expression are the new translating machines, built on the principle of statistical probability and the knowledge that human thought can be conveyed by a limited number of word combinations in a given language.

Though most of our knowledge about the kinship of language to thought is still supposition, it is impressive enough for us to realize how elemental a command of language is to "intelligence" or the ability to formulate and convey ideas. One psychologist has even gone so far as to declare that syntax (principles of word combinations) is one of the most important products of human cerebral action and that the "series of hierarchies of organization" in language—i.e., words, sentences, paragraphs, the total discourse—may finally give insight into the "physiology of logic." In simple terms, language is possibly the key to the secrets of man's distinctive physical and mental nature.

Though the psychological basis of man's use of language is still to be discovered, from the earliest period of written language men have set down their discoveries about human systems of thought and about the most effective uses of language. The discipline of *logic* is that branch of philosophy dealing with *the principles of thinking and testing thought. Rhetoric* is *the craft of language.* Traditionally, logic and rhetoric have been taught separately, often as though they were distinct and slightly contradictory fields. At times, "rhetoric" has been thought of as the techniques of eloquence that appeal to the emotions rather than to reason. As a result, some of us think of rhetoric as a "gift of gab" divorced from any orderly or systematic thinking; and others shudder at the idea of "cold," "strait-laced" logic with its formidable "rules" of thinking so remote from everyday behavior.

Of course logic cannot really be separated from rhetoric, since one is related to *what* you say and the other is related to the *way* you express it. Though it is possible in examining a piece of prose to emphasize form or content, one more than the other, form and content cannot truly be separated except as an academic exercise. Straight thinking demands clear expression, and verbal expression cannot be clear unless it embodies straight thinking. Neither is more important than the other, for neither can be effective without the other. Thomas Gray's famous phrase, "some mute, inglorious Milton," is a contradiction in terms, and so is the common excuse for vagueness, "I know what I mean, but I can't put it into words." Can a "glorious" thought be glorious if it stays unexpressed? (Check the meanings of "glory" and "glorious" in your dictionary.) And if the expression of an idea is inadequate in form, can the idea be considered to have adequate formulation or meaning?

Since, in fact, most communicated ideas are the fusion of a thought, developed by some mental process, with a combination of words following certain principles of language, it seems sensible to study ways of thinking and ways of writing as co-ordinate processes. Do we know what we think before we express it in words; or must we wait to hear ourselves speak before we know what we think? The question is moot and relatively unimportant. The point is that the logical system of thinking and the rhetorical system of using words correspond.

The chapters that lie ahead of you in this book postulate the reality and importance of the relationships between how we think, what we think, and how we convey thought through words. Each chapter explains some system of thinking that human beings have developed as a way to deal with the stubborn, often chaotic facts of existence, it points out the values and limitations of that system, and it shows how one or more types of rhetoric reflect that pattern of thought. Following each chapter, a group of essays illustrates the system of thinking and the patterns of writing that embody it. By seeing how individual writers develop and communicate ideas, you will learn new ways of thinking and new thoughts to think as well as how better to put thoughts into words.

If the foregoing emphasis on logic strikes you as stern and humorless in tone, or if you view with private alarm the prospect of producing one eloquently declamatory statement after another once you have finished studying this text, then relax. No one expects you to become a Thomas Aquinas and Demosthenes rolled into one during your freshman year in college. The human effort to be logical is subject to absurdities, and the desire to be eloquent often backfires, as Robert Benchley, S. J. Perelman, and other essayists will show you. The urge to become better thinkers and writers does not compel us to set our jaws in self-consciously heroic, grim lines. If clear thinking and writing are necessary to the understanding of the atomic bomb, demagoguery, and segregation, they are no less vital to discussions of jazz, dating, and television. The point to remember is that *all* experience—trivial as well as profound—is best appreciated by the clear mind and best embodied in controlled, proficient expression.

Since this book will be a fairly constant companion to you during your freshman English course, two cautionary comments should be kept in mind. This is an introductory text, and it does not profess to be an exhaustive treatment of intricate philosophical disciplines. Furthermore, because it is an elementary text, it sometimes makes basic assumptions which are not elaborately justified in the text itself. The course between a dogmatic, authoritarian tone and complete wishy-washiness is sometimes difficult to steer when a basic working knowledge of vastly complicated fields is involved. This book tries to show you the arbitrary nature of much logical and rhetorical practice without being opinionative or implying that arbitrary practices are necessarily meaningless. It is hoped that the thoughtful student will see for himself that certain basic assumptions are always open to question, and that he will learn something of the rudimentary techniques of asking and answering these questions even as they occur to him.

These, then, are your present aims: to learn to think logically, to write clearly, to read and evaluate for your intellectual profit the thought and writing of people accomplished as thinkers and writers, to come in contact with a broad sample of the areas of knowledge that are the material of your future education. This book and this course may not enable you to fulfill all these aims at once and completely, but they can indicate the direction toward eventual fulfillment and help you to make a start.

I. Questions for Review

Read the essays on "Thought and Language" on pp. 277 ff, and then answer these review questions:

1. What is a thought? How do the linguist, the philosopher, and the semanticist describe the thought process?
2. According to psychologists and linguists, do we think in pictures, words, or both? How do thoughts made of images and thoughts made of words differ in their purpose and application?
3. Can such animals as dogs and apes "think?" How do their thoughts differ from those of human beings? Can birds and animals express their thoughts in "language?"

4. What are the essential differences between human "language" and that of insects, birds, and animals?
5. If human language is the product of the human brain and its structure, why then do different groups of human beings speak different languages? What causes these differences in speech?
6. How do such speech "defects" as stammering and stuttering indicate the relationship between thought and language?
7. Does the logical pattern (grammar) of language correspond to some inherent biological or mental pattern? If so, why do languages change as they are used by successive generations?
8. What forces cause a language, such as English, to effect changes in its structure and vocabulary through the centuries?
9. Is it possible for a man to have a thought which the vocabulary of his own language cannot effectively express? Explain. As he learns "new" or different languages, does a man actually have to learn new ways of thinking?
10. We often say, "I know what I mean, but I can't put it into words." Is this state of affairs possible? Can we really have thoughts which cannot be verbalized?
11. Is it possible to express an idea without really thinking or consciously formulating that idea?

II. Exercises
1. Look up the following groups of words in several dictionaries and compare their meanings. Differentiate the shades of meaning between the words in each group:
   A. Thought, idea, concept
   B. Word, vocabulary, diction
   C. Grammar, syntax, rhetoric
   D. Articulation, enunciation, speech
2. Since you yourself are constantly engaged in thinking, make your mind the object of an examination of how thinking operates. Let your thoughts move at will for a minute or two, and then deliberately reconstruct your pattern of ideas, jotting down each idea as it occurs. With the memo before you, answer these questions:
   A. How are these ideas related to each other—through a time sequence, by emotional associations, by visual similarities, by some logical relationship; or are they connected at all?
   B. Do some of your ideas bear resemblance to others in some way; i.e., are they expressive of hope, fear, doubt, or anxiety; are they actions; or do they deal with the same period of time?
   C. Group together the separate ideas which appear somehow to be related to each other. What would you say was the reason for

your having these related ideas intermittently, that is, why do ideas of this kind recur in your mind? Are you trying to solve some problem? To clarify your opinion? To give an outlet to your emotion? To make plans?

D. Now set yourself some specific subject to think about for a few minutes: the War of the Roses, automobiles, Beethoven's music, your wardrobe, the United States Supreme Court. Jot down the sequence of your thoughts. Is there any difference between the way you thought when you were freely associating ideas and when you were attempting to think about one subject alone?

E. "Selective" or "concentrated" thinking on a specific subject is required of you when writing term papers, preparing reports, or taking examinations. From what you have just seen of your thought processes, is it possible to develop one's ability to think selectively whenever one wishes? Is it desirable to develop this way of thinking? Explain.

3. To see how the words in a language alter, look up the old English and Middle English versions of these words: silly, bird, health, lady, nose, lark. Which words changed form or meaning because of a condensation of two words into one? Which changed because of altered pronunciation? Which changed because of new dimensions of meaning attached to the idea represented in the word?

4. Words representing family relationships often are strikingly alike in languages which otherwise vary. In an unabridged dictionary or comprehensive lexicon, look up the words in several languages for mother, father, sister, and brother. Also, find the words for one, two, and three. What explanation can you think of to account for the similarity of words expressing blood relationships in different and sometimes unrelated languages?

5. In your dictionary, look up the word for each in as many languages as possible, tracing the development of the word from Greek to Latin to French to English, or German to Anglo-Saxon to Middle English to Modern: star, goose, wine, winter, fire. How would you account for the change in each word from language to language?

III. Questions for Thought, Discussion, and Writing

1. Can a language limited in vocabulary or grammar, such as Bantu or Fijian, prevent a culture from developing?

2. If it is true that the Hopi language is better suited to understanding theoretical physics than English is, then why has theoretical physics been developed by speakers of English rather than speakers of Hopi?

3. Is the person who thinks logically someone who automatically can then write clearly and logically? Why or why not?

4. Is a language most directly shaped by the masses who speak it, the educated people who write it, or teachers of grammar and makers of dictionaries?

5. Is it possible to designate specific uses of a language as "proper" or "correct" and other uses as improper or incorrect? Is it all right to maintain that since language is used to communicate, any utterance which communicates a meaning successfully, whether spoken or written, is "correct" even if it is ungrammatical and mispronounced or misspelled?

6. Write a theme on one of these topics as directed by your instructor:
   A. What I Think about Capital Punishment (or Buttons, or Education for a Profession, or Cats, or Adolf Hitler), and Why I Think It
   B. How to Study
   C. What to Do about a Bad Memory
   D. What Is Day-Dreaming?
   E. My Worst Fear
   F. An Intellectual Autobiography (Why I Think as I Do)

ORDER AND OUTLINING

"Order and simplification are the first steps toward the mastery of a subject—the actual enemy is the unknown."
THOMAS MANN, THE MAGIC MOUNTAIN

One of the most characteristic traits of human beings is their ability to conceive systems of arrangement and to impose these systems on different objects. Though you and I as individuals may have to struggle to maintain such superficial manifestations of order as tidy rooms and neatly combed hair, nevertheless, as human beings with rational intellects we constantly conceive mental relationships and *perceive* these relationships in stars or atoms, or we *arrange* things—from silverware to steel girders—in orderly patterns. It is scarcely inaccurate to say that all order is man-made, since whatever the absolute nature of non-human objects, all we as human beings can know about them is determined by our sensual and intellectual perceptions.

Order may be simply defined as *systematically established relationships.* Whether the relationship is between such intangibles as ideas or such concrete objects as bricks, the nature of that relationship, its *order,* is determined by the patterns of human thought. For this reason, the way we use the established relationships of language is very significant indication of the ability of the individual to think in an orderly way. The very principles by which words are combined to express thoughts arise from the basic ability of the mind to develop and use orderly systems.

Think for a second of how useless words alone are as a means of conveying a thought. "Day," "was," "in," "a," "built," "Rome," "not": listed in this particular sequence, the words mean very little, if anything. In fact, the only words able to raise some response in your mind are

11

probably "day" and "Rome," but what about them? "Rome was not built in a day." Following this established system of word usage, seven short words convey a thought which combines a geographical location, an action, and a period of time in such a way as to have reference and significance. The *word order* has produced a coherent unit, the sentence. In English, sentences commonly contain a reference to some doer (a person, place, or thing) and an action and sometimes a recipient of the action (another person, place, or thing). Thus, the *order* of the English sentence usually is the subject (a noun or pronoun), the verb, and the object (noun or pronoun).

Of course, different languages use different systems of word order. If you have studied German, you know that German verbs come after everything else in the sentence, a practice which Mark Twain has humorously attacked as "unreasonable" and "illogical." There is nothing illogical or disorderly about German word order to the Germans, who find English, with its insistence on a different system, a trifle absurd. Each language develops its own structure, or grammatical and syntactical orders, out of a variety of influences, as J. N. Hook and E. G. Mathews show; and though this order may be arbitrary or accidental, so long as it serves its users as a way to communicate ideas accurately and effectively, it is a valid system.

As the embodiment of human thought, rhetoric—spoken or written— employs virtually every type of order developed by man. One type of order, *alphabetical,* is peculiar to written language, having been developed largely by historical accident when men first translated spoken sounds into written characters representing those sounds. Just as the symbols themselves were probably spontaneous choices, so the sequence of the symbols in alphabetical order was accidental or arbitrary. The Latin alphabet used by English may seem so inevitable to you that you think of it as *the* alphabet with an inherent order, but it really has none. "G", for example, might come *before* "D", as it does in the Greek or Russian alphabets. Similarly, *numerical order,* the sequence of Arabic symbols to represent quantities, is purely arbitrary. Alphabetical and numerical order are often used as the skeleton of discourse in prose, and, as we shall see, they are indispensable to formal outlining.

Certain types of order, such as *spatial,* represent systems of arrangement perhaps more dependent upon one human sense than another. *Spatial order* is the arrangement of objects in space; it appeals primarily to the sense of vision. Maps are an obvious instance of the way a pattern of geographic relationships can be represented to the eye, and so are picture captions that identify objects "from right to left." Obviously, the act of reading depends on the adaptation of the eye to spatial arrangement; written rhetoric possesses a strong sense of spatial order.

Look at this page as a concrete object and you will see how important spatial order is to written prose. Before the printing press was invented, men wrote on papyrus, linen, or stone, and they filled every inch of the precious material with words. To decipher the clutter of a Rosetta Stone or Dead Sea scroll is, consequently, a feat of scholarship today. Typesetting changed the form of written prose in vital ways. It produced our conception of the paragraph as a group of sentences related to a central topic. It encouraged the development of punctuation, which had been a hit or miss device in earlier days. Such mechanical devices as periods (which indicate the conclusion of a complete unit of thought); commas (which show subdivisions of related and incomplete thoughts); semi-colons (which separate two related but independent thoughts); and colons (which introduce information related to a previous complete thought)—all these are arbitrary signs which help make written language more readily comprehensible. When you learn to make margins on a page and organize your sentences into paragraphs, you are mastering the elements of spatial order in rhetoric.

Spatial order is important in the *organization* of ideas as well as in their visible written *form*. The opening chapter of Genesis on page 34 is a case in point. You can see immediately upon looking at the chapter how important physical spacing is; but it takes some reflecting to see that the prose itself is concerned with the spatial order of the universe and follows a cosmic descriptive order from heaven to earth to seas to land and so on. The writer is literally describing the spatial arrangement of the universe, just as Sir James Jeans describes the arrangement of a part of the cosmos in his essay on "The Distances of Stars." These pieces of rhetoric typify the way writing and the sense of spatial order may be fused.

Still another basic type of order closely related to the senses is the *tonal*. Just as in music certain sequences or progressions of sounds produce an effect on the ear, so in spoken language the pitch, inflection, pace, and resonance of the voice affect the hearer's ear in a specific way to produce a reaction. And although written prose cannot have the same auditory effect as spoken prose, still it retains some of the rhythms it would have when spoken. Such devices as the "rhetorical question," which this and every textbook liberally uses, are examples of the way a device of punctuation (?) can make us "hear" the sentence on the upward inflection associated with interrogation. The sentence patterns called loose, periodic, balanced, and mixed, discussed in detail in the final chapter, are further instances of the reproduction of tonal patterns in written rhetoric. The word *tone* itself is borrowed from the fields of music and oratory to apply to the way written words may reflect a writer's attitude toward what he is saying, just as the inflections of his voice would convey that attitude if he were speaking instead.

The other types of order associated with the physical senses—i.e., gustatory order (sequence of taste), olfactory order (sequence of smell), and tactile order (sequence of sensation)—tend to appear in the kinds of rhetoric that deal with processes. The process is treated fully in the next chapter as an example of *chronological* order, which together with *logical* order encompasses the other chief systems of thinking and forms of rhetoric. Chronological and logical order are the subject matter that will occupy our attention for most of the following chapters.

For the time being, however, our new awareness of the importance of alphabetical, numerical, and spatial order can serve to introduce the matter of the *outline* as one of the basic ways of combining systematic thinking with well-planned writing. Though making outlines is admittedly an academic exercise, it is a good way not only to develop your awareness of the way your mind works but to improve the organization of your formally spoken or written ideas and to whet your critical appreciation for the writing of others.

Outlines are the visible link between organized thoughts on some subject and the piece of prose that expresses them. An *outline* is *a combination of alphabetical and numerical arrangement to emphasize thematically related ideas in a rhetorical composition.* As such, it shows quickly the central ideas of a piece of written prose, indicates their relationship to each other and to lesser, supporting ideas, and clarifies the line of development of the composition from start to finish. An outline may be made under two sets of circumstances: *before* the essay is written, in which case it becomes a working blueprint, or *after* the essay is written, when it acts as a means of testing in retrospect the effectiveness of structure and development of the essay.

Your own talents and limitations as a writer must determine whether you use the outline as a preliminary sketch for a future composition or as a skeletal summary of a completed essay. You—or your teacher—may prefer that the outline precede the writing of the composition; in this case you will use it to make a tentative expression of ideas and to establish the relative equality of these ideas through the use of parallelism. *Parallelism is use of the same grammatical structure to express ideas which are related and have a similar purpose.* Outlining before you write helps you to employ parallel groups of words for ideas equal in importance and thereby to understand ways of emphasizing (or de-emphasizing) some ideas and not others. It will also help you to write more precise and rhetorically balanced sentences and paragraphs. Finally, it will establish a line to follow in developing your ideas from beginning to end.

"Collecting your thoughts" on a given subject is the first step in outlining before you write. From the jumble of ideas in your head, you must sort out those related to the subject you want to treat. The exercise you saw at the end of the Introduction, which asked you to put down your thoughts and then identify a common characteristic, was a crude form of the selective thinking necessary for planning verbal discourse. Whether you are told to write a theme on butterflies, collective bargaining, or What You Did Last Summer, you must go through the same process of sifting out the ideas related to your basic topic. Jot these down so you will be working with tangible words on a page and not half-formed, vague ideas. Suppose, for instance, that your instructor (obviously an eccentric!) has told you to write a 600-word theme on Nursery Rhymes. From some source or other—your previous knowledge or diligent reading—you have amassed an impressive collection of information about nursery rhymes: some of them were really political and social commentaries; "Sing a Song of Sixpence" may be about Henry VIII; some rhymes were written by famous men; and so forth. You can outline your ideas in three different forms: the Topic or Paragraph Outline, the Phrase Outline, and the Sentence Outline. In each type, you will use a combination of Roman and Arabic numbers and Latin letters to indicate the relationship and order of your various ideas.

The Paragraph Outline is the most simple form; it consists of listing in order the topic sentences of each proposed paragraph in your essay. Here is a specimen:

Title "Nursery Rhymes as History"

Central idea: British history can be traced in some detail by examining the nursery rhymes of successive periods and explaining their political allusions.

I. Many nursery rhymes had a political origin and a political significance.

II. The Tudors were dealt with in a number of rhymes.

III. Fewer rhymes were directed at the Stuarts.

IV. Even the Hanovers found themselves the subjects of jingles.

  V. English history between 1550 and 1750 is indicated roughly by the jingles which are now songs for children.

    This paragraph outline shows in a very simple way the principle of order that the essay will follow. The Roman numerals stand for paragraphs; each topic sentence shows that the paragraph will discuss the rhymes about members of one of three royal families: the Tudors, Stuarts, and Hanovers; and the first and last paragraphs (I, V) serve as general introduction and summary. The order in which the royal families are taken up is historical or chronological. Even so simple an outline shows a direction of development and a plan of arrangement.

    The limits of the paragraph outline are that it does not show much in the way of proportion between its parts; it does not indicate transitions between groups of ideas; and it is not much help as a reminder of specific facts. Far more detailed is the Phrase Outline, which looks something like this.

Title "Nursery Rhymes as History"

    Central Idea: British history can be traced in some detail by examining the nursery rhymes of successive periods and explaining their political allusions.

    I. Opening comments

        A. Origin of jingles
        B. Purposes
        C. How written

   II. The Tudors

        A. Rhymes about Tudor Succession
           1. "War of the Roses"
           2. Others
        B. Rhymes about Henry VIII
           1. "Sing a Song of Sixpence"
           2. "Wives' Song"
           3. Others
        C. Rhymes about Edward and Mary

D. Elizabeth
  1. Her personal life
  2. Her political activities
     a. "Mary, Mary, Quite Contrary"
     b. "Little Bo-Peep"
     c. "The Rose Is Red, The Grass Is Green"

III. The Stuarts

  A. James I and Charles I
  B. Charles II and his court
     1. "Curleylocks, Curleylocks"
     2. Lord Rochester's "Epitaph"
  C. James II, William and Mary, Anne
     1. "Rock-a-bye, Baby"
     2. "Wee Willie Winkie"
     3. Others

IV. The Hanovers

  A. George I—"Georgy Porgy"
  B. George II and Caroline—"The Old Woman Who Lived in the Shoe"
  C. George III and George IV—"The Duke of York"

  V. Decline of the political jingle and conclusions

The basic arrangement of this phrase outline is the same as that of the paragraph outline: the Roman numerals indicate divisions set up on the basis of royal families, the sequence is chronological, and so on. But the phrase outline uses Latin capitals (A, B, C) for members of each of the families, and the Arabic numerals (1, 2, 3) indicate units of information (aspects of the ruler's life, in the case of Elizabeth, or specific rhymes, in the case of the Stuarts) about these members. This phrase outline is a better reminder of individual facts than the paragraph outline; moreover, it is a better way of planning the relative length of each section of your proposed essay. Obviously, your paper will contain more material on the Tudors than on the Hanovers, and thus you can write with a clearer understanding of which portions of your essay will assume the greatest importance through their length and use of details.

In some instances, you may be required to—or you may voluntarily— make out a Sentence Outline for a projected theme. This kind of outline is the most detailed of all; in making it, you will put down in their

entirety ideas you want to include in the finished essay, and you can
experiment with the wording or phrasing of your individual ideas as well
as their combination into paragraphs. A Sentence Outline might well
begin as follows:

Title "Victims of the Jingle"

Central Idea: The makers of certain Nursery Rhymes were irreverent critics
of the world who laughed at institutions, practices, and individuals for their
faults, pretensions, and affectations.

I. Many of the jingles which we now call "Nursery Rhymes" were actually
bits of topical verse or lampoons.

   A. Many scholars have written conjectures about the sources of such
   jingles.

      1. Robert Graves, Vera Sackville West, and E. K. Chambers have
      speculated about the rhymes.

      2. Iona and Peter Opie have made the most complete collection of
      the theories about the origins of nursery jingles in *The Oxford
      Dictionary of Nursery Rhymes*.

   B. A number of theories have been advanced about whether the rhymes
   had political significance or not.

      1. One theory discards all belief in a topical relevance in the verse
      of the fifteenth and sixteenth centuries.

      2. The Opies tend to be sceptical about political implications in the
      jingles but admit they cannot disprove contrary theories.

      3. Fanciful or not, the rhymes lend themselves to a political inter-
      pretation with surprising accuracy.

   C. There is a positive recorded evidence of political intention in the
   poems of a few well known writers.

      1. Lord Rochester's "Epitaph" on Charles II was written under amus-
      ing circumstances.

      2. John Dryden admittedly wrote verses to scorn his political enemies.

      3. Jonathan Swift and Alexander Pope used jingles for a pointed end.

II. One of the largest bodies of Nursery Rhymes attacks the rulers of England and the members of their Courts.

    A. The personal foibles of the King were often satirized.

        1. Charles II was laughed at for his curls and mistresses.

        2. George I was mocked for his amorous "adventures."

    B. Royal policy was frequently criticized.

        1. Henry VIII's suppression of the monasteries may have been the subject of "Sing a Song of Sixpence."

        2. Elizabeth I was criticized for her behavior toward Mary, Queen of the Scots, in "Mary, Mary, Quite Contrary."

    C. The actions of the King's ministers were sometimes ridiculed.

        1. Cardinal Wolsey was unpopular with several rhyme-makers.

        2. John Gay contributed some verses which were chanted in scorn of Sir Robert Walpole.

III. The Church was mocked in successive periods by the jinglers.

    A.

    B.

IV. Political parties and institutions were the subjects of a few verses, especially between 1700 and 1750.

    A.

    B.

V. The popularity of the jingle was due to several historical factors which shaped it into an effective critical instrument.

Although the outline is not completed after Section II, it would be easy to fill out Sections III–V with relevant details in the same way as the first two were expanded. A sentence outline, if painstakingly detailed and complete, may be used as the first draft of your essay; if you think carefully before you begin such an outline, you may in time be able to make on your first try a sentence outline which *is* a completed, well proportioned, and clearly written piece of prose.

Of course, your first attempts at making prefatory outlines may not result in the artfully balanced parallelism of the examples above. Probably the most careful outline you ever make will not be as detailed or as contrived as these. But a working outline, made to serve as a guide for a future composition, can prevent the sort of obvious muddles of ideas and grammar that often occur when we do not think something out before we formally deliver it in a speech or as a piece of writing. The hapless and befuddled Assistant Treasurer of Benchley's mild spoof on page 25 might have fared better if he had taken more time and given more preliminary thought to preparing his report.

Instead of outlining before you write, you may find it more helpful to read your completed composition and then set up its implicit schematic plan in a written analysis, using the numerical and alphabetical devices of the formal outline. This sort of outlining permits to you see which ideas are incompletely presented or poorly emphasized. It also should show you which points you have not supported with adequate details or supporting information. You may even find that your ideas do not follow a proper or reasonable line of development. Discovering these flaws in your writing gives you the opportunity to correct and improve. Moreover, the practice of analysing one composition and seeing its faults is likely to help you avoid similar faults the next time you write.

Margaret Mead's brief explanation of the subject matter of her full-length book, *Male and Female,* is a rather specialized use of the outline made after the completion of the work. Mrs. Mead's sketch of the main sections of her study, her description of the way she developed her central themes, and the organization of the parts of the book into a coherent unit are a preface for the reader even as they are a summary of the work to be read. Most formal prefaces to full-length books are the last part of the book to be written; as such they serve to test the author's accomplishment of his original aims and to re-examine the effectiveness of the actual written work rather than the imagined or envisioned work. Your use of an outline made after the writing of your themes can accomplish the same purposes for you.

Whether you outline before or after you write, certain steps are essential before you start putting the words of your composition down on paper. Here they are, in a terse form: 1. Understand clearly what subject you are to treat. If you have been told to write an autobiography, be clear as to what kind of autobiography is meant: physical, social, or intellectual. Or if you are writing on "the fraternity system," discern the aspect of that system—its social principles, its parliamentary procedure, or its economic structure. 2. Survey your knowledge of your subject. If you have amassed all the general information your memory and experience can provide and this material is scanty, then do some research. (You will, of course, indicate in your finished paper any sources that you had to consult to gather information.) 3. Decide upon the end that you want your treatment of the material to attain. What is your basic purpose in writing on the subject: to present facts, to express an opinion, to amuse your reader, to argue for some action, or to arrange material for your own understanding? 4. Select a central concept or *theme* for your essay. This central idea will be the organizing principle of your paper; unless you know clearly what major points you wish to bring out, your writing will lack direction. 5. Decide which parts of your material are relevant to your aim and theme. No matter how tempting an isolated fact or bit of information, unless it is related to your main purpose in writing and illustrates your central theme, toss it out. Or put it in a footnote. Having taken all these steps, you are reasonably ready to write a preliminary outline or the essay itself.

Whether or not you put down on paper the arrangement of ideas and words that constitute an outline, in thinking systematically about a given subject you are improving your understanding of it and thus increasing its usefulness for you. The routine activities of life demand the sort of organization ("planning") that outlining helps us to develop. If you consider the countless professions that involve the imposition of order or the act of arrangement and when you realize the devices of order that crowd our daily lives—from buttons to stop signs—you can see that order is the aim of much human activity.

In literary form, man's desire for order may be manifested in making outlines that are discarded once they have served their purpose. It may take a written form that embodies our highest aspirations toward regulating human society, as in the Bill of Rights. Or it may become a timeless record of man's desire to understand eternal mysteries, as it does in the Book of Genesis. The essays that follow show a progression from the fumbling, laughable efforts at organization by a fallible man like one of us to a piece of rhetoric depicting a conception of order that touches the divine.

I. *Questions for Review*
1. What are some possible definitions for the term *order*? Which of these do you consider the best? Why?
2. Can order be said to exist only in the human mind, or are there kinds of order in nature apart from man's perceptions? Explain.

3. What kind of order depends on human vision? Human hearing?
4. Is alphabetical order entirely accidental, or is there some reasonable principle inherent in the order of A, B, C . . . X, Y, Z? Explain.
5. How is an outline vital to rhetorical order?
6. What general types of order are used in a rhetorical outline?
7. What is parallelism? Look up the meanings of parallel as they are used by a geographer, electrician, musician, and printer.
8. What are the three basic kinds of outline? Enumerate the advantages and disadvantages of each type.
9. What steps should one go through to plan an essay before he makes an outline?
10. In the outlines given in this chapter, there are at least two parts for each division and sub-division (i.e., A, B, or I, II, or 1, 2). To observe the principle of parallelism in the outline, is it necessary always to have at least two divisions for each unit of ideas?

II. *Exercises*
1. Choose one of the essays at the end of the book, read it carefully, and make a sentence or phrase outline of it.
2. How would you go about outlining your knowledge of one or more of the following topics; what would be your purpose in writing an essay on each; what central idea would you develop; and how many major divisions would your outline have?
   A. Pre-historic Reptiles
   B. Drag Racing
   C. Guided Missiles
   D. Choosing a College
   E. Racial Discrimination
   F. Dating or Going Steady
   G. Classical Ballet
   H. Greek Architecture
   I. Renaissance Painting
   J. Fraternities
   K. Wombats
   L. Television Programs
3. Using the information given in the chapter plus any additional information you have or can locate, write an outline of a 600-word essay on nursery rhymes from a point of view other than those used in the previous outlines.
4. Word order in the sentence (syntax) can be varied within limits without changing the meaning of the sentence. This line from Thomas Gray's "Elegy Written in a Country Churchyard" can be written in a number of ways with the words in a different order: "The lowing

herd winds slowly o'er the lea." Which of the following convey a
different meaning from the original line, and which convey the same
meaning but with a different effect:
   A. The herd, lowing, winds o'er the lea slowly.
   B. O'er the lea slowly winds the lowing herd.
   C. Lowing o'er the lea slowly the herd winds.
   D. Slowly, lowing, the herd winds o'er the lea.
   E. O'er the lea winds the lowing herd, slowly.
5. Each of these sentences belongs in the same paragraph. In what order
   would you place them. Why? Can the order of the sentences be
   shifted without changing the pattern of logical development?
   A. At first it was far away and no one could tell what the noise was.
   B. The theatrical one of the two trackers stood up.
   C. We were sitting in the blind that Wanderobo hunters had built of
      twigs and branches at the edge of the salt-lick when we heard the
      motor-lorry coming.
   D. Then it moved slowly nearer, unmistakable now, louder and
      louder until, agonizing in a clank of loud irregular explosions, it
      passed close behind us to go on up the road.
   E. "It is finished," he said.
   F. Then it was stopped and we hoped it had been nothing or perhaps
      only the wind.

—Ernest Hemingway, *Green Hills of Africa*

III. *Questions for Thought, Discussion, and Writing*
   1. In the quotation from *The Magic Mountain* given at the head of
      Chapter I, Thomas Mann says that order and simplification are the
      first steps in mastering a subject. Are they the only way to master a sub-
      ject? Are they the best way?
   2. "The actual enemy is the unknown." Is this the same as "Ignorance
      is an enemy?" There is an old saw, "What you don't know won't
      hurt you." Discuss the validity of Mann's statement and the maxim in
      the light of your own thinking and experience.
   3. In a culture like that of the ancient Hebrews or the modern Hindus,
      is the unknown considered an enemy? Is the view that ignorance is
      harmful limited to Western European culture?
   4. Is there any purpose in knowing that some nursery rhymes had
      political significance? Is this knowledge "useful?" Explain.
   5. Most of our ideas about parallelism are based on the mathematical
      axioms about the nature of parallel lines. Is there such a thing as
      truly parallel lines? Are our notions of order based on parallelism
      false? Why?

6. Is the individual writer justified in ignoring conventional word order if he finds it difficult to follow established principles of syntax? Evaluate this sentence from Gertrude Stein's *Three Lives* in the light of your answer: " . . . because after all I do as simply as it can, as commonplacely as it can say, what everybody can and does do; I never know what they can do, I really do not know what they are, I do not think that anyone can think because if they do, then who is who? "

7. At the direction of your instructor, write a theme on one of the following topics:
   A. The Sentence Order of Lincoln's Gettysburg Address
   B. Varieties of Order in the Telephone Directory
   C. A Phrase Outline of the Book of Genesis, Chapter I
   D. Kinds of Tonal Order in Music
   E. The Order of Sensation: How a Disease Develops
   F. Planning a Menu or Gustatory Order
   G. A Paragraph, Phrase, or Sentence Outline of
      1. Howard Mumford Jones, "Undergraduates on Apronstrings"
      2. Fred Hoyle, "The Origin of the Earth and Planets"
      3. Walter Kaufmann, "The Faith of a Heretic"

Robert Benchley

THE TREASURER'S REPORT

THE REPORT IS DELIVERED BY AN ASSISTANT TREASURER WHO HAS BEEN *called in to pinch-hit for the regular Treasurer who is ill. He is not a very good public-speaker, this assistant, but after a few minutes of confusion is caught up by the spell of his own oratory and is hard to stop.*

I shall take but a very few moments of your time this evening, for I realize that you would much rather be listening to this interesting entertainment than to a dry financial statement . . . but I *am* reminded of a story—which you have probably all of you heard.

It seems that there were these two Irishmen walking down the street when they came to a—oh, I should have said in the first place that the parrot which was hanging out in *front* of the store—or rather belonging to one of these two fellows—the *first* Irishman, that is—was—well, *anyway,* this parrot——

(*After a slight cogitation, he realizes that, for all practical purposes, the story is as good as lost; so he abandons it entirely and, stepping forward, drops his facile, story-telling manner and assumes a quite spurious business-like air.*)

Now, in connection with reading this report, there are one or two points which Dr. Murnie wanted brought up in connection with it, and he has asked me to bring them up in connec—to bring them up.

In the first place, there is the question of the work which we are trying to do up there at our little place at Silver Lake, a work which we feel not only fills a very definite need in the community but also fills a very definite need —er—in the community. I don't think that many members of the Society realize just how big the work is that we are trying to do up there. For instance, I don't think that it is generally known that most of our boys are between the age of fourteen. We feel that, by taking the boy at this age, we can get closer to his real nature—for a boy *has* a very real nature, you may be sure—and bring him into closer touch not only with the school, the parents, and with each other, but also with the town in which they live, the country to whose flag they pay allegiance, and to the—ah—(*trailing off*) town in which they live.

Now the fourth point which Dr. Murnie wanted brought up was that in connection with the installation of the new furnace last Fall. There seems to have been considerable talk going around about this not having been done quite as economically as it might—have—been—done, when, as a matter of fact, the whole thing *was* done just as economically as possible—in fact, even *more* so. I have here a report of the Furnace Committee, showing just how the whole thing was handled from start to finish.

(*Reads from report, with considerable initial difficulty with the stiff covers.*)

Bids were submitted by the following firms of furnace contractors, with a clause stating that if we did not engage a firm to do the work for us we should pay them nothing for submitting the bids. This clause alone saved us a great deal of money.

The following firms, then, submitted bids:

Merkle, Wybigant Co., the Eureka Dust Bin and Shaker Co., The Elite Furnace Shop, and Harris, Birnbauer and Harris. The bid of Merkle, Wybigant being the lowest, Harris Birnbauer were selected to do the job.

(*Here a page is evidently missing from the report, and a hurried search is carried on through all the pages, without result.*)

Well, that pretty well clears up that end of the work.

Those of you who contributed so generously last year to the floating hospital have probably wondered what became of the money. I was speaking on this subject only last week at our up-town branch, and, after the meeting, a dear little old lady, dressed all in lavender, came up on the platform, and, laying her hand on my arm, said: "Mr. So-and-So (calling me by name) Mr. So-and-So, what the hell did you do with all the money we gave you last year?" Well, I just laughed and pushed her off the platform, but it has occurred to the committee that perhaps some of you, like that little old lady, would be interested in knowing the disposition of the funds.

Now, Mr. Rossiter, unfortunately our treasurer—or rather Mr. Rossiter our *treasurer, unfortunately* is confined at his home tonight with a bad head-cold and I have been asked (*he hears someone whispering at him from the wings, but decides to ignore it*) and I have been asked if I would (*the whisperer will not be denied, so he goes over to the entrance*

and receives a brief message, returning beaming and laughing to himself).
Well, the joke seems to be on *me!* Mr. Rossiter has *pneumonia!*

Following, then, is a summary of the Treasurer's Report:

(*Reads, in a very businesslike manner.*)

During the year 1929—and by that is meant 1928—the Choral Society
received the following in donations:

B. L. G.	$500
G. K. M.	500
Lottie and Nellie W.——	500
In memory of a happy summer at Rye Beach..........	10
Proceeds of a sale of coats and hats left in the boat-house...	14.55
And then the Junior League gave a performance of "Pinafore" for the benefit of the Fund, which, unfortunately, resulted in a deficit of	300
Then, from dues and charges	2,354.75
And, following the installation of the new furnace, a saving in coal amounting to $374.75—which made Dr. Murnie very happy, you may be sure.	
Making a total of receipts amounting to	$3,645.75

This is all, of course, reckoned as of June.

In the matter of expenditures, the Club has not been so fortunate. There
was the unsettled condition of business, and the late Spring, to contend
with, resulting in the following—er—rather discouraging figures, I am
afraid.

Expenditures	$23,574.85
Then there was a loss, owing to—several things—of	3,326.70
Car-fare	$ 4,452.25
And then, Mrs. Rawlins' expense account, when she went down to see the work they are doing in Baltimore, came to $256.50, but I am sure that you will all agree that it was worth it to find out—er—what they are doing in Baltimore	
And then, under the general head of Odds and Ends	2,537.50
Making a total disbursement of (*hurriedly*)	$416,546.75

or a net deficit of—ah—several thousand dollars.

Now, these figures bring us down only to October. In October my sister
was married, and the house was all torn up, and in the general confusion
we lost track of the figures for May and August. All those wishing the
approximate figures for May and August, however, may obtain them from

me in the vestry after the dinner, where I will be with pledge cards for those of you who wish to subscribe over and above your annual dues, and I hope that each and every one of you here tonight will look deep into his heart and (*archly*) into his pocketbook, and see if he can not find it there to help us to put this thing over with a bang (*accompanied by a wholly ineffectual gesture representing a bang*) and to help and make this just the biggest and best year the Armenians have ever had. . . . I thank you.

(*Exits, bumping into proscenium*)

In this essay, Benchley is fondly satirizing the inability of the average man to organize his thoughts for the sake of effective, complete presentation. Comic as he is, the inept Assistant Treasurer shows us negatively what a well organized report should be. Answer these questions in the light of what you have just learned about order and outlining:

1. What *should* have been the central theme and purpose of the Treasurer's Report? How many different purposes does the Treasurer try to carry out?
2. Point out instances in which careless word order changes the meaning of what the Treasurer wanted to say.
3. Which of the basic rules of preparing material did the Treasurer ignore? What are the consequences on the report itself?
4. Into how many divisions can the Report be made according to subject matter? How many divisions should there be?
5. In what order should the materials of the report be presented?
6. What characteristics of human thought is Benchley making fun of? Does he believe that Treasurers' reports must always be like this one? Explain.

Margaret Mead

MALE AND FEMALE, PART I

HOW ARE MEN AND WOMEN TO THINK ABOUT THEIR MALENESS AND THEIR femaleness in this twentieth century, in which so many of our old ideas must be made new? Have we over-domesticated men, denied their natural adventurousness, tied them down to machines that are after all only glorified spindles and looms, mortars and pestles and digging sticks, all of which were once women's work? Have we cut women off from their natural closeness to their children, taught them to look for a job instead of the touch of a child's hand, for status in a competitive world rather than a unique place by a glowing hearth? In educating women like men, have we done something disastrous to both men and women alike, or have we only taken one further step in the recurrent task of building more and better on our original human nature?

These are questions which are being asked in a hundred different ways in contemporary America. Polls and tracts and magazine articles speculate and fulminate and worry about the relationship between the sexes. In the moving pictures beautiful girls in tortoise-shell spectacles and flat-heeled shoes are first humiliated for competing with men, then they are forgiven, loved, and allowed to be glamorous only when they admit their error. In the advertisements on the billboards, men are now told how they, if they wear the right hat, may be the chosen one, the loved one—a rôle that used to be reserved for women. The old certainties of the past are gone, and everywhere there are signs of an attempt to build a new tradition, which like the old traditions that have been cast aside will again safely enfold growing boys and girls, so that they may grow up to choose each other, marry, and have children. The fashions bear the imprint of this uncertainty; the "new look" of 1947 partly captured the fleeting image of the mothers of a generation ago, the boys could again find the girls marriageable—as their mothers were—while those same girls gained a new femininity by suiting their swinging gait to the re-membered feeling of ruffled skirts like those their mothers once wore. In

From *Male and Female* by Margaret Mead, copyright 1949 by Margaret Mead, by permission of William Morrow and Company, Inc.

every pair of lovers the two are likely to find themselves wondering what the next steps are in a ballet between the sexes that no longer follows traditional lines, a ballet in which each couple must make up their steps as they go along. When he is insistent, should she yield, and how much? When she is demanding, should he resist, and how firmly? Who takes the next step forward or the next step back? What is it to be a man? What is it to be a woman?

No single book can hope to do more than touch a question that is so basic to human life. I have tried, in this book, to do three things. I try first to bring a greater awareness of the way in which the differences and the similarities in the bodies of human beings are the basis on which all our learnings about our sex, and our relationship to the other sex, are built. Talking about our bodies is a complex and difficult matter. We are so used to covering them up, to referring to them obliquely with slang terms or in a borrowed language, to hiding even infants' sex membership under blue and pink ribbons. It is difficult to become aware of those things about us which have been, and will always be, patterned by our own particular modesties and reticences. We reject, and very rightly, catalogues of caresses arranged in frequency tables, or accounts of childhood that read like a hospital chart. So to make it possible to think vividly, and yet at a comfortable distance, of the way in which our bodies have learned, throughout their lives, how to be male, how to be female, I draw—in the first part of this book—upon the seven South Sea cultures I have studied during the last quarter of a century. Their basic learnings are the same as our basic learnings; each human baby at its mother's breast must learn that it is either of the same sex, or of the opposite sex, from the mother who has borne it, from the father who fathered it. The boy may grow up to carry spears and bows and arrows instead of briefcases and fountain pens, but also he must woo and win and keep a woman. The women may wear the scantiest clothing, and spend their days in the simplest tasks, but in their acceptance of their husbands, and in their childbearing on some green mountain-side, sometimes not even sheltered from the rain, they face their essential womanhood as surely as the woman who bears her baby in a modern hospital. In following the steps by which their children learn about their sex membership, we can get some sense of the process of learning to be male, learning to be female, some recognition of how we ourselves arrived at our own sense of our own sex; so I have called this section, Part Two, "The Ways of the Body."

In the next section, "The Problems of Society," I draw not merely on the seven South Sea cultures I have studied myself, but on some of the knowledge we have of all human societies, as each has attempted to develop a myth of work, to bind men to women and children, to get the children fed and reared, and to settle the problems that arise whenever individual sex impulses must be disciplined into social forms. We can design forms of the family that fit our modern life better if we know what designs have been used in the past, what are the common elements that no society has yet found ways of ignoring, how rules about incest have made it possible to develop family life as we know it. What does the family do, how does it function, and what is the relationship between family life, with its strains and its prohibitions, its sacrifices and its rewards, and the natural springing potency of men and the spontaneous slower-flowering responsiveness of women? Each known human society has tried to come to grips with these problems, with the incompatibility between man's spontaneity and the monotony of the domestic hearth, with the over-compatibility between women's docility and the perpetuation of some tight, outworn tradition. In this age when millions of women are unmated and childless, or left alone to bring up their children, when so many men, restless and unsettled, wander again over the face of the earth, this old problem is as pressing as it ever has been, and as inescapable. No people who fail to meet it survive, as whole human beings.

In Part Four, "The Two Sexes in Contemporary America," I come back to the known, the familiar, and the concretely pressing, to the relationship between the sexes in America today, to childhood and courtship and marriage in these United States as it looks when seen comparatively—contrasted with the ways of other societies.

And finally, I try to suggest ways in which we, as a civilization, may make as full use of woman's special gifts as we have of man's, and in so doing develop forms of civilization that can make fuller use of all human gifts. Each of these main parts of the book stands by itself. The reader may begin with human childhood in the South Seas, or with the problems of sex in society, or with sex in the United States today—according to temperament and taste. All three parts stem from the same method, from the discipline of anthropology, the science of custom, in which we have learned to look at the patterned ways in which men have built upon their common biological inheritance different and challenging human cultures.

This excerpt from Mrs. Mead's introduction to *Male and Female* shows the general plan of development of her book, a full-scale discussion of the psychology and sociology of sexual attitudes in America.

1. What is the purpose of the rhetorical questions in the first three paragraphs? Do they fulfill their purpose or not?
2. What are the major divisions of Mrs. Mead's study of male and female characteristics? How are they related?
3. What are the sub-divisions of each of the major divisions? How are the sub-divisions related to each other and to the larger division?
4. The author suggests the reading order of the major divisions of the book can be reversed or rearranged by the reader. Is this an indication that the book is weak in organization? Explain.
5. If the major divisions of *Male and Female* are read in sequence from first to last, what kind of order, logically speaking, will be developed: Is Mrs. Mead moving spatially (geographically) from far places to America or temporally (in time) from past to present, or what?

THE BILL OF RIGHTS

ARTICLE I

CONGRESS SHALL MAKE NO LAW RESPECTING AN ESTABLISHMENT OF RELIGION, or prohibiting the free exercise thereof; or abridging the freedom of speech, or of the press; or the right of the people peaceably to assemble, and to petition the government for a redress of grievances.

ARTICLE II

A well regulated militia, being necessary to the security of a free State, the right of the people to keep and bear arms, shall not be infringed.

ARTICLE III

No soldier shall, in time of peace be quartered in any house, without the consent of the owner, nor in time of war, but in a manner to be prescribed by law.

ARTICLE IV

The right of the people to be secure in their persons, houses, papers, and effects, against unreasonable searches and seizures, shall not be violated, and no warrants shall issue, but upon probable cause, supported by oath or affirmation, and particularly describing the place to be searched, and the persons or things to be seized.

ARTICLE V

No person shall be held to answer for a capital, or otherwise infamous crime, unless on a presentment or indictment of a grand jury, except in cases arising in the land or naval forces, or in the militia, when in actual service in time of war or public danger; nor shall any person be subject for the same offense to be twice put in jeopardy of life or limb; nor shall be compelled in any criminal case to be a witness against himself, nor be deprived of life, liberty, or property, without due process of law; nor shall private property be taken for public use without just compensation.

ARTICLE VI

In all criminal prosecutions, the accused shall enjoy the right to a speedy and public trial, by an impartial jury of the State and district wherein the crime shall have been committed, which district shall have been previously ascertained by law, and to be informed of the nature and cause of the accusation; to be confronted with the witnesses against him; to have compulsory process for obtaining witnesses in his favor, and to have the assistance of counsel for his defense.

ARTICLE VII

In suits at common law, where the value in controversy shall exceed twenty dollars, the right of trial by jury shall be preserved, and no fact tried by a jury shall be otherwise reexamined in any court of the United States, than according to the rules of the common law.

ARTICLE VIII

Excessive bail shall not be required, nor excessive fines imposed, nor cruel and unusual punishments inflicted.

ARTICLE IX

The enumeration in the Constitution of certain rights shall not be construed to deny or disparage others retained by the people.

ARTICLE X

The powers not delegated to the United States by the Constitution, nor prohibited by it to the States, are reserved to the States respectively, or to the people.

The Bill of Rights, added to the United States Constitution, follows a numerical order in making its points, but there is a more implicit order involved.

1. What is the principle of order developed between Articles I and X?
2. Outline the arrangement of the Bill of Rights according to divisions of subject matter and indicate which articles are related to the same general topic.
3. Could Articles III and IV be combined in the same statement? What effect would such a combination of ideas have on the meaning of the Articles as they stand now?
4. Could the Bill of Rights be written with the Articles in reverse order (X, IX, VIII, etc.) and still maintain a logical pattern of development? Explain.
5. What is the effect of parallel phrasing in the parts of the Bill of Rights? Does this use of parallelism have any real advantages, or is it merely an affected style?

THE BOOK OF GENESIS

In the beginning God created the heaven and the earth. And the earth was without form and void; and darkness *was* upon the face of the deep. And the Spirit of God moved upon the face of the waters. And God said, Let there be light: and there was light. And God saw the light, that *it was* good: and God divided the light from the darkness. And God called the light Day, and the darkness he called Night. And the evening and the morning were the first day.

And God said, Let there be a firmament in the midst of the waters, and let it divide the waters from the waters. And God made the firmament, and divided the waters which *were* under the firmament from the waters which *were* above the firmament: and it was so. And God called the firmament Heaven. And the evening and the morning were the second day.

And God said, Let the waters under the heaven be gathered together unto one place, and let the dry *land* appear: and it was so. And God called the dry *land* Earth; and the gathering together of the waters called he Seas: and God saw that *it was* good. And God said, Let the earth bring forth grass, the herb yielding seed, *and* the fruit tree yielding fruit after his kind, whose seed *is* in itself, upon the earth: and it was so. And the earth brought forth grass, *and* herb yielding seed after his kind, and the tree yielding fruit, whose seed *was* in itself, after his kind: and God saw that *it was* good. And the evening and the morning were the third day.

And God said, Let there be lights in the firmament of the heaven to divide the day from the night; and let them be for signs, and for seasons, and for days, and years: And let them be for lights in the firmament of the heaven to give light upon the earth: and it was so. And God made two great lights; the greater light to rule the day, and the lesser light to rule the night: *he made* the stars also. And God set them in the firmament of the heaven to give light upon the earth, And to rule over the day and over the night, and to divide the light from the darkness: and God saw that *it was* good. And the evening and the morning were the fourth day.

And God said, Let the waters bring forth abundantly the moving creature that hath life, and fowl *that* may fly above the earth in the open firmament of heaven. And God created great whales, and every living creature that moveth, which the waters brought forth abundantly, after their kind, and every winged fowl after his kind: and God saw that *it was* good. And God blessed them, saying, Be fruitful, and multiply, and fill the waters in the seas, and let fowl multiply in the earth. And the evening and the morning were the fifth day.

And God said, Let the earth bring forth the living creature after his kind, cattle, and creeping thing, and beast of the earth after his kind: and it was so. And God made the beast of the earth after his kind, and cattle after their kind, and everything that creepeth upon the earth after his kind: And God saw that *it was* good.

And God said, Let us make man in our image, after our likeness: and let them have dominion over the fish of the sea, and over the fowl of the air, and over the cattle, and over all the earth, and over every creeping thing that creepeth upon the earth. So God created man in his *own* image, in the image of God created he him; male and female created he them. And God blessed them, and God said unto them, Be fruitful, and multiply, and replenish the earth, and subdue it: and have dominion over the fish of the sea, and over the fowl of the air, and over every living thing that moveth upon the earth.

And God said, Behold, I have given you every herb bearing seed, which *is* upon the face of all the earth, and every tree, in the which *is* the fruit of a tree yielding seed; to you it shall be for meat. And to every beast of the earth, and to every fowl of the air, and to every thing that creepeth upon the earth, wherein *there is* life, I *have given* every green herb for meat: and it was so. And God saw every thing that he had made, and, behold, *it was* very good. And the evening and the morning were the sixth day.

Thus the heavens and the earth were finished, and all the host of them. And on the seventh day God ended his work which he had made; and he rested on the seventh day from all his work which he had made. And God blessed the seventh day, and sanctified it: because that in it he had rested from all his work which God created and made.

1. Point out examples of parallelism of thoughts and phrases in this section of the Book of Genesis from the *Old Testament*.
2. Why is parallelism used so extensively in this translation?
3. What kinds of order are used in this account of the Creation of the World by God?
4. Which of the types of order is most basic to the account? Why?
5. In a very literal sense, the Book of Genesis is an outline. Write the first twenty-nine verses in a sentence outline form, using the conventional combination of letters and numbers. Into how many parts does the outline fit? To what do these correspond?

CHAPTER 2

CHRONOLOGICAL ORDER:
THE PROCESS; CAUSE AND EFFECT

"How long a time lies in one little word!"
WILLIAM SHAKESPEARE, *Richard II*, I.3.213

In the thought of Western civilization, there has always been a strong emphasis on time, which has grown, in our own day, to something of an obsession. In contemporary culture, vast industries—watch making, clock and calendar manufacture—have developed to appease our mass interest in time. Time is bought and sold in radio and television. Wages are paid on the basis of "hours" rather than quality or volume of work. As the sciences have developed, new ways of measuring time have been devised, so that there now exist numerous systems of *chronology* (or "time patterns"): geological, historical, astronomical, and psychological. We even can measure split seconds of time in electronic blips on a cathode tube.

As the upshot of this cultural emphasis, each of us has a sense of time almost as tangible as the watches we wear on our wrists. But what is time? Is it the rising and setting of the sun, the ebb and flow of ocean tides, or the rotation of the seasons? Is it the movement of a shadow on a sun dial, sand sifting in a glass, the 360-degree sweep of a needle, or the pattern on an oscilloscope? Perhaps it is the change in human emotions or the growth of our bodies? From St. Augustine to Albert Einstein, men have tried to define time with definitions ranging from the theological to the astrophysical. The definition of time that we will use is this one: *time is a system of measuring duration and sequence of events.* It is, therefore, an example of the arbitrary patterns of arrangement devised by the human mind.

When Einstein's theory was first made known, people were startled at his relative concept of time, but historical facts indicate that the system of

37

telling time has always been arbitrary and determined by man's sense of actions in a sequential order. The ancient Egyptians and the American Indians counted time as so many "moons" ago. The Greeks counted from the Olympic games. The Romans dated events "from the founding of the City." And our present designation of dates as years "Anno Domini" reflects the selection of a specific event, the birth of Jesus Christ, as the starting point of measurement. Orthodox Jewish dates, today as well as for thousands of past years, are based on the conjectured date of the Creation of the World as recounted in Genesis.

Our systems of measuring time are no less workable for being artificial. The man who throws away his alarm clock and becomes habitually tardy, in the belief that "his time" is as reasonable as any other arbitrary measurement, is likely to miss trains and subject himself to other, greater inconveniences. Since our system of measuring temporality operates to our communal benefit, there is no advantage in ignoring it or little point in trying to change it radically, but we need to realize that when we refer to *chronological order,* this order is not any absolute order apart from a succession of occurrences or events.

When we express in words the sequential patterns that we impose on events as a means of understanding their relationship better, we find that English as a language has usages strongly related to our time sense. The most ordinary verb in English has over one hundred forms—present, present progressive, past, past perfect, future, and so forth—to indicate *tense,* or time of occurrence, as well as duration and intensity of action. There is a multiplicity of conjunctions that serve to introduce conditions governing the time of action expressed by the verb: "since," "while," "when." And numerous adverbs—"ago," "formerly," "later," "soon,"—act to make tense even more precise and specific than verbs alone can do.

The combination of chronological order and language into prose discourse results in the recounting of events in sequence, or a narrative. Joseph Addison's reconstruction of the mythical life adventures of a shilling on page 50 is a clearcut example of prose that narrates or relates actions in sequence. From the instant of being removed as raw silver from a Peruvian mine in the sixteenth century to its re-smelting in eighteenth-century England, the shilling undergoes a sequence of happenings which constitute the rhetorical arrangement of Addison's essay. Addison's prose is dependent on the most basic kind of chronological order.

While "narrative" is a term usually given to the sort of writing which treats fictional or biographical events, there is a special name for chronological order as it appears in expository or informative rhetoric. This kind of prose treats the *process*.

The word *process* is derived from two Latin words (*pro*, "forward," and *cessus*, "movement" or "step"). It can be defined as *a succession of events tending to some specific end*. It is this imputed sense of purpose that characterizes a number of events as a unified process. We see within a sequence of actions an apparent principle which directs all these actions toward some final step or goal. Obviously, since actions must take place in a time sequence, every process is an example of chronological order, though not all examples of chronological order are processes. To list the succession of American Presidents from George Washington to John F. Kennedy is an obvious instance of chronological order, but the succession of Presidents is not a process, because the single events in time (their terms in office) do not constitute a movement toward some end step or goal.

Because we see processes taking place everywhere—even within our minds and bodies—much that is written is a reflection of this way of viewing events. The occurrences in the physical universe may become the basis for an essay such as Fred Hoyle's "The Origin of the Earth and Planets." The social rituals which grow up in a culture over a period of time are processes; Geoffrey Gorer treats American dating as just such a coherent, arbitrarily established sequence of actions. The operation of the mind is a process that you are familiar with through introspection and that has been rhetorically described in John Dewey's "How We Think." Walter Kaufmann's "The Faith of a Heretic" outlines the successive steps in converting the mind from one set of beliefs to another. Other processes, describing everything from how a civilization falls to how a bed collapsed one night, provide subject matter for writers like Stanley Casson and James Thurber.

Superficially, nothing seems easier than understanding a process and writing about it. In truth, since our concept of the process is flexible, adapting itself to all kinds of actions, formulating the steps and sequential order of a process and setting them down in prose holds some tricky surprises for the unwary writer. Is a recipe an example of a rhetorical treatment of a process or not? What about all of the do-it-yourself material that tells you how to accomplish everything from building a barbecue pit to cooking a wolf? What would be the first step taken up in an account of the origin of the universe, and at what point would the process be considered complete? A comparison of Genesis and Fred Hoyle's essay shows a difference of method as well as differences of assumption about the events in the process.

When you undertake to write about one, first decide what is the magnitude of the process, i.e., how many separate events does it include and over how long a period of time does it extend? You should not attempt to describe the fall of the Roman Empire in two pages; the magnitude of the events is too great to be covered adequately by so brief a treatment. Likewise, recounting the steps in tying a necktie ought not to take more than a few words of direction sufficient to prevent the neophyte from strangling himself with a Hangman's Noose of foulard. An extended discussion of tying a necktie is bound to be finicky and excessive.

Be sure whether the process you are describing is a *natural* or *artificial* one. Natural processes are founded in our awareness of the inherent nature of the physical world or the physiological nature of man: solar eclipses and hiccuping are natural processes. Artificial processes are made of steps established by accident or the volition of a single person: wedding ceremonies and dancing the Cha Cha are artificial processes. Do not treat artificial processes as though they were as fixed as natural ones.

Give careful thought to the event that you consider first in the process under examination. Deciding what was the first step in the event sequence making up a process is often difficult. Since the process is composed of events in time, some selectivity is necessary, for time is infinite and events occur incessantly, but not all time and not all events can be included in the discussion of processes. You must define the limits of the process by the principle of unity that you see within single events and determine the first step accordingly. Addison could have begun his discussion of the progress of a shilling with the formation of the silver vein in Peru or the earlier formation of the mountain or even the rising of the South American continent from the seas in primordial time. He chose, however, to begin the career of the coin from the moment of its extraction from the mountain rather than its first smelting or the prehistoric formation of its silver. Every rhetorical account of a process necessarily begins at some point after many previous, preparatory events have already happened.

Once you determine a starting point, be sure that your explanation of a process does not involve any unusual and undefined terms. S. J. Perelman's chaotic experience with a do-it-yourself set of instructions on page 54 stems in part from lack of understanding what terms mean. An explanation that starts, "Connect one wire from terminal 1 on the low-frequency speaker to solder lug 1 on the metal cover" is incomprehensible unless you define certain terms. Ordinary words need not be defined, but if the process demands a specialized terminology, the explanation must make meanings clear or fail to accomplish its purpose.

Follow strictly sequential order in listing the intermediate steps of a process. If you reverse the order of the steps or leave out an essential stage, you will lose your reader. Show the relationship between the steps and indicate the relative time necessary for each—if time is a direct factor. Also indicate how each step in sequence points to the final goal of the process.

The conclusion of a process may be just as arbitrary a point as the beginning. What is the final step in the expansion of a galaxy? Infinity, or annihilation, or what? In some instances, a tangible object—a lemon pie, or a steel pipe, or perhaps a letter of admission—is the end result of a process. In other processes, there is simply an alteration of conditions: washing dishes, swimming, and thinking are such processes. In your rhetorical explanation of a process, be clear as to what the events lead to and at what point in the sequence they may be considered terminated and the action fulfilled.

Prose dealing with processes is not a simple listing of a number of actions, one after another. To be truly effective and to communicate an understanding of how a process works, a rhetorical presentation must incorporate a fundamental awareness of chronological sequence and an interpretation of events as unified by some pervasive principle. Since the writer's job is to verbalize his own comprehension of these systems, unless he systematically examines the process before he writes and systematically translates the order of the process into the order of his prose composition, he will confuse rather than enlighten his reader.

CAUSE AND EFFECT

In many cases, chronological order involves a relationship between one event and another more intrinsic than that of mere succession in time. In such instances, the event preceding is so vital to the event following that its occurrence is necessary to the occurrence of its successor; in fact, the second event can take place *only* if the first does previously, and it must then occur as an inevitable consequence. This relationship is that of Cause and Effect, or Causation. It is the assumption that actions in time occur *because* of some initial event which induces another event which in turn induces a third, and so on.

The differences between the process and causation are often so slight as to be indistinguishable, but in general the process is composed of events loosely related to each other, sometimes existing independently, and unified by their total relationship to an end step or goal. In causation, however, each step is dependent upon the step preceding it, and no step can be removed from a causal sequence without destroying that sequence. Many natural processes (soil erosion, for example) involve causation; and it is scarcely an exaggeration to say that only the most artificially devised processes exist without some element of causality. Separating the causal sequence from the process is not mere pedantry, however, since real errors in thinking can result from automatically assuming they are one and the same.

A cause and effect sequence may be composed of two events only, one the action, situation, or condition which produces the other in due course. Or a causal relationship may involve several conditions which result in a new, single condition or effect. Perhaps one condition may have several separate consequences. Or, finally, one condition may produce another, which in turn produces a third, and perhaps more, in sequence. A carelessly thrown ball and a broken window would be a single cause and effect. A blaring radio, a screaming siren, and a neighboring piano might be multiple causes resulting in a single effect: a splitting headache. A drop in the stock market could be the sole cause of a loss of investments, a drop in wages, and several suicides. Or a match falling in a wastebasket, thus starting a fire in the paper, which in turn sets some drapes on fire, and so forth, is an instance of a causal chain. Diagrammed, the various causal relations could be represented like this:

A ——————— B	**Single Cause and Effect**
A ——————————┐	
C ——————— D	**Multiple Causes, Single Effect**
K ——————————┘	
┌——————— Y	
X	**Single Cause, Multiple Effects**
└——————— Z	
A ———B———D———X	**Causal Sequence**

Obviously, of the above types of causal relationships, the causal sequence is most likely to be identified with the process. In differentiating one from the other, remember that no variation in sequence is possible in a real cause and effect chain of events. Also, keep in mind the broad principle that the process is basically concerned with the How of events whereas causation is concerned with the Why.

Here is a case in point. Scrambling an egg is a process composed of several steps: getting a bowl, taking an egg from the refrigerator, breaking the egg into the bowl, stirring it with milk and salt, heating a pan, pouring the mixture into the pan, and stirring. Each step in this process is necessary only to the achievement of the end product: a scrambled egg. No one step takes place *because* of the previous step, and a good deal of alteration in the sequence of the steps is possible without affecting the validity of the process. Suppose, however, that you feel hungry, and therefore you decide to scramble yourself an egg. Accordingly, you go to the refrigerator to remove an egg, but as you open the door, a bottle of milk falls to the floor and breaks. In trying to avoid the resulting mess, you step on a piece of glass and cut your foot. In point of fact, every action in this unhappy sequence was caused by a previous condition or action—even your initial hunger was caused by something—and you actually cut your foot *because* you were hungry, far-fetched though it seems.

One of the most troublesome things about causation is that everything has some cause or other, every action resulting from some prior action as far back in time as time can be conceived of. Carried to an extreme, theories of causation can result in a philosophical determinism, the belief that each event occurs as an inevitable result (and simultaneous cause) of other events predetermined by the nature of the first occurrence eons ago. Another bothersome thing about causation is that the causal relationship may seem tangible enough—a window shattering when a ball strikes it is certainly a tangible event—but it may also be confusingly intangible. A window suddenly shattering without being struck by a visible object obviously breaks for some reason, but what could it be: heat pressure, sound waves, evil spirits?

The fact that causal relationships are often speculative serves to remind us that many relationships regarded as obvious cause and effect are really only *hypothetical*. When men observe some tangible data, or evidence (a set of circumstances, conditions, or events), they tend to try to explain the existence of these phenomena by ascribing some reason (or cause) for their being as they are. They construct a probable *hypothesis or conjectured explanation*. When the conjecture deals with probable reasons for present phenomena, the result is a hypothetical cause. When it anticipates the consequences of present phenomena, speculating as to probable future events, the conjecture treats a hypothetical result.

There are various forms of hypothesizing, both about possible causes and probable effects. The ancient tribal wise man who explained the observable phenomenon of rainbows by saying they were supernatural tokens of divine approval was hypothesizing, just as the modern scientist hypothesizes when he explains the rainbow as the refraction of light rays into component parts of the color spectrum through the action of moisture in the air. Similarly, the tribal witchdoctor who put a spell on a victim and predicted the victim's death was using a form of hypothesis, prophesying, which a modern physician uses when he predicts the future course of a disease by observing a patient's symptoms. Divination and prophecy, diagnosis and prediction—all are forms of hypothesizing or establishing causation.

The difference between a pure guess and a scientific hypothesis is this: guessing is a matter of intuition or hunches leading to a conjecture founded on little or no supporting evidence and following no reliable principles of inference. A scientific hypothesis is in part intuition, but it is also a systematic testing of conjecture against all available data or evidence and in the light of previous experience. The hypothesis most likely to prove right must do the following: 1. Include all known facts; 2. not over-emphasize any part of the evidence at the expense of the rest; 3. observe the laws of probability as established by previous investigation; 4. avoid logical contradictions; and 5. stay as simple as possible without ignoring any part of the evidence. Hypotheses which violate any one of these requirements are *Forced Hypotheses.*

Suppose, for example, that you find yourself terribly drowsy at 1:30 P.M. while you sit reading in the college library. You hypothesize that you have been bitten by a tsetse fly, and your lassitude is an indication that you are coming down with sleeping sickness. You are constructing two theories: one concerning the cause of your drowsiness and the other its possible consequences. Both hypotheses are forced, unless you happen to live in Africa. The causal hypothesis ignores relevant facts (you ate a heavy lunch; you slept only five hours the night before; you are reading a tedious book); it rests on no observable facts. Similarly, the consequential hypothesis rests on a false postulation, and thus is forced (your drowsiness cannot lead to sleeping sickness since it is unconnected with it).

Another erroneous treatment of causation is the *Post Hoc Fallacy.* This kind of wrong thinking is best described by its Latin name, *post hoc, ergo propter hoc:* "After this, therefore because of this." It is the belief that when two events follow in chronological order, the second is the result of the first. This general confusing of simple chronological order with causation appears often, in writing as well as conversation. The line of thinking runs like this: Women were given the vote in 1920; since then juvenile delinquency, dope addiction, prostitution, and organized crime have increased alarmingly; therefore, the granting of suffrage to women was responsible. To dispel such fuzzy *post hoc* thinking, we have only to realize that since 1920 a cure for poliomyelitis has been found, the Yankees have lost the pennant, and the average American income has risen to $2,200 a year . . . therefore what? Nothing. No cause and effect relationship exists in either set of chronological events. Finding causes which support our prejudices or desires is a simple but suspect act.

In prose discourse, the dividing line between basic chronological order, the process, and causal order is often a frail one, hard to see. In discriminating between one and another, you may rely with some confidence on the signposts of language that a writer uses. Some phrases almost always introduce an idea stated to be a cause: "because of," "due to," "if," "when," "since," "as a result of" are examples of the way causation is stated. Likewise, the phrases "therefore," "consequently," "hence," "as a result," and "thus" preface an assertion about effects.* In some instances, causal phrases may not appear, but a causal relationship may be implicitly stated anyway. "The effectiveness of the Northern blockade reduced the supply of arms to the Confederacy to a virtual trickle in the latter days of 1864." This statement shows cause and effect in the tense of the verb, "reduced," but it also suggests causation in the noun, "effectiveness." Even in the most innocuous assertion of causation, the careful reader will be able to see that a positive relationship is stated.

In the four essays following this discussion, you will see all of the basic rhetorical uses of chronological order. S. J. Perelman's wry evaluation of do-it-yourself prose and practice, Addison's simple delineation of sequential events in time, Ortega y Gasset's hypothesis about the present state of the novel, and Stanley Casson's combination of process writing and archeological hypothesizing—these illustrate the basic range of chronologically directed prose. In reading them, notice carefully how important precise use of verb tenses and adverbs is. Also watch how each writer indicates the passage of time through using adverbs and transitional phrases reflecting chronological sequence. Finally, heed the signpost words and phrases

---

* Sometimes these terms appear to indicate a causal relationship but do not, e.g., "She ought to make an excellent wife since she makes good fudge," or "Because he is near-sighted, he can never be President of the United States." If you look closely at these statements, you will see that the two parts have nothing to do with events in sequence but are related through a purely logical process called deduction. Deduction and its wrong uses are discussed in Chapter VII.

indicating causation, and test the causally connected ideas for any possible forced hypotheses and *post hoc* errors. By becoming aware of how other writers handle the rhetorical problems attending accounts of processes and causal sequences, you will be able to monitor your own chronological thinking better and test your writing more accurately for its presentation of this thought.

I. Questions for Review
1. What is time? What definitions of *time* does your dictionary give?
2. Define *chronological order*. What determines our concept of this order?
3. What is a process? How does it differ from chronological order?
4. What elements must be included in a rhetorical statement of a process?
5. What is causation? Are all cause and effect relationships a form of chronological order? Explain.
6. Can there be any process which does not involve some causation? Give examples, if possible. Can you think of any cause and effect relationships which do not also fit the definition of a process given in this chapter? Consider these: lightning, a suicide, a toothache, the wind, spontaneous combustion.
7. What is an hypothesis? What are the tests of a valid or correct hypothesis?
8. What is the difference between an hypothesis and a forced hypothesis?
9. What is a post hoc fallacy? Give some examples of it.
10. What kinds of writing necessarily involve use of chronological order, the process, and causation? Why?

II. Exercises
1. Which are processes and which are not?

A. Signing your signature
B. An automobile trip
C. Repairing a clock
D. Typing a term paper
E. Wishing
F. The Franco-Prussian War
G. A tidal wave
H. The origin of the earth
I. Winding a wristwatch
J. Telling time
K. Beethoven's *Fifth Symphony*
L. Osmosis
M. Smiling
N. Murder

2. What would be the major steps in each of these processes?

A. A date
B. Electrolysis
C. Washing the family car (or dishes)
D. Choosing a college
E. Electing the President of the U.S.
F. Conducting a fraternity meeting

G. Launching a rocket   I. Learning to swim
H. Studying for an exam   J. Registering to vote

3. Which are cause and effect, which are forced hypotheses, and which are post hoc fallacies?

A. The virtual extermination of the American Indian in the 19th century was due to many factors: the diminishing herds of wild game, the building of a railroad to the west coast, the inter-tribal warfare of the Indians themselves, and not least, the hostile policies of a series of Secretaries of Indian Affairs.

B. It's no wonder the natives of South Africa never developed any degree of civilization. Terrible tropical diseases such as leprosy, yaws, and encephalitis forced all the natives' energies into a struggle for survival so they had no time to develop in other ways.

C. Increased wages cause increased prices. In 1956, the Union of Bakery Workers struck for a three per cent wage increase. It was granted, and, by 1960, the cost of bread was up 12 per cent. Rises in bread costs were obviously the result of increased wages for bakery workers.

D. If Red China is admitted to the United Nations, a series of dis-asters will result. China's prestige will be strengthened so that her propaganda will become more effective, and former pro-Western nations, like Thailand and Pakistan, will be influenced to cast their lot with Communism.

E. Dolores has been having dreadful headaches lately. I *told* her she ought to stop using that cheap peroxide on her hair.

F. When I had that terribly sore, raw throat with some fever, my doctor diagnosed them as symptoms of pharyngeal influenza.

G. For want of a nail, a shoe was lost; for want of a shoe, a horse was lost; for want of a horse, a rider was lost; for want of a rider, a message was lost; for want of a message, a battle was lost; for want of a battle, a kingdom was lost . . . and all for the want of a nail.

H. Say what you like, but the world is better off with Stalin dead. Since he died, the American standard of living has improved, and the French economy is much stronger.

I. "Why do you suppose we've dropped so many football games this year?" "Are you kidding? Because our coach is no good, that's why!"

J. Isadora Duncan actually died because she had a sense of the dramatic. She insisted on wearing a long, red silk scarf while out riding in an open roadster. The scarf fluttered into an axle; and as the car started, the scarf twisted and broke her neck.

4. Which type of cause and effect (single, causal sequence, etc.) are the following:

A. An apple a day keeps the doctor away.

B. Not only has television revolutionized one industry (electronics) and diminished another (motion pictures); it has changed the family habits of Americans and influenced methods of education.

C. The lax morality of the Restoration Period of English history probably was due to many factors: a reaction against Puritanism; the new discoveries of the sciences; the materialistic philosophy current in the time; and the notorious examples set by Charles II and his courtiers.

D. In the town of Enterprise, Alabama, there is a monument to the boll weevil. Grateful farmers erected this tribute to the insect because it destroyed the cotton crops of so many years that farmers were forced to turn to new, diversified crops and thus revitalized Southern agricultural economy.

E. Good fences make good neighbors.

5. Below are several sets of conditions and a number of possible hypotheses to explain each set. Select the most likely hypothesis in each instance, and explain why the others are less probable.

A. You enter your living room in the morning to find the French doors forced open, mud on the rug, and a silver vase missing. (A) The neighbor's dog has gotten in. (B) There was an earthquake during the night which burst the doors open, spattered the rug with mud, and shook the vase from its usual place. (C) A burglar has broken in. (D) Your house is haunted.

B. You fail a physics exam dismally. (A) Your high school education did not prepare you adequately for college. (B) Your physics teacher dislikes you and is determined to flunk you. (C) You didn't study sufficiently. (D) You aren't smart enough to understand physics. (E) Only grinds and eggheads could have passed that test.

C. You are riding on a bus and see an intense, twenty-year-old man begin to read a copy of Hitler's *Mein Kampf*. (A) He is a local college student. (B) He is a Nazi war criminal. (C) He is an undercover agent for the F.B.I. (D) He is insane. (E) He is un-American.

D. A terrible earthquake in Chile destroys scores of villages and human lives. (A) The Aztec god, Quetzalcoatl, is angry and wishes to be appeased with a human sacrifice. (B) God is punishing the Chileans for their immorality. (C) The Russians have set off a secret H-Bomb test in the Pacific. (D) The earth's crust is shifting. (E) Engineers in Peru are blasting out a railroad bed.

E. The Boers of South Africa defend their policy of *apartheid* (or segregation) on the grounds that the Negro is biologically inferior. A more likely explanation is that: (A) *Apartheid* is more beneficial to the Negro than any other system. (B) It is a historical tradition impossible to change. (C) It is sanctioned by the *Bible*. (D) It is socially and economically advantageous to the Boers. (E) It is the only system that will work.

F. After four years of intense fighting, the Confederacy was defeated by the Union in the War of the Secession. The Confederacy lost because: (A) Agrarian societies cannot hope to win wars fought against industrial societies. (B) The cause of the Confederacy was morally wrong. (C) Union generals were better strategists than Confederate generals. (D) Confederate soldiers were cowardly. (E) Abraham Lincoln was President of the Union.

III. Questions for Thought, Discussion, and Writing

1. Make up a list of words denoting time (e.g., while, during, ago) and explain the meaning of each.

2. The Greek word for time is *chronos*. What do the following compound words mean and how are they related to a sense of time: chronological, chronaxie, chronic, chronicle, synchronize?

3. The social rituals which a sociologist calls *mores* and those which are called *manners* are really types of processes. Explain. Are these processes natural, artificial, or a combination of both?

4. Mathematicians, chemists, philosophers, and theologians all develop hypotheses to account for their views of life. Is the mathematician's hypothesis more demonstrable than the theologian's or the chemist's more than the philosopher's? Why?

5. Is it correct to say that all scientific experimentation is the attempt to develop or confirm hypotheses?

6. Read a generous sample of "Letters to the Editor" in your local paper and make a collection of the forced hypotheses and post hoc fallacies you find there.

7. Write a theme on one of these topics:
   A. A subject taken from II, 2 above
   B. The time conceptions of the Greeks (or the early Christians)
   C. The *Primum Mobile* of the Middle Ages
   D. The origins of the system of measuring time in minutes, hours, days, weeks, and months.
   E. A causal relationship of your own choosing.

Joseph Addison

THE PROGRESS OF A SHILLING

From my own Apartment, Nov. 10.

I WAS LAST NIGHT VISITED BY A FRIEND OF MINE WHO HAS AN INEXHAUStible fund of discourse, and never fails to entertain his company with a variety of thoughts and hints that are altogether new and uncommon. Whether it were in complaisance to my way of living, or his real opinion, he advanced the following paradox, that it required much greater talents to fill up and become a retired life than a life of business. Upon this occasion he rallied very agreeably the busy men of the age, who only valued themselves for being in motion, and passing through a series of trifling and insignificant actions. In the heat of his discourse, seeing a piece of money lying on my table, "I defy," says he, "any of these active persons to produce half the adventures that this twelvepenny-piece has been engaged in, were it possible for him to give us an account of his life."

My friend's talk made so odd an impression upon my mind, that soon after I was a-bed I fell insensibly into a most unaccountable reverie, that had neither moral nor design in it, and cannot be so properly called a dream as a delirium.

Methought the shilling that lay upon the table reared itself upon its edge, and turning the face towards me, opened its mouth, and in a soft silver sound gave me the following account of his life and adventures:

"I was born," says he, "on the side of a mountain, near a little village of Peru, and made a voyage to England in an ingot, under the convoy of Sir Francis Drake. I was, soon after my arrival, taken out of my Indian habit, refined, naturalised, and put into the British mode, with the face of Queen Elizabeth on one side, and the arms of the country on the other. Being thus equipped, I found in me a wonderful inclination to ramble, and visit all the parts of the new world into which I was brought. The people very much favoured my natural disposition, and shifted me so fast from hand to hand, that before I was five years old, I had travelled into almost every corner of the nation. But in the beginning of my sixth year, to my unspeakable grief, I fell into the hands of a miserable old fellow, who clapped

From *The Tatler,* No. 249 (Saturday, Nov. 11, 1710)

50

me into an iron chest, where I found five hundred more of my own quality who lay under the same confinement. The only relief we had, was to be taken out and counted over in the fresh air every morning and evening. After an imprisonment of several years, we heard somebody knocking at our chest, and breaking it open with a hammer. This we found was the old man's heir, who, as his father lay a-dying, was so good as to come to our release: he separated us that very day. What was the fate of my companions, I know not: as for myself, I was sent to the apothecary's shop for a pint of sack. The apothecary gave me to an herb-woman, the herb-woman to a butcher, the butcher to a brewer, and the brewer to his wife, who made a present of me to a nonconformist preacher. After this mannner I made my way merrily through the world; for, as I told you before, we shillings love nothing so much as travelling. I sometimes fetched in a shoulder of mutton, sometimes a play-book, and often had the satisfaction to treat a Templar at a twelvepenny ordinary, or carry him with three friends to Westminster Hall.

"In the midst of this pleasant progress which I made from place to place, I was arrested by a superstitious old woman, who shut me up in a greasy purse, in pursuance of a foolish saying, that while she kept a Queen Elizabeth's shilling about her, she should never be without money. I continued here a close prisoner for many months, till at last I was exchanged for eight-and-forty farthings.

"I thus rambled from pocket to pocket till the beginning of the Civil Wars, when, to my shame be it spoken, I was employed in raising soldiers against the King; for being of a very tempting breadth, a sergeant made use of me to inveigle country fellows, and list them in the service of the Parliament.

"As soon as he had made one man sure, his way was to oblige him to take a shilling of a more homely figure, and then practise the same trick upon another. Thus I continued doing great mischief to the Crown, till my officer chancing one morning to walk abroad earlier than ordinary, sacrificed me to his pleasures, and made use of me to seduce a milkmaid. This wench bent me, and gave me to her sweetheart, applying more properly than she intended the usual form of, 'To my love and from my love.' This ungenerous gallant marrying her within few days after, pawned me for a dram of brandy, and drinking me out next day, I was beaten flat with a hammer, and again set a-running.

"After many adventures, which it would be tedious to relate, I was sent to a young spendthrift, in company with the will of his deceased father.

The young fellow, who I found was very extravagant, gave great demonstrations of joy at the receiving the will; but opening it, he found himself disinherited and cut off from the possession of a fair estate, by virtue of my being made a present to him. This put him into such a passion, that after having taken me in his hand, and cursed me, he squirred me away from him as far as he could fling me. I chanced to light in an unfrequented place under a dead wall, where I lay undiscovered and useless during the usurpation of Oliver Cromwell.

"About a year after the King's return, a poor cavalier that was walking there about dinner-time fortunately cast his eye upon me, and, to the great joy of us both, carried me to a cook's-shop, where he dined upon me, and drank the King's health. When I came again into the world, I found that I had been happier in my retirement than I thought, having probably by that means escaped wearing a monstrous pair of breeches.

"Being now of great credit and antiquity, I was rather looked upon as a medal than an ordinary coin; for which reason a gamester laid hold of me, and converted me to a counter, having got together some dozens of us for that use. We led a melancholy life in his possession, being busy at those hours wherein current coin is at rest, and partaking the fate of our master, being in a few moments valued at a crown, a pound, or a sixpence, according to the situation in which the fortune of the cards placed us. I had at length the good luck to see my master break, by which means I was again sent abroad under my primitive denomination of a shilling.

"I shall pass over many other accidents of less moments, and hasten to that fatal catastrophe when I fell into the hands of an artist, who conveyed me under ground, and with an unmerciful pair of shears cut off my titles, clipped my brims, retrenched my shape, rubbed me to my inmost ring, and, in short, so spoiled and pillaged me, that he did not leave me worth a groat. You may think what a confusion I was in to see myself thus curtailed and disfigured. I should have been ashamed to have shown my head, had not all my old acquaintance been reduced to the same shameful figure, excepting some few that were punched through the belly. In the midst of this general calamity, when everybody thought our misfortune irretrievable, and our case desperate, we were thrown into the furnace together, and (as it often happens with cities rising out of a fire) appeared with greater beauty and lustre than we could ever boast of before. What has happened to me since the change of sex which you now see, I shall take some other opportunity to relate. In the meantime I shall only repeat two adventures, as being very extraordinary, and neither of them having ever happened to me above once in my life. The first was, my being in a poet's pocket, who was so taken with the brightness and novelty of my appearance, that it gave occasion to the finest burlesque poem in the British language, entitled from me, 'The Splendid Shilling.' The second adventure, which I must not omit, happened to me in the year 1703, when I was given away in charity to a blind man; but indeed this was by a mistake, the person who gave me having heedlessly thrown me into the hat among a pennyworth of farthings."

1. Is the progress of a shilling, as Addison described it, a chain of separate events or a series of causal relationships? Support your view by citing the text.
2. Is the process a natural or an artificial one? Why?
3. How is the progress of a shilling related to chronological order?
4. Besides the shilling itself, what ties the episodes of the process together? What does each episode illustrate about a basic theme?
5. How does Addison use hypothesis in this essay?

S. J. Perelman

INSERT FLAP A AND THROW AWAY

ONE STIFLING SUMMER AFTERNOON LAST AUGUST, IN THE ATTIC OF A TINY
stone house in Pennsylvania, I made a most interesting discovery: the
shortest, cheapest method of inducing a nervous breakdown ever perfected.
In this technique (eventually adopted by the psychology department of
Duke University, which will adopt anything), the subject is placed in a
sharply sloping attic heated to 340° F. and given a mothproof closet known
as the Jiffy-Cloz to assemble. The Jiffy-Cloz, procurable at any department
store or neighborhood insane asylum, consists of half a dozen gigantic
sheets of red cardboard, two plywood doors, a clothes rack, and a packet
of staples. With these is included a set of instructions mimeographed in
pale-violet ink, fruity with phrases like "Pass Section F through Slot AA,
taking care not to fold tabs behind washers (see Fig. 9)." The cardboard
is so processed that as the subject struggles convulsively to force the staple
through, it suddenly buckles, plunging the staple deep into his thumb.
He thereupon springs up with a dolorous cry and smites his knob (Section
K) on the rafters (RR). As a final demonic touch, the Jiffy-Cloz people
cunningly omit four of the staples necessary to finish the job, so that after
indescribable purgatory, the best the subject can possibly achieve is a
sleazy, capricious structure which would reduce any self-respecting moth to
helpless laughter. The cumulative frustration, the tropical heat, and the
soft, ghostly chuckling of the moths are calculated to unseat the strongest
mentality.

In a period of rapid technological change, however, it was inevitable
that a method as cumbersome as the Jiffy-Cloz would be superseded. It
was superseded at exactly nine-thirty Christmas morning by a device called
the Self-Running 10-Inch Scale-Model Delivery-Truck Kit Powered by
Magic Motor, costing twenty-nine cents. About nine on that particular
morning, I was spread-eagled on my bed, indulging in my favorite sport
of mouth-breathing, when a cork fired from a child's air gun mysteriously

lodged in my throat. The pellet proved awkward for a while, but I finally ejected it by flailing the little marksman (and his sister, for good measure) until their welkins rang, and sauntered in to breakfast. Before I could choke down a healing fruit juice, my consort, a tall, regal creature indistinguishable from Cornelia, the Mother of the Gracchi, except that her foot was entangled in a roller skate, swept in. She extended a large, unmistakable box covered with diagrams.

"Now don't start making excuses," she whined. "It's just a simple cardboard toy. The directions are on the back—"

"Look, dear," I interrupted, rising hurriedly and pulling on my overcoat, "it clean slipped my mind. I'm supposed to take a lesson in crosshatching at Zim's School of Cartooning today."

"On Christmas?" she asked suspiciously.

"Yes, it's the only time they could fit me in," I countered glibly. "This is the big week for crosshatching, you know, between Christmas and New Year's."

"Do you think you ought to go in your pajamas?" she asked.

"Oh, that's O.K.," I smiled. "We often work in our pajamas up at Zim's. Well, goodbye now. If I'm not home by Thursday, you'll find a cold snack in the safe-deposit box." My subterfuge, unluckily, went for naught, and in a trice I was sprawled on the nursery floor, surrounded by two lambkins and ninety-eight segments of the Self-Running, 10-Inch Scale-Model Delivery-Truck Construction Kit.

The theory of the kit was simplicity itself, easily intelligible to Kettering of General Motors, Professor Millikan, or any first-rate physicist. Taking as my starting point the only sentence I could comprehend, "Fold down on all lines marked 'fold down'; fold up on all lines marked 'fold up,'" I set the children to work and myself folded up with an album of views of Chili Williams. In a few moments, my skin was suffused with a delightful tingling sensation and I was ready for the second phase, lightly referred to in the directions as "Preparing the Spring Motor Unit." As nearly as I could determine after twenty minutes of mumbling, the Magic Motor ("No Electricity—No Batteries—Nothing to Wind—Motor Never Wears Out") was an accordion-pleated affair operating by torsion, attached to the axles. "It is necessary," said the text, "to cut a slight notch in each of the axles with a knife (see Fig C). To find the exact place to cut this notch, lay one of the axles over diagram at bottom of page."

"Well *now* we're getting someplace!" I boomed, with a false gusto that deceived nobody. "Here, Buster, run in and get Daddy a knife."

"I dowanna," quavered the boy, backing away. "You always cut yourself at this stage." I gave the wee fellow an indulgent pat on the head that flattened it slightly, to teach him civility, and commandeered a long, serrated bread knife from the kitchen. "Now watch me closely, children," I ordered. "We place the axle on the diagram as in Fig. C, applying a strong downward pressure in the knife handle at all times." The axle must have been a factory second, because an instant later I was in the bathroom grinding my teeth in agony and attempting to stanch the flow of blood. Ultimately, I succeeded in contriving a rough bandage and slipped back into the nursery without awakening the children's suspicions. An agreeable surprise awaited me. Displaying a mechanical aptitude clearly inherited from their sire, the rascals had put together the chassis of the delivery truck.

"Very good indeed," I complimented (naturally, one has to exaggerate praise to develop a child's self-confidence). "Let's see—what's the next step? Ah, yes. 'Lock into box shape by inserting tabs C, D, E, F, G, H, J, K, and L into slots C, D, E, F, G, H, J, K, and L. Ends of front axle should be pushed through holes A and B.'" While marshaling the indicated parts in their proper order, I emphasized to my rapt listeners the necessity of patience and perseverance. "Haste makes waste, you know," I reminded them. "Rome wasn't built in a day. Remember, your daddy isn't always going to be here to show you."

"Where *are* you going to be?" they demanded.

"In the movies if I can arrange it," I snarled. Poising tabs C, D, E, F, G, H, J, K and L in one hand and the corresponding slots in the other, I essayed a union of the two, but in vain. The moment I made one set fast and tackled another, tab and slot would part company, thumbing their noses at me. Although the children were too immature to understand, I saw in a flash where the trouble lay. Some idiotic employee at the factory had punched out the wrong design, probably out of sheer spite. So that was his game, eh? I set my lips in a grim line and, throwing one hundred and fifty-seven pounds of fighting fat into the effort, pounded the component parts into a homogeneous mass.

"There," I said with a gasp, "that's close enough. Now then, who wants candy? One, two, three—everybody off to the candy store!"

"We wanna finish the delivery truck!" they wailed. "Mummy, he won't let us finish the delivery truck!" Threats, cajolery, bribes were of no avail. In their jungle code, a twenty-nine-cent gewgaw bulked larger than a parent's love. Realizing that I was dealing with a pair of monomaniacs, I determined to show them who was master and wildly began locking the cardboard units helter-skelter, without any regard for the directions. When sections refused to fit, I gouged them with my nails and forced them together, cackling shrilly. The side panels collapsed; with a bestial oath, I drove a safety pin through them and lashed them to the roof. I used paper clips, bobby pins, anything I could lay my hands on. My fingers fairly flew and my breath whistled in my throat. "You want a delivery truck, do you?" I panted. "All right, I'll show you!" As merciful blackness closed in, I was on my hands and knees, bunting the infernal thing along with my nose and whinnying, "Roll, confound you, roll!"

"Absolute quiet," a carefully modulated voice was saying, "and fifteen of the white tablets every four hours." I opened my eyes carefully in the darkened room. Dimly I picked out a knifelike character actor in pince-nez lenses and a morning coat folding a stethoscope into his bag. "Yes," he added thoughtfully, "if we play our cards right, this ought to be a long, expensive recovery." From far away, I could hear my wife's voice bravely trying to control her anxiety.

"What if he becomes restless, Doctor?"

"Get him a detective story," returned the leech. "Or better still, a nice, soothing picture puzzle—something he can do with his hands."

1. In this humorously exaggerated account, Perelman is satirizing the do-it-yourself craze in America, among other things. How is this fad related to processes? Is Perelman satirizing the process as such?
2. What implicit criticism of process literature does this essay make? Explain.
3. The first paragraph refers to the "the shortest, cheapest method of inducing a nervous breakdown ever perfected." How is this statement related to the development of the essay and to its criticism of certain processes?
4. Are the processes in this essay natural or artificial? How does the nature of the process affect Perelman's specific points of complaint?
5. Like Robert Benchley, S. J. Perelman uses distorted syntax or unlikely word order for humorous effect. Point out examples. In what other ways do "The Treasurer's Report" and "Insert Flap A" resemble each other in theme and technique?

José Ortega y Gasset

THE DECLINE OF THE NOVEL

PUBLISHERS COMPLAIN THAT NOVELS DO NOT SELL WELL, AND IT IS TRUE that the reading public buys fewer novels while the demand for books of a theoretical character is relatively increasing. This statistical fact, even if there were no more intrinsic reasons, would suffice to make us suspect that something is amiss with the literary genre of the novel. When I hear a friend, particularly if he is a young writer, calmly announce that he is working on a novel, I am appalled, and I feel that in his case I should be trembling in my boots. Perhaps I am wrong, but I cannot help scenting behind such an equanimity an alarming dose of incomprehension. To produce a good novel has always been a difficult thing. But while, before, it was enough to have talent, the difficulty has now grown immeasurably, for to be a gifted novelist is no longer a guaranty for producing a good novel.

Unawareness of this fact is one component of the aforementioned incomprehension. Anyone who gives a little thought to the conditions of a work of art must admit that a literary genre may wear out. One cannot dismiss the subject by comfortably assuming that artistic creation depends on nothing but the artist's personal power called inspiration or talent—in which case decadence of a genre would be due exclusively to an accidental lack of talents, and the sudden appearance of a man of genius would at any time automatically turn the tide. Better beware of notions like genius and inspiration; they are a sort of magic wand and should be used sparingly by anybody who wants to see things clearly. Imagine a woodsman, the strongest of woodsmen, in the Sahara desert. What good are his bulging muscles and his sharp ax? A woodsman without woods is an abstraction. And the same applies to artists. Talent is but a subjective disposition that is brought to bear upon a certain material. The material is independent of individual gifts; and when it is lacking, genius and skill are of no avail.

Just as every animal belongs to a species, every literary work belongs to a genre. (The theory of Benedetto Croce, who denies the existence of literary forms in this sense, has left no trace in aesthetics.) A literary genre, the same as a zoological species, means a certain stock of possibilities; and since in art only those possibilities count which are different enough not to be considered replicas of one another, the resources of a literary genre are definitely limited. It is erroneous to think of the novel—and I refer to the modern novel in particular—as of an endless field capable of rendering ever new forms. Rather it may be compared to a vast but finite quarry. There exist a definite number of possible themes for the novel. The workmen of the primal hour had no trouble finding new blocks—new characters, new themes. But present-day writers face the fact that only narrow and concealed veins are left them.

With this stock of objective possibilities, which is the genre, the artistic talent works, and when the quarry is worked out talent, however great, can achieve nothing. Whether a genre is altogether done for can, of course, never be decided with mathematical rigor; but it can at times be decided with sufficient practical approximation. At least, that the material is getting scarce may appear frankly evident.

This, I believe, is now happening to the novel. It has become practically impossible to find new subjects. Here we come upon the first cause of the enormous difficulty, an objective not a personal difficulty, of writing an acceptable novel at this advanced stage.

During a certain period novels could thrive on the mere novelty of their subjects which gratuitously added an induced current, as it were, to the value proper of the material. Thus many novels seemed readable which we now think a bore. It is not for nothing that the novel is called "novel." The difficulty of finding new subjects is accompanied by another, perhaps more serious, dilemma. As the store of possible subjects is more and more depleted the sensibility of the reading public becomes subtler and more fastidious. Works that yesterday would still have passed, today are deemed insipid. Not only is the difficulty of finding new subjects steadily growing, but ever "newer" and more extraordinary ones are needed to impress the reader. This is the second cause of the difficulty with which the genre as such is faced in our time.

Proof that the present decline is due to more fundamental causes than a possibly inferior quality of contemporary novels is given by the fact that, as it becomes more difficult to write novels, the famous old or classical ones appear less good. Only a very few have escaped drowning in the reader's boredom.

This development is inevitable and need not dishearten the novelist. On the contrary; for they themselves are bringing it about. Little by little they train their public by sharpening the perception, and refining the taste, of their readers. Each work that is better than a previous one is detrimental to this and all others of the same level. Triumph cannot help being cruel. As the victor wins the battle at the cost of smashing the foe, thus the superior work automatically becomes the undoing of scores of other works that used to be highly thought of.

In short, I believe that the genre of the novel, if it is not yet irretrievably exhausted, has certainly entered its last phase, the scarcity of possible subjects being such that writers must make up for it by the exquisite quality of the other elements that compose the body of a novel.

1. Is this essay an example of process, cause and effect, hypothesis, or all three? Explain.
2. What is the basic data upon which Ortega y Gasset builds his ideas? Is this data supported by specific evidence? Or is the fact of the novel's decline a supposition in itself?
3. What is the hypothesis advanced in the essay? Is the causal relationship a single one, multiple cause and single effect, single cause and multiple effects, or a causal sequence?
4. Does the hypothesis meet the requirements of a valid hypothesis? Why or why not?
5. Are you prepared to accept Ortega y Gasset's explanation or not? Why?

Stanley Casson

CHALLENGE TO COMPLACENCY: WHAT
FUTURE ARCHAEOLOGISTS WILL THINK OF US

THE ARCHAEOLOGIST HAS A COLD AND CALLOUS EYE. IT LOOKS BACKWARD TO the past and forward to the future and seldom pauses on the present. Walking down Fifth Avenue or Regent Street, I cannot help letting my imagination leap forward a thousand years or so. How, in that remote future, will these wide streets and concrete palaces look? What problems will they hold for the excavator of a new world that has prospered in some distant part of the globe, who has sent his reconnaissance expedition to investigate the enormous mounds, smooth and rolling and grass-covered, that will then mark the sites of capital cities of an almost-forgotten civilization?

You smile! Surely that can never happen, you say. And so smiled the Minoans of Cnossus, the ancient Indians of the vast city of Mohendjodaro in the Indus Valley, and the Mayas in their indestructible palaces of Yucatan. Yet they were forgotten for thousands of years, and only the chance of excavation brought them to light. Of course it will happen to us, yet we live in the unshaken complacency of an immovable belief that we are permanent—like those ancient Agrigentines of whom a Greek once said that "they live as if they were to die tomorrow, and build as if they were to live forever."

When the crash comes and civilization decides to shift elsewhere, when London and New York are as forgotten as was Athens after the fall of Rome, or as Persepolis after Alexander had burned it, how will the change come about by which London and New York are transformed into those delectable grassy hillocks that delight the eye of the prospective excavator?

Of course one must make assumptions. Cnossus or Persepolis did not perish overnight. A mighty sacking or conflagration is not fatal. London in 1666 started at once to recover and rebuild; Cnossus was sacked and ruined, but not reduced to a heap of rubble. Persepolis could have been

This material originally appeared in *The Atlantic Monthly* (July, 1935). Reprinted by permission of *The Atlantic Monthly*.

remade and restored. One must assume certain political and social catastrophes that make it impossible for the inhabitants to return or to remake; some financial breakdown that forbids repair, upkeep, and restoration. And if in the dry and gentle climate of the Mediterranean, or in the dryer but hotter climate of India, several civilizations that in their bloom thought themselves as immutable as rock, as unforgettable as the sun, perished from the memory of man as utterly as if they consisted of mere squalid mud-hut villages, how much more shall London, New York, Paris, or Berlin be reduced to rolling hills of rubble under the impact of a climate that destroys with four times the speed of the climate of the Mediterranean or of India!

For what is the chief enemy of a great city, or, for that matter, of any building, but water? Water that seeps into cracks, water that freezes in those cracks and expands with a slow destructive force as great as dynamite, water that drips its way through ferro-concrete and oxidizes the immortal strength of iron and steel and reduces their power to heaps of red dust.

Let us look ahead. Imagine some devastating European-American war, a war in which the whole world is involved. Neglect grows as all energy is concentrated on the vigor of war. For a period of years there are no repairs done to cities and their buildings, no improvements, no strengthening, no painting of steel girders or refurbishing of stone surfaces. Imagine London or New York as was Vienna in 1919—paint peeling from walls, plaster cracking, encompassing grime and mildew in holes and crannies and corners. And then imagine a financial crash more desperate, more irremediable than any that the world has suffered in the last few years, a crash from which there is no escape, for the cure of which no Roosevelt appears like a *deus ex machina*. Fortune is not always so obliging as to produce a magician to move every rock, and we must assume an accumulation of rocks with no magician at all.

The financial breakdown is followed by political chaos, political chaos by public insecurity. Out of this chaos only one element will emerge organized, and that is crime. The criminal elements will feed like parasites on a tottering fabric of civilization in a way far more deadly than ever in history, if only because crime can now obtain weapons which make its offensive quality more deadly. Failure of means of communication provides just the conditions most suitable for the growth of criminal organization, which in any case has its own channels of communication. Then famine and perhaps disease reduce the population to a minimum, and so in the end develops a situation in which mass emigration has become a necessity.

The climate of the Northern States of America would force a population thus swiftly deprived of its ordinary means of subsistence steadily to the south, whether to South America or to the Southern States does not matter. But in any breakdown of organized civilization a move to a climate where the essential comforts of a primitive mode of existence are more easily obtainable becomes obvious. And so from a by now barbarized North would move upon a still stable South a horde of people virtually indistinguishable from the barbaric Europeans who moved southward upon the stable culture of the Mediterranean at various periods of history. Thus fell Mycenae and Troy, and thus many attempts were made from the north upon Constantinople, which failed only because of the immensely superior defenses of that city.

A similar situation in England would be less easily evaded by mass movement. For in chaotic conditions the English Channel would prove a tremendous obstacle, only to be crossed by small numbers aided by a few enterprising craft, the property of pirates out for gain. Only the relatively rich would escape, and the remainder would die of starvation far more rapidly than in America; although, on the other hand, the rigors of the climate would not be so fatal to humanity as in America.

Such gloomy prognostications as these rise to my mind when I look at the neat complacent buildings of Regent Street or of the long alleys of New York. Perhaps I am a pessimist, but then I am not such a fool as to imagine that the particular kind of world I live in will go on for more than its fair share of time. Just as the average Londoner or New Yorker is incredulous that his city should not be there ten thousand years hence, so to me it is incredible that it should. And, indeed, London all but faded out of existence after the Roman departure from Britain, while New York faced catastrophe only three years ago! And the ruins of Palmyra and Baalbek and Luxor cry loudly to the living that they are only leaseholders of property that will, after the 99 or 999 or 9999 years' lease is up, revert once more to the ground landlord.

1. What kind of hypothesis does Casson advance in this essay? Explain
2. Point out examples of valid causation in the description of the decline of New York.
3. Which of the possible hypotheses set forth do you think will be most likely to occur? Why?

4. In his opening paragraph, Casson says his essay results from a "leap" taken by his imagination. Is he merely guessing or does his hypothesis rest on scientific probability? Explain.
5. What causal words does Casson use to establish his hypothesis? Does he accept as facts ideas which are really conjecture?
6. Do you consider the hypothesis made in "Challenge to Complacency" a valid or likely one?

CHAPTER 3

LOGICAL ORDER: MACHINES, ORGANISMS, ORGANIZATIONS

"We are a machine made to live; we are organized for that purpose, and such is our nature. . . ."
NAPOLEON BONAPARTE, LETTER TO DR. ANTOMMARCHI,
October 14, 1820

Whereas chronological order is a way of looking at actions or events, *logical order is a way of arranging objects, tangible or intangible, to understand them better.* Taken from the Greek word *logos* ("pattern" or "plan"), logical order is, obviously, arrangement determined by the system of thought called logic. It is a means of conceiving the nature of single entities or relationships between several entities.

Whatever word you choose to refer to an entity—"thing," "object," "phenomenon"—basically you are conceiving of a structure with some principle of organic unity. This structure may be as concrete as a brick wall or as abstract as Plato's code of civic responsibility (see "Crito" on page 390), but you view it as a synthesis, or composite unity made up of parts into a recognizable whole. For our purposes, all composite unities are *organic structures;* these are either *tangible* or *intangible;* and tangible structures are either *active* (dynamic) or *passive* (non-dynamic). The same general principles of logical order apply as well to intangible organic structures as to tangible, but to avoid discussing matters not directly related to the rhetorical uses of logical order, we shall concern ourselves for now with concrete, or tangible, entities only.

Of the billions of tangible entities that lie within the range of human experience, the vast majority are *passive.* From the tiniest grain of sand to the moon, such structures are interesting primarily for the way their parts apparently constitute a whole rather than for the way they initiate and carry out some action. The passive *thing* may become the agent or instrument of some active structure and thus, like the moon, become involved in a process or even develop secondary qualities (gravitational pull, for instance). In general, however, passive entities remain inert, being lifeless and non-dynamic. Writing about them is relatively simple. Their parts are described and the arrangement of these parts is explained; sometimes the process that produced them is dealt with. An essay on a stalagmite, for example, would be likely to outline the way it was formed as well as to describe its form and composition. The *passive* organic structure is usually the *end product* of a process.

The active organic structure, on the other hand, instigates and carries out some process. Some structures—mechanical in nature—are created by human beings to function actively; others—biological by nature—are innately capable of carrying out certain processes. The type of logical order most closely related to chronological order is that treating such active organic structures. Similarly, the problems arising from writing about active entities are related to the problems of prose about processes. By way of transition from strictly chronological order and rhetoric to the logical methods of treating numbers of phenomena, we may look closely at the three chief kinds of active organic structures—machines, organisms, and organizations—and ways of thinking and writing about them.

MACHINES

There are several terms synonymous with *machine:* device, gadget, appliance, apparatus, mechanism. The distinctions in meaning between these are slight, and there is little point in trying to differentiate between them. For our purposes, a machine is a *combination of functioning parts into an apparatus that performs some work.* We may list the essential components of a machine as: two or more separate parts, each carrying on some action; an interrelation of such actions to form a coherent process; the accomplishment of work by this process.

The one thing all machines have in common is that they are *manufactured* (from the Latin phrase, "made by hand"). Every machine is devised by a human mind to carry on an action helpful to man, and its parts are arranged with this purpose in view. Even weirdly nonsensical machines— the "Rube Goldbergs"—exist for some purpose, perhaps to satirize the human love of gadgets or to solve a theoretical problem, such as perpetual motion. Devising machinery is the business of thousands of engineers, and manufacturing this machinery occupies the time and energy of millions of workers today. Countless hours are spent in operating machines. Consider, for instance, how many machines—from alarm clock to automobile—are involved in your daily life.

Even if you are never compelled to explain a machine in written prose, you can hardly avoid reading a good deal of such "technological" writing, though it may be nothing more than a car owner's manual or a washing machine booklet. If you become involved in engineering or manufacturing, however, you are likely to be writing about machines for the enlightenment of other people. In any case, improving your understanding of rhetorical ways of dealing with machines will be helpful to you, since effective writing about mechanisms depends on your awareness of the logical principles underlying the construction and operation of these artificial organic structures.

First of all, establish the *purpose* which the machine fulfills. Since all machines perform some sort of work, the work the machine does is the purpose of its being. Machines exist to wash dishes, to transport (automobiles), to alert (doorbells), to warn (sirens), and so forth. Since machines are contrived by people, the "purpose" of a machine should always be thought of as the human use to which it is put. Obviously, a machine can have primary and secondary uses: a dishwasher primarily exists to wash dishes, thought it can be used as a bin for potatoes, a platform, or a storage place for old shoes. The *purpose* of a machine is its *intended* use.

The actual way the parts of the machine carry out a process are the *function* of that machine. Function may be defined as *the interrelated actions performed by the parts of the machine*. By this definition, the *function* of a doorbell is the passing of alternating electrical current through a wire, once contact is made through a button, so that a metal clapper is pulled against a sounding object, and repeatedly released. *Function,* in speaking of a machine, is thus another way of indicating *its method of performing*.

Finally, any written explanation of a machine should deal with the *operative principle* it employs. Each machine has some source of energy that causes its parts to commence functioning and enables the machine to carry on its process. This source may be the muscle power of a man or animal, or it may be a natural force (wind, moving water, gravity, heat of the sun). *The way the source of energy is utilized by the machine* is its *operative principle*. Many different operative principles are used by modern machines. Leverage, gravitational pull, the magnetic field, exploding gases, metallic expansion, liquid pressure, creation of a vacuum—the fascinating variety of operative principles provides an interesting focal point for writing about machines, as well as being the primary interest of such fields as thermodynamics and hydraulics.

The specific facets of a machine which the writer selects to emphasize depend in large part on his own interests and the kind of audience he writes for. Ron Ross's article on the Geiger counter, on page 76, is an obviously popularized account of what the counter is for, how it is put together, and how it works. From its initial imitation of the sound of the Geiger counter to the last sentence, Ross's intention in his essay is always to create the physical presence of the mechanism even as he explains its more technical aspects, and he constantly "humanizes" the counter by describing its use by people and its effects on their lives. Although Ross presents vital information about the purpose, function, and operative principle as well as organic structure of the Geiger counter, his essay never becomes a listing of parts or steps in a process. Writing about a machine in prose which is neither so sprightly as to be inaccurate nor so systematic as to be boring is the true test of the technical writer.

ORGANISMS

In general, prose about machines is called technical writing, while rhetoric dealing with organisms is called scientific prose. The difference in root meanings between the two designations shows an important human attitude toward machines and organisms. *Technical* comes from the Greek word, *techne,* meaning *skill* or *craft,* and implying manual dexterity. *Scientific* comes from the Latin, *scio, to know* or *have wisdom,* thus to possess a true insight into the ultimate truth of things. Thus, writing about machines is prose that treats the *craft* or *manufacture* of one kind of organic structure (the non-living), while prose about organisms is scientific in that it deals with *living* organic structures and thus is delving into *vital* (literally, *life*) matters.

Not all writing about organisms is formal or pompous, however, as you will see when you recall that prose concerning organisms ranges from textbooks on chordate anatomy to John James Audubon's *Book of Birds* to a Burpee Seed Catalogue. Prose about the spinal column of a salamander and a paragraph about Queen Wilhelmina tulips may not seem to have much in common initially, but writing either requires something of the same ways of regarding organisms and planning good expository or informational prose about them.

The main qualities that distinguish organisms are these: they are animate (living); they do not require an external source of energy in the way a machine does to begin and continue functioning; they are capable of self-reproduction without human help; they are not manufactured, but constituted by natural processes not fully understood by men. Of course, these general statements need some qualification when you are writing with the utmost accuracy about organisms. To our knowledge, all life, vegetable and animal, requires *some* external energy in order to function. But in broad terms, the statements above are workable tests of organisms. In any event, it can be said that our understanding—and thus, explanations—of them must concern the *constitution* and the *function* of organisms rather than their purpose.

Though the centuries-old question of the *purpose* of certain vegetable and animal growths has tortured the human mind, we are not much closer today to reaching an answer than men ever were. "What is it *for?*" we like to ask; and it surprises us when certain common objects—the staphylococcus or the barnacle or poison ivy—cannot be said to have any "reason" for existing. Our human desire for "tidiness," for "order," is somehow offended, and we strive to think up "purposes" for things that do not require an imputed "purpose" or human application. Hypotheses range from the theological (All things exist to serve and glorify God) to the philosophically optimistic (All is for the best in this best of all possible worlds) to the "scientific" (All organisms exist for the sake of reproduction). In any case, what we actually know about organisms is how their parts are seemingly constituted to form an entity and how that entity carries out a process.

The dividing line between true organisms, which are alive and can reproduce themselves, and the organic compounds that concern the chemist may be a vague one, but generally we can say that the most simple organism is the organic cell, plant or animal. Since the cell is a tangible structure, made of component parts, prose about it can discuss those parts following some principle of spatial or logical order. An essay about the cell might describe the cell wall, chromatin, the nucleus, nucleolus, cytoplasm, etc., show their separate functions, and discuss the relationship of the cell as a whole to the larger body of which it is part. Such an essay combines information about the constitution and function of the cell in a perfectly comprehensible way. With more complex organisms—starfish or amphibians, for instance—a writer may be forced to assume a basic knowledge on his reader's part of structure and organic processes, or he may simplify his explanation to the reader's level of understanding. Theodore Roughley and John Kieran are two naturalists who have the ability to condense vast erudition in readable, informative prose. You can see how they do it on pages 81 and 104.

You will be encountering more complicated rhetorical discussions of organisms in many of your science courses—social and natural—and you will be required to write about them as well. In dealing with organisms, remember that our understanding of their nature or constitution depends to a great extent on the functions they perform; thus the organism is often defined in terms of the process it maintains. You should also remember that since the precise nature of "vital" processes is something of a mystery, many of the steps in the organic process are conjectured, and such hypothetical steps must be more tentatively handled than the steps in a mechanical process deliberately set up by human beings for an express purpose.

ORGANIZATIONS

When a number of self-governing, individual organisms are combined into a working arrangement that carries out established processes, the result is an *organization*. An organization is *a body of people or animals organized for some end or work*. By this definition, a swarm of bees is an organization, and so is your family. The rather troublesome thing about defining the organization is not its encompassing such widely diverse organisms as a gaggle of geese and a Boy Scout troop, but that it is oddly intangible. An organization is not the specific individuals who compose it, since the staff (or personnel or members) of an organization may change and the organization still maintain its distinctive character. In some cases, an organization has a legal existence completely separate from that of the people who make it up. A *corporation*—from the Latin *corpus*, "body"—has the same legal rights and obligations that the single person does, and though it is composed of individual people, no one person or specific group of people is equatable with the legal entity of the corporation.

The difference between the organization and the other kinds of organic structures (machines and organisms) is this: an organization is made up of self-governing, individual organisms complete in themselvse, and thus it cannot be a fusion of parts in the way other organic structures are. The cog in the machine or the nucleus in the cell are really partial identities; that is, they derive their distinctive character from their participation in the function of the organic structure, and their identities are submerged in the total structure. A cog is really nothing but a part of a machine and a nucleus nothing but a vital part of a cell, whereas the human member of an organization is a man or woman with a nature *not* dependent on the function of the organization.

The key to understanding a specific organization and thus to explaining it in prose lies in the *purpose* of that organization. As in the case of machines, the human use of the organization is its reason for existence, or *purpose,* and just as the parts of a machine are fitted together to effect actions performing some work, so the parts of an organization (its management, staff, equipment, and procedures) are put together to accomplish some end or perform some job. You should start your investigation of an organization with a clear understanding of the purpose of its existence.

There can be many purposes for an organization: mutual protection (NATO), self-preservation (a bee hive), administration (the city council), supervision (the P.T.A.), enhancing prestige (the Daughters of the American Revolution), propagating ideals (the Methodist Church), encouraging learning (the Guggenheim Foundation), and so on. Every organization, whether a pride of lions or a tribe of Bantu Kiriki, exists for some purpose, and its existence depends finally upon the successful attainment of its purpose.

The processes, or function, an organization carries on are determined by its reason for existing, and so are the interrelationships of staff members in the jobs they perform, the processes making up the job of each staff member, and the machinery required for these processes. To carry on functions that will attain its purpose, the human organization must possess certain basic resources: a number of people with varying talents; established methods of proceeding that have proved successful previously or appear likely to be successful in the future; an administrational hierarchy; certain basic machinery; and so forth. Obviously, a business organization can be as complex as the Standard Oil Company, functioning over several continents with personnel in the thousands and millions of dollars worth of equipment, or it can be a simple working group of a full-time yard man, his part-time helper, and a lawnmower.

In the last fifty years, writing about organizations has increased in volume and so changed in character that now it is "scientific" as often as not. When you read a study of a *kraal* system of the Africans or one on teenaged gangs in New York City, the arrangement of ideas is likely to be prescribed by the demands of the social sciences; its techniques of development and terminology will follow the uses of rhetoric developed by sociology, psychology, and anthropology. Even contemporary books on ant colonies or a motion picture documentary on a herd of deer follow scientifically methodical steps in explaining objectively the purpose, composition, and functions of organizations.

Martin Mayer's discussion of one segment of a Madison Avenue advertising agency—the sort of agency that "shapes a public image" of a product to sell it—uses some of the sociological techniques of examining an organization. It is taken from a full-length account of how advertising agencies are organized, and why and how they operate, and as you see the intricate interrelationship of one small part of the agency described in Mayer's account of supervising copywriters, you must remember that this is only a segment of a total organization. The highly involved relationships between the people in an organization, the complicated co-ordination of single jobs into an overall process, the numerous kinds of equipment necessary to the process—all these must be fully understood by the would-be interpreter, who is obliged to plan and write carefully if his explanation of the organization is to be intelligible.

Before you undertake to put into a prose composition information about an organization, first determine the nature of the organization. If you want to write about a group such as a lynch mob or a church choir, you had first better be sure that you are confronting a true organization. Ask yourself these questions:

1. Does the group have a reason for existing as a single unit?
2. Does each member of the group have a duty or function that relates to the work of the group as a whole?
3. Does the group carry out an established process?
4. Has the group performed (or is it likely to perform) this process over a period of some time?
5. Does this process have significance for the people who perform it, or for the society in which it takes place?

The answer to all of these questions must be "yes" for the group to be an apt subject for the sort of logical method set up to deal with organizations.

The specific problems of writing about organizations of people or animals reflect some of the matters already touched on in the discussion of machines and organisms. Which component parts should be treated and with what emphasis? Should the essay be "scientific" or "popular," and how much simplification of facts is advisable? What order of discussion will be most lucid for the reader? Answers to these problems must be determined by the nature of the organization, the writer's intention in treating it, and the reader he is aiming for.

Technology, the natural sciences, the social sciences—these vast areas of information depend on man's interest in the individual machine, organism, and organization. As different as they are, each shows the same fundamental preoccupation with organic structures, and each utilizes the same logical methods of investigation. The quantity of literature about machines, organisms, and organizations about us is the inevitable consequence of our living in a society that is industrial, scientific, and democratic. Understanding technological and scientific literature helps to give us specific information not only about *things* but also about the customary habits of thinking about things our society has adopted.

I. Questions for Review
   1. What is logical order? How does it differ from chronological order?
   2. What are organic structures? How do passive and active organic structures differ?
   3. What is a machine? What do these terms mean as related to machines: purpose, function, operative principle?
   4. What is an organism? How does it differ from a machine?
   5. Which is more important in organisms: purpose or function? Why?
   6. What is an organization? How does it differ from machines and organisms?
   7. What are the tests of an organization?
   8. What professions are most concerned with machines? With organisms?
   9. Give examples of literature dealing with machines, organisms, and organizations.

II. Exercises
   1. Which of the following are not machines? Why?

A. Slide rules	F. Ball point pens
B. Model airplanes	G. Kaleidoscopes
C. Portable radios	H. Ambulances
D. Sundials	I. Windshield wipers
E. Guillotines	J. Stethoscopes

2. Identify each as a mechanism, organism, or organization:
   A. A coral reef
   B. Penicillin
   C. The United Nations
   D. Racing punts
   E. Moss
   F. A colony of ants
   G. Orchids
   H. A cloud
   I. A flock of starlings
   J. Aphids
   K. The Boston Symphony Orchestra
   L. Sea anemones
   M. Bathyspheres
   N. Hospitals
   O. Bunsen burners
   P. The Volunteer Firemen of Winesburg, Ohio

3. Give the purpose, function, and operative principle of:
   A. Typewriters
   B. Electric sanders
   C. Refrigerators
   D. T.V. sets
   E. Neon signs
   F. Watermills
   G. Phonograph turntables
   H. Oil furnaces
   I. Sonar
   J. Radar

4. Are these organizations or not? Explain.
   A. A movie audience
   B. The history department of your college
   C. A filling station crew
   D. The employees of a supermarket
   E. The customers of a supermarket
   F. A herd of buffalo
   G. Jehovah's Witnesses
   H. The population of Louisville, Ky.
   I. A circus
   J. The St. Louis Zoo
   K. The residents of your dormitory
   L. Vegetarians
   M. The editors of *The New Yorker*
   N. The Independent Grocers of America
   O. The British Commonwealth

III. *Questions for Thought, Discussion, and Writing*
   1. Must all organic structures be related to a process, actively or passively? Explain.
   2. Can you think of any organic structures, aside from organizations, which are intangible? Would a field of study, such as fine art, or a musical composition qualify as intangible organic structures?
   3. Can you think of any machines which do not have a purpose?
   4. There are many organic structures—Rembrandt's paintings, men's neckties, a peacock's plumes, ragweed—which seem to have no practi-

cal "purpose" or "end." Can you think of any "purpose" which these examples may have?

5. Is it legitimate to say that men create some organic structures purely for aesthetic reasons and that these objects justify their existence by their aesthetic nature? Explain.

6. Dr. Albert Schweitzer, the great thinker and humanitarian, has declared that all life is sacred; yet he is a doctor who spends most of his time in trying to eradicate organisms which cause disease. Is this a contradiction or not? Discuss.

7. What justification for the existence of organisms is given by the philosopher Leibnitz? By Darwin, the naturalist? By the early Christian theologians? By such Oriental religious as Jain? With which, if any, do you agree? Why?

8. Some thinkers believe that all organizations are set up because the people in them are weak and afraid and seek protection in numbers. Among others, Thomas Hobbes has said organizations result from weakness and fear. Do you agree or not? Why?

9. Can there be a "reason" for an organization of animals in the same sense as there is a reason for a human organization? Can an organization therefore exist without a reason or purpose?

10. Write a theme on one of these subjects:
    A. My Family as an Organization
    B. The Purposes of Organizations That I Belong To
    C. The Human Body as a Machine
    D. A Comparison and Contrast between Organizations and Machines
    E. How a Clock (or some other mechanism) Is Put Together
    F. How a Bicycle (or some other machine) Operates
    G. The Structure of a Flower Petal (or some other organism)
    H. How Photosynthesis (or some other vital process) Works

Ron Ross

ATOMIC AGE ALARM

CLICK . . . CLICK . . . CLICK, CLICK, CLICK, CLICK—FASTER AND FASTER, AN ominous signal is heard. The atomic alarm has sounded. It can be a warning, in time, against atomic bombs—or it can be the death rattle of our civilization: a harsh, staccato noise emitted from an electronic device that scientists call a Geiger counter. It clicks out its warning of radiation, such as that emitted from radium, or more pertinently from the mother stuff of atomic bombs, uranium. Whenever dangerous radioactivity is sprayed out in radiations—X-ray-like gamma rays, alpha particles which are helium hearts, beta rays which are fleet electrons—the Geiger counter clicks.

Tomorrow, in a world deadly fearful of illicit atomic bombs or atomic materials, Geiger counters will be the unsleeping mechanical policemen of the atomic age. You may not read about it, but the chances are that every passenger who steps off an international airplane or debarks from a transoceanic steamer will be given the once-over with a Geiger counter. At the gateways to our public institutions, at the freight and package entrances to our critical and important offices, these warning devices will be on guard. Patrolling airplanes will carry them routinely to chart any unusual activity in the upper air. The alarm could be sounded if a radioactive gas attack seemed approaching. At critical and important places, such as 42nd and Broadway and atop the Golden Gate Bridge, the counters will be on watch. Just as radar will constantly scan our frontiers for incoming ships by air and sea, so the detectors of radioactivity will be part of the nation's defense.

The difference between life and death in the future may be a metallic tube. This tube is the heart of the Geiger counter. Tell-tale radiations from uranium, plutonium or other radioactive materials sound the atomic alarm when they strike the remarkable tube of the Geiger counter. These rays cannot be seen with our eyes and are not felt by our bodies. The most powerful ray from atomic bomb material is the gamma ray. This is a sort of shortwave X-ray. It is only one tenth as long as the shortest X-ray but it

From *Science News Letter*, June 14, 1947, 378–379. By permission of Science Service, Inc. and the author.

is usually many times as powerful. Beta rays are high speed electrons, the negatively charged particles which are a part of all atoms. They are not so penetrating as gamma rays, but are more powerful than alpha rays, which are composed of "stripped" helium atoms. Hiding, or shielding, the rays of uranium from the tube of the Geiger counter would require huge amounts of lead for even a small bit of material. Sneaking an atomic bomb or its materials into an area guarded by the counter will be difficult, if not impossible.

The Geiger counter was first developed nearly 40 years ago by a German professor, Hans Geiger, and the famous English physicist, Lord Rutherford. Later, Geiger and a German colleague, W. Mueller, improved the counter so that it could count large numbers of particles in a short time. The instrument is formally known as the Geiger-Mueller counter.

The counter is a million times more sensitive than most of the devices in scientific laboratories. It measures the ultimate particles of matter. A single particle of an atom triggers a click from the counter. Yet, this sensitive instrument is amazingly simple. A delicate electrical balance is set up inside the tube. When a bit of an atom, a ray given off from uranium or other radioactive material, penetrates the thin wall of the tube, it upsets this balance. An electrical charge is given off. This charge registers as a click for each ray entering the tube.

The metallic tube may be of many different sizes. Scientists at the National Bureau of Standards have developed a hypodermic needle type of counter tube. This is hardly bigger than a small needle and is used for radioactive tracer work. A novel counter was built from an empty tooth paste tube. More common types of counter use metal tubes an inch or more in diameter. The tube may be enclosed in glass or have a glass window. The thickness of the wall of the tube is important. This determines which rays will be detected by the counter. For spotting radioactive material, a metal tube which may block alpha and beta rays can be used. To detect uranium, a gamma ray counter is sufficient. These powerful rays can warn of radioactivity without help from beta and alpha radiations.

Inside the tube of the Geiger counter is a wire running the length of the tube. The wire connects insulating disks which seal the ends of the tube. The tube contains a gas at low pressure. High voltage is applied to establish a strong electrical field between the wire and the tube. The voltage is high enough so that the gas is just ready to "break down." This establishes the necessary delicate electrical balance. The balance is broken by a ray penetrating the tube. This penetrating ray rips the gas molecules and frees charged particles, called ions. This produces the electrical discharge. When the discharge is amplified by the Geiger counter, you hear a click. Each time a ray penetrates the tube, it sets off the electrical discharge and you hear a click.

Even away from uranium and other well-known radioactive materials, there is some clicking. Powerful cosmic rays from outer space penetrate the tube and cause clicks. Some materials which are not thought of as radioactive may send out some radiation which can produce some clicking. But normally, the clicking of the counter is irregular. You can count the clicks in a minute. When radioactive material is brought into the room near a counter, the clicks increase. They become a steady clicking, faster and faster as the material is brought closer. This is the atomic alarm system in action.

1. Do you consider "Atomic Age Alarm" a successful piece of explanatory prose? Why? What device does Ross use to make the Geiger counter interesting?
2. Point out passages which deal with the *function* of the mechanism. The *purpose*. The *operative principle*.
3. Which of the elements of mechanisms (structure, operative process, purpose) is Ross most concerned with in this essay? Explain.
4. Does this essay follow the order of dealing with mechanisms set up in the chapter? Why does Ross follow the one used?
5. Point out any examples of technical words not easily understood or not defined clearly. Is the essay as a whole intelligible to the layman? Discuss.

Sir James Jeans

THE DISTANCES OF STARS

THE SOLAR SYSTEM HAS OCCUPIED THE FOREGROUND OF OUR PICTURE OF the universe, because its members are incomparably nearer to us than other astronomical bodies. As a preliminary to filling in the rest of the picture let us imagine the various objects in the universe arranged in the order of their distances from the earth. Disregarding bodies much smaller than the earth, such as the moon, other planetary satellites and comets, we must give first place to the planets Venus and Mars, which approach to within 26 and 35 millions of miles of the earth respectively. Next in order comes Mercury with a closest approach of 47 million miles, and then the sun at about 93 million miles. Other planets follow in turn until we reach Neptune at a distance of 2800 million miles.

After this comes a great gap—the gap which divides the solar system from the rest of the universe. The first object on the far side of the gap is the faint star Proxima Centauri, at a distance of no less than 25,000,000 million miles, or more than 8000 times the distance of Neptune. Close upon this come the two components of the binary star α Centauri at 25,-300,000 million miles; these, with Proxima Centauri, form a triple system of stars which are not only near together in the sky, but are voyaging through space permanently in one another's company. After this come three faint stars, Munich 15,040, Wolf 359, and Lalande, 21,185, at 36, 47 and 49 million million miles respectively and then Sirius, the brightest star in the sky, at 51 million million miles. Comparing these distances with the distances of the planets, we see that the nearest stars are almost exactly a million times as remote as the nearest planets.

A simple scale model may help us to visualise the vastness of the gulf which divides the planets from the stars. If we represent the earth's orbit by a circle of the size of the full stops of the type used in this book (circles of a hundredth of an inch radius) the sun becomes an entirely invisible speck of dust and the earth an ultra-microscopic particle a millionth of an inch in diameter. On this same scale the distance to the nearest star, Proxima

Centauri, is about 75 yards, while that to Sirius is about 150 yards. We see vividly the isolation of the solar system in space and the immensity of the gap which separates the planets from the stars.

Before parting from this model, let us notice that the distance of one hundred million light-years to the farthest object so far discussed by astronomy is represented on the same scale by a distance of about a million miles. In this model, then, the universe is millions of miles in diameter, our sun shrinks to a speck of dust and the earth becomes less than a millionth part of a speck of dust. The inhabitant of the earth may well pause to consider the probable objective importance of this speck of dust to the scheme of the universe as a whole.

1. "The Distance of the Stars" is an explanation of a physical relationship. Does it treat a mechanism or an organization? Explain.
2. Is the universe, as a "structural object," a proper subject for the type of approach usually confined to machines, organisms, and organizations? Why?
3. Is a process treated in this essay, either directly or implicitly?
4. What method of logical order does Sir James use to help us conceive of the structure of the earth, its solar system, and the stars? Point out uses of familiar comparisons.
5. This explanation of the universe was written in 1929. Is it still valid according to modern theory? Is it a helpful example of the way a technical subject can be made understandable through a written exposition? How?

Theodore C. Roughley

STARFISH

STARFISH OF DIVERSE SIZES, FORMS, AND COLOURS ABOUND EVERYWHERE on the reef flats from the most northern to the most southern limits of the Barrier; in size they may vary from an inch or less to over a foot in diameter, from a fraction of an ounce to several pounds in weight; in form they range from kinds with small bodies and long, radiating arms to those with squat, bulky, cushion-shaped bodies and arms reduced to mere vestiges.

Undoubtedly the most common, most conspicuous and most widely distributed is a large blue starfish that abounds on almost every reef; it is conspicuous by its size, which varies from about eight to twelve inches across the arms (smaller ones are rarely if ever seen on the reef flats), and by its colour which is a cobalt blue of wonderful purity with inconspicuous lighter spots distributed everywhere over the surface. The body of this starfish is reduced to a minimum; it is formed by the junction of the five long arms which are almost three-quarters of an inch thick at their bases. Most starfish have a tendency to conceal themselves amongst the coral or under boulders in the daytime but this blue *Linckia* is usually found lying on the sand in most exposed situations.

Equally striking though far less abundant is a bright red species with a much larger body and with arms less well defined. Extending along the surface of each arm is a series of rounded black protuberances which add considerably to its beauty and help to throw it into even greater relief.

Far more substantial than either of the above is a species that has the arms reduced to bluntly triangular projections, while the body is extremely bulky and resembles a pentagonal cushion. It is known generally as the pincushion starfish and may attain a diameter of upwards of a foot and a weight of several pounds. Its colour is very variable, ranging from olive-green to reddish-brown, variously spotted and mottled on the upper surface.

Thus amongst the giants of the Barrier Reef starfish we have an extreme divergency of shape, and the multitude of smaller species will be found to conform more or less closely to one or another of them.

Looked at from above, starfish are seen to be covered with a hard, leathery integument, but if turned over they will be found to have a groove extending along the whole length of each arm and meeting at the centrally situated mouth. These grooves are bordered by a great number of small, muscular tubes that can be stretched out or withdrawn at will; they are known as tube-feet and by their means the starfish is able to crawl about, though always very sluggishly. The tube-feet are remarkable little structures, unique in the animal world on account of the fact that their activities are dependent on a supply of water for their expansion and contraction. When the animal requires them to expand it pumps them full of water which distends them greatly, and when it is necessary to contract them the water is withdrawn. Each is provided with a sucker-like extremity and walking is accomplished by pushing a series in the direction it is desired to take, attaching them to the surface and then contracting them to draw the body forward. The suction of the tube-feet is remarkably strong and if a starfish is pulled from a rock many of the feet will probably be found to remain adherent to it.

Equally characteristic are the feeding habits of starfish. Much of the food is conducted to the mouth by a sort of hand-to-hand movement of the tube-feet, but there are occasions when prey is encountered much too large to pass through the mouth. Under similar circumstances most other animals would bite or rasp the surface to remove pieces sufficiently small to handle, but the starfish has not the means at its disposal for doing either of these things and so it performs a far more remarkable feat—it forces its baggy stomach through its mouth, envelops the prey with it and digests it before again withdrawing its stomach into its interior.

In Europe and America certain species of starfish are a menace to oysters and do considerable damage to those lying loose on the beds. For a long time the manner in which the starfish opened the oyster remained a mystery, but it is now known to envelop itself round the shell and, attaching its tube-feet to both valves, it exerts a firm and steady pressure in opposite directions. The large adductor muscle which holds the two valves of the shell together, although very powerful, gradually tires under the continual strain and at last relaxes, allowing the valves of the shell to gape. The starfish then inserts its protrusible stomach into the oyster and dissolves away the flesh.

Naturally the oyster-growers wage war on the starfish. At one time, whenever one was brought up in the dredge it was promptly chopped in two and thrown overboard. Little did they realize that they were thereby increasing the pests they were so anxious to destroy, for each half is capable of developing into a complete starfish. Having learnt this, the oyster-growers now either take the starfish ashore or drown it in fresh waters. Fortunately there is no evidence of the killing of oysters by starfish in Australian waters.

The regenerative powers of starfish are very marked. If the arms are cut off with a portion of the central disk attached each will eventually develop into a fully-formed starfish; if an arm is broken off it at once begins to grow again, and it is very common to find on the Barrier Reef starfish that have been mutilated by fishes and others of their foes in various stages of redevelopment of the lost parts. One may even sometimes see an arm with a small central disk at one end and four buds beginning to grow out from its edge.

Some starfish of the Barrier habitually frequent the intertidal zone, and as the tide recedes they burrow just beneath the sand where their star-shaped contour may be betrayed by a slight bulge at the surface; thus they escape the attention of wading birds which are ever fossicking over the reef at low water.

Although the great majority of starfish possess five arms, some species commonly found on the reef are provided with six, seven, or even more.

1. "The organism is most often defined in terms of the process it carries out." Does this assertion apply to Roughley's essay?

2. What specific vital processes in the life of starfish does the author describe? Is his approach to these the same in every case?

3. Does Roughley suggest any *purpose* for the existence of starfish? What purposes might a starfish have?

4. Point out passages in which the organic structure or composition of the starfish is extensively described. What form of order does the author use in these sections?

5. Would you think this essay was written for highly trained marine biologists or for the non-technician? Why? Does the essay sacrifice thoroughness or accuracy to accomplish its ends?

Martin Mayer

A GREAT BIG AGENCY: MOSTLY
J. WALTER THOMPSON

As a rough rule, advertising agencies require ten to twelve employees to serve each million dollars of billings. Thompson, with something
like $225,000,000 of domestic billings, has about twenty-five hundred
people working for it in the United States, half of them in the "World
office" in New York. This relatively small staff represents a vast range of
human enterprise and talent: there are writers and artists for print and
drama, salesmen, sociologists, psychologists, economists, typographers, statis-
ticians, public relations flacks, stage and dress designers, electronic tech-
nicians, financial experts, space and time buyers (a fine, futuristic occupation, this), dietians, accountants, lawyers, photographers, engravers, geniuses, secretaries, stenographers, file clerks, comptometer operators, switchboard girls, and executives. They are all strapped together into a single
organization which operates, as president Sigurd Larmon of Young &
Rubicam says about his similar organization, "for one purpose—to help sell
goods and services for our clients."

Exactly how this strapping together is accomplished is one of the mysteries of advertising—especially at Thompson. Thompson has no "table of
organization," no set of "flow charts," no fixed system of work. Every once
in a while the agency becomes disturbed about its organizational fluidity
and wonders what its clients—most of whom have elaborate charts with
lines and boxes—must think of it. At these times somebody is sent off to
make still another attempt to draw a chart. All such attempts run into
Resor's deeply felt suspicion of "military systems" which inhibit creative
effort. Only once has he looked with pleasure on an organizational chart
drawn up for his inspection. This one, he said, was almost right; it needed
only one simple change, which he proceeded to effect. He picked up an
eraser and neatly removed all the lines that connected all the boxes.
Incidents like these lend weight to copywriter Dick Neff's remark that
"working for the Thompson company is like being in business for yourself."

Thompson's principle of organization is the "group system," with a separate group for each account. (An account at Thompson is a brand, not a client; there are separate groups for Lever's Lux and Lever's Rinso, Ford cars and Ford trucks.) Each tribe of Indians has two chiefs, a "group head" and an "account representative," and many tribes are gathered into a clan with an account supervisor as grand sachem. (The Thompson word for account supervisor is, for some reason, "backstop," but nobody except Resor himself uses it without embarrassment. "I hate that word," says one backstop, "because it implies that somebody is always dropping the ball, which isn't true.") There are about a dozen account supervisors for the eighty-odd major accounts serviced by the New York office.

The key man in each account group is the account representative (or account "executive," in non-Thompson terminology). All information from the client comes to him, and he presents to the client the agency's suggestions and the advertising campaigns prepared by the creative staff. In theory, at least, he is ultimately responsible for the quality of the work which Thompson does for the client and for Thompson's thorough understanding of what the client needs and wants from his advertising agency—keeping in mind, as a Thompson account supervisor puts it, "that what the client needs may be something different from what he wants." Basically, the account representative's specialty is personal relations, his ability to get along with the client's advertising people and with the people inside the agency who work on this account. There are account representatives who have no other talent whatever, at all agencies, and they get along. But the best representatives, the ones who become account supervisors, are also thoroughly trained advertising men (often with a background in copywriting, media or research) or shrewd businessmen who have been persuaded to try advertising. Stanley Resor, in a memorandum, put the nature of the job in its simplest terms: the account representative, he wrote, "will know what constitutes the best advertising for the produce in question."

Resor defined the task of the group head with equal simplicity in the same memorandum; group heads, he wrote, "must organize and stimulate the writers and artists with whom they work to obtain the most effective advertising that can be prepared in conformity with the standards of good taste." The group head is almost invariably a promoted copywriter, though it is not impossible for an artist to make the grade (Wally Elton, head of the Ford Car account group, the largest in the agency, came out of the art department). In most cases, he sees the client only rarely, when the representative feels that his presence at the conference table would help to sell the client an agency product or when he needs a piece of specialized information which the representative feels he could best get on his own. Representative and group head are coequal with the group, and, obviously, their responsibilities overlap: one must "know . . . the best advertising," the other must "obtain the most effective advertising." Disagreements arise, usually, says group head Ed Robinson, "because somebody has insufficient information. Not always. In case of dissension, the squabble is settled by the backstop."

Keeping the account all in one harness is the central job of the account supervisor; his central responsibility, says one of them grimly, is "holding the account." The supervisor at Thompson is usually, though not always, an older man; he can come out of almost any background at all. Garrit Lydecker, who supervises the work for Scott Paper (an important account, since Resor sits on Scott's board of directors), comes out of research and copy at Young & Rubicam and client contact at the Leo Burnett agency. Charles Rheinstrom, supervisor on Eastman Kodak, New York Central, Northeast Airlines, and Douglas Aircraft, was operations manager for American Airlines before he went into advertising. Kennet Hinks, who supervises all work for Lever Brothers, entered the Thompson company in 1921 as a copywriter, worked in the Chicago research department, managed Thompson's offices on the West Coast and then in Central Europe before he entered the client contact end of the business. The account supervisor maintains his own liaison with the client, usually at the level above that reached by the account representative. If the representative is working with a brand manager, the supervisor will talk with the vice-president in charge of advertising; he usually keeps on good terms with the client's sales manager, and at Thompson he often knows the people who own the business.

In one way, each account supervisor has his own separate advertising agency working under him. Each account group contains a permanent representative from the media, research and television programming departments (if television is used) and is serviced by regularly assigned engraving experts from the production department and clerical help from traffic control, accounting and billing. And it is the supervisor who, like the principal owner of a smaller agency, must make the decision about what goes to the client. But he has assets a small agency cannot command. He can call on specialized departments (a legal staff, a medical expert, a woman who does nothing but gather testimonials, an economist) whenever he feels the need for a specialist's opinion. If his own staff becomes overwhelmed with work, he can borrow junior assistants from elsewhere in the agency (checking first with the "traffic control" department) or call on top-priced talent, often men who are group heads on other accounts, to show his people the way out of a rut (checking first with Howard Kohl, Resor's personal assistant, who runs a traffic control system on senior personnel). And he never has the full authority of an agency head, because the work done by his groups is examined periodically by an *ad hoc* Review Board of senior men, most of them outside his authority. The Review Board has no powers of compulsion, and the account supervisor (especially if he knows the client is on his side) may disregard the board's advice; but, obviously, there is no future in doing so. . . .

1. This selection from *Madison Avenue, U.S.A.* describes the organization of a large advertising agency in New York City. Using the selection as a basis, what facts about the J. Walter Thompson Agency qualify it as a *bona fide* "organization?"
2. In describing the interrelationship of the Thompson staff, what principle of arrangement does the author follow?
3. What is the effect of using specific people to illustrate a general statement? Does this practice help to clarify the organization or not?
4. What is the purpose of an advertising agency? How does the organization of the Thompson Agency carry out this purpose?
5. What devices does the author use to "humanize" the large organization he is explaining? Does his attitude remain objective throughout his discussion? Support your opinion by citing the text.

CHAPTER 4

LOGICAL ORDER: CLASSIFICATION

"There are three classes of intellects: one which comprehends by itself; another which appreciates what others comprehend, and a third which neither comprehends by itself nor by the showing of others. . . ."
— NICCOLO MACHIAVELLI, *The Prince*

Quickly, without stopping to deliberate, can you tell what these objects have in common: whales, pigs, duck-billed platypuses, Alexander the Great, and dolphins? Can you think of a point of resemblance? What about grapes, tomatoes, cranberries, and bananas? Or unicorns, vampires, basilisks, sphinxes and centaurs? If you knew that the objects in the first group were all mammals, those in the second berries, and those in the third mythological animals, you were able to *classify*. Classification, the ability to discern likeness between seemingly unlike objects, is a prime aspect of man's capacity for logical thought.

Classification is not the work of scientists alone. Daily living involves constant classifying, and examples of writing based on classification range from the "classified" ads in the newspaper to Francis Bacon's famous classification of the "Idols of the Mind." When you think or speak of your clothes as "everyday," "Sunday," "work," and "play," you are classifying. When you use slang to evaluate your acquaintances— a "cat," a "doll"—you are classifying people. "Middle class," "high brow," "suburbanite," "white collar worker" are terms stemming from classification. So are residential "zones," literary "genres," blood "types," and school "grades."

Although classification is strongly identified with science, it is used continually in other areas of knowledge—by doctors, librarians, teachers, insurance salesmen, and people in dozens of other occupations. Classification is popular today partly because of our desire to be "scientific," but also because it is one of the best ways man has developed to organize and relate phenomena in order to increase his knowledge of them. Classification deals primarily with *things;* as an aid to comprehending the nature of objects, the kind of simplification and arrangement which constitute classification are invaluable.

There are certain principles of classification which we must follow if we want our classes to mean or explain anything. When we designate a number of objects, somewhat similar in nature, as a *family,* we must employ a consistent *categorical principle.* This is *the quality or characteristic which is shared by all the members of the same category.*

When we categorize whales, pigs, duck-billed platypuses, Alexander the Great, and dolphins as members of the *family* of *mammals,* we mean that they share the mammalian characteristics: they have spines, feed their young from the mother's breast, and have diaphragms. Grapes, tomatoes, cranberries, and bananas have in common the qualities of the *berry family:* they are simple fruits with pulpy polycarps in which seeds are embedded. As for our mythological animals—unicorns, sphinxes, vampires, and the rest—all of them have as their common principle the imaginary overlapping of natural categories of animals: a sphinx is part lion, part human; a centaur is part human, part horse; a basilisk is part animal, part reptile; and so forth. Their categorical principle might be considered to be the denial of the categories of the real animal world.

No matter how much alike the members of the category or family may be, there are bound to be dissimilarities as well. Thus we may subdivide a family into *species* (or sub-categories) on the basis of a *principle of division.* Whales, platypuses, men, and pigs may all be mammals, but there are great differences between them. Whales and dolphins are water-dwellers. Pigs and human beings are hairy and produce their young living. Platypuses lay eggs. Thus mammals may be subdivided on the basis of habitat, method of giving birth, skin covering, or some other principle of division. It is important to observe the same basis of division in setting up each species, or you will commit the error of *cross-ranking.* In cross-ranking, the species overlap so that the same member of a family belongs in more than one species. If you divide phonograph records (the family) into the species of 78 RPM, Decca, Dinah Shore, and Vinylite, you are cross-ranking. Conceivably the same record could belong in all these subclasses, since they are set up by playing speed, manufacturer, recording artist, and record composition. *Always keep to a single basis of division.*

When you discuss in the form of an essay or theme some large group of objects, you may find classification the most illuminating way to treat the group. Be sure that you find *the most effective* principle of division as the basis for setting up your species. There is little point in dividing cats into "Cats That Like Liver" and "Cats That Don't," for example, since the subgrouping tells us nothing new or illuminating about cats. Also be sure that your divisive principle will result in species that are *exhaustive;* that is, every member of the family under classification must be fitted into one species or another. The division of football players into centers, tackles, and guards on the basis of playing position or team function is not exhaustive: there are football players who do not fit into those categories. Furthermore, your subdivisions must be *mutually exclusive,* so that the same member of the family cannot be placed into more than one species. This is another way of saying: do not cross-rank.

If you are trying to set up categories to include all the members of some large family—say, human beings—you may find it difficult to establish tidy, mutually exclusive, and exhaustive categories which are illuminating as well. If you classify people as Negroid, Caucasoid, or Mongoloid on the principle of head and eye shapes or tooth and hair structure, you will find that you cannot place the Ainu of Japan or the Polynesians of Tahiti in any of these three species. Thus you must discover another principle of division which works better. Or you can simply group all members of a family which do not fit into the major categories in a category called "Miscellaneous" or "Others." Sometimes, a single member of a family of objects needs a species all to itself; in this case it is *sui generis,* "in a category by itself." Do not use the Miscellaneous and *Sui Generis* categories without care, however; you may find that your other species are established on some false or inane principle.

Classification can be of two types. The type discussed so far is Horizontal Classification: it is the kind in which a family, or group of similar objects, is subdivided *once* into species on the basis of a single principle of division. But remember that each of these species could be subdivided into another set of categories on another principle, and these in turn could be divided, and so on until we reach the smallest, *sui generis* category made up of a single object, say, a female, duck-billed platypus named Penelope in the Bronx Zoo. If the largest family of objects is divided and subdivided down to the individual member of that family, the result is *Vertical Classification*.* These diagrams should make the varieties of classification clear.

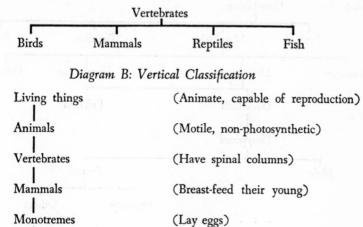

Diagram A: Horizontal Classification

Vertebrates

| Birds | Mammals | Reptiles | Fish |

Diagram B: Vertical Classification

Living things — (Animate, capable of reproduction)

Animals — (Motile, non-photosynthetic)

Vertebrates — (Have spinal columns)

Mammals — (Breast-feed their young)

Monotremes — (Lay eggs)

Duck-bills — (Have beaks)

Platypuses — (Web-footed)

Female Platypuses — (Bear the young)

Penelope

The horizontal classification of vertebrates obviously is based on some principle such as outer covering (birds have feathers, mammals have soft skins, reptiles have scaly skins, and fish have scales—usually). In the vertical classification, however, each of the sub-categories is established on a different principle; by understanding the categorical principles determining the groups to which she belongs, you can gain a fairly large amount of information about the nature and characteristics of Penelope. Obviously,

---

* The science of biology has developed specific designations for each of the divisions and subdivisions of vertical classificaton. From the largest inclusive group to the smallest, the categories are as follows: kingdom, phylum, class, subclass, family, tribe, genus, and species. For general purposes in this chapter, we have used "family" to refer to any group possessed of a similar set of characteristics, and "species" to refer to the subdivisions of a family.

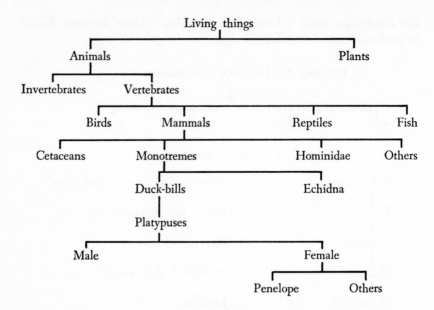

both horizontal and vertical classification are selected portions of a
larger, total classification, which looks, in part, like this: *

This diagram could be made sufficiently detailed to include all varieties
of plants, the sub-varieties of invertebrates, and so on. But as it stands,
it gives an indication of the relationship of horizontal classification to
vertical classification.

Whether horizontal or vertical, classification can be a very helpful
way of arranging subject matter for rhetorical presentation. William
Howells' essay on the problem of finding categorical principles for the
human race ("Various Views of Race" on page 466) actually classifies
approaches to classification and thereby uses classification both for its
subject and its method. Eric Berne's discussion of bodily differences in
human males employs a scientific classification to describe individual

---

* Halfway between a complete classification and a vertical classification is the
Dichotomous Classification, which uses a negative principle of division; thus, living
things would be divided into animals and non-animals; animals into vertebrates and
non-vertebrates; vertebrates into mammals and non-mammals, etc. The chief value
of the dichotomous classification is to remind us that a vertical classification is not
exhaustive in its categories; its chief fault is that it oversimplifies distinctions
between species and thus causes misunderstandings. Generally, it should be avoided
by neophyte logicians and writers who wish to be accurate.

temperaments. Francis Bacon makes habits of thinking more graspable by setting up arbitrary categories; Aaron Copland does something similar by using individual reactions to music to show how aesthetic responses may be classified. In each essay, things tangible or intangible are the subjects of rhetoric that is dependent on classification.

When you use classification to aid your own understanding of groups of objects, you may gain an insight that you want to preserve in written form. Some of the most entertaining as well as informative pieces of prose writing center in just such insights. Many groups of everyday objects—spoons, magazines, college students—have never been subjected to "scientific" classification; you may discover something revealing about the nature of these entities by classifying them and using your classification as the basis of an essay. In writing, remember to make your categories exhaustive, mutually exclusive, and based on a single (and illuminating) principle of division, if your classification is horizontal. If it is vertical, be sure your categories really add to an understanding of the object being classified.

One logician has said that classification is the means we use to make sense out of the hodge-podge of life. If you will remember that classification, like most logical systems, is arbitrary and must be changed or altered when new information is discovered or contradictions arise, you will be better able to appreciate the rôle it plays in understanding and learning. Classification is the first step in mastering a body of material; when you make an outline, as on nursery rhymes, you are actually classifying facts or ideas about a subject. An outline is not the final measure of comprehension of a subject, however; nor is classification, no matter how complete. Classification is a kind of complex description; if describing a thing by its surface qualities does not tell us all we need to know, at least we are making a logical start toward knowledge.*

I. *Questions for Review*
   1. What are some of the uses of classifications?
   2. What is the value of classification in non-scientific subjects?

* One of the main errors associated with classification is the *Hasty Generalization,* which stems from the wrong assumption that members of the same family share extensive characteristics simply because they share a categorical principle. Thus, if dolphins, men, and platypuses are all mammals, and if men are carnivorous (meat-eaters), dolphins, platypuses, and pigs are carnivorous, too. Not so. See Chapter VII for the *Hasty Generalization* and the ways to avoid associating specific individuals with the hazy mental association called up by general names.

3. What are the limitations of classification as a means to understanding a subject? What errors in thinking can classification lead to?
4. What is a categorical principle? What is a principle of division? What is a dichotomous principle of division?
5. What are the tests of proper species set up as subdivisions of a group, or "family," of objects?
6. What is cross-ranking? How does it come about and what are its defects?
7. How does vertical classification differ from horizontal classification? From complete classification? From dichotomous classification?
8. Why can no system of classification ever be said to be without flaws? Why must all categories be subject to change or corrections?
9. What is the meaning of *sui generis*? How it is used in classification?

II. *Exercises*
1. What principle of division would be used to divide each category into the species given:
   A. Musical instruments — strings, woodwinds, brass, percussion
   B. Rocks — igneous, sedimentary, metamorphic
   C. Pouring vessels — jugs, crocks, pitchers, ewers
   D. Eighteenth-century dances — sarabandes, gavottes, allemands, minuets
   E. Books — quarto, folio, octavo, duodecimo
   F. Shoes — leather, cloth, rubber, plastic
2. Which of these species are established on more than one principle of division, i.e., which commit cross-ranking:
   A. Roads — dirt, macadam, two-lane, concrete, blacktop, toll
   B. Commercial soaps — flakes, powder, detergent, liquid, cake
   C. Dogs — setters, wolfhounds, spaniels, mongrels, pekingese
   D. Houses — Cape Cod, Georgian, split-level, Frank Lloyd Wright, pre-fab
   E. Flowers — annuals, perennials, hybrid, hothouse
3. What categorical principle is shared by:
   A. Milk, ink, coffee, hydrochloric acid
   B. Napoleon, Marie Antoinette, Charles de Gaulle, Brigitte Bardot
   C. Bismuth, vanadium, mercury, graphite
   D. Judas Iscariot, Cassius, Benedict Arnold, Vidkun Quisling
   E. Flashlights, portable radios, walkie-talkies, automobiles
   F. Romantic, Neo-Classical, Baroque, Gothic
   G. Vampire bats, gliders, angels, pigeons
   H. Chrysanthemums, butter, lemons, sulphur
4. Which of the suggested principles of division do you consider best for separating the larger category into species? Justify your choice.

A. Magazines — frequency of publication, reading audience, publisher, contents, price, quality of paper printed on

B. College professors — subject taught, degree, methods of lecturing, way of dressing, I.Q., mannerisms

C. Books — publisher, date of publication, type of binding, author, subject matter, place of publication

D. Automobiles — manufacturer, price range, body type, place of manufacture, advertising appeal to buyer, color, use by owner

E. College sports — participants, equipment, nature of physical activity, kinds of spectators, cost of program

F. The population of Egypt — racial background, religion, marital status, sex, geographical distribution, degree of education, age

G. American politicians — region, party affiliation, office held, educational level, beliefs

III. *Questions for Thought, Discussion, and Writing*

1. In grammar, some nouns are called "common" and others "proper"; the latter are capitalized and the former are not. How are these related to the idea of classification? To *sui generis*?

2. Classification is a means of defining. How does your dictionary define each of these words and how is classification used: rampion, moa, yawl, thulium, ectomorph, Yahoo, goosander.

3. What separate principles of division are used in classifying human beings by: the anthropologist, sociologist, economist, politician, biologist, physician, geographer? Which is the most illuminating? Why?

4. Many items are classified. What principle of classification (or division) is used to classify: library books, mushrooms, human blood, American males over 18, television programs, murder, city areas?

5. How does classification help us in understanding machines, organisms, and organizations? Can classification be used on processes? Explain. How are classification and outlining related?

6. When a child is learning to talk, does he learn general or specific words first? How do you account for this? Is learning to talk at least in part the learning how to classify? Explain.

7. Even though the common use of general (or category) words may lead to vagueness of meaning or to wrong thinking, is it possible for us to speak or write in words which are not general?

8. Write a theme on one of these subjects:
   A. The Types in My Fraternity
   B. The Use of Slang in Typing People
   C. The Limitations of Classification Used in Psychology (or Sociology or Biology or English)

D. The Classifications an American Man Is Subject to Today
E. A Department Store as Spatial Classification
F. History as Chronological Classification
G. Select some subject not commonly classified, such as musical compositions, children, jewelry, or sports cars. Choose a principle of division and establish categories which you find illuminating; then write a composition explaining the subject and your classification of it.

Francis Bacon

IDOLS OF THE MIND

THE IDOLS AND FALSE NOTIONS WHICH ARE NOW IN POSSESSION OF THE
human understanding, and have taken deep root therein, not only so beset
men's minds that truth can hardly find entrance, but even after entrance
obtained, they will again in the very instauration of the sciences meet and
trouble us, unless men being forewarned of the danger fortify themselves
as far as may be against their assaults.

There are four classes of Idols which beset men's minds. To these for
distinction's sake I have assigned names,—calling the first class *Idols of the
Tribe;* the second, *Idols of the Cave;* the third, *Idols of the Marketplace;*
the fourth, *Idols of the Theatre.*

The formation of ideas and axioms by true induction is no doubt the
proper remedy to be applied for the keeping off and clearing away of idols.
To point them out, however, is of great use; for the doctrine of Idols
is to the Interpretation of Nature what the doctrine of the refutation of
Sophisms is to common Logic.

The Idols of the Tribe have their foundation in human nature itself, and
in the tribe or race of men. For it is a false assertion that the sense of man
is the measure of things. On the contrary, all perceptions as well of the
sense as of the mind are according to the measure of the individual and
not according to the measure of the universe. And the human understanding is like a false mirror, which, receiving rays irregularly, distorts and discolours the nature of things mingling its own nature with it.

The Idols of the Cave are the idols of the individual man. For every
one (besides the errors common to human nature in general) has a cave
or den of his own, which refracts and discolours the light of nature; owing
either to his own proper and peculiar nature; or to his education and conversation with others; or to the reading of books, and the authority of
those whom he esteems and admires; or to the differences of impressions,
accordingly as they take place in a mind preoccupied and predisposed

From the *Novum Organum,* 1620.

or in a mind indifferent and settled; or the like: So that the spirit of man (according as it is meted out to different individuals) is in fact a thing variable and full of perturbation, and governed as it were by chance. Whence it was well observed by Heraclitus that men look for sciences in their own lesser worlds, and not in the greater or common world.

There are also Idols formed by the intercourse and association of men with each other, which I call Idols of the Marketplace, on account of the commerce and consort of men there. For it is by discourse that men associate; and words are imposed according to the apprehension of the vulgar. And therefore the ill and unfit choice of words wonderfully obstructs the understanding. Nor do the definitions or explanations wherewith in some things learned men are wont to guard and defend themselves, by any means set the matter right. But words plainly force and overrule the understanding, and throw all into confusion, and lead men away into numberless empty controversies and idle fancies.

Lastly, there are Idols which have immigrated into men's minds from the various dogmas of philosophies, and also from wrong laws of demonstration. These I call Idols of the Theatre; because in my judgment all the received systems are but so many stage-plays, representing worlds of their own creation after an unreal and scenic fashion. Nor is it only of the systems now in vogue, or only of the ancient sects and philosophies, that I speak; for many more plays of the same kind may yet be composed and in like artificial manner set forth; seeing that errors the most widely different have nevertheless causes for the most part alike. Neither again do I mean this only of entire systems, but also of many principles and axioms in science, which by tradition, credulity, and negligence have come to be received.

But of these several kinds of Idols I must speak more largely and exactly, that the understanding may be duly cautioned.

1. Exactly what group of things is Bacon classifying here? Is the classification a horizontal or vertical one?
2. What principle of division is used to set up the various species of mental Idols? Could another principle have been used to better advantage?
3. Do the four categories meet the requirements of effective classification?
4. Think of some "mental Idols." Can you place these in one or another of Bacon's categories? Is any cross-ranking present?

5. Is Bacon's classification a helpful or illuminating one? What advantage, if any, is gained from classifying the Idols?
6. Can Bacon's views be reconciled with the ideas about thought in the essays of Dewey, Sapir, and Chase included at the end of this book? Discuss.

Eric Berne

CAN PEOPLE BE JUDGED BY THEIR APPEARANCE?

EVERYONE KNOWS THAT A HUMAN BEING, LIKE A CHICKEN, COMES FROM an egg. At a very early stage, the human embryo forms a three-layered tube, the inside layer of which grows into the stomach and lungs, the middle layer into bones, muscles, joints, and blood vessels, and the outside layer into the skin and nervous system.

Usually these three grow about equally, so that the average human being is a fair mixture of brains, muscles, and inward organs. In some eggs, however, one layer grows more than the others, and when the angels have finished putting the child together, he may have more gut than brain, or more brain than muscle. When this happens, the individual's activities will often be mostly with the overgrown layer.

We can thus say that while the average human being is a mixture, some people are mainly "digestion-minded," some "muscle-minded," and some "brain-minded," and correspondingly digestion-bodied, muscle-bodied, or brain-bodied. The digestion-bodied people look thick; the muscle-bodied people look wide; and the brain-bodied people look long. This does not mean the taller a man is the brainier he will be. It means that if a man, even a short man, looks long rather than wide or thick, he will often be more concerned about what goes on in his mind than about what he does or what he eats; but the key factor is slenderness and not height. On the other hand, a man who gives the impression of being thick rather than long or wide will usually be more interested in a good steak than in a good idea or a good long walk.

Medical men use Greek words to describe these types of body-build. For the man whose body shape mostly depends on the inside layer of the egg, they use the word *endomorph*. If it depends mostly upon the middle layer, they call him a *mesomorph*. If it depends upon the outside layer, they call him an *ectomorph*. We can see the same roots in our

English words "enter," "medium," and "exit," which might just as easily have been spelled "ender," "mesium," and "ectit."

Since the inside skin of the human egg, or endoderm, forms the inner organs of the belly, the viscera, the endomorph is usually belly-minded; since the middle skin forms the body tissues, or soma, the mesomorph is usually muscle-minded; and since the outside skin forms the brain, or cerebrum, the ectomorph is usually brain-minded. Translating this into Greek, we have the viscerotonic endomorph, the somatotonic mesomorph, and the cerebrotonic ectomorph.

Words are beautiful things to a cerebrotonic, but a viscerotonic knows you cannot eat a menu no matter what language it is printed in, and a somatotonic knows you cannot increase your chest expansion by reading a dictionary. So it is advisable to leave these words and see what kinds of people they actually apply to, remembering again that most individuals are fairly equal mixtures and that what we have to say concerns only the extremes. Up to the present, these types have been thoroughly studied only in the male sex.

Viscerotonic endomorph. If a man is definitely a thick type rather than a broad or long type, he is likely to be round and soft, with a big chest but a bigger belly. He would rather eat than breathe comfortably. He is likely to have a wide face, short, thick neck, big thighs and upper arms, and small hands and feet. He has overdeveloped breasts and looks as though he were blown up a little like a balloon. His skin is soft and smooth, and when he gets bald, as he does usually quite early, he loses the hair in the middle of his head first.

The short, jolly, thickset, red-faced politician with a cigar in his mouth, who always looks as though he were about to have a stroke, is the best example of this type. The reason he often makes a good politician is that he likes people, banquets, baths, and sleep; he is easygoing, soothing, and his feelings are easy to understand.

His abdomen is big because he has lots of intestines. He likes to take in things. He likes to take in food, and affection and approval as well. Going to a banquet with people who like him is his idea of a fine time. It is important for a psychiatrist to understand the natures of such men when they come to him for advice.

Somatotonic mesomorph. If a man is definitely a broad type rather than a thick or long type, he is likely to be rugged and have lots of muscle. He is apt to have big forearms and legs, and his chest and belly are well formed and firm, with the chest bigger than the belly. He would rather breathe than eat. He has a bony head, big shoulders, and a square jaw. His skin is thick, coarse, and elastic, and tans easily. If he gets bald, it usually starts on the front of the head.

Dick Tracy, Li'l Abner, and other men of action belong to this type. Such people make good lifeguards and construction workers. They like to put out energy. They have lots of muscles and they like to use them. They go in for adventure, exercise, fighting, and getting the upper hand. They are bold and unrestrained, and love to master the people and things around them. If the psychiatrist knows the things which give such people satisfaction, he is able to understand why they may be unhappy in certain situations.

Cerebrotonic ectomorph. The man who is definitely a long type is likely to have thin bones and muscles. His shoulders are apt to sag and he has a flat belly with a dropped stomach, and long, weak legs. His neck and fingers are long, and his face is shaped like a long egg. His skin is thin, dry, and pale, and he rarely gets bald. He looks like an absent-minded professor and often is one.

Though such people are jumpy, they like to keep their energy and don't fancy moving around much. They would rather sit quietly by themselves and keep out of difficulties. Trouble upsets them, and they run away from it. Their friends don't understand them very well. They move jerkily and feel jerkily. The psychiatrist who understands how easily they become anxious is often able to help them get along better in the sociable and aggressive world of endomorphs and mesomorphs.

In the special cases where people definitely belong to one type or another, then, one can tell a good deal about their personalities from their appearance. When the human mind is engaged in one of its struggles with itself or with the world outside, the individual's way of handling the struggle will be partly determined by his type. If he is a viscerotonic he will often want to go to a party where he can eat and drink and be in good company at a time when he might be better off attending to business; the somatotonic will want to go out and do something about it, master the situation, even if what he does is foolish and not properly figured out, while the cerebrotonic will go off by himself and think it over, when perhaps he would be better off doing something about it or seeking good company to try to forget it.

Since these personality characteristics depend on the growth of the layers of the little egg from which the person developed, they are very difficult to change. Nevertheless, it is important for the individual to know about these types, so that he can have at least an inkling of what to expect from those around him, and can make allowances for the different kinds of human nature, and so that he can become aware of and learn to control his own natural tendencies, which may sometimes guide him into making the same mistakes over and over again in handling his difficulties.

1. How does this essay use causation to help classification?
2. What category is the author classifying, and what principle of division does he use?
3. Must an endomorph always be viscerotonic, according to Berne? Are there actually two classifications rather than one in this essay? If so, do they over-lap or cross-rank?
4. Are the three Classes exhaustive? What other category (or categories) might you add to Berne's?
5. Are the classifications worthwhile? What information do we gain about human beings in seeing them so classified?

John Kieran

UNTAILED AMPHIBIANS OF NEW YORK CITY

As to the "untailed amphibians" within the city limits, meaning the frogs and toads, the most abundant is the familiar Spring Peeper already mentioned, which is a frog. Toads are more terrestrial and have warty skins as a rule and a glandular swelling behind each eye. Otherwise there is no important distinction between frogs and toads, and indeed one common resident of the region goes by either name. That is the little tree climber with the scientific name of *Hyla versicolor* and the choice of Treefrog or "Tree Toad" as a common name. Not only does it have two names but it comes in different colors: brown, green, gray, and almost white. But in any color they are equipped with toe pads or disks that exude a sticky substance enabling them to cling to smooth surfaces, even at a vertical angle. This is the explanation of their climbing exploits.

These really attractive little creatures grow to a length of two inches or so but more often the ones you may find will be smaller. They have a delicate trilling call or song almost birdlike in quality that they tune up in the dusk and continue intermittently through the warm nights of late spring and early summer. The best way to find one is to track it down as closely as possible by ear in the dusk or dark and then turn on a flashlight for the final search on a tree trunk or branch. If caught in the beam of a flashlight, a Treefrog usually remains motionless and, if approached slowly, may be picked off the tree by hand for closer inspection. If you capture one, be sure to look at its toe pads.

As a matter of fact—and as its scientific name *Hyla crucifer* indicates— the Spring Peeper is a close relative and a member of this family of climbing frogs. The Peepers, too, have toe pads, but they do not climb as high nor stray as far from water as do the Treefrogs. They more often utter their piping calls from the branch of a shrub or a plant stem sticking up out of the water. The Spring Peeper is only about an inch in length but its vocal equipment is so efficient that its shrill calls can be heard nearly a mile off on a quiet night. It is not as soft on the ear as the purring trill of the Treefrog but, when first lifted each year in the twilight "among the sallows and the windy gleams of March," it is cherished as the herald of spring and the promise of fresh greenery over a landscape drab and drear from the ravages of a retreating winter.

Another member of the same family and the smallest frog occurring in the area has toe pads so small and ineffective that it doesn't climb at all. It's the Southern Cricket Frog (*Acris gryllus*) that lives along the grassy edges of ponds and slow streams and gains its name from the notes the male gives off in the courting season, a series of *chirks* somewhat insect-like in quality. It is just over an inch in length at most, brownish of hue with a sprinkling of small dark spots, and it has a light green or yellowish line running down the middle of its back. It is by no means common in our area, which is close to the northeast limit of the range of the species, so if you come upon one within the city limits you may consider it something of a batrachian prize. For that matter, a searcher may have to comb the far reaches and lonelier sectors of Queens and the Bronx to find Treefrogs or even hear their thin trilling voices calling eerily in the twilight of a warm day in May.

It is not so with the Green Frog (*Rana clamitans*), however. While not nearly as abundant as the Spring Peeper, it is common in the ponds and park lakes of all five boroughs and plentiful along the borders of the swamps and streams in the outlying sections of the city. This is the frog, about 4 inches in length and green or greenish brown in color, that sits along the edge of a pond, lake, or stream and gives a squeaky croak as it jumps—plop!—into the water at your approach. Despite its small size it has a reputation for ferocity and voracity and even has been charged with "cannibalism" in the form of feeding on tadpoles of its own species. It rarely wanders on dry ground beyond reach of water in one jump, and often sits in the water with only its head exposed, from which point of vantage it occasionally gives off a resounding *tchung!*

Less plentiful but more majestic is the famous Bullfrog (*Rana catesbeiana*). Under cultivation this species is reputed to reach a length of 8 inches but in the park lakes and some of the larger ponds on the outskirts of the city a six-incher still would be exceptional. In fact, a five-incher at the northern end of the Van Cortlandt Park Lake will cause me to stop, look, and listen. To some listeners its deep voice grumpily calls for a *jug o' rum! jug o' rum!;* to my ears it never utters anything but a hoarse and meaningless *ker-r-rumppp!* Either way, its voice has an air of solidity and authority and its presence lends dignity to the scene where it lords it over lesser forms of batrachian life in our region.

The Bullfrog is truly aquatic and spends all its life in the water. A really adventurous little amphibian is the slim and graceful Wood Frog (*Rana sylvatica*) that often wanders far from its watery cradle. This is a handsome frog about 2 to 3 inches in length—the male is the smaller— and quite smooth of skin. It is marked to match the dead leaves of the forest floor along which it forages, a pattern of light and dark brown with a narrow black patch running backward from the eye. The eggs are deposited in some woodland pool in early spring and, after a tadpole stage varying from six weeks to about twice as long, depending on the weather and local conditions, the young emerge as tiny frogs that immediately start hunting for food in the undergrowth of the woods. It takes these frogs four years to reach full growth, such as it is. They are lively creatures and extraordinary jumpers for their size. It is easy to see one in motion when it leaps from under your foot but it's hard to find when it lands at the end of the jump, so well does it blend into the background of the woodland carpet. In the adult stage they have so little affinity with water (they go to it only to answer the mating call in spring) that their hind feet are only partially webbed and their front feet not at all. Since the woods within the city limits are now confined to scattered patches on Staten Island and in the outlying sections of Queens and the Bronx, the Wood Frogs of the area must be sought in such local refuges. Even there they are comparatively scarce and hard to find.

Some frog fanciers hold that the Northern Leopard Frog (*Rana pipiens*) is even more handsome than the Wood Frog. It's a matter of taste. The Leopard Frog is another wanderer from the water but it doesn't go as far as the Wood Frog. It is so frequently found in open grassy places that some persons prefer to call it the Meadow Frog. It has a bronze or green body studded with rows of roundish white-edged dark spots and though rarely exceeding 4 inches in length, it is so abundant in many parts of its wide range in North America and so easily caught that it is the main source of supply for the frogs' legs served up in restaurants. The slightly smaller Pickerel Frog (*Rana palustris*), rarely more than 3 inches in length, is somewhat similar in color and pattern, but the two rows of spots on its back are roughly rectangular and lack the conspicuous light edging of the Leopard Frog spots. Perhaps the easiest distinguishing mark is the brilliant orange color of the underside of the hind legs of the Pickerel Frog, which, incidentally, is not as abundant or as widespread as the Leopard Frog, nor does it travel as far from water.

Moving over to the toad department, there are two kinds of toad—and just possibly a third—that are still resident in the region. The well-known, dust-colored, warty-skinned, slow-moving American Toad (*Bufo americanus*) still thrives, though in decreasing numbers, in the public parks of the city and in outlying open ground. It doesn't attract much attention for several reasons, one being that it moves about and feeds mostly at night. Another is that it disappears at the first sign of cold weather, digging itself in for a long period of hibernation in a favorable spot. At full growth a female may be up to 4 inches in length. The males are smaller. Both sexes ordinarily are silent but the males give off low sweet trills when the sexes gather at the ponds wherein the females deposit their strings of eggs in May. The eggs hatch in about ten days and the tadpole stage takes up seven to nine weeks of the career of the American Toad. Once it develops legs and takes to dry ground, it never returns to the water except for annual spring reunion of the sexes at the ponds. Fowler's Toad (*Bufo woodhousei fowleri*), a trifle smaller but much similar to the American Toad in appearance except that it has a median light line down its dark-spotted warty back and generally has three warts instead of one or two in each dark spot on its back, is the more common species in some sections of the city. It has approximately the same habits and life cycle as the American Toad but it does not lift as melodic a note at the meeting of the sexes at the ponds in spring. The sound that Fowler's Toad gives off on such amorous occasions can only be described as a husky and ghostly *ur-r-r-r*.

Although the Eastern Spadefoot (*Scaphiopus holbrookii*) is fairly common over most of the eastern part of the United States, it is definitely a rarity on city territory. There has been only one report of its occurrence within the city limits in recent years and that came from Staten Island, where, strangely enough, the familiar American Toad doesn't occur at all. At least no report of its appearance has been filed. Fowler's Toad is the resident species. The Eastern Spadefoot owes its name to horny projections along the inside of the soles of its hind feet that help it to dig in soft ground the tunnels and burrows in which it lives and feeds. Since it is less than 3 inches long and rarely is seen above ground, doing most of its foraging under stones and logs, it often escapes notice even where it occurs in fair numbers; this can't be the case in our territory, or else expert searchers would be reporting it with regularity. It must be that the Spade-foot has been discouraged by the spread of reinforced concrete and other such hard surfaces within the city limits and has left permanently for unpaved ground.

It's our loss. Toads are useful creatures and helpful to Man, being active guardians of field crops and protectors of trees, flowers, fruits, and garden vegetables from the ravages of insects. The word toad applied as an epithet or a term of disapprobation is a libel on these gentle amphibians. Familiarity with them will not breed contempt—nor warts, as the ancient fable has it—rather, a deep respect and perhaps even a little affection for these possibly unhandsome but certainly quiet, friendly, and helpful creatures.

All this adds up to ten species of "untailed amphibians" that you might expect or at least hope to find resident on city territory and active in the warmer months of the year. Of these the Spring Peepers are by far the most numerous and widespread, and also the most insistently vociferous in season. Our Green Frogs and Bullfrogs also announce themselves in good strong tones where they are locally common in and around ponds and lakes. To come upon the wider ranging Pickerel Frogs, Northern Leopard Frogs, and Wood Frogs will be a harder task, and getting a good view of the little Southern Cricket Frog will be a real task. As for the Treefrog and the two resident species that are legally entitled to the name of "toad," the American and the Fowler's Toad, they are best sought after dark. All you need for a successful search is a good place, a good ear, a good flashlight—and a good deal of patience.

1. Kieran's classification of the frogs and toads in New York City uses what categorical principle for establishing the family? Does the author differentiate between the families of toads and frogs? What is his reason for establishing the categories he uses?

2. This classification deals with organisms (untailed amphibians). What special problems arise in classifying organisms, as this essay shows? How does the author solve them?

3. What principle of division does Kieran use in separating untailed amphibians into species? Illustrate your answer.

4. What are the Latin phrases used in describing each kind of frog? How are they related to the question of formal and informal classification in this essay?

5. What evidence—words, phrases, opinions—supports the view that the primary purpose of Kieran's classification is more popular than scientific? What end does Kieran hope to achieve in setting up these categories?

Aaron Copland

HOW WE LISTEN

WE ALL LISTEN TO MUSIC ACCORDING TO OUR SEPARATE CAPACITIES. BUT, for the sake of analysis, the whole listening process may become clearer if we break it up into its component parts, so to speak. In a certain sense we all listen to music on three separate planes. For lack of a better terminology, one might name these: (1) the sensuous plane, (2) the expressive plane, (3) the sheerly musical plane. The only advantage to be gained from mechanically splitting up the listening process into these hypothetical planes is the clearer view to be had of the way in which we listen.

The simplest way of listening to music is to listen for the sheer pleasure of the musical sound itself. That is the sensuous plane. It is the plane on which we hear music without thinking, without considering it in any way. One turns on the radio while doing something else and absent-mindedly bathes in the sound. A kind of brainless but attractive state of mind is engendered by the mere sound appeal of the music.

You may be sitting in a room reading this book. Imagine one note struck on the piano. Immediately that one note is enough to change the atmosphere of the room—proving that the sound element in music is a powerful and mysterious agent, which it would be foolish to deride or belittle.

The surprising thing is that many people who consider themselves qualified music lovers abuse that plane in listening. They go to concerts in order to lose themselves. They use music as a consolation or an escape. They enter an ideal world where one doesn't have to think of the realities of everyday life. Of course they aren't thinking about the music either. Music allows them to leave it, and they go off to a place to dream, dreaming because of and apropos of the music yet never quite listening to it.

Yes, the sound appeal of music is a potent and primitive force, but you must not allow it to usurp a disproportionate share of your interest. The sensuous plane is an important one in music, a very important one, but it does not constitute the whole story.

There is no need to digress further on the sensuous plane. Its appeal to every normal human being is self-evident. There is, however, such a thing as becoming more sensitive to the different kinds of sound stuff as used by various composers. For all composers do not use that sound stuff in the same way. Don't get the idea that the value of music is commensurate with its sensuous appeal or that the loveliest sounding music is made by the greatest composer. If that were so, Ravel would be a greater creator than Beethoven. The point is that the sound element varies with each composer, that his usage of sound forms an integral part of his style and must be taken into account when listening. The reader can see, therefore, that a more conscious approach is valuable even on this primary plane of music listening.

The second plane on which music exists is what I have called the expressive one. Here, immediately, we tread on controversial ground. Composers have a way of shying away from any discussion of music's expressive side. Did not Stravinsky himself proclaim that his music was an "object," a "thing," with a life of its own, and with no other meaning than its own purely musical existence? This intransigent attitude of Stravinsky's may be due to the fact that so many people have tried to read different meanings into so many pieces. Heaven knows it is difficult enough to say precisely what it is that a piece of music means, to say it definitely, to say it finally so that everyone is satisfied with your explanation. But that should not lead one to the other extreme of denying to music the right to be "expressive."

My own belief is that all music has an expressive power, some more and some less, but that all music has a certain meaning behind the notes and that that meaning behind the notes constitutes, after all, what the piece is saying, what the piece is about. This whole problem can be stated quite simply by asking, "Is there a meaning to music?" My answer to that would be, "Yes." And "Can you state in so many words what the meaning is?" My answer to that would be, "No." Therein lies the difficulty.

Simple-minded souls will never be satisfied with the answer to the second of these questions. They always want music to have a meaning, and the more concrete it is the better they like it. The more the music reminds them of a train, a storm, a funeral, or any other familiar conception the more expressive it appears to be to them. This popular idea of music's meaning—stimulated and abetted by the usual run of musical commentator—should be discouraged wherever and whenever it is met. One timid lady once confessed to me that she suspected something seriously lacking in her appreciation of music because of her inability to connect it with anything definite. That is getting the whole thing backward, of course.

Still, the question remains. How close should the intelligent music lover wish to come to pinning a definite meaning to any particular work? No closer than a general concept, I should say. Music expresses, at different moments, serenity or exuberance, regret or triumph, fury or delight. It expresses each of these moods, and many others, in a numberless variety of subtle shadings and differences. It may even express a state of meaning for which there exists no adequate word in any language. In that case, musicians often like to say that it has only a purely musical meaning. They sometimes go farther and say that *all* music has only a purely musical meaning. What they really mean is that no appropriate word can be found to express the music's meaning and that, even if it could, they do not feel the need of finding it.

But whatever the professional musician may hold, most musical novices still search for specific words with which to pin down their musical reactions. That is why they always find Tchaikovsky easier to "understand" than Beethoven. In the first place, it is easier to pin a meaning-word on a Tchaikovsky piece than on a Beethoven one. Much easier. Moreover, with the Russian composer, every time you come back to a piece of his it almost always says the same thing to you, whereas with Beethoven it is often quite difficult to put your finger right on what he is saying. And any musician will tell you that that is why Beethoven is the greater composer. Because music which always says the same thing to you will necessarily soon become dull music, but music whose meaning is slightly different with each hearing has a greater chance of remaining alive.

Listen, if you can, to the forty-eight fugue themes of Bach's *Well Tempered Clavichord*. Listen to each theme, one after another. You will soon realize that each theme mirrors a different world of feeling. You will also soon realize that the more beautiful a theme seems to you the harder it is to find any word that will describe it to your complete satisfaction. Yes, you will certainly know whether it is a gay theme or a sad one. You will be able, in other words, in your own mind, to draw a frame of emotional feeling around your theme. Now study the sad one a little closer. Try to pin down the exact quality of its sadness. Is it pessimistically sad or resignedly sad; is it fatefully sad or smilingly sad?

Let us suppose that you are fortunate and can describe to your own satisfaction in so many words the exact meaning of your chosen theme.

There is still no guarantee that anyone else will be satisfied. Nor need they be. The important thing is that each one feel for himself the specific expressive quality of a theme or, similarly, an entire piece of music. And if it is a great work of art, don't expect it to mean exactly the same thing to you each time you return to it.

Themes or pieces need not express only one emotion, of course. Take such a theme as the first main one of the *Ninth Symphony,* for example. It is clearly made up of different elements. It does not say only one thing. Yet anyone hearing it immediately gets a feeling of strength, a feeling of power. It isn't a power that comes simply because the theme is played loudly. It is a power inherent in the theme itself. The extraordinary strength and vigor of the theme results in the listener's receiving an impression that a forceful statement has been made. But one should never try to boil it down to "the fateful hammer of life," etc. That is where the trouble begins. The musician, in his exasperation, says it means nothing but the notes themselves, whereas the nonprofessional is only too anxious to hang on to any explanation that gives him the illusion of getting closer to the music's meaning.

Now, perhaps, the reader will know better what I mean when I say that music does have an expressive meaning but that we cannot say in so many words what that meaning is.

The third plane on which music exists is the sheerly musical plane. Besides the pleasurable sound of music and the expressive feeling that it gives off, music does exist in terms of the notes themselves and of their manipulation. Most listeners are not sufficiently conscious of this third plane. It will be largely the business of this book to make them more aware of music on this plane.

Professional musicians, on the other hand, are, if anything, too conscious of the mere notes themselves. They often fall into the error of becoming so engrossed with their arpeggios and staccatos that they forget the deeper aspects of the music they are performing. But from the layman's standpoint, it is not so much a matter of getting over bad habits on the sheerly musical plane as of increasing one's awareness of what is going on, in so far as the notes are concerned.

When the man in the street listens to the "notes themselves" with any degree of concentration, he is most likely to make some mention of the melody. Either he hears a pretty melody or he does not, and he generally lets it go at that. Rhythm is likely to gain his attention next, particularly if it seems exciting. But harmony and tone color are generally taken for granted, if they are thought of consciously at all. As for music's having a definite form of some kind, that idea seems never to have occurred to him.

It is very important for all of us to become more alive to music on its sheerly musical plane. After all, an actual musical material is being used. The intelligent listener must be prepared to increase his awareness of the musical material and what happens to it. He must hear the melodies, the rhythms, the harmonies, the tone colors in a more conscious fashion. But above all he must, in order to follow the line of the composer's thought, know something of the principles of musical form. Listening to all of these elements is listening on the sheerly musical plane.

Let me repeat that I have split up mechanically the three separate planes on which we listen merely for the sake of greater clarity. Actually, we never listen on one or the other of these planes. What we do is to correlate them—listening in all three ways at the same time. It takes no mental effort, for we do it instinctively.

Perhaps an analogy with what happens to us when we visit the theater will make this instinctive correlation clearer. In the theater, you are aware of the actors and actresses, costumes and sets, sounds and movements. All these give one the sense that the theater is a pleasant place to be in. They constitute the sensuous plane in our theatrical reactions.

The expressive plane in the theater would be derived from the feeling that you get from what is happening on the stage. You are moved to pity, excitement, or gayety. It is this general feeling, generated aside from the particular words being spoken, a certain emotional something which exists on the stage, that is analogous to the expressive quality in music.

The plot and plot development is equivalent to our sheerly musical plane. The playwright creates and develops a character in just the same way that a composer creates and develops a theme. According to the degree of your awareness of the way in which the artist in either field handles his material will you become a more intelligent listener.

It is easy enough to see that the theatergoer never is conscious of any of these elements separately. He is aware of them all at the same time. The same is true of music listening. We simultaneously and without thinking listen on all three planes.

In a sense, the ideal listener is both inside and outside the music at the same moment, judging it and enjoying it, wishing it would go one way and watching it go another—almost like the composer at the moment he composes it; because in order to write his music, the composer must also be inside and outside his music, carried away by it and yet coldly critical of it.

A subjective and objective attitude is implied in both creating and listening to music.

What the reader should strive for, then, is a more *active* kind of listening. Whether you listen to Mozart or Duke Ellington, you can deepen your understanding of music only by being a more conscious and aware listener —not someone who is just listening, but someone who is listening *for* something.

1. In this essay, Copland sets up three categories of "ways to listen to music." Is he actually classifying "planes" or something more tangible?
2. What principle of division results in the classifications that Copland makes?
3. Does the author's admission that a listener experiences all three planes of sensation at once result in cross-ranking? Explain.
4. How does this essay show the arbitrary nature of classification as an aid to understanding?

CHAPTER 5

LOGICAL ORDER: COMPARISON
AND CONTRAST

"Why is a raven like a writing desk?"
LEWIS CARROLL, *Alice in Wonderland*

When the Mad Hatter asked Alice his famous riddle about the similarity between ravens and writing desks in the Tea Party scene of *Alice in Wonderland,* he was indirectly pointing out the limitations of classification as a logical method. How *is* a raven like a writing desk? One is an organism, animate, feathered, carnivorous, and capable of flight; the other is inanimate, vegetable (wood), manufactured, stationary, and a container. Both are things, or structured objects, but this categorical principle tells us very little. As Lewis Carroll, a brilliant logician and mathematician, well knew, ravens and writing desks simply cannot be dealt with effectively by the methods of classification.

There *are* ways of dealing with highly dissimilar objects, however. One is to compare them through a clever verbal twist on similar sounding words, or *homonyms.* This is the technique of the riddle: unlike objects are equated through a pun. Ingenious though they may be, puns are more revealing of the nature of words than the objects words represent; the logical method of *comparison and contrast* is a somewhat more significant and helpful way of treating unlike things. As its name denotes, comparison and contrast is *a systematic way of establishing points of resemblance and difference.*

Superficially, comparison and contrast may not differ very much from classification, which is used to separate objects on the basis of likeness and unlikeness. There are important differences between the two, however. Classification emphasizes common characteristics of groups of things, usually tangible; comparison and contrast emphasizes dissimilarities between

116

individual things, often intangible, to distinguish the individual. Classification is concerned with surface, or physical, resemblances. Comparison and contrast is concerned with essential distinctions and thus is a more penetrating method of understanding the qualities of objects.

If the technique of classification were applied to rats, hamsters, and squirrels, for example, all of them would be lumped together in the family of *rodents*: furry mammals that nibble or gnaw. Such a grouping tells us very little about the nature of a hamster as opposed to a rat or a squirrel. A systematic comparison of a hamster and a squirrel, on the other hand, if methodically carried out, will provide a fuller and more accurate knowledge of both squirrels and hamsters.

It would be difficult to over-emphasize the importance of comparison and contrast in human thought, since it underlies our system of values, our conception of intangible qualities, the methods of scientific investigation— even our idea of progress. Our practice of evaluating one thing as "better" or "smaller" or "more (anything)" than something else depends on an arbitrary scale of measurement based on comparison and contrast. Such commonly used words as "hot," "dry," "sweet," and "solid" reflect the logical patterns of thought which seek to determine the *degree* or *extent* to which a quality is present in a combination of things. Scientific *data* are observed phenomena which are judged or evaluated by some comparative scale and then used as the basis for establishing a hypothesis, a process, or a classification. Our belief in progress or improvement depends on a value system determined by a comparison and contrast of present and past conditions. Even our language, with its use of comparative adjectives and adverbs (good, better, best; slowly, more slowly, very slowly) is permeated with comparisons and contrasts.*

Inevitably, since it plays such an important part in thinking, comparison and contrast appears often in written rhetoric. This technique can be employed to advantage when writing about actions, people or ideas. The Greek biographers—Xenophon among them—discovered long ago that one of the best ways to depict a man's character is to show how he is like and unlike men of comparable positions. The contemporary journalist Richard

---

* It should be noted here that many people make errors in language usage by illogically trying to compare words that have no comparative or superlative degrees of comparison. Any adjective which indicates a supreme or unique state cannot logically be compared, e.g., "one," "square," "dead," "unique." Often people say "very unique," which is redundant at best and foolish at worst. "Unique" means *sui generis,* in a class alone, and thus, incomparable.

Rovere uses the same technique in his portrait of the late Senator Mc-Carthy (see page 133). The ancient historian Herodotus compared and contrasted the customs and behavior of far-flung peoples of the Mediterranean world. Margaret Mead, a modern anthropologist, employs the same principles in her treatment of the Balinese and Samoans. Even such seemingly unlike fields as journalism and poetry may be profitably compared and contrasted in written prose, as Archibald MacLeish shows in his essay, "The Poet and the Press," on page 432.

If you wish to use the principles of comparison and contrast in developing your ideas and expressing them in literary form, first select the objects, persons, actions, cultures, or ideas you want to treat, and define the major categories to which each belongs. Enumerate to yourself the characteristics the *sui generis* object shows by its inclusion in larger classes, and then compare, or correlate, the common qualities between the objects of your investigation. Alexander the Great and Julius Caesar were both ancient generals, warriors, adventurers, and rulers of empires, for instance. Then go on to point out the chief points of disparity: e.g., Alexander was a Macedonian, Hellenic in temperament, a monomaniac, the son of a militarist, trained in logic by Aristotle, and a mystic; whereas Caesar was a Roman, thoroughly Latin in disposition, widespread in interests, a patrician and not royal, educated in the arts, and a pragmatic administrator. Choose the points of major likeness and unlikeness for special emphasis, remembering always that you wish to emphasize the distinctive nature of the individual. It is your purpose to convey certain factual information about the objects of your discourse and to develop a clearer understanding of the nature of these objects collectively and singly.

In writing a comparison and contrast, you are likely to use some of the specialized versions of the method, which have been developed through the centuries. Some of these uses are primarily verbal; others are intellectual or logical. Both are subject to misuse at times. Let us see some of the chief forms of comparison and contrast in rhetoric.

ᐱ FIGURATIVE LANGUAGE

You have already learned from reading some essays on Thought and Language that language is symbolic and abstract by nature. At times, it is difficult to state in words exactly what you mean, especially if your meaning concerns something intangible like an emotion or an abstract concept (truth, justice). At other times, you may have difficulty in conveying an idea about something tangible that holds for you a quality not immediately apparent to other people. *Figurative language is those words and phrases which compare objects as possessing a like characteristic.* (Tropes, or figures of speech,) are thus a precise way of designating otherwise elusive qualities.

One of the chief kinds of figurative language is the *simile*. A simile is the direct comparison of two objects, qualities, or concepts for the sake of attributing a characteristic of one to the other. A simile is an open or obvious comparison; it always uses the word "like" or "as." (The Latin word, *similis, simile*, means "like" or "as.") Thus, "My love is like a red, red rose" is a simile; so are "sly as a fox," "slow as Christmas," and "quick as a wink." In every simile, some reasonably tangible action or object (a rose, a fox, Christmas, a wink) is cited for an outstanding quality (beauty, sly-ness, slowness, quickness), and any object directly compared with one of these (e.g., "my love") is assumed to share that quality. Poets are fond of such comparisons, because they permit an extensive comparison in a few words. Burns's tribute to his sweetheart asserts that she is beautiful, fresh, young, and sweet-smelling, simply by comparing her to a "red, red rose," which presumably has all these qualities. Properly used, a simile can make many positive comparisons in a few words. Notice, for instance, the wide and precise range of qualities attributed to the godly man in Psalm I by the Psalmist's use of the tree simile (page 129).

The *metaphor* is a form of comparison, like the simile, but the compar-ison is covert or unstated. The words "like" and "as" do not appear; so metaphors tend to be more subtle than similes. A metaphoric comparison may be of several kinds. Two things, one concrete and the other abstract, may be linked together as in "a cloak of silence" or "a stream of traffic." (The similes would be "a cloak-like silence" or "traffic like a stream.") A metaphor may be a combination of a noun and a verb: "the sneeze erupted" or "the trees curtseyed." (The sneeze becomes a volcano and the trees polite ladies.) Or the metaphor may substitute one word in place of an-other: a political candidate is a "standard-bearer" or money becomes "lettuce." Dr. Johnson's well-known discussion of the poets Dryden and Pope, on page 130, shows how metaphoric language can convey a critical evaluation while making implicit comparisons.

Still another sort of figurative comparison is the *personification* of a non-human thing by attributing to it human qualities; e.g., "the wind sighed" or "the sun is smiling." The inherent comparison of a non-human thing to a person is the kind of thinking called anthropomorphism; we try to understand something better by seeing it in terms of human emotion. Personification in rhetoric ranges from Aesop's *Fables* to Pogo and Mickey Mouse, and even John Ruskin's attack on the error of personification in his essay on the pathetic fallacy (i.e., attributing feelings to that which cannot feel) has not been successful in destroying the popularity of this type of figurative comparison.

There are other tropes which involve a comparative principle: *metonymy* is an assumed comparison between an object and something to which it is logically related: e.g., "the pen (literature) is mightier than the sword (warfare)." A *synecdoche* uses a part of something to refer to the entire thing: "to ask for a girl's hand (her entire person) in marriage." Like similes and metaphors, these lesser rhetorical figures are ways of expressing somewhat tenuous qualities in a concrete fashion through comparison.

As invaluable as they are to poets and prose writers alike, figures of speech lend themselves to exploitation by those who use words to persuade or to sell rather than to inform or enlighten. Advertising writers try to be as adept as poets in the use of figurative language. More attention will be paid to these writers in the chapters on diction and slanting. For now, let us simply note that an advertisement which proclaims that "Atoll Cigarettes Are Fresh as a Mountain Flower" or "Guzzler's Gin—the Mother's Milk of Alcoholic Beverages" is using a simile and a metaphor to *impute* a quality to a product which may not have it. Similarly, the newspaper which reports that "Senator Cato rasped or bellowed his proposals for a new Tax Law" is deliberately making an uncomplimentary comparison between the Senator and a file or a fire bellows.

ℬ THE ANALOGY

An *anology* is an extended comparison for the sake of explanation or illustration. It is *the establishment of a point-by-point correspondence between two situations or objects for explanatory purposes.* If we wish to understand or to explain to others the arrangement and structure of the atom, for example, we may compare it to the structure of our solar system: the sun is like the nucleus, the planets are like electrons, and various other moons, comets, and planetary dust are like neutrinos, mesons, and so forth. An analogy in its simplest form could be stated as a simile—an atom is like the solar system—but it differs from a simile in that there is similarity or correspondence between several aspects of the compared objects rather than in a single aspect.

As a way to convey some idea of what things are or how they work, the analogy is enormously helpful. The human heart may be compared to a pump or the brain to a switchboard, so that these highly complicated organs and their general principle of operation can be grasped. But the comparison, however clever or illuminating, is *not* complete: there are great differences between a brain and a switchboard and we must not assume or assert that the similarities are more than partial. When we overemphasize the comparative aspects of the analogy and disregard the contrasts between the analogous objects, we are susceptible to the error of the *False Analogy*.

A false analogy may be of several kinds. It may be an extension of a limited analogy to cover *all* circumstances under which a comparison is made, the wrongful exaggeration of several points of similarity to a total correspondence. This kind of false analogy may be seen in the time-honored comparison of a government (the body politic) with human anatomy. The head is the chief of state; the arms are the military forces; the legs are the workers; and so on and on, until the stomach becomes the Treasury Department, or some such nonsense. These forced comparisons are a form of confusion rather than clarification. Another kind of false analogy is the comparison of two things with essentially unlike or irreconcilable natures. Communistic societies are sometimes compared with a beehive: mechanistic class structure, rigidly designated worker functions, the sharing of common goods. But people are *not* bees, and it is doubtful that an analogy between them sheds much true light.

Another kind of error, both in drawing mental comparisons or putting them down in prose, is the *Argument by Analogy*. Here the assumption is that limited points of similarity between analogous phenomena may be used to "prove" that what is true in the case of one must also be true in the case of the second. Children are like puppies, so the argument by analogy runs; the way to housebreak a puppy is to whip it; thus the way to "housebreak" a child is to whip him. Examples of argument by analogy surround us in our everyday lives; possibly even you and I are guilty of them. American civilization is doomed because it is materialistic as Rome was, and Rome fell. The atom bomb does not mean the end of the human race, because people said the same thing about the invention of gun powder, and gun powder has not ended the human race. Use Rosebud Soap, as the glamorous stars of Broadway do, and you too will be glamorous.

Analogies are perfectly legitimate and very useful forms of comparison so long as they clarify the complex or help to explain the intangible. The parables of Jesus in the New Testament or the allegories of Socrates in the writings of Plato show how splendid a device the analogy is in the hands of a fine teacher. Because it necessarily simplifies, however, the analogy is a limited intellectual tool, and it must be used with care. To use an analogy to argue a point of view, or as a substitute for a complete comprehension of a complex situation, is dubious thinking and specious writing.

C. ANTITHESIS

Antithesis is a combination of two Greek words—*anti*, "against"; *thesis*, "proposition"—and it is a way of thinking or writing in which one thing is pitted against another to show their basic dissimilarities. The systematic contrast of ravens and writing desks at the start of the chapter was an example of antithesis. We might make a similar list of contrasting points about soul and body, Classicism and Romanticism, or culture and anarchy. The antithesis is the reverse of the analogy, which stresses points of resemblance.

Antithetical thinking is not only the basis for understanding the differences between two phenomena; it also underlies the spoken and written techniques of objective analysis. We speak of "weighing the pro's and con's" of a situation, by which we mean we try to reach some conception of the degree of truth in a case by considering opposite points of view. The very premises of law and trial by jury depend on an antithetical process conducted by a prosecuting and defense attorney. A formal debate, with affirmative and negative sides, is another instance of antithesis. And even an account book, with its credits and debits, uses the contrasting technique of antithetical thinking.

Rhetorically, antithetical statements of ideas or opinions may be indicated by a number of single words: "but," "nevertheless," "versus," "against," "opposing," and "contrariwise" among them. Or a more fully developed antithesis may use a balanced structure of phrases indicating opposition: "on the one hand this, on the other hand that," or "positively this but negatively that." So long as antithesis is used to give information or explain by presenting opposing facts, it is a valuable aid to understanding. Sometimes, however, antithesis as a general type of logical order becomes a means of argument or persuasion, in which case it is called disjunction.

ℚ DISJUNCTION

Disjunction means separation; the meaning of the Latin root phrase ("to unyoke") indicates something of the nature of disjunctive thinking and disjunctive rhetoric. In disjunction, alternative assertions are made, of which only one is supposedly true. The sign of a disjunctive statement is the words "either . . . or . . .," as in the sentence, "Either Semiramis founded Babylon, or Ninus founded it." This statement not only denies any principle of similarity (such as "Like Ninus, Semiramis founded Babylon," or "Semiramis and Ninus founded Babylon"); it emphasizes antithesis to the extent that contradiction is implied ("It is impossible that both Semiramis and Ninus founded Babylon"), and that one alternative is true and the other is not. Thus the disjunctive statement indicates that, of two opposing ideas, only *one* can be valid.

In its use as a kind of deductive thinking, the disjunction can become very perplexing, as we shall see, but so long as it simply asserts alternatives and does not declare one of them false, it remains a type of exposition (or factual discourse). Even in this use, it may take one of several forms of expression; for instance:

> Either Hitler was a sadist or he was a masochist.
> If Hitler was not a masochist, then he was a sadist.
> Unless he was a masochist, Hitler was a sadist.

Any of these statements can be reduced to the "either . . . or . . ." format, where the choice is more obvious and the disjunction more apparent.

Since a disjunction is an assertion of alternatives (or two choices), it may become the wrong form of thinking or the erroneous sort of statement called the *False Dilemma*. This familiar phrase refers to such statements as:

> Either a piranha eats human flesh or it starves to death.
> Either Christopher Marlowe wrote *King Lear* or Thomas Ford did.
> Either you hate Khrushchev or you are a Communist.

In these statements, only a choice of two possibilities is given when other possibilities exist: a piranha eats other things when hapless swimmers are not available; neither Marlowe nor Ford wrote *King Lear;* and many people who are non-Communists do not hate Khrushchev. If a disjunction states only two choices when more exist, it is a false dilemma.

ℰ   THE NO DEGREE FALLACY

Since comparison and contrast is the basis for our ideas of *degree*, sometimes in our thinking we exaggerate the contrasts between two things to such a point that we view them as irreconcilable, diametrical extremes, and thus forget that they actually may simply be two points separated by a matter of extent or degree. None of us would be silly enough to declare that water must either be hot or else cold; it can be chilly, cool, tepid, or warm, and to assume that these graduations of heat do not exist is to simplify thought to a harmfully inaccurate extent. The illustration of hot or cold water may seem silly, but otherwise sensible people think and utter equally wrong examples of *No Degree* when they let their emotional urges conquer their logical ability.

"Set up Medical Care for the Aged, and America will soon have Socialized Medicine!" "Take that first drink, and you'll wind up an alcoholic!" "Let Alaska and Hawaii into the Union, and then Puerto Rico, Panama, and finally Tasmania will want in, too!" "Let the Russians hear one soft word from us, and they'll start bombing New York!" All of these commit the error of thinking there is no difference between one, limited action and an all-out process, or that one change cannot be admitted without admitting a large additional number of changes. Often the no degree fallacy is stated as a dilemma ("Either we keep Alaska out of the Union or *everybody* will want in"); but it is detectable in any form as a refusal to admit compromise or to seek for similarities where similarities exist.

In the guise of a written essay, antithetical and disjunctive statements often take on an authority they do not have, and even false analogies and dilemmas may slip by the reader's notice unless he takes care. Bertrand Russell's essay, "Co-existence or No Existence," expertly destroys such sophistical reasoning even as it shows the proper uses of antithesis and disjunction. Whether you agree with its fundamental assumptions or not, you will find Lord Russell's prose marvelously clear in its use of the techniques of comparative and contrasting thought and writing.

In summary of all the techniques of comparison and contrast, we may say that they enable us to understand one thing more clearly by likening it to or differentiating it from some other thing. So long as figures of speech present accurate comparisons, and analogies illustrate properly, they aid understanding. So long as antitheses and disjunction merely distinguish differences or point out alternatives, we may accept them as valid. If tropes are slanted to convince us of an untruth, however, or an analogy misrepresents to "prove" a contention; if antithesis is exaggerated until a choice is unduly limited or degrees of likeness are not admitted; then comparison and contrast is used to muddle thinking and to obfuscate rhetoric rather than to improve the one and guide the other.

I. Questions for Review
   1. What are the differences between classification and comparison and contrast? In what way does classification depend on the other technique?
   2. How does one go about writing an essay comparing and contrasting two things?
   3. What figures of speech employ comparison? What is the difference between these tropes?
   4. What is antithesis? Give examples of the ways it is used in social processes, in thinking, in literature.
   5. What is disjunction? What is the basic form of the disjunctive statement?
   6. What is a false dilemma? How does it differ from disjunction?
   7. What is an analogy? A false analogy? Argument by analogy?
   8. How are the analogy and the antithesis related?
   9. What is the fallacy of no degree? How does it differ from the false dilemma?
   10. What are the chief uses of comparison and contrast? How is it misused?

II. Exercises
   1. List the main points of similarity and difference between:
      A. Football and soccer
      B. Epicureanism and hedonism
      C. Stars and planets
      D. Dolls and puppets
      E. Helicopters and gliders
      F. Napoleon and Mussolini
      G. Stocks and bonds
      H. Mathematics and philosophy
      I. Revolutions and rebellions
      J. Wedgwood and Meissen china
   2. What figures of speech are the following:
      A. The fog comes on little cat feet.

B. Abraso Detergent is as mild, as kind to your hands as an expensive beauty lotion; buy some today.

C. If music be the food of love, play on.

D. Hurrah for the Red, White, and Blue!

E. Enjoy the springtime odor of an El Fungo Cigar.

F. He has a finger in every pie.

G. A poem should be palpable and mute as a globed fruit.

H. The hand that rocks the cradle rules the world.

I. Rumor walked through the land, whispering his secrets.

J. Ballerina maple leaves twirled in the autumn wind.

3. Are these analogies explanatory, false, or argumentative:

A. Language experts tell us that words symbolize sounds, which in turn represent ideas, so that language is a symbol of a symbol, just as a check is a symbol of paper money which symbolizes gold. It's clear from this that we ought not to use too many words, since the man who writes too many checks will overdraw his bank account.

B. In literature, words are like leaves: where you find the most words, you're likely to find the least fruit of sense.

C. When the Federal Government sent troops into Little Rock to enforce integration of the public school system, the governor of Arkansas attacked the action, saying that it was an act of brutal intervention as bad as the sending of troops by Russia into Hungary to squelch the Hungarians' rebellion. In both cases, the governor said, the rights of a freedom-loving, independent people were being violated.

D. America must wake up to its moral decadence before it's too late and we bring about our own destruction. The Hebrews were warned by the prophet Isaiah about their vice, luxury, immorality, and degeneracy, but they refused to listen; as a consequence they were conquered and sold into slavery by the Babylonians. The same thing will happen to us unless we reform ourselves and our nation.

E. A Chinese whirligig operates very much like a water mill wheel. The folds of the child's toy are set in spiral on a stick, like the paddles of a mill wheel are set on a shaft, and just as the moving current of water strikes the wheel, causing it to rotate, so the moving current of air spins the folds of the Whirligig.

F. Napoleon was a little bantam rooster of a man: he was short but cocky; he loved to strut about, looking important; he adored gaudy clothes and dazzling headpieces; he even kept a sort of harem of adoring ladies. And his willingness to crow about his achievements was legendary.

G. Dr. Manfred von Eisenstadt has conducted a series of significant experiments recently in which he has concluded that human beings can live longer by eating nothing but bananas and leafy vegetables and perhaps dried grasses. He has observed a herd of elephants for the last few years and concluded that their diet of such foods is the cause of their well-known longevity. By eating as elephants do, he suggests, a man may live to be ninety or a hundred years old.

H. Generals make the best presidents because they're used to making decisions and giving orders. After all, the government of the United States is organized like an army: the Cabinet members are seconds-in-command; senators and congressmen are majors and captains; and the vast corps of civil service workers—postmen, clerks, secretaries—are the privates. Who better than a general can command such an organization?

I. A vacuum cleaner is like a soda straw. You suck liquid through a straw by drawing out the air with your mouth, thus creating a vacuum which the liquid rises to fill. A vacuum cleaner empties its bag through the electrical creation of a vacuum, which dirt and air rush to fill through a nozzle and tube arrangement similar to the soda straw.

J. The human stomach is a combination storage bin, chemical plant, and pulverizing machine. It also has some of the characteristics of an elastic bag, a conveyer belt, and a sponge.

4. Are the following pairs analogous or antithetical? Why?
   A. Table silver and garden tools
   B. Jesus and Socrates
   C. Zero and infinity
   D. Catholicism and Communism
   E. Solids and gases
   F. Justice and vengeance
   G. Youth and ignorance
   H. Education and happiness
   I. Acids and bases
   J. Male and female

5. Are the following valid disjunctions, false dilemmas, or no degree fallacies?
   A. One thing is clear: either a man dies young or he grows old. There's no other possibility.
   B. Don't bite your fingernails. Once you start, you're bound to get appendicitis!
   C. Why send financial aid to Laos? If we do, then Vietnam will want a loan, then Afghanistan, then Israel, then Red China, and we'll bankrupt ourselves while helping others.
   D. If the government doesn't support the American button industry

by raising tariffs on imported buttons, it's the end of our free enterprise system.

E. If you aren't a theist, then you're an atheist—that's plain to see.

F. Never take a chance with food that may contain botuline. One taste means inevitable death!

III. Suggestions for Writing

1. Using a lexicon, grammar text, or some other source, make up a list of words which express degrees of qualities (e.g., "solid," "molten," "liquid," "gaseous"), and write an essay on the ways language expresses such a scale of degrees.

2. Look up the positive, comparative, and superlative forms of a number of "strong" adjectives (good, bad, many, etc.) and "weak" adjectives (strong, rich, fast) as well as a number of "absolute" or incomparable adjectives (whole, no, human, circular). Write an essay, classifying the sorts of qualities compared in each of the three ways.

3. Read through a history or physics textbook and note the author's use of analogy; then evaluate this use in a critical examination of several specific analogies.

4. Write an essay, using an analogy, to explain one of these topics:
   a. The operation of flying a kite
   b. Your reaction to music
   c. Color blindness
   d. The sensations of a head cold
   e. Ocean tides
   f. Sound waves
   g. Digestion

5. Read Plato's *Crito* at the end of the book, and write a critical discussion of Socrates' use of analogy.

6. Write a comparison and contrast of one of the subjects in II 1 above or a pair of subjects of your or your instructor's choosing.

THE BOOK OF PSALMS

PSALM I.

Blessed *is* the man that walketh not in the counsel of the ungodly,
Nor standeth in the way of sinners,
Nor sitteth in the seat of the scornful.

But his delight *is* in the Law of the LORD;
And in his Law doth he meditate day and night.
And he shall be like a tree planted by the rivers of water,
That bringeth forth his fruit in his season;   SIMILE
His leaf also shall not wither;
And whatsoever he doeth shall prosper.
The ungodly *are* not so:
But *are* like the chaff which the wind driveth away.
Therefore the ungodly shall not stand in the judgment,
Nor sinners in the Congregation of the righteous.
For the LORD knoweth the way of the righteous:
But the way of the ungodly shall perish.

1. What form of comparison is used in Psalm I; explain your answer.
2. What are the bases of comparison between the godly man and the tree? Do such a man and a tree have these qualities in common? Why?
3. Explain the form of comparison between the ungodly and chaff.
4. From what kind of cultural and economic background are the figures of speech in Psalm I taken? Cite evidence in the poem to support your view.
5. Are the comparisons in this Psalm effective? Are they accurate? Explain your answer. How are they related to the use of parallelism?

Dr. Samuel Johnson

THE LIFE OF ALEXANDER POPE

HE PROFESSED TO HAVE LEARNED HIS POETRY FROM DRYDEN, WHOM, whenever an opportunity was presented, he praised through his whole life with unvaried liberality; and perhaps his character may receive some illustration, if he be compared with his master.

Integrity of understanding and nicety of discernment were not allotted in a less proportion to Dryden than to Pope. The rectitude of Dryden's mind was sufficiently shewn by the dismission of his poetical prejudices, and the rejection of unnatural thoughts and rugged numbers. But Dryden never desired to apply all the judgement that he had. He wrote, and professed to write, merely for the people; and when he pleased others, he contented himself. He spent no time in struggles to rouse latent powers; he never attempted to make that better which was already good, nor often to mend what he must have known to be faulty. He wrote, as he tells us, with very little consideration; when occasion or necessity called upon him, he poured out what the present moment happened to supply, and, when once it had passed the press, ejected it from his mind; for when he had no pecuniary interest, he had no further solicitude.

Pope was not content to satisfy; he desired to excel, and therefore always endeavoured to do his best: he did not court the candour, but dared the judgement of his reader, and expecting no indulgence from others, he shewed none to himself. He examined lines and words with minute and punctilious observation, and retouched every part with indefatigable diligence, till he had left nothing to be forgiven.

For this reason he kept his pieces very long in his hands, while he considered and reconsidered them. The only poems which can be supposed to have been written with such regard to the times as might hasten their publication, were the two satires of *Thirty-eight*; of which Dodsley told me, that they were brought to him by the author, that they might be fairly copied. "Every line," said he, "was then written twice over; I gave him a clean transcript, which he sent some time afterwards to me for the press, with every line written twice over a second time."

From *The Lives of the Poets*, 1779–1781.

His declaration, that his care for his works ceased at their publication, was not strictly true. His parental attention never abandoned them; what he found amiss in the first edition, he silently corrected in those that followed. He appears to have revised the *Iliad*, and freed it from some of its imperfections; and the *Essay on Criticism* received many improvements after its first appearance. It will seldom be found that he altered without adding clearness, elegance, or vigour. Pope had perhaps the judgement of Dryden; but Dryden certainly wanted the diligence of Pope.

In acquired knowledge, the superiority must be allowed to Dryden, whose education was more scholastick, and who before he became an author had been allowed more time for study, with better means of information. His mind has a larger range, and he collects his images and illustrations from a more extensive circumference of science. Dryden knew more of man in his general nature, and Pope in his local manners. The notions of Dryden were formed by comprehensive speculation, and those of Pope by minute attention. There is more dignity in the knowledge of Dryden, and more certainty in that of Pope.

Poetry was not the sole praise of either; for both excelled likewise in prose; but Pope did not borrow his prose from his predecessor. The style of Dryden is capricious and varied, that of Pope is cautious and uniform; Dryden obeys the motions of his own mind, Pope constrains his mind to his own rules of composition. Dryden is sometimes vehement and rapid; Pope is always smooth, uniform, and gentle. Dryden's page is a natural field, rising into inequalities, and diversified by the varied exuberance of abundant vegetation; Pope's is a velvet lawn, shaven by the scythe, and levelled by the roller.

Of genius, that power which constitutes a poet; that quality without which judgement is cold and knowledge is inert; that energy which collects, combines, amplifies, and animates; the superiority must, with some hesitation, be allowed to Dryden. It is not to be inferred that of this poetical vigour Pope had only a little, because Dryden had more; for every other writer since Milton must give place to Pope; and even of Dryden it must be said, that if he has brighter paragraphs, he has not better poems. Dryden's performances were always hasty, either excited by some external occasion, or extorted by domestick necessity; he composed without consideration, and published without correction. What his mind could supply at call, or gather in one excursion, was all that he sought, and all that he gave. The dilatory caution of Pope enabled him to condense his sentiments, to multiply his images, and to accumulate all that study might produce, or chance might supply. If the flights of Dryden therefore are higher, Pope continues longer on the wing. If of Dryden's fire the blaze is brighter, of Pope's the heat is more regular and constant. Dryden often surpasses expectation, and Pope never falls below it. Dryden is read with frequent astonishment, and Pope with perpetual delight.

This parallel will, I hope, when it is well considered, be found just; and if the reader should suspect me, as I suspect myself, of some partial fondness for the memory of Dryden, let him not too hastily condemn me; for meditation and enquiry may, perhaps, shew him the reasonableness of my determination.

1. Who were John Dryden, Alexander Pope, and Dr. Johnson? Look up the basic facts about them in an encyclopaedia or the *Dictionary of National Biography*. What did they all have in common?
2. Identify the forms of comparison and contrast which Johnson uses in this passage. How many different kinds are there?
3. List the major points of comparison and difference which Johnson makes. Does each succeed in individualizing the two writers equally or does Johnson emphasize one writer more than the other? Explain.
4. Why do you suppose Johnson resorted to figures of speech to make his comparisons? What characteristics of the two writers is he able to convey through these tropes?
5. What other basis of comparison than that in the passage could Johnson have used to compare Dryden and Pope? Why did he select this one?

Richard Rovere

SENATOR JOE McCARTHY: WHAT HE WAS AND WHAT HE DID

BACK IN THOSE MELANCHOLY DAYS, MANY PEOPLE NOT EASILY GIVEN TO alarm feared that a day might come when McCarthy would not be breaking the laws but proclaiming them. World War II was not far in the past, and comparisons with Adolf Hitler came readily to mind. "When I think of McCarthy, I automatically think of Hitler," President Eisenhower's banker brother, Arthur, once said, to the consternation of the White House. "McCarthy's methods, to me, look like Hitler's," Eleanor Roosevelt wrote. Joseph C. Harsch reported in 1953 that when the Germans thought about McCarthy, they found "a release from [their] own sense of guilt about Hitler," and in Düsseldorf, Hjalmar Schacht, Hitler's financial prestidigitator, said to John Emmet Hughes, an adviser to Eisenhower, "Perhaps now you realize it is not so easy for a people to get rid of a demagogue just by wishing him to go away—no?" The comparisons were natural and not wholly without justice. Like Hitler McCarthy was a screamer, a political thug, a master of the mob, an exploiter of popular fears. He used the fear of Bolshevism as Hitler used it, with the difference that Hitler described Communism as a revolutionary menace to the state, while McCarthy described it as a conspiracy that had already achieved some of the ends it prized the most. McCarthy was not anti-Semitic, but in his demonology the Democratic leaders, the liberal intelligentsia, and a supposedly decadent Eastern aristocracy played the accomplice role that Hitler assigned to the Jews.

To be sure, there were points, and crucial ones, at which contrast was more striking than comparison. Hitler had a program for the coming millennium; McCarthy had no program for tomorrow morning. Hitler's aim was to win control of the machinery of the state; it is still arguable as to whether McCarthy was up to anything of quite this magnitude. He never encouraged direct action by his followers; he did not organize uni-

From *Senator Joe McCarthy*, © 1959, by Richard H. Rovere. Reprinted by permission of Harcourt, Brace & World, Inc.

formed groups or even raggle-taggle street fighters. Politically, he never tried to organize outside the existing party structure, and there are reasons for supposing that he never intended to do so. But he built within the system a large and dedicated following. It was larger than that of any demagogue of the past and the first movement of its kind ever to be national in scope. Though this country has produced many demagogues of proficiency, none of them, before McCarthy, had more than a regional or sectarian power.* Huey Long of Louisiana seemed on the verge of winning a national following when Dr. Carl A. Weiss's bullet found him in 1935, and Father Charles E. Coughlin of Michigan might have led a formidable movement if he had not been silenced by his ecclesiastical superiors at the start of the war. But neither of them made it, and neither of them had anything like McCarthy's influence on American life and institutions.

Because McCarthyism has no real grit and substance as a doctrine and no organization, it is difficult to deal with as a movement. Adherence was of many different sorts. There were those who accepted McCarthy's leadership and would have been happy to see him President. There were others who were indifferent to his person but receptive to what he had to say about the government. There were others still who put no particular stock in what he had to say and even believed it largely nonsense but felt that he was valuable anyway.

McCarthy drew into his following most of the zanies and zombies and compulsive haters who had followed earlier and lesser demagogues in the fascist and semifascist movements of the thirties and forties. At a typical McCarthy rally, there would be, seated in the front rows, thanks to early arrival, numbers of moon-struck souls wearing badges or carrying placards identifying them as Minute Women of the U.S.A., Sons of I Shall Return, members of the Alert Council for America, the Nationalist Action League, We the Mothers Mobilize, the Republoform, and so on. They knew all the words of "Nobody Loves Joe but the Pee-pul," and if this anthem was sung, their voices, generally on the shrill or reedy side, would be heard above the rest. But this was really the least part of it. McCarthy went far beyond the world of the daft and the frenzied—or, to put the matter another way, that world was greatly enlarged while he was

---

* In *The American Democrat,* published in 1828, James Fenimore Cooper wrote as if a demagogue was almost by definition a spokesman for a local interest against the common good. The only types he discussed—in a generally brilliant essay—were "the town demagogue" and "the county demagogue."

about. Into it came large numbers of regular Republicans who had coolly decided that there was no longer any respectable way of unhorsing the Democrats and that only McCarthy's wild and conscienceless politics could do the job. He built, as Samuel Lubell pointed out in *Revolt of the Moderates,* a coalition of the aggrieved—of men and women not deranged but deeply affronted by various tendencies over the preceding two or three decades: toward internationalism, and, in particular, toward closer ties with the British; toward classlessness; toward the welfare state. There were Roman Catholics, particularly those of Irish descent, who saw in this aggressive Hibernian the flaming avenger of their own humiliations of the past and who could not believe that the criticism he provoked was based on anything but hatred of his Church and his name. To these and many others he was a symbol of rebellion. And beyond all this, he simply persuaded a number of people that he was speaking the essential truth; he sent up such vast and billowing clouds of smoke that many men and women who were not abnormally gullible became convinced that there must be a fire beneath it all.

This is an excerpt from a full length work entitled *Senator Joe McCarthy.* Senator McCarthy was the junior Senator from Wisconsin, who in 1952 and 1953 created a sensation with his one-man investigation into alleged Communist infiltration of the State Department. According to Rovere, Senator McCarthy never actually proved that a single Communist agent was employed by the Department of State, in spite of all his accusations. McCarthy was officially censured by the United States Senate in 1954, and he died in 1957.

1. What characteristics does Rovere ascribe to Senator McCarthy in this passage? Which are imputed through comparison and which are directly stated?

2. Does Rovere consider the comparison of McCarthy with Hitler an accurate one? Explain.

3. Who are the other men with whom McCarthy is compared: Huey Long, Father Coughlin? What qualities does Rovere say they shared? How did they differ from McCarthy?

4. What would you say is Rovere's purpose in comparing McCarthy with Hitler and lesser demagogues? Is he attempting to discredit McCarthy or to explain him? Discuss.

5. Do the comparisons and contrasts in this essay result in the individualization of McCarthy or do they classify him? Why?

Bertrand Russell

CO-EXISTENCE OR NO EXISTENCE:
THE CHOICE IS OURS

THE RECENT CHANGES IN THE TECHNIQUE OF WAR HAVE PRODUCED A
situation which is wholly unprecedented. War has existed ever since there
were organized states, that is to say for some six thousand years. This ancient institution is now about to end. There are two ways in which the
end may come about: the first is the extinction of the human race; the
second is an agreement not to fight. I do not know which of these will be
chosen.

Neither the general public nor the majority of powerful statesmen have
as yet realized that war with modern weapons cannot serve the purposes of
any government in the world. It is of the first importance that this should
be realized by those who control policy both in the East and in the West.
It is generally conceded by those who are in a position to speak with authority that no complete defense against an H-bomb attack is possible. We
must, I think, consider it the most likely hypothesis that if a great war
broke out tomorrow each side would be successful in attack and unsuccessful in defense. This means that in the first days of such a war all the great
centers of population on each side would be obliterated. Those who survived this first disaster would perish slowly or quickly as a result of the
fall-out from radioactive cloud. Destruction of life from this cause would
not be confined to the belligerent countries. The winds would gradually
spread death throughout the world. This, at least, is what is to be feared. It
cannot be said that the worst outcome is certain, but it is sufficiently probable to deter any sane man from incurring the risk.

Apart from the totality of destruction, there is another new element in
the situation. In old days if you had a military advantage over your enemy,
you might hope to win in time. But now, if each side has enough H-bombs
to wipe out the other, there is no longer any advantage in having twice as
many as your adversary.

Both in the United States and in Great Britain there has been much

From *The Nation*, CLXXX, No. 25 (June 18, 1955). Copyright 1955 by *The
Nation*. Reprinted by permission of the author and of *The Nation*.

talk of civil defense. Russian military journals contain talk of the same kind. All such plans, I am convinced, show either ignorance or hypocrisy in those who advocate them. Deep shelters would enable a portion of the population to survive the first explosion, but sooner or later these people would have to emerge from their shelters into a radioactive world.

Although the H-bomb is the center of public attention at the moment, it is only one of the possibilities of destruction which science has put in the hands of irresponsible politicians. Chemical and bacteriological warfare are studied by all powerful states and may have consequences at least as horrifying as those of the H-bomb. There is no visible end to the methods of inflicting death that may be invented. Even if a portion of the human race were to survive a great war now, it cannot be doubted that the next war, if scientific technique survives, would complete what its predecessor had left unfinished.

There is therefore no escape from the choice that lies before us: Shall we renounce war, or shall we bring our species to an end? *NO DEGREE FALLACY*

ESCAPE FROM REALITY

If men realized that these are the only alternatives, no one can doubt that they would choose peace. But there are various ways in which people escape the realization of unpleasant facts. I have seen statements by Russians and Chinese that a thermonuclear war would of course destroy the rotten capitalistic civilization of the West but would not vitally injure the sturdy Communist nations of the East. I have also seen statements by American authorities claiming that the West would be victorious. Both seemed to me, if genuinely believed, to be mere fantasies of wish-fulfilment and, if not genuinely believed, to be part of the silly game of bluff which great nations have been allowing themselves. I hope that this is beginning to be understood. Recently there have been hopeful signs that neither side is willing to push issues to the point of war. And with every month that passes there is a better chance that statesmen both in the East and in the West will become aware of some of the important facts by which their policy ought to be guided.

Another widespread delusion is that perhaps in a great war H-bombs would not be employed. People point to the fact that gas was not employed in the Second World War. They forget that gas had not proved a decisive weapon even in the First World War and that in the meantime gas-masks had been provided which were a complete protection. Any analogy is therefore entirely misleading.

It is thought by many that the first step forward should be an international agreement not to use H-bombs in the event of war, and this is generally coupled with the suggestion that both sides should destroy their existing stock of these weapons. This suggestion has certain merits but also certain drawbacks. Its chief merit is that if the destruction of existing stocks were honestly carried out, the danger of a sudden attack in the style of Pearl Harbor would be lessened. Against this we must set the fact that no system of inspection can now make sure that bombs are not being manufactured. This is a new fact. At the time of the Baruch proposal it was still possible for an inspectorate to gain control of the raw materials, but this is so no longer. Each side would therefore suspect that the other side was manufacturing bombs surreptitiously, and this might make relations worse than if no agreement had been concluded. What is even more important is that, if war did break out, neither side would consider itself bound by the agreement, and after a certain number of months H-bomb warfare would be in full swing. Only by not making war can the danger be avoided. We must therefore turn our thoughts away from war to the methods by which peace can be made secure.

PEACE BY STAGES

The transition from the cold war to a condition of secure peace cannot be made in a day. But it can be made, and it must be made. It will have to be made by stages. The first stage will consist in persuading all powerful governments of the world that their aims, whatever they may be, cannot be achieved by war. In this first stage, scientists—not only nuclear physicists but also physiologists, geneticists, and bacteriologists—have a very important part to play. Their discoveries have created the dangers, and it is their obvious duty to arouse the public and the governments to a sense of the risks they are running. They may, in performing this duty, be compelled to take action of which their governments disapprove, but loyalty to mankind should be for them the paramount consideration. I am convinced that it is within their power to persuade the governments both of the East and of the West to look to negotiation rather than war for a solution of their problems.

The next stage must be to create temporary machinery to negotiate settlements of all the questions at present causing conflict between East and

West. It will be necessary to refer such questions to a body of negotiators in which East and West have equal representation and the balance of power is in the hands of the neutrals. I do not venture to suggest what solution should be reached on any of the vexed questions of the present. I think that a body constituted as I have suggested would avoid gross unfairness to either side, and subject to this condition almost any settlement would be preferable to a continuation of the present state of tension. A very important part of any settlement should of course be a drastic reduction of armaments. It is hardly to be supposed that the very delicate negotiations which will be required can be conducted successfully in the atmosphere of strained hostility that has existed during recent years. Each side will have to abandon perpetual abuse of the other and learn to practice that degree of toleration which after centuries of warfare was at last achieved between Christians and Moslems and between Catholics and Protestants. We cannot now wait for the slow operation of reason through the discouragements of long indecisive wars. We must learn in advance a manner of thinking and feeling which in the past has been learned slowly and through bitter experience. I will not pretend that this is easy. But if men can be made to realize the dreadful alternative I do not think it will prove impossible.

THE THIRD STEP

If the immediate problems that now divide East and West were settled in some such way, we could reach the third stage of progress toward secure peace. The international problems of our day are not the last that will ever arise. There will be new problems, perhaps dividing the world quite differently from the way in which it is now divided between Communist and anti-Communist blocs.[3] So long as there is not an established international authority capable of enforcing peace, the risk of war will remain, and with every advance in science the risk will become more terrible. The international anarchy resulting from a multitude of states with unrestricted sovereignty must be brought to an end. The international authority which is to end it will have to be federal and endowed with only such powers as are necessary for preserving the peace of the world. The most important of these powers, and also the most difficult to secure, will be an obvious preponderance of armed forces over those of any national state or alliance of states. The anarchic liberty at present enjoyed by sovereign states is dear to most people and will not be surrendered easily, but it will have to be surrendered if the human species is to survive. The process required is a continuation of that which occurred in the fifteenth and sixteenth centuries. Before that time powerful barons in their castles could defy national governments, and there was the same sort of anarchy within a nation as now exists between nations. Gunpowder and artillery put an end to internal anarchy in France, Spain, and England. The hydrogen bomb has the same part to play in ending international anarchy. The loss of liberty, though it may be distasteful, is precisely of the same kind as that which private individuals suffer by being forbidden to commit murder, for after all it is the right to murder which hitherto sovereign states will be asked to surrender.

LEGITIMATE HOPES

I have been speaking of dangers and how to avoid them, but there is another thing which it is just as important to emphasize, for while fears are at present unavoidable, hopes are equally legitimate. If we take the measures needed to end our fears, we shall thereby create a world capable of such well-being as has never been known and scarcely even imagined. Throughout the long ages since civilization began, the bulk of mankind have lived lives of misery and toil and bondage. All the long burden of misery that has darkened the slow progress of mankind has now become unnecessary. If we can learn to tolerate each other and to live in amity, poverty can be abolished everywhere more completely than it is now abolished in the most fortunate nations. Fear can be so much diminished that a new buoyancy and a new joy will brighten the daily lives of all. The work of science, which while war survives is largely evil, will become wholly beneficent. Nothing stands in the way but the darkness of atavistic evil passions. New technical possibilities of well-being exist, but the wisdom to make use of them has hitherto been lacking. Shall we collectively continue to turn our back upon the things that each one of us individually desires? We can make a world of light, or we can banish life from our planet. One or other we must do, and do soon. A great duty rests upon those who realize these alternatives, for it is they who must persuade mankind to make the better choice.

1. Is this essay an example of exposition (informative writing) or persuasion (argumentative writing)? Justify your answer.

2. What analogies does Lord Russell attack in his essay? Does he prove his points?

3. What basis for the two alternatives of his title does the author establish in the essay? Does he support with facts his contention that only two possibilities exist?

4. Point out all dilemmas and disjunctions in this essay. Are there any choices which are false?

5. List any hypotheses which Lord Russell advances. Are they valid? Why or why not?

6. Write a theme, either supporting or attacking Lord Russell's position in this essay; then evaluate your answer. How many disjunctions, analogies, and hypotheses do you use in making your points?

CHAPTER 6

LOGIC AND ARGUMENTATION

"Myself when young did eagerly frequent
"Doctor and Saint, and heard great argument
"About it, and about: but evermore
"Came out by the same door where in I went."

EDWARD FITZGERALD, *The Rubáiyát of Omar Khýyam*

By now, you are undoubtedly chafing at the repetition of such words as "regarded," "established," and "arbitrary" in our definitions of logical and rhetorical order. "Established by whom?" you must feel like asking, and it has probably occurred to you that such arbitrary constructs as organizations, classification, and the other forms of logical order which we have encountered so far must be something less than dogmatic. In fact, have you thought that all logical systems are open to question or subject to doubt?

They are. Any man-made arrangement, forms of logical order included, is liable to constant re-evaluation and criticism. Furthermore men of differing abilities and intellectual habits may argue repeatedly over the very principles by which thinking operates and literature records. Two eminent scientists may disagree violently over whether a newly discovered skeleton of a prehistoric man belongs in a certain classification or whether its discovery demands the establishment of an entirely new system of classifying. Several highly qualified men of letters may wage a verbal battle for years over the nature of syntax or the merits of a contemporary poem. Such disagreement is healthy and profitable, provided it stays within certain limits: each generation must re-examine the knowledge of the past in light of its own experience, and it must apply that knowledge or adapt it to present needs. Consequently, disagreements take place regularly in every field of knowledge; it is right that they should.

When we say that some "logical" system is "considered" or "regarded" as practicable, we mean that people who know about such matters are in general agreement about principles. It is not necessary that every one of the 2,500,000,000 people on earth reach a common accord about the proper forms of outlining or the use of a principle of division in classification. It is enough that a few experts who have made an extensive study of a matter make common cause as to methods of approach or thinking procedures. The validity of Einstein's formula of $E = MC^2$ does not depend upon a universal plebiscite but upon the concurrent testimony of experts in physics. Similarly, the laws of the United States depend less on popular sentiment than on the interpretation of the United States Constitution, drawn up by a very few men and constantly re-interpreted by nine judges on the Supreme Court.

Usually, then, we can assume that "arbitrary" logical systems have been established by "experts" in their field. An expert is a man with a specialized, comprehensive, first-hand knowledge of an area of study, whose judgment is respected by others in the field. If this man is capable of evaluating his own knowledge objectively, he is all the more an authority. In matters depending on first hand knowledge of *facts*—the height of the Andes Mountains or the names of the emperors of Byzantium—we may rely on the explorers who have tracked out the Andes or the scholars who have devoted themselves to Byzantine history. In matters of *opinion*, however, the experts themselves sometimes disagree, as we know, and laymen are forced to do their own thinking to arrive at the truth.

How can we tell a *fact* from an *opinion*? Or, to extend the problem, how can we differentiate between the kind of rhetoric which presents factual information (*exposition*) and that which tries to convince us of a certain point of view or attitude (*argumentation*)? Separating facts from beliefs and exposition from argumentation is not as easy as you might think. We know how difficult it is to distinguish such expository techniques as cause and effect from the persuasive forced hypothesis or the post hoc argument; similarly, the analogy often merges with argumentative analogy or antithesis with the disjunction. There *are* ways of separating purely factual knowledge from opinionative knowledge; furthermore, there are workable methods of pursuing differences of opinion in order to arrive at facts.

First of all, you must scrutinize the nature of the idea as it is stated in a sentence (or unit of complete thought). Only sentences which the grammarian calls *declarative* are *statements*; the *statement* is an assertion that something is true. Each of these declarative sentences is a statement, or assertion of truth:

> Herbert Hoover was born on August 10, 1874.
> Pablo Picasso is an Egyptian painter.
> There is no such thing as a purple cow.
> All water moccasins are poisonous.
> No permanent resident of Fargo, North Dakota,
> has red hair.

Not all of these declarative sentences are *true*; i.e., not all of them correspond to demonstrable reality or objective evidence, but all of them are statements. For our purposes here, we can define a statement of fact as one possessing a very high degree of public reliability. Only statements which are based on observable, corroborating evidence can be considered statements of *fact*. Obviously, sentences which ask questions (interrogations), give commands (imperatives), or exclaim (exclamations) cannot be statements of fact, because they do not assert anything.

2. Once you have determined that a sentence is an assertion or declaration, you must go about verifying the statement to see whether it is fact or not. In most of the sentences above, the word of an authority can be accepted as the basis of declaring the sentence true or false. The Town Clerk of Fargo, *Who's Who in America,* and a scholarly text on reptiles are acceptable sources of information for three of the statements. To be doubly sure, you might check with two or three authorities about the same matter just to be positive about the accuracy of supporting evidence. Remember that the Town Clerk of any city is a human being and subject to error or prejudice. Even the blandly dogmatic sentences of *Who's Who, Webster's Unabridged Dictionary,* and the *Encyclopaedia Britannica* were originally the products of a human brain, and thus susceptible to mistakes. The word of three authorities is likely to be a safer basis for a fact than the word of one alone; but three authorities *can* be mistaken—at one time *all* authorities believed the earth was flat.

In the case of a declaration such as "There is no such thing as a purple cow," you may rely with some confidence upon your firsthand knowledge in deciding whether it is true or not. If you have never seen a purple cow with your own eyes, talked to anyone who has seen one, or encountered one in works on cows, you may reasonably conclude that the statement is true. Remember that you possess approximately the same senses (taste, sight, hearing, etc.) that everybody else does; your own sensual experience is a workable basis (though not an exhaustive one) for deeming many statements true or false.

At the same time, you must recognize the possibility that your senses may not be as accurate as those of a gifted or specially trained person; a tone deaf man certainly does not have the accuracy of hearing that a "perfect pitch" musician has, and he should not rely on this sense when he knows it is deficient. Besides, the area of our firsthand knowledge is necessarily confined—few of us have visited Tibet, but we do not doubt that Tibet exists—so we must be realistic in the extent to which we test assertions by the data gathered by our own eyes and ears. In most cases, we can depend on a judicious combination of our own experiences and the word of experts to verify many ideas or rhetorical declarations.

There are, of course, some declarations which are not easily demonstrated to be true or false because they rest on incomplete evidence or they deal with the intangibles of logical relationships. Even personal experience and scores of authorities cannot serve in the case of these assertions to determine their truth. It is declarations of this kind which cause disagreements not happily ended by consulting an encyclopaedia:

The increased rate of illegitimacy in America during the 1950's was the result of the practice of "going steady."
Smoking causes lung cancer.
Capital punishment ought to be abolished in the United States.
Birth control should be made compulsory in over-populated nations like China and India.
High moral character is more commendable than intelligence in any man or woman.
Chess is a more intellectual pastime than bridge.
Everyone is morally entitled to a college education.
All men are created equal.

All of these sentences *assert* an idea as truth, but the statements remain *opinion* rather than facts.

Look closely at the nature of each pair of statements, and you will see why they are not demonstrable truths. The sentences about illegitimacy and lung cancer are hypotheses; each postulates a causal relationship, but neither rests on sufficient objective evidence to prove its validity. They may be true or not; at present, however, they remain tentative hypotheses which might very well prove false when more evidence is collected. The second pair of statements assert the necessity of a process to accomplish a desirable end. The third pair compares and contrasts two things and tenders judgment of relative values. Thus, the types of statement which assert *causation, obligation,* and *evaluation* are troublesome to distinguish as facts or opinions, as statements intended to provide objective information or to convince us of the worth of the speaker's belief.

In the last two statements above, those about education and equality, we are asked to accept a *generalization,* a statement which attributes a quality or characteristic to a category as a whole. In both declarations, the category is human beings ("men" being a synecdoche), and the assertion is made that every member of this class possesses the same right or quality of all the other members. Thus generalizations are statements which reflect *classification* and the categorical principle. In the next chapter, we shall see how generalizations are formed and how some of them are true while others are blatantly false. Now, let us simply note that generalizations are statements of opinion until they are proved true by objective evidence; therefore classification must join causation, the process, and comparison and contrast as logical systems which produce statements open to argument.

Now, of all the assertions made above, only one is likely to be accepted as a *fact* on its surface: all men are created equal. You may even have been shocked at the suggestion that this famous declaration is liable to question. If you will consider for a minute the basis upon which the statement is considered a fact, however, you may be surprised. Is it indeed true that all men are equal? Using our firsthand knowledge, we know that all human beings are not intellectually equal: an idiot is not the equal of a Socrates. Are human beings physically equal? No, since some of us are sickly or maimed and others are vigorous athletes. Perhaps men are equal in the eyes of the law? Segregation laws say not, and mentally defective people as well as criminals are not permitted to vote. Economically equal? No. Socially equal? Unfortunately not. Then are men equal in the sight of God? Possibly, but this is an unprovable hypothesis. And anyway, the Founding Fathers of this country declared that the truth of the equality of men is "self-evident." Is it, indeed? What *evidence* supports the assertion?

When forced to defend the truth of a statement, we first look to the authority of the man, or men, who made it. Were the Founding Fathers— human beings, after all—removed from all error in writing their views into the Constitution? They never claimed divine inspiration or superhuman wisdom. They were fallible men: Thomas Jefferson, Benjamin Franklin,

James Madison. Does our own reasoning permit us to question theirs? What do you think: Are all men created equal or not?

If you are troubled at the thought of a falsehood in our Constitution, be at peace. The emphasis of the statement, as we see by reading it within the context of the other sentences surrounding it, falls upon the word *created*. That is to say, at the moment of their conceptions, all human beings are theoretically equal to all other human beings, whatever the future limitations put upon them by circumstance. Moreover, the Constitution goes on to define equal rights as those of life, liberty, and the pursuit of happiness. Thus what seems to be a false generalization may be a part of a fuller combination of ideas; we must be careful in testing the validity of a statement to see the meaning of the statement as part of the larger meaning of related statements.

We must realize that a series of factual statements may be combined in such a way as to present an opinionative view or that a number of unproved assertions may result in a true or objectively verifiable conclusion. It is wrong to assume that if every individual declaration in an essay is a fact, then the essay as a whole must be true. Likewise, it is wrong to assume that a piece of reasoning which consists of unprovable assertions cannot result in a valid and testable view. A slanted news account may be factual in all it asserts and yet speak to persuade or inculcate an opinion; a philosophical dissertation may explain a tangible truth by a series of untestable hypothetical constructs. The points to keep in mind are these: 1. In a written form, the individual statement or the collective statements or both may be opinion rather than fact. 2. Therefore, all statements must be viewed singly *and* within their contexts and judged against objective evidence (the word of experts, the reader's personal experiences, or both) before they are accepted as *facts*.

The purpose of all argumentation should be to discover the truth, that is, to establish facts. Unless you assert your opinions more for the sake of testing them in open debate than for the sake of forcing them on someone else and proving to him that his own, contrary views are wrong, you are quarreling rather than conducting an argument. Of course, one purpose of much argument is to *persuade* another of the validity of your facts or interpretation of those facts and thus win his assent. Unless your basic purpose is to establish a common agreement on the grounds of true evidence, however, and not on your powers to cajole or coax your opponent into agreeing with you, the argument may persuade and still not be a particularly worthwhile one. Worthwhile argumentation, spoken or written,

must observe a few elementary ground rules if it is to accomplish its put
pose. Here they are:

1. Be sure that your statements are accurate representations of what
you really think. Unless your words assert clearly the opinions you hold,
you cannot convince anyone of your point of view nor can you test and
confirm that view for your own benefit. *Say what you believe.*

2. Define the areas of agreement and disagreement between yourself
and those whose views you oppose. Do not waste time arguing over things
you are really agreed upon.

3. Never, never argue about established facts. Look them up in one or
more authorities.

4. Be sure you know whether the argument is founded upon differences
of opinion concerning causation, obligation, evaluation, or generalization.
The evidence you present to support your view must be determined by
the nature of the disagreement.

5. Summon up from memory, collect from reliable sources, and compare
from common experiences between yourself and your opponent *all* relevant
data or evidence, not just evidence to support your point of view. You are
supposed to be finding out facts, not humiliating an enemy.

6. Keep yourself emotionally detached and stay cool. Lost tempers do
not win arguments. The tone of your voice or your written composition
must stay moderate and composed. Remember the Biblical injunction, "A
soft answer turneth away wrath."

7. Examine all evidence thoughtfully and objectively. Use what you
know about the principles of logical order to arrange and evaluate all information pertinent to the issue.

8. Stick to the issue or question under discussion. If you shift the
grounds of the argument or begin talking about some irrelevant matter,
you are guilty of *Ignoring the Question.* One of the chief forms of this
error is shifting the argument from the issue to the character of your opponent and attacking him rather than his evidence, data, or reasoning:
this is the *Argumentum ad hominem,* or *argument against the man.*
Begging the Question is assuming to be true the thing you are trying to
prove true. Do not assume to be a fact the very proposition that you are
testing.*

9. Do not appeal to the emotions of your opponent or your readers when
you find yourself being tested intellectually. It is fallacious argument to

* Examples of arguments committing these fallacies may be seen in the Exercises
(II 5) below.

resort to tear-jerking (the Appeal to Pity), scare tactics (Appeal to Fear), flag-waving (Appeal to Patriotism), or "Just Plain Folks" approaches (Identification of Speaker with Audience). Your listeners cannot view the issues calmly and thoughtfully if you stir them up emotionally; the wrongness of such tactics is shown in their popularity with dictators and demagogues.

10. Reach whatever conclusions seem justified by the evidence calmly considered. If you think the evidence insufficient, then postpone your decision until more evidence is available. It is not the sign of a weak character if you do not have a positive, dogmatic opinion about everything— better indecision than an irrevocable, wrong decision.

11. If you decide your original opinion was wrong, admit it and accept the right one. No one loses face by admitting his mistakes. Remember Ralph Waldo Emerson's remark, "A foolish consistency is the hobgoblin of little minds."

Even if you observe all of these ground rules in stating your opinions— and if you can, you are something of a saint—do not expect to become a model of prudent rationality. We all make mistakes constantly, and only our awareness of our susceptibility to error makes us search for ways of thinking and acting which will correct past mistakes and prevent future ones. Our very willingness to formulate private, sometimes foolish or baseless beliefs in words and thus expose them to examination—to argue about our ideas—is the means by which we develop our intellectual powers.

In addition to its personal advantages, argumentation results in widespread social benefit as well. All of the blessings of civilization which we take for granted today were once the subject of violent and sometimes bloody disagreement: innoculation against smallpox, universal voting privileges, freedom of the press, trial by jury, higher education. Each was a hotly contested issue at one time or another. That there is such unanimity of opinion about them today shows that as long as people are willing to discuss their differences thoughtfully and objectively, blind quarrels will give way to argumentation, and so at last to persuasion and agreement, partial or total.

I. Questions for Review
   1. What is argumentation? How is it related to exposition? To persuasion?
   2. Is it possible to argue about such matters as processes? Machines? Organisms? Classification? What causes differences of opinion about such examples of logical order?

3. Why is argumentation necessary before agreement can be reached?
4. What is an opinion? A statement? A fact?
5. What qualities make a person an authority in his field?
6. Why must we be wary of relying entirely on our personal experience for evidence as to the truth or falsity of an opinion?
7. What are statements of causation, obligation, and evaluation?
8. How is a generalization related to classification?
9. Can you think of any types of argumentative statement which are not causation, obligation, evaluation, or generalization?
10. What is the nature of these fallacies in argument: Ignoring the Question, *Ad Hominem*, Appeal to Fear, Appeal to Pity, Appeal to Patriotism, Audience Identification, Begging the Question?

II. Exercises
1. Which of the members of each list are likely to be the best and most reliable authorities on the indicated subject? Why?
   A. Discrimination in college fraternities: the national secretary of a fraternity, a college man who is non-fraternity, the dean of a college which has fraternities, the parents of a fraternity man, a professor of sociology in an Ivy League college.
   B. The cleansing properties of Blurb Toothpaste: the chemist who developed Blurb, the U. S. Testing Service, the manufacturer of Blurb, a movie actress who endorses Blurb, a housewife who uses Blurb, the American Dental Association.
   C. The foreign policy of the United States: the editorial writer of the *Atlanta Constitution,* the Under Secretary of State, the American representative to the United Nations, the political correspondent for the *New York Times,* a professor of political science in a midwestern university.
   D. The character of Benjamin Franklin: a modern British historian, a modern American historian, Franklin's *Autobiography,* the contemporary account of Franklin written by a French countess, Franklin's great-great-grandnephew.
   E. Your inferiority complex: you, your mother, your family doctor, your dearest friend, your favorite high school teacher, the resident adviser in your dormitory, the college psychologist.
   F. Contemporary American painting: a well known French art critic, *An Encyclopedia of American Art* (published in 1925), a modern American painter, the art critic of the *Chicago Tribune,* the director of the Cleveland Museum of Art, a professor of art at Vassar College.
   G. Caesar's campaign against Gaul: Caesar's *Commentaries,* Cicero's orations, the histories of Livy, an eighteenth-century British play

about Caesar, a twentieth-century history of Rome written by a professor of Classics at Columbia University, a Hollywood version of Shakespeare's play about Caesar.

2. Are the following sentences statements or not?
    A. In fourteen hundred and ninety-two, Columbus sailed the ocean blue.
    B. What is the cube root of 3,408?
    C. Early to bed, early to rise, makes a man healthy, wealthy, and wise.
    D. Once upon a time there was a beautiful princess named Snow White.
    E. A horse! A horse! My kingdom for a horse!
    F. In the beginning, God created the heavens and the earth.
    G. How doth the little crocodile improve his shining tail?
    H. A little learning is a dangerous thing.
    I. Drink deep or taste not the Pierian Spring.
    J. A home is a place where, when you have to go there, they have to take you in.

3. Which are facts (true statements) and which are not?
    A. No biped has four legs.
    B. East is east and west is west and never the twain shall meet.
    C. Once in the Land of Never-Was, there lived three billy goats gruff.
    D. The cube root of 3,408 is 34.5.
    E. John James Audubon, the famous naturalist, was said to have been the Lost Dauphin of France, the infant son of Louis XVI and Marie Antoinette who disappeared during the Revolution.
    F. All fruit trees are deciduous.
    G. Polydactilism is hereditary.
    H. Stuff a cold and you'll starve a fever.
    I. There is no such thing as a bad boy; there are only unloved boys.
    J. Chaucer died in 1400.

4. Which statements are causal, which obligatory, which evaluative, and which generalizations?
    A. No one loses face by admitting his mistakes.
    B. Every American must rally to the polls on Election Day.
    C. If Napoleon hadn't invaded Russia, he'd never have lost the French throne.
    D. Absence makes the heart grow fonder.
    E. There ought to be a law against drivers who go less than 35 miles an hour on superhighways.
    F. Vote for Homer U. McDancey for the Senate? Why, he isn't fit to run for Garbage Collector!
    G. Americans have the finest standard of living on earth.

H. No wonder juvenile delinquency is on the increase! With so many mothers working, it's a wonder there isn't more.

I. Doctors are all money mad nowadays; all they think of is getting rich.

J. It's better to make one true friend in college than to make Phi Beta Kappa.

5. Each of the following is a fallacious argument of one kind or another. Identify each as Begging the Question, Ignoring the Question, Ad Hominem, Appeal to Pity, Appeal to Fear, Appeal to Patriotism, Audience Identification.

A. To those who argue that Tasmanians are the intellectual, biological, social, and moral equals of Americans, I have but one reply: I do not want *my* sister to marry a Tasmanian.

B. Some of my enemies have accused me of accepting money and other favors during my campaign for the Senate. I readily admit that a little, fuzzy puppy named Backgammon was given to my little boys; but I have no intention of giving him back. Would my enemies want to make me break my children's hearts by depriving them of their pet?

C. Insofar as our position in the missile race is concerned, Professor Niles Smyth-Bradston, the British missile expert, has declared that the United States is far behind the Russians. But we need not be too concerned over what Smyth-Bradston says. He's notorious as an atheist and free-thinker, and he's been divorced three times. The man's an obvious neurotic.

D. Buy insurance today. A horrible, crippling accident may happen to you tomorrow: a skidding car, a fall down the stairs, a lingering illness. A Megalopolitan Insurance Policy stands between you and Disaster.

E. The reign of the Hanover kings in England during the eighteenth century was wise and judicious. Those who declare the Hanovers ignorant and stupid are overlooking the lovely architecture of the period, the graceful furniture, and such masterpieces of literature as *The Decline and Fall of the Roman Empire.*

F. A vote for our opponents, the Mugwumps, is a vote for certain atomic war with inevitable destruction of our great land and the death of you and your loved ones.

G. It's a real pleasure for me to be here in Gopher Prairie again with my many friends to talk a little about the proposed highway project. And as I look about at your friendly faces, I know I'm among homefolks who are going to see eye to eye with me about this outrageous proposal.

H. Won't you give generously to the Fund for the Widow of the Unknown Soldier? Think of this poor war widow, deprived of the love and care of her husband. Think of her poor, fatherless children, hungry for the food and warmth that *your* dollars could provide for them.

I. Certainly Walter has been two-timing Imogene! Where there's smoke, there's fire, you know; people wouldn't say he was a two-timer unless he was, would they?

J. What do you mean, money can't buy happiness? Are you opposed to the capitalist system? What are you—a Communist or something?

III. *Suggestions for Writing*

1. Read one of the argumentative essays at the end of the book: "Undergraduates on Apronstrings," "Stranger in the Village," "The Poet and the Press," or "The Faith of a Heretic." Then write a critical examination of the organization and major points of the essay and assess its techniques, use of appeals, reliance on authority, and the other elements of argumentation.

2. Select one of the essays in this book with which you disagree, and write an argumentative essay in reply.

3. Choose an argumentative essay from a worthwhile periodical, such as *Harper's, The Atlantic Monthly, Virginia Quarterly,* or *The Nation.* Read it carefully; then write a critical estimate of it or write an essay opposing its arguments.

4. Think about one of these topics; organize your opinions about it in essay form; then evaluate these opinions objectively as facts, as types of statements, as systems of logical thinking, and as arguments:

A. Birth control
B. Mercy killings
C. Segregation
D. Universal college education
E. Abolishment of fraternities
F. Welfare aid to illegitimate children
G. Protective tariffs
H. Federal aid to private schools
I. American foreign policy toward Russia

Katherine Anne Porter

THE FUTURE IS NOW

NOT SO LONG AGO I WAS READING IN A MAGAZINE WITH AN ENORMOUS circulation some instructions as to how to behave if and when we see that flash brighter than the sun which means that the atom bomb has arrived. I read of course with the intense interest of one who has everything to learn on this subject; but at the end, the advice dwindled to this: the only real safety seems to lie in simply being somewhere else at the time, the farther away the better; the next best, failing access to deep shelters, bomb-proof cellars and all, is to get under a stout table—that is, just what you might do if someone were throwing bricks through your window and you were too nervous to throw them back.

This comic anticlimax to what I had been taking as a serious educational piece surprised me into real laughter, hearty and carefree. It is such a re-lief to be told the truth, or even just the facts, so pleasant not to be coddled with unreasonable hopes. That very evening I was drawn away from my work table to my fifth-story window by one of those shrill terror-screaming sirens which our excitement-loving city government used then to affect for so many occasions: A fire? Police chasing a gangster? Somebody being got to the hospital in a hurry? Some distinguished public guest being transferred from one point to another? Strange aircraft coming over, maybe? Under the lights of the corner crossing of the great avenue, a huge closed vehicle whizzed past, screaming. I never knew what it was, had not in fact expected to know; no one I could possible ask would know. Now that we have bells clamoring away instead for such events, we all have one doubt less, if perhaps one expectancy more. The single siren's voice means to tell us only one thing.

But at that doubtful moment, framed in a lighted window level with mine in the apartment house across the street, I saw a young man in a white T-shirt and white shorts at work polishing a long, beautiful dark table top. It was obviously his own table in his own flat, and he was en-joying his occupation. He was bent over in perfect concentration, rubbing, sandpapering, running the flat of his palm over the surface, standing back now and then to get the sheen of light on the fine wood. I am sure he had not even raised his head at the noise of the siren, much less had he come to the window. I stood there admiring his workmanlike devotion to a good job worth doing, and there flashed through me one of those pure fallacies of feeling which suddenly overleap reason: surely all that effort and energy so irreproachably employed were not going to be wasted on a table that was to be used merely for crawling under at some unspecified date. Then why take all those pains to make it beautiful? Any sort of old board would do.

I was so shocked at this treachery of the lurking Foul Fiend (despair is a foul fiend, and this was despair) I stood a moment longer, looking out and around, trying to collect my feelings, trying to think a little. Two windows away and a floor down in the house across the street, a young woman was lolling in a deep chair, reading and eating fruit from a little basket. On the sidewalk, a boy and a girl dressed alike in checkerboard cotton shirts and skin-tight blue denims, a costume which displayed acutely the structural differences of their shapes, strolled along with their arms around each other. I believe this custom of lovers walking enwreathed in public was imported by our soldiers of the First World War from France, from Paris indeed. "You didn't see that sort of thing here before," certain members of the older generation were heard to remark quite often, in a tone of voice. Well, one sees quite a lot of it now, and it is a very pretty, reassuring sight. Other citizens of all sizes and kinds and ages were crossing back and forth; lights flashed red and green, punctually. Motors zoomed by, and over the great city—but where am I going? I never read other peoples' descriptions of great cities, more particularly if it is a great city I know. It doesn't belong here anyway, except that I had again that quieting sense of the continuity of human experience on this earth, its perpetual aspirations, set-backs, failures and re-beginnings in eternal hope; and that, with some appreciable differences of dress, customs and means of conveyance, so people have lived and moved in the cities they have built for more millennia than we are yet able to account for, and will no doubt build and live for as many more.

Why did this console me? I cannot say; my mind is of the sort that can often be soothed with large generalities of that nature. The silence of the spaces between the stars does not affright me, as it did Pascal, because I am unable to imagine it except poetically; and my awe is not for the silence and space of the endless universe but for the inspired imagination of man, who can think and feel so, and turn a phrase like that to communicate it to us. Then too, I like the kind of honesty and directness of the young soldier who lately answered someone who asked him if he knew what he was fighting for. "I sure do," he said, "I am fighting to live." And as for the future, I was once reading the first writings of a young girl, an apprentice author, who was quite impatient to get on with the business and find her way into print. There is very little one can say of use in such matters, but I advised her against haste—she could so easily regret it. "Give yourself time," I said, "the future will take care of itself." This opinionated young person looked down her little nose at me and said, "The future is now." She may have heard the phrase somewhere and liked it, or she may just have naturally belonged to that school of metaphysics; I am sure she was too young to have investigated the thought deeply. But maybe she was right and the future does arrive every day and it is all we have, from one second to the next.

So I glanced again at the young man at work, a proper-looking candidate for the armed services, and realized the plain, homely fact: he was not preparing a possible shelter, something to cower under trembling; he was restoring a beautiful surface to put his books and papers on, to serve his plates from, to hold his cocktail tray and his lamp. He was full of the deep, right, instinctive, human belief that he and the table were going to be around together for a long time. Even if he is off to the army next week, it will be there when he gets back. At the very least, he is doing something he feels is worth doing now, and that is no small thing.

At once the difficulty, and the hope, of our special time in this world of Western Europe and America is that we have been brought up for many generations in the belief, however tacit, that all humanity was almost unanimously engaged in going forward, naturally to better things and to higher reaches. Since the eighteenth century at least when the Encyclopedists seized upon the Platonic theory that the highest pleasure of mankind was pursuit of the good, the true, and the beautiful, progress, in precisely the sense of perpetual, gradual amelioration of the hard human lot, has been taught popularly not just as theory of possibility but as an article of faith and the groundwork of a whole political doctrine. Mr. Toynbee has even simplified this view for us with picture diagrams of various sections of humanity, each in its own cycle rising to its own height, struggling beautifully on from craggy level to level, but always upward. Whole peoples are arrested at certain points, and perish there, but others go on. There is also the school of thought, Oriental and very ancient, which gives to life the spiral shape, and the spiral moves by nature upward. Even adherents of the circular or recurring-cycle school, also ancient and honorable, somehow do finally allow that the circle is a thread that spins itself out one layer above another, so that even though it is perpetually at every moment passing over a place it has been before, yet by its own width it will have risen just so much higher.

These are admirable attempts to get a little meaning and order into our view of our destiny, in that same spirit which moves the artist to labor with his little handful of chaos, bringing it to coherency within a frame; but on the visible evidence we must admit that in human nature the spirit of contradiction more than holds its own. Mankind has always built a little more than he has hitherto been able or willing to destroy; got more children than he has been able to kill; invented more laws and customs than he had any intention of observing; founded more religions than he was able to practice or even to believe in; made in general many more promises than he could keep; and has been known more than once to commit suicide through mere fear of death. Now in our time, in his pride to explore his universe to its unimaginable limits and to exceed his possible powers, he has at last produced an embarrassing series of engines too powerful for their containers and too tricky for their mechanicians; millions of labor-saving gadgets which can be rendered totally useless by the mere failure of the public power plants, and has reduced himself to such helplessness that a dozen or less of the enemy could disable a whole city by throwing a few switches. This paradoxical creature has committed all these extravagances and created all these dangers and sufferings in a quest—we are told —for peace and security.

How much of this are we to believe, when with the pride of Lucifer, the recklessness of Icarus, the boldness of Prometheus and the intellectual curiosity of Adam and Eve (yes, intellectual; the serpent promised them wisdom if . . .) man has obviously outreached himself, to the point where he cannot understand his own science or control his own inventions. Indeed he has become as the gods, who have over and over again suffered defeat and downfall at the hands of their creatures. Having devised the most exquisite and instantaneous means of communication to all corners of the earth, for years upon years friends were unable even to get a post-card message to each other across national frontiers. The newspapers assure us that from the kitchen tap there flows a chemical, cheap and available, to make a bomb more disturbing to the imagination even than the one we so appallingly have; yet no machine has been invented to purify that water so that it will not spoil even the best tea or coffee. Or at any rate, it is not in use. We are the proud possessors of rocket bombs that go higher and farther and faster than any ever before, and there is some talk of a rocket ship shortly to take off for the moon. (My plan is to stow away.) We may indeed reach the moon some day, and I dare predict that will happen before we have devised a decent system of city garbage disposal.

This lunatic atom bomb has succeeded in rousing the people of all nations to the highest point of unanimous moral dudgeon; great numbers of persons are frightened who never really had much cause to be frightened before. This world has always been a desperately dangerous place to live for the greater part of the earth's inhabitants; it was, however reluctantly, endured as the natural state of affairs. Yet the invention of every new weapon of war has always been greeted with horror and righteous indignation, especially by those who failed to invent it, or who were threatened with it first . . . bows and arrows, stone cannon balls, gunpowder, flintlocks, pistols, the dumdum bullet, the Maxim silencer, the machine gun, poison gas, armored tanks, and on and on to the grand climax—if it should prove to be—of the experiment on Hiroshima. Nagasaki was bombed too, remember? Or were we already growing accustomed to the idea? And as for Hiroshima, surely it could not have been the notion of sudden death of others that shocked us? How could it be, when in two great wars within one generation we have become familiar with millions of shocking deaths, by sudden violence of most cruel devices, and by agonies prolonged for years in prisons and hospitals and concentration camps. We take with apparent calmness the news of the deaths of millions by flood, famine, plague —no, all the frontiers of danger are down now, no one is safe, no one, and that, alas, really means all of us. It is our own deaths we fear, and so let's out with it and give up our fine debauch of moralistic frenzy over Hiroshima. I fail entirely to see why it is more criminal to kill a few thousand persons in one instant than it is to kill the same number slowly over a given stretch of time. If I have a choice, I'd as lief be killed by an atom bomb as by a hand grenade or a flame thrower. If dropping the atom bomb is an immoral act, then the making of it was too; and writing of the formula was a crime, since those who wrote it must have known what such a contrivance was good for. So, morally speaking, the bomb is only a magnified hand grenade, and the crime, if crime it is, is still murder. It was never anything else. Our protocriminal then was the man who first struck fire from flint, for from that moment we have been coming steadily to this day and this weapon and this use of it. What would you have advised instead? That the human race should have gone on sitting in caves gnawing raw meat and beating each other over the head with the bones?

And yet it may be that what we have is a world not on the verge of flying apart, but an uncreated one—still in shapeless fragments waiting to be put together properly. I imagine that when we want something better, we may have it: at perhaps no greater price than we have already paid for the worse.

1. This essay, which appears to be a formal, expository essay, is really an argument. Exactly what is the question under discussion and what position does Miss Porter take toward it?
2. Outline the major propositions or the successive steps in Miss Porter's argument. What proof does she offer to support each?
3. Point out examples in "The Future Is Now" of opinions which appear to be statements of fact or facts which seem to be opinion. How can they be told apart? How can they be tested?
4. Does Miss Porter cite any authorities to support her views? How does she support her statements mainly?
5. Does Miss Porter observe the ground rules of proper argumentation? Justify your answer.

Jonathan Swift

A MODEST PROPOSAL

For Preventing the Children of Poor People From Being A Burthen to Their Parents or Country, and for Making Them Beneficial to the Public.

IT IS A MELANCHOLY OBJECT TO THOSE WHO WALK THROUGH THIS GREAT town, or travel in the country, when they see the streets, the roads, and cabin-doors crowded with beggars of the female sex, followed by three, four, or six children, *all in rags,* and importuning every passenger for an alms. These mothers, instead of being able to work for their honest livelihood, are forced to employ all their time in strolling, to beg sustenance for their helpless infants, who, as they grow up, either turn thieves for want of work, or leave their dear Native Country to fight for the Pretender in Spain, or sell themselves to the Barbadoes.

I think it is agreed by all parties that this prodigious number of children, in the arms, or on the backs, or at the heels of their mothers, and frequently of their fathers, is in the present deplorable state of the kingdom a very great additional grievance; and therefore whoever could find out a fair, cheap, and easy method of making these children sound useful members of the commonwealth would deserve so well of the public as to have his statue set up for a preserver of the nation.

But my intention is very far from being confined to provide only for the children of professed beggars; it is of a much greater extent, and shall take in the whole number of infants at a certain age who are born of parents in effect as little able to support them as those who demand our charity in the streets.

As to my own part, having turned my thoughts, for many years, upon this important subject, and maturely weighed the several schemes of other projectors, I have always found them grossly mistaken in their computation. It is true a child, just dropped from its dam, may be supported by her milk for a solar year with little other nourishment, at most not above the value

First published in 1727.

160

of two shillings, which the mother may certainly get, or the value in scraps, by her lawful occupation of begging, and it is exactly at one year old that I propose to provide for them, in such a manner as, instead of being a charge upon their parents, or the parish, or wanting food and raiment for the rest of their lives, they shall, on the contrary, contribute to the feeding and partly to the clothing of many thousands.

There is likewise another great advantage in my scheme, that it will prevent those voluntary abortions, and that horrid practice of women murdering their bastard children, alas, too frequent among us, sacrificing the poor innocent babes, I doubt, more to avoid the expense than the shame, which would move tears and pity in the most savage and inhuman breast.

The number of souls in this kingdom being usually reckoned one million and a half, of these I calculate there may be about two hundred thousand couple whose wives are breeders, from which number I subtract thirty thousand couple who are able to maintain their own children, although I apprehend there cannot be so many under the present distresses of the kingdom, but this being granted, there will remain an hundred and seventy thousand breeders. I again subtract fifty thousand for those women who miscarry, or whose children die by accident or disease within the year. There only remain an hundred and twenty thousand children of poor parents annually born: The question therefore is, how this number shall be reared, and provided for, which, as I have already said, under the present situation of affairs, is utterly impossible by all the methods hitherto proposed, for we can neither employ them in handicraft, or agriculture; we neither build houses (I mean in the country), nor cultivate land: they can very seldom pick up a livelihood by stealing till they arrive at six years old, except where they are of towardly parts, although, I confess they learn the rudiments much earlier, during which time they can however be properly looked upon only as *probationers,* as I have been informed by a principal gentleman in the County of Cavan, who protested to me that he never knew above one or two instances under the age of six, even in a part of the kingdom so renowned for the quickest proficiency in that art.

I am assured by our merchants that a boy or a girl, before twelve years old, is no saleable commodity, and even when they come to this age, they will not yield above three pounds, or three pounds and half-a-crown at most on the Exchange, which cannot turn to account either to the parents or the kingdom, the charge of nutriment and rags having been at least four times that value.

I shall now therefore humbly propose my own thoughts, which I hope will not be liable to the least objection.

I have been assured by a very knowing American of my acquaintance in London, that a young healthy child well nursed is at a year old a most delicious, nourishing, and wholesome food, whether stewed, roasted, baked, or boiled, and I make no doubt that it will equally serve in a fricassee, or a ragout.

I do therefore humbly offer it to public consideration, that of the hundred and twenty thousand children already computed, twenty thousand may be reserved for breed, whereof only one fourth part to be males, which is more than we allow to sheep, black-cattle, or swine, and my reason is that these children are seldom the fruits of marriage, a circumstance not much regarded by our savages, therefore one male will be sufficient to serve four females. That the remaining hundred thousand may at a year old be offered in sale to the persons of quality, and fortune, through the kingdom, always advising the mother to let them suck plentifully in the last month, so as to render them plump, and fat for a good table. A child will make two dishes at an entertainment for friends, and when the family dines alone, the fore or hind quarter will make a reasonable dish, and seasoned with a little pepper or salt will be very good boiled on the fourth day, especially in winter.

I have reckoned upon a medium, that a child just born will weigh 12 pounds, and in a solar year if tolerably nursed increaseth to 28 pounds.

I grant this food will be somewhat dear, and therefore very proper for landlords, who, as they have already devoured most of the parents, seem to have the best title to the children.

Infants' flesh will be in season throughout the year, but more plentiful in March, and a little before and after, for we are told by a grave author, an eminent French physician, that fish being a prolific diet, there are more children born in Roman Catholic countries about nine months after Lent than at any other season; therefore reckoning a year after Lent, the markets will be more glutted than usual, because the number of Popish infants is at least three to one in this kingdom, and therefore it will have one other collateral advantage by lessening the number of Papists among us.

I have already computed the charge of nursing a beggar's child (in which list I reckon all cottagers, labourers, and four-fifths of the farmers) to be about two shillings *per annum*, rags included, and I believe no gentleman would repine to give ten shillings for the carcass of a good fat child, which, as I have said, will make four dishes of excellent nutritive meat, when he hath only some particular friend or his own family to dine with him. Thus the Squire will learn to be a good landlord, and grow popular among his tenants, the mother will have eight shillings net profit, and be fit for work till she produces another child.

Those who are more thrifty (as I must confess the times require) may flay the carcass; the skin of which, artificially dressed, will make admirable gloves for ladies, and summer boots for fine gentlemen.

As to our City of Dublin, shambles may be appointed for this purpose, in the most convenient parts of it, and butchers we may be assured will not be wanting, although I rather recommend buying the children alive, and dressing them hot from the knife, as we do roasting pigs.

A very worthy person, a true lover of this country, and whose virtues I highly esteem, was lately pleased, in discoursing on this matter, to offer a refinement upon my scheme. He said that many gentlemen of this king- dom, having of late destroyed their deer, he conceived that the want of venison might be well supplied by the bodies of young lads and maidens, not exceeding fourteen years of age, nor under twelve, so great a number of both sexes in every country being now ready to starve, for want of work and service: and these to be disposed of by their parents if alive, or other- wise by their nearest relations. But with due deference to so excellent a friend, and so deserving a patriot, I cannot be altogether in his sentiments; for as to the males, my American acquaintance assured me from frequent experience that their flesh was generally tough and lean, like that of our schoolboys, by continual exercise, and their taste disagreeable, and to fatten them would not answer the charge. Then as to the females, it would, I think with humble submission, be a loss to the public, because they soon would become breeders themselves: And besides, it is not improbable that some scrupulous people might be apt to censure such a practice (although indeed very unjustly) as a little bordering upon cruelty, which, I confess, hath always been with me the strongest objection against my project, how- ever so well intended.

But in order to justify my friend, he confessed that this expedient was put into his head by the famous Psalmanazar, a native of the island For- mosa, who came from thence to London, above twenty years ago, and in conversation told my friend that in his country when any young person happened to be put to death, the executioner sold the carcass to persons of quality, as a prime dainty, and that, in his time, the body of a plump girl of fifteen, who was crucified for an attempt to poison the emperor, was sold to his Imperial Majesty's Prime Minister of State, and other great

Mandarins of the Court, in joints from the gibbet, at four hundred crowns. Neither indeed can I deny that if the same use were made of several plump young girls in this town, who, without one single groat to their fortunes, cannot stir abroad without a chair, and appear at the playhouse, and assemblies in foreign fineries, which they never will pay for, the kingdom would not be the worse.

Some persons of a desponding spirit are in great concern about that vast number of poor people, who are aged, diseased, or maimed, and I have been desired to employ my thoughts what course may be taken to ease the nation of so grievous an encumbrance. But I am not in the least pain upon that matter, because it is very well known that they are every day dying, and rotting, by cold, and famine, and filth, and vermin, as fast as can be reasonably expected. And as to the younger labourers they are now in almost as hopeful a condition. They cannot get work, and consequently pine away for want of nourishment, to a degree, that if at any time they are accidentally hired to common labour, they have not strength to perform it; and thus the country and themselves are happily delivered from the evils to come.

I have too long digressed, and therefore shall return to my subject. I think the advantages by the proposal which I have made are obvious and many, as well as of the highest importance.

For first, as I have already observed, it would greatly lessen the number of Papists, with whom we are yearly over-run, being the principal breeders of the nation, as well as our most dangerous enemies, and who stay at home on purpose with a design to deliver the kingdom to the Pretender, hoping to take their advantage by the absence of so many good Protestants, who have chosen rather to leave their country than stay at home, and pay tithes against their conscience to an Episcopal curate.

Secondly, The poorer tenants will have something valuable of their own, which by law be made liable to distress, and help to pay their landlord's rent, their corn and cattle being already seized, and *money a thing unknown.*

Thirdly, Whereas the maintenance of an hundred thousand children, from two years old, and upwards, cannot be computed at less than ten shillings a piece *per annum,* the nation's stock will be thereby increased fifty thousand pounds *per annum,* besides the profit of a new dish, introduced to the tables of all gentlemen of fortune in the kingdom, who have any refinement in taste, and the money will circulate among ourselves, the goods being entirely of our own growth and manufacture.

Fourthly, The constant breeders, besides the gain of eight shillings sterling *per annum,* by the sale of their children, will be rid of the charge of maintaining them after the first year.

Fifthly, This food would likewise bring great custom to taverns, where the vintners will certainly be so prudent as to procure the best receipts for dressing it to perfection, and consequently have their houses frequented by all the fine gentlemen, who justly value themselves upon their knowledge in good eating; and a skilful cook, who understands how to oblige his guests, will contrive to make it as expensive as they please.

Sixthly, This would be a great inducement to marriage, which all wise nations have either encouraged by rewards, or enforced by laws and penalties. It would increase the care and tenderness of mothers toward their children, when they were sure of a settlement for life, to the poor babes, provided in some sort by the public to their annual profit instead of expense. We should see an honest emulation among the married women, which of them could bring the fattest child to the market, men would become as fond of their wives, during the time of their pregnancy, as they are now of their mares in foal, their cows in calf, or sows when they are ready to farrow, nor offer to beat or kick them (as it is too frequent a practice) for fear of a miscarriage.

Many other advantages might be enumerated: For instance, the addition of some thousand carcasses in our exportation of barrelled beef; the propagation of swine's flesh, and improvement in the art of making good bacon, so much wanted among us by the great destruction of pigs, too frequent at our tables, which are no way comparable in taste or magnificence to a well-grown, fat yearling child, which roasted whole will make a considerable figure at a Lord Mayor's feast, or any other public entertainment. But this and many others I omit, being studious of brevity.

Supposing that one thousand families in this city would be constant customers for infants' flesh, besides others who might have it at merry-meetings, particularly weddings and christenings, I compute that Dublin would take off annually about twenty thousand carcasses, and the rest of the kingdom (where probably they will be sold somewhat cheaper) the remaining eighty thousand.

I can think of no one objection that will possibly be raised against this proposal, unless it should be urged that the number of people will be thereby much lessened in the kingdom. This I freely own, and was indeed one principal design in offering it to the world. I desire the reader will observe, that I calculate my remedy for this one individual *Kingdom of*

Ireland, and for no other that ever was, is, or, I think, ever can be upon earth. Therefore let no man talk to me of other expedients: *Of taxing our absentees at five shillings a pound: Of using neither clothes, nor household furniture, except what is of our own growth and manufacture: Of utterly rejecting the materials and instruments that promote foreign luxury: Of curing the expensiveness of pride, vanity, idleness, and gaming in our women: Of introducing a vein of parsimony, prudence, and temperance: Of learning to love our Country, wherein we differ even from* LAPLANDERS, *and the inhabitants of* TOPINAMBOO: *Of quitting our animosities and factions, nor act any longer like the Jews, who were murdering one another at the very moment their city was taken: Of being a little cautious not to sell our country and consciences for nothing: Of teaching landlords to have at least one degree of mercy toward their tenants. Lastly, of putting a spirit of honesty, industry, and skill into our shopkeepers, who, if a resolution could now be taken to buy only our native goods, would immediately unite to cheat and exact upon us in the price, the measure, and the goodness, nor could ever yet be brought to make one fair proposal of just dealing, though often and earnestly invited to it.*

Therefore I repeat, let no man talk to me of these and the like expedients, till he hath at least some glimpse of hope that there will ever be some hearty and sincere attempt to put them in practice.

But as to myself, having been wearied out for many years with offering vain, idle, visionary thoughts, and at length utterly despairing of success, I fortunately fell upon this proposal, which as it is wholly new, so it hath something solid and real, of no expense and little trouble, full in our own power, and whereby we can incur no danger in *disobliging* ENGLAND. For this kind of commodity will not bear exportation, the flesh being of too tender a consistence to admit a long continuance in salt, *although perhaps I could name a country which would be glad to eat up our whole nation without it.*

After all I am not so violently bent upon my own opinion as to reject any offer, proposed by wise men, which shall be found equally innocent, cheap, easy, and effectual. But before something of that kind shall be advanced in contradiction to my scheme, and offering a better, I desire the author, or authors, will be pleased maturely to consider two points. First, as things now stand, how they will be able to find food and raiment for an hundred thousand useless mouths and backs. And secondly, there being a round million of creatures in human figure, throughout this kingdom, whose whole subsistence put into a common stock would leave them in debt two millions of pounds sterling; adding those, who are beggars by profession, to the bulk of farmers, cottagers, and labourers with their wives and children, who are beggars in effect. I desire those politicians, who dislike my overture, and may perhaps be so bold to attempt an answer, that they will first ask the parents of these mortals whether they would not at this day think it a great happiness to have been sold for food at a year old, in the manner I prescribe, and thereby have avoided such a perpetual scene of misfortunes as they have since gone through, by the oppression of landlords, the impossibility of paying rent without money or trade, the want of common sustenance, with neither house nor clothes to cover them from the inclemencies of the weather, and the most inevitable prospect of entailing the like, or greater miseries upon their breed for ever.

I profess in the sincerity of my heart that I have not the least personal interest in endeavouring to promote this necessary work, having no other motive than the *public good of my country, by advancing our trade, providing for infants, relieving the poor, and giving some pleasure to the rich.* I have no children by which I can propose to get a single penny; the youngest being nine years old, and my wife past child-bearing.

1. "A Modest Proposal" is a satiric argument, set forth in accordance with all the conventions of proper argumentation. What exactly is Swift's projector arguing for? What is Swift arguing for?
2. Outline the argument in its major phases.
3. What about the projector's calculations in support of his proposal: are they accurate? What refutation can you make against them?
4. What are the assumed propositions that the projector argues from in this essay? Are they facts or not? Explain.
5. Are the authorities cited by the projector proper ones or not? Why?
6. What evidence of improper use of emotional language can you find in Swift's essay? What effect has this upon the argument?

CHAPTER 7

LOGICAL THINKING

"Safe upon the solid rock the ugly houses stand:
Come and see my shining palace built upon the sand!"
EDNA ST. VINCENT MILLAY, *A Few Figs from Thistles**

Thoughts, Ideas, Conceptions—we do not know why the brain functions as it does to produce these; but we know, largely from the word of experts who have observed and tested their way into knowledge, that our verbal thoughts form in three discernible ways. Of course, there are other ways that non-verbal ideas develop: association of sensation, memory, reverie, and so on. Edna St. Vincent Millay's couplet above reminds us, however, that if we want to build upon something more solid than whim or mood, we must abandon castles in the air and take to the hard-rock base of logic. The intellectual processes which underpin logical thought are Inductive Thinking, Deductive Thinking, and what we can call Reductive Thinking (or Simplification).

INDUCTIVE THOUGHT

"Induction" comes from the Latin words *in* and *duco,* which mean "lead into" or "lead up to." As a form of thinking or reasoning, it is *the process of weighing observed evidence in order to arrive at a proposition governing that evidence.* When we observe through our physical senses some situation, set of circumstances, objects, or other *data,* we try to understand these by conjecturing a proposition that either *explains* the data or *applies* the data to other, similar data. In the first case, we construct a probable cause or *hypothesis;* in the second, we are universalizing about the category to

* From *Collected Poems,* Harper & Brothers. Copyright 1918–1945 by Edna St. Vincent Millay. Permission of Norma Millay Ellis.

which the data belongs and therefore making a _generalization_. We are already somewhat familiar with the ways these forms of induction are used in causation and classification.

You will remember that in forming a hypothesis, we first observe certain evidence or phenomena; we then assume these facts were _caused_ by something; and finally, using our previous experience and the laws of probability, we surmise the nature of the unknown cause. In arriving at the hypothesis, we are reasoning _inductively_ and passing from the known into the unknown. Any time we use the observable to conjecture about the unobservable or use the factual as the basis of the possible or probable, we jump from facts to assumptions. Sometimes this necessary step is "guessing;" sometimes, if it follows the established tests of valid induction, it becomes the somewhat more dignified but still risky _inductive leap_.

In the other form of inductive thinking, _generalizing_, we know that limited data about members of the same category are expanded to be applied to _all_ the members of that category. The characteristics present in a few instances are postulated to be present in all instances; thus a categorical principle is extended to cover unknown members of the category. It is in the going from the few to the totality that a generalization takes the inductive leap. T. H. Huxley's famous example of the man who bites successively into three hard, green apples, only to discover that each is sour, and then concludes that _all_ hard, green apples are sour is an instance of generalization in daily usage.

Though much of human knowledge is a store of inductively developed generalizations—all men must die, and so on—the inductive leap necessary in making a generalization sometimes causes us to slip and fall into mistakes. Just as a hypothesis can be a false one, so a generalization can be false, too. Erroneous generalizations are usually called _Hasty Generalizations_; they are caused by universalizing from too few examples or attributing the characteristic of a few objects to other like objects which differ in that particular respect. The man who buys a Powhatan automobile only to find that it has a malfunctioning carburetor, and thereupon declares that all Powhatans are junk, is guilty of hasty generalization. Or the woman who hires a Mexican cook, also a thief by trade, is generalizing wrongly if she then decides that _all_ Mexicans are thieves. The human tendency to exaggerate often takes the form of a hasty generalization.

What constitutes sufficient evidence to serve as the basis for a valid generalization? If one Powhatan is not enough, then are ten? Fifty? A thousand? How many green apples must a man eat before he can decide whether or not every green apple is sour? Obviously, the more examples you have to illustrate the truth of your generalization, the better the generalization is. But even if you have six million hard, green apples that are sour and only one that is not, you cannot properly generalize about *all* hard green apples. You must generalize that "most," "many," or "some" green apples are sour. As long as you generalize about every member of a class, unknown as well as known, you can never be positive that your generalization is true in *all* instances.

Since generalizations are by nature *assertions* rather than *facts*, it is wise when you read someone else's generalizations or when you write your own to establish upon how large a sampling of members of a category each generalization is based. The famous study of *Sexual Behavior in the Human Male* made many assertions and painstakingly charted percentages to prove certain "facts" about human males as a total category, but the study actually was based on the cases of slightly over 5,000 men, many of them college students from Ohio, Indiana, and Illinois. Perhaps this sampling is large enough to be accurate; it certainly is larger than the samplings which appear in newspapers as Public Opinion Polls or Television Rating Surveys. Many a high sounding generalization—"With medical experts, Goddard's Drops are the favorites, two to one"—sounds absurd when reduced to actual figures—"Ten doctors we talked to liked Goddard's Drops, but five didn't." Never accept, or use, the flimsy phrase "Statistics tell us . . ." as a substitute for the data supporting a generalization.

If you feel that generalizations are rather suspect, you are right. At the same time, it is true that facts are generalizations for which there is a large amount of supporting and no contradictory evidence. All men must die. Tomatoes are edible. Dodos are extinct. Any of these facts could be made into erroneous generalizations with the appearance of one immortal man, one poisonous tomato, or one live dodo. To keep our generalizations extensive and yet accurate is one of the difficulties of using our inductive powers to advantage.

Perhaps one of the most direct ways to understand types of generalizations is to see how they derive from classification. Do you recall the classification we made of duck-billed platypuses? It ran in part like this:

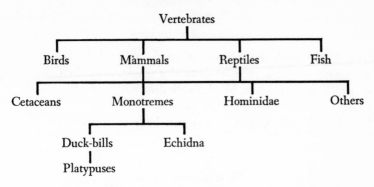

Now, if you look carefully at the categories and sub-categories on this classification chart, you can see at once that certain generalizations can be made, such as:

> All monotremes are mammals
> All platypuses are vertebrates
> No birds are reptiles
> No cetaceans are monotremes
> Some vertebrates are fish
> Some mammals are platypuses
> Some vertebrates are not mammals
> Some mammals are not hominidae

Clearly, when we generalize about objects in their categorical relationships, there are four types of statement we can make:

> All .... are ...... (Categorical Affirmative)
> No .... are ...... (Categorical Negative)
> Some .. are ...... (Limited Affirmative)
> Some .. are not ... (Limited Negative)

Even such statements as "Bears hibernate in the winter" or "A few moles are brown" can be put in the form of one of these types, as: "All bears are creatures that hibernate" or "Some moles are brown objects."

All generalizations deal with a whole group of objects or a part of a group (even if the group is "things"). If the statement declares that something is true or not true of a group as a whole, it is a *categorical statement*. The statement applies to every member of the group; thus the group is said to be *distributed*. In a Categorical Affirmative such as

X
All snarks are boojums

we are dealing with the category of snarks as a whole, but we are *not* dealing with the category of boojums as a whole, since there may be boojums which are not snarks. We indicate distribution of categories by placing an (x) over the distributed category.

In a Categorical Negative statement, both of the categories are distributed:

X   X
No snarks are boojums
X   X
Boojums are not snarks

In these statements the total categories (snarks and boojums) completely exclude each other; thus we are dealing with both categories as wholes.

In the Case of limited statements, the term preceded by "some" shows us at once that the category is only partially dealt with, and we can see that in a Limited Affirmative statement, the second category is not treated as a whole either.

Some snarks are boojums

This is the equivalent of saying

Some boojums are snarks

and though the categories overlap, neither is distributed.

So to the Limited Negative statement, which is perplexing unless you think carefully. In a Limited Negative statement such as

X
Some snarks are not boojums

it is obvious that we not treating the entire category of snarks since we specify only "some." But we *are* dealing with the category of boojums as a whole because the statement says that this category *excludes* a specific portion of the category of snarks. If we reverse the statement, it would read

X
No boojums are some snarks

Thus in a Limited Negative statement, the first (or subject) category is not distributed, but the second (or predicate) category *is* distributed.

If you find the matter of distribution confusing, then simply memorize this chart of generalizations and distribution. Distributed terms are marked with an (x). For those who want to speculate a bit more on why each of the four kinds of generalization deals with whole or partial categories, each generalization is reversed in parentheses, showing equivalent statements that illustrate why predicate categories are or are not treated as a whole (distributed).

    X
All boys are human beings.   (Some human beings are boys)   Cat. Aff.
   X   X
No boys are girls.   (No girls are boys)   Cat. Neg.
Some boys are athletes.   (Some athletes are boys)   Lim. Aff.
           X
Some boys are not athletes.   (No athletes are some boys)   Lim. Neg.

When we accept certain generalizations as *facts,* we must be positive that the generalization is accurately formulated and precisely stated. Otherwise when we try to apply them to actual situations, we will make grievous mistakes. If we think that *all* Italians are musical or *all* dogs are friendly, we may find ourselves suffering through a concert by a tone deaf Roman or taking anti-rabies shots. If you know *several* non-musical Italians or you consider most dogs friendly, state your conviction as a limited generalization. Whether you say "a few," "many," "almost all," or "99 44/100 per cent," phrase the generalization as a Limited Affirmative or Limited Negative statement. You will then be using generalizations in their only effective way.

DEDUCTIVE THOUGHT

If human beings simply observed data, hypothesized or generalized about them, and tucked the resulting inductive thought away in the back of their heads, never to be used again, we would not have to worry about whether the induction is valid or not. But each of us constantly uses inductive "truths" as the starting point of another thought process. This process is *deduction,* from the Latin *de* and *duco,* "lead down from." Deduction is *the application of a generalization to a specific instance, thereby reaching a conclusion.*

We employ deduction any time we confront a situation slightly different from, yet resembling, situations we have faced before. When you approach a strange door, you automatically look for a knob to turn because your previous experience has left you with a generalization: doors are opened by turning knobs. Your "first impression" of a new acquaintance is determined in part by deduction. You try to place him in a category of familiar personalities; thus you categorize him and impute qualities of the category to him. You meet an insurance salesman; all insurance salesmen are brash, so this fellow is probably brash, too. Deduction is the essence of most argumentation, and it is virtually impossible to read a topical essay in which deduction does not play a major part.

The most formal and complete type of deduction is the *syllogism,* which is a three-step thought process. These steps are the Major Premise, which predicates a generalization about members of a category; the Minor Premise, which identifies a specific object as a member of that category; and the Conclusion, which applies the categorical principle to the specific object. Here is an example:

All human beings must die	(Major Premise)
The King of Ethiopia is human	(Minor Premise)
The King will die	(Conclusion)

Obviously, in these three steps a specific object (the King) is connected with a category (human beings) which has a common characteristic (mortality). Whether our deduction is worth anything depends on: 1. the truth of each of the statements, and 2. the way these statements are treated in relationship to each other. To test the validity of our syllogism, we should rephrase it so that the categories are clear, thus:

X	
All human beings are mortal creatures	(Major Premise)
X	
The King of Ethiopia is a human being	(Minor Premise)
X	
The King of Ethiopia is a mortal creature	(Conclusion)

The x's indicate distributed categories in each statement. Notice that the first (subject) term in the minor premise is a categorical affirmative one. The King is an individual who makes up the total category—there is only *one* King of Ethiopia—so he is *sui generis,* in a class by himself. Any statement about a *sui generis* category necessarily is a categorical one.

These are the tests of a valid syllogistic relationship:

1. The syllogism must consist of three statements, each relating two categories.

2. One category, and only one, must appear in *both* the major and minor premises. It must be distributed at least once.

3. In the entire syllogism a total of only three categories must be used. Each category appears twice, once in each of any two of the three statements.

4. There must be no category distributed in the conclusion which has not been distributed in one of the premises.

5. There must not be two negative premises. If there are, no conclusion can be made. Two negatives cannot be logically related.

Applying these tests, we find that our syllogism about the mortality of the King of Ethiopia is logically valid; it has not violated any basic principles of deduction. There are only three terms in all; both premises are positive (or affirmative); the category common to the two premises is distributed in the major premise; and the only term distributed in the conclusion (King of Ethiopia) was distributed in the minor premise. The syllogism is *valid* as a logical process; if each of the premises is true, then our conclusion must be true too.

If your taste for the mediaeval practice of solving syllogisms has been whetted, you will find some to occupy you in the Exercises at the end of the chapter. Before you sample the syllogistic fare, however, you must be warned about the *disjunctive syllogism.* You know the disjunction is a type of antithetical statement containing two ideas in an "either. . . . or. . . ." relationship. In the disjunction, a choice of alternatives is given. If a disjunctive statement is used as the major premise of a syllogism, one of the alternatives *denied* in the minor premise and the remaining statement taken as a conclusion, the result is deduction in syllogistic form, as in:

> Either Rudolph Valentino is dead or else he has retired from films
>
> He has not retired
> _____
> He must be dead

Or we could have denied the first alternative and concluded that the second was true. Our disjunctive syllogism would have been just as *valid* logically, though it might not have been *true.*

On the other hand, if two alternatives are established in a disjunctive major premise and then one is affirmed in the minor premise, as

> Either the Grettla-saga was Icelandic or else it was Finnish
> It was Icelandic
> _____
> It was not Finnish

then the syllogism is guilty of a *false disjunction*. The minor premise must always *deny* one of the alternatives, never affirm. The reasons for this are subtle ones, and your best course is to take this principle on faith—or sign up for a course in Logic. Either you will sign up for the course or accept the rule on faith; but you probably will not sign up for Logic; therefore . . . what?

Unfortunately, deductive thinking does not always take the easily examinable form of the syllogism. More often, one of the three logical steps in deduction is omitted, with the result of a partial syllogism or *enthymeme*. The following are enthymemes:

> She's bound to be sophisticated; she lives in New York.
> Students who don't study fail exams, and you didn't study.
> Ectomorphs are highly nervous, so of course Wilbur is nervous.
> Certainly Nehru is a pacifist. He's an Indian, isn't he?

Each of these two-part deductions leaves out an essential statement:

> All people who live in New York are sophisticated. (Major Premise)
> You failed. (Conclusion)
> Wilbur is an ectomorph. (Minor Premise)
> All Indians are pacifists. (Major Premise)

Because the enthymeme assumes an essential statement, it can appear to be a reasonable piece of deduction when it actually is fusty thinking. The logical errors called *non-sequiturs* are really enthymemes which rest upon an assumed and erroneous major premise. At first glance, a *non-sequitur* may look like the error we met long ago: the *post hoc* fallacy. But a *post hoc fallacy* correlates two events in sequence and a *non-sequitur* applies an unspoken generalization to a specific object. It is such apparent "causal" words as "because," "since," and so on, that blur our perception of the *non-sequitur* and make us think it something else.

In statements using such causal terms, a substitution of "therefore" in the proper place will mark it clearly as a piece of deduction. For instance:

> "Joe will never marry because he's so homely" becomes "Joe is homely; therefore he'll never marry."

"Gertrude ought to get a job with the State Department; she reads Sanskrit" becomes "Gertrude reads Sanskrit; therefore she ought to get a job with the State Department."

"Naturally, Vermeer was a great painter. He lived in 17th century Holland" becomes "Vermeer lived in 17th century Holland; therefore he was a great painter."

Each of these pairs of statements is an enthymeme composed of a minor premise (a specific object) and a conclusion (the application of a categorical principle to it). The reconstruction of the assumed major premise in each enthymeme shows what nonsense the deduction is made upon:

Homely people never marry.
People who read Sanskrit ought to get jobs with the State Department.
All people living in 17th century Holland were great painters.

Of course, not all enthymemes are false. These are valid and true:

Being human, Aristotle made mistakes at times.
Lotus Flower is a Siamese cat, so she has blue eyes.
Obviously canaries lay eggs; they're birds.
Abelard wrote in Latin because he was a scholastic.

When you think or write, using deduction—whether in syllogistic, enthymemic, or disjunctive form—remember that not only must your deductions be valid (logically accurate in method) but your individual generalizations must be true (or facts). Unless deductive thought is both true and valid, it does not amount to much.

REDUCTIVE THOUGHT

Although "reductive" is not an established term like "inductive" or "deductive," it is a helpful word to indicate the third major way by which we form our verbal thoughts. As we use it, *reductive thinking is simplification for the sake of initial understanding*. It is the method of comprehension which Thomas Mann has urged us to adopt as the first step toward mastery of the unknown, and we have already encountered the chief forms of it.

Obviously, the simplification of data or relationships may be made in two ways: 1. Only the outstanding pieces of information about a topic are dealt with, the lesser known or understood being relegated to a position of unimportance, or 2. the data or relationship is understood in terms of some other, more tangible data or relationship. With these kinds of simplification in view, we have no trouble in identifying *outlines, disjunctions,* and *generalizations* as variations of the first sort and *analogies* and *figures of speech* as examples of the second. The technique of simplification is used to an extent in all of these types of logical arrangement, and we already have investigated the proper ways of developing and applying these in thinking and writing.

The main trouble with reductive thinking is that it often tends to *oversimplify,* reducing something to the point at which the essential nature of the data or relationship is distorted or ignored. This is a type of *reductio ad absurdum,* which is a logical term applied to disproving a proposition by showing the logical consequences of an assumption. As we use the term, however, it means what it literally says, "reduce (or simplify) to an absurdity:" thinkers and writers who oversimplify ideas, whether to convey "information" or "argue a point," may not be aware of the logical ridiculousness of their assertions, but they are in fact refuting their own arguments by reducing them to restricted and narrow interpretations. The oversimplification chooses to ignore certain data in order to make a point, or it refuses to admit that an exact equation cannot exist between two separate sets of conditions. Forms of oversimplification which we have looked at include the *hasty generalization, argument by analogy, false analogy, false dilemma,* and *post hoc fallacy.* Even the *forced hypothesis* may be counted as a form of oversimplification if it ignores some of the data it purports to account for.

Simplification is quite an acceptable way of *beginning* to master a subject, but many areas of knowledge in life are by nature complex and unsusceptible to much simplification. Theoretical physics or mathematics, philosophy, history—none is a "simple" subject; when you try to understand or explain human emotions and actions, the causes and effects of subjectivity, it is downright dangerous to assume that *any* data are irrelevant or any relationship easily simplified. Yet, most of us cling tenaciously to the simplified explanations we learned as children when we think our thoughts or speak our opinions. In written rhetoric, too, ideas often come forth in the form of simplified assertions which are highly suspect.

Whether an assertion is one of causation, obligation, evaluation, or generalization, it is liable to oversimplification. Take these declarative sentences, for instance:

"Stop juvenile delinquency? It's easy. All we have to do is throw every one of those young hoodlums in jail until they see the light."

"Alcoholism is simple self-indulgence. Alcoholics are people who just don't exercise any self-control."

"Why all this jabbering over a conference table with foreigners? We should go ahead and drop a bomb on Moscow and all the rest of those Communist countries. After all, it's them or us, isn't it?"

"Once artificial class structures are eliminated, everyone will live together in peace and harmony with sufficient goods for all."

Each of these sentences can be classified as a type of assertion posing as a fact. Each ignores a complex relationship or ignores vital data. All are oversimplification to a dangerous degree. The speaker of each statement is assuming that the very intricate fields of sociology, psychology, international politics, and economics can be reduced to so-called "common sense." As a form of simplified thinking, common sense is all right; but as a basis for comprehending anything but the most uninvolved, obvious facts, common sense is too common to be trusted.

Like induction and deduction, reductive thought is a fundamental method of developing and applying ideas. Actually, in our minds all three processes are so intertwined as to be inseparable; the rhetorical presentation of ideas is likely to reflect this intertwining with a combination of ways of developing its central themes. In our artificial separation of the elementary kinds of thinking into such logical and rhetorical forms as the process, causation, organic structures, classification, and comparison and contrast, we have been isolating (and thus simplifying) aspects of logical relationships. The specimens of prose illustrating these different aspects have been dominantly indicative of one approach, though elements of more than one sort of logical order can be found in all of them. The thing to keep in mind is that any attempt to isolate a "pure" example of logic or a "clearcut" rhetorical example is largely academic. In our minds and our writing, we combine various ways of thinking to arrive at our view of truth.

Now that we have looked at various arbitrary chronological and logical patterns of thinking and at the three fundamental ways of developing thoughts supporting these patterns, we must examine the basic unit linking logic to rhetoric: words and their uses.

I. *Questions for Review*
   1. What are the differences between inductive, deductive, and reductive thinking?

2. What are the two main forms of inductive thinking? How do they differ? How are they alike?
3. How can we tell a generalization from a hasty generalization?
4. Why is no generalization ever absolutely beyond doubt?
5. What are the four kinds of generalized statement? Give examples.
6. What is distribution? Which terms are distributed in each of the four kinds of generalized statements? Why?
7. What is a syllogism? A disjunctive syllogism? An enthymeme?
8. What are the tests of a valid syllogism?
9. Can a piece of deduction be valid without being true? Can it be true without being valid? Distinguish between truth and logical validity.
10. What is a *non-sequitur*? How does it differ from a *post hoc fallacy*? Give examples.
11. What are the limitations of reductive thinking? What are its advantages?

II. *Exercises*

1. Are the following hypotheses or generalizations?
   A. Moliere's plays are marvelously funny! I just read *Tartuffe* and it's hilarious, and so is *The Imaginary Invalid*.
   B. The Irish are all just as quaint and superstitious as they can be. My neighbor, Sean O'Flannery, actually believes in leprechauns.
   C. I don't feel very well today. I think I've caught some kind of virus.
   D. The stock market dropped five points today. Probably the collapse of the latest Summit Conference a few days ago has shaken the investor's confidence in the world market.
   E. Aren't parakeets delightful? They're just as perky and lively as they can be. And they really talk quite well.
   F. The Department of Alchemy in this college is really terrible. Last year my Alchemy teacher spoke in a monotone, and this year my quiz leader stutters.
   G. Diamonds are a girl's best friend.
   H. That telephone operator is away from the switchboard. I've tried five times in the last ten minutes to get her on the line, and she doesn't answer.
   I. Caviar always gives me heartburn. I've eaten it three times now, and every single time, I've gotten heartburn.
   J. Certainly the Abominable Snowman exists! They've found those tracks of a huge foot up in the Himalayas, haven't they? Many of the Sherpas believe in the *Yeti*, as they're called. Books have been written about them. How could all these things happen unless the Snowmen existed?

2. Are the following syllogisms valid? Are they true? Why?

  A. Some human beings are cannibals.
  You are a human being.
  ___
  You are a cannibal.

  B. No Yankees have Southern drawls.
  No people with Southern drawls are integrationists.
  ___
  Yankees are integrationists.

  C. Some gourmets are not fat.
  No fat people are healthy.
  ___
  Some gourmets are healthy.

  D. Some college teachers are not paupers.
  All paupers are indigent.
  ___
  Some college teachers are not indigent.

  E. No true Catholics are Communist.
  All Communists are pro-Russian.
  ___
  No true Catholics are pro-Russian.

  F. All Phi Betes are odd balls.
  Connie is a Phi Bete.
  ___
  Connie is an odd ball.

  G. Some Democrats are not liberals.
  Jim is a liberal.
  ___
  Jim is not a Democrat.

  H. All boojums are voracious.
  All snarks are boojums.
  ___
  All snarks are voracious.

  I. College students are revolutionaries in ideas.
  Communists are revolutionaries in ideas.
  ___
  College students are Communists.

  J. College students are revolutionaries.
  Communists are revolutionaries.
  ___
  College students are Communists.

3. Embedded in each of these expository and argumentative paragraphs is a piece of deduction. Examine each paragraph carefully and construct the deduction in syllogistic form. Mark each distributed category with an (x) and then apply the validity tests. Say whether each syllogism is valid or not and whether it is true or not.

  A. Concerning the religion of the Meroitic and Kushite cultures, not much is known. In other nations of Central Africa, small statues of the Egyptian sun-god, Amun Rē, have been found, and it is clear that these nations held to a form of religious polytheism derived from that of Egypt. In Meroë and Kush, a few heads of Amun Rē have also been found; so it may be concluded that Meroitic culture had a religion polytheistic in nature and Egyptian in derivation. Beyond this, not much can be said.

B. Some action must be taken by Congress at once to insure the continued well-being of American industry. All Americans benefit from high tariffs on foreign-made goods that compete with American-made goods. The reason is obvious: all people with high standards of living are better off with the best-made goods; Americans have the highest standard of living in the world; therefore, Americans are better off with American-made goods, which are the best in the world. Congress must raise import taxes on the shoddy, foreign-made products that compete with our own superlative products.

C. The Tuaregs of the Sahara area are Hamitic in racial origin. Both the Tuaregs and the Berbers have brown skins, blue eyes, thin noses, and rounded heads. It has been shown beyond all doubt that the Berbers are Hamites, so the Tuaregs must be Hamites too. All Hamites possess the qualities best typified by the Berbers.

D. Bodily studies carried out over an extended period of time have proved that endomorphs (fat, round people) tend to be viscerotonic, or dominated by their digestive tracts. On the other hand, the ectomorphs (long, tall individuals) are never viscerotonic but are cerebrotonic, or dominated by their nervous systems. Clearly, no endomorphs could ever be cerebrotonic.

E. It is difficult to deny that the moon has a strange and unknown influence over human beings, just as it does over the earth. Our word *lunatic* means "moon-struck," and the effect of the moon on lovers has been well documented through the centuries. The most obvious effects of the moon may be seen in the ebb and flow of ocean tides; all such tidal movements are moon-controlled. Thus it is apparent that the cycle of fertility in human females, the great tidal movement of life, is also determined by the moon.

F. According to the so-called Chinese Peoples Government, any aristocrat of the old Manchu Dynasty was to be held an enemy of the people. It is interesting in the light of this pronouncement to hear that Henry Pu-Yi, the last Manchu ruler and the grandson of the great Manchu Dowager Empress, has been declared not an enemy of the people because technically he is no longer an aristocrat.

G. Some of Dickens' admirers are sentimentalists, of course. But many sentimentalists are people of great intelligence. Many instances could be cited of men with brilliant minds who weep readily at slight provocation. So we must not assume that nobody with a brain admires Dickens. On the contrary, a great many brainy people are devoted to him.

H. It is ironic that our best athletes are prevented from taking part in the Olympic games. Only amateurs are eligible for the Olympics; but of course it is the athletes who have progressed beyond their amateur standing and become professionals who are best in their fields. Since none of our best athletes are amateurs, none of them are eligible for the Games.

I. No Incan in the grandest days of the Inca Empire would have questioned the supreme might of their solar gods; but oddly, some of the priests of the Empire were not Incans, but Toltecs and Olmecs. It is entirely conceivable that the Incans were led by men who doubted the very gods they professed to worship.

J. The ancient Romans believed in the existence of werewolves. In his *Satyricon*, Petronius Arbiter recounts a tale of a soldier who became a werewolf before the eyes of his companions. No Roman ever *saw* a werewolf himself (or reported it if he did); but plenty of self-acknowledged witnesses to werewolves showed up in Rome from time to time, and it was generally agreed that if they had been exposed to such exotic sights, they *must* be Romans, since the gods revealed their wonders to Romans alone.

K. As far as the foreign policy of the United States is concerned, our choice in the Northern Hemisphere is clear. Either we support the Monroe Doctrine of nonintervention in hemispheric affairs or we open the gate to the invasion of Communism, as in Fidel Castro's Cuba. However, we *will* support the Monroe Doctrine to the utmost limit of our power and determination; and by so doing, we will prevent the infiltration of world Communism into North and South America. The gate will stay closed.

4. Supply the missing statement in each enthymeme. Is the deduction valid or not?

A. Most of Ingmar Bergman's movies are tremendously interesting pictorially, so *Wild Strawberries* ought to be interesting too.

B. Those butterfly sling chairs are dreadfully uncomfortable, so I just refuse to go to Merton's apartment anymore, since all his chairs are sling types.

C. Gaylord must be crazy; all of those Sutpens are.

D. Well, if you're a redhead, you may as well resign yourself to be freckled, I say.

E. When we were in Miami Beach, we steered clear of the Chez Pompano Restaurant. All of those places on Biscayne Boulevard are expensive, so we knew *it* was.

F. If you read it in the *Clarion,* it's so.

G. All I can say is, no excessively emotional music appeals to me, and Wagner writes the most emotional music of all.

H. Socrates was fortunate to live during the reign of Pericles; in fact, all Athenians were.

5. Are the following over-simplifications or not? Explain.

A. If scientists want to create life artificially, they must first learn to synthesize protoplasm, since protoplasm *is* life.

B. "How could Swift write a thing like *A Modest Proposal,* do you suppose?" "Why, he was obviously insane, that's why."

C. I could make good grades if I wanted to take the time to study. I I just don't want to take the time, that's all.

D. "Bobby, don't climb on that coffee table!"
"Why?"
"Because I say not to, that's why."

E. There's one sure way to save money. Put it in the bank as soon as you get it, then it won't be available. You can't spend what you don't have.

F. Boys, if you want to grow up to be a big league baseball star like Homer Wallop, just eat a big bowl of Gristles Corn Pops every morning. Homer eats Gristles every day; they supply him with the high protein food energy that a big league hitter needs.

G. If you want to make a nation of free men into a race of slaves, just close the schools. No nation with a high illiteracy rate can ever be a true democracy.

H. Why worry about over-population of the world? All we have to do is find ways to increase food production and the earth can supply an infinite number of people.

I. What's difficult about dealing with mercy killings? Whether it's called euthanasia or not, it's deliberate murder and anybody who commits it, for whatever reason, has to be treated as a murderer.

J. Certainly, euthanasia is morally right. It is nothing but common humanity to relieve suffering; if the only way to end suffering is through a mercy killing, then I say go ahead. You don't let an animal suffer with old age or hopeless injuries, do you? Then, why make a human being suffer more than an animal?

III. Suggestions for Writing

1. Choose an essay which you have already been graded on—in English or another subject—and subject it to a logical examination. Point out types of assertions, the basic kind of thinking used, and all examples of logical fallacies.

2. Write a theme analyzing the forms of thought involved in a group of essays following one of the earlier chapters of this book.
3. Choose two essays, either from the selections in this book or from a reputable periodical, one expository and the other argumentative. Examine the forms of thought used in each and the ways they are used; then write a theme comparing and contrasting the techniques of exposition and argumentation.
4. Read a lengthy editorial from your local newspaper. Analyze it for logical fallacies, and write a logical critique of the piece.

C. S. Lewis

IS CRITICISM POSSIBLE?

Amicus Plato, *my father would say, construing the words to my
uncle Toby as he went along,* Amicus Plato; *that is, Dinah was my aunt*
—sed magis amica veritas—*but truth is my sister.*

Tristram Shandy, Vol. I, cap. 21.

BUT, FIRST, A NECESSARY DIGRESSION. A RECENT REMARK OF MR. ELIOT'S
poses for us at the outset the fundamental question whether we (mere
critics) have any right to talk about Milton at all. Mr. Eliot says bluntly
and frankly that the best contemporary practising poets are the only 'jury
of judgment' whose verdict on his own views of *Paradise Lost* he will accept. And Mr. Eliot is here simply rendering explicit a notion that has
become increasingly prevalent for about a hundred years—the notion that
poets are the only judges of poetry. If I make Mr. Eliot's words the peg on
which to hang a discussion of this notion it must not, therefore, be assumed that this is, for me, more than a convenience, still less that I wish
to attack him *quâ* Mr. Eliot. Why should I? I agree with him about matters
of such moment that all literary questions are, in comparison, trivial.

Let us consider what would follow if we took Mr. Eliot's view seriously.
The first result is that I, not being one of the best contemporary poets, cannot judge Mr. Eliot's criticism at all. What then shall I do? Shall I go to
the best contemporary poets, who can, and ask them whether Mr. Eliot is
right? But in order to go to them I must first know who they are. And this,
by hypothesis, I cannot find out; the same lack of poethood which renders
my critical opinions on Milton worthless renders my opinions on Mr.
Pound or Mr. Auden equally worthless. Shall I then go to Mr. Eliot and
ask him to tell me who the best contemporary poets are? But this, again,

From *A Preface to Paradise Lost* by C. S. Lewis. Reprinted by permission of the
Oxford University Press.

will be useless. I personally may think Mr. Eliot a poet—in fact, I do—but then, as he has explained to me, my thoughts on such a point are worthless. I cannot find out whether Mr. Eliot is a poet or not; and until I have found out I cannot know whether his testimony to the poethood of Mr. Pound and Mr. Auden is valid. And for the same reason I cannot find out whether *their* testimony to *his* poethood is valid. Poets become on this view an unrecognizable society (an Invisible Church), and their mutual criticism goes on within a closed circle which no outsider can possibly break into at any point.

But even within the circle it is no better. Mr. Eliot is ready to accept the verdict of the best contemporary poets on his criticism. But how does *he* recognize them as poets? Clearly, because he is a poet himself; for if he is not, his opinion is worthless. At the basis of his whole critical edifice, then, lies the judgement 'I am a poet.' But this is a critical judgement. It therefore follows that when Mr. Eliot asks himself, 'Am I a poet?' he has to *assume* the answer 'I am' before he can *find* the answer 'I am'; for the answer, being a piece of criticism, is valuable only *if* he is a poet. He is thus compelled to beg the question before he can get started at all. Similarly Mr. Auden and Mr. Pound must beg the question before *they* get started. But since no man of high intellectual honour can base his thought on an exposed *petitio* the real result is that no such man can criticize poetry at all, neither his own poetry nor that of his neighbour. The republic of letters resolves itself into an aggregate of uncommunicating and unwindowed monads; each has unawares crowned and mitred himself Pope and King of Pointland.

In answer to this Mr. Eliot may properly plead that the same apparently vicious circle meets us in other maxims which I should find it less easy to reject: as when we say that only a good man can judge goodness, or only a rational man can judge reasonings, or only a doctor can judge medical skill. But we must beware of false parallels. (1) In the *moral* sphere, though insight and performance are not strictly equal (which would make both guilt and aspiration impossible), yet it is true that continued disobedience to conscience makes conscience blind. But disobedience to conscience is voluntary; bad poetry, on the other hand, is usually not made on purpose. The writer was trying to make good poetry. He was endeavouring to follow such lights as he had—a procedure which in the moral sphere is the pledge of progress, but not in poetry. Again, a man may fall outside the class of 'good poets' not by being a bad poet, but by writing no poetry at all, whereas at every moment of his waking life he is either obeying or breaking the moral law. The moral blindness consequent on being a bad man must therefore fall on every one who is not a good man, whereas the critical blindness (if any) due to being a bad poet need by no means fall on every one who is not a good poet. (2) *Reasoning* is never, like poetry, judged *from the outside* at all. The critique of a chain of reasoning is itself a chain of reasoning; the critique of a tragedy is not itself a tragedy. To say that only the rational man can judge reasonings is, therefore, to make the merely analytical proposition 'Only the rational man can reason', parallel to 'only the poet can make poetry', or 'only the critic can criticize', and not at all parallel to the synthetic proposition 'only the poet can criticize'. (3) As regards a *skill*, such as medicine or engineering, we must distinguish. Only the skilled can judge the skilfulness, but that is not the same as judging the value of the result. It is for cooks to say whether a given dish proves skill in the cook; but whether the product on which this skill has been lavished is worth eating or no is a question on which a cook's opinion is of no particular value. We may therefore allow poets to tell us (at least if they are experienced in the same *kind* of composition) whether it is easy or difficult to write like Milton, but not whether the reading of Milton is a valuable experience. For who can endure a doctrine which would allow only dentists to say whether our teeth were aching, only cobblers to say whether our shoes hurt us, and only governments to tell us whether we were being well governed?

Such are the results if we take the position in its full rigour. But of course if it is only meant that a good poet, other things being equal (which they often are not), is reasonably likely, in talking about the kinds of poetry he has himself written well and read with delight, to say something more worth hearing than another, then we need not deny it.

1. The "Mr. Eliot" of this essay is T. S. Eliot, the highly regarded contemporary poet and critic. What statement of Eliot's is C. S. Lewis attacking? According to this essay, what fallacy does Eliot's assertion commit?
2. What are the chief kinds of reasoning used by Lewis to refute Eliot's premise? Trace the logical development of the argument.
3. Isolate all examples of enthymemes and syllogisms in the essay, and test their validity. Are they valid? Are they true?

4. What argument by analogy does Lewis claim Eliot has committed? How does Lewis refute this argument? Does Lewis himself argue by analogy? Explain.
5. How is Lewis' final statement related to T. S. Eliot's original assertion? What kind of statement is it? Is it a fact (true statement)? Explain.

Lewis Carroll

THE QUEEN'S EXAMINATION

"WELL, THIS *is* GRAND!" SAID ALICE. "I NEVER EXPECTED I SHOULD BE A Queen so soon—and I'll tell you what it is, your Majesty," she went on, in a severe tone (she was always rather fond of scolding herself), "it'll never do for you to be lolling about on the grass like that! Queens have to be dignified, you know!"

So she got up and walked about—rather stiffly just at first, as she was afraid that the crown might come off: but she confronted herself with the thought that there was nobody to see her, "and if I really am a Queen," she said as she sat down again, "I shall be able to manage it quite well in time."

Everything was happening so oddly that she didn't feel a bit surprised at finding the Red Queen and the White Queen sitting close to her, one on each side: she would have liked very much to ask them how they came there, but she feared it would not be quite civil. However, there would be no harm, she thought, in asking if the game was over. "Please, would you tell me——" she began, looking timidly at the Red Queen.

"Speak when you're spoken to!" the Queen sharply interrupted her.

"But if everybody obeyed that rule," said Alice, who was always ready for a little argument, "and if you only spoke when you were spoken to, and the other person always waited for *you* to begin, you see nobody would ever say anything, so that——"

"Ridiculous!" cried the Queen. "Why, don't you see, child——" here she broke off with a frown, and, after thinking for a minute, suddenly changed the subject of the conversation. "What do you mean by 'If you really are a Queen'? What right have you to call yourself so? You ca'n't be a Queen, you know, till you've passed the proper examination. And the sooner we begin it, the better."

"I only said 'if'!" poor Alice pleaded in a piteous tone.

The two Queens looked at each other, and the Red Queen remarked, with a little shudder, "She *says* she only said 'if'——"

From *Alice Through the Looking Glass,* 1872.

"But she said a great deal more than that!" the White Queen moaned, wringing her hands. "Oh, ever much more than that!"

"So you did, you know," the Red Queen said to Alice. "Always speak the truth—think before you speak—and write it down afterwards."

"I'm sure I didn't mean——" Alice was beginning, but the Red Queen interrupted her impatiently.

"That's just what I complain of! You *should* have meant! What do you suppose is the use of a child without any meaning? Even a joke should have some meaning—and a child's more important than a joke, I hope. You couldn't deny that, even if you tried with both hands."

"I don't deny things with my *hands*," Alice objected.

"Nobody said you did," said the Red Queen. "I said you couldn't if you tried."

"She's in that state of mind," said the White Queen, "that she wants to deny *something*—only she doesn't know what to deny!"

"A nasty, vicious temper," the Red Queen remarked; and then there was an uncomfortable silence for a minute or two.

The Red Queen broke the silence by saying, to the White Queen, "I invite you to Alice's dinner-party this afternoon."

The White Queen smiled feebly, and said "And I invite *you*."

"I didn't know I was to have a party at all," said Alice; "but, if there *is* to be one, I think *I* ought to invite the guests."

"We gave you the opportunity of doing it," the Red Queen remarked: "but I daresay you've not had many lessons in manners yet?"

"Manners are not taught in lessons," said Alice. "Lessons teach you to do sums, and thing of that sort."

"Can you do Addition?" the White Queen asked. "What's one and one and one and one and one and one and one and one and one and one?"

"I don't know," said Alice. "I lost count."

"She ca'n't do Addition," the Red Queen interrupted. "Can you do Subtraction? Take nine from eight."

"Nine from eight I ca'n't, you know," Alice replied very readily: "but——"

"She ca'n't do Subtraction," said the White Queen. "Can you do Division? Divide a loaf by a knife—what's the answer to *that*?"

"I suppose——" Alice was beginning, but the Red Queen answered for her. "Bread-and-butter, of course. Try another Subtraction sum. Take a bone from a dog: what remains?"

Alice considered. "The bone wouldn't remain, of course, if I took it—and the dog wouldn't remain: it would come to bite me—and I'm sure *I* shouldn't remain!"

"Then you think nothing would remain?" said the Red Queen.

"I think that's the answer."

"Wrong, as usual," said the Red Queen: "the dog's temper would remain."

"But I don't see how——"

"Why, look here!" the Red Queen cried. "The dog would lose its temper, wouldn't it?"

"Perhaps it would," Alice replied cautiously.

"Then if the dog went away, its temper would remain!" the Queen exclaimed triumphantly.

Alice said, as gravely as she could, "They might go different ways." But she couldn't help thinking to herself "What dreadful nonsense we *are* talking!"

"She ca'n't do sums a *bit!*" the Queens said together, with great emphasis.

"Can *you* do sums?" Alice said, turning suddenly on the White Queen, for she didn't like being found fault with so much.

The Queen gasped and shut her eyes. "I can do Addition," she said, "if you give me time—but I ca'n't do Subtraction under *any* circumstances!"

"Of course you know your *ABC?*" said the Red Queen.

"To be sure I do," said Alice.

"So do I," the White Queen whispered: "we'll often say it over together, dear. And I'll tell you a secret—I can read words of one letter! Isn't *that* grand? However, don't be discouraged. You'll come to it in time."

Here the Red Queen began again. "Can you answer useful questions?" she said. "How is bread made?"

"I know *that!*" Alice cried eagerly. "You take some flour——"

"Where do you pick the flower?" the White Queen asked. "In a garden or in the hedges?"

"Well, it isn't *picked* at all," Alice explained: "it's *ground*——"

"How many acres of ground?" said the White Queen. "You mustn't leave out so many things."

"Fan her head!" the Red Queen anxiously interrupted. "She'll be feverish after so much thinking." So they set to work and fanned her with bunches of leaves, till she had to beg them to leave off, it blew her hair about so.

"She's all right again now," said the Red Queen. "Do you know Languages? What's the French for fiddle-de-dee?"

"Fiddle-de-dee's not English," Alice replied gravely.

"Who ever said it was?" said the Red Queen.

Alice thought she saw a way out of the difficulty, this time. "If you'll tell me what language 'fiddle-de-dee' is, I'll tell you the French for it!" she exclaimed triumphantly.

But the Red Queen drew herself up rather stiffly, and said "Queens never make bargains."

"I wish Queens never asked questions," Alice thought to herself.

"Don't let us quarrel," the White Queen said in an anxious tone. "What is the cause of lightning?"

"The cause of lightning," Alice said very decidedly, for she felt quite certain about this, "is the thunder——no, no!" she hastily corrected herself. "I meant the other way."

"It's too late to correct it," said the Red Queen: "when you've once said a thing, that fixes it, and you must take the consequences."

"Which reminds me——" the White Queen said, looking down and nervously clasping and unclasping her hands, "we had *such* a thunderstorm last Tuesday—I mean one of the last set of Tuesdays, you know."

Alice was puzzled. "In *our* country," she remarked, "there's only one day at a time."

The Red Queen said "That's a poor thin way of doing things. Now *here,* we mostly have days and nights two or three at a time, and sometimes in the winter we take as many as five nights together—for warmth you know."

"Are five nights warmer than one night, then?" Alice ventured to ask.

"Five times as warm, of course."

"But they should be five times as *cold,* by the same rule——"

"Just so!" cried the Red Queen. "Five times as warm, *and* five times as cold—just as I'm five times as rich as you are, *and* five times as clever!"

Alice sighed and gave it up. "It's exactly like a riddle with no answer!" she thought.

This excerpt comes from the final chapter of Carroll's *Alice Through the Looking Glass,* which, together with *Alice's Adventures in Wonderland,* is perhaps the most pointed—and the funniest—work ever written about the ways of thoughts and words. Carroll's disclosure of how close sense is to nonsense alerts the perceptive reader to how important words are to logical thinking.

1. Point out examples of Hasty Generalizations. Which are used as bases for deductive thinking in the "examination?"
2. Find the enthymemic statements used to reach some deductive conclusion. What part of the total syllogism is omitted? Are the conclusions valid or not?
3. Certain statements—e.g., "You couldn't deny that, even if you tried with both hands"—*imply* other assertions. How does Alice typify the human tendency to leap to conclusions, and how does Carroll treat this tendency?
4. Puns, homonyms, and equivocation are favorite verbal tricks of the Red Queen. Cite examples. How are these uses of words related to the problem of thinking logically, according to Carroll?
5. What forms of logical order (comparison and contrast, cause and effect, the process, etc.) are humorously treated in this excerpt? Is Carroll saying that all logical methodology leads to nonsense? Discuss.

CHAPTER 8

DICTION: WORD LEVELS
AND MEANINGS

Polonius: *What do you read, my Lord?*
Hamlet: *Words, words, words!*
WILLIAM SHAKESPEARE, *Hamlet*, II.2.195

Like Hamlet, all of us read words, words, words. We also speak them and write them—thousands of them in all. We take them for granted; they are a "human habit," but they are also abstractions, patterns of sounds, and the basic unit of communication. All of these broad definitions have sustained us until now; but in our gradual narrowing of attention from general problems of organization to methods of logical arrangement, to single statements, we have been inevitably approaching a more intensive examination of the very stuff of which most human communication is made—words. Whether we explain or argue, we use words, and our understanding of the essential nature of logical and rhetorical patterns depends finally on our basic ability to know and use words.

Nobody knows for certain how many words make up the vocabulary of the English language, but experts estimate that there are about 500,000. They also estimate that no one person knows more than 200,000 of these words, or about forty percent. Even to know one-fifth of the words in English, a man would have to be educated or above average; the man in the street is supposed to know from 35,000 to 75,000 words, which is a great many, if you try to visualize it. Of course, Richard Roe may not have a very precise idea of what all these words mean, but he can recognize them and use them with an approximation of meaning, even if he does confuse "affect" and "effect" or "overt" and "covert" at times.

One may wonder how English can be composed of 500,000 words, if no one person ever knows more than forty percent of them. Who uses the other sixty percent of the vocabulary, the part even a well-educated man does not recognize? The answer lies in the levels of diction used by the several hundred million people who speak English. (Diction comes from the Latin dictum, or "word.") When you consider the wide selection of words used by a garage mechanic that are virtually unknown to a housewife ("differential," "piston," "lug wrench"), or when you think of the words used by housewives that a garage mechanic is ignorant of ("pinking shears," "baste," "brisket of beef"), you get an inkling of the extent to which language propagates and words develop to suit particular needs. Like many other things, a language such as English, with thousands of words, can be better understood by classification. All words in English can be put in one of four categories: Standard, Technical, Formal, and Informal. About standard diction, not much is to be said except that it is the accepted, "educated" set of words used on formal or semi-formal occasions. The language used by the nationwide news broadcaster or the reportorial columns of *The New York Times* are examples of standard diction. The other three categories supplement standard diction.

TECHNICAL WORDS

These are words which have a highly specific application to a particular craft or occupation. Naturally, any craft is going to use certain instruments, processes, and methods developed to its ends; consequently it must have terms for these. Take the field of electronics, for instance. It is founded in a set of concepts derived from physics; therefore it begins with a set of technical terms borrowed from physics: "sound waves," "high frequency," "amplitude," "capacitance." It has evolved specialized equipment that has designations to distinguish it from other, similar equipment: "galvanometer," "rectifier," "capacitor general," "cathode," "thermistor." Finally, it has adapted procedures to its uses and applied specific names to these: "strip and tin," "insulate," "dress," "solder." If you want to learn about electronics, you must first develop a new vocabulary expressly designed for use in that field.

Almost every profession has special terms for the equipment and processes necessary to it. Mathematics has its sines, sequents, sigmas, theorems, and parallaxes; medicine has its endemias, embolisms, toxins, and contusions; music has its staffs, counterpoint, fugues, diatonics, and hemi-demi-semi-quavers. Many occupations use the same word to designate quite different things: consider what the term "drill" means to a machinist, a dentist, a soldier, an armsmaker, a seamstress, a farmer, and a zoologist, for example. If you compile a list of the terms used by one profession or occupation alone, a single set of technical words, you can easily see how English acquires its impressive vocabulary.

The term *jargon* is sometimes used to refer to the set of words or phrases particular to a job or occupation. Although the meaning of "jargon" varies according to the dictionary or handbook you consult, generally *jargon is the set of informal terms used by members of an occupation to refer to their work.* It differs from technical language in that it is informal rather than formal, it tends to be metaphoric rather than literal, and it implies a certain attitude toward the thing it designates rather than simply designating it for what it is. It is a sort of humanized technical language.

All professions and trades seem to develop their own jargons, but some are richer in jargon than others. The Navy, for instance, has a set of technical terms for its personnel, equipment, and procedures; but through the centuries, Navy men have developed a parallel set of jargon words. Thus the gold braid on an officer's cap becomes "scrambled eggs," the four-year enlistment stripe is a "hash mark" or "stupidity stripe," a radio operator is a "sparks," and a loudspeaker or intercommunications system is a "squawk box." Jazz musicians have developed an extensive jargon during the fifty years of jazz history, many of their words becoming an integral part of the English language: "swing," "take off," "vamp," and "down beat." You yourself as a college student employ a jargon when you speak of quizzes, finals, passes, flunks, and averages.

Sometimes the word "jargon" is used to refer to an overly pretentious technical set of words which might easily be replaced by a more common set. In this instance, *jargon is an excessively specialized use of terms peculiar to an occupation.* Physicians will sometimes call nosebleeds "nasal hemorrhages;" lawyers will talk about selling a house as a "transference of property and chattel from the party of the first part to the party of the second part;" and insurance agents will stupify their clients with notations that "assignment of interest under this endorsement shall not bind the company herein named until its consent is endorsed hereon." The human desire to appear important by parading one's technical knowledge before other people causes such absurd and unnecessary double-talk.

Technical words, then, are one of the main categories of diction, being used in highly specialized occupations and serving very limited professional needs. Excessively technical language and informal technical language alike become jargon. Thus technical diction can be sub-divided into Excessive, Expressive, and Degraded (Excessive and Degraded being the two forms of jargon, and Expressive being the terms vital to the understanding of the profession). We shall see that the other two main categories of words may be likewise sub-divided.

FORMAL DICTION

Formal words are those used by people of education in situations calling for prescribed behavior. Just as we dress ourselves in certain clothes to attend a reception or a stockholder's meeting, so we use formal language on those occasions when we are dealing with relative strangers or people worthy of courtesy and respect. If this description of formal language strikes you as redolent of Lord Chesterfield's letters to his son on gentlemanly conduct, just remember that many of our dealings are with strangers, and, in order to communicate our ideas to them, we must choose our words with care and attention to the traditional use of the language. Formal language is the language of educated people, but not all educated people are stuffy.

Certain overformal or excessively formal diction may seem stuffy. Chief of the excessive types of formal words are *circumlocutions,* which literally "talk around" something instead of going to the heart of the matter. Circumlocutions are used to impress listeners, just as jargon sometimes is. The man who refers to fish as "denizens of the deep" or to natives as "aboriginal inhabitants" is being pompous and self-important. Someone once said of Dr. Samuel Johnson, the first dictionary-maker, that he made little fishes talk like great whales; when we read of Johnson that he stopped going to the theater because the actresses "excited his amorous propensities," and that he referred to birds building nests as "ornithological nidification," we may grant his critic the point. Such Latinate circumlocutions, no matter how learned they were in the eighteenth century, strike us today as affected.

Very close to the circumlocution is the *euphemism;* in fact, some experts consider euphemisms a sub-type of circumlocution. *Euphemism* comes from two Greek words meaning "to speak well;" a euphemism is a polite or delicate way of expressing something that may otherwise be offensive. At times, euphemisms may be so overly sensitive and delicate as to appear prissy-prim or affected. Such Victorian euphemisms as "limb" for "leg" (even when referring to tables), "indisposed" for "ill," "in a delicate condition" for "pregnant," or "glow" for "perspire" seem silly or fussy nowadays. But some euphemisms are necessary to avoid hurting others needlessly; it is crude to tell someone recently bereaved that you're "sorry to hear his sister died." Euphemisms such as "passed away" or "your loss" may help prevent suffering in someone grieved by a recent death, though "die" and "death" are *not* harsh or cruel words in themselves. The most common sort of euphemism is the use of Latin derivatives to refer to bodily functions which also have Anglo-Saxon names that have come to be thought vulgar. Actually the Anglo-Saxon words are highly poetic when viewed objectively; the term for procreation, for example, means "to plant the seed." But because of changing social attitudes, the Anglo-Saxon words for many physical processes are considered less acceptable than the rather high-flown Latin euphemisms—"expectorate," or "evacuate"—that mean the same thing.

One of the chief forms of useful or expressive formal diction is the *idiom*. Idioms are *words or phrases, peculiar to a language, in which the literal meaning differs from the understood meaning*. If you have ever struggled to learn French, German, or any other language, you know how troublesome idioms can be. Closely related to the word *idiot,* an idiom is "strange" or "odd" too. Often it appears to make no sense when viewed literally. English idioms are similarly strange to foreigners. Why should we "board" a train or plane, "get on" a bus, and "get in" an automobile, for instance, when we are in essence performing the same operation in each case? Why should we "take" a walk in English (Where do we "take" it?) when the Germans "make" a walk and the Spanish "give" a walk? And why should rain "fall" in English when it "walks" in Russian? The next time you tell someone to "face the music" or "take his medicine" or "pay the piper," think of how different your meaning is from what you are saying, and you will see that not only foreign languages but English contain conventional, formal phrases that make sense only idiomatically.

Another perfectly acceptable kind of Expressive formal diction is the *conventional phrase*. These are the ready-made phrases that help us out as conversational gambits or serve an established purpose. Chief among them are "Miss _____, may I present Mr. _____?" "How do you do?" "I'm pleased to have met you" and so on. Birth, wedding, and death announcements follow a conventional phraseology, largely because it would be silly to try to think of witty or original ways to describe social processes. If you will glance at the society and obituary columns in any newspaper, you will see the conventional phrase in the height of its use-fulness.

The dividing line between conventional phrases and *clichés* is sometimes slight, but generally we can say that the former is useful because it fulfills a definite and recognized need, whereas the latter is an attempt to be clever and original by using some word or phrase worn out by needless repetition. *Clichés* are examples of Degraded formal language. Because of the mass media that fill our world, clichés are all too prevalent: "the glamorous star of stage, screen, and television," "the distinguished Senator from," "the beautiful state of," "our fair city," "this is bigger than both of us," "the champagne bubbles tickle my nose," and on and on. When a series of stale, worn-out words and phrases are combined to express trite, unoriginal ideas, the result is *cant* (derived from the Latin "to sing" or "to chant"). Such stereotyped sentences as these are cant: "New York is a wonderful place to visit, but I wouldn't want to live there;" "It's not the heat that bothers me; it's the humidity;" "Some of my best friends are Jews," *et cetera.* Such word combinations are within the limits of formal diction, but it is of a degraded sort.

INFORMAL DICTION

Informal diction is the assortment of words and phrases that we use in ordinary, daily conversation with our friends and families. We cannot be at our most elegant and polite all the time, either in clothing and manners *or* in speech. The informal terms we use are generally shorter than formal terms; they tend to "sound" less precise than formal words; they are more widely used than formal diction, since uneducated people as well as educated people employ them; they have less importance in literary usage. The chief kind of informal Expressive—or useful—words are *contractions,* the condensations of several words into one: e.g., "doesn't" for "does not;" "I'll" for "I will;" "can't" for "cannot," and so forth. Contractions are quite all right in speaking but should generally be avoided in formal writing. Other common types of informal diction are *colloquialisms,* which are words appropriate to ordinary speech but not to formal writing. Contractions are often considered a type of colloquialism; other examples of colloquial words are "car" for "automobile," "pants" for "trousers," "coat" for "jacket," "T.V." for "television," "sick" for "ill," "dime" for "ten cents," and "phone" for "telephone." You can supply numerous other examples from your own daily speech.

Do not confuse colloquialisms with *localisms*. *Localisms* are *informal words or phrases used in the common speech of a particular region.* Whereas the colloquialism is present in the speech of a people as a whole, the localism is confined to a very limited area or a segment of the population. Such regional expressions as "you all," "over yonder," and "little old" (South), or "stay to home" and "pick up the house" (New England), or "Howdy" (the Southwest) are *localisms.* If the total speech of a group is composed of localisms, the speech is called *patois.* The famous Gullah speech of South Carolina and the Cajun speech of the Louisiana swamps are specimens of such extreme use of localisms.

Somewhat less acceptable than colloquialisms and localisms as informal diction is *slang*. Dear to the hearts of adolescents, college students, and jazz fans, *slang is diction markedly colloquial in character which is essentially poetic in origin and usually short-lived.* Slang is often vivid, colorful, and clever; but it is overused and rapidly loses its flavor and originality. Groups of people develop slang as a sort of private language to bind themselves together. Thus the Beatniks have their "pads" (rooms), "chicks" (girls), "like crazy" (excellent); Army men have their "sacks" (beds), "chicken bird-dogs" (martinet officers), "chow time" (meal time); musicians have their "Daddy-O" (mentor), "licorice stick" (clarinet), "real George" (highly satisfactory); and collegians have their "gut courses" (undemanding courses), "snowed" (overwhelmed), "book-shook" (mental fatigue), and "clutched" (frightened). Slang is originated by some basically poetically-minded person who wishes to speak metaphorically to convey his ideas. If you will look at such terms as these—"go ape," "hit the sack," "get off my back," "passion pit," "stoned"—you will see they are all metaphors. Other slang ("like crazy") is simile. In fact, every slang term can be classified as some figure of speech. G. K. Chesterton once remarked that all slang is metaphor, and all metaphor is poetry. What, then, may we deduce?

Occasionally, slang terms may become so generally accepted over a period of time that they are dignified by becoming acceptable colloquialisms. "Mob" and "fizz" were thought to be vulgar in the eighteenth century but are proper colloquialisms today. More often, slang becomes obsolete; nothing sounds more archaic than the slang of a decade ago. Think of the "sheik," "sheba," and "cootchy coo" of the 1920's, for instance, or the "hubba, hubba," "cutie," "queen," and "battle bitter" of the 1940's. Very frequently slang is truly vulgar or obscene in nature, and as a whole it must be termed a degraded type of informal diction.

Even more socially unacceptable than slang is *argot,* which is the language of the lower or criminal classes. Thanks to motion pictures and television, everyone is now familiar with such words as "bull" (policeman), "chopper" (machine gun), "chippie" (prostitute), "tea" (heroin), "snow" (cocaine), and "to rat" (inform). But *argot* remains a form of sub-language and a prime example of degraded informal speech.

Finally, there is the *Vulgarism,* or the Illiteracy, which is low, vulgar words written out and commonly misspelled. Profanity is usually called a vulgarism; so are those Anglo-Saxon words we spoke of. Other vulgarisms include such uses as "eats" for "food," "gents" for "gentlemen," "thru" for "through," "humans" for "human beings," "nite" for "night," "rite" for "right," and so on. Modern advertising, with its phonetically spelled trade names, has increased the spread of vulgarisms. When a child is confronted with such misspellings as "qwik," "tite," "glo," "duz," and "holsum" on commercial products in place of "quick," "tight," "glow," "does," and "wholesome," it is small wonder that vulgarisms abound. Some of them, like "thru" and "humans," are now appearing in otherwise reputable newspapers and magazines and may eventually become proper spellings.

So far, we have not given any examples of informal diction which is excessive. There are two main types: the Elegant Illiteracy and the Malapropism. The Elegant Illiteracy is committed by people wishing to appear highly correct and proper in their speech but not having a very good sense of what is correct and what is not. Such horrors as "My sister and myself went to the theater last week" and "My father took my brother and myself fishing" are examples of Elegant Illiteracy. Malapropisms are words misused for other words which they resemble in sound; thus, "In his fall, he suffered lubrications and confusions" (for "lacerations and contusions") or "That bowl of flowers is attractively deranged."

These are the chief types of the major classifications of words into Standard, Technical, Formal and Informal Diction. Remember that, like all classifications, the above is something of a simplification. A case could be made for placing Malapropisms under formal rather than informal diction; certain other alterations might be made as well. Furthermore, many words belong in more than one category, according to the varying meanings which they have. This arbitrary schematization, therefore, should be read as a general and simplified description rather than as a rigidly prescriptive outline of language. (See the diagram on the page following.)

In general, the role played by words in written discourse is that of a means to an end: i.e., expressing what the writer wants to say. But some specialized prose is concerned with the nature of words in themselves, and prose about language may be informative, entertaining, or both. Frank Sullivan's parody of an interview between a questioner and a "cliché expert" shows how a writer sharply attuned to uses of words can write originally and wittily even while he reveals the unoriginal thought and phrasing of others. Sheridan's *The Rivals* first revealed to the world the elegantly ignorant Mrs. Malaprop, who has given her name to a kind of misuse of words. Geoffrey Hellman's essay on page 249 also emphasizes words as words. In these articles, diction *per se* is the topic of investigation. In Chapter 10 below, you will learn more fully how levels of diction are important in all rhetoric and how writers use the levels implicitly to reenforce their ideas.

DEFINITION

We have spent a good deal of time talking about levels of diction partly to show the way the total vocabulary of English is compiled, partly to show the rich variety of words and their use, but mostly to demonstrate how our understanding of word meanings necessarily involves understanding the category to which words belong. When you consult a dictionary (*dictionary* is a *diction*-ary, or word collection, just as an aviary is a bird collection), one of the things you are told about a word is the level of diction to which it is consigned. Words are indicated as colloquialisms, slang, idioms, or one of the other types, according to their usage and the evaluation of this usage by language experts. Our entire understanding of the meaning of a word is tied to our awareness of the proper occasions on which to use it.

Since a dictionary reflects the current state of language, and since languages are constantly changing, adding some words and dropping others, the same word may be classified as being in two dictional levels. "Poke" is a perfectly common informal verb meaning "to jab," but it is also used as a noun in the Southern localism, "a pig in a poke," where "poke" means "bag" or "sack." The dictionary will give you the various meanings attached to the same word; your intelligent use of the word must take into account the variational meanings. Sometimes a word such as "wrought," "drear," or "hath" is indicated as archaic or obsolete, in which case it has largely dropped out of the language. Since English is spoken by British peoples as well as Americans, and since differences in meaning and spelling exist, the dictionary will indicate these: the British spell "wagon" with two "g's," for instance, and "gray" with an "e." These spellings are acceptable in American English but are not preferred use. Also, your use of such common

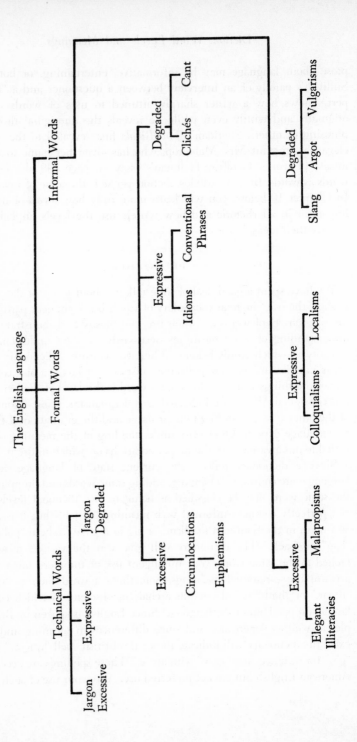

LEVELS OF DICTION

The English Language

Technical Words
  Jargon Excessive
  Expressive
  Jargon Degraded

Formal Words
  Excessive
    Circumlocutions
    Euphemisms
  Expressive
    Idioms
    Conventional Phrases
  Degraded
    Clichés
    Cant

Informal Words
  Excessive
    Elegant Illiteracies
    Malapropisms
  Expressive
    Colloquialisms
    Localisms
  Degraded
    Slang
    Argot
    Vulgarisms

American colloquialisms as "piddle," "bum," and "bloody" would be considered offensive in Britain—such words are vulgarisms—and the dictionary often indicates this fact. Remember that word meanings tend to vary within their contexts and from region to region or even person to person.

So that we will not become a race of Humpty-Dumptys, each of us insisting that a word means what *he* wants it to mean, we consult compilations of words which tell us how a word is commonly used by other people; that is, the word is *defined* for us. *Defined* comes from the Latin word for *limit;* that is precisely what a definition does: limit the meaning or use of the word. It effectively draws boundary lines around the area of meanings to which that word can be applied, so that we will know when we use it just what specific range of meanings a word will have for our listeners. Of course, many of us have only vague ideas of what certain words mean, so we toss them about loosely and never convey very much to our listeners. If you do not know exactly what other people understand "disinterested," "liberal," or "democracy" to mean, then you had better clear up your terms at the start of your discussion by defining the words you use. This step is vital for arguments: unless you are agreed on word meanings, you and your opponent will never reach an agreement or even a basic understanding of what each is talking about. Some semanticists (people who specialize in word meanings) feel that much of the present world tension is due to misunderstandings arising from the use of word definitions; when we see both the United States and Russia claiming to be champions of liberty, democracy, and freedom, but acting in opposite ways, we may agree. Obviously, both we and the Russians must define what we mean by "freedom," "liberty," and "democracy" before we can reach an understanding on how to achieve it.

There are five basic ways of defining. We will examine each of these in turn:

1. *Definition by root meaning.* This is the method used often in this book. Since English is derived from Latin, Greek, Anglo-Saxon, French, German, and other languages, many of our words can be defined and their meanings made clear by breaking them down into the foreign words that are their roots, thus:

> Defenestrate—Latin, *de,* out, *fenestra,* window, "to throw
> out of the window"
> Pathology—Greek, *pathe,* disease, *logos,* study, "the study
> of diseases"

> Kindergarten—German, *kinder,* children, *garten,* garden,
> "a garden of children"
> Wife—Anglo-Saxon, *wif,* woman, "a married woman"

The trouble with defining words by their root meanings is that word meanings change and the present use of the word may be quite different from the original meaning, as in

> Chocolate—Aztec, *chocolatl,* bitter water
> Lord—Anglo-Saxon, *hlaf weard,* loaf keeper
> Squirrel—Greek, *skia ouros,* shadow tail

Root meanings are always interesting to anyone with an ear for words, but they are limited in helpfulness to people who want to know the current use rather than the origins of words.

2. *Definition by synonym.* While somewhat limited, this method of defining is the most direct and simple. It consists of giving the meaning of the term to be defined by equating it with another word of almost the same meaning. Often, definition by synonym consists of translating the word from one language into another, as in

> Cerumen—earwax
> Axilla—armpit
> Faux pas—error

Sometimes a close synonym can be found which adequately conveys the meaning in the same language:

> Fool—simpleton
> Parcel—package
> Jabber—chatter
> Itinerary—route

Since it is impossible to find a close synonym for all words, the next method is far more commonly used; it is

3. *Definition by classification.* Sometimes this method is called definition by *genus* and *differentia,* but it is the same technique. We said that classification was a complex description, and the same could be said about some definitions. To define a thing by classification, we place it in a class or category of objects, and then point out its differences from other objects in the category. For instance:

> Goliard — one of a class of wandering students in Germany, France, and England, chiefly in the 12th and 13th centuries, noted for their rioting and intemperance and their satirical Latin verse.

The class into which the term is put is "students"; the differentia are all the other particular qualities which separate the Goliards from other types of students. The definition by classification may be expressed in various ways. In the following definitions, the genus or class is underlined once and the differentia are underlined twice:

Goosander— a saw-billed fish-eating duck

Ciborium— a permanent canopy placed over an altar

Macerate— to soften, or separate the parts of a substance by steeping in a liquid, with or without heat.

Notice that the method of defining by classifying can be used even in the case of verbs (action words), as "macerate" above. In the case of gerunds (action words used as nouns) such as "spinning" or "gyrating" the genus part of the definition may be "the act" and the differentia a particularized description of the action process. Most standard dictionaries use the form of definition by classification for every word, though in some instances definition by synonym may be used.

4. *Definition by illustration.* Usually it is considered poor practice to define by giving an example of the term to be defined. In such apparent definitions as:

A mirage is when you see something that isn't there

a double fault is committed: the "definition" is grammatically clumsy (It uses a dependent clause as a noun), and it limits the definition of a class of objects (mirages) to a specific instance. In such a "definition" by example as this,

Altruism is giving all your money to the poor

the definition gives a single instance of altruism and identifies all altruism with this one act. Consequently, *definition by example* is weak and fallacious. Definition by illustration, on the other hand, is necessary in the case of intangibles, which cannot be easily defined by another method. Here are samples of definition by illustration:

Yellow—of a bright color like that of butter,
lemons, etc.
Sour—having an acid taste, such as that of
vinegar, lemon juice, etc.

Broil—to cook by direct heat, as on a gridiron
Hardy—fitted for enduring fatigue, hardship,
exposure, etc.: *hardy animals*

Notice in the last definition that an example of usage of the term *hardy*
is given which is not a part of the definition proper. In the other definitions, however, in order for the full meaning of the word to be clear,
a tangible instance is given to particularize a vague or intangible initial
description, thus "a bright color *like*. . . ," "an acid taste, *such as* . . . ," and
"to cook, *as on* . . ." You will recognize these definitions as using the
technique of comparison which we have seen in an earlier chapter. Sometimes the only way to make meaningful a definition of an intangible is to
express it through a comparison with something that helps us to visualize it.
Thus words expressing actions (verbs, gerunds), qualities (adjectives), or
manner (adverbs) are at times best defined through illustration.

5. *Definition by Negation.* In some cases, words are defined in terms of
what they are not or characteristics they do not possess. Definitions of this
type are called definitions by negation, and they include obvious terms
which have the prefixes "un," "in," and "a"; e.g.,

Unacceptable—not acceptable
Inept—not suitable
Amorphous—lacking shape or form

In certain instances, however, the word to be defined is antithetical to a
positive or material concept and therefore must be defined in a negative
way, as

Vacuum—a space entirely devoid of matter
Zero—the symbol of absence of numerical quantity
Death—total and permanent cessation of all vital
functions of an animal or plant.

The total number of words which can be defined only by negation is
probably not very many. This method of defining is usually a supple-
mentary way of giving meaning to a term properly defined by another
method.

If you scan a dictionary, you will see that all of the five basic ways of
defining are sometimes used to give the complete signification of a single
word. In the case of such complex words as "life" or such words with
varying uses as "light," variations and combinations of the five methods of
defining are essential to convey the true meanings of the terms as they

are used and understood. For a formal, authoritative definition, always refer to a good, preferably an unabridged dictionary.

In written discourse, terms are frequently defined in the brief fashion of the five types we have looked at. On occasion, however, when a writer is dealing with a really complicated or abstract or arbitrary term he may write an *extended definition*. Such a definition will include all of the varieties of definition that a dictionary uses, plus others: different meanings in different periods of time; definitions made by authorities in disagreement; definitions through numerous illustrations. Barry Ulanov's definition of jazz, included in the selections at the end of the chapter, is an extended one, set forth to make clear the extent and nature of a subject he proposes to treat at length. Carl Jung's extended definition of "soul" serves as a preface to a detailed investigation of the nature of the subconscious. Similarly, a writer discoursing on the Renaissance, love, the Hellenistic Age, or Socialism cannot be satisfied with a brief dictionary definition of his topic. Often the very words we take most for granted— e.g., "life," "literature," "sin," "ambition"—are the very ones that need to be defined in detail for the sake of precision of meaning.

On certain occasions, we may not need a formal or standard definition of a word; we may prefer for the sake of discussion or for a specific set of circumstances to make our own *informal* or *impromptu definition*. The informal definition may be used in an argument or in expository discourse; usually it is more simplified than the formal meaning of the same word, and care must be taken to make the informal definition as clear and accurate as possible. Here are cases in which an informal definition could be used:

Speaker A: "The main trouble with Doris is that she's a nonconformist. It gets irritating the way she's always working to appear different."

Speaker B: "Oh, I don't think she *tries* to be different; she acts naturally enough according to her own personality."

Speaker A: "But that's just what I mean. It may be 'natural' for her, but it isn't natural for anyone else."

Speaker B: "The point is that she doesn't *work* at being the way she is; she's spontaneous. If by 'nonconformist' you mean someone who values spontaneous behavior more than socially prescribed behavior, then Doris is a nonconformist."

Speaker A: "O.K., I'll go along with that."

Or this example of an informal definition in informative discourses:

> When I refer to "artists," I do not mean musicians, dancers, or actors; though all of these groups are legitimately people of the arts, they are not the "craftsmen" who work with material or plastic substance in the true sense of artistry. To be an artist, one must impose his ideas on some external substance tangible to the viewer. By "artists" I mean painters, sculptors, and architects.

Obviously, unless one's audience agrees with his informal definition, the definition is valueless so far as accomplishing understanding is concerned. Yet the informal definition is sometimes more practical than the formal one in conveying information or reaching an agreement. Once you have made an informal definition, be sure to stay with it and not let it shift or alter meaning; if this happens, you are guilty of *equivocation*. Equivocation (Latin *equi*, "equal," *voco*, "to call or name," hence "to call equal") is the use of more than one meaning for the same word within a context where only one meaning is understood. In the heat of an argument, equivocation becomes a dodge easy to slip into, or it may be a way of begging the question. Look at this argument as a case in point:

A: "It's really frightening the way America is declining morally."

B: "What do you mean 'declining'? "

A: "Oh, the way we've lost our sense of values and become so greedy and materialistic."

B: "Do you really think we're greedy, with our foreign aid plans, the millions of dollars we give to charities like the Red Cross and Community Chest, exchange scholarships, Federal slum clearance, and all the other humanitarian services we finance with taxes and donations? Certainly Americans today are more generous than our ancestors were in the eighteenth and nineteenth centuries."

A: "That's just what I mean: we've declined by abandoning the principles of our ancestors!"

In this exchange, A is equivocating by defining "decline" first as "greed and materialism" and then "abandonment of our ancestral principles."

Unless he is caught short by B and forced to stand by his original definition, the argument must end in a morass of confusion.

Whether your definition is formal or informal, you must be careful to keep it from committing the fallacies of inclusion and exclusion. If you define a word too broadly, the definition may cover examples that do not legitimately come within the limits of that term. Here are definitions that are too *inclusive*:

> Chair—a piece of furniture designed to be sat on (This definition would include such non-chairs as sofas, benches, ottomans, and stools.)

> College—an institution established for the purpose of spreading knowledge (This definition would wrongly include primary and secondary schools as well as professional institutes.)

On the other hand, a definition may be so narrow as to leave out certain objects which rightly belong in the defined term. In these cases, the definition is said to be too *exclusive*:

> Boat—a water-going vessel, propelled by oars or paddles (This definition leaves out sail boats, motor boats, and steam boats.)

> Chair—a piece of furniture consisting of an upholstered seat resting upon four legs and supporting a padded back and arms, to be used for sitting (This excludes wooden, plastic, and metal chairs, chairs without arms, chairs with three legs, and sling chairs.)

In a few cases, a definition may be both too inclusive and too exclusive, as in the following:

> Shoe—a foot covering consisting of a leather sole with a leather piece fitted over the arch and heel (This definition could include sandals, moccasins, and slippers; but it excludes shoes made of materials other than leather.)

To be sure you know the proper meaning (or signification) of a word, check your definition against this list of qualities necessary for accurate definition:

1. Is the term to be defined clearly understood and removed from any confusing context (i.e., a phrase or clause)? Is a single word or a group of words the term to be defined? If the term is a group of words, which

is the word in question (e.g., the definition of "motor boat" must emphasize the characteristics of the "motored" boat as distinguished from other boat types)?

2. Are the terms to be defined and the definition the same or equivalent grammatical constructions? Verbs must be defined by verbs (i.e., infinitives), nouns by nouns, and so on. Always use parallel units of syntax to define your terms.

3. Which of the five basic methods of definition is used? Is this the best method for the word under examination?

4. Is the definition too inclusive? Too exclusive?

5. Is the definition more clear and simple than the term to be defined? (Never give a more complicated definition than the word itself, e.g., "hermit" means "anchorite.")

6. Does the term to be defined appear in the definition? If so, the definition is *circular* and fallacious. (If the term to be defined is a phrase, a part of the phrase may appear in the definition; e.g., "eyebrow" means "the arch or ridge over the eye.")

Once you have realized the necessity for defining the words vital to the ideas you express in conversation or writing, and when you have mastered the logical methods of defining, you will possess the means to clear thinking and clear expression. Because words are so numerous, so varied, and so widely used, they have characteristics other than the fundamental ones of dictional level and signification, but an awareness of the importance of word levels and meaning underlies all of the other things we must learn about words to be qualified as able users of English.

I. Questions for Review

1. What is the meaning of *diction?* What are the chief levels of diction treated in this chapter? On what principle of division are they established?

2. What are the two kinds of jargon? How are they related to technical language? How do they differ from it?

3. What are the main types of formal diction? Which are the most useful? Why? Why are certain kinds of formal diction "excessive"?

4. What is the difference between these types of informal diction: contractions, colloquialisms, localisms? Which, if any, are acceptable in "formal" writing? Explain.

5. How do slang and argot differ? Look up a definition of slang and of jargon in your dictionary. Could slang be properly termed a sort of jargon? Discuss.

6. What is definition? What are the five basic types of definition? What are the advantages and disadvantages of each?

7. What are the uses of the extended definition?

8. How is an impromptu definition used?

9. What is equivocation? Give examples and show how they are used in expository and argumentative writing.

10. How is diction related to the problem of thinking logically? Explain.

II. Exercises

1. Make up a list of words illustrating each of these levels of diction: idioms, slang, clichés, jargon (degraded).

2. Identify the level of diction to which each belongs:

   A. Jam session
   B. Set the table
   C. Tastee-Kreme
   D. Goof off
   E. Bo'sun (for Boatswain)
   F. Ice (for diamonds)
   G. Go steady
   H. Socks (for stockings)
   I. Sidewinder (for rattlesnake)
   J. To razz (or give the raspberry)
   K. Request the pleasure
   L. Our gracious and charming hostess
   M. Baby-sitter
   N. Fan (for admirer or devotee)
   O. Gas (for gasoline)
   P. Roger and Over
   Q. Hardware (for firearms)
   R. R. S. V. P.
   S. Dynamometer
   T. Keelhaul
   U. Meanwhile, back at the ranch . . . .
   V. His sister is a sinister (for spinster)
   W. Take a ride
   X. Bar-B-Q
   Y. Take him for a ride

3. Translate the following statements into correct, formal English. Identify the dictional level of each in its present form.

A. A triplicity of astigmatic rodents; observe their mode of travel. They collectively pursued an agriculturist's spouse, who amputated their caudal appendages with a paring utensil.

B. This kook from way out in Squaresville took a dog to a dive and got bombed on joy juice.

C. The D. J. spun three platters before he found out the mike was dead and the switchman asleep.

D. The motivational factors of the culture, added to environmental elements and a low interest threshold, have resulted in a noncompetitive spirit in group activities.

E. This snow-bird was pulling a two-finger to get the scratch for a fix, when the pie-wagon showed and a badge sneezed him.

4. Look up the root meanings for these words in your dictionary.

A. Heliotrope	K. Cinch
B. Mister	L. Pedagogue
C. Candidate	M. Ambidextrous
D. Superfluous	N. Groom
E. Blitzkrieg	O. Starch
F. Napkin	P. Hydrocephalic
G. Grisly	Q. Prison
H. Phonograph	R. Dandelion
I. Chute	S. Algebra
J. Grotto	T. Vamoose

5. What would be the best method of defining these words:

A. Scarlet	F. Appendage
B. Prism	G. Puerile
C. Ocelot	H. Cold (noun)
D. Minus	I. Anhydrous
E. Agile	J. Gyrate

6. What is wrong with these definitions?

A. Dog—a domesticated, carniverous quadruped.

B. A carpet is a rectangular piece of heavy cloth, woven in a warp and woof fashion and used as a floor covering.

C. Ceramics is taking some clay and molding it and then baking it in a kiln or oven.

D. Sabotage is the deliberate injury to tools, machinery, work; the underhanded interference with production by enemy agents during wartime; the destruction by employees of equipment during a strike; or any other act of sabotage.

E. Lyre—a musical instrument of ancient Greece, consisting of a sound box (usually a turtle shell), with two curving arms carrying a cross bar (yoke) from which strings are stretched to the body, used to accompany the voice in singing and recitation.

F. Hibernate—the process that bears observe in the winter.

G. A borogrove is a thin, shabby-looking bird with its feathers sticking out all round—something like a live mop.

H. Home is a place where, when you have to go there, they have to take you in.

I. A mother-in-law is a woman whose mouth is always open and whose purse is always shut.

J. Candy—confections made of sugar combined with other ingredients.

III. *Suggestions for Writing*

1. Write an essay on the relationship of definition to classification or comparison and contrast.

2. Quickly scan the definitions in the early chapters of the book and categorize them as being of one of the five basic types. How is definition used in expository writing? Using this book as example, write a theme discussing definition and exposition.

3. Read one of the selections at the end of the book: Newman's "What Is a University?" Sapir's "Dialect," or Edith Hamilton's "The Idea of Tragedy," and then write an analysis of its use of the techniques of definition.

4. Write an extended definition of one of these terms:

A. Liberty	F. Justice
B. Beauty	G. Society
C. History	H. Civilization (or Culture)
D. Music	I. Honor
E. Art	J. Education

Barry Ulanov

WHAT IS JAZZ?

IN *The American Scene*, HENRY JAMES SAID OF AMERICAN CITIES, "So there it all is; arrange it as you can. Poor dear bad bold beauty; there must indeed be something about her . . .!" The same thing can be said of American jazz.

On the surface there is disorder and conflict in jazz. No common definition of this music has been reached. It resists dictionary definition, and its musicians splutter nervously and take refuge in the colorful ambiguities of its argot. Nonetheless, its beauty can be probed; its badness can be separated from its boldness. The process is a difficult one, as it is in any art, and in jazz two arts, the composing and the performing arts, are joined together. But if one goes beneath the surface and does not allow the contradictions and the confusions of appearances to put one off, much becomes clear, and the mystery at the center is seen to be the central mystery of all the arts.

the outer layer

The cortex of jazz consists of several layers, alternately hard and soft, complex in structure, and hard to take apart. It is compounded of the history of the music and of the many styles of jazz. At first the history seems disjointed and the styles contradictory. One marks a confounding series of shifts in place and person and style. One finds a music dominated by Negroes in New Orleans, by white musicians in Chicago, by important but apparently unrelated figures in New York. One discovers a disastrous split in jazz inaugurated by the swing era and intensified during the days of bebop and so-called progressive jazz. But then one looks and listens more closely, and order and continuity appear.

Americans have long been wedded to the boom-and-bust cycle, and their culture reflects that dizzying course. Jazz is not like that; it has no cycles; it doesn't spiral. Whether you adopt the approach of the economic historian, the cultural anthropologist, or the aesthetic philosopher, you will not find an easy reflection of a theory in jazz. While much of America

—crises and ecstasies and even a moment or two of exaltation—has found its way into jazz, the history of jazz is a curiously even one, chaotic at any instant, but always moving ahead in what is for an art form almost a straight line.

For most of its history, jazz, rejected in its homeland, has had consciously to seek survival, conscientiously to explain and defend its existence. From its early homes, the Ozark hills, the Louisiana bayous, the Carolina cotton fields, the Virginia plantations, through the New Orleans bordellos and barrelhouses to its latter-day efflorescence it has been alternately condemned and misunderstood. Variously banned and bullied and sometimes cheered beyond its merits, jazz has led a lonely life but a full one. It is still with us and looks to be around for quite a while.

No matter what the fortunes of jazz, its nucleus has remained constant, little touched by extravagances of opinion, sympathetic or unsympathetic. The nucleus of jazz—as differentiated from its cortex—contains its nerve center, its source of life, and here are its mystery and meaning. The nucleus of jazz is made up of melody, harmony, and rhythm, the triune qualities of the art of music which, as everybody knows, can be fairly simply defined. In bare definition, melody is any succession of notes, harmony any simultaneity of tones, rhythm the arithmetic measure of notes or tones. In closer examination, melody appears as a vast variety of things, ranging from so simple a tune as "Yankee Doodle" to the complexity of one of Arnold Schoenberg's constructions. In more detailed analysis, harmony shows up as a vertical ordering of a Bach fugue, or a tight structuring based entirely on whole tones in the impressionism of Debussy. But bewildering as the complications of melody and harmony can be, they are easier to analyze and verbalize than rhythm or any of its parts, and rhythm is the most important of the three in jazz.

Before attempting a synoptic definition of jazz as a noun (or discussing the misuse of "jazz" as a verb and "jazzy" as an adjective), and of the various corollary terms that explain the meaning of this music, it might be instructive to examine definitions by musicians themselves. The following definitions were made by jazz musicians in 1935, when their music was undergoing a revival as a result of the then current vogue for the jazz that went by the new name of swing. Benny Goodman was a great success, and jam sessions had become public again. Musicians themselves found it difficult to define "swing," by which of course they merely meant the 1935 version of jazz, which wasn't very different from the 1930 or 1925 music. Let us examine the definitions.

WINGY MANONE: "Feeling an increase in tempo though you're still playing at the same tempo."

MARSHALL STEARNS AND JOHN HAMMOND   (jazz authorities) AND BENNY GOODMAN: "A band swings when its collective improvisation is rhythmically integrated."

GENE KRUPA: "Complete and inspired freedom of rhythmic interpretation."

JESS STACY: "Syncopated syncopation."

MORTON KAHN AND PAYSON RE: "Feeling a multitude of subdivisions in each beat and playing or implying the accents that you feel; that is, if the tune is played at the proper tempo, so that when you're playing it, you'll feel it inside."

GLENN MILLER: "Something that you have to feel; a sensation that can be conveyed to others."

FRANKIE FROEBA: "A steady tempo, causing lightness and relaxation and a feeling of floating."

TERRY SHAND: "A synthetic co-operation of two or more instruments helping along or giving feeling to the soloist performing."

OZZIE NELSON: "A vague something that you seem to feel pulsating from a danceable orchestra. To me it is a solidity and compactness of attack by which the rhythm instruments combine with the others to create within the listeners the desire to dance."

CHICK WEBB: "It's like lovin' a gal, and havin' a fight, and then seein' her again."

LOUIS ARMSTRONG: "My idea how a tune should go."

ELLA FITZGERALD: "Why, er—swing is—well, you sort of feel—uh—uh—I don't know—you just swing!"

These musicians were looking for a new set of terms that would catch the beat so basic to jazz; they were stumped for the words to describe the kind of improvisation necessary to jazz.

In the simple, compressed, sometimes too elliptic vocabulary of the jazz musician, one learns a great deal about the music he plays. One learns that "jazz" is a noun, that it is not American popular music (as it has often been thought to be), that the jazz musician is most interested in the rhythmic connotation of the word and in little else. If you tell him that some say the term comes from the phonetic spelling of the abbreviation of a jazz musician named Charles (Charles, Chas., Jass, Jazz), he is not in the least interested. If you tell him that there is a great deal of substance to the claim that the word comes from the French word *jaser*—to pep up, to exhilarate—he may nod his head with a degree of interest but ask you, "What about the beat?" You will learn from the jazz musician that "swing" is no longer a noun, in spite of the fact that it was first so used in the title of a Duke Ellington recording in 1931, "It Don't Mean a Thing if It Ain't Got that Swing," which gives it a kind of ex cathedra endorsement. You will learn that "swing" is a verb, a way of describing the beat, even as Ellington's title for another tune, "Bouncing Buoyancy," is a description of the same beat, even as the term "jump" is, even as "leaps" is, even as the description of jazz as "music that goes" is, even as in the thirties the compliment of "solid" to performer or performance was like "gone," "crazy," "craziest," "the end," and "cool" today. They are descriptions of the beat.

From an examination of jazz musicians' own words, it is possible to glean the subtle, unruly, and almost mystical concept of the jazz spirit, or feeling, or thinking—it is all these things and is so understood by the jazz musician himself. The jazzman has his own way of getting at the center of his music, and thus he formulates his own musical language. Also he converts the musical language into a verbal dialect of his own. In his own set of terms, musical and verbal, he thinks, he feels; he rehearses, he performs; he scores, he improvises; he gets a beat.

To get that elusive beat, a jazzman will do anything. Without it, he cannot do anything. With it, he is playing jazz, and that is a large and satisfying enough accomplishment. When a jazzman picks up a familiar tune, banal or too well-known through much repetition, and alters its rhythmic pattern in favor of a steady if sometimes monotonous beat, and varies its melodies and maybe even changes its chords, he is working freely, easily, and with as much spontaneity as he can bring to his music. That freedom, ease, and spontaneity brought him to jazz; within those determining limits he will find a place for himself or get out, or join one of the bands whose frightening parodies of jazz are so often more popular than the real thing. It is by his formal understanding of certain definite values that the jazz musician has conceived, organized, and developed his art. It has been hot; it has become cool. It has jumped and swung; it has sauntered. It has borrowed; it has originated. It has effected a change, a literal transformation; inherited conventions have gradually been restated, reorganized, and ultimately restructured as a new expression. It may be that jazz musicians have simply rediscovered a controlling factor in music, the improvising performer. Without any awareness of what he has done, the jazzman may have gone back to some of the beginnings of music, tapping once more the creative roots which nourished ancient Greek music, the plain chant, the musical baroque and its immediate successors and predecessors. We know that seventeenth- and eighteenth-century composers were improvisers and that when they brought their scores to other musicians they left the interpretation of parts to the discretion of the performers, even as an arranger for a jazz band does today.

But the jazz musician has brought more than procedures, composing conceptions, and improvisation to his music. Techniques have been developed that have broadened the resources and intensified the disciplines of certain instruments far beyond their use in other music. Colors have been added to solo instruments and to various combinations and numbers of instruments that are utterly unlike any others in music. New textures have emerged from a conception of tonality and of pitch that is not original but is entirely fresh in its application. The improvising jazz musician has a different and more responsible and rewarding position from that of his counterparts in earlier art and folk music. The rhythmic base of music has been reinterpreted, making the central pulse at once more primitive than it has been before in Western music, and more sophisticated in its variety.

This, then, is how one might define jazz: it is a new music of a certain distinct rhythmic and melodic character, one that constantly involves improvisation—of a minor sort of adjusting accents and phrases of the tune at hand, of a major sort in creating music extemporaneously, on the spot. In the course of creating jazz, a melody or its underlying chords may be altered. The rhythmic valuations of notes may be lengthened or shortened according to a regular scheme, syncopated or not, or there may be no consistent pattern of rhythmic variations so long as a steady beat remains implicit or explicit. The beat is usually four quarter-notes to the bar, serving as a solid rhythmic base for the improvisation of soloists or groups playing eight or twelve measures, or some multiple or dividend thereof.

These things are the means. The ends are the ends of all art, the expression of the universal and the particular, the specific and the indirect and the intangible. In its short history, jazz has generally been restricted to short forms and it has often been directed toward the ephemeral and the trivial, but so too has it looked toward the lasting perception and the meaningful conclusion. Much of the time jazz musicians have sought and obtained an unashamed aphrodisiac effect; they have also worshiped in their music, variously devout before the one God and the unnamed gods. Like poets and painters, they are of all faiths, their doctrines are many; but they are united in one conviction, that they have found a creative form for themselves, for their time, for their place.

At the opening of the *Gradus ad Parnassum,* the dialogue offered as a study of counterpoint by Johann Josef Fux in 1725, the music master Aloysius warns the student Josef: "You must try to remember whether or not you felt a strong natural inclination to this art even in childhood." The student answers: "Yes, most deeply. Even before I could reason, I was overcome by the force of this strange enthusiasm and I turned all my thoughts and feelings to music. And now the burning desire to understand it possesses me, drives me almost against my will, and day and night lovely melodies seem to sound around me. Therefore I think I no longer have reason to doubt my inclination. Nor do the difficulties of the work discourage me, and I hope that with the help of good health I shall be able to master it." Several jazz musicians have read Fux, even as Haydn and Beethoven did, though perhaps with less immediate application. They have, however, echoed the pupil's "strange enthusiasm"; that, these jazzmen said, was their experience, their "burning desire." Following the "inclination," jazz musicians have not had much of the help of good health; some of them have flaunted their doggedly unreasonable living habits and suffered the personal and public consequences of the habits and of the flaunting. All this their music has reflected, and sometimes it is noisy and grotesque as a result. More often it has a fullness and richness of expression. Slowly, clearly, the music is maturing, and, for it and with it and by it, so are the musicians.

1. Ulanov's book *A History of Jazz in America* opens with this discussion. Is this a proper or effective opening? Why?
2. How many different kinds of definition appear here? What are they? Which is the most helpful in understanding the meaning of "jazz?"
3. Are any fallacious definitions given? Which are they?
4. What is wrong with the definitions of Wingy Manone, Jess Stacy, Glenn Miller, and Ella Fitzgerald? Why?
5. If Ulanov's discussion is typical of the extended definition, what elements would you say are necessary to such a definition?

Carl Jung

CONCERNING THE WORD "SPIRIT"

THE WORD "SPIRIT" POSSESSES SUCH A WIDE RANGE OF APPLICATION THAT it requires considerable effort to make clear to oneself all the things it can mean. Spirit, we say, is the principle that stands in opposition to matter. By this we understand an immaterial substance or form of existence which on the highest and most universal level is called "God." We imagine this immaterial substance also as the vehicle of psychic phenomena or even of life itself. In contradiction to this view there stands the opposition: spirit and nature. Here the concept of spirit is restricted to the supernatural or antinatural, and has lost its substantial connection with psyche and life. A similar restriction is implied in Spinoza's view that spirit is an attribute of the One Substance. Hylozoism goes even further, taking spirit to be a quality of matter.

A very widespread view conceives spirit as a higher and psyche as a lower principle of activity, and conversely the alchemists thought of spirit as the *ligamentum animae et corporis*, obviously regarding it as a *spiritus vegetativus* (the later life spirit or nerve spirit). Equally common is the view that spirit and psyche are essentially the same and can be separated only arbitrarily. Wundt takes spirit as "the inner being, regardless of any connection with an outer being." Others restrict spirit to certain psychic capacities or functions or qualities, such as the capacity to think and reason in contradistinction to the more "psychic" sentiments. Here spirit means the sum total of all the phenomena of rational thought, or of the intellect, including the will, memory, imagination, creative power, and aspirations motivated by ideals. Spirit has the further connotation of *sprightliness*, as when we say that a person is "spirited," meaning that he is versatile and full of ideas, with a brilliant, witty, and surprising turn of mind. Again, spirit denotes a certain attitude or the principle underlying it; for instance, one is "educated in the spirit of Pestalozzi," or one says that the "spirit of Weimar is the immortal German heritage." A special instance is the time spirit, or spirit of the age, which stands for the principle and motive force

From *Spirit and Nature*, Papers from the Eranos Yearbooks, Bollingen Series XXX.1 (Pantheon Books), Bollingen Foundation, New York, 1954.

behind certain views, judgments, and actions of a collective nature. Then there is the "objective spirit," by which is meant the whole stock of man's cultural possessions with particular regard to his intellectual and religious achievements.

As linguistic usage shows, spirit in the sense of an attitude has unmistakable leanings towards personification: the spirit of Pestalozzi can also be taken concretistically as his ghost or imago, just as the spirits of Weimar are the personal specters of Goethe and Schiller; for spirit still has the spookish meaning of the soul and of one departed. The "cold breath of the spirits" points on the one hand to the ancient affinity of *psyche* with *psychros* and *psychos,* which both mean "cold," and on the other hand to the original meaning of *pneuma,* which simply denoted "air in motion"; and in the same way animus and anima were connected with *animos,* "wind." The Germans word *Geist* probably has more to do with something frothing, effervescing, or fermenting; hence affinities with *Gischt* (foam), *Gäscht* (yeast), "ghost," "gas," and also with the emotional "ghastly" and "aghast," are not to be rejected. From time immemorial emotion has been regarded as possession, which is why we still say today, of a hot-tempered person, that he is possessed of a devil or that an evil spirit has entered into him.

Just as, according to the old view, the spirits or souls of the dead are of a subtle disposition like a vapor or a smoke, so to the alchemist *spiritus* was a subtle, volatile, active, and vivifying essence, such as alcohol was understood to be, and all the arcane substances. On this level, spirit includes spirits of salts, spirits of ammonia, formic spirit, etc.

This score or so of meanings and shades of meaning attributable to the word "spirit" makes it difficult for the psychologist to delimit his subject conceptually, but on the other hand they lighten the task of describing it, since the many different aspects go to form a vivid and concrete picture of the phenomenon in question. We are concerned with a functional complex which originally, on the primitive level, was apprehended as an invisible, breathlike "presence." William James has given us a lively account of this primordial phenomenon in his *Varieties of Religious Experience.* Another well-known example is the wind of the Pentecostal miracle. The primitive mentality finds it quite natural to personify the invisible presence as a ghost or demon. The souls or spirits of the dead are identical with the psychic activity of the living; they merely continue it. The view that the psyche is a spirit is implicit in this. When therefore something psychic happens in the individual which he feels as belonging to himself, that something is his own spirit. But if anything psychic happens which seems to him strange, then it is somebody else's spirit, and it may be causing a possession. The spirit in the first case corresponds to the subjective attitude, in the latter case to public opinion, to the time spirit, or to the original, not yet human, anthropoid disposition which we also call the *unconscious*.

In keeping with its original wind-nature, spirit is always an active, winged, swift-moving being as well as that which vivifies, stimulates, incites, fires, and inspires. To put it in modern language, spirit is the dynamic principle, forming for that very reason the classical antithesis of matter— the antithesis, that is, of its stasis and inertia. Basically it is the contrast between life and death. The subsequent differentiation of this contrast leads to the actually very remarkable opposition of spirit and nature. Even though spirit is regarded as essentially alive and enlivening, one cannot really feel nature as unspiritual and dead. We must therefore be dealing here with the (Christian) postulate of a spirit whose life is so vastly superior to the life of nature that in comparison with it the latter is no better than death.

1. What type of definition would you call Jung's discussion of the word "spirit:" formal or impromptu? Why?
2. What methods of definition appear in this selection?
3. Which method of definition do you consider best of those Jung uses? Why?
4. What are Jung's reasons for giving so many definitions of "spirit?" How are the definitions related to his later purpose?

Frank Sullivan

THE CLICHÉ EXPERT REVEALS HIMSELF
IN HIS TRUE COLORS

Q: MR. ARBUTHNOT, WOULD YOU MIND TELLING US TODAY HOW YOU HAP-
pened to become a cliché expert? Was it easy?

A: Easy! Don't make me laugh, Mr. Crouse. It was an uphill climb. A
cliché novitiate is no bed of roses, and if anyone ever tells you it is, do you
know how I want you to take his statement?

Q: How?

A: With a grain of salt. I shall tell you about my career, since you insist, and as a special treat, I shall describe it to you entirely in terms of the
seesaw cliché.

Q: The seesaw cliché?

A: You'll see what I mean. Before I made my mark as a cliché expert,
I had my ups and downs. Sometimes, when everything was at sixes and
sevens, it almost seemed as though my dearest ambitions were going to
wrack and ruin. I had moments when I was almost tempted to believe that
everything was a snare and a delusion. Even my own flesh and blood discouraged me, in spite of the fact that I was their pride and joy . . . You
aren't listening, Mr. Crouse.

Q: Yes I am. I just closed my eyes because the light hurt. You were
saying that your own kith and kin discouraged you.

A: I didn't say kith and kin, but it doesn't matter. For a considerable
period of time it was nip and tuck whether I would sink or swim. If I had
not been hale and hearty, and well equipped for a rough-and-tumble
struggle, I wouldn't have come through. But I kept at it, hammer and
tongs. I gave 'em tit for tat . . . Mr. Crouse, you *are* asleep.

Q: No, I'm not, Mr. Arbuthnot. You were saying you went after your
goal hard and fast.

A: I did. I eschewed wine, woman, and song—

Reprinted by permission of the author. This material appeared in *A Pearl in
Every Oyster* by Frank Sullivan, published by Little, Brown & Company, 1938.

Q: Ah, but wine, woman, and song is not a seesaw cliché, Mr. Arbuthnot.

A: Yes it is, too. Woman is standing in the middle, balancing. I worked morning, noon, and night, and kept to the straight and narrow. The consequence was that in the due course of time—

Q: And tide?

A: Please! In the due course of time things began to come my way by fits and starts, and a little later by leaps and bounds. Now, I'm fine and dandy.

Q: High, wide, and handsome, eh?

A: I wish I had said that, Mr. Crouse.

Q: You—

A: Will, Oscar. Had you there, Mr. Crouse, didn't I, ha ha! When I started I was free, white, and twenty-one. Now I'm fat, fair, and forty, and I venture to predict that no man, without regard to race, creed, or color, is a better master of the cliché than your servant—your *humble* servant— Magnus Arbuthnot. So much for my life story in terms of the seesaw cliché.

Q: It certainly is an interesting story, Mr. Arbuthnot—by and large.

A: Well, in all due modesty, I suppose it is, although sometimes, to tell you the truth, I think there is neither rhyme nor reason to it.

Q: Where were you born, Mr. Arbuthnot?

A: In the altogether.

Q: I see. How?

A: On the impulse of the moment.

Q: And when?

A: In the nick of time.

Q: It is agreeable to find a man so frank about himself, Mr. Arbuthnot.

A: Why not? You asked me a question. You know what kind of question it was?

Q: Impertinent?

A: Oh, my dear man, no.

Q: Personal?

A: Civil. You asked me a civil question. I answered you by telling you the truth. I gave it to you, if I may be permitted to say so, straight from the shoulder. I revealed myself to you in my—

Q: True colors?

A: Ah, someone told you. Rather, someone *went* and told you.

Q: Were you ever in love, Mr. Arbuthnot, or am I out of order in asking that?

A: Not at all. I have had my romances.

Q: How nice.

A: Ah, you wouldn't say so if you knew what kind of romances they were.

Q: What kind were they?

A: Blighted romances, all of 'em. I kept trying to combine single blessedness with wedded bliss. It didn't work. I had a sweetheart in every port, and I worshiped the ground they walked on, each and every one of them. This ground amounts to a matter of 18,467 acres, as of my latest blighted romance.

Q: Hm! You must have been quite a pedestrian.

A: Well, those are the figures when the tide was out; only 16,468 acres at the neap. I was land-poor at the end. And you take the advice of a sadder—

Q: And a wiser man.

A: That's what I was going to say. And never trust the weaker sex, or you'll have an awakening. You seem to be so smart, interrupting me all the while, maybe you can tell me what kind of awakening.

Q: Awakening? Awakening? I'm afraid you have me.

A: Rude awakening.

Q: Oh, of course. Now, I don't think your story would be complete, Mr. Arbuthnot, without some statement from you regarding your material circumstances. Are you well-to-do, or are you—

A: Hard pressed for cash? No, I'm solvent. I'm well paid.

Q: You mean you get a handsome salary?

A: I prefer to call it a princely stipend. You know what kind of coin I'm paid in?

Q: No. What?

A: Coin of the realm. Not that I give a hoot for money. You know how I refer to money?

Q: As the root of all evil?

A: No, but you have a talking point there. I call it lucre—filthy lucre.

Q: On the whole, you seem to have a pretty good time, Mr. Arbuthnot.

A: Oh, I'm not complaining. I'm as snug as a bug in a rug. I'm clear as crystal—when I'm not dull as dishwater. I'm cool as a cucumber, quick as a flash, fresh as a daisy, pleased as Punch, good as my word, regular as clockwork, and I suppose at the end of my declining years, when I'm gathered to my ancestors, I'll be dead as a doornail.

Q: *Eh bien! C'est la vie!*

A: *Mais oui, mon vieux.* I manage. I'm the glass of fashion and the mold of form. I have a finger in every pie, all except this finger. I use it for pointing with scorn. When I go in for malice, it is always malice aforethought. My nods are significant. My offers are standing. I am at cross-purposes and in dire straits. My motives are ulterior, my circles are vicious, my retainers are faithful, and my hopefuls are young. My suspicions are sneaking, my glee is fiendish, my stories are likely. I am drunk.

Q: Drunk?

A: Yes, with power. You know where?

Q: Where?

A: Behind the throne. I am emotional. My mercies are tender, and when I cry, I cry quits. I am lost in thought and up in arms. I am a square shooter with my trusty revolver. My courage is vaunted and my shame is crying, but I don't care—a rap. I have been in the depths of despair, when a watery grave in the briny deep seemed attractive. Eventually I want to marry and settle down, but the woman I marry must be clever.

Q: Clever?

A: With the needle.

Q: Well, I'd certainly call you a man who has led a full life, Mr. Arbuthnot, and a likable chap, too.

A: Yes, I'm a peach of a fellow. I'm a diamond in the rough, all wool and a yard wide. I'm too funny for words and too full for utterance. I'm a gay dog, and I like to trip the light fantastic and burn the candle at both ends with motley throngs of boon companions. I may be foolish but my folly is at least sheer.

Q: I think you certainly have run—

A: I certainly have. The entire gamut of human emotions. I know the facts of life. I'm afraid I've got to go now, Mr. Crouse. I'm due back at my abode. Do you know what kind of abode I live in?

Q: Humble, Mr. Arbuthnot?

A: Certainly not. Palatial! Goodbye, my little periwinkle!

1. Is there such a thing as a cliché expert? What is the author satirizing?
2. What is a seesaw cliché? Is this an effective way to describe a particular kind of worn-out phrase? What do such phrases have in common?

3. What figures of speech have become seesaw clichés? Why do you think these particular phrases have been overused?
4. From what fields (law, medicine, etc.) are the clichés taken? Discuss.
5. What qualities of the cliché (apart from its triteness) does Sullivan criticize in this essay?

Richard Brinsley Sheridan

MRS. MALAPROP ON EDUCATION

Enter MRS. MALAPROP, *and* SIR ANTHONY ABSOLUTE

MRS. MAL. There, Sir Anthony, there sits the deliberate simpleton who wants to disgrace her family, and lavish herself on a fellow not worth a shilling!

LYD. Madam, I though you once—

MRS. MAL. You thought, Miss! I don't know any business you have to think at all. Thought does not become a young woman. But the point we would request of you is, that you will promise to forget this fellow—to illiterate him, I say, quite from your memory.

LYD. Ah! Madam! our memories are independent of our wills. It is not so easy to forget.

MRS. MAL. But I say it is, Miss; there is nothing on earth so easy as to *forget,* if a person chooses to set about it. I'm sure I have as much forgot your poor dear uncle as if he had never existed—and I thought it my duty so to do; and let me tell you, Lydia, these violent memories don't become a young woman.

SIR ANTH. Why sure she won't pretend to remember what she's ordered not!—aye, this comes of her reading!

LYD. What crime, Madam, have I committed to be treated thus?

MRS. MAL. Now don't attempt to extirpate yourself from the matter; you know I have proof controvertible of it. But tell me, will you promise to do as you're bid? Will you take a husband of your friend's choosing?

LYD. Madam, I must tell you plainly, that had I no preference for anyone else, the choice you have made would be my aversion.

MRS. MAL. What business have you, Miss, with *preference* and *aversion?* They don't become a young woman; and you ought to know, that as both always wear off, 'tis safest in matrimony to begin with a little *aversion.* I am sure I hated your poor dear uncle before marriage as if he'd been a blackamoor—and yet, Miss, you are sensible what I wife I made!— and when it pleased heaven to release me from him, 'tis unknown what

From *The Rivals,* first acted in 1775.

tears I shed! But suppose we were going to give you another choice, will you promise us to give up this Beverley?

LYD. Could I belie my thoughts so far as to give that promise, my actions would certainly as far belie my words.

MRS. MAL. Take yourself to your room. You are fit company for nothing but your own ill-humours.

LYD. Willingly, Ma'am—I cannot change for the worse.

(*Exit* LYDIA)

MRS. MAL. There's a little intricate hussy for you!

SIR ANTH. It is not to be wondered at, Ma'am—all this is the natural consequence of teaching girls to read. Had I a thousand daughters, by heaven! I'd as soon have them taught the black art as their alphabet!

MRS. MAL. Nay, nay, Sir Anthony, you are an absolute misanthropy.

SIR ANTH. In my way hither, Mrs. Malaprop, I observed your niece's maid coming forth from a circulating library! She had a book in each hand—they were half-bound volumes, with marble covers! From that moment I guessed how full of duty I should see her mistress!

MRS. MAL. Those are vile places, indeed!

SIR ANTH. Madam, a circulating library in a town is as an evergreen tree of diabolical knowledge! It blossoms through the year! And depend on it, Mrs. Malaprop, that they who are so fond of handling the leaves, will long for the fruit at last.

MRS. MAL. Fie, fie, Sir Anthony, you surely speak laconically!

SIR ANTH. Why, Mrs. Malaprop, in moderation, now, what would you have a woman know?

MRS. MAL. Observe me, Sir Anthony. I would by no means wish a daughter of mine to be a progeny of learning; I don't think so much learning becomes a young woman; for instance—I would never let her meddle with Greek, or Hebrew, or Algebra, or Simony, or Fluxions, or Paradoxes, or such inflammatory branches of learning—neither would it be necessary for her to handle any of your mathematical, astronomical, diabolical instruments;—but, Sir Anthony, I would send her, at nine years old, to a boarding-school, in order to learn a little ingenuity and artifice. Then, Sir, she should have a supercilious knowledge in accounts—and as she grew up, I would have her instructed in geometry, that she might know something of the contagious countries—but above all, Sir Anthony, she should be mistress of orthodoxy, that she might not misspell, and mispronounce words so shamefully as girls usually do; and likewise that she might reprehend the true meaning of what she is saying. This, Sir Anthony, is what I would have a woman know—and I don't think there is a superstitious article in it.

SIR ANTH. Well, well, Mrs. Malaprop, I will dispute the point no further with you; though I must confess that you are a truly moderate and polite arguer, for almost every third word you say is on my side of the question.

1. The term "malapropism" was taken from the character of Mrs. Malaprop in Sheridan's eighteenth-century comedy, *The Rivals.* What does "malaprop" come from and what does it mean?
2. Point out examples of specific malapropisms and tell what words should have been used.
3. How do you account for someone's using malapropisms? How can they be prevented?
4. Generally, what level of diction is used by the characters in this scene from *The Rivals* (i.e., Lydia, Sir Anthony)? Why? Is diction of this level used today? Where?
5. Look up the root meanings of "fie" and "nay." Are these terms, common in the eighteenth century, ever used today?

CHAPTER 9

DICTION: SIGNIFYING, EVOKING, SLANTING

"A name! What's in a name? That which we call a rose, by any other name would smell as sweet."
WILLIAM SHAKESPEARE, *Romeo and Juliet*, II. 2.43

When Romeo was trying to persuade Juliet that the hostility between their families, the Montagues and Capulets, did not affect his love for her, he used the argument that names are mere sounds and practically meaningless: a rose by any other name would smell as sweet. Though Juliet, in her infatuation, was convinced, no one who has ever looked closely at the emotional properties of language would find Romeo's point very defensible. What's in a name? A very great deal, as any hapless person named "Percival," "Adolf," "Jezebel," or "Judas" can tell you.

Of course, it is quite true that the flower known as a rose would not change its physical nature if it were called a peony, cabbage, or ragweed, but the reactions that we have upon hearing the flower called something other than "rose" would be very different. Just think of reading Burns' line as "My love is like a red, red cabbage." Our entire emotional reaction changes because the words "rose" and "cabbage" make us respond in different ways. As words, "rose" and "cabbage" are equally worthy: both are of the formal level of diction, each has honorable and ancient root words (Greek and Old French), each has an exact botanical meaning and can be defined by classification. The only differences between the words are those which lie not in their basic, or primary, meanings but in their secondary or associational meanings.

It may seem a bit frustrating to you that a word can be precisely located in a level of diction and logically defined, and then still be elusive in meaning, yet words can be just that. To define "cabbage" in one of the five fundamental ways may tell us what the word signifies or *denotes;* but it does not tell us what associations, or *connotations,* the word has acquired for people. Through a long period of eating cabbage (or avoiding it), smelling cabbage, reading stories in which tenement houses are said to "reek with cabbage-like odors," discovering how other people feel about cabbage, and seeing that cabbage prices are generally low because cabbage is plentiful, we may decide, consciously or not, that cabbage is inelegant, vulgar, and unappetizing, or an unimaginative food. Attitudes spread, and then phrases like "cabbage-head" or "cabbage-shaped" spring up to indicate contempt or scorn; thus the poor cabbage—and the rather pleasant sounding word representing it—convey ridiculous or vulgar emotional impressions to the hearer. Compare your reactions to the words "cabbage," "sauerkraut," and "slaw": all represent the same thing in one form or another, but your associations differ as your "taste" differs.

To see how extensive your emotional reactions are to ordinary words, read the following list and note your reaction to each word as favorable, indifferent or unfavorable:

1. Paper
2. Blood
3. Vanilla
4. Glass
5. Benedict Arnold
6. Cat
7. Tulip
8. Chalk
9. Cadillac
10. Slime
11. Crystal
12. Russian
13. Diamond
14. Thirteen
15. Love

Of these, some few words (paper, glass) are likely to leave you indifferent, since they name common objects with few strong associations, favorable or unfavorable. If "glass" makes you think of broken glass, however, and thus of an accident or injury, your reaction may be negative or unfavorable; compare your reactions to "glass" and "crystal," which are two words for the same thing, in essence. Probably, "crystal" impresses you favorably, whatever your reaction to "glass." Certain of the above words usually are displeasing in their connotations: Benedict Arnold, slime, thirteen, and (possibly) blood. Words with favorable associations are vanilla, tulip, diamond, and love. Other words depend for their associations on your private experiences: cat, Cadillac, chalk, Russian. In a few cases, a word that has pleasant associations for most people (vanilla, Cadillac) will repel you because you are allergic to vanilla or find Cadillacs ostentatious. But the similarity of response to words among a majority of people is amazing until you remember that most of us see the same motion pictures, watch the same television programs, hear the same radio broadcasts, read the same best-sellers, and consult the same magazines. We are conditioned to respond by the same stimuli; so it is not surprising that we find ourselves similar in our reactions to things and the words for them.

Even in cases of departure from a standard response to a single word, the individual will probably react to a combination of words—or phrases—very much the way other people do, and the way the originator of that phrase wants us to.* Your reaction to the word "blood" may be favorable with secondary emotional impressions of life, health, vigor, but if you hear the phrase "oozing blood," your reactions are probably quite different. This phrase conjures up impressions of disease, injury, and possibly death, or at least pain; therefore, most people will respond negatively to the words. On the other hand, if "cabbage" is usually negative in connotation, the addition of a word or two can alter the connotations; e.g., "crisp cabbage," "fluffy cabbage leaves," or "cabbage-plump." Even words with the strongest favorable secondary meanings—love, mother—can develop unpleasant undertones emotionally with the addition of other strongly connotative words: "step-mother," "illicit love," "unnatural mother," "incestuous love," or "love nest."

These observations on the association of words, both singly and in context, remind us of the way words form in our minds as a means of transferring our thoughts through speech or writing. If our minds were able to deal with verbal thoughts separately from the thoughts arising out of our senses and emotions, we might be able to use language in a purely objective fashion. Words would have referents and we could use those words to refer to actions, people, things, or qualities rather than to our subjective feelings about actions, etc. But we know that our thoughts are a mixture

---

* The widespread use of clichés is related to the tendency of most people to react emotionally rather than logically to words. Clichés are phrases which originally had a strong appeal to patriotism, piety, filial love, friendship, or some other set of emotions. Unoriginal or unscrupulous speakers and writers siezed upon the phrase to evoke a standard response. Phrases like "the dog, man's best friend" or "Southern Womanhood" or "the patter of little footsteps" are clichés which became overworked and trite in attempts to benefit from conditioned emotional responses. In time, overuse kills the response which the cliché strives for, and a new set of clichés arises.

of verbal and non-verbal conceptions; they occur simultaneously; and it is impossible for words to exist without being somewhat colored by the intellectual personality of the man who uses them. Before you deplore such a personalization of words as an obstruction to communication, remember that each of us uses words to objectify and communicate our private selves and our interactions, emotionally as well as intellectually, with things outside ourselves. It is the *function* of language to express the awareness of the individual, and though words primarily convey verbal thoughts, these thoughts are ultimately inseparable from some emotional coloration.

Almost all words have two sets of meanings which reinforce each other. These are the *signification* of the word (its primary, formal definition, which is objectively descriptive) and the *evocation* of the word (its secondary, associational meanings, which are subjective, emotional, and often private). Sometimes the evocation is called the *connotative* or *intensive* meaning. It does not matter what set of terms you use so long as you understand the difference between the primary and secondary meaning of words. We will use *evocation* to indicate secondary meaning, because this meaning *evokes*, or "calls forth," our associations and emotional attitudes connected with the word. Often you will find secondary meanings for words listed along with primary meanings in your dictionary; but it is only when secondary meanings become common or widespread that such a listing is made. When the evocations of a word are still private, limited to a small group, or unrecognized, it is impossible for any dictionary maker who is not clairvoyant to cite these meanings. Obviously, then, the evocative qualities of words must be less precisely understood than the significatory qualities, though they are even more important, as psychologists have learned through their word association tests.

Words take on evocative meanings partly because they are used by human beings with emotions, but also because words signify different kinds of things, some being too nebulous to define tangibly. They signify people and objects (nouns), actions (verbs), qualities or characteristics (adjectives and adverbs), degree (adverbs), relationships (prepositions), and emotions (interjections), and some are artificial words that exist to hold other words together in the sentence in coherent syntax (articles, conjunctions). Even one category of words, nouns, may be sub-divided on the basis of the kinds of people or objects they stand for. *Proper nouns* are names of individual (or *sui generis*) persons, places, or things (Dwight D. Eisenhower, Calcutta, the Bible), and *common nouns* are names of groups of things (man, city, book). Some nouns are *collective* because they refer to groups acting as a single unit (family, agency, organization); some are *abstract*, because they refer to intangible things (pity, duty, infinity); and others are *concrete* because they refer to tangibles (hat, appendix, steel). Some nouns refer to categories, and thus are *class* words (dwelling, furniture, artist), and others are *species* words that refer to particular types within a class (house, sofa, sculptor). These divisions often overlap; in the case of the word "Vatican," for example (the center of Roman Catholicism), we would have to classify it as a proper, concrete, collective, species word.

Since classification proves to be little help in telling what the evocative meanings of a word are, the only way we can deal with word meanings effectively is to compare and contrast certain groups of words as they are used within our own experience. Because English is a language with a large vocabulary, we have recourse to many words which generally represent the same quality or object. Though the various levels of diction account for the multiplicity of synonyms in some instances, in other cases a variety of formal words may exist as synonyms for a term but possess slight, though significant, connotative meanings. Here are some examples:

In the case of the noun "disagreement," various types or degrees of disagreement are indicated by the synonyms "quarrel," "contention," "conflict," "difference of opinion," "dissent."

The state of being overweight may be indicated by "plump," "stout," "corpulent," "endomorphic," "fleshy," "fat," "obese."

A person of unusual intelligence may be termed a "genius," "intellectual," "brain," "highbrow," or "egghead."

Though the above lists of synonymous terms differ in some ways, they have in common a graduation in associational meanings from relatively favorable to obviously unfavorable. If you wish to minimize a disagreement, you would be likely to refer to it as a "difference of opinion" whereas if you wanted to indicate a sharp disagreement and your unfavorable evaluation of it, you would probably call it a "quarrel." Similarly, if you think highly of intelligence and the person possessing it, you will call such a man an "intellectual" rather than an "egghead," which is a slang term decidedly derogatory in implication. Though the difference in degree between "stout" and "plump" may be imperceptible, there is an apparent difference in the use of "stout" and "fat" to describe someone who is overweight. In our very choice of a synonym, or our instinctive use of a word, we tend to convey some evaluations of our own by the word we choose to represent the subject under discussion.

If we deliberately set out to present our private opinions of something by the emotionally evocative words we select in speaking of it, then we are *slanting* our discourse; that is, we are sacrificing objectivity for the sake of persuading our listener or reader of the validity of our views. Slanting is always an emotional device, and though some slanting is inevitable in our conversation or writing—a man's "style" or way of using words to express himself is one aspect of slanting—still we should feel obliged, for the sake of getting at the truth, to keep such practice at a minimum. If we are discussing the question of re-arming West Germany, for instance, we would certainly refrain from such emotionally freighted terms as "Prussian stiff-necks," "krauts," "blood-thirsty Huns," or "Nazi butchers." Such terms merely blind us emotionally and obscure the real issues involved in the question.

We saw in the chapter on comparison and contrast how such figures of speech as similes and metaphors could be used to slant discourse for the purpose of convincing emotionally rather than logically. Advertisements are an omnipresent example of slanting, but there are other kinds of literature and speech characteristically slanted for one reason or another. Political speeches are universally slanted. Newspapers almost inevitably engage in slanting, largely because they want to sell papers, raise their circulation, and thus attract advertisers. The assumption is that the best way to raise circulation is to "emphasize" the news that will appeal to the reading public. Such "emphasis" takes the form of eliminating certain news items, "blowing up" others, or writing headlines which will catch the reader's eye and attention. Really unscrupulous periodicals unashamedly use strongly evocative words to describe commonplace situations even though such use could enflame public opinion and create a national crisis. "Reds Slam U.S. Policy" reads a headline over a newspaper story that describes how a Russian magazine has criticized the practice of the American Department of State in refusing travel visas to Communist sympathizers. Or "Race Riots Erupt in Detroit" may preface an account of clash between two teen-aged gangs which was quickly controlled by the police.

If all language is expressive of the thoughts of an individual, and every individual's thoughts are affected by his emotions, then should we not conclude deductively that all language is emotionally "slanted?" In general, we must admit that language inherently is "slanted" by a man's use of it; but we need not commit the no degree fallacy by asserting that all uses of language are "slanted" in the same way or for the same purpose. There are instances in which a writer may use emotionally evocative language for highly commendable reasons. Generally, the writer of fiction (or non-factual prose) is legitimately entitled to emphasize the connotative qualities of language, because he is dealing with the subjective aspects of our lives. To fulfill his purpose of conveying to us through the artificial medium of words such intangibles as sensation, emotion, and imagery, he employs powerfully evocative single words and the qualities of figurative language so that we, the readers, may experience something of the writer's own feelings and attitudes. So long as a writer uses this kind of "slanting" to embody certain non-logical aspects of life, he is quite within his aesthetic rights. On the other hand, if a writer purports to be conveying *facts* or verifiably objective truths, and he uses strongly evocative language which implicitly interprets these facts, he is slanting. Or the writer who argues by stating his views, his reasoning, and his data in such a way as to appeal to emotion rather than to logic is illegitimately slanting. We cannot simplify the question of slanting by reducing it to a matter of the writer's intention, since writers may slant without being consciously aware that they are doing so. Proper or improper use of evocative language depends on the nature and purpose of the discourse itself: if it claims to present verifiable facts or to argue logically from data to some conclusion, emotional language should be kept to the barest minimum. If the writer is overtly presenting non-facts (or fiction), he is entitled to use language in whatever way he desires so long as it effectively achieves his purpose of creating an aesthetically, intellectually, and emotionally valid view of human experience. If he seeks to persuade us of the validity of his inductive, deductive, or reductive opinions by appealing to our emotions rather than our capacity for logic, he is slanting in the least defensible fashion.

The following three acounts of an automobile accident may illustrate the variational uses of language. The first is a "factual" newspaper account; the second, a "human interest" account, improperly slanted to inculcate a view in the reader; and the third is a fictional accident serving as the basis for a poet's reflections on the uncertainty of human life and our reaction to anything reminding us we are mortal:

ACCOUNT A

Driver Hurt In Collision

One driver was injured in a two-car crash on Plymouth Avenue North near Brown Street shortly after 10 A.M. today.

Robert N. Norman, 63, of 52 Jackson Boulevard, Woodhaven, suffered neck and shoulder injuries. He was given first aid treatment at Municipal Hospital. The other driver was Walter Chattham, 32, of 60 Berkeley Place.

ACCOUNT B

Tipsy Driving Charge Lodged

Walter Chattham, 32, of 60 Berkeley Place, was arrested after his car forced the car of a neighbor homeward-bound from church over a curb and severely injured Robert N. Norman, 63, of 52 Jackson Boulevard, Woodhaven. Chattham will be arraigned in City Court tomorrow on a charge of drunken driving.

Police reported that Chattham's car struck a motorist stopped for a stop sign about 10 A.M. at Plymouth Avenue and Brown Street. The impact forced the car over a curb where the elderly Norman stood waiting for a bus. Norman was dragged several feet and severely injured. He was rushed by ambulance to the Municipal Hospital, where he underwent emergency treatment.

Patrolmen Angelo Piresi and Robert Prior said there was extensive damage to the stopped car, owned by Nicholas M. Adams of 43 Berkeley Place, a neighbor of Chattham's.

ACCOUNT C

"Auto Wreck" by Karl Shapiro*

Its quick soft silver bell beating, beating,
And down the dark one ruby flare
Pulsing out red light like an artery,
The ambulance at top speed floating down
Past beacons and illuminated clocks
Wings in a heavy curve, dips down,

* Copyright 1941 by Karl Shapiro. Reprinted from *Poems 1940–1953,* by Karl Shapiro, by permission of Random House, Inc.

And brakes speed, entering the crowd.
The doors leap open, emptying light;
Stretchers are laid out, the mangled lifted
And stowed into the little hospital.
Then the bell, breaking the hush, tolls once,
And the ambulance with its terrible cargo
Rocking, slightly rocking, moves away,
As the doors, an afterthought, are closed.

Though it is unlikely that you will ever have occasion to write either a newspaper account or a reflective lyric poem, nontheless you have the responsibilities that the reporter and the poet do. As a human being anxious to learn as much of the truth about yourself and your cosmos as you possibly can, you are compelled to use language honestly. This means that you must gauge, in your conversation and writing, your own thoughts and their bases, and adapt your verbalization to the thought you want to express. When you profess to explain or argue, keep your diction as unslanted as possible; when listening to others, always hear what they *say* and not what you *want* to hear.

Our ability to forestall or minimize slanting in our own speech and writing and to recognize it in the discourse of others, depends upon our self-conscious awareness of words and a sensitiveness to their implications. To separate a fact from an opinion, an assertion from a declaration, an hypothesis from a true cause, we must listen carefully to spoken words and read printed words with close attention. So long as we remain ignorant of the devices of language and the innate qualities of words, we are subject to manipulation by language jugglers. In a vital sense, knowledge is the mastery of language, and intellectual freedom is the ability to equate your words with your thoughts.

I. *Questions for Review*

1. What is the difference between the primary and secondary meaning of words? Which is more important? Why?
2. How does a word develop secondary meanings?
3. Is it possible, considering that they are used by human beings, for any body of words to remain purely significatory through prolonged usage?
4. Are technical words without evocative meanings?

5. What, exactly, is slanting? Under what circumstances is slanting justifiable and when is it not?

II. *Exercises*

1. In the following sets of statements, how do the connotations of the underlined word differ?

   A. My mistress' brow is marble; her cheeks are lilies; her lips are cherries.

      Alas, my mistress has a heart of purest marble.

   B. April showers bring May flowers.

      The rain enfolds the hills like an April shroud.

      April is the cruelest month, mixing memory and desire.

   C. Nature, red in fang and claw.

      Red sails in the sunset.

      I saw red.

   D. God bless you and keep you, Mother Machree

      Mother love is smother love.

   E. The cut was as slight as a henpeck.

      Bishop Proudie was a henpecked husband.

   F. If the shoe fits, wear it.

      His smile was as comfortable as an old shoe.

   G. The dishwasher that scalds your dishes.

      Boiling water can scald the careless.

   H. Be it ever so humble, there's no place like home.

      Is your home protected against fire?

      Home, home on the range.

      A house is not a home.

2. In each list of three synonymous terms, which is the most complimentary, which the least complimentary, and which the most neutral? Explain your choice.

   A. Criminal, social deviate, victim of Society.

   B. Spouse, little woman, wife.

   C. Job, profession, trade.

   D. Energetic, hectic, busy.

   E. Project, chore, duty.

   F. Inebriate, drunk, alcoholic.

   G. Surgeon, sawbones, doctor.

   H. Attractive, spacious, ingratiating.

    I. Teacher, pedagogue, schoolmaster.

    J. Cabinet maker, carpenter, woodworker.

    K. Janitor, cleaning man, custodian.

    L. Embalmer, mortician, undertaker.

    M. Show, movie, cinema.

    N. Verse, poem, doggerel.

    O. Debutante, belle, party girl.

3. Make up a list of terms synonymous with each of the following, arrange the terms in a descending order from complimentary, and identify the level of diction to which each term belongs. (Example: automobile [formal], car [colloquial], jalopy [slang]). Do the same for each of these terms: lawyer, politician, doctor, woman, fraternity, newspaper, party (social), party (political), athlete.

4. Read the following carefully and point out all instances of slanting through word choice.

    A. Inhabitants of the French Riviera were startled last week to see Broadwayite Carol Charming making a tour of their gambling palaces, clad in spectacular red slacks and trailing International Playboy Pedro Salmanazar. Tagged by curious reporters, who wondered what she was doing in the company of Salmanazar while still married to wealthy Industrialist J. P. Monroe, Carol burbled, "We're both sun-worshippers, and what place is better than the Riviera for that?"

    B. The scheme for handing over private concerns to a powerful central government may look good to Harvard professors, fellow-travellers, and other fuzzy thinkers; but the salvation of America lies not in more, but less, government control.

    C. Noble, erect, his white beard jutting from his chin, George Bernard Shaw stood straight before his appreciative audience and showed that age has not dimmed his keen wit. His frisky, impertinent answers to questions from the floor kept his listeners buzzing with delight.

    D. The driverless truck then caromed over a curb, striking down pretty, three-year-old Judy Tucker, who had been innocently playing with her dolls on the sidewalk before her home.

    E. While waiting for the jury to finish its deliberations, the defendant sat puffing nervously on a cigarette and avoiding the questions of reporters by shifting his eyes away to look at the vacant jury box. His hands trembled at times, and occasionally he cleared his throat deliberately.

5. Collect a group of articles from magazines and newspapers. Note carefully examples of slanting and indicate the purpose of such slanting.

III. *Suggestions for Writing*

    1. Read Archibald MacLeish's "The Poet and the Press." Write an essay commenting on MacLeish's views and expressing your own views as to the differences in language used by journalists and creative writers.

    2. Reread some of the selections at the ends of previous chapters—Richard Rovere's essay on Senator McCarthy or Martin Meyer's piece on the Thompson Agency. Write an analysis of the use of language in one.

    3. Write a brief statement on some subject such as birth control, politics, religion, or another subject about which you feel strongly. Make your statement as free of slanting as possible. Then go back and mark any evocative words you have used and re-write your essay to make it more objective and unslanted.

Vance Packard

CURES FOR OUR HIDDEN AVERSIONS

"The prune is a joyless Puritan. . . . We found it needed rediscovering."
ERNEST DICHTER, PRESIDENT, INSTITUTE FOR MOTIVATIONAL
RESEARCH, INC.

ONE AREA WHERE THE INSIGHTS OF THE MOTIVATIONAL ANALYSTS WERE
most gracefully received was in helping marketers cope with our hidden
resistance to their products. Often our resistance seemed blindly unreason-
ing and could not be dislodged by standard dosages of persuasion. The
doctors of commerce, using their diagnostic skills, were called upon to get
to the roots of our resistance and prescribe corrective measures.

Many of these hidden resistances, it developed, were based on our unreasoned, or seemingly unreasoned, prejudice against certain products
offered for sale. These products develop a sort of inferiority complex. They
become burdened with "psychological limitations," to use Dr. Dichter's
phrase. Some of the proudest triumphs of Dr. Dichter's institute have
involved "rediscovering" products or commodities thus burdened with inferiority complexes. Following are some of the more dramatic cases of
psychological limitation diagnosed by the depth experts, and the couch
treatment applied, to give the unfortunate patients a new chance in the
battle for our dollars.

Old maids and boardinghouses. The diagnosis and remodeling Dr.
Dichter performed on the poor, inferiority-ridden prune constitutes one of
the classic achievements of motivation research.

The merchandisers of prunes had become exceedingly discouraged in
their efforts to persuade Americans to eat prunes, even in the quantities
consumed in former years. With something akin to desperation the California Prune Advisory Board turned to the Institute for Motivational Research for counsel. Dr. Dichter, perhaps naturally, suspected that sub-

conscious resistances were working against the prune. (A nonsubconscious factor might be the problem of coping with pits while eating prunes.) The variety of hidden meanings the prune held to Americans, however, astonished even his case workers. The prune's image was ridden with meanings, all unfortunate.

When word-association tests were tried on people, the first thoughts that came to the surface of their minds in reference to prunes were such thoughts as "old maid," "dried up." In his studies of the place the word prune had in the English language he came upon such phrases as "old prune face" and "dried-up old prune." When his investigators conducted their depth interviews they found that prunes were thought of as a symbol of decreptitude and devitalization. Others thought of prunes in terms of parental authority. They remembered that as children they were often directed to eat prunes because they "ought to" or because "prunes are good for you." Prunes were associated with boardinghouses where they were served by parsimonious landladies, with stingy, ungiving people, with joyless puritans. The black murky color of prunes as commonly served was commented upon unpleasantly. The color black was considered somehow symbolically sinister, and in at least one case the poor prune was associated with witches.

Pervading all of these associations and dominating the image of prunes was still another meaning. The prune was thought of primarily as a laxative. In word-association tests when people were asked to write in the first word they thought of in connection with prunes, many wrote "constipation." Now this laxative image was not entirely unfortunate. In fact the prune people had once prospered when the prune's laxative powers first became common knowledge. By the mid-fifties, however, the laxative market was crowded, and the prune's laxative connotations were felt by Dr. Dichter to be a mixed blessing even though the prune people were still stressing the laxative aspect in their advertising. Dr. Dichter felt this was giving the prune such an unfavorable image that it was blocking efforts to get the prune widely accepted as a food. "The taste story," he felt, "had become lost." He found that when a grocer asked a housewife if she wanted prunes she was saying to herself, "No. I don't want the laxative."

James Vicary got into the prune problem, I should mention, from another angle, for another client. His particular interest was in profiling the typical prune buyer. When he found that a great many of them suffered from constipation, he proceeded to build up a psychological profile of the constipated type. He found that a person who is constipated typically is more apt to be an ungiving type of person. It is not easy for such a person, for example, to give gifts.

All this should indicate the dreadful state the poor prune had gotten itself into. What should be done? The various depth probers couldn't agree among themselves on how to handle the laxative angle. One M.R. firm felt the laxative connotations had become a mental block in people's thinking about prunes so that they had to be faced, in a selling message, right at the start and brought out into the open. It found in tests that when the laxative aspect was stated at the outset "anxiety of the respondents was measurably reduced and favorable attitudes toward prunes were increased."

Dr. Dichter disagreed. He felt that what was needed was a top-to-bottom surgery job on the public's image of the prune so that the public could "rediscover" it as a brand-new fruit. The prune, he decided, would be the new "wonder fruit." The whole concept of the prune as a dried-out fruit for people in need of a laxative was recast into a more "dynamic" image under his guidance by the California prune people. The aim in stressing "new wonder fruit" was to reassure housewives that it was now perfectly acceptable to serve people prunes.

Overnight the prune became a delightful, sweet fruit, almost a candy, if you were to believe the ads. The new imagery showed prunes in a setting as far away as you could get from the dark, murky, old-maidish look of old in which four black prunes were shown floating in a dark fluid. In the new ads gay, bright colors were used, and childish figures were shown playing. Later the image figures of "youth" gradually changed from children to pretty girls figure skating or playing tennis. And where prunes were shown they were in bright, gay-colored dishes or shown against white cottage cheese. With the pictures were jingles saying, "Put Wings on Your Feet" and "Get That Top of the World Feeling." One ad said, "Prunes help bring color to your blood and a glow to your face." In its public image the prune became a true-life Cinderella!

As for the laxative angle it was now mentioned in passing near the bottom of the message. One ad showing the cute figure skater concluded with these words: "—and, a gentle aid to regularity. When you feel good, good things happen to you. So start eating prunes today till you have energy to spare."

The rediscovered prune soon was enjoying a spurt in sales. By 1955, a few years after Dr. Dichter began his couch treatment, the prune was being hailed in the press as "the exception" in the farm dilemma.

While price and consumption of most food crops were dropping, both the consumption and price to the grower of prunes were rising. Industry spokesmen attributed this phenomenon to "the new and very real interest in prunes among consumers."

1. Vance Packard's *The Hidden Persuaders* is an account of how advertising agencies influence the public to buy products by hiring psychologists to explain the subconscious forces which motivate our buying. What causes you to buy a product: your considered and objective examination of the merit of the product, advertisements, the opinions of other people, or something else?
2. What is your own attitude toward prunes? Why do you feel that way?
3. Does Packard explain in this selection why many people felt an aversion for prunes? Were the advertisers interested in causes for the aversion? Why?
4. What devices did advertisers use to change the "public image" of the prune? Why were these successful?
5. Make a collection of advertisements in magazines and classify the nature of the basic appeals which they make. What emotions in the buyer are they slanted toward?

Geoffrey T. Hellman

"TIME" LUMBERS ON

You can't always put your finger on what it is that makes a person attractive. The people in *Time* have long seemed unusually attractive to me, and I have sometimes wondered why this was so, since they are, by and large, the same bunch you find in the papers and in *Newsweek*, where they seem O.K. but not as compelling. I have gone to some pains to analyze the matter by studying *Time* carefully for the past several months, and I think the chief source of their charm is the way their voltage gets stepped up once they get into *Time*. Most of the people in *Time* are men. What steps up men's voltage? Girls. The biggest category on *Time's* masthead of two hundred and nineteen names is that of its sixty-two girl editorial researchers. I suspect that it's largely the presence of these ladies—especially the ones with the wonderful names like Bernadine Beerheide, Harriet Ben Ezra, Quinera Sarita King, Danuta Reszke-Birk, Deirdre Mead Ryan, and Yi Ying Sung—that peps up *Time's* denizens. *Newsweek* has far fewer girls, and their names aren't quite as stimulating. No offense, I hope. Mrs. Reid is the only girl on the *Herald Tribune's* masthead, and as for the *Times*, it's Arthur Hays Sulzberger, Julius Ochs Adler, Orvil E. Dryfoos, Amory H. Bradford, Francis A. Cox all the way. Confidence-inspiring, but not pulse-quickening.

Be that as it may (and what isn't?), the people in *Time* are possessed of an unusual vigor, which is reflected in their gait, in the pace of their vehicles, and in their conversation. Take President Eisenhower, for example. He rarely walks in *Time;* he strides. "A smiling Dwight Eisenhower . . . strode to the rostrum" in the January 17th *Time*. More recently, in the February 28th issue, he "strode into the Congressional Room of Washington's Statler Hotel." To stride, according to Webster, means "to walk with long steps, esp. in a measured or pompous manner." *Time* is a patriotic magazine, and I have a feeling that when the President strides in its pages he is doing it in a measured rather than a pompous manner. Furthermore, when he writes a letter, he doesn't dictate it lackadaisically and then glue it up in an envelope with a lacklustre lick; he treats it like a fire-cracker, or a twenty-one-gun salute: "Last week Ike fired off a new letter to CAB."

Another February 28th *Time* strider, and a man whose vehicular pace is well calculated to make Quinera and Danuta sit up and take notice, is Colonel Marcos Pérez Jiménez, President of Venezuela. "Stopping the procession," *Time* states, "he strode over to the Mercedes-Benz." Pérez Jiménez is playing ball with us when it comes to oil, and I'm glad to learn that a strider rather than a sidler, he. It's good to know, too, that when he gets into a car he doesn't just drive; he snakes, streaks off, swerves along, speeds away, flashes by, hurries dustily on, and coasts. What a delightfully spirited Good Neighbor he is! "In gullied wastelands, the shriek of [his] tires and the stench of scorched rubber filled entire valleys." Can this be? Can one man stink up an entire valley? No matter. The concept is gargantuan; the Colonel is my boy.

Still another *Time* strider, and also a fast man on wheels, is Harlow H. Curtice, president of General Motors. "Into a large, cluttered Detroit studio one day 18 months ago strode a trim, lean man with the suave good looks of an ambassador and the cheery smile of a salesman," *Time* writes. Most people would pick their way in a cluttered studio, but not Curtice. As if striding, and looking as suave as Clare Boothe Luce, weren't enough to make you love the man, *Time* calls him "Red" seven times in one article. (Red is Harlow's nickname, not a crack.) When Red travels, he doesn't drive, or fly, or take a train; he swings. "Curtice swung around the country getting to know his harried dealers." This sounds as though he had a prehensile tail, which I, for one, find attractive, though I suppose it might harry a conventional Cadillac dealer. I don't mean to make a monkey out of Red; according to *Time,* he is closer to a Cadillac than to a marmoset:

> His bright blue eyes sparkle like a newly polished car [*Time* writes], his smile is as broad as a Cadillac grille. His voice is quiet, his manner calm. But under the Curtice hood there throbs a machine with the tireless power of one of his own 260-h.p. engines.

Curtice's voice may be quiet but his conversation is forceful. When he announces an expansion program, he does it "boldly"; his predictions are "right on the button"; "on weekends he likes to drop in on the nearby Buick division, shoot the breeze with anyone from a sweeper to a foreman." *Time* gets a little mixed up about Red—he "never seems to be in a hurry," it says, and, two paragraphs later, "Curtice has a hot-rodder's feeling for cars . . . likes to dash around his home town of Flint in a sporty grey-blue Buick Skylark"—but, all in all, the picture of a bold, hooded, throbbing, breeze-shooting, skylarking president is an engaging one.

For a while after reading about Curtice, Eisenhower, and Pérez Jiménez, I had the idea that only presidents strode in *Time*. Not at all. Look at Scotland's Roman Catholic Father Sydney MacEwan, "a white-haired but boyish-looking priest in a knee-length clerical coat [who] strode to the dais in the Waldorf-Astoria's Jade Room." But I regret to state that striders don't always stay boyish-looking; sometimes their strides give out, and they are reduced to walking. "An old man climbed aboard United Air Lines flight 709 in New York . . . to fly to Los Angeles," *Time* writes of General Douglas MacArthur. "His famous stride had become a careful step, his hands looked transparent and his skin like parchment. . . ."

This brings me to another attractive locomotive trait of *Time's* cast of characters. They don't *get* into vehicles; they *climb* into them, which sounds more manly. They also climb out of them. When MacArthur got to Los Angeles, he "climbed out." John Foster Dulles is forever climbing in and out of planes in *Time*, and President René Coty, of France, "climbed from his bed to confer with pouchy-eyed politicians," while his wife, whose movements also eschew the humdrum, "padded about the palace kitchen . . . serving endless cups of coffee." Did Coty climb *up* from his bed or *down* from it? Up, I guess; those politicians were hanging from the ceiling, and were pouchy-eyed from looking down on their recumbent leader. My favorite *Time* climber is Coty's compatriot Pierre Mendès-France, who "climbed into his black Citroën." This is a real feat, even for a Frenchman who has stunted his growth by drinking milk.

I'm sorry that Mendès-France is out of office, and therefore presumably out, or relatively out, of the pages of *Time*. He will be missed. When he wasn't climbing in *Time*, he was hurrying out or walking briskly, and when he talked, he snapped. "*Eh bien*," he once snapped in *Time*, "I seem to have plenty of friends but few supporters." His downfall is clearly attributable to overexercise. He got so bushed bustling about *Time's* Foreign News department that he was too exhausted to repair his political fences.

Time's snappers girdle the globe. " 'We are not prepared to accept the proposition that because the Soviet Union and the U.S. are agreed, all problems are solved,' snapped [India's Krishna] Menon," while the Americas abound in snappers:

"It's unanimous!" snapped Congressman William Dawson.

Private Schine snapped: "I have stopped speaking to newspapermen."

Joe [McCarthy] snapped back: "They have been shooting at me, and I've got to get back at them."

"I am here to apply the law and you ask me to break it!" snapped Café Filho [President of Brazil].

Asked by waiting newsmen about his intentions, [Marlon Brando] snapped: "It is not a publicity stunt, and I do intend to marry the girl."

Brando's girl, by the way, burbles, which makes for a nice combination. They can play burble-and-snap:

"I know I am going to start a new life with the help of Marlon, and it will be different from what I have done so far," burbled she.

When the two of them get into a vehicle in *Time*, they hop on and chug off, and when he leaves her, he speeds off.

McCarthy's snaps sometimes cause other Senators to gruff:

But when he heard of McCarthy's statement, Colorado's tough, burly [Edwin C.] Johnson gruffed: "This is the first time I've ever been called a hand-maiden."

McCarthy not only snaps, he also ambles, lumbers, elbows, and careens:

A scowling, puffy-eyed McCarthy . . . lumbered into the hearing room . . . then he ambled out. . . . McCarthy elbowed his way through the crowd . . .

Careening about his old stamping grounds in his home town of Appleton, Wisconsin's Senator Joseph R. McCarthy . . .

McCarthy's closest locomotive parallel is Ernest Hemingway:

Rolling to starboard like an old freighter, Ernest Hemingway lumbered about his weather-beaten manor. . . .

Not so peppy, perhaps, but a novelty. And when it comes to the girls on *Time's* masthead, Hemingway knows what he's doing; he married one of them.

A more athletic note is struck by Governor Craig of Indiana, Admiral Halsey, and Nehru:

Having vaulted into the governor's office in a hurry, George Craig landed running, has been in a hurry ever since.

After the game . . . Fleet Admiral (ret.) William F. ("Bull") Halsey . . . bounced around like a midshipman . . .

A slender man with jodhpured legs and a rose-bud in his buttonhole scooted about the diplomatic conference rooms of London with whispered propositions on his lips. India's Jawaharlal Nehru wanted to be helpful.

But don't think that Nehru always scoots around whispering in *Time;* sometimes he croaks:

"Since the dawn of history," croaked Nehru throatily . . .

As in the case of McCarthy's snaps, one colorful *Time* vocalization often begets another. Nehru's croaks are followed by conversational chuckles from his colleagues:

Pudgy Rafi Ahmad Kidwai, 60, Minister of Food and Agriculture . . . chuckled: "That will make Nehru think twice."

And here's a pounce that flushed a weasel:

His interrogator pounced: "But you did say it! Why?" Weaseled (Alfred) Hitchcock uneasily: "It depends what press it was."

Before going on to some of the other ways in which the people in *Time* exercise their vocal chords, let us observe how certain ladies among them move:

Mrs. George Malone . . . flounced from the banquet hall.

One day Oveta Culp Hobby clicked in with a bundle of charts.

Very well. Back to *Time's* conversationalists. In addition to snapping, snorting, burbling, chuckling, croaking, pouncing, weaseling, and shooting the breeze, they groan, coo, snarl, taunt, thunder, chortle, crack, intone, growl, drawl, sneer, grumble, rumble, blurt, smirk, purr, husk, rasp, bubble, beam, smile, grin, drone, roar amid guffaws, sigh, worry, and spit entire sentences and even paragraphs. I have all the documentation at hand, but suffice it to bellow that Billy Graham and Senator Irving M. Ives thunder; Frank Lloyd Wright chortles; Konrad Adenauer growls; Winston Churchill growls, rumbles, and worries (he is also a snapper); Georgia's Governor Marvin Griffin drawls genially; Montgomery Ward Chairman Sewell Avery smiles "Do you know anyone who has $600 million all wrapped up in a bundle?;" Nat (King) Cole, a singer, husks, while shrugging, "Dialogue is just lyrics that don't rhyme"; and a "disgruntled hotelman" sighs "That is a sight that Pondicherry will not again see."

Adenauer, incidentally, whistle-stops when he takes a train, while Senator Ives, in a Caddy, roars down (without guffaws) to Manhattan. I've found only one man in *Time* who makes a really poor vehicular showing— Senator Wayne Morse:

> One jungle-hot afternoon a weathered Model T lurched down the 1600 block of Pennsylvania Avenue. . . . Out popped Wayne Morse.

Time is a Republican magazine, so perhaps Morse, who reneged on the Republicans, doesn't feel at home in it. He lurches and pops out, instead of roaring and climbing, because he's ill at ease.

Well, I think I'll gruff my analysis to a close, but first I want to point to a character trait that enhances the attractiveness of *Time* people all over the world: dutifulness. They do everything from talking dutifully to marrying dutifully:

> Said Maurine [Neuberger, wife of the Senator from Oregon] dutifully: she will retire from politics to help her husband in Washington.

> [Matyas] Rakosi [former Premier of Hungary] dutifully sent word that he agreed completely with the newest New Course.

> Pérez Jiménez [remember the old strider, dusty hurrier, and stinker-upper?] dutifully put down a dozen or so minor uprisings.

> Queen Elizabeth II's younger sister dutifully attended to the routine chores of visiting royalty.

> On [the Queen Mother's] arrival at the center, bystanding neighborhood ragamoppets applauded her dutifully.

> Crown Prince of Rumania . . . Carol Hohenzollern . . . dutifully married Princess Helen of Greece.

> Dutifully, Faure tried.

Faure, of course, is Mendès-France's successor, and in *Time* he's dutifully trying to get the support of the Socialists for a left-center coalition. He didn't succeed (some ragamoppets grimaced him down), but what can you expect of a man who—so far, at any rate—hasn't stridden, vaulted, bounced, or *entrechatted* his way into a conference room? I never heard of a Frenchman who didn't want to get on the good side, or sides, of sixty-two girls. Faure is warming up. He sighed in the March 28th issue of *Time*, and as of April 4th he is credited with a seven-sentence snap. I hear he's hired a drive-yourself Renault, and that we may hope for a shrieking-tired ricochet any week.

1. What is the significance of Hellman's title for this satiric criticism of slanting in a news magazine?
2. What are the chief ways of slanting that Hellman points out? How are they related to figurative language?
3. Point out instances of evocative language which the author himself uses to make his point.
4. What justification could be made by *Time* for its "peppy" style? Do you think the use of evocative language is appropriate in a news magazine? Explain.

THREE VIEWS OF SPUTNIK

ACCOUNT A: THE RED CONQUEST

IN THE CONQUEST OF SPACE—AND ALL THE MASTERY THAT IT IMPLIES IN the affairs of men on earth—the Russians had made a mighty move. Late on Friday, Oct. 4, Soviet rocket experts announced man's greatest technological triumph since the atomic bomb first flashed over the American desert. Their success was a shiny antenna-rigged sphere, the exterior of which closely resembles the one which U.S. rocket men have been developing for two years on the ground. The Red sphere was blasted into orbit some 300 miles above the Caspian Sea. Flying faster than any sizable object ever before fashioned by man, the sphere, a second eerie moon, revolved around the earth at a speed of about 18,000 miles per hour, or 5 miles per second. At least three times each day, it glided over almost every populated spot on earth, at incredible altitudes from 300 to 560 miles.

A total surprise to virtually every non-Russian scientist in the world, the news was announced with assured calmness by Radio Moscow, and received in New York at 6:30 p.m. The first confirmation was made by radio operators of the Radio Corp. of America in Riverhead, L.I., who picked up the measured "beep . . . beep . . . beep . . ." of the satellite's radio as it swept over the Eastern U.S. These uneasy tones were soon entering U.S. living rooms via radio and television news flashes, an ominous reminder that the Russian entry into space, well ahead of American plans, could mark a crucial turning point in history.

ACCOUNT B: RED MOON OVER THE U.S.

HURTLING UNSEEN, HUNDREDS OF MILES FROM THE EARTH, A POLISHED metal sphere the size of a beach ball passed over the world's continents and oceans one day last week. As it circled the globe for the first time, traveling at 18,000 m.p.h., the U.S. was blissfully unaware that a new era in history had begun, opening a bright new chapter in mankind's conquest of the natural environment and a grim new chapter in the cold war.

From *Newsweek* Magazine (October 14, 1957).
From *Time* Magazine (October 14, 1957).

The news came in a broadcast by Moscow radio, and it got to Washington in an ironic way. At the Soviet embassy on 16th Street that evening, some 50 scientists of 13 nations, members of the International Geophysical Year rocket and satellite conference, were gathered at a cocktail party. After the vodka, Scotch and bourbon started to flow, New York *Times* Reporter Walter Sullivan got an urgent phone call from his paper, hurried back to whisper in the ear of a U.S. scientist. A moment later Physicist Lloyd Berkner rapped on the hors d'oeuvre table until the hubbub quieted. "I wish to make an announcement," he said. "I am informed by the New York *Times* that a satellite is in orbit at an elevation of 900 kilometers [559 miles]. I wish to congratulate our Soviet colleagues on their achievement."

Sputnik's Pulse. By then, the world's communication systems were already crackling with the story that the Russians had launched history's first man-made earth satellite, and scientists across the U.S. were being routed out by newspapers and colleagues. The Russians called it *sputnik;* it weighed 184.3 lbs., they said, and was sending continuous radio signals.

ACCOUNT C

To judge from the shrieking headlines and comments in some of the most respectable pro-administration publications, October 4, 1957, might be called a day that will live in infamy. We hasten to say that we can find no such significance in the day on which the Russian-launched satellite started whirling around the earth. The event has been called "disastrous" by some, "defeat" by others. Disaster and defeat may lie ahead, but only if our nation fails to act. Those "beeps" are the ticking of a clock that Soviet technology has given the American people, who can certainly put the Russian timepiece to good use.

It is not in the grain of a democracy, particularly when it is both powerful and wealthy, to go through an emergency of unlimited duration. But now, from October 4 on, we can time our effort and measure the energy, the sacrifices that are asked of us. The asking must be done by our government, for the government alone has access to all the relevant information. Yet we, the citizens, have been learning a great deal since that timepiece started to tick. We have learned how most of our leaders, with the remarkable exception of Vice-President Nixon, are trying to befuddle us. One of them,

From *The Reporter* (October 31, 1957).

now fortunately retired, has called Sputnik "a neat, scientific trick"; others, the President included, seem to consider it a peculiar Muscovite way of celebrating the International Geophysical Year, and of luring us into a technological duel that we are too proud to fight. Yet not even the White House and the Pentagon together, disturbed as they have been, have succeeded in classifying Sputnik.

1. Which of the three periodical accounts above do you consider the most slanted? The least slanted?
2. Point out instances of unnecessarily evocative words in any one of the pieces. What effect do these words have on our attitude toward the events described?
3. Re-write the article which you consider the most slanted to make it as objective as possible. Examine your rewritten account for any strongly flavored words indicating your own views.

CHAPTER 10

RHETORIC: THE CRITICAL ANALYSIS

"The whole is the equal to the sum of its parts"
CLAVIUS

Many pages back, *rhetoric* was defined as "the craft of language;" and the term has appeared often in our spiral of investigation inward and downward from the broad question of how we think to matters of organizing and testing thought to the function of words. Since language is the instrument of thought, rhetoric has been treated as the verbal embodiment of systematized (or "logical") thinking. Now it is time to deal somewhat more extensively with the qualities of traditional rhetoric, or *the art of specially literary uses of language.*

Unfortunately, most of us tend to associate traditionally "literary" rhetoric with Fourth of July oratory or the more floreated speeches of some United States Senators. These unfavorable secondary associations have caused the makers of dictionaries to define *rhetoric,* in some cases, as "the use of exaggeration or display" or "artificial elegance of language." Actually, however, all spoken or written language is "rhetoric;" and the most carefully constructed prose is the very kind of rhetoric which abhors exaggeration, display, and artificial elegance. The writer who consciously employs rhetorical "art" is the thinker whose ideas are most lucidly expressed.

You may be surprised to know that most of the "specially literary uses of language" which make up the rhetorical art are already familiar to you from foregoing chapters. Figurative language (metaphors, similes), parallelism, antithesis, and evocative diction are the essence of effective writing; each has been discussed in detail. The remaining elements of written prose—its tonal and structural patterns and its specialized uses— may be seen best by employing one last type of logical order: the analysis. Just as we have previously been unable to separate thought from language, content from form, logic from rhetoric, so now we again must use the techniques of one to explain the other. In the present instance, a logical *analysis* of rhetorical practice enables us to develop a critical system for reading and evaluating the writing of others as well as our own.

Analysis is a word often encountered in our scientific age. As a matter of course, physical scientists *analyze* various objects; such abstract things as news events, the condition of the stock market, and even the human psyche are "analyzed" by other kinds of experts. *Analysis* is taken from the Greek words for "breaking up;" it is *the separation of a whole, whether a material substance or any matter of thought, into its constituent elements.* Thus it is the reverse process of the synthesis. Like other forms of logical order, it is concerned with relationships, but it seeks to understand the totality by breaking it down into its component parts.

For some inexplicable reason, many people are appalled at the thought of "analyzing" a piece of literature—most often poetry but frequently prose as well. "We murder to dissect," such self-styled aesthetes declare, thereby illogically arguing by analogy and begging the question all at once. The fact of the matter is that we cannot fully understand, much less completely appreciate and enjoy, a piece of prose unless we make ourselves aware of the writer's "style" through a systematic examination of his rhetorical techniques. What the writer says is inseparable from the *way* he says it.

> True wit is nature to advantage dressed,
> What oft was thought, but ne'er so well expressed,

so Alexander Pope tells us in his *Essay on Criticism*. It would seem that a true understanding of the thought of a rhetorical composition can come about only when we as readers appreciate the precision and imagination the author has used in expressing his ideas.

Since words, sentences, paragraphs are the "parts" which compose the "whole" rhetorical work, and since our understanding of the total work depends on our comprehension of successively greater units of it, we may may set up a method of analysis by reversing the spiral of the first nine chapters of the book. The tonal and structural patterns of rhetoric, and the specialized uses made by certain prose genres, are most clearly explained by looking first at words, then their combination into sentences, the relationship of sentences in the paragraph, and finally the combination of paragraphs into the work as a whole. First,

WORDS

The *tone* of a piece of writing is established within the first few words by the level of diction used. *Tone is the way the author's attitude toward his subject is reflected in his choice of words.* There are as many kinds of tone in written language as there are in spoken: angry, serious, playful, ironic, bantering, didactic, caustic, and so forth. Where spoken language depends on facial expressions, gestures, pitch and volume of the voice, and the nuances of inflection, written language depends on words alone and in combination. The writer must rely on his selection of words to convey to the reader his intellectual personality and his attitude toward the subject of his composition.

Of course, one man may use different tones in different works. Here, for instance, are three statements by the same rhetorician:

1. "Labor is prior to, and independent of, capital. Capital is only the fruit of labor, and could never have existed if labor had not first existed."

2. "With malice toward none; with charity for all; with firmness in the right, as God gives us to see the right, let us strive on to finish the work we are in. . . ."

3. "I don't s'pose anybody on earth likes gingerbread better'n I do—and gets less'n I do."

Abraham Lincoln is the author of all three statements. The same intelligence formulated each set of sentences, but the tone is different for each. In the first statement, Lincoln was addressing Congress on economic policy: the use of such technical terms as "capital" and "labor" as well as the legalistic phrase "prior to, and independent of" indicate the formality and technical nature of the address. The second statement is from the Second Inaugural Address in 1865. The high moral tone of the speech is emphasized by the standard level of diction and such abstractions as "malice," "charity," and "right." Notice, too, the use of parallel syntax. The third statement, full of colloquialisms and using a humorous antithesis, sets the tone of folksy earthiness and informality for which Lincoln was noted.

A writer's style is in part identifiable with his vocabulary: his knowledge of words and the general dictional levels that they represent. A formal writer, such as Dr. Samuel Johnson or Joseph Addison, uses a good many polysyllabic words—"amplification," "dilatory," "solicitude"—and often em-

ploys euphemisms or circumlocutions. An informal writer—Robert Benchley, for instance—uses informal words and colloquial or even slang terms.
The effective writer on a technical subject keeps jargonistic words to a nonexistent level and lightens his tone by inserting idiomatic expressions; see
the selections from William Laurence or Fred Hoyle in the present text.

Although few writers adhere to one level of diction only, the best
rhetoricians adapt their words to their subject matter and purpose in
writing. Jonathan Swift's horrifying proposition in "A Modest Proposal"
in calculated to shock us, and does, by describing child murder in an
elaborate set of euphemisms, occasionally lapsing into brutal technical
words: "strip," "carcass." Generalizations about "proper" style in writing or
"proper" word usage are dangerous to make, but we may say rather
broadly that the effective writer selects one level of diction—standard,
formal, informal, or technical—and varies or modifies it only for limited
and specific purposes.

A vital element in good writing is the clarification of terms; unusual or
difficult words must be defined or their meanings made clear in context. If
the writer is using a term in a different or personal way, he must give an
extended or impromptu definition, or his writing will convey very little
to the reader. Another important thing to guard against as a reader is the
acceptance of equivocation (shifting word meanings). The author who
tosses words about vaguely, changing meanings without notifying his
reader, is guilty of loose (or crafty) thinking and confused writing.

SENTENCES

Words are combined into complete thoughts, which in verbalized form
are sentences. By the inductive rules of grammar, there are four basic types
of sentences, each depending on the number of complete or partial thoughts
included in a single group of words. These are the Simple, Compound,
Complex, and Compound-Complex sentences. A single complete thought
("To err is human") is a simple sentence. Two complete thoughts or more
in a single grammatical unit ("Beauty is Truth and Truth is Beauty")
compose a compound sentence. One independent statement and one or
more dependent statements make up a complex sentence ("Fame is the
spur that the clear spirit doth raise"). And a combination of two or more
complete thoughts and one or more dependent thoughts is a compound-
complex sentence ("If at first you don't succeed, try, then try again"). Ob-

viously, the kinds of ideas a writer wants to express will affect the grammatical forms of his sentences. Simple mental relations between a thing and an action will take the form of simple sentences; more involved ones will take more intricate forms.

Almost as a matter of course, a writer will vary his sentence patterns. If he does not, the repetitiousness of his sentences in form will begin to bore and then irritate the reader. You know the sort of first reader style which repeats the same kind of simple sentence pattern over and over: "I see the house. The house is brown. It is a big house. Do you see the house?" Repetition may be an effective device for teaching small children to read. It may even be an effective device in poetry or specialized types of factual prose (instruction manuals, for example), but in general it should be avoided. Variation may be found by using different grammatical types of sentences or by inverting the regular sentence order (subject and modifiers, verb and modifiers, object and modifiers) to produce different kinds of *rhetorical patterns*.

Rhetorically, sentences may be of four types. (Do not confuse these rhetorical classifications with the grammatical classifications above; they do not correspond.) According to the way the sentence elements (words and phrases) are disposed, a sentence rhetorically is Loose, Periodic, Balanced or Mixed. These categories sound familiar to you because you encountered them in Chapter I as examples of the influence of sound order on written prose. A spoken sentence has a certain rhythm and inflection. Written down, the sentence preserves something of its aura of sound for the reader. The symbol (?) at the end of a sentence automatically makes us "hear" the sentence end on the upward inflection of a question; a period or exclamation mark (.) or (!) terminates the statement firmly and finally on a level or downward inflection. Punctuation and paragraphing aid the eye and the mind in grasping the meaning of written language; since all language is originally vocal, written language causes us to retain some of the reactions we would have to the same sentence if it were spoken.

Rhetorically, a sentence which is graspable in meaning after the first few words is a loose sentence. Generally, the action word (verb) and subject (noun or pronoun) come near the start of the loose sentence. In this sentence, for example,

Not so long ago I was reading in a magazine with an enormous circulation some instructions as to how to behave if and when we see that flash brighter than the sun which means that the atom bomb has arrived.

there are forty words, but after reading only seven, we have grasped the central actor ("I") and action ("was reading") of the statement. Everything else in the sentence expands and qualifies the situation of the first few words. In a sentence like this one, however, we must read almost the entire sentence before the central action, thus meaning, is apparent:

As to my own part, having turned my thoughts, for many years, upon this important subject, and maturely weighed the several schemes of other projectors, I have always found them grossly mistaken in their computation.

This periodic sentence must be read almost to the end before the central idea ("I have always found them") is apparent. The periodic sentence is a fine way to hold your reader's attention and add weight and importance to what you are saying, but it can become exasperating if used too often. Several periodic sentences strung together result often in a ponderous style and a pontifical tone.

In a balanced sentence, the sentence elements are placed with equal emphasis on either side of the central statement, which comes halfway. This is a balanced sentence:

If I were asked to describe as briefly and popularly as I could, what a University was, I should draw my answer from its ancient designation of a *Stadium Generale* or "School of Universal Learning."

Here the subject and verb ("I should draw") are counterbalanced by the qualifying clause at the beginning of the sentence and the series of phrases toward the end. The final kind of rhetorical sentence, the mixed, is the compound or compound-complex sentence in which one complete statement is of one sort of rhetorical pattern and the other of some different kind. Here is an example:

The reverence due to writings that have long subsisted arises, therefore, not from any credulous confidence in the superior wisdom of past ages or gloomy persuasion of the degeneracy of mankind, but is the consequence of acknowledged and indubitable positions; that what has been longest known has been most considered, and what is most considered is best understood.

You need not be a famous prose writer like Katherine Anne Porter, Jonathan Swift, Cardinal Newman, or Dr. Samuel Johnson to use the four types of rhetorical sentence. Any sentence you speak or write can be classified grammatically and rhetorically. If you become *aware* of the grammatical and syntactical rhythms of your own prose, you can then learn to utilize these rhythms to produce the tone you wish and to use the tonal qualities of literature to re-enforce your meaning.

PARAGRAPHS

We already know that paragraphs are largely the effect of the invention of printing, being an attempt to impose spatial order on a body of words for clearer communication. But the paragraph has developed into something more than a mere mechanical device in the centuries of written English prose. Now the paragraph is a body of closely related ideas (or sentences) grouped together in a rhetorically effective and logically appropriate unit.

Every paragraph should contain a central theme or concept which is implicitly expanded in each sentence of that paragraph. The syntactic unit expressing this theme is the Topic Sentence; though some paragraphs may not embody a central theme in a single statement, every well-written and coherent paragraph inherently develops a basic concept. If the central theme is stated in sentence form, it may appear anywhere in the paragraph that the writer's principle of arrangement demands that it be. The topic sentence of *this* paragraph, for instance, is the first one, but in the previous paragraph, the second sentence states the basic concept.

Depending on the nature of the central idea to be expressed, the paragraph may be developed in many ways: through definition, comparison and contrast, classification, cause and effect, illustration, induction, deduction, narration (the process), or analysis. The techniques of each of these are familiar to you through your study of the thought patterns underlying each method and through the specimens of prose illustrating previous chapters.

Whatever method of development it uses, the paragraph is made coherent implicitly through the logical plan it follows and explicitly through the devices of *transition*. Transition, from the Latin "go across," is linkage between sentences in a paragraph or between paragraphs. There are a number of forms of transition. Certain parts of speech—adverbs and conjunctions especially—are useful connections between one sentence and the next: "however," "so," "then," "next," "therefore," "thus" as well as all of the causal words we have already examined. Another useful kind of transition is the pronoun, which refers to a noun in the previous sentence. "This," "those," "it," "that," "he"—these and other pronouns overtly refer to something named earlier and thereby link the ideas of successive sentences. Likewise, adjectives like "such," "each," or "some" pick up a reference and continue a thought from sentence to sentence. One obvious form of linkage is the repetition of a key word. The first three sentences of this paragraph, for example, are joined by the repetition of the word "transition," which in the fourth sentence appears in the synonym, "connections." Repetition as a transitional device should be used carefully, however, since it tends to induce monotony. A judicious combination of the many kinds of connectives is probably a better way of uniting your paragraphs than a reliance on one or two transitional devices for everything.

There can be no set number of sentences required in a paragraph, since paragraphs vary in purpose and method. Probably the best way to see something of the range of variation in paragraphs is to look at several paragraphs similar in intention, tone, and technique. The first are from Philip Wylie's notorious description of Mom in *Generation of Vipers;* the second from the Old Testament Book of Isaiah:

Reading #1

Mom, however, is a great little guy. Pulling pants onto her by these words, let us look at mom.

She is a middle-aged puffin with an eye like a hawk that has just seen a rabbit twitch far below. She is about twenty-five pounds overweight, with no sprint, but sharp heels and a hard backhand which she does not regard as a foul but a womanly defense. In a thousand of her there is not sex appeal enough to budge a hermit ten paces off a rock ledge. She none the less spends several hundred dollars a year on permanents and transformations, pomades, cleansers, rouges, lipsticks, and the like—and fools nobody except herself. If a man kisses her with any earnestness, it is time for mom to feel for her pocketbook, and this occasionally does happen.

She smokes thirty cigarettes a day, chews gum, and consumes tons of bonbons and *petit fours*. The shortening in the latter, stripped from pigs, sheep and cattle, shortens mom. She plays bridge with the stupid voracity of a hammerhead shark, which cannot see what it is trying to gobble but never stops snapping its jaws and roiling the waves with its tail. She drinks moderately, which is to say, two or three cocktails before dinner every night and a brandy and a couple of highballs afterward. She doesn't count the two cocktails she takes before lunch when she lunches out, which is every day she can. On Saturday nights, at the club or in the juke joint, she loses count of her drinks and is liable to get a little tiddly, which is to say, shot or blind. But it is her man who worries about where to acquire the money while she worries only about how to spend it, so he has the ulcers and colitis and she has the guts of a bear; she can get pretty stiff before she topples.

Her sports are all spectator sports.

Reading #2

Moreover the Lord saith. Because the daughters of Zion are haughty, and walk with stretched forth necks and wanton eyes, walking and mincing *as* they go, and making a tinkling with their feet: therefore the Lord will smite with a scab the crown of the head of the daughters of Zion, and the Lord will discover their secret parts. In that day the Lord will take away the bravery of *their* tinkling ornaments *about their feet,* and *their* cauls, and *their* round tires like the moon, the chains, and the bracelets, and the mufflers, the bonnets, and the ornaments of the legs, and the headbands, and the tablets, and the earrings, the rings, and nose jewels, the changeable suits of apparel, and the mantles, and the wimples, and the crisping pins, the glasses, and the fine linen, and the hoods, and the veils. And it shall come to pass, *that* instead of sweet smell there shall be stink; and instead of a girdle a rent; and instead of well set hair baldness; and instead of a stomacher a girding of sackcloth; *and* burning instead of beauty. Thy men shall fall by the sword, and thy mighty in the war. And her gates shall lament and mourn; and she *being* desolate shall sit upon the ground.

These two vehement attacks on women are separated by a period of over 2,500 years; the two excerpts above are specimens of English prose about 350 years apart. Yet the paragraphs are strikingly similar: each *catalogues* qualities, piling up data to serve as the basis for a limited generalization (i.e., Certain women are vain, luxurious, wicked creatures, contributing to the downfall of civilization); each uses highly evocative words; each depends on comparison and contrast; each hypothesizes. Wylie's description, however, depends on the isolated detail, while Isaiah's relates similar details in a series of phrases. Wylie's sentences are related primarily by the use of the word "she;" Isaiah's sentences (in this translation) are linked by time references ("will," "on that day," "shall"). All of the statements in Isaiah's prophecy are summed up in the first, or topic, sentence of the paragraph; Wylie's paragraphs either contain no topic sentence or nothing but a topic sentence. Our discussion could be extended, but you can already see that stylistic differences between writers make the distinction between two expressions of essentially the same idea.

When you are examining the paragraphs in a work of non-fictional prose, after you have discerned the author's dictional level and uses and discovered his grammatical and rhetorical patterns, silently ask yourself these questions. 1. What is the central idea of the paragraph; in what sentence is it stated? 2. How is each sentence related to the development of this theme? 3. What transitional devices hold the sentences together? 4. What logical principle of development holds the ideas in the sentences together? 5. How is the paragraph related to the overall plan of the discourse?

THE WORK AS A WHOLE

Conventionally, all written prose is divided into Exposition, Argumentation, Narration, and Description. Like most classifications, these categories are oversimplified, perhaps to the point of not being very helpful. We know the difficulties involved in separating exposition (facts) from argumentation (opinions) already. No less difficult is separating exposition from description: classification and comparison and contrast are expository techniques, but both are used in description as well. Classification, in fact, was defined as a sort of complex description. Exposition and narration are easily confused when a process is being dealt with: does the man writing about his wartime experiences "expound" or "narrate?" Sometimes, narration and description are terms applied to fictional or imaginative prose, while exposition and argumentation are applied to non-fictional rhetoric. We have made this distinction in our discussion so far.

We should realize, however, that all rhetoric uses a combination of logical and literary techniques rather than a pure form of each. Evaluating a prose work becomes, therefore, a matter of *investigating how and why* various logical and rhetorical methods are combined rather than simply *identifying* a single method with a name tag. If we try to classify all written prose into categories, using a consistent principle of division, we invariably must give up in despair. Effective rhetoric is the prose work which combines clear thinking with good writing—not the work which observes all the "rules" of one arbitrary way of thinking or writing.

When evaluating a prose work as a whole, after viewing separately its rhetorical parts and its logical techniques, you must then consider it as a fusion of thought and the language embodying that thought. This being so, every prose work must be examined on its own merits. You should beware of the error of establishing some one prose writer as a "model" and judging all other writers by his style. You would not expect every writer to hold precisely the same views or to know the same facts as some "model" writer. Why, then, should you insist that the style of Addison or Thoreau ought to be imitated by other writers? *"Le style est l'homme même,"* remember. "Style is the man himself."

Just as the best way to learn to think logically is to be made to think rigorously and systematically, so the best way to learn to write well is to write much yourself and to read the writing of others. By a sort of intellectual osmosis, effective rhetoric leaves the imprint of its form as well as its content on the mind. The collection of essays at the end of this volume is a ready-made prose terrain for you to explore and acclimate yourself to. You will find all of the major ways of thinking which you have studied, and there will be some new variations of rhetorical forms—the Report, Letter, Informal Essay, Dialogue, and so forth—for you to explore. You have at your command the basic techniques of literary and logical exploration. The development of the ultimate awareness of the unique way a really good writer fuses his thought and form must be the next step. It is up to you to develop your own "feel" for literature.

I. Questions for Review
   1. What is rhetoric? Give several definitions which dictionaries make. What are the chief differences in meaning in these? Which are the most honorific and which are most derogatory?
   2. Can effective rhetoric be separated from logical thinking? Explain.
   3. What is analysis, in the logical sense? How does it operate? Give several varied examples of the use of analysis.
   4. What is meant by rhetorical tone? How is it achieved in speech? In writing?
   5. How are vocabulary and level of diction used to produce tone by a rhetorician? Explain and give examples.
   6. What are the grammatical classes in which sentences may be placed? On what basis are these categories set up?
   7. What are the four main types of rhetorical classifications for sentences? What is their principle of division?
   8. What are the advantages rhetorically of loose sentences? Periodic sentences? Which is more commonly used? How do you account for this fact?
   9. What is a paragraph? In what ways may a paragraph be developed?
   10. What devices hold the paragraph together?
   11. Into what divisions is rhetoric usually placed? What are the limitations of these categories?

II. Exercises
   1. Take one of your own themes or term papers and analyze it rhetorically. Examine the diction, grammatical and rhetorical sentence patterns,

methods of paragraph development, and so on. What is the tone of the work? Do you manage to achieve a fusion of what you meant to say with the way you said it? Why?

2. Discuss the diction, sentences (grammatically and rhetorically), and method of paragraph development in each of the following:

A. Those who have handled sciences have been either men of experiment or men of dogmas. The men of experiment are like the ant; they only collect and use: the reasoners resemble spiders, who make cobwebs out of their own substance. But the bee takes a middle course, it gathers its material from the flowers of the garden and of the field, but transforms and digests it by a power of its own. Not unlike this is the true business of philosophy; for it neither relies solely or chiefly on the powers of the mind, not does it take the matter which it gathers from natural history and mechanical experiments and lay it up in the memory whole, as it finds it; but lays it up in the understanding altered and digested. Therefore from a closer and purer league between these two faculties, the experimental and the rational, (such as has never yet been made) much may be hoped.

— Francis Bacon, *Novum Organum* (1620)

B. Sir Thomas More, Lord Chancellour: his Countreyhowse was at Chelsey, in Middlesex, where Sir John Danvers built his howse. Where the gate is now, adorned with two noble Pyramids, there stood anciently a Gate-house, which was flatt on the top, leaded, from whence there is a most pleasant prospect of the Thames and the fields beyond. On this place the Lord Chancellour More was wont to recreate himselfe and contemplate. It happened one time that a Tom of Bedlam came up to him, and had a Mind to have throwne him from the battlements, saying Leap, Tom, Leap. The Chancellour was in his gowne, and besides ancient and not able to struggle with such a strong fellowe. My Lord had a little dog. Sayd he, Let us first throwe the dog downe, and see what sporte that will be. So the dog was throwne over. This is a very fine sport, sayd my Lord, Let us fetch him up, and try once more. While the mad man was goeing downe, my lord fastened the dore, and called for help, but ever after kept the dore shutt.

— John Aubrey, *Brief Lives* (c. 1670)

C. Man is, in general, made up of contradictory qualities; and these will ever show themselves in strange succession, where a consistency in appearance at least, if not in reality, has not been attained by long habits of philosophical discipline. In proportion to the native vigour of the mind, the contradictory qualities will be the more prominent, and more difficult to be adjusted; and, therefore, we are not to wonder that, Samuel Johnson exhibited an eminent example of this remark which I have made upon human nature. At different times, he seemed a different man in some respects; not, however, in any great or essential article, upon which he had fully employed his mind, and settled certain principles of duty, but only in his manners, and in the display of argument and fancy in his talk. He was prone to superstition but not to credulity. Though his imagination might incline him to a belief of the marvelous and the mysterious, his vigorous reason examined the evidence with jealousy. He was a sincere and zealous Christian, of high Church-of-England and monarchical principles, which he would not tamely suffer to be questioned; and had, perhaps, at an early period, narrowed his mind somewhat too much, both as to religion and politics.

— James Boswell, *Life of Samuel Johnson* (1792)

D. My dearest Girl,

Indeed I will not deceive you with respect to my Health. This is the fact as far as I know. I have been confined three weeks and am not yet well—this proves that there is something wrong about me which my constitution will either conquer or give way to. Let us hope for the best. Do you hear the Thrush singing over the field? I think it is a sign of mild weather—so much the better for me. Like all Sinners now I am ill I philosophise aye out of my attachment to every thing, Trees, Flowers, Thrushes, Spring, Summer, Claret &c &c—aye everything but you—my Sister would be glad of my company a little longer. That Thrush is a fine fellow. I hope he was fortunate in his choice this year. Do not send any more of my Books home. I have a great pleasure in the thought of you looking on them.

Ever yours, my sweet Fanny

— John Keats, Letter to Fanny Brawne (February 24, 1820)

E. Dear Mrs. Abbey,

We are very unhappy at the non-arrival of our eggs and are full of delicacy, at the same time, as to inquiring about them. Is the egg crop failing? Have the animals struck? Are we and they all victims of agricultural depression? I fear it, and if the disaster is at last upon us, won't you very kindly let me know the worst? I have been wanting yet fearing to write to you. Today at last I seem to find courage just to twitch the hem of your garment. I seem also to myself to have divined that you most naturally can't be any longer bothered by the bugbear of my breakfasts. It would indeed break down the patience of the angels. Nevertheless, a still, small hope does flicker in my breast. May we at any rate have news? News would be good, but eggs would be better. I shall hope for the best, but, after one tragic sob, I shall completely enter into the worst. With love to the Master, Yours, Mrs. Abbey, in affectionate suspense,

> — Henry James, Letter to Mrs. Edwin Abbey
> (November 1, 1894)

F. *Internecine* has suffered an odd fate; being mainly a literary or educated man's word, it is yet neither pronounced in the scholarly way nor allowed its Latin meaning. It should be called ĭntĕr nīsĭn, & is called internē´ sĭn. And the sense has had the Kilkenney-cat notion imported into it because mutuality is the idea conveyed by *inter* in English, the Latin word meant merely of or to exter-mination (cf. *intereo* perish, *intercidio* slay, *interimo* destroy) without implying that of both parties. The imported notion, how-ever, is what gives the word its only value, since there are plenty of substitutes for it in its true sense—*destructive, slaughterous, murderous, bloody, sanguinary, mortal* & so forth. The scholar may therefore use or abstain from the word as he chooses, but it will be vain for him to attempt correcting other people's conception of the meaning.

> — H. W. Fowler, *A Dictionary of Modern English
> Usage* (1926)

G. The chief difference is that when, at sixteen or even twenty, I said "faith," I meant the Catholic faith; and when now I oppose "faith" to reason I mean faith in the existence and order of nature, a faith in the assumptions made inevitably in daily life; yet I see far more clearly than I did in my youth that pure reason, a reason that is not based on irrational postulates and presuppositions, is perfectly impotent. It is not "smoky" or indistinct: on the contrary, it is mathematically precise, but abstract and in the air. What I had in mind then when I spoke of "knowledge" was the common sense and science of the day, which in fact were uncritically based on animal faith and empirical presumption, and which I, with a solipsistic breath, could at once reduce to a dream, not to say a nightmare. For that reason, I call them "smoky," at once ugly, obscure, and unsubstantial. But it was immature of me to wish, lackadaisically and hopelessly, to substitute a religious myth for that sensuous obsession.

— George Santayana, *Persons and Places* (1944)

H. Now that Jack Frost's magic brush has made every dell a delight with delicate traceries of ice and snow, inviting each of us to turn Wandervögel and roam the woodland path with a dog in his haversack, what pulse does not quicken? *My* pulse, sweetie, and don't forget it. If anything, it slows down to a dead stop at the mere thought. It is on days like these that I barricade the door with my bureau, heap my stout walking shoes and parka on the coals, and settle down by the oven with a plate of cookies and the current issue of either *The Cracker Baker* or *Metronome*. Whatever energy I burn turning their pages is replaced by the cookies, which in turn are replaced by more cookies.

— S. J. Perelman, *The Best of Perelman* (1947)

I. We dare not forget today that we are the heirs of that first revolution. Let the word go forth from this time and place, to friend and foe alike, that the torch has been passed to a new generation of Americans—born in this century, tempered by war, disciplined by a hard and bitter peace, proud of our ancient heritage—and unwilling to witness or permit the slow undoing of those human rights to which this nation has always been committed, and to which we are committed today at home and around the world.

— John F. Kennedy, *Inaugural Address* (1961)

3. Each of the following essays is a specialized type of rhetoric. Read one or more, and discuss the ways each author has adapted basic logical and rhetorical techniques to his purpose and audience.
   A. Edward Sapir, "Dialect" (Encyclopaedia Article)
   B. Henry Thoreau, "Where I Lived and What I Lived For" (Autobiography)
   C. Lord Chesterfield, "To His Son" (Letter)
   D. McCrea Hazlett, "The Liberal Arts and the Liberal Virtues" (Speech)
   E. Oliver Goldsmith, "The Englishman" (Periodical Essay)

F. Xenophon, "Socrates" (Biographical Sketch)
G. Plato, "Crito" (Dialogue)
H. Wolfenstein and Leites, "British, French, and American Films" (Criticism)

III. Suggestions for Writing
1. Write a rhetorical analysis of one of your own essays previously composed for English or some other college course.
2. Read a selection from one of these famous examples of rhetoric of the past and write a rhetorical and logical analysis of it:
   A. Pericles' "Funeral Oration to the Athenians" in Thucydides' *History of the Peloponnesean Wars* (Benjamin Jowett, trans.)
   B. Cicero's *Oration Against Verres* (Greenwood or Yonge trans.)
   C. Mark Anthony's "Oration" in Shakespeare's *Julius Caesar,* III.2.79
   D. Sir Thomas Browne, *Urn-Burial*
   E. Jonathan Swift, "Digression upon Madness," from *Tale of a Tub*
   F. Edmund Burke, *Reflections on the French Revolution*
   G. Benjamin Franklin's *Letters*
   H. Abraham Lincoln, *Second Inaugural Address, Letter to Mrs. Bixby*
3. Write a rhetorical analysis of a work by some well-known and admired twentieth-century writer or speaker, e.g. William Faulkner's "Nobel Prize Acceptance Speech" (1950), John F. Kennedy's "Inaugural Address" (1961).

PART II

THOUGHT AND LANGUAGE

John Dewey

WHAT IS THINKING?*

I. DIFFERENT MEANINGS OF THOUGHT

NO ONE CAN TELL ANOTHER PERSON IN ANY DEFINITE WAY HOW HE *should* think, any more than how he ought to breathe or to have his blood circulate. But the various ways in which men *do* think can be told and can be described in their general features. Some of these ways are better than others; the reasons why they are better can be set forth. The person who understands what the better ways of thinking are and why they are better can, if he will, change his own personal ways until they become more effective; until, that is to say, they do better the work that thinking can do and that other mental operations cannot do so well. The better way of thinking that is to be considered in this book is called reflective thinking: the kind of thinking that consists in turning a subject over in the mind and giving it serious and consecutive consideration. Before we take up this main theme, we shall, however, first take note briefly of some other mental processes to which the name *thought* is sometimes given.

All the time we are awake and sometimes when we are asleep, something is, as we say, going through our heads. When we are asleep we call that kind of sequence "dreaming." We also have daydreams, reveries, castles built in the air, and mental streams that are even more idle and chaotic. To this uncontrolled coursing of ideas through our heads the name of "thinking" is sometimes given. It is automatic and unregulated. Many a child has

From *How We Think,* 1933. Reprinted by permission of D. C. Heath and Company.

277

attempted to see whether he could not "stop thinking"—that is, stop this procession of mental states through his mind—and in vain. More of our waking life than most of us would care to admit is whiled away in this inconsequential trifling with mental pictures, random recollections, pleasant but unfounded hopes, flitting, half-developed impressions. Hence it is that he who offers "a penny for your thoughts" does not expect to drive any great bargain if his offer is taken; he will only find out what happens to be "going through the mind" and what "goes" in this fashion rarely leaves much that is worth while behind.

In this sense, silly folk and dullards *think*. The story is told of a man in slight repute for intelligence, who, desiring to be chosen selectman in his New England town, addressed a knot of neighbors in this wise: "I hear you don't believe I know enough to hold office. I wish you to understand that I am thinking about something or other most of the time." Now, reflective thought is like this random coursing of things through the mind in that it consists of a succession of things thought of, but it is unlike in that the mere chance occurrence of any chance "something or other" in an irregular sequence does not suffice. Reflection involves not simply a sequence of ideas, but a *con*-sequence—a consecutive ordering in such a way that each determines the next as its proper outcome, while each outcome in turn leans back on, or refers to, its predecessors. The successive portions of a reflective thought grow out of one another and support one another; they do not come and go in a medley. Each phase is a step from something to something—technically speaking, it is a *term* of thought. Each term leaves a deposit that is utilized in the next term. The stream of flow becomes a train or chain. There are in any reflective thought definite units that are linked together so that there is a sustained movement to a common end.

The second meaning of thinking limits it to things not sensed or directly perceived, to things *not* seen, heard, touched, smelt, or tasted. We ask the man telling a story if he saw a certain incident happen, and his reply may be, "No, I only thought of it." A note of invention, as distinct from faithful record of observation, is present. Most important in this class are successions of imaginative incidents and episodes that have a certain coherence, hang together on a continuous thread, and thus lie between kaleidoscopic flights of fancy and considerations deliberately employed to establish a conclusion. The imaginative stories poured forth by children possess all degrees of internal congruity; some are disjointed, some are articulated. When connected, they simulate reflective thought; indeed,

they usually occur in minds of logical capacity. These imaginative enter-
prises often precede thinking of the close-knit type and prepare the way for
it. In this sense, a thought or idea is a mental picture of something not
actually present, and thinking is the succession of such pictures.

In contrast, reflective thinking has a purpose beyond the entertainment
afforded by the train of agreeable mental inventions and pictures. The train
must lead somewhere; it must tend to a conclusion that can be substantiated
outside the course of the images. A story of a giant may satisfy merely because of the story itself; a reflective conclusion that a giant lived at a certain
date and place on the earth would have to have some justification outside
of the chain of ideas in order to be a valid or sound conclusion. This contrasting element is probably best conveyed in the ordinary saying: "Think
it *out*." The phrase suggests an entanglement to be straightened out,
something obscure to be cleared up through the application of thought.
There is a goal to be reached, and this end sets a task that controls the
sequence of ideas.

A third meaning of thought is practically synonymous with *belief*. "I
think it is going to be colder tomorrow," or "I think Hungary is larger
than Jugo-Slavia" is equivalent to "I believe so-and-so." When we say,
"Men used to think the world was flat," we obviously refer to a belief that
was held by our ancestors. This meaning of thought is narrower than those
previously mentioned. A belief refers to something beyond itself by which
its value is tested; it makes an assertion about some matter of fact or some
principle or law. It means that a specified state of fact or law is accepted
or rejected, that it is something proper to be affirmed or at least acquiesced
in. It is hardly necessary to lay stress upon the importance of belief. It
covers all the matters of which we have no sure knowledge and yet which
we are sufficiently confident of to act upon and also the matters that we
now accept as certainly true, as knowledge, but which nevertheless may be
questioned in the future—just as much that passed as knowledge in the
past has now passed into the limbo of mere opinion or of error.

There is nothing in the mere fact of thought as identical with belief that
reveals whether the belief is well founded or not. Two different men say,
"I believe the world is spherical." One man, if challenged, could produce
little or no evidence for thinking as he does. It is an idea that he has picked
up from others and that he accepts because the idea is generally current,
not because he has examined into the matter and not because his own
mind has taken any active part in reaching and framing the belief.

Such "thoughts" grow up unconsciously. They are picked up—we know not how. From obscure sources and by unnoticed channels they insinuate themselves into the mind and become unconsciously a part of our mental furniture. Tradition, instruction, imitation—all of which depend upon authority in some form, or appeal to our own advantage, or fall in with a strong passion—are responsible for them. Such thoughts are prejudices; that is, prejudgments, not conclusions reached as the result of personal mental activity, such as observing, collecting, and examining evidence. Even when they happen to be correct, their correctness is a matter of accident as far as the person who entertains them is concerned.

Thus we are brought again, by way of contrast, to the particular kind of thinking that we are to study in this volume, *reflective thinking*. Thought, in the two first senses mentioned, may be harmful to the mind because it distracts attention from the real world, and because it may be a waste of time. On the other hand, if indulged in judiciously these thoughts may afford genuine enjoyment and also be a source of needed recreation. But in either case they can make no claim to truth; they cannot hold themselves up as something that the mind should accept, assert, and be willing to act upon. They may involve a kind of emotional commitment, but not intellectual and practical commitment. Beliefs, on the other hand, do involve precisely this commitment and consequently sooner or later they demand our investigation to find out upon what grounds they rest. To think of a cloud as a whale or a camel—in the sense of to "fancy"—does not commit one to the conclusion that the person having the idea would ride the camel or extract oil from the whale. But when Columbus "thought" the world was round, in the sense of "believed it to be so," he and his followers were thereby committed to a series of other beliefs and actions: to beliefs about routes to India, about what would happen if ships traveled far westward on the Atlantic, etc., precisely as thinking that the world was flat had committed those who held it to belief in the impossibility of circumnavigation, and in the limitation of the earth to regions in the small civilized part of it Europeans were already acquainted with, etc.

The earlier thought, belief in the flatness of the earth, had some foundation in evidence; it rested upon what men could see easily within the limits of their vision. But this evidence was not further looked into; it was not checked by considering other evidence; there was no search for new evidence. Ultimately the belief rested on laziness, inertia, custom, absence of courage and energy in investigation. The later belief rests upon careful and extensive study, upon purposeful widening of the area of observation, upon reasoning out the conclusions of alternative conceptions to see what would follow in case one or the other were adopted for belief. As distinct from the first kind of thinking there was an orderly chain of ideas; as distinct from the second, there was a controlling purpose and end; as distinct from the third, there was personal examination, scrutiny, inquiry.

Because Columbus did not accept unhesitantly the current traditional theory, because he doubted and inquired, he arrived at his thought. Skeptical of what, from long habit, seemed most certain, and credulous of what seemed impossible, he went on thinking until he could produce evidence for both his confidence and his disbelief. Even if his conclusion had finally turned out wrong, it would have been a different sort of belief from those it antagonized, because it was reached by a different method. *Active, persistent, and careful consideration of any belief or supposed form of knowledge in the light of the grounds that support it and the further conclusions to which it tends* constitutes reflective thought. Any one of the first three kinds of thought may elicit this type; but once begun, it includes a conscious and voluntary effort to establish belief upon a firm basis of evidence and rationality.

II. THE CENTRAL FACTOR IN THINKING

There are, however, no sharp lines of demarcation between the various operations just outlined. The problem of attaining correct habits of reflection would be much easier than it is, did not the different modes of thinking blend insensibly into one another. So far, we have considered rather extreme instances of each kind in order to get the field clearly before us. Let us now reverse this operation; let us consider a rudimentary case of thinking, lying between careful examination of evidence and a mere irresponsible stream of fancies. A man is walking on a warm day. The sky was clear the last time he observed it; but presently he notes, while occupied primarily with other things, that the air is cooler. It occurs to him that it is probably going to rain; looking up, he sees a dark cloud between him and the sun, and he then quickens his steps. What, if anything, in such a situation can be called thought? Neither the act of walking nor the noting of the cold is a thought. Walking in one direction of activity; looking and noting are other modes of activity. The likelihood that it will rain is, however, something *suggested*. The pedestrian *feels* the cold; first he *thinks* of clouds, then he looks and perceives them, and then he thinks of something he does not see: a storm. This *suggested possibility* is the idea, the thought. If it is believed in as a genuine possibility which may occur, it is the kind of thought which falls within the scope of knowledge and which requires reflective consideration.

Up to a certain point there is the same sort of situation as when one who looks at a cloud is reminded of a human figure and face. Thinking in both of these cases (the cases of belief and of fancy) involves noting or perceiving a fact, followed by something else that is not observed but that is brought to mind, suggested by the thing seen. One thing reminds us, as we say, of the other. Side by side, however, with this factor of agreement in the two cases of suggestion is a factor of marked disagreement. We do not *believe* in the face suggested by the cloud; we do not consider at all the probability of its being a fact. There is no *reflective* thought. The danger of rain, on the contrary, presents itself to us as a genuine possibility—a fact of the same nature as the observed coolness. Put differently, we do not regard the cloud as meaning or indicating a face, but merely as suggesting it, while we do consider that the coolness may *mean* rain. In the first case, on seeing an object, we just happen, as we say, to think of something else; in the second, we consider the *possibility and nature of the connection between the object seen and the object suggested.* The seen thing is regarded as in some way *the ground or basis of belief* in the suggested thing; it possesses the quality of *evidence.*

This function whereby one thing signifies or indicates another, thus leading us to consider how far the one may be regarded as warrant for belief in the other, is, then, the central factor in all reflective or distinctively intellectual thinking. By calling up various situations to which such terms as *signifies* and *indicates* apply, the student will realize for himself the actual facts denoted. Synonyms for these terms are: points to, tells of, betokens, prognosticates, represents, stands for, implies.* We also say one thing portends another, is ominous of another, or a symptom of it, or a key to it, or (if the connection is quite obscure) that it gives a hint, clue, or intimation. Reflection is not identical with the mere fact that one thing indicates, means, another thing. It commences when we begin to inquire into the reliability, the worth, of any particular indication; when we try to test its value and see what guarantee there is that the existing data *really* point to the idea that is suggested in such a way as to *justify* acceptance of the latter.

---

* *Implies* is more often used when a principle or general truth brings about belief in some other truth; the other phrases are more frequently used to denote the cases in which a fact or event leads us to believe in some other fact or in a law.

Reflection thus implies that something is believed in (or disbelieved in), not on its own direct account, but through something else which stands as witness, evidence, proof, voucher, warrant; that is, as *ground of belief*. At one time, rain is actually felt or directly experienced; at another time, we *infer* that it has rained from the appearance of the grass and trees, or that it is going to rain because of the condition of the air or the state of the barometer. At one time, we see a man (or suppose we do) without any intermediary fact; at another time, we are not quite sure what we see, and hunt for accompanying facts that will serve as signs, indications, tokens of what we are to believe.

Thinking, for the purposes of this inquiry, is accordingly defined as *that operation in which present facts suggest other facts (or truths) in such a way as to induce belief in what is suggested on the ground of real relation in the things themselves,* a relation between what suggests and what is suggested. A cloud *suggests* a weasel or a whale; it does not *mean* the latter, because there is no tie, or bond, in the things themselves between what is seen and what is suggested. Ashes not merely suggest a previous fire, but they signify there has been a fire, because ashes are produced by combustion and, if they are genuine ashes, only by combustion. It is an objective connection, the link in actual things, that makes one thing the ground, warrant, evidence, for believing in something else.

III. PHASES OF REFLECTIVE THINKING

We may carry our account further by noting that *reflective* thinking, in distinction from other operations to which we apply the name of thought, involves (1) a state of doubt, hesitation, perplexity, mental difficulty, in which thinking originates, and (2) an act of searching, hunting, inquiring, to find material that will resolve the doubt, settle and dispose of the perplexity.

In our illustration, the shock of coolness generated confusion and suspended belief, at least momentarily. Because it was unexpected, it was a shock or an interruption needing to be accounted for, identified, or placed. To say that the abrupt occurrence of the change of temperature constitutes a problem may sound forced and artificial; but if we are willing to extend the meaning of the word *problem* to whatever—no matter how slight and commonplace in character—perplexes and challenges the mind so that it makes belief at all uncertain, there is a genuine problem, or question, involved in an experience of sudden change.

The turning of the head, the lifting of the eyes, the scanning of the heavens, are activities adapted to bring to recognition facts that will answer the question presented by the sudden coolness. The facts as they first presented themselves were perplexing; they suggested, however, clouds. The act of looking was an act to discover whether this suggested explanation held good. It may again seem forced to speak of this looking, almost automatic, as an act of research, or inquiry. But once more, if we are willing to generalize our conceptions of our mental operations to include the trivial and ordinary as well as the technical and recondite, there is no good reason for refusing to give this title to the act of looking. For the result of the act is to bring facts before the mind that enable a person to reach a conclusion on the basis of evidence. In so far, then, as the act of looking was deliberate, was performed with the intention of getting an external basis on which to rest a belief, it exemplifies in an elementary way the operation of hunting, searching, inquiring, involved in any reflective operation.

Another instance, commonplace also, yet not quite so trivial, may enforce this lesson. A man traveling in an unfamiliar region comes to a branching of the road. Having no sure knowledge to fall back upon, he is brought to a standstill of hesitation and suspense. Which road is right? And how shall his perplexity be resolved? There are but two alternatives: he must either blindly and arbitrarily take his course, trusting to luck for the outcome, or he must discover grounds for the conclusion that a given road is right. Any attempt to decide the matter by thinking will involve inquiring into other facts, whether brought to mind by memory, or by further observation, or by both. The perplexed wayfarer must carefully scrutinize what is before him and he must cudgel his memory. He looks for evidence that will support belief in favor of either of the roads—for evidence that will weight down one suggestion. He may climb a tree; he may go first in this direction, then in that, looking, in either case, for signs, clues, indications. He wants something in the nature of a signboard or a map, and *his reflection is aimed at the discovery of facts that will serve this purpose.*

The foregoing illustration may be generalized. Thinking begins in what may fairly enough be called a *forked-road* situation, a situation that is ambiguous, that presents a dilemma, that proposes alternatives. As long as our activity glides smoothly along from one thing to another, or as long as we permit our imagination to entertain fancies at pleasure, there is no call for reflection. Difficulty or obstruction in the way of reaching a belief brings us, however, to a pause. In the suspense of uncertainty, we metaphorically climb a tree; we try to find some standpoint from which we may survey additional facts and, getting a more commanding view of the situation, decide how the facts stand related to one another.

Demand for the solution of a perplexity is the steadying and guiding factor in the entire process of reflection. Where there is no question of a problem to be solved or a difficulty to be surmounted, the course of suggestions flows on at random; we have the first type of thought described. If the stream of suggestions is controlled simply by their emotional congruity, their fitting agreeably into a single picture or story, we have the second type. But a question to be answered, an ambiguity to be resolved, sets up an end and holds the current of ideas to a definite channel. Every suggested conclusion is tested by its reference to this regulating end, by its pertinence to the problem in hand. This need of straightening out a perplexity also controls the kind of inquiry undertaken. A traveler whose end is the most beautiful path will look for other signs and will test suggestions on another basis than if he wishes to discover the way to a given city. *The nature of the problem fixes the end of thought,* and *the end controls the process of thinking.*

IV. SUMMARY

We may recapitulate by saying that the origin of thinking is some perplexity, confusion, or doubt. Thinking is not a case of spontaneous combustion; it does not occur just on "general principles." There is something that occasions and evokes it. General appeals to a child (or a grown-up) to think, irrespective of the existence in his own experience of some difficulty that troubles him and disturbs his equilibrium, are as futile as advice to lift himself by his bootstraps.

Given a difficulty, the next step is suggestion of some way out—the formation of some tentative plan or project, the entertaining of some theory that will account for the peculiarities in question, the consideration of some solution for the problem. The data at hand cannot supply the solution; they can only suggest it. What, then, are the sources of the suggestions? Clearly, past experience and a fund of relevant knowledge at one's command. If the person has had some acquaintance with similar situations, if he has dealt with material of the same sort before, suggestions more or less apt and helpful will arise. But unless there has been some analogous experience, confusion remains mere confusion. Even when a child (or grown-up) has a problem, it is wholly futile to urge him to think when he has no prior experiences that involve some of the same conditions.

There may, however, be a state of perplexity and also previous experience out of which suggestions emerge, and yet thinking need not be reflective. For the person may not be sufficiently *critical* about the ideas that occur to him. He may jump at a conclusion without weighing the grounds on which it rests; he may forego or unduly shorten the act of hunting, inquiring; he may take the first "answer," or solution, that comes to him because of mental sloth, torpor, impatience to get something settled. One can think reflectively only when one is willing to endure suspense and to undergo the trouble of searching. To many persons both suspense of judgment and intellectual search are disagreeable; they want to get them ended as soon as possible. They cultivate an over-positive and dogmatic habit of mind, or feel perhaps that a condition of doubt will be regarded as evidence of mental inferiority. It is at the point where examination and test enter into investigation that the difference between reflective thought and bad thinking comes in. To be genuinely thoughtful, we must be willing to sustain and protract that state of doubt which is the stimulus to thorough inquiry, so as not to accept an idea or make positive assertion of a belief until justifying reasons have been found.

Susanne K. Langer

FROM "THE LORD OF CREATION"

OF ALL BORN CREATURES, MAN IS THE ONLY ONE THAT CANNOT LIVE BY bread alone. He lives as much by symbols as by sense report, in a realm compounded of tangible things and virtual images, of actual events and ominous portents, always between fact and fiction. For he sees not only actualities but meanings. He has, indeed, all the impulses and interests of animal nature; he eats, sleeps, mates, seeks comfort and safety, flees pain, falls sick and dies, just as cats and bears and fishes and butterflies do. But

From "The Lord of Creation," by Susanne K. Langer. This material originally appeared in *Fortune Magazine* (January, 1944). Courtesy of *Fortune Magazine*.

he has something more in his repertoire, too—he has laws and religions, theories and dogmas, because he lives not only through sense but through symbols. That is the special asset of his mind, which makes him the master of earth and all its progeny.

By the agency of symbols—marks, words, mental images, and icons of all sorts—he can hold his ideas for contemplation long after their original causes have passed away. Therefore, he can think of things that are not presented or even suggested by his actual environment. By associating symbols in his mind, he combines things and events that were never together in the real world. This gives him the power we call imagination. Further, he can symbolize only part of an idea and let the rest go out of consciousness; this gives him the faculty that has been his pride throughout the ages—the power of abstraction. The combined effect of these two powers is inestimable. They are the roots of his supreme talent, the gift of reason.

In the war of each against all, which is the course of nature, man has an unfair advantage over his animal brethren; for he can see what is not yet there to be seen, know events that happened before his birth, and take possession of more than he actually eats; he can kill at a distance; and by rational design he can enslave other creatures to live and act for him instead of for themselves.

Yet this mastermind has strange aberrations. For in the whole animal kingdom there is no such unreason, no such folly and impracticality as man displays. He alone is hounded by imaginary fears, beset by ghosts and devils, frightened by mere images of things. No other creature wastes time in unprofitable ritual or builds nests for dead specimens of its race. Animals are always realists. They have intelligence in varying degrees—chickens are stupid, elephants are said to be very clever—but, bright or foolish, animals react only to reality. They may be fooled by appearance, by pictures or reflections, but once they know them as such, they promptly lose interest. Distance and darkness and silence are not fearful to them, filled with voices or forms, or invisible presences. Sheep in the pasture do not seem to fear phantom sheep beyond the fence, mice don't look for mouse goblins in the clock, birds do not worship a divine thunderbird.

But oddly enough, men do. They think of all these things and guard against them, worshiping animals and monsters even before they conceive of divinities in their own image. Men are essentially unrealistic. With all their extraordinary intelligence, they alone go in for patently impractical actions—magic and exorcism and holocausts—rites that have no connection with common-sense methods of self-preservation, such as a highly intelligent animal might use. In fact, the rites and sacrifices by which primitive man claims to control nature are sometimes fatal to the performers. Indian puberty rites are almost always intensely painful, and African natives have sometimes died during initiations into honorary societies.

We usually assume that very primitive tribes of men are closer to animal estate than highly civilized races; but in respect of practical attitudes, this is not true. The more primitive man's mind, the more fantastic it seems to be; only with high intellectual discipline do we gradually approach the realistic outlook of intelligent animals.

Yet this human mind, so beclouded by phantoms and superstitions, is probably the only mind on earth that can reach out to an awareness of things beyond its practical environment and can also conceive of such notions as truth, beauty, justice, majesty, space and time and creation.

THE PARADOX OF MORALITY AND CRUELTY

There is another paradox in man's relationship with other creatures: namely, that those very qualities he calls animalian—"brutal," "bestial," "inhuman"—are peculiarly his own. No other animal is so deliberately cruel as man. No other creature intentionally imprisons its own kind, or invents special instruments of torture such as racks and thumbscrews for the sole purpose of punishment. No other animal keeps its own brethren in slavery; so far as we know, the lower animals do not commit anything like the acts of pure sadism that figure rather largely in our newspapers. There is no torment, spite, or cruelty for its own sake among beasts, as there is among men. A cat plays with its prey, but does not conquer and torture smaller cats. But man, who knows good and evil, is cruel for cruelty's sake; he who has a moral law is more brutal than the brutes, who have none; he alone inflicts suffering on his fellows with malice aforethought.

If man's mind is really a higher form of the animal mind, his morality a specialized form of herd instinct, then where in the course of evolution did he lose the realism of a clever animal and fall prey to subjective fears? And why should he take pleasure in torturing helpless members of his own race?

THE GREAT PROJECTOR

The answer is, I think, that man's mind is *not* a direct evolution from the beast's mind, but is a unique variant and therefore has had a meteoric and startling career very different from any other animal history. The trait that sets human mentality apart from every other is its preoccupation with symbols, with images and names that *mean* things, rather than with things themselves. This trait may have been a mere sport of nature once upon a time. Certain creatures do develop tricks and interests that seem biologically unimportant. Pack rats, for instance, and some birds of the crow family take a capricious pleasure in bright objects and carry away such things for which they have, presumably, no earthly use. Perhaps man's tendency to see certain forms as *images,* to hear certain sounds not only as signals but as expressive tones, and to be excited by sunset colors or starlight, was originally just a peculiar sensitivity in a rather highly developed brain. But whatever its cause, the ultimate destiny of this trait was momentous; for all human activity is based on the appreciation and use of symbols. Language, religion, mathematics, all learning, all science and superstition, even right and wrong, are products of symbolic expression rather than direct experience. Our commonest words, such as "house" and "red" and "walking," are symbols; the pyramids of Egypt and the mysterious circles of Stonehenge are symbols; so are dominions and empires and astronomical universes. We live in a mind-made world, where the things of prime importance are images or words that embody ideas and feelings and attitudes.

The animal mind is like a telephone exchange; it receives stimuli from outside through the sense organs and sends out appropriate responses through the nerves that govern muscles, glands, and other parts of the body. The organism is constantly interacting with its surroundings, receiving messages and acting on the new state of affairs that the messages signify.

But the human mind is not a simple transmitter like a telephone exchange. It is more like a great projector; for instead of merely mediating between an event in the outer world and a creature's responsive action, it transforms or, if you will, distorts the event into an image to be looked at, retained, and contemplated. For the images of things that we remember are not exact and faithful transcriptions even of our actual sense impressions. They are made as much by what we think as by what we see. It is a well-known fact that if you ask several people the size of the moon's disk as they look at it, their estimates will vary from the area of a dime to that of a barrel top. Like a magic lantern, the mind projects its ideas of things on the screen of what we call "memory"; but like all projections, these ideas are transformations of actual things. They are, in fact, *symbols* of reality, not pieces of it.

SIGNS AND SYMBOLS

A symbol is not the same thing as a sign; that is a fact that psychologists and philosophers often overlook. All intelligent animals use signs; so do we. To them as well as to us sounds and smells and motions are signs of food, danger, the presence of other beings, or of rain or storm. Furthermore, some animals not only attend to signs but produce them for the benefit of others. Dogs bark at the door to be let in; rabbits thump to call each other; the cooing of doves and the growl of a wolf defending his kill are unequivocal signs of feelings and intentions to be reckoned with by other creatures.

We use signs just as animals do, though with considerably more elaboration. We stop at red lights and go on green; we answer calls and bells, watch the sky for coming storms, read trouble or promise or anger in each other's eyes. That is animal intelligence raised to the human level. Those of us who are dog lovers can probably all tell wonderful stories of how high our dogs have sometimes risen in the scale of clever sign interpretation and sign using.

A sign is anything that announces the existence or the imminence of some event, the presence of a thing or a person, or a change in a state of affairs. There are signs of the weather, signs of danger, signs of future good or evil, signs of what the past has been. In every case a sign is closely bound up with something to be noted or expected in experience. It is always a part of the situation to which it refers, though the reference may be remote in space and time. In so far as we are led to note or expect the signified event we are making correct use of a sign. This is the essence of rational behavior, which animals show in varying degrees. It is entirely realistic, being closely bound up with the actual objective course of history —learned by experience, and cashed in or voided by further experience.

If man had kept to the straight and narrow path of sign using, he would be like the other animals, though perhaps a little brighter. He would not talk, but grunt and gesticulate and point. He would make his wishes known, give warnings, perhaps develop a social system like that of bees and ants, with such a wonderful efficiency of communal enterprise that all men would have plenty to eat, warm apartments—all exactly alike and perfectly convenient—to live in, and everybody could and would sit in the sun or by the fire, as the climate demanded, not talking but just basking, with every want satisfied, most of his life. The young would romp and make love, the old would sleep, the middle-aged would do the routine work almost unconsciously and eat a great deal. But that would be the life of a social, superintelligent, purely sign-using animal.

To us who are human, it does not sound very glorious. We want to go places and do things, own all sorts of gadgets that we do not absolutely need, and when we sit down to take it easy we want to talk. Rights and property, social position, special talents and virtues, and above all our ideas, are what we live for. We have gone off on a tangent that takes us far away from the mere biological cycle that animal generations accomplish; and that is because we can use not only signs but symbols.

A symbol differs from a sign in that it does not announce the presence of the object, the being, condition, or whatnot, which is its meaning, but merely *brings this thing to mind.* It is not a mere "substitute sign" to which we react as though it were the object itself. The fact is that our reaction to hearing a person's name is quite different from our reaction to the person himself. There are certain rare cases where a symbol stands directly for its meaning: in religious experience, for instance, the Host is not only a symbol but a Presence. But symbols in the ordinary sense are not mystic. They are the same sort of thing that ordinary signs are; only they do not call our attention to something necessarily present or to be physically dealt with—they call up merely a conception of the thing they "mean."

The difference between a sign and a symbol is, in brief, that a sign causes us to think or act *in face of* the thing signified, whereas a symbol causes us to think *about* the thing symbolized. Therein lies the great importance of symbolism for human life, its power to make this life so different from any other animal biography that generations of men have found it incredible to suppose that they were of purely zoological origin. A sign is always embedded in reality, in a present that emerges from the actual past and stretches to the future; but a symbol may be divorced from reality altogether. It may refer to what is *not* the case, to a mere idea, a figment, a dream. It serves, therefore, to liberate thought from the immediate stimuli of a physically present world; and that liberation marks the essential difference between human and nonhuman mentality. Animals think, but they think *of* and *at* things; men think primarily *about* things. Words, pictures, and memory images are symbols that may be combined and varied in a thousand ways. The result is a symbolic structure whose meaning is a complex of all their respective meanings, and this kaleidoscope of *ideas* is the typical product of the human brain that we call the "stream of thought."

THE NEED OF SYMBOLIC EXPRESSION

The process of transforming all direct experience into imagery or into that supreme mode of symbolic expression, language, has so completely taken possession of the human mind that it is not only a special talent but a dominant, organic need. All our sense impressions leave their traces in our memory not only as signs disposing our practical reactions in the future but also as symbols, images representing our *ideas* of things; and the tendency to manipulate ideas, to combine and abstract, mix and extend them by playing with symbols, is man's outstanding characteristic. It seems to be what his brain most naturally and spontaneously does. Therefore his primitive mental function is not judging reality, but *dreaming his desires*.

Dreaming is apparently a basic function of human brains, for it is free and unexhausting like our metabolism, heartbeat, and breath. It is easier to dream than not to dream, as it is easier to breathe than to refrain from breathing. The symbolic character of dreams is fairly well established. Symbol mongering, on this ineffectual, uncritical level, seems to be instinctive, the fulfillment of an elementary need rather than the purposeful exercise of a high and difficult talent.

The special power of man's mind rests on the evolution of this special activity, not on any transcendently high development of animal intelligence. We are not immeasurably higher than other animals; we are different. We have a biological need and with it a biological gift that they do not share.

Because man has not only the ability but the constant need of *conceiving* what has happened to him, what surrounds him, what is demanded of him—in short, of symbolizing nature, himself, and his hopes and fears— he has a constant and crying need of *expression*. What he cannot express, he cannot conceive; what he cannot conceive is chaos, and fills him with terror.

If we bear in mind this all-important craving for expression we get a new picture of man's behavior; for from this trait spring his powers and his weaknesses. The process of symbolic transformation that all our experiences undergo is nothing more nor less than the process of *conception*, which underlies the human faculties of abstraction and imagination.

When we are faced with a strange or difficult situation, we cannot react directly, as other creatures do, with flight, aggression, or any such simple instinctive pattern. Our whole reaction depends on how we manage to conceive the situation—whether we cast it in a definite dramatic form, whether we see it as a disaster, a challenge, a fulfillment of doom, or a fiat of the Divine Will. In words or dreamlike images, in artistic or religious or even in cynical form, we must *construe* the events of life. There is great virtue in the figure of speech, "I can *make* nothing of it," to express a failure to understand something. Thought and memory are processes of *making* the thought content and the memory image; the pattern of our ideas is given by the symbols through which we express them. And in the course of manipulating those symbols we inevitably distort the original experience, as we abstract certain features of it, embroider and reinforce those features with other ideas, until the conception we project on the screen of memory is quite different from anything in our real history.

Conception is a necessary and elementary process; what we do with our conceptions is another story. That is the entire history of human culture— of intelligence and morality, folly and superstition, ritual, language, and the arts—all the phenomena that set man apart from, and above, the rest of the animal kingdom. As the religious mind has to make all human history a drama of sin and salvation in order to define its own moral attitudes, so a scientist wrestles with the mere presentation of "the facts" before he can reason about them. The process of *envisaging* facts, values, hopes, and fears underlies our whole behavior pattern; and this process is reflected in the evolution of an extraordinary phenomenon found always, and only, in human societies—the phenomenon of language.

THE LANGUAGE LINE

Language is the highest and most amazing achievement of the symbolistic human mind. The power it bestows is almost inestimable, for without it anything properly called "thought" is impossible. The birth of language is the dawn of humanity. The line between man and beast—between the highest ape and the lowest savage—is the language line. Whether the primitive Neanderthal man was anthropoid or human depends less on his cranial capacity, his upright posture, or even his use of tools and fire, than on one issue we shall probably never be able to settle—whether or not he spoke.

In all physical traits and practical responses, such as skills and visual judgments, we can find a certain continuity between animal and human mentality. Sign using is an ever evolving, ever improving function throughout the whole animal kingdom, from the lowly worm that shrinks into his hole at the sound of an approaching foot, to the dog obeying his master's command, and even to the learned scientist who watches the movements of an index needle.

This continuity of the sign-using talent has led psychologists to the belief that language is evolved from the vocal expressions, grunts and coos and cries, whereby animals vent their feelings or signal their fellows; that man has elaborated this sort of communion to the point where it makes a perfect exchange of ideas possible.

I do not believe that this doctrine of the origin of language is correct. The essence of language is symbolic, not signific; we use it first and most vitally to formulate and hold ideas in our own minds. Conception, not social control, is its first and foremost benefit.

Watch a young child that is just learning to speak play with a toy; he says the name of the object, e.g.: "Horsey! horsey! horsey!" over and over again, looks at the object, moves it, always saying the name to himself or to the world at large. It is quite a time before he talks to anyone in particular; he talks first of all to himself. This is his way of forming and fixing the *conception* of the object in his mind, and around this conception all his knowledge of it grows. *Names* are the essence of language; for the *name* is what abstracts the conception of the horse from the horse itself, and lets the mere idea recur at the speaking of the name. This permits the conception gathered from one horse experience to be exemplified again by another instance of a horse, so that the notion embodied in the name is a general notion.

To this end, the baby uses a word long before he *asks for* the object; when he wants his horsey he is likely to cry and fret, because he is reacting to an actual environment, not forming ideas. He uses the animal language of *signs* for his wants; talking is still a purely symbolic process—its practical value has not really impressed him yet.

Language need not be vocal; it may be purely visual, like written language, or even tactual, like the deaf-mute system of speech; but it *must be denotative*. The sounds, intended or unintended, whereby animals communicate do not constitute a language, because they are signs, not names. They never fall into an organic pattern, a meaningful syntax of even the most rudimentary sort, as all language seems to do with a sort of driving necessity. That is because signs refer to actual situations, in which things have obvious relations to each other that require only to be noted; but symbols refer to ideas, which are not physically there for inspection, so their connections and features have to be represented. This gives all true language a natural tendency toward growth and development, which seems almost like a life of its own. Languages are not invented; they grow with our need for expression.

In contrast, animal "speech" never has a structure. It is merely an emotional response. Apes may greet their ration of yams with a shout of "Nga!" But they do not say "Nga" between meals. If they could *talk about* their yams instead of just saluting them, they would be the most primitive men instead of the most anthropoid of beasts. They would have ideas, and tell each other things true or false, rational or irrational; they would make plans and invent laws and sing their own praises, as men do.

Stuart Chase

HOW LANGUAGE SHAPES OUR THOUGHTS

IN THE CURRENT MASS OF TALK ABOUT TALK, COMMUNICATION ABOUT communication, the emphasis is generally on the talker's power over his language, and thus over people who hear his words. Students are coached to increase their vocabulary, improve their delivery, and so control their audience. Commentators view with alarm the propaganda victories of Hitler, McCarthy, the Moscow radio.

The reverse of the process is seldom mentioned—the power which language exerts over the talker. The talker (or writer) never feels this power. His is as unconscious of it as of the circulation of his blood. He assumes that he is in command of his thoughts and of the words in which they are clothed.

The idea that the structure of the language we use affects our thought, may even be prior to thought, is beyond the purview of most of us. The first serious modern student to realize the power of a language over its speakers was probably Benjamin Lee Whorf. He was a linguist with imagination.

There are at least a dozen disciplines now contributing to the scientific study of communication—semantics, cybernetics, the mathematical theory of Claude Shannon, the perception theory of Ames and Cantril, and so on. Central in the whole complex is linguistics, probably the most exact of all the social sciences. Developed by Bloomfield, Sapir, Jesperson, and others, both here and abroad, linguistics begins by analyzing the sounds we make, of which the simplest unit is called a *phoneme*. It finds the actual patterns of spoken sounds in a given language, follows their combinations into words, and so to sentences and to syntax—the basic grammatical structure that carries meaning.

To collect a new language, the exploring linguist goes into the field like an anthropologist, settles in a native community, establishes a working relationship with the head man, and proceeds to record the sounds the villagers make. He often begins with numbers. "How do you say *one, two, three* in this village?" If he can get these wild flowers of speech upon a sound track, his delight knows no bounds. Many native languages, like the trumpeter swan, are in grave danger of extinction.

The linguist recognizes, as the classical grammarian did not, that people talked long before they wrote. "Noises made with the face" antedated "scratches made with the fist" by a hundred thousand years or more. He begins his researches, accordingly, at the more rewarding end—with live speech. In analyzing the sounds made by speakers of English, for instance, the linguist develops a formula—in a special code looking like algebra—which sums up every combination that one-syllable words, or word-like forms, may have, and bars out every combination they do not, and *cannot*, have. MPST, for example, can be pronounced, as in "glimpsed"; KSTHS, as in "sixths." On the other hand, the formula for English speakers rejects sound combinations readily pronounceable in other languages, such as LITK, FPAT, NWENG, DZOGB.

An advertising man in his cubicle on Madison Avenue, after a week of dreaming, may christen a new breakfast food "crunchy, vitamin-packed THRUB," but he cannot call it DLUB, not in English he can't. If he tried to name it NFPK, a common sound in other tongues, he would undoubtedly be fired. Again English permits no words to begin with NG, but Eskimo is full of them.

FROM ENGINEERING TO METALINGUISTICS

Some linguists, having mastered their phonemes and field work, go on to a new dimension in communication. They call it *meta*linguistics, or superlinguistics. After syntax, said Whorf, "then on to further planes still, the full import of which may some day stagger us." I will not deny that, as a student of semantics, their import staggers me. Metalinguistics is the top rung of communication study; it throws the longest shadow. It may be doing for language what relativity did for physics. Furthermore, it is based on linguistic relativity. Metalinguists ask: How does a given language shape the thought of the speaker and his view of nature and the world? How does the structure of English, say, differ from that of Maya, and what are the comparative effects on speakers of the two?

Whorf, had he lived, might have become another William James or Franz Boas, so brilliant were his powers of projecting scientific observations into fruitful generalizations.

Actually, thinking [he says] is most mysterious, and by far the greatest light upon it that we have, is thrown by the study of language. This study shows that the forms of a person's thoughts are controlled by inexorable laws of pattern, of which he is unconscious. These patterns are the unperceived intricate systematizations of his own language—shown readily enough by a candid comparison and contrast with other languages, especially those of a different linguistic family. His thinking itself is in a language—in English, in Sanskrit, in Chinese. And every language is a vast pattern-system, different from others, in which are culturally ordained the forms and categories by which the personality not only communicates, but analyzes nature, notices or neglects types of relationship, channels his reasoning, and builds the house of his consciousness. This doctrine is new to Western science, but it stands on unimpeachable evidence.

Whorf was born in Boston in 1897, and graduated from MIT as a chemical engineer in 1918. He took a job with a large insurance company in Hartford as a specialist on fire prevention in chemical industries, and remained with the company until his death in 1941. While still in school he developed an interest in language and how it was put together. At Hartford he spent long hours in the Watkinson Library which specializes in Amerindian languages, and his intensive program of independent study won him scientific recognition by 1928. He deciphered certain Aztec inscriptions for the first time. In 1930 he took leave of absence to go to Mexico under a grant from the Social Science Research Council, to study Aztec and Maya inscriptions at first hand. Later he published a brilliant paper on the deciphering of Maya codices.

He spent the best part of two years on the Hopi language, and as we shall see, based some of his most daring speculations upon its remarkable structure. His only book, unfinished and, alas, unpublished, now in the possession of Clyde Kluckhohn, is a Hopi-English dictionary. All this work, remember, was done as an avocation; daytimes he was a chemical engineer.

He often visited Yale, where he became a firm friend of Edward Sapir, the great Amerindian scholar. Sapir encouraged him to carry linguistics into broader fields. At Yale he did his only formal academic work, giving a course of lectures on his consuming interest.

After mastering, through library and field work, the accumulated knowledge in linguistics, he wrote a famous essay in the *Technology Review*, entitled "Linguistics as an Exact Science." In it the reader will find ample justification for the view that prediction fares better here than in the other social sciences. The power to predict, of course, is the test of any science. But linguistics was a foundation stone on which he stood to lift his eyes. Only a unique combination of the scientific method and an imagination almost poetic could have produced his great contribution to the study of communication.

In addition to the dictionary, Whorf left a score of papers, upon which I am principally basing this essay. The core of his thinking can be found in "Four Articles on Metalinguistics," issued in reprint form by the Foreign Service Institute in Washington in 1950. The Institute, a kind of university in the State Department, prepares young career men for government service overseas with courses in languages, comparative cultures, economic geography, and so on. In addition, it operates an active research center in linguistics, directed by George Trager and Henry Lee Smith, Jr. (You remember Dr. Smith, the man on the radio who could tell by your accent exactly in what corner of the country you were reared.)

Language, more than any other trait, makes us human, distinguishes us from all other creatures. The opposed thumb we share with the great apes. We are born with a relatively large area in the brain for manipulating tongue, larynx, and the speech apparatus. We are also endowed with a drive to talk: but the words and the language structure have to be learned. Curiously enough, the first word normally learned in English, "mamma," is a sound heard around the world. Many other languages have similar phonemes for mother.

Of all the tens of thousands of behavior patterns and belief systems we learn from the culture, language is far and away the most important. It has long been recognized that every man alive—or who ever lived for that matter—is culture-bound. It remained for Whorf and his group to demonstrate that every one of us is language-bound.

Speech, says Whorf, is the best show man puts on. "It is his own particular act on the stage of evolution, in which he comes before the cosmic backdrop" to play his part. Julian Huxley hazards the guess that culture and language may be displacing evolution in the case of man.

The metalinguists demonstrate that the forms of a person's thoughts are controlled by patterns learned early, of which he is mostly unconscious. Thinking is a language process, whether in English, Russian, or Hopi. Every language is a complex system, with three main functions:

(1) To communicate with other persons.
(2) To communicate with oneself, or, as we say, think.
(3) To mold one's whole outlook on life.

Thinking follows the tracks laid down in one's own language; these tracks will converge on certain phases of "reality," and completely bypass phases which may be explored in other languages. In English, for instance, we say "Look at that wave." But a wave in nature never occurs as a single phenomenon. In the Hopi language they say, "Look at that slosh." The Hopi word, whose nearest equivalent in English is "slosh," gives a closer fit to the actual physics of wave motion, connoting movements in a mass.

Most of us were brought up to believe that talking is merely a tool which something deeper called "thinking" puts to work. Thinking, we have assumed, depends on laws of reason and logic common to all mankind. These laws are said to be implicit in the mental machinery of human beings, whether they speak English or Choctaw. Languages, it follows, are simply parallel methods for expressing this universal logic. On this assumption it also follows that any logical idea can be translated unbroken, or even unbent, into any language. A few minutes in the glass palace of the United Nations in New York will quickly disabuse one of this quaint notion. Even such a common concept as "democracy" may not survive translation.

OUR LOVE AFFAIR WITH TIME

Another set of assumptions underlying Western culture, says Whorf, imposes upon the universe two grand cosmic forms: *space* and *time*. *Space* in our thinking is static, three-dimensional, and infinite; beyond the last area is always another area. *Time* is kinetic and one-dimensional, flowing perpetually and smoothly from the past to the present and into the future. It took the genius of Einstein to correct these cosmic assumptions, and most of us are still firmly wedded to them.

Linguistic relativity makes it clear that Newton took his concepts of

Absolute Space and Absolute Time, not so much out of profound cogitation, as out of the language he spoke. They had been lying there for thousands of years. Both "time" and "space" affect the behavior of every one in Western culture. "Time," especially, causes us to be oriented towards calendars, dates, "the course of history," time tables, clocks, time wages, races against time, accounting, compound interest, actuarial statistics, annals, diaries, the age of the rocks, of the earth, of the solar system, of the universe. The book of Genesis gets the cosmos launched in 4004 B.C. It is difficult for Westerners to conceive of what Fred Hoyle, the astronomer, calls "continuous creation," for we want to start things moving at a definite date, and build up from there. Time impels us to look ahead in planning programs, schedules, appropriations, balanced budgets. Our love affair with time causes other cultures whose languages permit a less hurried outlook, say the Chinese, to regard us as somewhat mad.

The assumptions underlying the culture of the Hopi also impose two grand cosmic forms upon the universe: the *objective* and the *subjective;* the manifest and the unmanifest. The first is everything accessible to the human senses, without distinction between past and present. The second is "the realm of expectancy, of desire and purpose, of vitalizing life, of efficient causes, of thought thinking itself out . . . into manifestation." It exists in the hearts and minds of animals, plants, mountains, as well as men. This subjective realm is intensely real to a Hopi, "quivering with life, power, and potency."

All languages contain terms of cosmic grandeur. English includes "reality," "matter," "substance," "causation," as well as "space" and "time." Hopi includes the cosmic term *tunátya,* meaning a special and exalted kind of "hope." It is a verb, not a noun—the action of hoping, the stirring toward hope—and is bound up with communal ceremonies, like prayers for the harvest, and for the forming of rain clouds.

The ancient Greeks, with their belief in a universal rule of reason, nevertheless did their thinking in Greek, which, like all Indo-European tongues, followed what is called the "subject-predicate" form. If there is a verb there must be a noun to make it work; it could not often exist in its own right as pure action. The ancient Greeks, as well as all Western peoples today, say, "The light flashed." Something has to be there to make the flash; "light" is the subject; "flash" is the predicate. The whole trend of modern physics, however, with its emphasis on the *field,* or the whole process, is away from subject-predicate propositions. A Hopi Indian, accordingly, is the better physicist when he says, "*Reh-pi*"—"flash!"—one word for the whole performance, no subject, no predicate, and no time element. (Children tend to do this too.) In Western languages we are constantly reading into nature ghostly entities which flash and perform other acts. Do we supply them because our verbs require substantives in front of them?

Again, the Hopi language does not raise the tough question whether things in a distant village exist at the same present moment as things in one's own village. Thus it avoids the idea of *simultaneity,* which has plagued Western scientists for generations, and was only banished by relativity. The thoughts of a Hopi about events always include *both* space and time, for neither is found alone in his world view. Thus his language gets along adequately without tenses for its verbs, and permits him to think habitually in terms of space-time. For you or me really to understand relativity, we must abandon our spoken tongue altogether and take to the special language of calculus. But a Hopi, Whorf implies, has a sort of calculus built into him.

No human being is free to describe nature with strict objectivity, for he is a prisoner of his language. A trained linguist can do better because he, at least, is aware of the bondage, and can look at nature through a variety of frames. A physicist can do better by using the language of mathematics. Semanticists are now painfully learning how to do better. It is not easy for anybody. Says Whorf:

We are thus introduced to a new principle of relativity, which holds that all observers are not led by the same physical evidence to the same picture of the universe, unless their linguistic backgrounds are similar, or can in some way be calibrated.

Indo-European languages can be calibrated with each other: English, Italian, Spanish, French, Russian, German, Latin, Greek, and the rest, back to Indo-Hittite all use the subject-predicate form. All speakers of these languages are capable of observing the world in a roughly similar way, at least on the high levels of "time," "space," and "matter." Hopi cannot be calibrated with them; neither can Chinese, nor thousands of other languages, living and dead.

THE PATHS OF CHINESE LOGIC

Speakers of Chinese dissect nature and the universe very differently than Western speakers, with a profound effect upon their systems of belief.

A Chinese writer, Chang Tung-Sun, vigorously supports the thesis of linguistic relativity in a monograph reprinted in the semantic quarterly *ETC.*

Kant imagined that he was dealing in universal categories in *The Critique of Pure Reason,* but actually, says Chang, he was only discussing standard forms of Western thought, a very limited approach. Kant's logic was one of the subject-predicate variety, which is not normal in Chinese. An intelligent Chinese gentleman does not know what Kant is talking about—unless he learns some Western tongue in which to read Kant's words.

Our Western verb "to be," observes Chang, used with an adjective predicate, implies the existence of the adjective as an independent quality. When we say, "This is yellow and hard," we tend to assume the existence of two qualities, "yellowness" and "hardness," which suggests to a Chinese something Chang calls a "cosmic substance." "The substance is characterized by its attributes, and the attributes are attributed to the substance," observes Chang, in considerable astonishment at such a circular performance. The verb "to be" creates great congeries of identities, and blossoms in Aristotle's laws of logic, of which the first is the law of identity, "A is A." This "law" is causing a lot of trouble today in charges of guilt by association.

No such law is possible in the Chinese language, where logic follows a quite different path. In Chinese, one does not attribute existence to "yellowness" and "hardness," or to polar words like "longness" and "shortness." Rather one says: "the long and the short are mutually related"; "the difficult and easy are mutually complementary;" "the front and the rear are mutually accompanying."

In the West we say, "This is the front of the car, and that is the rear, and let's have no more nonsense about it!" But in the Chinese view, Westerners are guilty of considerable nonsense in creating "frontness" and "rearness" as entities. Even a Westerner can see that if a car is torn in two in a crash, the part with the radiator grille becomes the "front," and the part toward the now severed windshield becomes the "rear"—*of that segment.* We can see, if we work hard enough, that there are no such entities as "frontness" or "rearness," "difficulty" or "easiness," "longness" or "shortness," by themselves out there. The Chinese language has this useful correction built in; we Westerners have to sweat it out with the help of linguistics, semantics, and mathematics.

Linguists have also emphasized that Chinese is a "multi-valued" language, not primarily two-valued like English and Western languages generally. We say that things must be "good" or "bad," "right" or "wrong," "clean" or "dirty," "black" or "white"—ignoring shades of gray. When an economist talks about a middle road between "socialism" and "capitalism," both camps vie in their ferocity to tear him apart. (I have been that unhappy economist.)

Speakers of Chinese set up no such grim dichotomies; they see most situations in shades of gray, and have no difficulty in grasping the significance of a variety of middle roads. As a result, Chinese thought has been traditionally tolerant, not given to the fanatical ideologies of the West. Racial, religious, and doctrinal conflicts have been hard to maintain in China, because a Chinese speaker does not possess an unshakable confidence that he is totally right and that his opponent is totally wrong. Observe that this is not a moral judgment, but structual in the language.

This happy lack of two-valued thinking raises an interesting question. Communism, as formulated by Marx and developed by Lenin, is rigidly two-valued. The heroic worker stands against the wicked capitalist and one or the other must go down. There is no place for shades of gray or for innocent bystanders. Those who are not with us are against us. Which side are you on?

Russian is an Indo-European language, and the two-sided choice is readily accepted by its speakers. The choice is accepted, too, by top leaders of the Chinese Communists today, for they went to Moscow to be indoctrinated, and to learn the Russian language. But four hundred million Chinese have not been to Moscow or learned Russian, or any other Indo-European language, and there is small prospect of their doing so. How, then, can the Chinese people become good ideological Communists, since it is difficult if not impossible for them to take seriously the central dialectic of Marxism? The structure of their language seems to forbid the idea.

"REH-PI! IT METEORS."

The Wintu Indians of North America are even more shy of the law of identity than the Chinese, says D. D. Lee, writing in the *International Journal of American Linguistics*. We say, "This *is* bread," but in Wintu they say, "We call this bread." They avoid the "is of identity," and so are less likely to confuse words with things. When a Wintu speaks of an event not within his own experience, he never affirms it but only suggests, "Perhaps it is so." When Mrs. Lee asked her informant the word for "body," she was given a term signifying "the whole person." Thus the Wintus seem to have antedated the psychosomatic school.

The Coeur d'Alene Indians of Idaho have long antedated other modern scientists. They do not speak in terms of simple cause-and-effect relations as we do, but rather in terms of *process,* as Western scientists are now painfully learning to do. Their language requires speakers to discriminate between three causal processes, denoted by three verb forms: growth, addition, secondary addition. "If, given a more sophisticated culture," says Whorf, "their thinkers erected these now unconscious discriminations into a theory of triadic causality, fitted to scientific observations, they might thereby produce a valuable intellectual tool for science." Our specialists can do this by taking thought, fortified with mathematics but the Coeur d'Alenes seem to do it automatically.

Eskimo breaks our single term "snow" into many words for different kinds of snow—a procedure which all skiers can applaud. Aztec, however, goes in the opposite direction; here we find one word for "snow," "ice," and "cold." In Hopi, "wave," "flame," "meteor," and "lightning" are all verbs, suiting their dynamic quality. Looking into the August sky, a Hopi says: "*Reh-pi!* It meteors." (Observe how in English we need a djin called "it" to power the meteor.)

It is easier and clearer to recite the story of William Tell in the Algonquin language than in English or French, because it is equipped with enough possessive pronouns to distinguish easily between "his" as applied to Tell, and as applied to his son. Writing in English I must continually watch my step with pronouns, lest I attach them to the wrong person or thing.

Chichewa, spoken by a tribe of unlettered Negroes in East Africa, has two past tenses, one for events which continue to influence the present, and one for events which do not. With this structure, says Whorf, "a new view of time opens before us. . . . It may be that these primitive folks are equipped with a language which, if they were to become philosophers or mathematicians, could make them our foremost thinkers upon *time.*"

LANGUAGE LINKS MANKIND

The metalinguists cause us to realize that language is not a tool with which to uncover a deeper vein of reason, universal to all thinkers, but a shaper of thought itself. Shaping the thought, it helps to shape the culture, as in the Western cult of the Adoration of Time. They are making us realize that we get our view of the world, our *Weltanschauung,* as much from words inside our heads as from independent observation. When, as scientists, we try to become independent observers, the words may distort the readings, unless we take special precautions. Einstein could not accurately talk about relativity in German or English, he had to talk about it in the calculus of tensors. There is no reason to suppose that English, German, Russian, or any Indo-European language, with its two-valued logic, its monster-making subject-predicate form, is the ultimate in communication.

The structure, or grammar, of each language, says Whorf, "is not merely a reproducing instrument for voicing ideas but rather is itself the shaper of ideas, the program and guide for the individual's mental activity, for his analysis of impressions." The world is presented to us in a kaleidoscopic flux of impressions which must be organized by our minds, which means by the linguistic system built into our minds. We cut up the seamless web of nature, gather the pieces into concepts, because, within our speech community, we are parties to an agreement to organize things that way, an agreement codified in the patterns of language. This agreement is, of course, an unstated one, but "its terms are absolutely obligatory"; we cannot talk at all except by subscribing to the rules. People who try to avoid them land in mental hospitals.

"A sort of Copernican revolution in communication" is implied by metalinguistics, according to John B. Carroll in his book, *The Study of Language.* Sober scientists are shy of revolutions and we find considerable skepticism among contemporary linguists and social scientists for the *Weltanschauung* view. They may note a trend in that direction, but they want more research—say, the time concept isolated and compared in a hundred different languages. Whorf, one suspects, would be the first to welcome such a project.

Criticism comes too from the intellectuals and the literati. It is directed not only at metalinguistics, but at all serious attempts to analyze language, and linguistic relativity, except those inaugurated by classical grammarians. As a student of semantics, and author of *The Tyranny of Words,* I have felt the sting of this criticism. Some men show a strong disposition, says Whorf, to make a virtue of ignorance and denounce any effort to understand the machinery of the mind. To them language is given, and no one more pries into it than into the financial affairs of one's friends.

I doubt whether language makes people of different cultures perceive the space-time world very differently. An Eskimo, I suspect, sees an iceberg about the way I do—though in more detail, with all its food signals clear. Rather, as Carroll suggests, the particular language we learn causes us to pay attention to some things more than to others; it shifts the emphasis of our perception. Also it certainly influences large, high-order concepts like "time," and gives an illiterate Hopi Indian a better aptitude for grasping the fourth dimension than, say, your author. A multivalued language like Chinese helps maintain ideological tolerance, and it may be that Chinese speakers will be unable to absorb Marxism in consequence. But we shall have to wait for a while for proof of that.

Metalinguistics may or may not produce a Copernican revolution, but it will be an important consideration in any workable plan for One World; in the engineering of an acceptable international language; in an understanding of people living in cultures other than our own. (The linguists find serious difficulties with Basic English, Esperanto, and other preliminary attempts.)

There are no languages properly to be termed "primitive." The living standards of Australian bushfellows may leave something to be desired, but the structure of their language is more complicated than English. Though systems differ widely, yet in their order, harmony, and subtle powers of apprehending reality, they demonstrate the link which binds all men together. "The crudest savage," says Whorf, "may unconsciously manipulate with effortless ease a linguistic system so intricate, manifoldly systematized, and intellectually difficult, that it requires the lifetime study of our greatest scholars to describe its workings."

A Papuan head-hunter, similarly conditioned, could mathematize as well as physicists from Princeton, and, conversely, scientist and yokel, scholar and tribesman, may all fall into similar kinds of logical impasse. "They are as unaware of the beautiful and inexorable systems that control them, as a cowherd is of cosmic rays."

Metalinguistics has gone far enough to build a fire under anyone interested in communication. One hopes that other students in many cultures will take up the torch which Whorf laid down.

Edward Sapir

DIALECT

THE TERM "DIALECT" HAS A CONNOTATION IN TECHNICAL LINGUISTIC USAGE which is somewhat different from its ordinary meaning. To the linguist there is no real difference between a "dialect" and a "language" which can be shown to be related, however remotely, to another language. By preference the term is restricted to a form of speech which does not differ sufficiently from another form of speech to be unintelligible to the speakers of the latter. Thus, Great Russian and White Russian are said to be dialects of the same language. Similarly, Alsatian, Swabian, and Swiss German are dialects or groups of dialects of a common folk speech. Literal mutual intelligibility, however, is not a criterion of great interest to the linguist, who is more concerned with the fact and order of historical relationships in speech. To him Venetian and Sicilian are equally dialects of Italian, although as far as mutual intelligibility is concerned these two might as well be called independent languages. Russian, Polish, Czech, Bulgarian, and Serbian, conventionally considered independent languages because of their national affiliations, are no less truly dialects of a common Slavic speech or linguistic prototype than Venetian and Sicilian are dialects of a supposedly common Italian language. If two obviously related forms of speech are spoken at the same time, the linguist does not say that one of them is a dialect of the other but that both are sister dialects of some common prototype, known or inferred. When they diverge so far as not only to be mutually unintelligible but no longer to be too obviously related to each other, the term "language" is more freely used than "dialect," but in principle there is no difference between the two. Thus, in a sense, all Romance languages, all Celtic languages, all Germanic languages, all Slavic languages, and all Indo-Aryan vernaculars are merely dialect groups of a common Aryan or Indo-European language.

A group of dialects is merely the socialized form of the universal tendency to individual variation in speech. These variations affect the phonetic form of the language, its formal characteristics, vocabulary, and such

From *Encyclopedia of the Social Sciences,* Vol. V, Copyright 1931 by The Macmillan Company, and used with its permission.

prosodic features as intonation and stress. No known language, unless it be artificially preserved for liturgical or other non-popular uses, has ever been known to resist the tendency to split up into dialects, any one of which may, in the long run, assume the status of an independent language. From dialects formed by inherent differentiation one may distinguish dialects which owe their origin to speech transfers. A community which takes on a language that is different from the one to which it has originally been accustomed will unconsciously carry over into the adopted language peculiarities of its own form of speech which are pronounced enough to give its use of the foreign language a dialectic tinge. Many linguists attach much importance to the influence of superseded languages in the formation of dialects. Thus some of the distinctive peculiarities of both Celtic and Germanic are supposed to be due to the retention of phonetic peculiarities of pre-Aryan languages.

In less technical or frankly popular usage the term "dialect" has somewhat different connotations. Human speech is supposed to be differentiated and standardized in a number of approved forms known as "languages," and each of these in turn has a number of subvarieties of lesser value known as "dialects." A dialect is looked upon as a departure from the standard norm, in many cases even as a corruption of it. Historically, this view is unsound, because the vast majority of so-called dialects are merely the regular, differentiated development of earlier forms of speech which antedate the recognized languages. Popular confusion on the subject is chiefly due to the fact that the question of language has become secondarily identified with that of nationality in the larger cultural and ethnic group which, in course of time, absorbs the local tradition. The language of such a nationality is generally based on a local dialect and spreads at the expense of other dialects which were originally of as great prestige as the culturally more powerful one.

Of the large number of dialects spoken in Germany, German Switzerland, and Austria, for example, very few, if any, can be considered as modified forms of the culturally accepted *Hochdeutsch* of literature, the pulpit, the stage, and cultural activity generally. The dialects of the German-speaking folk go back unbrokenly to the Old High German of early medieval times, a German which was even then richly differentiated into dialects. The present standardized German of the schools arose comparatively late in the history of German speech as a result of the fixing of one of the Upper Saxon dialects as the recognized medium of official communication within the German-speaking dominions. Luther's Bible helped considerably in the diffusion of this form of German as the recognized standard. It has taken a long time, however, for *Hochdeutsch* to take on a recognized phonetic form and to be looked upon as a well standardized form of oral communication, and to this day a large proportion of Germans, including the educated ranks, are bilingual in the sense that they use the standardized German for formal purposes but employ the local dialect for more familiar uses.

The history of German is paralleled more or less by the history of all the other national languages of Europe and of other parts of the world. As a result of cultural reasons of one kind or another a local dialect gets accepted as the favored or desirable form of speech within a linguistic community that is cut up into a large number of dialects. This approved local dialect becomes the symbol of cultural values and spreads at the expense of other local forms of speech. The standardized form of speech becomes more and more set in its vocabulary, form, and eventually pronunciation. The speakers of local dialects begin to be ashamed of their peculiar forms of speech because these have not the prestige value of the standardized language; and finally the illusion is created of a primary language, belonging to the large area which is the territory of a nation or nationality, and of the many local forms of speech as uncultured or degenerated variants of the primary norm. As it is well known, these variations from the standard norm are sometimes much more archaic, historically speaking, than the norm from which they are supposed to depart.

Local dialects are, in a sense, minority languages, but the term "minority language" should be reserved for a completely distinct form of speech that is used by a minority nationality living within the political framework of a nation. An example of such a minority language would be the Basque of southwestern France and northern Spain or the Breton of Brittany. These languages are not dialects of French and Spanish but historically distinct languages that have come to occupy culturally secondary positions.

There is naturally no hard and fast line between a dialect and a local variation of a minor nature such as New England English as contrasted with middle western English. In the older dialects the connection with the standardized speech is quite secondary, whereas in such local variations as New England versus middle western American speech standard English, however loosely defined, is present in the minds of all as the natural background for these variations, which are thus psychologically, if not altogether historically, variations from the primary or standard norm. It would be possible for the speaker of a local Swiss dialect or of Yorkshire English to build up a nationalistic gospel around his local dialect in opposition to the accepted speech of the cultured group, but the attempt to do this for middle western English in America would have something intrinsically absurd about it because of the feeling that this form of English is, at best, but a belated departure from an earlier norm. As usual in social phenomena, however, it is the symbolism of attitude that counts in these matters rather than the objective facts of history.

Ever since the formation of the great national languages of Europe toward the end of the medieval period there have been many social and political influences at work to imperil the status of the local dialects. As the power of the sovereign grew, the language of the court gained in prestige and tended to diffuse through all the ramifications of the official world. Meanwhile, although the Roman Catholic and Greek churches, with their sacred liturgical languages, were little interested in the question of folk versus standardized speech, the Protestant sects, with their concern for a more direct relation between God and His worshippers, naturally emphasized the dignity of folk speech and lent their aid to the diffusion of a selected form of folk speech over a larger area. The influence of such documents as Luther's Bible and King James's Authorized Version in the standardization of English and German has often been referred to. In more recent days, the increase of popular education and the growing demand for ready intelligibility in the business world have given a tremendous impetus to the spread of standardized forms of speech.

In spite of all these standardizing influences, however, local dialects, particularly in Europe, have persisted with a vitality that is little short of amazing. Obviously the question of the conservatism of dialect is not altogether a negative matter of the inertia of speech and of the failure of overriding cultural influences to permeate into all corners of a given territory. It is, to a very significant degree, a positive matter of the resistance of the local dialects to something which is vaguely felt as hostile. This is easily understood if we look upon languages and dialects not as intrinsically good or bad forms of speech but as symbols of social attitudes. Before the growth of modern industrialism culture tended to be intensely local in character in spite of the uniformizing influences of government, religion, education, and business. The culture that gradually seeped in from the great urban centers was felt as something alien and superficial in spite of the prestige that unavoidably attached to it. The home speech was associated with kinship ties and with the earliest emotional experiences of the individual. Hence the learning of a standardized language could hardly seem natural except in the few centers in which the higher culture seemed properly at home, and even in these there generally developed a hiatus between the standardized language of the cultured classes and the folk speech of the local residents. Hence cockney is as far removed psychologically from standard British English as is a peasant dialect of Yorkshire or Devon. On the continent of Europe, particularly in Germany and Italy, the culture represented by, say, standardized German or standardized Italian was, until very recent days, an exceedingly thin psychological structure, and its official speech could hardly take on the task of adequately symbolizing the highly differentiated folk cultures of German-speaking and Italian-speaking regions.

The Age of Enlightenment in the eighteenth century was, on the whole, hostile to the persistence of dialects, but the Romantic movement which followed it gave to folk speech a glamour which has probably had something to do with the idealization of localized languages as symbols of national solidarity and territorial integrity. Few writers of the seventeenth or eighteenth centuries would have taken seriously the use of dialect in literature. It was only later that Lowland Scotch could be romantically restored in the lyrics of Robert Burns, that Fritz Reuter could strive to establish a Low German (*Plattdeutsch*) literary language, and that Mistral could attempt to revive the long lost glory of Provençal. One may suspect that this renewed emphasis on linguistic differences is but a passing phase in the history of modern man. Be that as it may, it has had much to do with the emergence of new nationalisms in recent time. It is doubtful if such countries as Lithuania, Esthonia, and Czechoslovakia could have so easily proved their right to exist if it had not come to be felt that just as every nationality needs its language, so every unattached language needs its nationality and territorial independence to fulfill its inherent mission. Perhaps the best example of what might be called linguistic romanticism is the attempt of the Irish nationalists to renew the vitality of Gaelic, a form of speech which has never been standardized for literary, let alone folk, purposes and which is profoundly alien to the majority of the more articulate of Irish nationalists.

No doubt the respect for local forms of speech has received assistance from scientific linguistics and its tendency to view all languages and dialects as of equal historical importance. It is very doubtful, however, if linguistic localism can win out in the long run. The modern mind is increasingly realistic and pragmatic in the world of action and conceptualistic or normative in the world of thought. Both of these attitudes are intrinsically hostile to linguistic localism of any sort, and necessarily therefore to dialectic conservatism. Compulsory education, compulsory military service, modern means of communication, and urbanization are some of the more obvious factors in the spread of these attitudes, which, so far as language is concerned, may be defined by the thesis that words should either lead to unambiguous action among the members of as large a group as is held together culturally or, in the domain of thought, should aim to attach themselves to concepts which are less and less purely local in their application. In the long run therefore it seems fairly safe to hazard the guess that such movements as the Gaelic revival in Ireland and the attempt to save as many minority languages and dialects from cultural extinction as possible will come to be looked upon as little more than eddies in the more powerful stream of standardization of speech that set in at the close of the medieval period. The modern problem is more complex than the classical or medieval problem because the modern mind insists on having the process of standardization take the form of a democratic rather than an aristocratic process.

A word may be added in regard to the social psychology of dialectic forms of speech. In the main, markedly dialectic peculiarities have been looked upon as symbols of inferiority of status, but if local sentiment is strongly marked and if the significance of the local group for the larger life of the nation as a whole allows, a local dialect may become the symbol of a kind of inverted pride. We thus have the singular spectacle of Lowland Scotch as an approved and beautiful linguistic instrument and of cockney as an undesirable ugly one. These judgments are extrinsic facts of language themselves but they are none the less decisive in the world of cultural symbolisms.

If an individual is brought up in a community that has its characteristic dialect and if he becomes identified later in life with another community which has a second mode of speech, some very interesting personality problems arise which involve the status symbolism or affectional symbolism of these differing forms of speech. Individuals who vacillate somewhat in their conception of their own role in society may often be detected unconsciously betraying this feeling of insecurity in a vacillating pronunciation or intonation or choice of words. When, under the influence of an emotional crisis, such individuals are thrown back upon their earliest emotional experiences—"regress," in short—they are likely to relapse into early dialectic habits of speech. It is suggested that the question of the relation of the individual to the various dialects and languages to which he has been subjected from time to time is of far more anecdotal interest, that it constitutes, as a matter of fact, a very important approach to the problem of personality subjected to the strains of cultural change.

J. N. Hook and E. G. Mathews

CHANGES IN THE ENGLISH LANGUAGE

EXAMPLES OF OLD ENGLISH

AT FIRST GLANCE A SELECTION FROM OLD ENGLISH APPEARS TO BE IN A foreign tongue. More careful scrutiny reveals that some of the words are almost the same as ours, that others have undergone considerable change, and that still others have vanished. Modern English has lost some of the grammatical constructions that formerly existed.

Here is the Lord's Prayer in the Old English (West Saxon) version of approximately a thousand years ago:

> Fæder ūre þū þe eart on heofonum sī þin nama gehālgod. Tō becume þīn rīce. Gewurþe ðin willa on eorðan swā swā on heofonum. Ūrne gedæghwāmlīcan hlāf syle ūs tō dæg. And forgyf ūs ūre gyltas swā swā wē forgyfað ūrum gyltendum. And ne gelæd þū ūs on costnunge ac ālȳs ūs of yfele. Sōþlīce.

Detailed comment on these few lines would fill many pages; here we shall look at only a few words and constructions. Word order was much less fixed in Old English than it is today: notice the Old English forms of *Father our* and *be thy name hallowed* as examples. Case endings are used with nouns, as in *heofonum* (heaven), *eorðan* (earth), *gyltas* (debts), and *gyltendum* (debtors). Adjectives had to agree in case, number, and gender with their nouns: *ūre, ūrne,* and *ūrum* are today simply *our*. The word *rīce* is now translated as *kingdom,* but it is actually a cognate of *Reich* which survives in German. The symbols þ (thorn) and ð (eth) were both used for *th*. Since Old English times some words have been reduced in the number of syllables: *gehālgod* (hallowed), *gedæghwāmlīcan* (daily), *forgyfað* (forgive). Spelling was much more phonetic than that of today;

in general, there were no silent letters. In pronunciation, vowel sounds were more similar to those found in modern continental languages than to those in Modern English; and consonant sounds were not much different from those of Modern English. Punctuation marks other than periods were rare, and even periods were not used very systematically by the scribes.

As a second example consider the following lines from the epic poem *Beowulf*. The manuscript is generally believed to be in the hand of a scribe of the late tenth century. This passage tells of King Hrothgar's sorrow over the killing of his friend and follower by a hideous demon:

Hrothgar spoke
Hrōðgar maþelode
Not ask thou about happiness.
Ne frīn þū æfter sælum
of the Danes for the people
Denigea lēodum
Irmenlaf's
Yrmenlāfes
my confidant
mīn rūnwita
shoulder-companion
eaxlgestealla
head protected
hafelan weredon
boar-helmets struck
eoferas cnysedan
nobleman good from old times
æþeling ærgōd

defender of the Scyldings
helm Scyldinga:
Sorrow is renewed
Sorh is genīwod
Dead is Aeschere
Dēad is Æschere
elder brother
yldra brōþor
and my counselor
ond mīn rædbora
when we in battle
ðonne wē on orlege
when clashed together troops
þonne hniton fēþan
Such should hero be
Swylc scolde eorl wesan
as Aeschere was.
swylc Æschere wæs.

Even the literal translation of this passage does not seem very clear today. A more free translation might go like this: "Hrothgar, the defender of the Scyldings, spoke: 'Do not ask about happiness, because sorrow has come again to the Danish people. Aeschere is dead. He was Irmenlaf's older brother and my confidant and counselor. He stood at my shoulder when in battle we protected our heads and hewed the boar-helmets as troops clashed. Every hero should be as Aeschere was, a nobleman good to recall from old times.'"

Notice, in comparing these translations, how word order has changed. Observe also how large a proportion of the Old English words have dropped out of the language. Some of them remain, however, in recognizable form: *helm* is a cousin of our *helmets, æfter* is *after, dēad* has changed only its pronunciation, *yldra broþor* is still recognizable, *þonne* has become *then, wē* and *in* are unchanged in spelling, *scolde* is similar to *should, eorl* has altered its meaning and become *earl, ærgōd* contains the ancestors of *ere* and *good,* and *wæs* is obviously *was.*

Inflectional endings are much more important in Old English than in Modern: for example, *Scyldinga* (genitive plural) requires here a three-word translation, *of the Scyldings;* and *lēodum* also requires either a three-word translation, *for* (or *to*) *the people,* or a revised word order. The endings of such words as *rūnwita, fēþan,* and *eoferas* help, along with the context, to show whether the word is to be regarded as a subject or an object. In Modern English we depend more upon word order and upon "function words" such as prepositions than we do upon inflections.

Old English grammar may be made a subject for special study. Here you have seen illustrated only a few of its most obvious characteristics.

EXAMPLE OF MIDDLE ENGLISH

When we move forward about four hundred years, from the late tenth to the late fourteenth century, we see that the language has changed rather drastically. Here are lines from the Prologue of Chaucer's *Canterbury Tales,* describing the squire, son of the knight:

> With him ther was his sone a yong Squyer
> (lover)   (aspirant to knighthood)
> A lovyere and a lusty bacheler
> (curly)   (as if)
> With lokkes crulle as they were leyd in presse.
> Of twenty yeer of age he was I gesse.
>
> .   .   .
>
> (Embroidered)   (meadow)
> Embrouded was he, as it were a mede
> (flowers)
> Al ful of fresshe floures whyte and rede.
> (playing the flute)
> Singinge he was or floyting al the day.
> He was as fresh as is the month of May.
> Short was his goune with sleves long and wyde.
> (excellently)
> Wel coude he sitte on hors and faire ryde.
> (compose the words)
> He coude songes make and wel endyte

<small>(Joust)　　(also)　　　　　　　　　　(draw)</small>
Juste and eek daunce and wel purtreye and wryte.
<small>(hotly)　　　　　　　　　　　(in the night-time)</small>
So hote he lovede that by nightertale
He sleep namore than dooth a nightingale.

This passage is closer to Modern English in word order than most Old English was. Only in two or three places, such as "He coude songes make," does the order seem very strange to us. Inflectional endings of Middle English were considerably reduced from Old English. In a noun an -s or -es usually signified either a genitive singular or any case of the plural. (The battle between an -s and an -en plural was almost decided by Chaucer's time, although in a few words such as *oxen* the -en plural never surrendered.) Adjectival forms had in general been reduced to two, one for the "strong" singular, and a second for the strong plural and the "weak" singular and plural. Verbs were somewhat simplified also; in the past tense no distinction was retained between singular and plural or between first, second, and third person, and the past tense and past participle were often identical, as they are in most verbs today.

Of all the things that have happened to English, the reduction of inflectional endings and the increased inflexibility of word order have been most important in giving the language its modern characteristics. Although these changes were not completed in Middle English and will never be completed while the language lives, they were far advanced by the year 1500, a date chosen rather arbitrarily as the beginning of Modern English.

SOME OF THE DEVELOPMENTS IN MODERN ENGLISH

Since 1500 English word order has become still more fixed, and living inflections have been reduced to seven: an -s or -es plural for nearly all nouns, an -s ending for most third person singular verbs in the present tense, an -ed ending for most verbs in the past tense, an -ing form for verbs, a special past participle for some verbs, and -er ending for the comparative degree of many adjectives and some adverbs, and an -est ending for the superlative degree of the same words.

In other ways grammar has changed only slightly. Representative of the many comparatively small changes are the use of *do* in questions (*Does he consent?* rather than Elizabethan *Consents he?*) and the growth in frequency of the progressive tenses (*He was speaking,* for instance, often replacing *He spoke*). Steadily increasing reliance upon prepositional phrases, greater employment of subordinate clauses, the increase in verb-adverb (or verb-preposition) combinations ("I *ran into* an old friend"), and a tendency to use almost any word as more than one part of speech—these are but a few of the Modern English developments that later will be treated in more detail.

In the eighteenth century some grammarians, failing to recognize the inevitability of linguistic change, strove to stop or at least retard it. They believed that change in a language is undesirable; since Latin was the most highly regarded language, and since Latin had not changed much in fifteen hundred years or so, change must be bad. (Those who held this theory failed to realize that Latin would probably have changed a great deal if it had not become a dead language, and that in monks' Latin it actually did change considerably.) They believed also that the loss of inflections should be stopped to prevent further "deterioration."

The results of the efforts of these few grammarians may be illustrated by referring to a couple of pronouns and a few verbs. The distinction between *who* and *whom*, which is not essential for clarity, was erratically observed during the eighteenth century. But under pressure from pre-scriptive grammarians, teachers and editors began to insist upon strict main-tenance of *whom* as an object. Several verbs, including *blow, know,* and *throw,* were moving toward a "weak" or "regular" past tense and past participle: *blow, blowed, blowed,* and so on. They were thus following other verbs that had made the shift without hurting the language: as examples, *help* once had *healp* as one past form and *holpen* as the past participle; *climb* had *clamb* and *clumben; chew* had *ceaw* and *cowen.* Certainly *blowed* would be no worse than *climbed* or *chewed,* but the prescribers wanted no more "deterioration." As a result of their efforts and those of their intellectual descendants the use of *blowed, knowed,* and *throwed* may even today keep an able person from being employed for a white collar position.

Similarly, in the eighteenth century, a tendency toward identical forms for past tense and past participle was noticeable. The verb *sing* was tending toward *sing, sung, sung; write* toward *write, wrote, wrote.* The original title of Thomas Gray's most famous poem was "Elegy Wrote in a Country Churchyard." But once more the reactionaries went to work, and the schools ever since have insisted upon different forms for the past tense and past participle of *drink, give, ride, shrink, sing, sink, write,* and other verbs. How many million child-hours have been spent on mastering these forms is beyond calculation. Totally false conceptions of "correctness" have resulted from this wasted effort.

Perhaps the most noticeable change that has occurred since 1500 is not in grammar but in vocabulary. Through borrowings from dead Latin, dead Greek, and most of the important living languages of the world, English has multiplied its store of words manyfold. Since no one can precisely define what a word is, no one can say how many words are now in the language. One clue to the number is that unabridged dictionaries have about 600,000 entries. But since no lexicographer would claim that his dictionary lists every existing word in the language, the total may be much larger.

WHY THE LANGUAGE HAS CHANGED

A language changes because things happen to people. If we could imagine the impossible—a society in which nothing happened—there would be no changes in language. But except possibly in a cemetery, things are constantly happening to people: they eat, drink, sleep, talk, make love, meet strangers, struggle against natural perils, and fight against one another. They slowly adapt their language to meet the changing conditions of their lives. Although the changes made in one generation may be small, those made in a dozen generations may enormously affect the language. The big and little phases of history—fashions, fads, inventions, the influence of a leader, a war or two, an invasion or two, travel to a foreign land, the demands of business intercourse—may alter a language so much that a Rip Van Winkle who slept two or three hundred years might have trouble in making himself understood when he awoke. Even in a relatively quiet society, linguistic change proceeds inexorably.

Think, if you will, of the English language as a river. Its headwaters are the closely interrelated Teutonic languages of the Angles, Saxons, and Jutes, who lived mainly in the northern part of what is now Germany. They provided the basic grammatical structure of the language that we call English; they provided most of its linguistic heritage; they provided its basic words, the common everyday words that still are the most important in our simple communications. But to the basic elements brought in by these Teutonic peoples many additions have been made.

When the Teutons began invading and settling in the British Isles in 449 A.D., they found in possession the Celts, who previously had been pushed about by Roman soldiers for several centuries. The Teutons pushed the Celts about some more, finally tending to localize them in what we now call Ireland, Wales, and parts of Scotland. But the Teutonic language was influenced somewhat by the Celtic and indirectly by the Latin which the Celts had fragmentarily learned. So in English we have words of Celtic ancestry such as *brat, cairn,* and *crag,* and the place names *Aberdeen* (*Aber* = river mouth), *Avon*(river), *Caerleon, Cardiff, Carlyle* (*caer* or *car* = fortress), *Dundee, Dunbarton, Dunbar* (*dun* = hill), *Inchcape* (*inch* = island), *Kildare, Kilpatrick* (*kill* = church). And as a result of the early and indirect Latin tributary (which existed on the Continent even before the invasions of Britain) we have *wall* and *street* and *port,* words that give promise of enduring even longer than the Roman constructions that they name; and we have place names: Roman *Londinium* (originally Celtic) is now *London, Eboracum* (also once Celtic) has undergone considerable transformation to appear as *York,* and Latin *castra,* a military camp, appears both in England and the United States in *Lancaster, Worcester, Leicester, Gloucester, Chester, Dorchester, Rochester.* Thus Latin and Celtic are early tributaries of English.

By the end of the sixth century Latin was to renew its influence upon English. In 597 Roman missionaries began coming to the British Isles in an attempt to Christianize the inhabitants. They introduced such church words as *altar, creed, mass,* and *nun* and some homely words such as *beet, pine, cheese,* and *cup.* Some of the words that the priests brought over had been borrowed by Latin from Greek: *bishop, deacon, martyr, church, devil, priest, monk, pope, psalm, dish* and *plum.* So once more a double tributary entered the river of the English language.

In the seventh and most of the eighth centuries the Anglo-Saxon inhabitants of the British Isles lived a relatively peaceful existence—simple by modern standards but maybe happier than a more complex society can be. But starting in about 790, "Northmen" or Danes began to invade the islands. They were rough and vigorous; in 793, "the heathen men miserably destroyed God's church at Lindisfarne with rapine and slaughter," a contemporary account says. The forays grew into expeditions; the Danes began to colonize; Alfred the Great for a while paid them tribute but then organized military forces and compelled the invaders to sign a peace treaty. One of the terms of the treaty was that the Danes accept Christianity. Since the chief difference between the Danes and the Anglo-Saxons had been in religion, this concession meant that the two groups, already speaking kindred and often mutually intelligible languages, would merge. However, attacks by new groups of Danes, not covered by the treaty, continued, and early in the eleventh century a Danish king, Cnut, ruled in England.

It is often difficult to separate the linguistic contributions of the Danes from the closely related Anglo-Saxon, but apparently we owe to Danish such words as *fellow, husband, law, wrong,* and a number of words with an *sk* sound, as *skill, scale, scare, skirt* (*shirt,* a cognate form, is from Anglo-Saxon), *skin, sky, score,* and *bask.* Numerous English place names are Danish in origin. Danish *thwaite* (piece of ground) appears in many names such as *Stonethwaite, Hallthwaite; thorp* (village) is in names like *Lowthorpe* and *Northorpe; by* (town) is in *Derby, Kirby, Selby, Whitby,* etc.; *toft* (a clearing) is in *Lowestoft.*

The next big tributary came from north via east. Northmen, later called Normans, had begun moving into France at about the time that the Danes invaded England. They were flexible people who adopted French as their language, changing it somewhat in the process. They made of Normandy one of the most vigorous and ambitious states of Europe. In 1066, after the death of England's Edward the Confessor, the Duke of Normandy decided that he would attempt to gain the crown of his late cousin, and at Hastings he earned the more glorious title of William the Conqueror. His people moved into the British Isles, relegated natives to the rank of second-class citizens, and eventually concentrated their grip upon England as they lost their continental footholds.

Now began the period of greatest linguistic turmoil that English has known. England was a country of two languages: the Norman French of the ruling classes and the English of the conquered. The Bishop of Worcester was deposed in 1095 because he was "an idiot who did not know French." French was used in the churches, in the courts, in important business transactions, and in the schools. But inevitably the two groups had to meet. A French landowner had to give instructions to his tenants; an English farmer or smith to try to sell his goods or his skills; intermarriage became frequent. Each group picked up words from the other. However, just as American occupation troops learned only the rudiments of German, Italian, and Japanese after World War II, the Normans did not learn the intricacies of English nor did the English learn the intricacies of Norman French. Each group learned only the fundamentals.

Before the Norman conquest there had been signs that grammatical inflections were being reduced—the dative and accusative cases, for instance, were blending their forms. But the coming of the Normans seems to have expedited such change. At any rate, after the Normans had been in England for about three centuries, English inflections were not nearly so numerous.

The two groups gradually blended. So did their vocabularies, and to a much smaller extent their grammar, although the impact of Norman French upon English was less than one might think. But partly as a result of that impact, and more largely as a result of other, less tangible causes, grammatical gender was replaced by natural gender, word order became less free as inflections were reduced, pronunciations changed, and many words from Norman French, French, and Latin entered the language.

Chaucer's contemporary, John Gower, in the fourteenth century wrote three major works—one in English, one in French, and one in Latin. He chose three languages because he was not sure which language would become standard in England, and he wanted one of his works to be in the language that endured. Had he lived fifty years later, he would have had no difficulty in seeing that English was going to be the winner.

During the Renaissance two more large tributaries entered English. These, of course, were in the form of additional Latin and Greek contributions. Thousands of words came into the English vocabulary during this period, including huge numbers of relatively useless terms that lived briefly and were then buried in soon-to-be-forgotten graves. English spellings were also influenced by the new interest in the Classical languages. Learned men perhaps foolishly proclaimed that the orthography of English words should reveal their Latin backgrounds. They therefore recommended the spellings *debt* and *doubt,* even though the *b*'s in these words were not pronounced, and even though the French, from whom the English had borrowed both words, had already dropped the *b*'s that existed in Latin. A number of words with *tio,* like *nation,* had also been taken from the French, which often used a phonetically accurate *c* instead of *t;* in English the sound in question was pronounced as *s* or *sh,* but Renaissance scholars insisted that the Latin *t* be retained. Many other of our present illogical spellings may be attributed to the scholars of the Renaissance.

During the Renaissance period and later, the feeling grew that English grammar should be described in the terminology of Latin grammar. Sometimes that procedure was not objectionable, for many elements of the two languages were similar. But when the grammarians insisted upon finding in English everything that existed in Latin, when they made of Latin a procrustean bed into which English must be in some way fitted, and when they ignored the fact that English was basically a Teutonic and not an Italic language, they did irreparable harm to many generations of persons who wanted to acquire a clear understanding of the structure and peculiarities of the language.

Since the Renaissance, many small tributaries have enlarged the stream of English. These cannot be listed in chronological order. Latin has kept appearing, as have French and Greek. Italian has contributed many of the technical terms of music. Dutch has given sailing terms like *ahoy, boom, deck, hoist, skipper, sloop,* and *yacht.* Spanish has given, directly or indirectly, miscellaneous words like *matador, vanilla, armada, alligator,* and *mosquito.* North American Indian has contributed such words as *hominy, Mississippi* (an Algonquin word meaning "big river," not "Father of Waters"), *moccasin, moose, opossum, papoose, pemmican, raccoon, skunk, squaw, toboggan, tomahawk, wampum,* and *wigwam.* Among other contributing languages, with one or two representative words from each, have been Bengali (*bungalow*); Persian (*azure*); Slavic (*polka, vampire, mammoth*); Hebrew (*amen, hallelujah, behemoth*); Hungarian (*goulash*); Tartar (*khan*); Malay (*amuck, gong, cockatoo*); Indian (*rajah, nabob, khaki, yogi*); Australian (*boomerang, kangaroo*); South American Indian (*alpaca, condor, jaguar, quinine*); Polynesian (*taboo, tattoo*); African (*gumbo, mumbo jumbo, okra*). Even Chinese has given us some words (*tea, typhoon, chop suey,* and *chow mein*); Chinese Pidgin English has contributed the familiar *chopstick;* Japanese has given us *tycoon, kimono, judo,* and *ju-jitsu.*

The borrowing has of course gone the other way, also, although the details need not concern us here. English and American gastronomic and athletic terms, for instance, have been incorporated in many European languages. An American can use the terms *cocktail* and *beefsteak* with satisfactory results in almost any European restaurant.

Why did English change? Simply because many things happened to many people in many countries. Had the Angles, Saxons, and Jutes moved southeast instead of southwest, the language of the British Isles might never have been Teutonic. Had Harold defeated William the Conqueror at Hastings in 1066, the language of today might have been considerably different, perhaps more complicated in morphology, more simple in syntax. Had the English been stay-at-homes, their language might have lacked some of the versatility, the expressiveness, and the color that we believe it now has.

Jacques Barzun

ENGLISH AS SHE'S NOT TAUGHT

AT AN EDUCATIONAL CONFERENCE HELD IN VANCOUVER LAST SUMMER, leaders of the Canadian school system generally agreed that from half to three quarters of their students in the first year of college were incompetent in grammar, syntax, and analysis of thought. What was notable in the discussion was that nearly every participant used the English language with uncommon force and precision. Any looseness or jargon heard there came from the three American guests, of whom I was one. Most of our hosts—Canadian teachers, principals, supervisors, and university instructors —had obviously gone through the mill of a classical education; the chairman made a mild pun involving Latin and was rewarded with an immediate laugh. Yet they declared themselves unable to pass on their linguistic accomplishment to the present school generation, and they wanted to know why.

In the United States the same complaint and inquiry has been endemic, commonplace, for quite a while. You come across it in the papers. You hear parents, school people, editors and publishers, lawyers and ministers, men of science and of business, lamenting the fact that their charges or their offspring or their employees can neither spell nor write "decent English." The deplorers blame the modern progressive school or the comics or TV; they feel that in school and outside, something which they call discipline is lacking, and they vaguely connect this lack with a supposed decline in morality, an upsurge of "crisis." Like everything else, bad English is attributed to our bad times, and the past (which came to an end with the speaker's graduation from college) is credited with one more virtue, that of literary elegance.

The facts seem to me quite different, the causes much more tangled, and the explanation of our linguistic state at once more complex and less vague. For many years now I have been concerned with the art of writing and kept busy at the invidious task of improving other people's utterance, and I cannot see that performance has deteriorated. The level is low but it has not fallen. As a reader of history I am steadily reminded that the

This article originally appeared in *The Atlantic Monthly* (December, 1953)
Used by permission of the author.

writing of any language has always been a hit-and-miss affair. Here is Amos Barrett, our chief source on the battles of Concord and Lexington: "It wont long before their was other minit Compneys . . . We marched Down about a mild or a mild half and we see them acomming . . ." And so on. An illiterate New England farmer? Not so, since he could write; he had been taught and in some way represents "the past." The question he poses is, how do people write who are not professionals or accomplished amateurs? The answer is: badly, at all times.

Writing is at the very least a knack, like drawing or being facile on the piano. Because everybody can speak and form letters, we mistakenly suppose that good, plain, simple writing is within everybody's power. Would we say this of good, straightforward, accurate drawing? Would we say it of melodic sense and correct, fluent harmonizing at the keyboard? Surely not. We say these are "gifts." Well, so is writing, even the writing of a bread-and-butter note or a simple public notice; and this last suggests that something has happened within the last hundred years to change the relation of the written word to daily life.

Whether it is the records we have to keep in every business and profession or the ceaseless communicating at a distance which modern transport and industry require, the world's work is now unmanageable, unthinkable, without *literature*. Just see how many steps you can take without being confronted with something written or with the necessity of writing something yourself. Having been away for a couple of weeks during the summer, I find a bill from the window washer, who luckily came on a day when the cleaning woman was in the apartment. He has therefore scribbled below the date: "The windows have been cleaned Wed. 12:30 P.M. Your maid was their to veryfey the statement"—perfectly clear and adequate. One can even appreciate the change of tenses as his mind went from the job just finished to the future when I would be reading this message from the past.

Call this bad writing if you like, it remains perfectly harmless. The danger to the language, if any, does not come from such trifles. It comes rather from the college-bred millions who regularly write and who in the course of their daily work circulate the prevailing mixture of jargon, cant, vogue words, and loose syntax that passes for prose. And the greater part of this verbiage is published, circulated, presumably read. A committee won't sit if its drivelings are not destined for print. Even an interoffice memo goes out in sixteen copies and the schoolchildren's compositions appear verbatim in a mimeographed magazine. Multiply these cultural facts by the huge number of activities which (it would seem) exist only to bombard us with paper, and you have found the source of the belief in a "decline" in writing ability—no decline at all, simply the infinite duplication of dufferism. This it is which leads us into false comparisons and gloomy thoughts.

II

The apparent deterioration of language is a general phenomenon which is denounced throughout Western Europe. One had only to read the Catalogue of the British Exhibition of 1951 to see the common symptoms in England. Sir Ernest Gowers's excellent little book of a few years earlier, *Plain Words*, was an attempt to cure the universal disease in one congested spot, the Civil Service, which is presumably the most highly educated professional group in Britain.

In France, the newspapers, the reports of Parliamentary debates, and the literary reviews show to what extent ignorance of forms and insensitivity to usage can successfully compete against a training obsessively aimed at verbal competence. And by way of confirmation, M. Jean Delorme, a native observer of the language in French Canada, recently declared the classic speech "infected" on this side of the Atlantic too. As for Germany, a foreign colleague and correspondent of mine, a person of catholic tastes and broad judgment, volunteers the opinion that "people who cultivate good pure German are nowadays generally unpopular, especially among the devotees of newspaper fiction and articles. The universal barbarism of language has already gone well into the grotesque."

So much for the democratic reality. But great as has been the effect of enlarged "literacy," it does not alone account for what is now seen as linguistic decadence. The educated, in fact the leaders of modern thought, have done as much if not more to confuse the judgment. For what is meant by the misnomer "pure speech" is simply a habit of respect toward usage, which insures a certain fixity in vocabulary, forms, and syntax. Language cannot stand still, but it can change more or less rapidly and violently. During the last hundred years, nearly every intellectual force has worked, in all innocence, against language. The strongest, science and technology, did two damaging things: they poured quantities of awkward new words into the language and this in turn persuaded everybody that each new thing must have a name, preferably "scientific." These new words, technical or commercial, were fashioned to impress, an air of profundity being imparted by the particularly scientific letters *k*, *x*, and *o* = Kodak, Kleenex, Sapolio. The new technological words that came in were sinful hybrids like "electrocute" and "triphibian," or misunderstood phrases like "personal equation," "*n*th degree," or "psychological moment"—brain addlers of the greatest potency.

The passion for jargon was soon at its height, from which it shows no sign of descending. Every real or pseudo science poured new verbiage into the street, every separate school or -ism did likewise, without shame or restraint. We can gauge the result from the disappearance of the Dictionary properly so called. Consult the most recent and in many ways the best of them, *Webster's New World Dictionary,* and what you find is a miniature encyclopedia filled with the explanation of initials, proper names, and entries like "macrosporangium" or "abhenry," which are not and never will be words of the English language.

Under the spate of awe-inspiring vocables, the layman naturally felt that he too must dignify his doings and not be left behind in the race for prestige. Common acts must suggest a technical process. Thus we get "contact" and "funnel" as workaday verbs—and "process" itself: "we'll process your application"—as if it were necessary to name the steps or choices of daily life with scientific generality. I know a young businessman who makes jottings of his business thoughts; when he has enough on one topic he *folderizes* them.

What is wrong with all this is not merely that it is new, heedless, vulgar, and unnecessary (all signs of harmful vice in a language) but that jargon swamps thought. The habit of talking through cant words destroys the power of seeing things plain. "I'll contact you to finalize the agreement." What does it mean? The drift is plain enough, but compare: "I'll call at your office to sign the contract." The former raises no clear image or expectation, the latter does. Moreover, the former smells of inflated ego, it fills the mouth in a silly bumptious way.

But who cares? Why fuss?—good questions both. Nobody cares much because—we all think—it's the deed (or the thing) that counts, not the words. This conviction, too, is a product of modern technology, and its effect is great though unremarked. The power of words over nature, which has played such a role in human history, is now an exploded belief, a dead emotion. Far from words controlling things, it is now things that dictate words. As soon as science was able to chop up the physical world and recombine it in new forms, language followed suit; and this not only among scientists making up new vocables, but among the supposed guardians of the language, the poets and men of letters. It is highly significant that around 1860 writers deliberately began to defy usage and turn syntax upside down. Lewis Carroll and Edward Lear made good fun with it; "obscure" poets such as Rimbaud sought new depths of meaning. There was in this a strong impulse to destroy all convention, for Victorian moralism had made the idea of conventionality at once suspect and hateful. The revolt succeeded and its spirit is still alive; novelty-hunting is now a linguistic virtue, or to express it differently, a common influence is at work in Jabberwocky and James Joyce, in the scientist's lingo and in the advertiser's "Dynaflow," "Hydramatic," or "Frigidaire"—which end by becoming household words. In short, modern man is feeling his oats as the manipulator of objects and he shows it in his manhandling of words.

This helps to explain why the predominant fault of the bad English encountered today is not the crude vulgarism of the untaught but the blithe irresponsibility of the taught. The language is no longer regarded as a common treasure to be hoarded and protected as far as possible. Rather, it is loot from the enemy to be played with, squandered, plastered on for one's adornment. Literary words imperfectly grasped, meanings assumed from bare inspection, monsters spawned for a trivial cause—these are but a few of the signs of squandering. To give examples: the hotel clerk giving me a good room feels bound to mention the well-known person whom "we last hospitalized in that room." Not to lag behind Joyce, the advertiser bids you "slip your feet into these easy-going *leisuals* and breathe a sigh of real comfort."

Undoubtedly these strange desires are often born of the need to ram an idea down unwilling throats. We all fear our neighbor's wandering attention and try to keep him awake by little shocks of singularity, or again by an overdose of meaning. Unfortunately, novelty-hunting proceeds from the known to the unknown by a leap of faith. "It was pleasant," writes the author of very workmanlike detective stories, "to watch her face and find his resentment *vitiate* as he made excuses for her."

III

The notable fact is that all this occurs in printed books, written by writers, published (usually) by first-rate firms that employ editors. In speech, the same blunders and distortions come from educated people. It is all very well to say, as one expert has confidently done, that "what certain words really mean is moving toward what they seem to mean," the implication being that after a while everything will be in place. Actually, this leaves meaning nowhere, if only because we're not all moving in step. The *New Yorker* spotted a movie theater sign on which "adultery" was used to mean "adulthood." From an English periodical I learn that some new houses "*affront* the opposite side of the street." If Mrs. Malaprop is going to become the patron saint of English, what is going to prevent "contention" from meaning the same thing as "contentment" or the maker of woodcuts from being called a woodcutter?

There is no getting around it: meaning implies convention, and the discovery that meanings change does not alter the fact that when convention is broken misunderstanding and chaos are close at hand. Mr. Churchill has told how Allied leaders nearly came to blows because of the single word "table," a verb which to the Americans meant dismiss from the discussion, whereas to the English, on the contrary, it meant put on the agenda. This is an extraordinary instance, and the vagaries of those who pervert good words to careless misuse may be thought more often ludicrous than harmful. This would be true if language, like a great maw, could digest anything and dispose of it in time. But language is not a kind of ostrich. Language is alive only by a metaphor drawn from the life of its users. Hence every defect in the language is a defect in somebody.

For language is either the incarnation of our thoughts and feelings or a cloak for their absence. When the ordinary man who has prepared a report on sales up to June 30 rumbles on about "the frame of reference in which the co-ordination campaign was conceived," he is filling the air with noises, not thoughts.

For self-protection, no doubt, the contemporary mind is opposed to all this quibbling. It speaks with the backing of popular approval when it says: "Stop it! You understand perfectly well what all these people mean. Don't be a dirty purist looking under the surface and meddling with democratic self-expression." To haggle over language *is* quibbling, of course. All precision is quibbling, whether about decimals in mathematics or grains of drugs in prescriptions—fairly important quibbles. The question is whether in language the results justify the quibble. Well, the public is here the best judge, and it is evidence that as a consumer of the written word, the public is always complaining that it cannot understand what it is asked to read: the government blanks, the instructions on the bottle or gadget, the gobbledygook of every trade, the highbrow jargon of the educators, psychiatrists, and social workers, and—one must also add—the prose of literary critics. The great cry today is for improved communication, mass communication, the arts of communication, and yet under the pretext of being free and easy and above quibbling, those who do the most talking and writing indulge themselves in the very obscurities and ambiguities that cause the outcry.

They are abetted, moreover, by another offspring of the scientific spirit, the professional student of language. In his modern embodiment, the linguist takes the view that whatever occurs in anybody's speech is a fact of language and must not be tampered with, but only caught in flight and pinned on a card. This is "scientific detachment," and it has gone so far that under its influence in many schools all the categories of grammar, syntax, and rhetoric have been discarded. The modern way to learn English or a foreign language is to absorb a phrase-by-phrase enumeration of all that might conceivably be said in ordinary talk—a directory instead of a grammar.

This brings us back to our first difficulty, how to teach the millions the use of their mother tongue *in composition*. We have made nearly everybody literate in the sense of able to read and write words. But that is not writing. Even those who profess disdain for the literary art and the literary quibbles respond automatically to good writing, which they find unexpectedly easy to read and retain, mysteriously "pleasant" as compared with their neighbors' matted prose. The linguists themselves pay lip service to "effective" speech, approving the end while forbidding discrimination among the means.

Now many thousands of people in the United States today exercise this discrimination; there is amid the garbage a steady supply of good writing, modestly done and published—in every newspaper and magazine, over TV and radio, in millions of ads and public notices, in railroad timetables, travel booklets, and printed instructions on objects of daily use. Good writing is good writing wherever it occurs, and some of the impugned comics which are supposed to defile the native well of English in our young are far better than acceptable.

It is therefore idle and erroneous to condemn "the newspapers" or "the radio" en masse. Here too one must discriminate, and the failure to do so is one cause of the trouble—the strange cultural trait whose origin I have sketched and which makes us at once indifferent to our language, full of complaints about it, and irresponsible about mangling it still more. In these conditions people who write well learn to do so by virtue of a strong desire, developed usually under necessity: their job requires lucidity, precision, brevity. If they write advertising copy they must not only make it fit the space but make the words yield the tone.

Tone—that is the starting point of any teaching in composition. What effect are you producing and at what cost of words? The fewer the words, and the more transparent they are, the easier they will be to understand. The closer the ideas they stand for and the more natural their linkage, the more easily will the meaning be retained. Simple in appearance, this formula is yet extremely difficult to apply, and even more arduous to teach. You cannot work on more than one pupil at a time and you must be willing to observe and enter into his mind. On his part, the discipline calls for a thorough immersion in the medium. He must form the habit of attending to words, constructions, accents, and etymologies in everything he reads or hears—just as the painter unceasingly notes line and color and the musician tones. The would-be writer has the harder task because words are entangled with the business of life and he must stand off from it to look at them, hearing at the same time their harmonies and discords. It is an endless duty, which finally becomes automatic. The ideal writer would mentally recast his own death sentence as he was reading it—if it was a bad sentence.

IV

Now such a discipline cannot be imposed from without, and not everybody needs it in full. But its principle, which suffices for ordinary purposes, should be made clear to every beginner, child or adult. Unfortunately, the school system, even when progressive, makes writing an irrational chore approached in the mood of rebellion. The school does this in two ways: by requiring length and by concentrating on correctness. I know very well that correctness was supposedly given up long ago. The modern teacher does not mention it. But if the teacher marks spelling and grammatical errors and speaks of little else, what is a child to think? He gets a mark with the comment "imaginative" or "not imaginative enough" and most often: "too short," and he is left with no more idea of composition than a cow in a field has of landscape painting. How *does* one judge the right length and get it out of a reluctant brain? Nobody answers, except perhaps with the word "creative," which has brought unmerited gloom to many a cheerful child. Who can be creative on demand, by next Tuesday, and in the requisite amount? In all but a few chatterboxes, mental frostbite is the only result.

Meanwhile the things that are teachable, the ways of translating the flashes of thought into consecutive sentences, are neglected. They have been, most often, neglected in the teachers themselves. How do *they* write or speak, what do *they* read? If they read and write educational literature, as they often must for advancement, are they fit to teach composition? And what of the teachers of other subjects, whose professional jargon also infects their speech, what is their countervailing effect on a child to whom a good English teacher has just imparted a notion of the writer's craft? Suppose the teacher of a course on family life has just been reading *Social Casework* and his mind is irradiated with this: "Familial societality is already a settled question biologically, structured in our inherited bodies and physiology, but the answer to those other questions are not yet safely and irrevocably anatomized." Unless this is immediately thrown up like the nux vomica it is, it will contaminate everybody it touches from pupil to public—in fact the whole blooming familial societality.

The cure is harsh and likely to be unpopular, for it must start with self-denial. It can be initiated by the school but it must not stop there. As many of us as possible must work out of our system, first, all the vogue words that almost always means nothing but temporary vacancy of mind—such words as "basic," "major," "over-all," "personal," "values," "exciting" (everything from a new handbag to a new baby); then all the wormy expressions indicative of bad conscience, false modesty, and genteelism, as in: "Frankly, I don't know too much about it"—a typical formula which tries through candor and whining to minimize ignorance while claiming a kind of merit for it; finally, all the tribal adornments which being cast off may disclose the plain man we would like to be: no frames of reference, field theories, or apperception protocols; no texture, prior to, or in terms of; and the least amount of co-ordination, dynamics, and concepts.

After the vocabulary has been cleansed, the patient is ready for what our Canadian friends at the Vancouver conference deplored the lack of in the modern undergraduate: analysis of thought. To show what is meant and let criticism begin at home, I choose an example from a New York City report of 1952 entitled "The English Language Arts." It begins: "Because language arts or English is so—" Stop right there! What are language arts?—A perfectly unnecessary phrase of the pseudo-scientific kind which tries to "cover." Besides, "language arts or English" is nonsense: ever hear of another language? Moreover, "language arts . . . is" doesn't sound like a happy opening for a report by and to English teachers. Let us go on: English is so what? Well, "language arts or English is so intimately connected with all knowledge and all living, it is the subject which most often bursts the dikes separating it from others." What do you mean, language is *connected* with living? And how does English connect with *all* knowledge and *all* living? Is the practical knowledge of the Russian engineer intimately connected with English? Do the amoebas speak English? And if this intimacy does exist, then what are these dikes that separate English from other subjects? Are these subjects no part of "all knowledge" with which English is connected—or rather, of which it too is a part?

Cruel work, but necessary if anything akin to thought is to arise from the written word. The Neanderthal glimmer from which the quoted sentence sprang is irrecoverable but its developed form should run something like this: "English, being a medium of communication, cannot be confined with set limits like other subjects; to the peoples whose speech it is, all theoretical knowledge, and indeed most of life, is inseparable from its use."

And this is so true that it justifies the operation just performed on the specimen of non-thought. For although it is possible to think without words and to communicate by signs, our civilization depends, as I said before, on the written word. Writing is embodied thought, and the thought is clear or muddy, graspable or fugitive, according to the purity of the medium. Communication means one thought held in common. What could be more practical than to try making that thought unmistakable?

As for the receiver, the reader, his pleasure or grief is in direct proportion to the pains taken by the writer; to which one can add that the taking of pains brings its special pleasure. I do not mean the satisfaction of vanity, for after a bout of careful writing one is too tired to care; I mean the new perceptions—sensuous or intellectual or comic—to be held all day long in one's encounters with language. Imagine the fun people miss who find nothing remarkable in the sentence (from Sax Rohmer): "The woman's emotions were too tropical for analysis"; or, who, trusting too far my disallowance of "contact" as a verb, miss the chance of using it at the hottest, stickiest time of year: "On a day like this, I wouldn't contact anybody for the world."

EDUCATION

Philip Stanhope, Lord Chesterfield

THE ART OF PLEASING

LONDON, OCTOBER 16, O.S. 1747

Dear Boy,

The art of pleasing is a very necessary one to possess; but a very difficult one to acquire. It can hardly be reduced to rules; and your own good sense and observation will teach you more of it than I can. Do as you would be done by, is the surest method that I know of pleasing. Observe carefully what pleases you in others, and probably the same things in you will please others. If you are pleased with the complaisance and attention of others to your humours, your tastes, or your weaknesses, depend upon it the same complaisance and attention, on your part to theirs, will equally please them. Take the tone of the company that you are in, and do not pretend to give it; be serious, gay, or even trifling, as you find the present humour of the company; this is an attention due from every individual to the majority. Do not tell stories in company; there is nothing more tedious and disagreeable; if by chance you know a very short story, and exceedingly applicable to the present subject of conversation, tell it in as few words as possible; and even then, throw out that you do not love to tell stories, but that the shortness of it tempted you. Of all things, banish the egotism out of your conversation, and never think of entertaining people with your own personal concerns or private affairs; though they are interesting to you they are tedious and impertinent to everybody else; besides that, one cannot keep one's own private affairs too secret. Whatever you think your own

From *Letters*, first published in 1774.

333

excellencies may be, do not affectedly display them in company; nor labour, as many people do, to give that turn to the conversation, which may supply you with an opportunity of exhibiting them. If they are real, they will infallibly be discovered, without your pointing them out yourself, and with much more advantage. Never maintain an argument with heat and clamour, though you think or know yourself to be in the right; but give your opinion modestly and coolly, which is the only way to convince; and, if that does not do, try to change the conversation, by saying, with good-humour, "We shall hardly convince one another; nor is it necessary that we should, so let us talk of something else."

Remember that there is a local propriety to be observed in all companies; and that what is extremely proper in one company, may be, and often is, highly improper in another.

The jokes, the *bons mots,* the little adventures, which may do very well in one company, will seem flat and tedious when related in another. The particular character, the habits, the cant of one company, may give credit to a word, or a gesture, which would have none at all if divested of those accidental circumstances. Here people very commonly err; and fond of something that has entertained them in one company, and in certain circumstances, repeat it with emphasis in another, where it is either insipid, or, it may be, offensive, by being ill-timed or misplaced. Nay, they often do it with this silly preamble: "I will tell you an excellent thing"; or, "the best thing in the world." This raises expectations, which, when absolutely disappointed, make the relator of this excellent thing look, very deservedly, like a fool.

If you would particularly gain the affection and friendship of particular people, whether men or women, endeavour to find out their predominant excellency, if they have one, and their prevailing weakness, which everybody has; and do justice to the one, and something more than justice to the other. Men have various objects in which they may excel, or at least would be thought to excel; and, though they love to hear justice done to them, where they know that they excel, yet they are most and best flattered upon those points where they wish to excel, and yet are doubtful whether they do or not. As, for example: Cardinal Richelieu, who was undoubtedly the ablest statesman of his time, or perhaps of any other, had the idle vanity of being thought the best poet too: he envied the great Corneille his reputation, and ordered a criticism to be written upon the *Cid.* Those, therefore, who flattered skilfully, said little to him of his abilities in state affairs, or at least but *en passant,* and as it might naturally occur. But the incense which they gave him, the smoke of which they knew would turn his head in their favour, was as a *bel esprit* and a poet. Why? Because he was sure of one excellency, and distrustful as to the other. You will easily discover every man's prevailing vanity, by observing his favourite topic of conversation; for every man talks most of what he has most a mind to be thought to excel in. Touch him but there, and you touch him to the quick. The late Sir Robert Walpole (who was certainly an able man) was little open to flattery upon that head; for he was in no doubt himself about it; but his prevailing weakness was, to be thought to have a polite and happy turn to gallantry—of which he had undoubtedly less than any man living: it was his favourite and frequent subject of conversation; which proved, to those who had any penetration, that it was his prevailing weakness. And they applied to it with success.

Women have, in general, but one object, which is their beauty; upon which, scarce any flattery is too gross for them to swallow. Nature has hardly formed a woman ugly enough to be insensible to flattery upon her person; if her face is so shocking, that she must in some degree be conscious of it, her figure and air, she trusts, make ample amends for it. If her figure is deformed, her face, she thinks, counterbalances it. If they are both bad, she comforts herself that she has graces; a certain manner; a *je ne sçais quoi*, still more engaging than beauty. This truth is evident, from the studied and elaborate dress of the ugliest women in the world. An undoubted, uncontested, conscious beauty is, of all women, the least sensible of flattery upon that head; she knows that it is her due, and is therefore obliged to nobody for giving it her. She must be flattered upon her understanding; which, though she may possibly not doubt of herself, yet she suspects that men may distrust.

Do not mistake me, and think that I mean to recommend to you abject and criminal flattery: no; flatter nobody's vices or crimes: on the contrary, abhor and discourage them. But there is no living in the world without a complaisant indulgence for people's weaknesses, and innocent, though ridiculous, vanities. If a man has a mind to be thought wiser, and a woman handsomer, than they really are, their error is a comfortable one to themselves, and an innocent one with regard to other people; and I would rather make them my friends, by indulging them in it, than my enemies, by endeauvouring (and that to no purpose) to undeceive them.

There are little attentions likewise, which are infinitely engaging, and which sensibly affect that degree of pride and self-love, which is inseparable from human nature; as they are unquestionable proofs of the regard and consideration which we have for the persons to whom we pay them. As, for example, to observe the little habits, the likings, the antipathies, and the tastes of those whom we would gain; and then take care to provide them with the one, and to secure them from the other; giving them, genteelly, to understand, that you had observed they liked such a dish, or such a room; for which reason you had prepared it: or, on the contrary, that having observed they had an aversion to such a dish, a dislike to such a person, etc., you had taken care to avoid presenting them. Such attention to such trifles flatters self-love much more than greater things, as it makes people think themselves almost the only objects of your thoughts and care.

These are some of the *arcana* necessary for your initiation in the great society of the world. I wish I had known them better at your age; I have paid the price of three and fifty years for them, and shall not grudge it, if you reap the advantage. Adieu.

Henry David Thoreau

WHERE I LIVED AND WHAT I LIVED FOR

At a certain season of our life we are accustomed to consider every spot as the possible site of a house. I have thus surveyed the country on every side within a dozen miles of where I live. In imagination I have bought all the farms in succession, for all were to be bought, and I knew their price. I walked over each farmer's premises, tasted his wild apples, discoursed on husbandry with him, took his farm at his price, at any price, mortgaging it to him in my mind; even put a higher price on it,—took everything but a deed of it,—took his word for his deed, for I dearly love to talk,—cultivated it, and him too to some extent, I trust, and withdraw when I had enjoyed it long enough, leaving him to carry it on. This experience entitled me to be regarded as a sort of real-estate broker by my friends. Wherever I sat, there I might live, and the landscape radiated from me accordingly. What is a house but a *sedes*, a seat?—better if a country seat. I discovered many a site for a house not likely to be soon improved, which some might have thought too far from the village, but to my eyes

From *Walden*, by Henry David Thoreau. First published in 1854.

the village was too far from it. Well, there I might live, I said; and there I did live, for an hour, a summer and a winter life; saw how I could let the years run off, buffet the winter through, and see the spring come in. The future inhabitants of this region, wherever they may place their houses, may be sure that they have been anticipated. An afternoon sufficed to lay out the land into orchard, woodlot, and pasture, and to decide what fine oaks or pines should be left to stand before the door, and whence each blasted tree could be seen to the best advantage; and then I let it lie, fallow perchance, for a man is rich in proportion to the number of things which he can afford to let alone.

My imagination carried me so far that I even had the refusal of several farms,—the refusal was all I wanted,—but I never got my fingers burned by actual possession. The nearest that I came to actual possession was when I bought the Hollowell place, and had begun to sort my seeds, and collected materials with which to make a wheelbarrow to carry it on or off with; but before the owner gave me a deed of it, his wife—every man has such a wife—changed her mind and wished to keep it, and he offered me ten dollars to release him. Now, to speak the truth, I had but ten cents in the world, and it surpassed my arithmetic to tell, if I was that man who had ten cents, or who had a farm, or ten dollars, or all together. However, I let him keep the ten dollars and the farm too, for I had carried it far enough; or rather, to be generous, I sold him the farm for just what I gave for it, and, as he was not a rich man, made him a present of ten dollars, and still had my ten cents, and seeds, and materials for a wheelbarrow left. I found thus that I had been a rich man without any damage to my poverty. But I retained the landscape, and I have since annually carried off what it yielded without a wheelbarrow. With respect to landscapes,—

> "I am monarch of all I *survey,*
> My right there is none to dispute."

I have frequently seen a poet withdraw, having enjoyed the most valuable part of a farm, while the crusty farmer supposed that he had got a few wild apples only. Why, the owner does not know it for many years when a poet has put his farm in rhyme, the most admirable kind of invisible fence, has fairly impounded it, milked it, skimmed it, and got all the cream, and left the farmer only the skimmed milk.

The real attractions of the Hollowell farm, to me, were; its complete retirement, being about two miles from the village, half a mile from the nearest neighbor, and separated from the highway by a broad field; its bounding on the river, which the owner said protected it by its fogs from frosts in the spring, though that was nothing to me; the gray color and ruinous state of the house and barn, and the dilapidated fences, which put such an interval between me and the last occupant; the hollow and lichen-covered apple trees, gnawed by rabbits, showing what kind of neighbors I should have; but above all, the recollection I had of it from my earliest voyages up the river, when the house was concealed behind a dense grove of red maples, through which I heard the house-dog bark. I was in haste to buy it, before the proprietor finished getting out some rocks, cutting down the hollow apple trees, and grubbing up some young birches which had sprung up in the pasture, or, in short, had made any more of his improvements. To enjoy these advantages I was ready to carry it on; like Atlas, to take the world on my shoulders,—I never heard what compensation he received for that,—and do all those things which had no other motive or excuse but that I might pay for it and be unmolested in my possession of it; for I knew all the while that it would yield the most abundant crop of the kind I wanted if I could only afford to let it alone. But it turned out as I have said.

All that I could say, then, with respect to farming on a large scale, (I have always cultivated a garden,) was, that I had had my seeds ready. Many think that seeds improve with age. I have no doubt that time discriminates between the good and the bad: and when at last I shall plant, I shall be less likely to be disappointed. But I would say to my fellows, once for all, As long as possible live free and uncommitted. It makes but little difference whether you are committed to a farm or the county jail.

Old Cato, whose "De Re Rustica" is my "Cultivator," says, and the only translation I have seen makes sheer nonsense of the passage, "When you think of getting a farm, turn it thus in your mind, not to buy greedily; nor spare your pains to look at it, and do not think it enough to go around it once. The oftener you go there the more it will please you, if it is good." I think I shall not buy greedily, but go round and round it as long as I live, and be buried in it first, that it may please me the more at last.

The present was my next experiment of this kind, which I purpose to describe more at length; for convenience, putting the experience of two years into one. As I have said, I do not propose to write an ode to dejection, but to brag as lustily as chanticleer in the morning, standing on his roost, if only to wake my neighbors up.

When first I took up my abode in the woods, that is, began to spend my nights as well as days there, which, by accident, was on Independence day, or the fourth of July, 1845, my house was not finished for winter, but was merely a defence against the rain, without plastering or chimney, the walls being of rough weather-stained boards, with wide chinks, which made it cool at night. The upright white hewn studs and freshly planed door and window casings gave it a clean airy look, especially in the morning, when its timbers were saturated with dew, so that I fancied that by noon some sweet gum would exude from them. To my imagination it retained throughout the day more or less of this auroral character, reminding me of a certain house on a mountain which I had visited the year before. This was an airy and unplastered cabin, fit to entertain a travelling god, and where a goddess might trail her garments. The winds which passed over my dwelling were such as sweep over the ridges of mountains, bearing the broken strains, or celestial parts only, of terrestrial music. The morning wind forever blows, the poem of creation is uninterrupted; but few are the ears that hear it. Olympus is but the outside of the earth everywhere.

The only house I had been the owner of before, if I except a boat, was a tent, which I used occasionally when making excursions in the summer, and this is still rolled up in my garret; but the boat, after passing from hand to hand, has gone down the stream of time. With this more substantial shelter about me, I had made some progress toward settling in the world. This frame, so slightly clad, was a sort of crystallization around me, and reacted on the builder. It was suggestive somewhat as a picture in outlines. I did not need to go out doors to take the air, for the atmosphere within had lost none of its freshness. It was not so much within doors as behind a door where I sat, even in the rainiest weather. The Harivansa says, "An abode without birds is like a meat without seasoning." Such was not my abode, for I found myself suddenly neighbor to the birds; not by having imprisoned one, but having caged myself near them. I was not only nearer to some of those which commonly frequent the garden and the orchard, but to those wilder and more thrilling songsters of the forest which never, or rarely, serenade a villager,—the woodthrush, the veery, the scarlet tanager, the field-sparrow, the whippoorwill, and many others.

I was seated by the shore of a small pond, about a mile and a half south of the village of Concord and somewhat higher than it, in the midst of an extensive wood between that town and Lincoln, and about two miles south of that our only field known to fame, Concord Battle Ground; but I was so low in the woods that the opposite shore, half a mile off, like the rest, covered with wood, was my most distant horizon. For the first week, whenever I looked out on the pond it impressed me like a tarn high up on the side of a mountain, its bottom far above the surface of other lakes, and, as the sun arose, I saw it throwing off its nightly clothing of mist, and here and there, by degrees, its soft ripples or its smooth reflecting surface was revealed, while the mists, like ghosts, were stealthily withdrawing in every direction into the woods, as at the breaking up of some nocturnal conventicle. The very dew seemed to hang upon the trees later into the day than usual, as on the sides of mountains.

This small lake was of most value as a neighbor in the intervals of a gentle rain storm in August, when, both air and water being perfectly still, but the sky overcast, mid-afternoon had all the serenity of evening, and the woodthrush sang around, and was heard from shore to shore. A lake like this is never smoother than at such a time; and the clear portion of the air above it being shallow and darkened by clouds, the water, full of light and reflections, becomes a lower heaven itself so much the more important. From a hill top near by, where the wood had been recently cut off, there was a pleasing vista southward across the pond, through a wide indentation in the hills which form the shore there, where their opposite sides sloping toward each other suggested a stream flowing out in that direction through a wooded valley, but stream there was none. That way I looked between and over the near green hills to some distant and higher ones in the horizon, tinged with blue. Indeed, by standing on tiptoe I could catch a glimpse of some of the peaks of the still bluer and more distant mountain ranges in the northwest, those true-blue coins from heaven's own mint, and also of some portion of the village. But in other directions, even from this point, I could not see over or beyond the woods which surrounded me. It is well to have some water in your neighborhood, to give buoyancy to and float the earth. One value even of the smallest well is, that when you look into it you see that earth is not continent but insular. This is as important as that it keeps butter cool. When I looked across the pond from this peak toward the Sudbury meadows, which in time of flood I distinguished elevated perhaps by a mirage in their seething valley, like a coin in a basin, all the earth beyond the pond appeared like a thin crust insulated and floated even by this small sheet in intervening water, and I was reminded that this on which I dwelt was but *dry land*.

Though the view from my door was still more contracted, I did not feel crowded or confined in the least. There was pasture enough for my imagination. The low shrub-oak plateau to which the opposite shore arose, stretched away toward the prairies of the West and the steppes of Tartary, affording ample room for all the roving families of men. "There are none happy in the world but beings who enjoy freely a vast horizon,"—said Damodara, when his herds required new and larger pastures.

Both place and time were changed, and I dwelt nearer to those parts of the universe and to those eras in history which had most attracted me. Where I lived was as far off as many a region viewed nightly by astronomers. We are wont to imagine rare and delectable places in some remote and more celestial corner of the system, behind the constellation of Cassiopeia's Chair, far from noise and disturbance. I discovered that my house actually had its site in such a withdrawn, but forever new and unprofaned, part of the universe. If it were worth the while to settle in those parts near to the Pleiades or the Hyades, to Aldebaran or Altair, then I was really there, or at an equal remoteness from the life which I had left behind, dwindled and twinkling with as fine a ray to my nearest neighbor, and to be seen only in moonless nights by him. Such was that part of creation where I had squatted;—

> "There was a shepherd that did live,
> And held his thoughts as high
> As were the mounts whereon his flocks
> Did hourly feed him by;"

What should we think of the shepherd's life if his flocks always wandered to higher pastures than his thoughts?

Every morning was a cheerful invitation to make my life of equal simplicity, and I may say innocence, with Nature herself. I have been as sincere a worshipper of Aurora as the Greeks. I got up early and bathed in the pond; that was a religious exercise, and one of the best things which I did. They say that characters were engraven on the bathing tub of king Tching-thang to this effect: "Renew thyself completely each day; do it again and again, and forever again." I can understand that. Morning brings back the heroic ages. I was as much affected by the faint hum of a mosquito making its invisible and unimaginable tour through my apartments at earliest dawn, when I was sitting with door and windows open, as I could be by any trumpet that ever sang of fame. It was Homer's requiem; itself an Iliad and Odyssey in the air, singing its own wrath and wanderings. There was something cosmical about it; a standing advertisement, till forbidden, of the everlasting vigor and fertility of the world. The morning, which is the most memorable season of the day, is the awakening hour.

Then there is least somnolence in us; and for an hour, at least, some part of us awakes which slumbers all the rest of the day and night. Little is to be expected of that day, if it can be called a day, to which we are not awakened by our Genius, but by the mechanical nudgings of some servitor, are not awakened by our own newly-acquired force and aspirations from within, accompanied by the undulations of celestial music, instead of factory bells, and a fragrance filling the air—to a higher life than we fell asleep from; and thus the darkness bear its fruit, and prove itself to be good, no less than the light. That man who does not believe that each day contains an earlier, more sacred, and auroral hour than he has yet pro-faned, has despaired of life, and is pursuing a descending and darkening way. After a partial cessation of his sensuous life, the soul of man, or its organs rather, are reinvigorated each day, and his Genius tries again what noble life it can make. All memorable events, I should say, transpire in morning time and in a morning atmosphere. The Vedas say, "All intelli-gences awake with the morning." Poetry and art, and the fairest and most memorable of the actions of men, date from such an hour. All poets and heroes, like Memnon, are the children of Aurora, and emit their music at sunrise. To him whose elastic and vigorous thought keeps pace with the sun, the day is a perpetual morning. It matters not what the clocks say or the attitudes and labors of men. Morning is when I am awake and there is a dawn in me. Moral reform is the effort to throw off sleep. Why is it that men give so poor an account of their day if they have not been slum-bering? They are not such poor calculators. If they had not been overcome with drowsiness they would have performed something. The millions are awake enough for physical labor; but only one in a million is awake enough for effective intellectual exertion, only one in a hundred millions to a poetic or divine life. To be awake is to be alive. I have never yet met a man who was quite awake. How could I have looked him in the face?

We must learn to reawaken and keep ourselves awake, not by mechani-cal aids, but by an infinite expectation of the dawn, which does not forsake us in our soundest sleep. I know of no more encouraging fact than the un-questionable ability of man to elevate his life by a conscious endeavor. It is something to be able to paint a particular picture, or to carve a statue, and so to make a few objects beautiful; but it is far more glorious to carve and paint the very atmosphere and medium through which we look, which morally we can do. To affect the quality of the day, that is the highest of arts. Every man is tasked to make his life, even in its details, worthy of the contemplation of his most elevated and critical hour. If we refused, or rather used up, such paltry information as we get, the oracles would distinctly inform us how this might be done.

I went to the woods because I wished to live deliberately, to front only the essential facts of life, and see if I could not learn what it had to teach, and not, when I came to die, discover that I had not lived. I did not wish to live what was not life, living is so dear; nor did I wish to practise resignation, unless it was quite necessary. I wanted to live deep and suck out all the marrow of life, to live so sturdily and Spartan-like as to put to rout all that was not life, to cut a broad swath and shave close, to drive life into a corner, and reduce it to its lowest terms, and, if it proved to be mean, why then to get the whole and genuine meanness of it, and publish its meanness to the world; or if it were sublime, to know it by experience, and be able to give a true account of it in my next excursion. For most men, it appears to me, are in a strange uncertainty about it, whether it is of the devil or of God, and have *somewhat hastily* concluded that it is the chief end of man here to "glorify God and enjoy him forever."

Still we live meanly, like ants; though the fable tells us that we were long ago changed into men; like pygmies we fight with cranes; it is error upon error, and clout upon clout, and our best virtue has for its occasion a superfluous and evitable wretchedness. Our life is frittered away by detail. An honest man has hardly need to count more than his ten fingers, or in extreme cases he may add his ten toes, and lump the rest. Simplicity, simplicity, simplicity! I say, let your affairs be as two or three, and not a hundred or a thousand; instead of a million count half a dozen, and keep your accounts on your thumb nail. In the midst of this chopping sea of civilized life, such are the clouds and storms and quicksands and thousand-and-one items to be allowed for, that a man has to live, if he would not founder and go to the bottom and not make his port at all, by dead reckoning, and he must be a great calculator indeed who succeeds. Simplify, simplify. Instead of three meals a day, if it be necessary eat but one; instead of a hundred dishes, five; and reduce other things in proportion. Our life is like a German Confederacy, made up of petty states, with its boundary forever fluctuating, so that even a German cannot tell you how it is bounded at any moment. The nation itself, with all its so called internal improvements, which, by the way, are all external and superficial, is just such an unwieldy and overgrown establishment, cluttered with furniture and tripped up by its own traps, ruined by luxury and heedless expense, by want of calculation and a worthy aim, as the million households in the land; and the only cure for it as for them is in a rigid economy, a stern and more than Spartan simplicity of life and elevation of purpose. It lives too fast. Men think that it is essential that the *Nation* have commerce, and export ice, and talk through a telegraph, and ride thirty miles an hour, without a doubt, whether *they* do or not; but whether we should live like baboons or like men, is a little uncertain. If we do not get out sleepers, and forge rails, and devote days and nights to the work, but go to tinkering upon our *lives* to improve *them,* who will build railroads? And if railroads are not built, how shall we get to heaven in season? But if we stay at home and mind our business, who will want railroads? We do not ride on the railroad; it rides upon us. Did you ever think what those sleepers are that underlie the railroad? Each one is a man, an Irishman, or a Yankee man. The rails are laid on them, and they are covered with sand, and the cars run smoothly over them. They are sound sleepers I assure you. And every few years a new lot is laid down and run over; so that, if some have the pleasure of riding on a rail, others have the misfortune to be ridden upon. And when they run over a man that is walking in his sleep, a supernumerary sleeper in the wrong position, and wake him up, they suddenly stop the cars, and make a hue and cry about it, as if this were an exception. I am glad to know that it takes a gang of men for every five miles to keep the sleepers down and level in their beds as it is, for this is a sign that they may sometime get up again.

Why should we live with such hurry and waste of life? We are determined to be starved before we are hungry. Men say that a stitch in time saves nine, and so they take a thousand stitches today to save nine tomorrow. As for *work,* we haven't any of any consequence. We have the Saint Vitus' dance, and cannot possibly keep our heads still. If I should only give a few pulls at the parish bell-rope, as for a fire, that is, without setting the bell, there is hardly a man on his farm in the outskirts of Concord, notwithstanding that press of engagements which was his excuse so many times this morning, nor a boy, nor a woman, I might almost say, but would forsake all and follow that sound, not mainly to save property from the flames, but, if we will confess the truth, much more to see it burn, since burn it must, and we, be it known, did not set it on fire,—or to see it put out, and have a hand in it, if that is done as handsomely; yes, even if it were the parish church itself. Hardly a man takes a half hour's nap after dinner but when he wakes he holds up his head and asks, "What's the news?" as if the rest of mankind has stood his sentinels. Some give directions to be waked every half hour, doubtless for no other purpose; and then, to pay for it, they tell what they have dreamed. After a night's sleep the news is as indispensable as the breakfast. "Pray tell me any thing new that has happened to a man any where on this globe,"—and he reads it over his coffee and rolls, that a man has had his eyes gouged out this morning on the Wachito River; never dreaming the while that he lives in the dark unfathomed mammoth cave of this world, and has but the rudiment of an eye himself.

For my part, I could easily do without the post-office. I think that there are very few important communications made through it. To speak critically, I never received more than one or two letters in my life—I wrote this some years ago—that were worth the postage. The penny-post is, commonly, an institution through which you seriously offer a man that penny for his thoughts which is too often safely offered in jest. And I am sure that I never read any memorable news in a newspaper. If we read of one man robbed, or murdered, or killed by accident, or one house burned, or one vessel wrecked, or one steamboat blown up, or one cow run over on the Western Railroad, or one mad dog killed, or one lot of grasshoppers in the winter,—we never need read of another. One is enough. If you are acquainted with the principle, what do you care for a myriad instances and applications? To a philosopher all *news,* as it is called, is gossip, and they who edit and read it are old women over their tea. Yet not a few are greedy after this gossip. There was such a rush, as I hear, the other day at one of the offices to learn the foreign news by the last arrival, that several large squares of plate glass belonging to the establishment were broken by the pressure,—news which I seriously think a ready wit might write a twelvemonth, or twelve years, beforehand with sufficient accuracy. As for Spain, for instance, if you know how to throw in Don Carlos and the Infanta, and Don Pedro and Seville and Granada, from time to time in the right proportions,—they may have changed the names a little since I saw the paper,—and serve up a bull-fight when other entertainments fail, it will be true to the letter, and give us as good an idea of the exact state or ruin of things in Spain as the most succinct and lucid reports under this head in the newspapers; and as for England, almost the last significant scrap of news from that quarter was the revolution of 1649; and if you have learned the history of her crops for an average year, you never need attend to that thing again, unless your speculations are of a merely pecuniary character. If one may judge who rarely looks into the newspapers, nothing new does ever happen in foreign parts, a French revolution not excepted.

What news! how much more important to know what that is which was never old! "Kieou-he-yu (great dignitary of the state of Wei) sent a

man to Khoung-tseu to know his news. Khoung-tseu caused the messenger to be seated near him, and questioned him in these terms: What is
your master doing? The messenger answered with respect: My master
desires to diminish the number of his faults, but he cannot come to the end
of them. The messenger being gone, the philosopher remarked: What a
worthy messenger! What a worthy messenger!" The preacher, instead of
vexing the ears of drowsy farmers on their day of rest at the end of the
week,—for *Sunday is the fit conclusion of an ill-spent week, and not the
fresh and brave beginning of a new one,*—with this one other draggletail
of a sermon, should shout with thundering voice,—"Pause! Avast! Why
so seeming fast, but deadly slow?"

Shams and delusions are esteemed for soundest truths, while reality is
fabulous. If men would steadily observe realities only, and not allow themselves to be deluded, life, to compare it with such things as we know,
would be like a fairy tale and the Arabian Nights' Entertainments. If we
respected only what is inevitable and has a right to be, music and poetry
would resound along the streets. When we are unhurried and wise, we
perceive that only great and worthy things have any permanent and absolute existence,—that petty fears and petty pleasures are but the shadow
of the reality. This is always exhilarating and sublime. By closing the eyes
and slumbering, and consenting to be deceived by shows, men establish
and confirm their daily life of routine and habit everywhere, which still is
built on purely illusory foundations. Children, who play life, discern its
true law and relations more clearly than men, who fail to live it worthily,
but who think that they are wiser by experience, that is, by failure. I have
read in a Hindoo book, that "there was a king's son, who, being expelled
in infancy from his native city, was brought up by a forester, and, growing up to maturity in that state, imagined himself to belong to the bar-
barous race with which he lived. One of his father's ministers having discovered him, revealed to him what he was, and the misconception of his
character was removed, and he knew himself to be a prince. So the soul,"
continues the Hindoo philosopher, "from the circumstances in which it is
placed, mistakes its own character, until the truth is revealed to it by some
holy teacher, and then it knows itself to be *Brahme.*" I perceive that we inhabitants of New England live this mean life that we do because our
vision does not penetrate the surface of things. (We think that that *is*
which *appears* to be.) If a man should walk through this town and see only
the reality, where, think you, would the "Mill-dam" go to? If he should
give us an account of the realities he beheld there, we should not recognize

the place in his description. Look at a meeting-house, or a court-house, or a jail, or a shop, or a dwelling-house, and say what that thing really is before a true gaze, and they would all go to pieces in your account of them. Men esteem truth remote, in the outskirts of the system, behind the farthest star, before Adam and after the last man. In eternity there is indeed something true and sublime. But all these times and places and occasions are now and here. God himself culminates in the present moment, and will never be more divine in the lapse of all the ages. And we are enabled to apprehend at all what is sublime and noble only by the perpetual instilling and drenching of the reality that surrounds us. The universe constantly and obediently answers to our conceptions; whether we travel fast or slow, the track is laid for us. Let us spend our lives in conceiving them. The poet or the artist never yet had so fair and noble a design but some of his posterity at least could accomplish it.

Let us spend one day as deliberately as Nature, and not be thrown off the track by every nutshell and mosquito's wing that falls on the rails. Let us rise early and fast, or breakfast, gently and without perturbation; let company come and let company go, let the bells ring and the children cry, —determined to make a day of it. Why should we knock under and go with the stream? Let us not be upset and overwhelmed in that terrible rapid and whirlpool called a dinner, situated in the meridian shallows. Weather this danger and you are safe, for the rest of the way is down hill. With unrelaxed nerves, with morning vigor, sail by it, looking another way, tied to the mast like Ulysses. If the engine whistles, let it whistle till it is hoarse for its pains. If the bell rings, why should we run? We will consider what kind of music they are like. Let us settle ourselves, and work and wedge our feet downward through the mud and slush of opinion, and prejudice, and tradition, and delusion, and appearances, that alluvion which covers the globe, through Paris and London, through New York and Boston and Concord, through church and state, through poetry and philosophy and religion, till we come to a hard bottom and rocks in place, which we can call *reality,* and say, This is, and no mistake; and then begin, having a *point d'appui,* below freshet and frost and fire, a place where you might found a wall or a state, or set a lamp-post safely, or perhaps a gauge, not a Nilometer, but a Realometer, that future ages might know how deep a freshet of shams and appearances had gathered from time to time. If you stand right fronting and face to face to a fact, you will see the sun glimmer on both its surfaces, as if it were a scimiter, and feel its sweet edges dividing you through the heart and marrow, and so you will happily conclude your mortal career. Be it life or death, we crave only reality. If we are really dying, let us hear the rattle in our throats and feel cold in the extremities; if we are alive, let us go about our business.

Time is but the stream I go a-fishing in. I drink at it; but while I drink I see the sandy bottom and detect how shallow it is. Its thin current slides away, but eternity remains. I would drink deeper; fish in the sky, whose bottom is pebbly with stars. I cannot count one. I know not the first letter of the alphabet. I have always been regretting that I was not as wise as the day I was born. The intellect is a cleaver; it discerns and rifts its way into the secret of things. I do not wish to be any more busy with my hands than is necessary. My head is hands and feet. I feel all my best faculties concentrated in it. My instinct tells me that my head is an organ for burrowing, as some creatures use their snout and fore-paws, and with it I would mine and burrow my way through these hills. I think that the richest vein is somewhere hereabouts; so by the divining rod and thin rising vapors I judge; and here I will begin to mine.

John Henry Newman

WHAT IS A UNIVERSITY?

IF I WERE ASKED TO DESCRIBE AS BRIEFLY AND POPULARLY AS I COULD, what a University was, I should draw my answer from its ancient designation of a *Studium Generale* or "School of Universal Learning." This description implies the assemblage of strangers from all parts in one spot;— *from all parts;* else, how will you find professors and students for every department of knowledge? and *in one spot;* else, how can there be any school at all? Accordingly, in its simple and rudimental form, it is a school of knowledge of every kind, consisting of teachers and learners from every quarter. Many things are requisite to complete and satisfy the idea embodied in this description; but such as this a University seems to be in its essence, a place for the communication and circulation of thought, by means of personal intercourse, through a wide extent of country.

There is nothing far-fetched or unreasonable in the idea thus presented

From *Lectures on Universities,* by John Henry Newman, 1859.

to us; and if this be a University, then a University does but contemplate a necessity of our nature, and is but one specimen in a particular medium, out of many which might be adduced in others, of a provision for that necessity. Mutual education, in a large sense of the word, is one of the great and incessant occupations of human society, carried on partly with set purpose, and partly not. One generation forms another; and the existing generation is ever acting and reacting upon itself in the persons of its individual members. Now, in this process, books, I need scarcely say, that is, the *litera scripta,* are one special instrument. It is true; and emphatically so in this age. Considering the prodigious powers of the press, and how they are developed at this time in the never-intermitting issue of periodicals, tracts, pamphlets, works in series, and light literature, we must allow there never was a time which promised fairer for dispensing with every other means of information and instruction. What can we want more, you will say, for the intellectual education of the whole man, and for every man, than so exuberant and diversified and persistent a promulgation of all kinds of knowledge? Why, you will ask, need we go up to knowledge, when knowledge comes down to us? The Sibyl wrote her prophecies upon the leaves of the forest, and wasted them; but here such careless profusion might be prudently indulged, for it can be afforded without loss, in consequence of the almost fabulous fecundity of the instrument which these latter ages have invented. We have sermons in stones, and books in the running brooks; works larger and more comprehensive than those which have gained for ancients an immortality, issue forth every morning, and are projected onwards to the ends of the earth at the rate of hundreds of miles a day. Our seats are strewed, our pavements are powdered, with swarms of little tracts; and the very bricks of our city walls preach wisdom, by informing us by their placards where we can at once cheaply purchase it.

I allow all this, and much more; such certainly is our popular education, and its effects are remarkable. Nevertheless, after all, even in this age, whenever men are really serious about getting what, in the language of trade, is called "a good article," when they aim at something precise, something refined, something really luminous, something really large, something choice, they go to another market; they avail themselves, in some shape or other, of the rival method, the ancient method, of oral instruction, of present communication between man and man, of teachers instead of learning, of the personal influence of a master, and the humble initiation of a disciple, and, in consequence, of great centres of pilgrimage and throng, which such a method of education necessarily involves. This, I think, will be found to hold good in all those departments or aspects of society, which possess an interest sufficient to bind men together, or to constitute what is called "a world." It holds in the political world, and in the high world, and in the religious world; and it holds also in the literary and scientific world.

If the actions of men may be taken as any test of their convictions, then we have reason for saying this, viz.—that the province and the inestimable benefit of the *litera scripta* is that of being a record of truth, and an authority of appeal, and an instrument of teaching in the hands of a teacher; but that, if we wish to become exact and fully furnished in any branch of knowledge which is diversified and complicated, we must consult the living man and listen to his living voice. I am not bound to investigate the cause of this, and anything I may say will, I am conscious, be short of its full analysis—perhaps we may suggest, that no books can get through the number of minute questions which it is possible to ask on any extended subject, or can hit upon the very difficulties which are severally felt by each reader in succession. Or again, that no book can convey the special spirit and delicate peculiarities of its subject with that rapidity and certainty which attend on the sympathy of mind with mind, through the eyes, the look, the accent, and the manner, in casual expressions thrown off at the moment, and the unstudied turns of familiar conversation. But I am already dwelling too long on what is but an incidental portion of my main subject. Whatever be the cause, the fact is undeniable. The general principles of any study you may learn by books at home; but the detail, the colour, the tone, the air, the life which makes it live in us, you must catch all these from those in whom it lives already. You must imitate the student in French or German, who is not content with his grammar, but goes to Paris or Dresden: you must take example from the young artist, who aspires to visit the great Masters in Florence and in Rome. Till we have discovered some intellectual daguerreotype, which takes off the course of thought, and the form, lineaments, and features of truth, as completely and minutely, as the optical instrument reproduces the sensible object, we must come to the teachers of wisdom to learn wisdom, we must repair to the fountain, and drink there. Portions of it may go from thence to the ends of the earth by means of books; but the fulness is in one place alone. It is in such assemblages and congregations of intellect that books themselves, the masterpieces of human genius, are written, or at least originated.

The principle on which I have been insisting is so obvious, and in-

stances in point are so ready, that I should think it tiresome to proceed
with the subject, except that one or two illustrations may serve to explain
my own language about it, which may not have done justice to the doctrine which it has been intended to enforce.

For instance, the polished manners and high-bred bearing which are so
difficult of attainment, and so strictly personal when attained,—which
are so much admired in society, from society are acquired. All that goes to
constitute a gentleman—the carriage, gait, address, gestures, voice; the
ease, the self-possession, the courtesy, the power of conversing, the talent
of not offending; the lofty principle, the delicacy of thought, the happiness of expression, the taste and propriety, the generosity and forebearance,
the candour and consideration, the openness of hand;—these qualities,
some of them come by nature, some of them may be found in any rank,
some of them are a direct precept of Christianity; but the full assemblage
of them, bound up in the unity of an individual character, do we expect
they can be learned from books? Are they not necessarily acquired, where
they are to be found, in high society? The very nature of the case leads us
to say so; you cannot fence without an antagonist, nor challenge all comers
in disputation before you have supported a thesis; and in like manner, it
stands to reason, you cannot learn to converse till you have the world to
converse with; you cannot unlearn your natural bashfulness, or awkward-
ness, or stiffness, or other besetting deformity, till you serve your time in
some school of manners. Well, and is it not so in matter of fact? The metropolis, the court, the great houses of the land, are the centres to which at
stated times the country comes up, as to shrines of refinement and good
taste; and then in due time the country goes back again home, enriched
with a portion of the social accomplishments, which those very visits serve
to call out and heighten in the gracious dispensers of them. We are unable
to conceive how the "gentlemanlike" can otherwise be maintained; and
maintained in this way it is.

And now a second instance: and here too I am going to speak without
personal experience of the subject I am introducing. I admit I have not
been in Parliament, any more than I have figured in the *beau monde;*
yet I cannot but think that statesmanship, as well as high breeding, is
learned, not by books, but in certain centres of education. If it be not
presumption to say so, Parliament puts a clever man *au courant* with
politics and affairs of state in a way surprising to himself. A member of
the Legislature, if tolerably observant, begins to see things with new eyes,
even though his views undergo no change. Words have a meaning now,

and ideas a reality, such as they had not before. He hears a vast deal in public speeches and private conversation, which is never put into print. The bearings of measures and events, the action of parties, and the persons of friends and enemies, are brought out to the man who is in the midst of them with a distinctness, which the most diligent perusal of newspapers will fail to impart to them. It is access to the fountain-heads of political wisdom and experience, it is daily intercourse, of one kind or another, with the multitude who go up to them, it is familiarity with business, it is access to the contributions of fact and opinion thrown together by many witnesses from many quarters, which does this for him. However, I need not account for a fact, to which it is sufficient to appeal; that the Houses of Parliament and the atmosphere around them are a sort of University of politics.

As regards the world of science, we find a remarkable instance of the principle which I am illustrating, in the periodical meetings for its advance, which have arisen in the course of the last twenty years, such as the British Association. Such gatherings would to many persons appear at first sight simply preposterous. Above all subjects of study, Science is conveyed, is propagated, by books, or by private teaching; experiments and investigations are conducted in silence; discoveries are made in solitude. What have philosophers to do with festive celebrities, and panegyrical solemnities with mathematical and physical truth? Yet on a closer attention to the subject, it is found that not even scientific thought can dispense with the suggestions, the instruction, the simulus, the sympathy, the intercourse with mankind on a large scale, which such meetings secure. A fine time of year is chosen, when days are long, skies are bright, the earth smiles, and all nature rejoices; a city or town is taken by turns, of ancient name or modern opulence, where buildings are spacious and hospitality hearty. The novelty of place and circumstance, the excitement of strange, or the refreshment of well-known faces, the majesty of rank or of genius, the amiable charities of men pleased both with themselves and with each other; the elevated spirits, the circulation of thought, the curiosity; the morning sections, the outdoor exercise, the well-furnished, well-earned board, the not ungraceful hilarity, the evening circle; the brilliant lecture, the discussions or collisions or guesses of great men one with another, the narratives of scientific processes, of hopes, disappointments, conflicts, and successes, the splendid eulogistic orations; these and the like constituents of the annual celebration, are considered to do something real and substantial for the advance of knowledge which can be done in no other way. Of course they can but be occasional; they answer to the annual Act, or Commencement, or Commemoration of a University, not to its ordinary condition; but they are of a University nature; and I can well believe in their utility. They issue in the promotion of a certain living and, as it were, bodily communication of knowledge from one to another, of a general interchange of ideas, and a comparison and adjustment of science with science, of an enlargement of mind, intellectual and social, of an ardent love of the particular study, which may be chosen by each individual, and a noble devotion to its interests.

Such meetings, I repeat, are but periodical, and only partially represent the idea of a University. The bustle and whirl which are their usual concomitants, are in ill keeping with the order and gravity of earnest intellectual education. We desiderate means of instruction which involve no interruption of our ordinary habits; nor need we seek it long, for the natural course of things bring it about, while we debate over it. In every great country, the metropolis itself becomes a sort of necessary University, whether we will or no. As the chief city is the seat of the court, of high society, of politics, and of law, so as a matter of course is it the seat of letters also; and at this time, for a long term of years, London and Paris are in fact and in operation Universities. . . . The newspapers, magazines, reviews, journals, and periodicals of all kinds, the publishing trade, the libraries, museums, and academies there found, the learned and scientific societies, necessarily invest [London] with the functions of a University; and that atmosphere of intellect, which in a former age hung over Oxford or Bologna or Salamanca, has, with the change of times, moved away to the centre of civil government. Thither come up youths from all parts of the country, the students of law, medicine, and the fine arts, and the *employés* and *attachés* of literature. There they live, as chance determines; and they are satisfied with their temporary home, for they find in it all that was promised to them there. They have not come in vain, as far as their own object in coming is concerned. They have not learned any particular religion, but they have learned their own particular profession well. They have, moreover, become acquainted with the habits, manners, and opinions of their place of sojourn, and done their part in maintaining the tradition of them. We cannot then be without virtual Universities; a metropolis is such: the simple question is, whether the education sought and given should be based on principle, formed upon rule, directed to the highest ends, or left to the random succession of masters and schools, one after another, with a melancholy waste of thought and an extreme hazard of truth.

Religious teaching itself affords us an illustration of our subject to a certain point. It does not indeed seat itself merely in centres of the world; this is impossible from the nature of the case. It is intended for the many not the few; its subject matter is truth necessary for us, not truth recondite and rare; but it concurs in the principle of a University so far as this, that its great instrument, or rather organ, has ever been that which nature prescribes in all education, the personal presence of a teacher, or, in theological language, Oral Tradition. It is the living voice, the breathing form, the expressive countenance, which preaches, which catechises. Truth, a subtle, invisible, manifold spirit, is poured into the mind of the scholar by his eyes and ears, through his affections, imagination, and reason; it is poured into his mind and is sealed up there in perpetuity, by propounding and repeating it, by questioning and requestioning, by correcting and explaining, by progressing and then recurring to first principles, by all those ways which are implied in the word "catechising." In the first ages, it was a work of long time; months, sometimes years, were devoted to the arduous task of disabusing the mind of the incipient Christian of its pagan errors, and of moulding it upon the Christian faith. The Scriptures indeed were at hand for the study of those who could avail themselves of them; but St. Irenæus does not hesitate to speak of whole races, who had been converted to Christianity, without being able to read them. To be unable to read or write was in those times no evidence of want of learning: the hermits of the desert were, in this sense of the word, illiterate; yet the great St. Anthony, though he knew not letters, was a match in disputation for the learned philosophers who came to try him. Didymus again, the great Alexandrian theologian, was blind. The ancient discipline, called the *Disciplina Arcani,* involved the same principle. The more sacred doctrines of Revelation were not committed to books but passed on by successive tradition. The teaching on the Blessed Trinity and the Eucharist appears to have been so handed down for some hundred years; and when at length reduced to writing, it has filled many folios, yet has not been exhausted.

But I have said more than enough in illustration; I end as I began—a University is a place of concourse, whither students come from every quarter for every kind of knowledge. You cannot have the best of every kind everywhere; you must go to some great city or emporium for it. There you have all the choicest productions of nature and art all together, which you find each in its own separate place elsewhere. All the riches of the land, and of the earth, are carried up thither; there are the best markets, and there the best workmen. It is the centre of trade, the supreme court of fashion, the umpire of rival talents, and the standard of things rare and precious. It is the place for seeing galleries of first-rate pictures, and for hearing wonderful voices and performers of transcendent skill. It is the place for great preachers, great orators, great nobles, great statesmen. In the nature of things, greatness and unity go together; excellence implies a centre. And such, for the third or fourth time, is a University; I hope I do not weary out the reader by repeating it. It is the place to which a thousand schools make contributions; in which the intellect may safely range and speculate, sure to find its equal in some antagonist activity, and its judge in the tribunal of truth. It is a place where inquiry is pushed forward, and discoveries verified and perfected, and rashness rendered innocuous, and error exposed, by the collision of mind with mind, and knowledge with knowledge. It is the place where the professor becomes eloquent, and is a missionary and a preacher, displaying his science in its most complete and most winning form, pouring it forth with the zeal of enthusiasm, and lighting up his own love of it in the breasts of his hearers. It is the place where the catechist makes good his ground as he goes, treading in the truth day by day into the ready memory, and wedging and tightening it into the expanding reason. It is a place which wins the admiration of the young by its celebrity, kindles the affections of the middle-aged by its beauty, and rivets the fidelity of the old by its associations. It is a seat of wisdom, a light of the world, a minister of the faith, an Alma Mater of the rising generation. It is this and a great deal more, and demands a somewhat better head and hand than mine to describe it well.

Such is a University in its idea and in its purpose. . . .

Howard Mumford Jones

UNDERGRADUATES ON APRONSTRINGS

I WISH TO ARGUE AN UNPOPULAR CAUSE: THE CAUSE OF THE OLD, FREE elective system in the academic world, or the untrammeled right of the undergraduate to make his own mistakes. Doubtless my case is one-sided and prejudiced, though it seems to me the case for controlled education is

This article first appeared in *The Atlantic Monthly* (October, 1955). Reprinted by permission of the author.

equally one-sided; nor does the fact that controlled education is just now in the ascendant make the present system eternal. Doubtless also there was a vast deal of waste in the old system. But as I have seen no study of waste under the present controlled system, I am prepared to hazard the guess that the present philosophy, though it produces bright, interchangeable students in quantity with almost no pain, is not inevitably the philosophy of education that will preserve this republic unto the latest generation.

I take it everybody knows what is meant by the old, free elective system. It was common in American colleges and universities in the last decades of the nineteenth century, and it lasted into the twentieth. In its time it was heralded as a tremendous advance over an older form of educational control. Theoretically everything was wrong with it, if you are to believe the twentieth-century diagnosticians. It was, they pontificate, the quintessence of laissez-faire. It encouraged individualism—rugged or otherwise. It let the student choose his courses and his instructors, something that he had come to college to do. It permitted the lazy man to be lazy and it permitted the student who had found, or thought he had found, his vocation, to concentrate on that vocation—that is, in the jargon of the present hour, to "narrow" his education by electing courses that seemed to him to fit his own particular case. The theory of the old, free elective system was a function of an obsolescent notion of the college and of the university, a notion advanced by Ezra Cornell, who wanted to found a university in which anybody could study anything. Nobody has ever made it clear to me why this idea is a product of the Old Nick himself.

Manifold objections were raised to the old, free elective system as practiced, for example, at Harvard under President Charles W. Eliot. It was argued that when an undergraduate could choose chemistry for fourteen out of his sixteen courses required for the bachelor's degree, he was not receiving a proper education. Whether the youth in question was merely eccentric I do not know—he may have been a genius, though I do not see how the authorities could tell; and all I can say is that, if you put college credits aside and look at the thing in terms of self-development, he was following the path originally trodden by persons like Thomas A. Edison, Henry Ford, John Stuart Mill, and Napoleon. The last was so bored by ordinary courses he showed no ability at Brienne except in matters that had to do with his genius for war. I have sometimes speculated what another Napoleon or Edison would do in our carefully calculated courses in general education. Is it at all conceivable that in setting up these required patterns of instruction we are either postponing or obliterating the expression of talent? This is, of course, the century of the common man. But I wonder what Leonardo da Vinci would do in the century of the common man.

It is also argued that the old, free elective system was, as I have indicated, a godsend to the lazy. I do not dispute it. I only want to know what the lazy are doing in the present well-regulated systems of general education. Have they disappeared from the college campus? Are these courses—overviews of the history of Western Man, for the most part—so exciting that the lazy now automatically catch fire and kindle to intellectual challenge? Am I to infer that pedagogical skill has so vastly increased, the lazy have ceased to be? I have lately been rereading Vincent Sheean's *Personal History*, including the wonderful passage in which he narrates how and why the University of Chicago taught him nothing in particular and taught it very well. But nobody later than Mr. Sheean seems to have confessed. All I know has to do with the complaints of English teachers about the indifference of students to ordinary requirements in prose.

Another customary charge against the old, free elective system is that it overcompensated the "popular" teacher and ignored the specialist who really knew. Perhaps it did. But has the situation altered under the present controlled system? As I watch the ebb and flow of enrollment in various courses nowadays, I wonder whether the world of the campus has changed. I seem to see, cynical fellow that I am, the same fashions at work—a surge into psychology or social anthropology, a surge into Russian, a surge into modern poetry. I see, or dream I see, the idols of the campus drawing their usual full houses while the classrooms of essential scholars have their modest quotas where the real work of the university is done. I venture to doubt that the "popular" teacher has somehow miraculously dissolved into the smooth, impersonal fabric of required courses in general education.

Products of the free elective system, graduating any year between 1895 and 1915 (my dates are approximate, or, as the New Critics would say, symbolical only), came into social or economic or cultural or political power in this republic some ten or twenty years after being graduated. They fought World War I. They carried forward the technological revolution that accompanied or followed that catastrophe. They were in the saddle during the administrations of Wilson, Harding, and Coolidge, and you can, if you like, say they are responsible for the twenties, for the stock-market crash of 1929, and for a variety of other sins. Perhaps I have no defense. All I can murmur is that American literature, American art, American music, American science, and American technology came of age during this quarter-century; and though I am as ready as the next historian to admit that 1929 was a catastrophic year, I am not persuaded that the world-wide depression setting in at the end of the twenties was the direct result of the old, free elective system.

It is also argued that the free elective system did not produce an informed citizenry, aware of the glorious history of the United States, alert to the significance of Western culture, and alive to the philosophic values of democracy. I dare say some part of the charge is true. But as I think of the careers of Robert M. La Follette, Frederick Jackson Turner, Robert Morss Lovett, Edward A. Ross, Charles E. Merriam, Frank Norris, Albert Bushnell Hart, and a variety of other persons associated with education in those years, I wonder where these characters and others like them picked up their singular dedication to civic virtue, and I speculate also on the immaculate morality of American public life when, some twenty or twenty-five years from now, graduates of the present controlled theories of education shall have completed their labors in the way of loyalty oaths and filled all the key posts of the republic with pure and righteous men. I seem to recall that teachers such as Royce with his doctrine of loyalty to the Great Community, James with his philosophy of the average man trying it on, and Dewey with his notion that if you want democracy you begin with the young—I seem to recall, I say, that these gentlemen had a particular knowledge of the democratic process. It would be vulgar of me to say that a crisp version of this philosophy may be found on the postcard which said: "Live every day so that you can look any man in the face and tell him to go to hell." On this assumption Mr. Lincoln Steffens seemed to think that there was something to be said even for the corrupt political boss, and Rev. Walter Rauschenbusch seemed to believe there might be something that Christian ethics had to offer society. Nowadays we have the disciples of Freud and the neo-Calvinists.

II

Well, it may be asked, what have we substituted for the old, free elective system? The substitution is not altogether bad. We have many, many more undergraduates in our colleges than we had in 1880 or 1900, and we have to do something with them; otherwise they will be disappointed of a degree, and the consequences may be disastrous for college financing. And inasmuch as ours is an excessively mobile population, we have invented for education what we invented for industry—a beautiful system of interchangeable parts. You may start your education in California and finish it in North Carolina, but it will not be much of a jar as you move, say, from Stanford to Duke. If Harvard has courses in general education, so do several hundred other colleges. If Wisconsin has a student radio, so do scores of other universities. If Iowa has a student theater, so do Michigan, Yale, Texas, and, for all I know, The Greater Southwest Teachers College State University. The philosophy of rugged individualism, which in its time gave a unique flavor to the new Johns Hopkins University, has now so far passed from favor that when they instituted Brandeis University in Waltham, Massachusetts, they ignored the opportunity to make an institution dedicated to intellectual excitement and created a school as much like the other schools around it as they could.

Putting intellectual matters aside, I submit that the motto of our present prevailing system of interchangeable parts is "adjustment." The freshman "adjusts" to his college. The sophomore "adjusts" to his professors, and by and by the senior is supposed to "adjust" to the outside world, nobody asks why. I doubt that "adjustment" would have made much sense to Emerson or Thorstein Veblen or Edgar Allan Poe or John Sloan or Jonathan Edwards or Frank Lloyd Wright or Carlson of Chicago or Einstein of Princeton. In my observation the world adjusts to the genius, not the genius to the world; and if Woodrow Wilson was right in saying that the principal purpose of a liberal education is to enable you to know a good man when you see him, I doubt that psychological testing is a proper telescope. Of course it can be argued that the thousands who annually pass through the American college are not geniuses, and this is true. But what about the genius who would like to be trained in his calling? Are we keeping paths open for the lonely talents who really shape culture and who are not content to imitate culture in others? Or are we so universally bent on "adjustment," all in the interests of a smoothly running society, we propose to break or smother the John Reeds and the Thorstein Veblens before they develop into dangerous reds?

Adjustment operates, in the jargon of the day, on two levels: the intellectual and the personal. Intellectual adjustment begins as required courses for freshmen (and sometimes sophomores) who have commonly just escaped from a good many required courses in the secondary school. And these required courses are the products of the kindest thoughts and a considerable administrative skill. Their instructors are hand-picked and, being selected, brood conscientiously over Great Books, The Development of Western Man, Humanism. and other well-meant exercises supposed to replace the old, pernicious survey course in English literature or the history of Europe. Commonly, however, inspection shows that the new required courses are simply the old courses blown up out of all manageable size. I may call them processing courses; and like all processing, they are directed at the average, the medium, the median, or the mean, whatever one's statistical philosophy devises. The difficulty is that in these enormous surveys instruction, like the radius vector of the planets, sweeps over equal areas in equal times. Meanwhile those who are not average are bored.

But the precious ointment in our sight is not intellectual adjustment but personal adjustment, and this is a sacred cause—so sacred that we have invented a weird and unique hierarchy of secular priests to see that the student forever "adjusts." There is on the face of the civilized globe no other group like it. We have deans, tutors, counselors, vocational guides, counselors on marriage, alumni advisers, medical men, and psychiatrists. We have orientation week, campus week, the reading period, religious retreats, and summer camps. I am not prepared to argue down the validity of any one of these inventions taken singly; all I am prepared to say is that, taken as a whole, they befog the idea that higher education is an intellectual exercise. Higher education becomes adjustment. And what these well-meant therapeutic devices do is to postpone decision-making. The symbol of this refusal to face the fact that in life as in war there are final occasions is the make-up examination.

Under the old, free elective system, when a youth went off to college, he went off to a mysterious place where he had to learn the rules by himself or suffer the consequences of not knowing them. This situation, however naïve in terms of "adjustment," had one big advantage: he was at last Away From Home. Going to college was like Bar Mitzvah in Hebrew tradition: once past it, you not only entered upon man's estate, but, moreover, there was no return. You had cut the leading strings; and the fiction of the nineties that pictures the Yale undergraduate with his bulldog and his pipe was true to the facts. Today we do not cut the leading strings, we merely lengthen them. It is not true that an American lad cannot make a significant mistake as a young collegian, but it is true to say that an entire battery of adjusters is happily at work to see that his mistakes shall never, never harm him. Mistakes should not be harmless. Experience, said Oscar Wilde, is the name we give to our mistakes. Take away the mistakes, and what good is the experience?

American college life is, or has become, a wan attempt to prolong adolescence as far as it can be stretched. If this seems excessive, look at any alumni reunion. To the intent of keeping the young idea in "adjustment" this regiment of supervisors dedicates a zealous professional activity. And their intent could not be more laudable. The intent is to promote the unalienable right to happiness. The intent is to do away with waste. The intent is, in the name of democracy, to see that the son or daughter of any or every taxpayer shall not fail. In order not to fail, the offspring must "get something" out of a college education. This, of course, puts an excessive strain upon the advisory staff, which forever demands more recruits, just as it puts an excessive strain upon the intellectual staff, and partly as a means of reducing this strain it has proved easier to channel young America into true and tried educational courses, usually set forth as required work in general education.

General education proves in fact to be a reduction in the classroom for average consumption of a certain average quantum of information about the behavior of Western Man. Why does this sort of thing represent an advance on my zealous scientific undergraduate who, inspired with enthusiasm for chemistry, took seven eighths of his work in what he came to college to find out? I cheerfully grant that, however superior as a chemist, he may have been a poor citizen, but are we turning out better citizens? The hope of the republic rests upon an informed citizenry. All the investigations into the book-reading habits of Americans, college graduates included, reveal that the reading of books drops sharply at the school-leaving age, and that we read fewer books in proportion to our population than does any other nation of the West.

The ancient fable of Mark Hopkins on a log is only a fable, and I do not favor the log. But I do favor Mark Hopkins. That is to say, I think there is a good deal to be said for the lopsided zealot, on fire with fanatical enthusiasm for the first crusade, aerodynamics, quaternions, the Federal Reserve system, or the superiority of William Butler Yeats to all other recent poets. I do not expect him to transmit this enthusiasm to the sad average, but I should like to give him the opportunity to collogue with his younger kind. In Blake's words, the way to the palace of wisdom leads through excess. I suggest that our well-meant hope that waste may be reduced may mean that excellence is reduced also. I suggest that the purpose of an academic institution is, or ought to be, to produce men of singular and exceptional talent, not merely conformable citizens. I am not quite clear, and never have been, why everybody has to be exposed to equal parts of Euripides and Beethoven, the Middle Ages and modern times, biology and mathematics. Like Mr. James Thurber, all I could ever see in the microscope they gave me in botany was a reflection of my own eye.

But of course this is merely an exercise in dissent.

McCrea Hazlett

THE LIBERAL ARTS AND THE LIBERAL VIRTUES

DURING THE NEXT FOUR YEARS I HOPE THAT MOST OF US WILL BECOME well acquainted. Yet however often we may meet, our encounters may be too casual or too businesslike, and I doubt that we will have many opportunities to discuss systematically and seriously *why we are here*: the most important and often the most forgotten question which the students and faculty of a university can ask. Because I fear that we may never get back to this question, I am going to spend my few minutes tonight talking about it. If they were worthy of a title, my remarks could be called, "The Liberal Arts and the Liberal Virtues."

I think I shall begin with my grandmother's cat. When I was a boy, my very good friend Orris Lynch, a town boy without the obvious advantages of having grandparents who lived on a farm, decided that he wanted a cat. Since my grandparents did live on a farm, and since Orris knew that my grandmother had numerous cats, he asked me to get one for him. I asked my parents, and one day they and Orris and I went to the country to get Orris his pet. My grandmother's cats were wild creatures who prowled the farm, exterminating rodents wherever they could find them. Consequently, there was no place where one could go at a particular time and be sure of locating his cat. These cats had to be rounded up, like western jack rabbits. The hired men and several of my uncles were summoned, we formed a semi-circle around the barnyard, beat the bushes with sticks, made a great racket, and moved toward the barn. The cats performed several strategic retreats, finally took refuge in the barn, and were locked inside. The hired men and uncles entered the barn; there were scuffles and howls, and presently the door opened and one of the youngest and most agile of the uncles emerged holding a squirming and

Used by permission of the author and the University of Rochester *Newsletter*.

very frightened calico cat at a safe distance. The cat was popped into a box, tied securely with a baling twine, and carried to the car. We took Orris home and immediately left, though I would have liked to stay.

As I heard it later the unboxing of the cat was more exciting for Orris than gratifying. The cat understood nothing about the new home he had found or the affection which was to be lavished upon him, and he was very upset by the treatment he had received. When Orris opened the box, the cat leaped out of his grasp, dashed up the rainspout, and disappeared, permanently, over the roof of the house. Orris, when I saw him next, was a very crestfallen former cat owner.

The positive connection between the liberal arts, the liberal virtues, and the cat may seem to be very slim. And indeed it is. The cat will serve us as a negative example; his behavior, judged by what one expects of the liberally educated man or woman, leaves much to be desired.

In the first place, he did not reveal any familiarity with the subject matter of the liberal arts. He did not understand the actions of men in such a way as to permit him to distinguish between the behavior of his captor, my uncle, and his benefactor, my friend. He did not understand the ideals and aspirations of men as exemplified in the desire of my friend Orris to lavish affection upon him. He did not understand the complex nature of society, and the mutually beneficial relationships which can exist between its members. Finally, he did not exhibit any particular understanding of the nature of the physical and biological worlds which surrounded him and of which he was part. This cat had not studied widely in the humanities, the social sciences, or the biological and physical sciences, all of which form the subject-matter of the liberal arts. He had not supplemented a broad general education with the mastery of a special field of concentration which would have focused his knowledge and drawn together its separate parts.

My grandmother's cat had not mastered the disciplines of a liberal education. He had not been required to organize his intellectual activities, to formulate and solve intellectual problems for himself. He had missed the discipline derived from close study of great systems of thought, ancient and modern, and from training in the understanding and employment of these works of the mind. He had not experienced the excitement imparted by learned and enthusiastic teachers and scholars, who stand at the frontiers of human knowledge, and who are imbued with a passion for teaching and research.

Finally, this cat did not embody the liberal virtues, in any complete sense.

Self-reliance he seems to have possessed, and courage, but they were the self-reliance and the courage of a wild beast, more determined by glandular secretion than by rational self-determination. He was not a cat of principle. His behavior was not motivated by a disinterested sense of duty and responsibility. He was not a tolerant or an inquiring cat. He exhibited no desire to inquire into the opinions of others and weigh them objectively before judging them.

We now dismiss my grandmother's cat with gratitude and with apologies. We are grateful to him for permitting us to use him as a vehicle for defining the liberal arts and the liberal virtues. From him we have learned that the liberal arts are those subjects for study and those intellectual disciplines which, when properly mastered, provide us with breadth of knowledge and depth of understanding. From him we have learned that the liberal virtues are self-reliance, principle, tolerance and curiosity. The two have no simple interrelationships. The liberal virtues are, in a sense, necessary to the mastery of the liberal arts. The liberal arts contribute to the development of the liberal virtues. Each is a cause and simultaneously an effect. Men and women who have mastered the liberal arts and developed the liberal virtues have an immense and intelligent curiosity regarding the universe in which they live; they approach new situations and new experiences gladly and imaginatively; they are part of their own society, but are not intolerant or unprincipled in their adherence to it; they are the only people who can create and maintain a free government; they are men and women whose spiritual resources sustain them, who live by the positive virtues, not merely the negative ones; they are virtuous rather than merely moral.

We apologize to my grandmother's cat for implying that he should be something that he could never have been: a rational human being. At the same time we note that the sufficient excuses for his deficiencies do not exist for us. In this gloomy century man has explored thoroughly the animal and irrational characteristics of human beings. We have acquired new perspective regarding our subconscious motivations and our compulsive acts. These discoveries, however, may have obscured but they have not destroyed the facts that there is a vast gulf between my grandmother's cat and me, that the essential differences include my capacity to reason and to follow rationally the implications of that reasoning, and that I cannot excuse my behavior by asserting that the cat and I are of the same nature. Unlike him, I am a creature for whom the liberal arts are ideal activities and for whom the liberal virtues are ideal canons of behavior.

There are many good reasons for coming to college: to prepare yourself to make money, to meet a husband or wife, to play games, to have a good time, or to rest in a protected atmosphere until you are old enough to go out into the world. Let me emphasize that each of these purposes is good. We were cast in the divine mold and therefore should aspire to spiritual things, but we were also given bodies and placed in a material universe. So long as money is necessary for the maintenance of our lives, the acquisition of it is essential. Husbands, wives, and children are necessary to well-regulated families, and the comfort, solace, and joy of marriage are very desirable. Games and other physical activities are important in the discipline of the mind and the acquisition of the liberal virtues. Having a good time, which usually refers to social life, is a pleasant part of college. And shelter from the violent blows of life until we are mature enough to withstand them is undoubtedly useful.

Yes, all of these are good reasons for going to college, but none of them is *the* reason for going to college. The only necessary reason for your being here is to study the subject-matter, and acquire the discipline of the liberal arts, and to develop the liberal virtues. It is this reason which controls and informs all the other reasons, renders them meaningful, and enriches your lives. And it is the purpose of the faculty and staff of this University to assist you in your pursuit of the liberal arts. As the miasma of novelty and confusion which you are now living in clears, you will, I hope, come gradually to realize that no matter how distant from the academic life some of our concerns may appear to be, and no matter how trivial and arbitrary some of our actions may appear to be, we are attempting to assist you in all the ways we can to master the liberal arts and acquire the liberal virtues.

On the fourth of July, 1845, Henry Thoreau, whom I believe to be one of the most significant of American writers, went to live by himself in a small hut on the shores of Walden Pond, two miles from his home in Concord, Massachusetts, and began making those notes which later formed his book *Walden*. He went to Walden Pond, not because he wished to retire permanently from society, but because he wished, for a while, to pursue the liberal arts and the liberal virtues, and finish some transcendental chores. "Both place and time were changed," he says in describing his reasons for moving to Walden, "and I dwelt nearer to those parts of the universe and to those eras in history which had most attracted me. . . . I went to the woods because I wished to live deliberately, to front only the essential facts of life, and see if I could not learn what it had to teach. . . . I wanted to live deep and suck all the marrow of life, to live so sturdily . . . as to put to rout all that was not life, to cut a broad swath and shave close, to drive life into a corner." In another place he says, " . . . my head is an organ for burrowing, as some creatures use their snout and forepaws, and with it I would mine and burrow my way through these hills. I think that the richest vein is somewhere hereabouts. . . . Time is but a stream to go a-fishing in. I drink at it; but while I drink I see the sandy bottom and detect how shallow it is. Its thin current slides away, but eternity remains; fish in the sky, whose bottom is pebbly with stars."

In spirit, if not in detail, your purpose at the University should be similar to Thoreau's. You have come away from the familiar society in which you have lived, and are dwelling now, in an intellectual sense, on the shores of Walden Pond, somewhat nearer the stars. I hope you have come resolved to live deliberately and to confront the essential facts of life. You must, while you are here, burrow with your intellect for a vein of wisdom, and go a-fishing in the stream of eternity. If you come with these purposes, if you pursue the liberal arts and the liberal virtues with all your vigor, the University will be an exciting and satisfying place for you, and you will acquire here knowledge and moral strength and spiritual vision which will support and refresh and give meaning to your entire lives. If you come with any less noble resolution, or if you permit "every nutshell and mosquito's wing," to use another of Thoreau's phrases, to deflect you, you will be denying yourselves membership in this society of scholars, squandering your intellectual and moral resources, and almost certainly preparing yourselves to speak, at some time in your lives, your own version of this piteous lament of Milton's Samson:

> "O glorious strength
> Put to the labor of a beast, debast
> Lower than bondslave. Promise was that I
> Should Israel from Philistian yoke deliver;
> Ask for this great deliverer now, and find him
> Eyeless in Gaza at the mill with slaves."

PEOPLE, SINGLY AND COLLECTIVELY

James Thurber

THE NIGHT THE BED FELL

I suppose that the high-water mark of my youth in Columbus, Ohio, was the night the bed fell on my father. It makes a better recitation (unless, as some friends of mine have said, one has heard it five or six times) than it does a piece of writing, for it is almost necessary to throw furniture around, shake doors, and bark like a dog, to lend the proper atmosphere and verisimilitude to what is admittedly a somewhat incredible tale. Still, it did take place.

It happened, then, that my father had decided to sleep in the attic one night, to be away where he could think. My mother opposed the notion strongly because, she said, the old wooden bed up there was unsafe; it was wobbly and the heavy headboard would crash down on father's head in case the bed fell, and kill him. There was no dissuading him, however, and at a quarter past ten he closed the attic door behind him and went up the narrow twisting stairs. We later heard ominous creakings as he crawled into bed. Grandfather, who usually slept in the attic bed when he was with us, had disappeared some days before. (On these occasions he was usually gone six or eight days and returned growling and out of temper, with the news that the federal Union was run by a passel of block-heads and that the Army of the Potomac didn't have any more chance than a fiddler's bitch.)

We had visiting us at this time a nervous first cousin of mine named Briggs Beall, who believed that he was likely to cease breathing when he was asleep. It was his feeling that if he were not awakened every hour during the night, he might die of suffocation. He had been accustomed to setting an alarm clock to ring at intervals until morning, but I persuaded him to abandon this. He slept in my room and I told him that I was such a light sleeper that if anybody quit breathing in the same room with me, I would wake instantly. He tested me the first night—which I had suspected he would—by holding his breath after my regular breathing had convinced him I was asleep. I was not asleep, however, and called to him. This seemed to allay his fears a little, but he took the precaution of putting a glass of spirits of camphor on a little table at the head of his bed. In case I didn't arouse him until he was almost gone, he said, he would sniff the camphor, a powerful reviver. Briggs was not the only member of his family who had his crotchets. Old Aunt Melissa Beall (who could whistle like a man, with two fingers in her mouth) suffered under the premonition that she was destined to die on South High Street, because she had been born on South High Street and married on South High Street. Then there was Aunt Sarah Shoaf, who never went to bed at night without the fear that a burglar was going to get in and blow chloroform under her door through a tube. To avert this calamity—for she was in greater dread of anesthetics than of losing her household goods—she always piled her money, silverware, and other valuables in a neat stack just outside her bedroom, with a note reading: "This is all I have. Please take it and do not use your chloroform, as this is all I have." Aunt Gracie Shoaf also had a burglar phobia, but she met it with more fortitude. She was confident that burglars had been getting into her house every night for forty years. The fact that she never missed anything was to her no proof to the contrary. She always claimed that she scared them off before they could take anything, by throwing shoes down the hallway. When she went to bed she piled, where she could get at them handily, all the shoes there were about her house. Five minutes after she had turned off the light, she would sit up in bed and say "Hark!" Her husband, who had learned to ignore the whole situation as long ago as 1903, would either be sound asleep or pretend to be sound asleep. In either case he would not respond to her tugging and pulling, so that presently she would arise, tiptoe to the door, open it slightly and heave a shoe down the hall in one direction, and its mate down the hall in the other direction. Some nights she threw them all, some nights only a couple of pair.

But I am straying from the remarkable incidents that took place during the night that the bed fell on father. By midnight we were all in bed. The layout of the rooms and the disposition of their occupants is important to an understanding of what later occurred. In the front room upstairs (just under father's attic bedroom) were my mother and my brother Herman, who sometimes sang in his sleep, usually "Marching Through Georgia" or "Onward, Christian Soldiers." Briggs Beall and myself were in a room adjoining this one. My brother Roy was in a room across the hall from ours. Our bull terrier, Rex, slept in the hall.

My bed was an army cot, one of those affairs which are made wide enough to sleep on comfortably only by putting up, flat with the middle section, the two sides which ordinarily hang down like the sideboards of a drop-leaf table. When these sides are up, it is perilous to roll too far toward the edge, for then the cot is likely to tip completely over, bringing the whole bed down on top of one, with a tremendous banging crash. This, in fact, is precisely what happened, about two o'clock in the morning. (It was my mother who, in recalling the scene later, first referred to it as "the night the bed fell on your father.")

Always a deep sleeper, slow to arouse (I had lied to Briggs), I was at first unconscious of what had happened when the iron cot rolled me onto the floor and toppled over on me. It left me still warmly bundled up and unhurt, for the bed rested above me like a canopy. Hence I did not wake up, only reached the edge of consciousness and went back. The racket, however, instantly awakened my mother, in the next room, who came to the immediate conclusion that her worst dread was realized: the big wooden bed upstairs had fallen on father. She therefore screamed, "Let's go to your poor father!" It was this shout, rather than the noise of my cot falling, that awakened Herman, in the same room with her. He thought that mother had become, for no apparent reason, hysterical. "You're all right, Mamma!" he shouted, trying to calm her. They exchanged shout for shout for perhaps ten seconds: "Let's go to your poor father!" and "You're all right!" That woke up Briggs. By this time I was conscious of what was going on, in a vague way, but did not yet realize that I was under my bed instead of on it. Briggs, awakening in the midst of loud shouts of fear and apprehension, came to the quick conclusion that he was suffocating and that we were all trying to "bring him out." With a low moan, he grasped the glass of camphor at the head of his bed and instead of sniffing it poured it over himself. The room reeked of camphor. "Ugf, ahfg," choked Briggs, like a drowning man, for he had almost succeeded in stopping his breath under the deluge of pungent spirits. He leaped out of bed and groped toward the open window, but he came up against one that was closed. With his hand, he beat out the glass, and I could hear it crash and tinkle on the alleyway below. It was at this juncture that I, in trying to get up, had the uncanny sensation of feeling my bed above me! Foggy with sleep, I now suspected, in my turn, that the whole uproar was being made in a frantic endeavor to extricate me from what must be an unheard-of and perilous situation. "Get me out of this!" I bawled. "Get me out!" I think I had the nightmarish belief that I was entombed in a mine. "Gugh," gasped Briggs, floundering in his camphor.

By this time my mother, still shouting, pursued by Herman, still shouting, was trying to open the door to the attic, in order to go up and get my father's body out of the wreckage. The door was stuck, however, and wouldn't yield. Her frantic pulls on it only added to the general banging and confusion. Roy and the dog were now up, the one shouting questions, the other barking.

Father, farthest away and soundest sleeper of all, had by this time been awakened by the battering on the attic door. He decided that the house was on fire. "I'm coming, I'm coming!" he wailed in a slow, sleepy voice— it took him many minutes to regain full consciousness. My mother, still believing he was caught under the bed, detected in his "I'm coming!" the mournful, resigned note of one who is preparing to meet his Maker. "He's dying!" she shouted.

"I'm all right!" Briggs yelled to reassure her. "I'm all right!" He still believed that it was his own closeness to death that was worrying mother. I found at last the light switch in my room, unlocked the door, and Briggs and I joined the others at the attic door. The dog, who never did like Briggs, jumped for him—assuming that he was the culprit in whatever was going on—and Roy had to throw Rex and hold him. We could hear father crawling out of bed upstairs. Roy pulled the attic door open, with a mighty jerk, and father came down the stairs, sleepy and irritable but safe and sound. My mother began to weep when she saw him. Rex began to howl. "What in the name of God is going on here?" asked father.

The situation was finally put together like a gigantic jig-saw puzzle. Father caught a cold from prowling around in his bare feet but there were no other bad results. "I'm glad," said mother, who always looked on the bright side of things, "that your grandfather wasn't here."

Oliver Goldsmith

THE ENGLISHMAN

LETTER IV. FROM LIEN CHI ALTANGI, TO THE CARE OF
FIPSIHI, RESIDENT IN MOSCOW, TO BE FORWARDED BY THE
RUSSIAN CARAVAN TO FUM HOAM, FIRST PRESIDENT OF
THE CEREMONIAL ACADEMY AT PEKIN, IN CHINA.

THE ENGLISH SEEM AS SILENT AS THE JAPANESE, YET VAINER THAN THE
inhabitants of Siam. Upon my arrival I attributed that reserve to modesty,
which I now find has its origin in pride. Condescend to address them
first, and you are sure of their acquaintance; stoop to flattery, and you con-
ciliate their friendship and esteem. They bear hunger, cold, fatigue, and
all the miseries of life, without shrinking; danger only calls forth their
fortitude; they even exult in calamity; but contempt is what they cannot
bear. An Englishman fears contempt more than death; he often flies to
death as a refuge from its pressure; and dies when he fancies the world has
ceased to esteem him.

Pride seems the source not only of their national vices, but of their
national virtues also. An Englishman is taught to love his king as his
friend, but to acknowledge no other master than the laws which himself
has contributed to enact. He despises those nations, who, that one may be
free, are all content to be slaves; who first lift a tyrant into terror, and then
shrink under his power as if delegated from heaven. Liberty is echoed
in all their assemblies; and thousands might be found ready to offer up
their lives for the sound, though perhaps not one of all the number understands its meaning. The lowest mechanic, however, looks upon it as his
duty to be a watchful guardian of his country's freedom, and often uses a
language that might seem haughty, even in the mouth of the great
emperor who traces his ancestry to the moon.

A few days ago, passing by one of their prisons, I could not avoid stopping, in order to listen to a dialogue, which I thought might afford me
some entertainment. The conversation was carried on between a debtor,
through the grate of his prison, a porter, who had stopped to rest his
burthen, and a soldier at the window. The subject was upon a threatened

From *Letters from a Citizen of the World* by Oliver Goldsmith. First published
in 1762.

invasion from France, and each seemed extremely anxious to rescue his country from the impending danger. *For my part*, cries the prisoner, *the greatest of my apprehensions is for our freedom; if the French should conquer, what would become of English liberty? My dear friends, liberty is the Englishman's prerogative; we must preserve that at the expense of our lives; of that the French shall never deprive us. It is not to be expected that men who are slaves themselves would preserve our freedom should they happen to conquer.* "Ay, slaves," cries the porter, "they are all slaves, fit only to carry burthens, every one of them. Before I would stoop to slavery, may this be my poison (and he held the goblet in his hand), may this be my poison—but I would sooner 'list for a soldier."

The soldier, taking the goblet from his friend, with much awe fervently cried out, *It is not so such our liberties as our religion that would suffer by such a change; ay, our religion, my lads. May the devil sink me into flames* (such was the solemnity of his adjuration), *if the French should come over, but our religion would be utterly undone.* So saying, instead of a libation, he applied the goblet to his lips, and confirmed his sentiments with a ceremony of the most persevering devotion.

In short, every man here pretends to be a politician; even the fair sex are sometimes found to mix the severity of national altercation with the blandishments of love, and often become conquerors by more weapons of destruction than their eyes.

This universal passion for politics is gratified by Daily Gazettes, as with us in China. But as in ours the Emperor endeavours to instruct his people, in theirs the people endeavour to instruct the administration. You must not, however, imagine, that they who compile these papers have any actual knowledge of the politics or the government of a state; they only collect their materials from the oracle of some coffee-house, which oracle has himself gathered them the night before from a beau at a gaming-table who has pillaged his knowledge from a great man's porter, who has had his information from the great man's gentleman, who has invented the whole story for his own amusement the night preceding.

The English in general seem fonder of gaining the esteem than the love of those they converse with. This gives a formality to their amusements: their gayest conversations have something too wise for innocent relaxation: though in company you are seldom disgusted with the absurdity of a fool, you are seldom lifted into rapture by those strokes of vivacity which give instant, though not permanent, pleasure.

What they want, however, in gaiety, they make up in politeness. You smile at hearing me praise the English for their politeness; you who have heard very different accounts from the missionaries at Pekin, who have seen such a different behaviour in their merchants and seamen at home. But I must still repeat it, the English seem more polite than any of their neighbours: their great art in this respect lies in endeavouring, while they oblige, to lessen the force of the favour. Other countries are fond of obliging a stranger; but seem desirous that he should be sensible of the obligation. The English confer their kindness with an appearance of indifference, and give away benefits with an air as if they despised them.

Walking, a few days ago, between an English and a Frenchman into the suburbs of the city, we were overtaken by a heavy shower of rain. I was unprepared; but they had each large coats, which defended them from what seemed to be a perfect inundation. The Englishman, seeing me shrink from the weather, accosted me thus: *Psha, man, what dost shrink at? here, take this coat; I don't want it; I find it no way useful to me; I had as lief be without it.* The Frenchman began to show his politeness in turn. *My dear friend,* cries he, *why won't you oblige me by making use of my coat? you see how well it defends me from the rain; I should not choose to part with it to others, but to such a friend as you I could even part with my skin to do him service.*

From such minute instances as these, most reverend Fum Hoam, I am sensible your sagacity will collect instruction. The volume of nature is the book of knowledge; and he becomes most wise who makes the most judicious selection. Farewell!

James Baldwin

STRANGER IN THE VILLAGE

FROM ALL AVAILABLE EVIDENCE NO BLACK MAN HAD EVER SET FOOT IN THIS tiny Swiss village before I came. I was told before arriving that I would probably be a "sight" for the village; I took this to mean that people of

From *Notes of a Native Son* by James Baldwin. Reprinted by permission of the Beacon Press.

my complexion were rarely seen in Switzerland, and also that city people are always something of a "sight" outside of the city. It did not occur to me—possibly because I am an American—that there could be people anywhere who had never seen a Negro.

It is a fact which cannot be explained on the basis of the inaccessibility of the village. The village is very high, but it is only four hours from Milan and three hours from Lausanne. It is true that it is virtually unknown. Few people making plans for a holiday would elect to come here. On the other hand, the villagers are able, presumably, to come and go as they please— which they do: to another town at the foot of the mountain, with a population of approximately five thousand, the nearest place to see a movie or to go to the bank. In the village there is no movie house, no bank, no library, no theater; very few radios, one jeep, one station wagon; and, at the moment, one typewriter, mine, an invention which the woman next door to me here had never seen. There are about six hundred people living here, all Catholic—I conclude this from the fact that the Catholic church is open all year round, whereas the Protestant chapel, set off on a hill a little removed from the village, is open only in the summertime when the tourists arrive. There are four or five hotels, all closed now, and four or five *bistros,* of which, however, only two do any business during the winter. These two do not do a great deal, for life in the village seems to end around nine or ten o'clock. There are a few stores, butcher, baker, *épicerie,* a hardware store, and a money-changer—who cannot change travelers checks, but must send them down to the bank, an operation which takes two or three days. There is something called the *Ballet Haus,* closed in the winter and used for God knows what, certainly not ballet, during the summer. There seems to be only one schoolhouse in the village, and this for the quite young children; I suppose this to mean that their older brothers and sisters at some point descend from these mountains in order to complete their education—possibly, again, to the town just below. The landscape is absolutely forbidding, mountains towering on all four sides, ice and snow as far as the eye can reach. In this white wilderness, men and women and children move all day, carrying washing, wood, buckets of milk or water, sometimes skiing on Sunday afternoons. All week long boys and young men are to be seen shoveling snow off the rooftops, or dragging wood down from the forest in sleds.

The village's only real attraction, which explains the tourist season, is the hot spring water. A disquietingly high proportion of these tourists are cripples, or semi-cripples, who come year after year—from other parts of Switzerland, usually—to take the waters. This lends the village, at the height of the season, a rather terrifying air of sanctity, as though it were a lesser Lourdes. There is often something beautiful, there is always something awful, in the spectacle of a person who has lost one of his faculties, a faculty he never questioned until it was gone, and who struggles to recover it. Yet people remain people, on crutches or indeed on deathbeds; and wherever I passed, the first summer I was here, among the native villagers, or among the lame, a wind passed with me—of astonishment, curiosity, amusement, and outrage. That first summer I stayed two weeks and never intended to return. But I did return in the winter, to work; the village offers, obviously, no distractions whatever and has the further advantage of being extremely cheap. Now it is winter again, a year later, and I am here again. Everyone in the village knows my name, though they scarcely ever use it, knows that I come from America—though, this, apparently, they will never really believe: black men come from Africa—and everyone knows that I am the friend of the son of a woman who was born here, and that I am staying in their chalet. But I remain as much a stranger today as I was the first day I arrived, and the children shout *Neger! Neger!* as I walk along the streets.

It must be admitted that in the beginning I was far too shocked to have any real reaction. In so far as I reacted at all, I reacted by trying to be pleasant—it being a great part of the American Negro's education (long before he goes to school) that he must make people "like" him. This smile-and-the-world-smiles-with-you routine worked about as well in this situation as it had in the situation for which it was designed, which is to say that it did not work at all. No one, after all, can be liked whose human weight and complexity cannot be, or has not been, admitted. My smile was simply another unheard-of phenomenon which allowed them to see my teeth—they did not, really, see my smile and I began to think that, should I take to snarling, no one would notice any difference. All of the physical characteristics of the Negro which had caused me, in America, a very different and almost forgotten pain were nothing less than miraculous—or infernal—in the eyes of the village people. Some thought my hair was the color of tar, that it had the texture of wire, or the texture of cotton. It was jocularly suggested that I might let it all grow long and make myself a winter coat. If I sat in the sun for more than five minutes some daring creature was certain to come along and gingerly put his fingers on my hair, as though he were afraid of an electric shock, or put his hand on my hand, astonished that the color did not rub off. In all of this, in which it must be conceded there was yet no suggestion that I was human: I was simply a living wonder.

I knew that they did not mean to be unkind, and I know it now; it is necessary, nevertheless, for me to repeat this to myself each time that I walk out of the chalet. The children who shout *Neger!* have no way of knowing the echoes this sound raises in me. They are brimming with good humor and the more daring swell with pride when I stop to speak with them. Just the same, there are days when I cannot pause and smile, when I have no heart to play with them; when, indeed, I mutter sourly to myself, exactly as I muttered on the streets of a city these children have never seen, when I was no bigger than these children are now: *Your* mother was a *nigger.* Joyce is right about history being a nightmare— but it may be the nightmare from which no one *can* awaken. People are trapped in history and history is trapped in them.

II

There is a custom in the village—I am told it is repeated in many villages—of "buying" African natives for the purpose of converting them to Christianity. There stands in the church all year round a small box with a slot for money, decorated with a black figurine, and into this box the villagers drop their francs. During the *carnaval* which precedes Lent, two village children have their faces blackened—out of which bloodless darkness their blue eyes shine like ice—and fantastic horsehair wigs are placed on their blond heads: thus disguised, they solicit among the villagers for money for the missionaries in Africa. Between the box in the church and the blackened children, the village bought last year six or eight African natives. This was reported to me with pride by the wife of one of the *bistro* owners and I was careful to express astonishment and pleasure at the solicitude shown by the village for the souls of black folks. The *bistro* owner's wife beamed with a pleasure far more genuine than my own and seemed to feel that I might now breathe more easily concerning the souls of at least six of my kinsmen.

I tried not to think of these so lately baptized kinsmen, of the price they themselves would pay, and said nothing about my father, who having taken his own conversion too literally, never, at bottom, forgave the white world (which he described as heathen) for having saddled him with a Christ in whom, to judge at least from their treatment of him, they themselves no longer believed. I thought of white men arriving for the first time in an African village, strangers there, as I am a stranger here, and tried to imagine the astounded populace touching their hair and marveling at the color of their skin. But there is a great difference between being the first white man to be seen by Africans and being the first black man to be seen by whites. The white man takes the astonishment as tribute, for he arrives to conquer and to convert the natives, whose inferiority in relation to himself is not even to be questioned; whereas I, without a thought of conquest, find myself among a people whose culture controls me, has even, in a sense, created me, people who have cost me more in anguish and rage than they will ever know, who yet do not even know of my existence. The astonishment with which I might have greeted them, should they have stumbled into my African village a few hundred years ago, might have rejoiced their hearts. But the astonishment with which they greet me today can only poison mine.

And this is so despite everything I may do to feel differently, despite my friendly conversations with the *bistro* owner's wife, despite their three-year-old son who has at last become my friend, despite the *saluts* and *bonsoirs* which I exchange with people as I walk, despite the fact that I know that no individual can be taken to task for what history is doing, or has done. I say that the culture of these people controls me—but they can scarcely be held responsible for European culture. America comes out of Europe, but these people have never seen America, nor have most of them seen more of Europe than the hamlet at the foot of their mountain. Yet, they move with an authority which I shall never have, and they regard me, quite rightly, not only as a stranger in their village but as a suspect latecomer, bearing no credentials, to everything they have—however unconsciously—inherited.

For this village, even were it incomparably more remote and incredibly more primitive, is the West, the West onto which I have been so strangely grafted. These people cannot be, from the point of view of power, strangers anywhere in the world: they have made the modern world, in effect, even if they do not know it. The most illiterate among them is related, in a way that I am not, to Dante, Shakespeare, Michelangelo, Aeschylus, Da Vinci, Rembrandt, and Racine; the cathedral at Chartres says something to them which it cannot say to me, as indeed would New York's Empire State Building, should anyone here ever see it. Out of their hymns and dances come Beethoven and Bach. Go back a few centuries and they are in their full glory—but I am in Africa, watching the conquerors arrive.

The rage of the disesteemed is personally fruitless, but it is also absolutely inevitable; this rage, so generally discounted, so little understood even among the people whose daily bread it is, is one of the things that makes history. Rage can only with difficulty, and never entirely, be brought under the domination of the intelligence and is therefore not susceptible to any arguments whatever. This is a fact which ordinary representatives of the *Herrenvolk*, having never felt this rage and being unable to imagine it, quite fail to understand. Also, rage cannot be hidden, it can only be dissembled. This dissembling deludes the thoughtless, and strengthens rage, and adds to rage, contempt. There are, no doubt, as many ways of coping with the resulting complex of tensions as there are black men in the world, but no black man can hope ever to be entirely liberated from this internal warfare—rage, dissembling, and contempt having inevitably accompanied his first realization of the power of white men. What is crucial here is that, since white men represent in the black man's world so heavy a weight, white men have for black men a reality which is far from being reciprocal; and hence all black men have toward all white men an attitude which is designed, really, either to rob the white man of the jewel of his naïveté, or else to make it cost him dear.

The black man insists, by whatever means he finds at his disposal, that the white man cease to regard him as an exotic rarity and recognize him as a human being. This is a very charged and difficult moment, for there is a great deal of will power involved in the white man's naïveté. Most people are not naturally reflective any more than they are naturally malicious, and the white man prefers to keep the black man at a certain human remove because it is easier for him thus to preserve his simplicity and avoid being called to account for crimes committed by his forefathers, or his neighbors. He is inescapably aware, nevertheless, that he is in a better position in the world than black men are, nor can he quite put to death the suspicion that he is hated by black men therefore. He does not wish to be hated, neither does he wish to change places, at this point in his uneasiness he can scarcely avoid having recourse to those legends which white men have created about black men, the most usual effect of which is that the white man finds himself enmeshed, so to speak, in his own language which describes hell, as well as the attributes which lead one to hell, as being as black as night.

Every legend, moreover, contains its residuum of truth, and the root function of language is to control the universe by describing it. It is of quite considerable significance that black men remain, in the imagination, and in overwhelming numbers in fact, beyond the disciplines of salvation; and this despite the fact that the West has been "buying" African natives for centuries. There is, I should hazard, an instantaneous necessity to be divorced from this so visibly unsaved stranger, in whose heart, moreover, one cannot guess what dreams of vengeance are being nourished; and, at the same time, there are few things on earth more attractive than the idea of the unspeakable liberty which is allowed the unredeemed. When, beneath the black mask, a human being begins to make himself felt one cannot escape a certain awful wonder as to what kind of human being it is. What one's imagination makes of other people is dictated, of course, by the laws of one's own personality and it is one of the ironies of black-white relations that, by means of what the white man imagines the black man to be, the black man is enabled to know who the white man is.

I have said, for example, that I am as much a stranger in this village today as I was the first summer I arrived, but this is not quite true. The villagers wonder less about the texture of my hair than they did then, and wonder rather more about me. And the fact that their wonder now exists on another level is reflected in their attitudes and in their eyes. There are the children who make those delightful, hilarious, sometimes astonishingly grave overtures of friendship in the unpredictable fashion of children; other children, having been taught that the devil is a black man, scream in genuine anguish as I approach. Some of the older women never pass without a friendly greeting, never pass, indeed, if it seems that they will be able to engage me in conversation; other women look down or look away or rather contemptuously smirk. Some of the men drink with me and suggest that I learn to ski—partly, I gather, because they cannot imagine what I would look like on skis—and want to know if I am married, and ask questions about my *métier*. But some of the men have accused *le sale nègre*—behind my back—of stealing wood and there is already in the eyes of some of them that peculiar, intent, paranoiac malevolence which one sometimes surprises in the eyes of American white men when, out walking with their Sunday girl, they see a Negro male approach.

There is a dreadful abyss between the streets of this village and the streets of the city in which I was born, between the children who shout *Neger!* today and those who shouted *Nigger!* yesterday—the abyss is experience, the American experience. The syllable hurled behind me today expresses, above all, wonder; I am a stranger here. But I am not a stranger in America and the same syllable riding on the American air expresses the war my presence has occasioned in the American soul.

III

For this village brings home to me this fact: that there was a day, and not really a very distant day, when Americans were scarcely Americans at all but discontented Europeans, facing a great unconquered continent and strolling, say, into a marketplace and seeing black men for the first time. The shock this spectacle afforded is suggested, surely, by the promptness with which they decided that these black men were not really men but cattle. It is true that the necessity on the part of the settlers of the New World of reconciling their moral assumptions with the fact—and the necessity—of slavery enhanced immensely the charm of this idea, and it is also true that this idea expresses, with a truly American bluntness, the attitude which to varying extents all masters have had toward all slaves.

But between all former slaves and slave-owners and the drama which begins for Americans over three hundred years ago at Jamestown, there are at least two differences to be observed. The American Negro slave could not suppose, for one thing, as slaves in past epochs had supposed and often done, that he would ever be able to wrest the power from his master's hands. This was a supposition which the modern era, which was to bring about such vast changes in the aims and dimensions of power, put to death; it only begins, in unprecedented fashion, and with dreadful implications, to be resurrected today. But even had this supposition persisted with undiminished force, the American Negro slave could not have used it to lend his condition dignity, for the reason that this supposition rests on another: that the slave in exile yet remains related to his past, has some means—if only in memory—of revering and sustaining the forms of his former life, is able, in short, to maintain his identity.

This was not the case with the American Negro slave. He is unique among the black men of the world in that his past was taken from him, almost literally, at one blow. One wonders what on earth the first slave found to say to the first dark child he bore. I am told that there are Haitians able to trace their ancestry back to African kings, but any American Negro wishing to go back so far will find his journey through time abruptly arrested by the signature on the bill of sale which served as the entrance paper for his ancestor. At the time—to say nothing of the circumstances—of the enslavement of the captive black man who was to become the American Negro, there was not the remotest possibility that he would ever take power from his master's hands. There was no reason to suppose that his situation would ever change, nor was there, shortly, anything to indicate that his situation had ever been different. It was his necessity, in the words of E. Franklin Frazier, to find a "motive for living under American culture or die." The identity of the American Negro comes out of this extreme situation, and the evolution of this identity was a source of the most intolerable anxiety in the minds and the lives of his masters.

For the history of the American Negro is unique also in this: that the question of his humanity, and of his rights therefore as a human being, became a burning one for several generations of Americans, so burning a question that it ultimately became one of those used to divide the nation. It is out of this argument that the venom of the epithet *Nigger!* is derived. It is an argument which Europe has never had, and hence Europe quite sincerely fails to understand how or why the argument arose in the first place, why its effects are so frequently disastrous and always so unpredictable, why it refuses until today to be entirely settled. Europe's black possessions remained—and do remain—in Europe's colonies, at which remove they represented no threat whatever to European identity. If they posed any problem at all for the European conscience, it was a problem which remained comfortingly abstract: in effect, the black man, *as a man,* did not exist for Europe. But in America, even as a slave, he was an inescapable part of the general social fabric and no American could escape having an attitude toward him. Americans attempt until today to make an abstraction of the Negro, but the very nature of these abstractions reveals the tremendous effects the presence of the Negro has had on the American character.

When one considers the history of the Negro in America it is of the greatest importance to recognize that the moral beliefs of a person, or a people, are never really as tenuous as life—which is not moral—very often causes them to appear; these create for them a frame of reference and a necessary hope, the hope being that when life has done its worst they will be enabled to rise above themselves and to triumph over life. Life would scarcely be bearable if this hope did not exist. Again, even when the worst has been said, to betray a belief is not by any means to have put oneself beyond its power; the betrayal of a belief is not the same thing as ceasing to believe. If this were not so there would be no moral standards in the world at all. Yet one must also recognize that morality is based on ideas and that all ideas are dangerous—dangerous because ideas can only lead to action and where the action leads no man can say. And dangerous in this respect: that confronted with the impossibility of remaining faithful to one's beliefs, and the equal impossibility of becoming free of them, one can be driven to the most inhuman excesses. The ideas on which American beliefs are based are not, though Americans often seem to think so, ideas which originated in America. They came out of Europe. And the establishment of democracy on the American continent was scarcely as radical a break with the past as was the necessity, which Americans faced, of broadening this concept to include black men.

This was, literally, a hard necessity. It was impossible, for one thing, for Americans to abandon their beliefs, not only because these beliefs alone seemed able to justify the sacrifices they had endured and the blood that they had spilled, but also because these beliefs afforded them their only bulwark against a moral chaos as absolute as the physical chaos of the continent it was their destiny to conquer. But in the situation in which Americans found themselves, these beliefs threatened an idea which, whether or not one likes to think so, is the very warp and woof of the heritage of the West, the idea of white supremacy.

Americans have made themselves notorious by the shrillness and the brutality with which they have insisted on this idea, but they did not invent it; and it has escaped the world's notice that those very excesses of which Americans have been guilty imply a certain, unprecedented uneasiness over the idea's life and power, if not, indeed, the idea's validity. The idea of white supremacy rests simply on the fact that white men are the creators of civilization (the present civilization, which is the only one that matters; all previous civilizations are simply "contributions" to our own) and are therefore civilization's guardians and defenders. Thus it was impossible for Americans to accept the black men as one of themselves, for to do so was to jeopardize their status as white men. But not so to accept him was to deny his human reality, his human weight and complexity, and the strain of denying the overwhelmingly undeniable forced Americans into rationalizations so fantastic that they approached the pathological.

At the root of the American Negro problem is the necessity of the American white man to find a way of living with the Negro in order to be able to live with himself. And the history of this problem can be reduced to the means used by Americans—lynch law and law, segregation and legal acceptance, terrorization and concession—either to come to terms with this necessity, or to find a way around it, or (most usually) to find a way of doing both these things at once. The resulting spectacle, at once foolish and dreadful, led someone to make the quite accurate observation that "the Negro-in-America is a form of insanity which overtakes white men."

In this long battle, a battle by no means finished, the unforeseeable effects of which will be felt by many future generations, the white man's motive was the protection of his identity; the black man was motivated by the need to establish an identity. And despite the terrorization which the Negro in America endured and endures sporadically until today, despite the cruel and totally inescapable ambivalence of his status in his country, the battle for his identity has long ago been won. He is not a visitor to the West, but a citizen there, an American; as American as the Americans who despise him, the Americans who fear him, the Americans who love him—the Americans who became less than themselves, or rose to be greater than themselves by virtue of the fact that the challenge he represented was inescapable. He is perhaps the only black man in the world whose relationship to white men is more terrible, more subtle, and more meaningful than the relationship of bitter possessed to uncertain possessor. His survival depended, and his development depends, on his ability to turn his peculiar status in the Western world to his own advantage and, it may be, to the very great advantage of that world. It remains for him to fashion out of his experience that which will give him sustenance, and a voice.

The cathedral at Chartres, I have said, says something to the people of this village which it cannot say to me; but it is important to understand that this cathedral says something to me which it cannot say to them. Perhaps they are struck by the power of the spires, the glory of the windows; but they have known God, after all, longer than I have known him, and in a different way, and I am terrified by the slippery bottomless well to be found in the crypt, down which heretics were hurled to death, and by the obscene, inescapable gargoyles jutting out of the stone and seeming to say that God and the devil can never be divorced. I doubt that the villagers think of the devil when they face a cathedral because they have never been identified with the devil. But I must accept the status which myth, if nothing else, gives me in the West before I can hope to change the myth.

Yet, if the American Negro has arrived at his identity by virtue of the absoluteness of this estrangement from his past, American white men still nourish the illusion that there is some means of recovering the European innocence, of returning to a state in which black men do not exist. This is one of the greatest errors Americans can make. The identity they fought so hard to protect has, by virtue of that battle, undergone a change: Americans are as unlike any other white people in the world as it is possible to be. I do not think, for example, that it is too much to suggest that the American vision of the world—which allows so little reality, generally speaking, for any of the darker forces in human life, which tends until today to paint issues in glaring black and white—owes a great deal to the battle waged by Americans to maintain between themselves and black men a human separation which could not be bridged. It is only now beginning to be borne in on us—very faintly, it must be admitted, very slowly, and very much against our will—that this vision of the world is dangerously inaccurate; and perfectly useless. For it protects our moral high-mindedness at the terrible expense of weakening our grasp of reality. People who shut their eyes to reality simply invite their own destruction, and anyone who insists on remaining in a state of innocence long after that innocence is dead turns himself into a monster.

The time has come to realize that the inter-racial drama acted out on the American continent has not only created a new black man, it has created a new white man, too. No road whatever will lead Americans back to the simplicity of this European village where white men still have the luxury of looking on me as a stranger. I am not really a stranger any longer for any American alive. One of the things that distinguishes Americans from other people is that no other people has ever been so deeply involved in the lives of black men, and vice versa. This fact faced, with all its implications, it can be seen that the history of the American Negro problem is not merely shameful, it is also something of an achievement. For even when the worst has been said, it must also be added that the perpetual challenge posed by this problem was always, somehow, perpetually met. It is precisely this black-white experience which may prove of indispensable value to us in the world we face today. This world is white no longer, and it will never be white again.

Xenophon

SOCRATES

I HAVE OFTEN WONDERED BY WHAT ARGUMENTS THOSE WHO DREW UP THE indictment against Socrates could persuade the Athenians that his life was forfeit to the state. The indictment against him was to this effect: *Socrates is guilty of rejecting the gods acknowledged by the state and of bringing in strange deities: he is also guilty of corrupting the youth.*

First then, that he rejected the gods acknowledged by the state—what evidence did they produce of that? He offered sacrifices constantly, and made no secret of it, now in his home, now at the altars of the state temples, and he made use of divination with as little secrecy. Indeed it had become notorious that Socrates claimed to be guided by 'the deity': it was out of this claim, I think, that the charge of bringing in strange deities arose. He was no more bringing in anything strange than are other believers in divination, who rely on augury, oracles, coincidences and sacrifices. For these men's belief is not that the birds or the folk met by accident know what profits the inquirer, but that they are the instruments by which the gods make this known; and that was Socrates' belief too. Only, whereas most men say that the birds or the folk they meet dissuade or encourage them, Socrates said what he meant: for he said that the deity gave him a sign. Many of his companions were counselled by him to do this or not to do that in accordance with the warnings of the deity: and those who followed his advice prospered, and those who rejected it had cause for regret. And yet who would not admit that he wished to appear neither a knave nor a fool to his companions? but he would have been thought both, had he proved to be mistaken when he alleged that his counsel was in accordance with divine revelation. Obviously, then, he would not have given the counsel if he had not been confident that what he said would come true. And who could have inspired him with that confidence but a god? And since he had confidence in the gods, how can he have disbelieved in the existence of the gods? Another way he had of dealing with intimate friends was this: if there was no room for doubt,

Reprinted by permission of the publishers and The Loeb Classical Library from Xenophon's *Memorabilia*, translated by E. C. Marchant. Cambridge, Mass.: Harvard University Press, 1923.

he advised them to act as they thought best; but if the consequences could not be foreseen, he sent them to the oracle to inquire whether the thing ought to be done. Those who intended to control a house or a city, he said, needed the help of divination. For the craft of carpenter, smith, farmer or ruler, and the theory of such crafts, and arithmetic and economics and generalship might be learned and mastered by the application of human powers; but the deepest secrets of these matters the gods reserved to themselves; they were dark to men. You may plant a field well; but you know not who shall gather the fruits: you may build a house well; but you know not who shall dwell in it: able to command, you cannot know whether it is profitable to command: versed in statecraft, you know not whether it is profitable to guide the state: though, for your delight, you marry a pretty woman, you cannot tell whether she will bring you sorrow: though you form a party among men mighty in the state, you know not whether they will cause you to be driven from the state. If any man thinks that these matters are wholly within the grasp of the human mind and nothing in them is beyond our reason, that man, he said, is irrational. But it is no less irrational to seek the guidance of heaven in matters which men are permitted by the gods to decide for themselves by study: to ask, for instance, Is it better to get an experienced coachman to drive my carriage or a man without experience? Is it better to get an experienced seaman to steer my ship or a man without experience? So too with that we may know by reckoning, measurement or weighing. To put such questions to the gods seemed to his mind profane. In short, what the gods have granted us to do by help of learning, we must learn; what is hidden from mortals we should try to find out from the gods by divination: for to him that is in their grace the gods grant a sign.

Moreover, Socrates lived ever in the open; for early in the morning he went to the public promenades and training-grounds; in the forenoon he was seen in the market; and the rest of the day he passed just where most people were to be met: he was generally talking, and anyone might listen. Yet none ever knew him to offend against piety and religion in deed or word. He did not even discuss that topic so favoured by other talkers, "the Nature of the Universe": and avoided speculation on the so-called "Cosmos" of the Professors, how it works, and on the laws that govern the phenomena of the heaven: indeed he would argue that to trouble one's mind with such problems is sheer folly. In the first place, he would inquire, did these thinkers suppose that their knowledge of human affairs was so complete that they must seek these new fields for the exercise of their brains; or that it was their duty to neglect human affairs and consider only things divine? Moreover, he marvelled at their blindness in not seeing that man cannot solve these riddles; since even the most conceited talkers on these problems did not agree in their theories, but behaved to one another like madmen. As some madmen have no fear of danger and others are afraid where there is nothing to be afraid of, as some will do or say anything in a crowd with no sense of shame, while others shrink even from going abroad among men, some respect neither temple nor altar nor any other sacred thing, others worship stocks and stones and beasts, so is it, he held, with those who worry with "Universal Nature." Some hold that *What is* is one, others that it is infinite in number: some that all things are in perpetual motion, others that nothing can ever be moved at any time: some that all life is birth and decay, others that nothing can ever be born or ever die. Nor were those the only questions he asked about such theorists. Students of human nature, he said, think that they will apply their knowledge in due course for the good of themselves and any others they choose. Do those who pry into heavenly phenomena imagine that, once they have discovered the laws by which these are produced, they will create at their will winds, waters, seasons and such things to their need? Or have they no such expectation, and are they satisfied with knowing the causes of these various phenomena?

Such, then, was his criticism of those who meddle with these matters. His own conversation was ever of human things. The problems he discussed were, What is godly, what is ungodly; what is beautiful, what is ugly; what is just, what is unjust; what is prudence, what is madness; what is courage, what is cowardice; what is a state, what is a statesman; what is government, and what is a governor;—these and others like them, of which the knowledge made a "gentleman," in his estimation, while ignorance should involve the reproach of "slavishness."

So, in pronouncing on opinions of his that were unknown to them it is not surprising that the jury erred: but is it not astonishing that they should have ignored matters of common knowledge? For instance, when he was on the Council and had taken the counsellor's oath by which he bound himself to give counsel in accordance with the laws, it fell to his lot to preside in the Assembly when the people wanted to condemn Thrasyllus and Erasinides and their colleagues to death by a single vote. That was illegal, and he refused the motion in spite of popular rancour and the threats of many powerful persons. It was more to him that he should keep his oath than that he should humour the people in an unjust demand and shield himself from threats. For, like most men, indeed, he believed that the gods are heedful of mankind, but with an important difference; for whereas they do not believe in the omniscience of the gods, Socrates thought that they know all things, our words and deeds and secret purposes; that they are present everywhere, and grant signs to men of all that concerns man.

I wonder, then, how the Athenians can have been persuaded that Socrates was a freethinker, when he never said or did anything contrary to sound religion, and his utterances about the gods and his behaviour towards them were the words and actions of a man who is truly religious and deserves to be thought so.

II. No less wonderful is it to me that some believed the charge brought against Socrates of corrupting the youth. In the first place, apart from what I have said, in control of his own passions and appetites he was the strictest of men; further, in endurance of cold and heat and every kind of toil he was most resolute; and besides, his needs were so schooled to moderation that having very little he was yet very content. Such was his own character: how then can he have led others into impiety, crime, gluttony, lust, or sloth? On the contrary, he cured these vices in many, by putting into them a desire for goodness, and by giving them confidence that self-discipline would make them gentlemen. To be sure he never professed to teach this; but, by letting his own light shine, he led his disciples to hope that they through imitation of him would attain to such excellence. Furthermore, he himself never neglected the body, and reproved such neglect in others. Thus over-eating followed by over-exertion he disapproved. But he approved of taking as much hard exercise as is agreeable to the soul; for the habit not only insured good health, but did not hamper the care of the soul. On the other hand, he disliked foppery and pretentiousness in the fashion of clothes or shoes or in behaviour. Nor, again, did he encourage love of money in his companions. For while he checked their other desires, he would not make money himself out of their desire for his companionship. He held that this self-denying ordinance insured his liberty. Those who charged a fee for their society he denounced for selling themselves into bondage; since they were bound to converse with all from whom they took the fee. He marvelled that anyone should make money by the profession of virtue, and should not reflect that his highest reward would be the gain of a good friend; as though he who became a true gentleman could fail to feel deep gratitude for a benefit so great. Socrates indeed never promised any such boon to anyone; but he was confident that those of his companions who adopted his principles of conduct would throughout life be good friends to him and to one another. How, then, should such a man "corrupt the youth"? Unless, perchance, it be corruption to foster virtue.

But, said his accuser, he taught his companions to despise the established laws by insisting on the folly of appointing public officials by lot, when none would choose a pilot or builder or flautist by lot, nor any other craftsman for work in which mistakes are far less disastrous than mistakes in statecraft. Such sayings, he argued, led the young to despise the established constitution and made them violent. But I hold that they who cultivate wisdom and think they will be able to guide the people in prudent policy never lapse into violence: they know that enmities and dangers are inseparable from violence, but persuasion produces the same results safely and amicably. For violence, by making its victims sensible of loss, rouses their hatred: but persuasion, by seeming to confer a favour, wins goodwill. It is not, then, cultivation of wisdom that leads to violent methods, but the possession of power without prudence. Besides, many supporters are necessary to him who ventures to use force: but he who can persuade needs no confederate, having confidence in his own unaided power of persuasion. And such a man has no occasion to shed blood; for who would rather take a man's life than have a live and willing follower?

But his accuser argued thus. Among the associates of Socrates were Critias and Alcibiades; and none wrought so many evils to the state. For Critias in the days of the oligarchy bore the palm for greed and violence: Alcibiades, for his part, exceeded all in licentiousness and insolence under the democracy. Now I have no intention of excusing the wrong these two men wrought the state; but I will explain how they came to be with Socrates. Ambition was the very life-blood of both: no Athenian was ever like them. They were eager to get control of everything and to outstrip every rival in notoriety. They knew that Socrates was living on very little, and yet was wholly independent; that he was strictly moderate in all his pleasures; and that in argument he could do what he liked with any disputant. Sharing this knowledge and the principles I have indicated, is it to be supposed that these two men wanted to adopt the simple life of Socrates, and with this object in view sought his society? Did they not rather think that by associating with him they would attain the utmost proficiency in speech and action? For my part I believe that, had heaven granted them the choice between the life they saw Socrates leading and death, they would have chosen rather to die. Their conduct betrayed their purpose; for as soon as they thought themselves superior to their fellow-disciples they sprang away from Socrates and took to politics; it was for political ends that they had wanted Socrates.

Plato

CRITO

WHY HAVE YOU COME AT THIS HOUR, CRITO? IT MUST BE QUITE EARLY?

CRITO: Yes, certainly.

SOCRATES: What is the exact time?

CRITO: The dawn is breaking.

SOCRATES: I wonder that the keeper of the prison would let you in.

CRITO: He knows me, because I often come, Socrates; moreover, I have done him a kindness.

SOCRATES: And are you only just arrived?

CRITO: No, I came some time ago.

SOCRATES: Then why did you sit and say nothing, instead of at once awakening me?

CRITO: I should not have liked myself, Socrates, to be in such great trouble and unrest as you are—indeed I should not: I have been watching with amazement your peaceful slumbers; and for that reason I did not awake you, because I wished to minimize the pain. I have always thought you to be of a happy disposition; but never did I see anything like the easy, tranquil manner in which you bear this calamity.

SOCRATES: Why, Crito, when a man has reached my age he ought not to be repining at the approach of death.

CRITO: And yet other old men find themselves in similar misfortunes, and age does not prevent them from repining.

SOCRATES: That is true. But you have not told me why you come at this early hour.

CRITO: I come to bring you a message which is sad and painful; not, as I believe, to yourself, but to all of us who are your friends, and saddest of all to me.

Jowett translation.

SOCRATES: What? Has the ship come from Delos, on the arrival of which I am to die?

CRITO: No, the ship has not actually arrived, but she will probably be here today, as persons who have come from Sunius tell me that they left her there; and therefore tomorrow, Socrates, will be the last day of your life.

SOCRATES: Very well, Crito; if such is the will of God, I am willing; but my belief is that there will be a delay of a day.

CRITO: Why do you think so?

SOCRATES: I will tell you. I am to die on the day after the arrival of the ship.

CRITO: Yes; that is what the authorities say.

SOCRATES: But I do not think that the ship will be here until tomorrow; this I infer from a vision which I had last night, or rather only just now, when you fortunately allowed me to sleep.

CRITO: And what was the nature of the vision?

SOCRATES: There appeared to me the likeness of a woman, fair and comely, clothed in bright raiment, who called to me and said: O Socrates,

The third day hence to fertile Phthia shalt thou go.

CRITO: What a singular dream, Socrates!

SOCRATES: There can be no doubt about the meaning, Crito, I think.

CRITO: Yes, the meaning is only too clear. But, oh! my beloved Socrates, let me entreat you once more to take my advice and escape. For if you die I shall not only lose a friend who can never be replaced, but there is another evil: people who do not know you and me will believe that I might have saved you if I had been willing to give money, but that I did not care. Now, can there be a worse disgrace than this—that I should be thought to value money more than the life of a friend? For the many will not be persuaded that I wanted you to escape, and that you refused.

SOCRATES: But why, my dear Crito, should we care about the opinion of the many? Good men, and they are the only persons who are worth considering, will think of these things truly as they occurred.

CRITO: But you see, Socrates, that the opinion of the many must be regarded, for what is now happening shows that they can do the greatest evil to anyone who has lost their good opinion.

SOCRATES: I only wish it were so, Crito; and that the many could do the greatest evil; for then they would also be able to do the greatest good— and what a fine thing this could be! But in reality they can do neither; for they cannot make a man either wise or foolish; and whatever they do is the result of chance.

CRITO: Well, I will not dispute with you; but please to tell me, Socrates, whether you are not acting out of regard to me and your other friends: are you not afraid that if you escape from prison we may get into trouble with the informers for having stolen you away, and lose either the whole or a great part of our property; or that even a worse evil may happen to us? Now, if you fear on our account, be at ease; for in order to save you, we ought surely to run this, or even a greater risk; be persuaded, then, and do as I say.

SOCRATES: Yes, Crito, that is one fear which you mention, but by no means the only one.

CRITO: Fear not—there are persons who are willing to get you out of prison at no great cost; and as for the informers, they are far from being exorbitant in their demands—a little money will satisfy them. My means, which are certainly ample, are at your service, and if you have a scruple about spending all mine, here are strangers who will give you the use of theirs; and one of them, Simmias the Theban, has brought a large sum of money for this very purpose; and Cebes and many others are prepared to spend their money in helping you to escape. I say, therefore, do not hesitate on our account, and do not say, as you did in the court, that you will have a difficulty in knowing what to do with yourself anywhere else. For men will love you in other places to which you may go, and not in Athens only; there are friends of mine in Thessaly, if you like to go to them, who will value and protect you, and no Thessalian will give you any trouble. Nor can I think that you are at all justified, Socrates, in betraying your own life when you might be saved; in acting thus you are playing into the hands of your enemies, who are hurrying on your destruction. And further I should say that you are deserting your own children; for you might bring them up and educate them; instead of which you go away and leave them, and they will have to take their chance; and if they do not meet with the usual fate of orphans, there will be small thanks to you. No man should bring children into the world who is unwilling to persevere to the end in their nurture and education. But you appear to be choosing the easier part, not the better and manlier, which would have been more becoming in one who professes to care for virtue in all his actions, like yourself. And indeed, I am ashamed not only of you, but of us who are your friends, when I reflect that the whole business will be attributed entirely to our want of courage. The trial need never have come on, or might have been managed differently; and this last act, or crowning folly, will seem to have occurred through our negligence and cowardice, who might have saved you, if we had been good for anything; and you might have saved yourself, for there was no difficulty at all. See now, Socrates, how sad and discreditable are the consequences, both to us and you. Make up your mind then, or rather have your mind already made up, for the time of deliberation is over, and there is only one thing to be done, which must be done this very night, and, if we delay at all, will be no longer practicable or possible; I beseech you therefore, Socrates, be persuaded by me, and do as I say.

SOCRATES: Dear Crito, your zeal is invaluable, if a right one; but if wrong, the greater the zeal the greater the danger; and therefore we ought to consider whether I shall or shall not do as you say. For I am and always have been one of those natures who must be guided by reason, whatever the reason may be which upon reflection appears to me to be the best; and now that this chance has befallen me, I cannot repudiate my own words: the principles which I have hitherto honored and revered I still honor, and unless we can at once find other and better principles, I am certain not to agree with you; no, not even if the power of the multitude could inflict many more imprisonments, confiscations, deaths, frightening us like children with hobgoblin terrors. What will be the fairest way of considering the question? Shall I return to your old argument about the opinions of men?—we were saying that some of them are to be regarded, and others not. Now were we right in maintaining this before I was condemned? And has the argument which was once good now proved to be talk for the sake of talking—mere childish nonsense? That is what I want to consider with your help, Crito: whether, under my present circumstances, the argument appears to be in any way different or not; and is to be allowed by me or disallowed. That argument, which, as I believe, is maintained by many persons of authority, was to the effect, as I was saying, that the opinions of some men are to be regarded, and of other men not to be regarded. Now you, Crito, are not going to die tomorrow—at least, there is no human probability of this—and therefore you are disinterested and not liable to be deceived by the circumstances in which you are placed. Tell me then, whether I am right in saying that some opinions, and the opinions of some men only, are to be valued, and that other opinions, and the opinions of other men, are not to be valued. I ask you whether I was right in maintaining this?

CRITO: Certainly.

SOCRATES: The good are to be regarded, and not the bad?

CRITO: Yes.

SOCRATES: And the opinions of the wise are good, and the opinions of the unwise are evil?

CRITO: Certainly.

SOCRATES: And what was said about another matter? Is the pupil who devotes himself to the practice of gymnastics supposed to attend to the praise and blame and opinion of every man, or of one man only—his physician or trainer, whoever he may be?

CRITO: Of one man only.

SOCRATES: And he ought to fear the censure and welcome the praise of that one only, and not of the many?

CRITO: Clearly so.

SOCRATES: And he ought to act and train, and eat and drink in the way which seems good to his single master who has understanding, rather than according to the opinion of all other men put together?

CRITO: True.

SOCRATES: And if he disobeys and disregards the opinion and approval of the one, and regards the opinion of the many who have no understanding, will he not suffer evil?

CRITO: Certainly he will.

SOCRATES: And what will the evil be, whither tending and what affecting, in the disobedient person?

CRITO: Clearly, affecting the body; that is what is destroyed by the evil.

SOCRATES: Very good; and is not this true, Crito, of other things which we need not separately enumerate? In questions of just and unjust, fair and foul, good and evil, which are the subjects of our present consultation, ought we to follow the opinion of the many and to fear them; or the opinion of the one man who has understanding? ought we not to fear and reverence him more than all the rest of the world: and if we desert him shall we not destroy and injure that principle in us which may be assumed to be improved by justice and deteriorated by injustice—there is such a principle?

CRITO: Certainly there is, Socrates.

SOCRATES: Take a parallel instance: if, acting under the advice of those who have no understanding, we destroy that which is improved by health and is deteriorated by disease, would life be worth having? And that which has been destroyed is—the body?

CRITO: Yes.

SOCRATES: Could we live, having an evil and corrupted body?

CRITO: Certainly not.

SOCRATES: And will life be worth having, if that higher part of man be destroyed, which is improved by justice and depraved by injustice? Do we suppose that principle, whatever it may be in man, which has to do with justice and injustice, to be inferior to the body?

CRITO: Certainly not.

SOCRATES: More honorable than the body?

CRITO: Far more.

SOCRATES: Then, my friend, we must not regard what the many say of us; but what he, the one man who has understanding of just and unjust, will say, and what the truth will say. And therefore you begin in error when you advise that we should regard the opinion of the many about just and unjust, good and evil, honorable and dishonorable.—"Well," someone will say, "but the many can kill us."

CRITO: Yes, Socrates; that will clearly be the answer.

SOCRATES: And it is true: but still I find with surprise that the old argument is unshaken as ever. And I should like to know whether I may say the same of another proposition—that not life, but a good life, is to be chiefly valued?

CRITO: Yes, that also remains unshaken.

SOCRATES: And a good life is equivalent to a just and honorable one—that holds also?

CRITO: Yes, it does.

SOCRATES: From these premises I proceed to argue the question whether I ought or ought not to try and escape without the consent of the Athenians: and if I am clearly right in escaping, then I will make the attempt; but if not, I will abstain. The other considerations which you mention, of money and loss of character and the duty of educating one's children, are, I fear, only the doctrines of the multitude, who would be as ready to restore people to life, if they were able, as they are to put them to death—and with as little reason. But now, since the argument has thus far prevailed, the only question which remains to be considered is whether we shall do right either in escaping or in suffering others to aid in our escape and paying them in money and thanks, or whether in reality we shall not do rightly; and if the latter, then death or any other calamity which may ensue on my remaining here must not be allowed to enter into the calculation.

CRITO: I think that you are right, Socrates; how then shall we proceed?

SOCRATES: Let us consider the matter together, and do you either refute me if you can, and I will be convinced; or else cease, my dear friend, from repeating to me that I ought to escape against the wishes of the Athenians: for I highly value your attempts to persuade me to do so, but I may not be persuaded against my own better judgment. And now please to consider my first position, and try how you can best answer me.

CRITO: I will.

SOCRATES: Are we to say that we are never intentionally to do wrong, or that in one way we ought and in another way we ought not to do wrong, or is doing wrong always evil and dishonorable, as I was just now saying, and as has been already acknowledged by us? Are all our former admissions which were made within a few days to be thrown away? And have we, at our age, been earnestly discoursing with one another all our life long only to discover that we are no better than children? Or, in spite of the opinion of the many, and in spite of consequences whether better or worse, shall we insist on the truth of what was then said, that injustice is always an evil and dishonor to him who acts unjustly? Shall we say so or not?

CRITO: Yes.

SOCRATES: Then we must do no wrong?

CRITO: Certainly not.

SOCRATES: Nor, when injured, injure in return, as the many imagine; for we must injure no one at all?

CRITO: Clearly not.

SOCRATES: Again, Crito, may we do evil?

CRITO: Surely not, Socrates.

SOCRATES: And what of doing evil in return for evil, which is the morality of the many—is that just or not?

CRITO: Not just.

SOCRATES: For doing evil to another is the same as injuring him?

CRITO: Very true.

SOCRATES: Then we ought not to retaliate or render evil for evil to anyone, whatever evil we may have suffered from him. But I would have you consider, Crito, whether you really mean what you are saying. For this opinion has never been held, and never will be held, by any considerable number of persons; and those who are agreed and those who are not agreed upon this point have no common ground, and can only despise one another when they see how widely they differ. Tell me, then, whether you agree with and assent to my first principle, that neither injury nor retaliation nor warding off evil by evil is ever right. And shall that be the premise of our argument? Or do you decline and dissent from this? For so I have ever thought, and continue to think; but, if you are of another opinion, let me hear what you have to say. If, however, you remain of the same mind as formerly, I will proceed to the next step.

CRITO: You may proceed, for I have not changed my mind.

SOCRATES: Then I will go on to the next point, which may be put in the form of a question: Ought a man to do what he admits to be right, or ought he to betray the right?

CRITO: He ought to do what he thinks right.

SOCRATES: But if this is true, what is the application? In leaving the prison against the will of the Athenians, do I wrong any? or rather do I not wrong those whom I ought least to wrong? Do I not desert the principles which were acknowledged by us to be just—what do you say?

CRITO: I cannot tell, Socrates; for I do not know.

SOCRATES: Then consider the matter in this way: Imagine that I am about to play truant (you may call the proceeding by any name which you like), and the laws and the government come and interrogate me: "Tell us, Socrates," they say; "what are you about? are you not going by an act of yours to overturn us—the laws, and the whole state, as far as in you lies? Do you imagine that a state can subsist and not be overthrown, in which the decisions of law have no power, but are set aside and trampled upon by individuals?"—What will be our answer, Crito, to these and the like words? Anyone, and especially a rhetorician, will have a good deal to say on behalf of the law which requires a sentence to be carried out. He will argue that this law should not be set aside; and shall we reply, "Yes; but the state has injured us and given an unjust sentence." Suppose I say that?

CRITO: Very good, Socrates.

SOCRATES: "And was that our agreement with you?" the law would answer; "or were you to abide by the sentences of the state?" And if I were to express my astonishment at their words, the law would probably add: "Answer, Socrates, instead of opening your eyes: you are in the habit of asking and answering questions. Tell us: What complaint have you to make against us which justifies you in attempting to destroy us and the state? In the first place did we not bring you into existence? Your father married your mother by our aid and begat you. Say whether you have any objection to urge against those of us who regulate marriage?" None, I should reply. "Or against those of us who after birth regulate the nurture and education of children, in which you also were trained? Were not the laws, which have the charge of education, right in commanding your father to train you in music and gymnastic?" Right, I should reply. "Well then, since you were brought into the world and nurtured and educated by us, can you deny in the first place that you are our child and slave, as your fathers were before you? And if this is true you are not on equal terms with us; nor can you think that you have a right to do to us what we are doing to you. Would you have any right to strike or revile or do any other evil to your father or your master, if you had one, because you have been struck or reviled by him, or received some other evil at his hands? You would not say this. And because we think right to destroy you, do you think that you have the right to destroy us in return, and your country as far as in you lies? Will you, O professor of true virtue, pretend that you are justified in this? Has a philosopher like you failed to discover that our country is more to be valued and higher and holier far than mother or father or any ancestor, and more to be regarded in the eyes of the gods and of men of understanding? also to be soothed, and gently and reverently entreated when angry, even more than a father, and either to be persuaded, or if not persuaded, to be obeyed? And when we are punished by her, whether with imprisonment or stripes, the punishment is to be endured in silence; and if she lead us to wounds or death in battle, thither we follow as is right; neither may anyone yield or retreat or leave his rank, but whether in battle or in a court of law, or in any other place, he must do what his city and his country order him; or he must change their views of what is just: and if he may do no violence to his father or mother, much less may he do violence to his country." What answer shall we make to this, Crito? Do the laws speak truly, or do they not?

CRITO: I think that they do.

SOCRATES: Then the laws will say: "Consider, Socrates, if we are speaking truly that in your present attempt you are going to do us an injury. For, having brought you into the world, and nurtured and educated you, and given you and every other citizen a share in every good which we had to give, we further proclaim to any Athenian by the liberty which we allow him, that if he does not like us when he has become of age and has seen the ways of the city, and made our acquaintance, he may go where he pleases and take his goods with him. None of us laws will forbid him or interfere with him. Anyone who does not like us and the city, and who wants to emigrate to a colony or to any other city, may go where he likes, retaining his property. But he who has experience of the manner in which we order justice and administer the state, and still remains, has entered into an implied contract that he will do as we command him. And he who disobeys us is, as we maintain, thrice wrong; first, because in disobeying us he is disobeying his parents; secondly, because we are the authors of his education; thirdly, because he has made an agreement with us that he will duly obey our commands; and he neither obeys them nor convinces us that our commands are unjust; and we do not rudely impose them, but give him the alternative of obeying or convincing us; that is what we offer, and he does neither. These are the sort of accusations to which, as we were saying, you, Socrates, will be exposed if you accomplish your intentions; you, above all other Athenians."

Suppose now I ask, why I rather than anybody else? They will justly retort upon me that I above all other men have acknowledged the agreement. "There is clear proof," they will say, "Socrates, that we and the city were not displeasing to you. Of all Athenians you have been the most constant resident in the city, which, as you never leave, you may be supposed to love. For you never went out of the city either to see the games, except once when you went to the Isthmus, or to any other place unless when you were on military service; nor did you travel as other men do. Nor had you any curiosity to know other states or their laws: your affections did not go beyond us and our state; we were your special favorites, and you acquiesced in our government of you; and here in this city you begat your children, which is a proof of your satisfaction. Moreover, you might in the course of the trial, if you had liked, have fixed the penalty at banishment; the state which refuses to let you go now would have let you go then. But you pretended that you preferred death to exile, and that you were not unwilling to die. And now you have forgotten these fine sentiments, and pay no respect to us, the laws, of whom you are the destroyer; and are doing what only a miserable slave would do, running away and turning your back upon the compacts and agreements which you made as a citizen. And, first of all, answer this very question: Are we right in saying that you agreed to be governed according to us in deed, and not in word only? Is that true or not?" How shall we answer, Crito? Must we not assent?

CRITO: We cannot help it, Socrates.

SOCRATES: Then will they not say: "You, Socrates, are breaking the covenants and agreements which you made with us at your leisure, not in any haste or under any compulsion or deception, but after you have had seventy years to think of them, during which time you were at liberty to leave the city, if we were not to your mind, or if our covenants appeared to you to be unfair. You had your choice, and might have gone either to Lacedaemon or Crete, both which states are often praised by you for their good government, or to some other Hellenic or foreign state. Whereas you, above all other Athenians, seemed to be so fond of the state, or, in other words, of us, her laws (and who would care about a state which has no laws?), that you never stirred out of her; the halt, the blind, the maimed were not more stationary in her than you were. And now you run away and forsake your agreements. Not so, Socrates, if you will take our advice; do not make yourself ridiculous by escaping out of the city.

"For just consider, if you transgress and err in this sort of way, what good will you do either to yourself or to your friends? That your friends will be driven into exile and deprived of citizenship, or will lose their property, is tolerably certain; and you yourself, if you fly to one of the neighboring cities, as, for example, Thebes or Megara, both of which are well governed, will come to them as an enemy, Socrates, and their government will be against you, and all patriotic citizens will cast an evil eye upon you as a subverter of the laws, and you will confirm in the minds of the judges the justice of their own condemnation of you. For he who is a corrupter of the laws is more likely to be a corrupter of the young and foolish portion of mankind. Will you then flee from well-ordered cities and virtuous men? and is existence worth having on these terms? Or will you go to them without shame, and talk to them, Socrates? And what will you say to them? What you say here about virtue and justice and institutions and laws being the best things among men? Would that be decent of you? Surely not. But if you go away from well-governed states to Crito's friends in Thessaly, where there is great disorder and license, they will be charmed to hear the tale of your escape from prison, set off with ludicrous particulars of the manner in which you were wrapped in a goatskin or some other disguise, and metamorphosed as the manner is of runaways; but will there be no one to remind you that in your old age you were not ashamed to violate the most sacred laws from a miserable desire of a little more life? Perhaps not, if you keep them in a good temper; but if they are out of temper you will hear many degrading things; you will live, but how?—as the flatterer of all men, and the servant of all men; and doing what?— eating and drinking in Thessaly, having gone abroad in order that you may get a dinner. And where will be your fine sentiments about justice and virtue? Say that you wish to live for the sake of your children—you want to bring them up and educate them—will you take them into Thessaly and deprive them of Athenian citizenship? Is this the benefit which you will confer upon them? Or are you under the impression that they will be better cared for and educated here if you are still alive, although absent from them; for your friends will take care of them? Do you fancy that if you are an inhabitant of Thessaly they will take care of them, and if you are an inhabitant of the other world that they will not take care of them? Nay; but if they who call themselves friends are good for anything, they will—to be sure they will.

"Listen, then, Socrates, to us who have brought you up. Think not of life and children first, and of justice afterwards, but of justice first, that you may be justified before the princes of the world below. For neither will you nor any that belong to you be happier or holier or juster in this life, or happier in another, if you do as Crito bids. Now you depart in innocence, a sufferer and not a doer of evil; a victim, not of the laws, but of men. But if you go forth, returning evil for evil, and injury for injury, breaking the covenants and agreements which you have made with us, and wronging those whom you ought least of all to wrong, that is to say, yourself, your friends, your country, and us, we shall be angry with you while you live, and our brethren, the laws in the world below, will receive you as an enemy; for they will know that you have done your best to destroy us. Listen then, to us and not to Crito."

This, dear Citro, is the voice which I seem to hear murmuring in my ears, like the sound of the flute in the ears of the mystic; that voice, I say, is humming in my ears, and prevents me from hearing any other. And I know that anything more which you may say will be vain. Yet speak, if you have anything to say.

CRITO: I have nothing to say, Socrates.

SOCRATES: Leave me then, Crito, to fulfill the will of God, and to follow whither he leads.

THE ARTS, FINE AND OTHERWISE

Gilbert Seldes

A CLINICAL ANALYSIS OF T.V.

When H. G. Wells was in New York on his last visit I asked him what television could do in "the race between education and catastrophe," and to my dismay he answered that it would be useless if not actively damaging. "You'll have nothing but parades," he said; "an endless newsreel of parades and sports."

He was wrong. So were many others. To strike a trial balance as TV approaches its tenth year of commercial operation, it might be helpful to recall what people hoped and feared and expected when it began.

A few months after my talk with Wells, Paul Kesten, then the executive vice president of C.B.S. for whom I was working, took me to lunch to explain the facts of life. Kesten is one of the few authentic geniuses of the business world and he interprets figures the way a virtuoso interprets "The Devil's Trill." Before my dazzled eyes he set the *proof* that no matter how many TV sets were sold, no matter how much you charged the sponsor, television could *never* pay its way.

Other predictions were that television would put an end to reading but would reunite the family (without conversation) around the 21-inch hearth, that it would make adult education popular, that it would be the decisive factor in the choice of Presidential candidates.

All things are possible, if not likely, and these forecasts may yet prove sound. Already taking its place beside Mr. Hoover's prediction (in the Twenties) that the American people would not stand for commercials on the air is the wishful thought that TV commercials would be less aggres-

Used by permission of the author and The New York Times Magazine.

sive because the sponsor's product would be visible. The strangest prediction of all is one in which the entire industry took part—that television wouldn't be more than a chemical "trace" in the broadcasting business for a long time to come.

Regardless of what the various managements wanted, they had a rough calendar at the back of their minds which allotted about two years after the war to regular AM radio (replacement of obsolete equipment, production of programs held up by the war); then Frequency Modulation would come in and occupy us for a decade, during which the apparatus and the techniques of television would be developed; and then TV, launched in black and white in the mid-Fifties, would hold us for another ten years, so that about 1965 the country would be ready for gorgeous color.

This is really the essential fact about television: It is ten years ahead of itself. A combination of economic pressures and technical advances resulted in the appearance of reasonably priced sets with a fairly clear and steady picture soon after the war ended, and the installation of large screens in cafes and roadhouses gave the business a sort of final push. The result was that the entire country became aware of television through cartoons and jokes about it even before Milton Berle arrived in 1948. Since then it has been an obsession with the American people. Even the eggheads and intellectuals (probably subversives every one of them) and the snobs who boast of never having seen a TV show are concerned with what television can do to them, to their fellowmen, to the economy, to the nation.

What has it done?

It has knocked off Ibsen's "A Doll's House" in 22½ minutes and it has also done stage-length versions of Shakespeare with intelligence and skill. It turned "Author Meets the Critics" into a brawl and back into civilized discussion. It has presented and still presents over a hundred separate acts of criminal violence a week, many of them seen by children, and at various times it presents serious studies in the cause of crime. In collaboration with colleges and universities, the commercial networks have carried studies in archaeology, in the dramatic arts and in history, and have had brilliant and popular educators on the air, yet the TV stereotypes of the teacher, of the man of science, of the educated woman, are almost ridiculous or disagreeable.

For a time it seemed as if the Comic Spirit were to be incarnated in Berle and that our last view of Fred Allen would be with a pig in his arms (this is called a "sight gag" and when you've seen one you know how appropriate the name is). It has urged children to eat a "superatomic" bread and presented a thirty-minute filmed advertisement for a scalp treatment (which was shown every night for weeks and was more popular than many programs), and it has also let us see productions from which the sponsors have voluntarily omitted their commercials. It has exploited the depths of human misery and mocked at native ignorance while it has collected hundreds of millions to alleviate suffering and has made great men and women known to millions, presenting their thoughts and their emotions simply and effectively.

It has brought advertising into the great ritual of democracy so that only the actual ceremony of the Presidential Inauguration is now unsponsored and, at great expense to themselves, the two less prosperous networks carried the Army-McCarthy hearings. It has been a godsend to the half-talented, promoting them into "personalities," and it has degraded or failed to use finer talents; it put over Liberace after the Continental and sent Victor Borge back to the theatre. It has the vigor of youth and is as pestiferous as a precocious child; it is a monster and a Medici.

The most honorable accomplishments of television have been in the hour-long play and in the handling of actuality.

The various dramatic series resemble one another, particularly in being uneven in quality from week to week, but rarely falling below a reasonably high level. The productions of Fred Coe have a special interest because he has surrounded himself with a group of writers who have actually created a style of drama which is neither theatre nor movie and definitely is television. It took the movies twenty years to escape from the wrong style— photographing a stage play—and almost as long again to create in cinematic terms.

Among the dramatists in the Coe group, Horton Foote, N. Richard Nash, and Paddy Chayefsky have reworked their TV plays for the theatre or for the movies, but their plays were originally shaped for production in a studio to be seen by two or three people at home. They and Robert Alan Arthur, Sumner Locke Elliott, Tad Mosel and David Shaw, who complete the group, concentrate on character, letting plot rise out of the hopes and fears and habits of human beings without over-projection, with intensity and passion. Their predilection for the "downbeat" or sad ending got Mr. Coe into trouble last season, but these writers are still writing the kind of TV plays which have their special quality.

In the area of straight communications, television reached a surprising maturity when the Kefauver Committee hearings were transmitted and the standards of TV reporting were established (by the directors and crews of the independent station WPIX). Not for a single moment were the cameras used to dramatize or to comment; dispassionate separation of fact from editorial opinion was not an abstract ideal, but a fact. The industry can be proud of having arrived at this point so early in its career.

Vastly to its credit also is the demonstration, led by Edward R. Murrow, of the value of courage on the air. His controversy with Senator McCarthy also demonstrated the emptiness of the old formula, "equal time to reply," because in television the time may be mathematically equal, but without equal money and skill, as well as the prestige of the program on which the attack is made, the reply cannot be effective.

The right to use television for controversies in which individuals are attacked and the right of stations and networks to editorialize about broadcasting or about other public issues are being discussed by the managers of the industry and it is a hopeful sign that Frank Stanton, the head of C.B.S. and Gen. David Sarnoff, of R.C.A.-N.B.C., are not at all agreed on some fundamental principles—the clash of opinion is all to the good.

Not quite so good is the industry's habit of making decisions affecting the public without inviting public discussion. Motor car manufacturers and makers of candy bars do this, but they are not required by law to operate in the public interest and the broadcasters are. More and more citizens, wondering what television may be doing to them, finding the managers of the business not responsive to anything but boycotts, organized phone calls and other pressures, turn to their Congressmen and now television finds itself on the defensive, facing investigations and threats.

Most of these arise from that part of the program schedule usually held as the industry's worst—its endless stream of crime shows, many of them available to children, bringing even lower the average, uninspiring to begin with, of programs for the young. Their standard is negative: "So long as no one can prove that harm comes from a program we have the right to show it."

Proof is lacking that crime shows contribute to juvenile delinquency, but television at this point has been lumped with the horror "comic" books and is sharing the odium they have deserved. The outcry against the networks has been going on for years and during this time the number of crime programs has steadily increased. The impression becomes strong that broadcasters are indifferent to unorganized complaints and this is matched by the broadcasters' confidence in the indifference of a great majority of their listener-viewers. It is not a good foundation for mutual respect and helpfulness.

Beyond the actual or potential damage done by any single type of program, more serious in the long run is what television does by filling so much of the air with the innocuous, the merely acceptable. I am thinking of dozens of half-hour series, all alike, all imitating one of two or three originals which in turn begin to imitate their followers, as "I Love Lucy" did, with all its individual cock-a-doodle-do lost and with Lucille Ball, a superlative comedienne, not using nine-tenths of her talents. And if they are not comedy programs outright, they are "situations" and you can't tell one from another because the star of one may be a lady orthodontist and of the other a boy veterinarian. In the end they all do the same thing: there's a mixup, see, and just before the middle commercial he (she) gets mad (drunk) and in comes . . .

No one believes in these things any more. They are produced without conviction and received with a kind of low-order apathy, and, anyhow, if someone got really tired of them he could turn to spelling bees and parlor games and exhibitions of personalities, all pleasant, most of them amusing, the people on them retreating farther and farther behind the masks of themselves, so that when a personality suddenly remembers that it belongs to a human being and something with bite or tang is spoken on the air seven people protest and the man's fired.

The willing suspension of all real wanting, the readiness to take whatever is given, is the consequence of routine schedules (which are, I think, inevitable) and routine thinking (not inevitable) which brings too many programs to a single level—not only of intelligence and education but also of emotional maturity. They all are looking for the same responses—a quick laugh, a quick jolt. A vast "so what" suffuses the atmosphere and people turn away from exceptional single shows to follow the favorites where they can see the same things being done this week as they saw last week. Giving the people what they want has degenerated into giving them what they are ready to accept for nothing without protest—and without passion.

Into focus floats Jimmy Durante, the great spirit of comedy of our time—and others: there are Burns and Allen, as good in television as they've ever been, and the most underrated, the shrewdest comedy of American domestic manners, "Ethel and Albert"; there is Benny, whom the screen hasn't intimidated; there are "Kukla, Fran and Ollie," now held down to the quarter-hours which are just right for them; there is "Omnibus," which fumbles at times but is still an act of faith; there is even a newcomer named George Gobel who has freshness and wit; there are special programs —opera commissioned for television and great events.

You begin to list these special people, these triumphs of a medium of communication and entertainment which only began to open its eyes in 1945, and it seems ungrateful to pick faults. But without criticism television may go further than it has—against its own best direction.

By 1950 critics were complaining that the new season's new programs were copies of all the others. This year a program called "Medic" duplicates the style (as artificial as blank verse) of "Dragnet," as if childbirth in which a mother must be sacrificed to save a child is somehow the same thing as tracking down a firebug. Next year we shall have, in clipped tones, after three bars of a hymn: "My name is Arthur Dimmesdale. (Pause) I'm a minister. (Pause) Working out of Boston, mostly. (Pause) Tuesday afternoon—routine check on Hester Prynne—charged with being an A-girl. (Pause) Not wearing her letter. . . ."

It is ungrateful to bring up such things, but the lack of pungent characters, of variety, of the excitement of discovery, all trace back to the principle of playing safe by imitating whatever has been successful. This is the cyclical method of Hollywood, which did more than television to keep people away from the movie houses. The complaints of the critics become almost routine as the programs against which they protest. Them, as Durante says, them's the conditions that prevail.

It is a fair guess that within a few years some form of pay-TV will arrive, perhaps in the home, perhaps in theatres, using new movies and specially produced plays, bringing exclusive events in sport. Ten cents each from one-tenth of all the TV set owners in the country will provide a stupendous budget for production, and if the FCC allots any frequencies to this type of transmission they will be side by side with another kind of competition: the educational stations.

Between them these two may siphon off so large a segment of the audience that the commercial broadcasters who now have everything their own way will have to compete, not with one another, which fatally leads downward in the search for common denominators, but with new concepts of "the public interest."

Then, perhaps, we shall have a truly democratic television service, in which the wants of the majority are neither neglected nor basely exploited, while the legitimate wants of all substantial minorities are satisfied without snobbishness or pedantry.

Robert Rice

THE FURY: MORT SAHL

MORT SAHL, A DARK AND SAVAGE WIT WHO SPENDS MOST OF HIS WORKING life fulminating through the haze, late at night, from the stage of one night club or another, is almost certainly the most widely acclaimed and best-paid nihilist ever produced by Western civilization. Unlike most men in the upper tax brackets, he is against practically everything. During one recent forty-five-minute night-club monologue, he disparaged, sometimes at length and sometimes merely in passing, the following persons, places, objects, institutions, and ideas, in the following order: Charles de Gaulle; Dwight Eisenhower; segregation; Shelley Berman; trade unions; "Marty;" jazz; New York City; Berkeley, California; Samuel Beckett; newspapers; coffeehouses; sandals; J. D. Salinger; soiled raincoats; natural-shoulder suits; women; filter-tip cigarettes; capital punishment; Zen Buddhism; the Chinese Nationalists; the Chinese Communists; Candlestick Park; atheism; policemen; Chicago; the Moskvich automobile; advertising; the Edsel automobile; "Death of a Salesman;" the Daughters of the American Revolution; the Woman's Christian Temperance Union; movies; the concept of guilt; astronauts; Josephine Baker; the hydrogen bomb; the State Department; Senator George Smathers; Cuba; Israel; Fidel Castro; Richard Nixon; Dave Garroway; John Kennedy; birth control; "On the Beach;" Dick Clark; American youth; schoolteachers; Christmas; German radios; corruption; Charles Van Doren; Adlai Stevenson; the Columbia Broadcasting System; prostitution; drug manufacturers; Elizabeth Arden; cheating on examinations; John Steinbeck; Norman Cousins; the Russians; *Fortune;* Miami; multiple-choice questions; the Federal Bureau of Investigation; the Pacific Gas & Electric Co.; Dave Brubeck; the Taft-Hartley

Act; former Governor Earl Long; Disneyland; Arturo Frondizi; the Diners' Club; the foreign-aid bill; Ezra Taft Benson; and the *Saturday Evening Post*. That didn't nearly exhaust the list of his animosities, of course; on the evening in question he didn't get around to a number of his favorite targets, like Christian Herter, sports cars, Billy Graham, civil defense, California freeways, psychoanalysis, General Motors, Tennessee Williams, the Strategic Air Command, *Playboy*, the American Medical Association, and beards.

Sahl's manner is as uncompromising as his matter. He hurls his words ferociously at his listeners, almost without pausing to breathe. He has big white teeth, which, when he says something destructive enough to amuse even him, suddenly glare from his lean and sardonic face in a wolfish grin, and if he becomes truly transported by the damage he is doing, he erupts into a staccato two-syllable bark of triumph. Though his basic idiom is accurate and cultivated English, he decorates it defiantly with some of the most repellent jargon of hipsters and of Ph.D.s. Sahl's words are meant to be heard, not read, and to get an idea of his style one must remember that passages like the one that follows are delivered at top speed and with passionate earnestness: "You know, chicks dig psychoanalysis the most—much better than guys. That's a generalization, of course. I do generalize a lot without specific knowledge. The head of psychoanalytic research at Mount Sinai Hospital—the same hospital that gave you Oscar Levant, kids—said he liked the way I could focus on a group, like advertising men, and talk about nailed-down collars and thin ties with stickpins through the body and wrought-iron glasses. He said, 'With a minimal distribution of energy, you focus on their mores and level them.' Of course, what he doesn't understand is that I have no specific knowledge of the subject, and that I generalize and use stereotypes, so if I weren't perceptive I could be a bigot." Talk like that can't be what an expense-account hedonist, intent on getting away from it all for an evening, expects to hear when he wanders into one of the night clubs where Sahl performs—the hungry i, in San Francisco, say, or Basin Street East, in New York; Mister Kelly's, in Chicago; the Crescendo, in Los Angeles; the Americana, in Miami Beach; or the Flamingo, in Los Vegas. Still, Sahl has never been hooted off the stage. On the contrary, large numbers of people apparently enjoy having their intellects, their sensibilities, and their beliefs pummelled by him. ("Are there any groups I haven't offended?" is one sentence that he often uses to get offstage. "I congratulate you on your attention span" is another.) They show up in sufficient force at whatever club he is performing in to enable the club to turn over to him from five thousand to seventy-five hundred dollars a week. The secret of his success is by no means mysterious. A lot of the time Sahl is very funny, as only a very serious man can be.

The subject that Sahl is best known for making serious jokes about is politics—perhaps because it is the least esoteric of the matters that he ordinarily deals with. (Actually, he devotes more words to another topic— women. But women as described by Sahl are apt to be so esoteric as to be unrecognizable. " 'What do you see in the moon?' she asks me. Chicks are always using the moon as a kind of a Rorschach," he may say, or "This chick smokes a lot, which is a sign that she's very advanced. She smokes filter-tip mentholated cigarettes through a holder with a filter in it. She wants to change the world, but she doesn't want to get a sore throat.") Sahl's attitude toward politics, like his other attitudes, is entirely negative. "I'm not so much interested in politics as I am in overthrowing the government," he often says, and he also often laments, "I wish I had a cause, because I've got a lot of enthusiasm." While nonpartisan ridicule of the actions and personalities of politicians goes back at least to the birth of the republic, it is doubtful whether anyone has ever practiced it with more zeal than Sahl, who has told his audience, "I don't tell jokes, I give little lectures." Some of the lectures, little as they are, contain as much meat as most orations. "Kennedy is trying to buy the country and Nixon is trying to sell it," Sahl will say. Or "Eisenhower is for integration, but gradually; Stevenson, on the other hand, is for integration, but moderately. It should be possible to compromise between those extremes." Or "For a while, every time the Russians threw an American in jail, the Un-American Activities Committee would retaliate by throwing an American in jail, too." Or " 'On the Beach' is an escapist film; it takes your mind off birth control." Since a reputation for having a sense of humor is considered a political asset in this country, the butts of Sahl's political jokes tend to laugh at them more heartily—if not always more sincerely—than anyone else, and Sahl has become a sort of fixture on the hundred-dollar-a-plate dinner circuit, where he has publicly convulsed the likes of Harry Truman, Henry Cabot Lodge, Herbert Lehman, Carmine De Sapio, and Jacob Javits. Some politicians have even been impelled to enter into private relations with him. He has discussed what to do about American humor and the State Department backstage at Mister Kelly's with Hubert Humphrey; he has exchanged more or less portentous small talk with John Kennedy at a number of

Hollywood parties; and he has maintained fairly brisk communication with Adlai Stevenson, who was one of his first admirers.

Since Sahl talks so much about politics, he has inevitably been compared to Will Rogers, the only other major entertainer in recent history who ventured to trespass on that territory. It is characteristic of Sahl that this annoys him; he feels that he alone has the right to choose the people he is mentioned in the same breath with. Some years ago, he told a reporter for this magazine that he had "a Christlike image" of himself. The remark attracted considerable attention, not all of it favorable, and Sahl presently began telling his night-club audiences, "I won't cop out; I said it. I think if you're going to model yourself on someone, you ought to really come on." (Sahl is as hostile to religion as he is to everything else, and only slightly more reticent about showing it; naturally, he is against agnostics and atheists, too.) In any case, Sahl certainly isn't much like Will Rogers. Whereas Rogers assumed the role of a yokel who questioned the common sense of the educated men managing the government, Sahl is an intellectual who is scornful of the government because he feels that it is managed by yokels whose sense is all too common. Indeed, intellect, which, by long tradition is contraband in the area of show business where Sahl customarily operates, is one of the qualities that have earned him renown. As the first entertainer in years who contrived to smuggle his brains past a velvet rope, he has been a pathfinder for a stimulating new generation of comedians, including Shelley Berman, Mike Nichols and Elaine May, Lenny Bruce, and Bob Newhart, most of whom have little in common with Sahl except that they are bright and therefore suspect. Sahl has also heartened that substantial section of the public that has a normal desire to drink too much, spend too much money, and stay up too late but hesitates to do any of those things if the only available excuse is a chanteuse, a pair of adagio dancers, or Jerry Lewis. Perhaps the most eloquent testimony to the intellectual rigor of Sahl's act has been given, admiringly, by Dave Brubeck, whose quartet appeared with Sahl at the Crescendo a few years ago. The Brubeck group headed the bill and therefore went on after Sahl. It was an arrangement that Brubeck found frustrating. "Mort's impossible to follow," he recently said. "He demands so much of an audience that it hasn't the strength for anyone else."

A second un-Rogerslike quality of Sahl's is his perpetual and comprehensive indignation. A few of the people who know him well—among them his mother and the motion-picture producer Jerry Wald—profess to believe that at heart Sahl is just a wholesome American boy who wants to get ahead in show business, and that what he says is all in fun, like Jack Benny pretending he's stingy. Wald likes to be quoted as saying, "They call Mort an Angry Young Man, but I don't call Mort an Angry Young Man. I call Mort a Funny Young Man." There is little doubt that Sahl wants to get ahead in show business, but there is even less doubt that he means just about every word he says to his audiences. Privately as well as professionally, he is appalled by the world he lives in. "If this were a movie, there would now be a dissolve, but unfortunately my life has no dissolves. I have to live every agonizing moment of it," he has said, in performance after performance. A few weeks ago, a night-club owner who has seen a lot of him on and off the stage said, "Make no mistake, Mort's Hostility City all the way."

If Sahl's intellect has moved intellectuals to admiration, his discontent has provoked enthusiasm among the discontented, a considerably larger group. For a section of the college population, especially, Sahl has been not so much an entertainer as a spokesman. When he began to perform, the era of Joe McCarthy had not yet come to an end; it was a time when indignation, though it doubtless smoldered in many breasts, was seldom expressed with much vehemence in places like night clubs, where it might be overheard. As a matter of fact, Sahl was given his first job, at seventy-five dollars a week, by Enrico Banducci, the proprietor of the hungry i— then an extraordinarily dim cellar in which the San Francisco Fire Department allowed no more than eighty-three beatniks to assemble at any one time—on the strength of a McCarthy joke. "The rest of Mort's audition was terrible, but that joke killed me," says Banducci, whose club is still in a cellar, but a roomy one about which Sahl has nothing more derogatory to say than that it reminds him of the ruins of Frankfurt. (He has never been in Frankfurt.) The McCarthy joke, an elaborate affair, started with a detailed description of an Eisenhower jacket equipped with what Sahl called, in his carefree way, "multi-directional zippers," and ended with a suggestion for an improved model, a McCarthy jacket, with an extra zipper to go across the mouth. The news of such audacity at such a time rapidly reached the campuses in the San Francisco area, and the hungry i's regular clientele soon found itself competing for those eighty-three places with college students, who were delighted not only with Sahl's boldness but with his working costume—a sweater over a shirt with an unbuttoned collar—and with the knowing way he spoke about jazz, psychiatry, sports cars, Christmas-vacation jobs at the post office, and other matters close to their hearts. They recognized him at once as a battle-scarred member of their tribe.

Sahl's scars are evidently many and deep, though the precise nature of the battles in which he won them is not clear. It is only under some duress that he is willing to reminisce at all about the first twenty-three years of his life, from May, 1927, when he was born in Montreal, to June, 1950, when he graduated, as a Bachelor of Science who had specialized in city management, from the School of Public Administration of the University of Southern California. When he is persuaded to dwell briefly on those years, his exposition of the facts is littered with obscure asides, like "Lenin said, 'You have to destroy before you can build,'" or "Society was yelling in my ear, 'You're a cripple because you have ability.'" or, more simply, when he is feeling blander and more lucid than usual, "I wasn't an organization cat." Sahl's father, a New Yorker who is now retired, devoted most of his career to working as a civil servant in various departments of the federal government. Once, however, he took a four-year leave of absence from government, during which he made an unrewarding attempt to operate a tobacco shop in Montreal, the city his wife comes from, and it was at that time that Morton Lyon, the couple's only child, was born. Sahl grew up in a number of cities besides Montreal, among them Washington, Chattanooga, and Honolulu, but if any place on earth can properly be called his home, it is Los Angeles, where the family moved when he was seven, and which remained its base from then on. ("Los Angeles isn't a home town; it's a weather-observation satellite somewhere out in space," a friend of Sahl's remarked a while ago. "No wonder Mort's a displaced person.") As his mother remembers it, he started to talk at the age of seven months. "When he was ten," she says, "he spoke like a man of thirty." It was in his early teens that he began to season his talk heavily with imitations and jokes; "I found people looked better to me when they smiled," he has explained. At the various public schools he attended, he apparently neither had nor took much trouble with his studies. At high school, R.O.T.C. was his chief interest—"I was a martinet as a kid," he has said—and at the end of his sophomore year, when he was fifteen, he persuaded an Army recruiting officer that he was eighteen, and became a soldier. He did have the grace to leave a note behind, so his mother was able to locate him, at Fort MacArthur, near Los Angeles, and retrieve him after a couple of weeks of active duty. "Gee, Mom, why do you have to spoil everything?" he said on that occasion, or so she recalls it. For the next two years, he more or less docilely attended his classes, and then, when he graduated, he enlisted in the Army Air Forces. By this time, he had ceased to be a martinet, and had become an insurrectionist, and he remained a private during his entire period of service—thirty-one months, a good part of them spent at Elmendorf Field, in Anchorage, Alaska. At one point, he says—in what may be one of his characteristic evocations of the mood, rather than the facts of his life—he was given K.P. duty for eighty-three straight days for publishing various insubordinate remarks about his commanding officer in a paper he was editing, called *Poop from the Group*.

Sahl came out of the Air Force with a strong desire to tell the world what was wrong with it, preferably by writing and performing, but with no notion of how to make the world listen. Consequently, he deferred to his father's wishes and continued his studies, under the G.I. Bill, at Compton Junior College. With his mustering-out pay, he realized a long-cherished dream by buying a car, which he describes as "a Model-A roadster, chopped, with the frame zeed in and a suicide front end." The description seems to convey a vivid picture to his fellow-tribesmen, if to no one else. Even with the suicide front end, Sahl's college years—two at Compton and two at Southern California—were not satisfactory to him. He tinkered with his car, listened to jazz, dated as many girls as he could, and was careful neither to attend any more classes than he had to nor to take any courses scheduled earlier than eleven in the morning, but he was simply not very happy. Then, one day in the fall of 1950, just after his graduation from U.S.C., he drove up to Berkeley in his latest car—a forty-dollar Chevrolet—to visit a girl who was doing graduate work at the University of California. (Eventually, Sahl married the girl, but after two years they were divorced, and he has not been married since.) The physical beauty of the San Francisco area and the intellectual ferment on the Berkeley campus so invigorated Sahl that he abandoned once and for all any idea of becoming a traffic engineer or a city manager. "I was born in San Francisco," he often says.

During the next three years, he concentrated on writing and performing —activities from which he earned, by his calculation, one hundred and eighteen dollars. Among his arenas were an obscure Hollywood outfit called Theatre X—the initial stood for "experimental," not, as it might well have, for "unknown"—and a magazine published by the Altruistic Artists Foundation, for which he wrote movie reviews, editorials, and an article entitled "Art and Poetry, the Siamese Twins of Beauty." Occasionally, when his finances were particularly desperate, he would settle down for a week or two as a messenger or a used-car salesman in Los Angeles, but he spent as much time as he could lurking on or about the Berkeley campus as a member of a nocturnal, poverty-stricken, exuberant band of poets, Trotskyites, Nietzsche-lovers, and other advanced types. He is often overcome by nostalgia for those days, when he customarily slept on a window seat in the apartment of three girls he knew, and for one period of some weeks subsisted mainly on leftover pies from an all-night hamburger joint where one of the Nietzsche-lovers was a short-order cook. "Things were simple then," he told an audience not long ago. "All there was to worry about was man's destiny." Finally, Banducci gave him the job at the hungry i, and, as a friend noted not long ago, "Right then and there was when Mort became a success; after all, there's a hell of a lot more difference between seventy-five dollars a week and nothing than there is between seventy-five and seventy-five hundred."

Sahl's excellent credentials as a rebellious youth have been strongly reinforced by his convoluted and self-deriding manner of expressing his rebellion. It is a manner that apparently gives accurate expression to the way many of his contemporaries and juniors—or, as he often calls them, "my people"—look at themselves and the world. "After all, if we couldn't laugh about these things, we might do something about them," he sometimes says. If ever a sentence called for exegesis, that one does, so it may be pardonable, if ponderous, to note that it can be taken in the following eight ways, at least:

It is a joke, in classic, surprise-ending form.

It is a piece of sarcasm aimed at the folklore that extolls a sense of humor above all other virtues.

It is an analysis of the origin and function of humor.

It is a general condemnation of society.

It is a denunciation of the audience for being in a night club instead of on the barricades.

It is a plea to the audience that he be given serious attention.

It is a confession that his work is unlikely to change things.

It is a characteristic defensive maneuver designed to disarm his critics in advance.

Sahl feels that intricacies of this sort are the crux of his work. He is fairly sure that audiences in Las Vegas or Miami Beach, say, are not up to coping with them, and therefore he isn't able to give his best shows in such places. He is at his very best, he thinks, when he makes one of his infrequent appearances on a campus, before an audience of his people. Not long ago, in conversation with a friend, he compared his act to an archipelago, completely submerged except for a few mountain peaks—his surefire gags. When he plays a college, he says, the waters recede, the lowlands become visible, and the country lies open to exploration. Those who have explored it—his people—can testify that Sahl country offers them little cover. What surrounds the celebrated gags about Richard Nixon, General Motors, the Strategic Air Command, Chiang Kai-shek, and the rest of his people's favorite enemies is a ceaseless and unsparing attack on his people themselves, or, to put it another way, on Sahl himself. He excoriates their mating habits, their avocations, and their intellectual attitudes. He keeps up a drumfire against almost everything they are attracted to—coffeehouses, earnest young women, sports cars, stereophonic jazz, even "Pogo." ("What kind of civilization are we living in when a possum says something and we all say, 'I wish I'd said that'?") His very language, with its thick overlay of jazz and academic jargon, is a deliberate parody of the way his people talk. Perhaps the most famous of his early routines described the notes passed between a group of college men who were trying to hold up the Fairmont Hotel in San Francisco—what they planned to do with the money was live in the hotel for the rest of their lives—and the hotel cashier, also a college man: "Give us the money and act normal." "First you must define your terms. What do you mean by normal?" "This is not a debating society. Give us the money." And so forth. Sahl's people, naturally, favored Adlai Stevenson for the Presidency, and so, just as naturally, Sahl has made Stevenson the target of some of his most carefully squeezed-off shots. A routine he used a good deal this spring was a rundown of public men in terms of the sort of relatives they appeared to him to resemble. Eisenhower, he said, was not so much a father as a stepfather; Nixon was an uncle; Kennedy was a kid brother; Symington was a very distant relation; and Stevenson was a rich uncle who would keep bringing you presents as long as you got good marks. Just before the Democratic Convention, he went on television with newsreels of the candidates arriving at the Los Angeles airport. He had his own version of what they said as they got off their planes:

Kennedy: "I am here to accept the nomination."

Johnson: "I am a candidate, but I can't be here because I have to run the country."

Stevenson: "I am not a candidate and I am not here."

Because a rolled-up newspaper is an essential part of Sahl's working gear, because he often starts a show by commenting on some of the day's news, and because his talk bristles with references to published matter ranging from Nietzsche epigrams to *Hot Rod*, his supporters assume that he is a voluminous reader. It is true that any quarters he occupies—his home, in Hollywood, or a hotel room on the road—are likely to contain all the local papers, the *Times, Playboy, Fortune, Variety, Newsweek*, the Manchester *Guardian, TV Guide, Down Beat, Life*, and a dozen other magazines, plus an assortment of books, which recently included "Cuba: Island of Paradox," James MacGregor Burns' biography of Kennedy, Adlai Stevenson's "Putting First Things First," Norman Mailer's "Advertisements for Myself," Irwin Shaw's "Two Weeks in Another Town," a volume of Nietzche, a couple of Henry James novels, and Theodor Reik's "Creation of Woman." Actually, though, Sahl is a voluminous skimmer. His imagination responds so energetically to just about any sentence his eye happens to catch that—for professional purposes, at least—he never needs to finish a paragraph. (The entertainment section is the one part of any daily paper that he does read from beginning to end, to the disillusionment of many new acquaintances, who would not have believed that he would ever choose Winchell over Lippmann. Even when he was living on pies in Berkeley, he managed, most weeks, to find a quarter for *Variety*.) His hotel-robbery routine was suggested by a newspaper headline about an attempt to hold up the Fairmont, to be sure, but the routine had nothing to do with the actual story, which he may not even have read. In a Russian-spy routine that he first used at the Village Vanguard, he used the name of Colonel Rudolf Abel, but except for the name he totally ignored the facts. His Colonel Abel lived in Greenwich Village; the two New York addresses that the real Colonel Abel maintained were a studio on Fulton Street in Brooklyn and a room in a hotel in the East Twenties. The reason Sahl moved Abel to the Village was typically complex. In the routine, F.B.I. men asked the spy's neighbors how it was that they hadn't known what he was up to, and they answered that they had known and had thought of notifying the F.B.I., but then they had figured, "That's the Village." There are endless instances of Sahl's disregard for the facts—as opposed to what he feels is the essence—of the news. Only a few weeks ago, for the sake of a little lecture, he said that Secretary of State Herter was in Geneva, when one of the day's principal stories was about a conference that Herter was attending in Washington. In general, Sahl doesn't so much comment on

what the news is as on what he thinks it is. As he says, if he weren't perceptive he'd be a bigot.

Sahl's method of working up his act is as unorthodox as the act itself.
None of his material is composed by anyone but himself, none of it is
written down, and very little of it is ever repeated word for word. "I'm
overcommunicative, as Riesman would say," he remarked recently. (He is
forever trying to implicate some more or less innocent bystander—Riesman,
Freud, the government, society, civilization—in what he does.) He even
says he doesn't utter a word that was not conceived right onstage—a statement that, like so many of the other things he says, is only approximately
factual. To many of his acquaintances, it appears that he spends most of the
non-working part of every day in a sort of low-pressure rehearsal that
consists of flipping through whatever reading matter happens to be around,
studying whatever environment he happens to be in, and trying out the
ideas he gets from these activities on whoever happens to be handy. It is
quite true, though, that he is never sure which of the ideas to keep, which
to modify, and which to discard until he is in the process of putting them
before an audience. Like any congenital performer, he lives more intensely
when he is onstage than at any other time; it is not merely that audience
reaction gives him a clue to the worth of his notions but that he himself
does not really hear what he says until he says it in public. Quite often
he says something that doesn't sound funny to the audience but does to
him. On those occasions, he tends to become stubborn and to repeat the
remark, with variations, night after night until he either succeeds in
making his listeners like it or grudgingly decides that he never will
succeed. Each of his regular routines began with a stray, embryonic thought
that was well received by both the audience and himself; in successive
performances, Sahl would force-feed such a thought until it had developed
into a routine—a process that usually takes him two or three weeks. Once
a routine has matured fully, Sahl tends to lose interest in it, and though
he keeps it in his head as what he calls a "saver" for nights when he and
the audience are not getting along well, he uses it less and less, and seldom
to its best effect. Paul Desmond, the saxophonist of the Brubeck quartet,
is one of Sahl's closest friends. (Their relationship is described by the
inscription on a cigarette lighter Sahl once gave Desmond: "To the sound
from the fury.") Now and then over the years, Desmond has had occasion
to see Sahl perform every night for a week or two at a stretch. "It's like
watching a garden in time-lapse photography" is the way he describes
the waxing and waning of a Sahl routine.

Desmond and Brubeck, among other jazz musicians, are fascinated by Sahl, because they feel that he improvises in much the way they do, first stating a theme and them letting his mind or his feelings vary it ad lib. Certainly jazz is part of Sahl's fibre. Ever since his teens, when he discovered Stan Kenton—to whom he now refers as "a father figure," apparently in an attempt to implicate Freud in his fondness for music— it seems to have provided him with the only reliable escape he has been able to find from his black musings about his own problems and the world's. He is undeniably a jazz connoisseur, and his memory for what he has heard is so prodigious that he has no trouble abashing Desmond, say, by singing, with complete accuracy, a Desmond chorus from a record Desmond made ten years before and has forgotten about. Whether or not Sahl consciously uses a jazz technique, his show, like any worthwhile jazz outfit's, changes so much from night to night, and even between ten in the evening and two in the morning, and is so vivid a reflection of his mood of the moment, that some employees and habitués of the clubs he works at watch every one of his performances obsessively. Many such adepts look forward to his late, late show on a Friday or Saturday night, when the audience has drunk itself into semi-insensibility and Sahl is tired and querulous. "That's when Mort's entrails really show," one of them said gleefully a few weeks ago, and went on to recall that during one such performance in May, just before his thirty-third birthday, Sahl, in the course of discussing the theory that he had achieved a good deal for a young man, said bitterly, "Look at Castro. *He's* thirty-two and he has a country. It kills me." Sahl probably thinks he's entitled to a country, too—a large one, like the United States of America—but saying so was an indiscretion of the kind he has enough grace not to commit when he is in full control of his feelings; however much it delighted the adept, it provoked a titter, rather than a laugh, from the rest of the audience, and he probably hasn't repeated it. A while ago, one of his friends, leading an informal symposium on Sahl's character, said, "What I admire most about Mort is that, angry and frustrated and sometimes childish as he is, he tries so hard, and usually so well, not to put anything but the best of himself into his work. And, believe me, for Mort it *is* hard. It takes real heroism for a multiple schizoid like him to keep so many of his neuroses out of his act."

For a star performer, an ordinary night-club week comprises between thirteen and eighteen shows, each of them lasting forty or fifty minutes;

Saturday is always a three-show night, Friday often is, and there are either two or three shows on four other nights, depending on local custom and the fine print in the star's contract. This sort of schedule exhausts even the conventional comedian, each of whose shows is pretty much a verbatim repetition of the one before it, or whose repertory, at best, includes three standard shows, to avoid repeating one on any given night. For Sahl, every night is, in his phrase, a lifetime. Though he clearly has enough nervous energy for a troupe, and must have considerable stamina, too, brawn is not one of his assets. He is neither very tall nor very broad, standing about five feet ten and weighing no more than a hundred and fifty. He is wiry, though; eight or ten years ago, as a result of a program of weight-lifting, he put an inch on his biceps in two weeks—of all his accomplishments, the one of which he is probably vainest. Every couple of years he comes down with mononucleosis, a disease that is generally attributed to fatigue, and it keeps him in bed for several weeks. He doesn't smoke and he doesn't drink ("We're living in a society in which girls drink and I don't," he complained recently, attempting to implicate society in the problems he has when he is out on a date), and he doesn't eat much, either. He drinks coffee in quantities so large that once a week or so he has to switch to tea for a day to get the taste of it out of his mouth. He has a headache most of the time, and after a night's work his legs and back ache, too; it takes him several hours to unwind to the point of being able to sleep. He spends those hours in coffeehouses, or driving a sports car with or without company, or just lying on a couch listening to old Kenton records. Whenever possible, in fact, he has a phonograph or a radio going, preferably loud. If it is a radio, he insists that it be FM; his ear is so sensitive, or he likes to think it is, that he can't endure the inaccuracies of AM broadcasting. Since he spends so much time driving, he regards the perfecting of an FM automobile radio as perhaps the only encouraging development in the recent history of the United States. Finding a place to stay that is either without neighbors or with neighbors who will accept Kenton records at top volume at four in the morning is a recurrent problem in his life.

Next to listening to jazz, the activity that relaxes him most is buying things, and in his view the ability to gratify his eccentric acquisitive impulses is the chief blessing of having as much money as he now has. The objects sold by stationery or hardware or sporting-goods or music stores appeal to him particularly, and his pleasure seems to come rather from the act of buying than from the fact of ownership. (One psychiatrically oriented acquaintance attributes what he calls "Mort's purchase compul-

sion" to the fact that Sahl grew up in a family that had almost no possessions—not even furniture or crockery—since, owing to his father's migra-
tory habits, the Sahls usually lived in furnished apartments.) A friend
who knew Sahl on the Berkeley campus recalls that in those days he
could pass an absorbed and contented half hour picking out the lead pencil
he had decided to spend his last nickel on. When he began making a little
money, he started laying in ball-point pens, and as he became increasingly
affluent he branched out into sunglasses, transistor radios, clocks and
watches, binoculars, high-fidelity sets, and, finally, sports cars. He also likes
maps and charts and logs and timetables—"anything that will guide me
through the day," as he puts it. When he is in New York, he gravitates
toward the nearest Hoffritz cutlery store, into whose window he can gaze
raptly for what seems to be an eternity, or toward the nearest Liberty
Music Shop, where he may survey the latest Japanese issue of transistor
radios, or toward the Scandinavian Ski & Sport Shop, where, on his last
visit, he ordered a fancy assortment of sunglasses. A lot of what he buys
he gives away, but he keeps a lot, too, and there is no telling how many of
each of the objects of his affection—even cars—he has at any moment.

Sahl finds it less easy to enjoy some of the other aspects of his success.
Since the end of April, for example, he has been a corporation chartered by
the State of California, and thus, possibly, the sort of respectable institution that, by his own canon, ought to be overthrown. He is quite able to
see the joke in a man who is famous for refusing to wear a jacket or a
tie in public yet supports an agent, a press agent, a personal manager, a
business manager, a lawyer, and a tax man. (He wants to change the
world, but he doesn't want to get second billing.) Perhaps that is the
reason he has lately taken to going around town, or even appearing onstage
once in a while, fashionably dressed in a narrow suit. On the other hand,
this sartorial reconditioning, which started smashingly two years ago when
he put on full dress for an appearance on the Academy Awards television
show ("My people will think I've gone over to the enemy," he said
lugubriously), may be part of a larger strategy. Sahl wants to withdraw as
fast as he can afford to from night-club work and infiltrate television, with,
if possible, a regular show, which he visualizes as "a bright March of
Time." Among the numerous reasons Sahl is eager to have a television
show of his own—good money, easier working conditions, wider recognition—is that he thinks of himself as an apostle, whose mission is to
bring his anti-gospel, if that is the word for bad tidings, to as many people
as possible. When he is asked why he takes dates in places like Miami

Beach, Las Vegas, and the Copacabana in New York, he says, "I can't let those audiences go by default." He also keeps saying, "History will absolve me."

So far, Sahl's experiences with television have been mainly frustrating, largely because network executives and advertising-agency chiefs, even if they are interested in him, feel that a man who has his mind on being absolved by history instead of by Trendex is too "special" or too "controversial" to appear as a regular performer. In 1954, at the beginning of his career, he was under contract for thirteen weeks to the Columbia Broadcasting System, and never got on the air. In 1956, the National Broadcasting Company signed him for a year and, after letting him work once on something called the "Colgate Comedy Hour," confined him to a scattering of shows late at night or early in the afternoon. He has been the guest (as who hasn't?) of Steve Allen and Jack Paar on a number of occasions, and of Eddie Fisher once. (That show produced a moment that Sahl fans cherish. Fisher gave him an effusive introduction, the burden of which was that Sahl was one of the funniest people alive, and then said, "Say something funny, Mort," whereupon Sahl strode purposefully front and center, stopped, glared at the camera, and said slowly and distinctly, "John Foster Dulles.") And last season he was the central figure in a pair of unspectacular spectaculars. What exasperates him about television more than any of these not especially memorable appearances is that the same network officials who consider him too "special" or "cerebral" frequently beg him to work at staff lunches and dinners. Sahl asserts, with some show of logic, that if N.B.C.'s sales force can understand him, its audience certainly can.

Since Sahl wants so badly to be given the opportunity to compete with "Father Knows Best," "The Untouchables," and professional wrestlers, and has had so much trouble getting it, he has resorted, in his most recent guest appearances on television, to what he has always found the most reliable technique for making himself heard: appealing to the audience over the head of the program director—or, as one of his friends describes the method, "Whatever the smart money says, do the opposite." The smart money thinks Sahl should be bland and jolly and tolerant—qualities that frequently get compressed into the opaque adjective "human"—if he wants to reach and hold a national audience, and therefore Sahl has been even more fierce and censorious than usual. In June, he was on the Steve Allen show for eight minutes, and in that brief period he delivered a number of little lectures that were ferocious even by his standards. Among them was a description of a typically cheerful domestic scene at the Nixons', with Mrs. Nixon sitting in a rocker knitting an American flag, and a discussion of the U-2 episode that concluded with Captain Beach, the commander of the round-the-world nuclear submarine Triton, being decorated at the White House as the one officer whose whereabouts the President always knew. Whether direct assault will work as well for Sahl on television as it has worked in night clubs remains to be seen, but one thing that seems clear is that he is in no danger of becoming mellow. Not long ago, one of John Kennedy's henchmen—presumably without Kennedy's knowledge—suggested privately to Sahl that since he obviously liked Kennedy personally, he might, as a friendly gesture, drop the "Kennedy's trying to buy the country" joke. Sahl became so enraged that in his next show he used every Kennedy joke he had ever thought up. "You don't have to worry that Mort will learn to keep his temper," a man who knows him well said a few weeks ago. "All you've got to do to find out how serene he's feeling is to look up the casualty list of his business associates. He's on his fourth personal manager, I guess, and his second agent and second press agent. I don't see him more than once a year or so, and when I do I look at the entourage he travels with, and, you know, the people are always the same but the faces are different. When he begins getting along with his associates, I'll believe he's gone into a decline, but I'm not going to hold my breath till it happens. If a guy has a persecution complex, he'll keep on feeling persecuted no matter how many pairs of sunglasses he can afford."

As long as there is one other angry person in the world, Sahl, with his overcommunicativeness, will continue to be a spokesman for somebody. His ability to make so many of his listeners feel that he has the same hopes and fears, the same ideas, problems, and tastes, that they have is perhaps the most impressive—and most inexplicable—of his gifts. Of course, he has a line that deals with that situation, too: "People tell me there are a lot of guys like me, which doesn't explain why I'm lonely."

Martha Wolfenstein and Nathan Leites

BRITISH, FRENCH, AND AMERICAN FILMS

Dramatic productions may show human fate in various ways. The story may be of love and we may see the happy lovers joined as in a dream while seeming obstacles melt away before them. Or love may contend with other powerful motives in the lover, or be opposed by strong antagonists. Love may overstep the bounds of licit choice. Lovers who defy the law to come together may be overwhelmed by punishers who overtake them or by their own conscience. Or conscience may run on ahead of longing, chastening their wishes and sending them apart without their ever having been together. Rivals in love may be brought into deadly conflict, or to renunciation. The lover may find he is not loved in return; his love may change to rage or self-destruction, or he may find someone else. And so again confusion may be sorted out and each one find a partner.

Thus wishes working their way through various hazards may win happy fulfilment, may be denied, or may by being fulfilled bring down hard penalties. The plot may be of violence, and we may see the hero carrying out acts we wish but dread to do. He commits the dreamed-of crime but also bears its awful recompense. Or injury may justify his deeds, or call for deeds he cannot bring himself to do. Battles may be won or lost; victory may be dimmed by regrets for the loser, or gladdened by assurance of a righteous cause. Justice may be done or may miscarry. We may feel both triumph and pain as we see the hero undergo inevitable punishment for his rash deeds. Or we may see the fallibility of human justice as misplaced penalties fall on the innocent.

The world may appear in various aspects, as beautiful or dangerous or sordid, ruled over by benign or punitive gods or none at all. The main point of the drama may be not to exhibit conflicts between protagonists who may win or lose but to show the opposition of human wishes to the nature of life itself. The contest becomes one in which we all lose in the end, and the aim of the drama may be to reconcile us to this eventuality.

The dramatic productions of a particular culture at a particular time, or even over a considerable period, tend to exhibit a distinctive plot

From *Movies: A Psychological Study* by Martha Wolfenstein and Nathan Leites. Reprinted by permission of The Free Press, Glencoe, Illinois.

configuration. This configuration gives the various individual dramas the distinctive atmosphere which we can recognize as pervading them all. Obviously a group of plots or even a single plot is exceedingly complex. Nevertheless a certain basic plan may be discerned; we can see that one pattern from among the range of dramatic alternatives has been chosen for major emphasis.

Looking back over the films which we have been discussing, we shall now indicate briefly the essential plot configuration which distinguishes each of the three groups of films with which we have been concerned, the British, the French, and the American.

The essential plot in British films is that of the conflict of forbidden impulses with conscience. Either one of the contending forces may win out and we may follow the guilt-ridden course of the wrong-doer or experience the regrets of the lost opportunity virtuously renounced. In the happy instance, wishes may coincide with the demands of virtue and a fatherly fate will reward the good children. The world is presided over by authorities who are wise and good and against whom the wilful and unlucky may contend. But the counterpart of these authorities is also implanted in the individual soul; the evil-doer will be self-condemned as well as pursued by the authorities.

British films evoke the feeling that danger lies in ourselves, especially in our impulses of destructiveness. In a cautionary way they show what happens if these impulses break through, particularly where the weak become the victims. Thus they afford a catharsis at the same time that they demonstrate the value of defenses by showing the consequences of their giving way. The character who embodies dangerous impulses is apt to be a superior person, one who should be able to control his own destructiveness, and in whom it is all the more terrible to see it get out of hand. Violence is not simply a destructive force but a breaking both of the pattern within the individual personality and of the order which prevails in his world. The complete murderer is one who disputes the rule of just authorities, in his pride setting himself up as an arbiter of life and death, and doomed by his own struggle. While violence is on one side related to a whole social framework, it has also another side of intimacy and isolation. The act of violence is slowly prepared and may be preceded by special closeness between murderer and victim. Violence is thus often pervaded by the tenderness which in ordinary circumstances serves to ward it off.

Self-accusation is prominent in British films and may be evoked by wishes no less than by acts. Characters feel guilty when circumstances beyond their control produce fatalities coinciding with unconscious wishes. Lovers tempted to overstep lawful bounds draw back alarmed by guilty apprehensions. However, the pure in heart find that the authorities of this world and the next are their allies. The hero, temporarily distressed by a false charge, discovers that the police know all along that he is innocent and are quietly working side by side with him. The fine young couple who for the moment fear that fate has brought them together only to separate them learn that even death can be set aside so that they can be joined.

British films preserve, in a modern idiom (the peculiarities of which we shall not analyze here), many of the themes of Shakespearean drama. There are heroes who like Macbeth are carried away by criminal impulses and then punished; heroes who like Hamlet suffer pangs of conscience for crimes they did not commit. And there are young couples briefly and playfully threatened by the same fate which intended all along to wed them as Prospero did with his daughter and Ferdinand. The image of a perfect father, like Hamlet Sr., still presides over the scene, and constitutes the model for an exacting conscience.

In the major plot configuration of French films, human wishes are opposed by the nature of life itself. The main issue is not one of inner or outer conflicts in which we may win or lose, be virtuous or get penalized. It is a contest in which we all lose in the end and the problem is to learn to accept it. There are inevitable love disappointments, the world is not arranged to collaborate with our wishes, people grow older, lovers become fathers, the old must give way to the young, and eventually everyone dies. The desire for justice is ranged alongside other human wishes which are more likely than not to be frustrated. French films repeatedly present these aspects of life so that we may inure ourselves to them and master the pain they cause us. It is the Mithridates principle of taking a little poison every day so that by and by one becomes less vulnerable to it.

It is in keeping with this tendency that French films so often take as their central character an aging man. He is not the triumphant hero whom we wish to become nor the criminal hero whom we fear to become, but simply what we must become: old. In him we see concentrated disappointment, lost hopes, change, decline of physical powers, and imminent death. We can observe his sadly comic struggle against his fate as he refuses to realize that he is no longer eligible to be the lover of a young girl, or learn from him the compensations of later life as he renounces the role of lover for that of father. He helps to reconcile us both to our past and to our future. We see in him our own father no longer dominant and powerful but a sharer of our common human fate. He who was in possession of things which we as children were denied is now seen suffering disappointments more grievous than we suffered then. In making peace with him we also make peace with our own future.

The young hero no less than the aging one in French films is likely to be disappointed. We see him in his pursuit of a beloved woman about whom he gradually learns much that is contrary to his wishes. He is not spared the discovery that this woman is involved with another man, and we in following his fate may work through our own similar disillusionments. Knowledge which at first glance increases sorrow in the end mitigates the pain which, we see, could not be avoided.

We must learn that the world is not arranged to fulfil our demands for justice any more than to satisfy our longings for happiness. Human agencies of justice are obtuse and inefficient, and there are no divine ones. We are shown how the innocent are convicted, how the guilty are exonerated; they may even confess without being believed. Where justice is done, it is made clear that this is a happy accident. A clue uncovered by chance a moment earlier or later makes the difference between life and death for an innocent man. No one is watching over him, nor is he able to be the master of his own fate. Things may turn out happily. The suicidal bullet misses, the brain tumor may be operable, the hostages facing execution may be rescued at the last moment, the aging couple may find an unexpected revival of pleasure in life. The pleasure, no less sweet for that, is tinged with sadness; we know it is only a reprieve.

The major plot configuration in American films contrasts with both the British and the French. Winning is terrifically important and always possible though it may be a tough fight. The conflict is not an internal one; it is not our own impulses which endanger us nor our own scruples that stand in our way. The hazards are all external, but they are not rooted in the nature of life itself. They are the hazards of a particular situation with which we find ourselves confronted. The hero is typically in a strange town where there are apt to be dangerous men and women of ambiguous character and where the forces of law and order are not to be relied on. If he sizes up the situation correctly, if he does not go off half-cocked but is still able to beat the other fellow to the punch once he is sure who the enemy is, if he relies on no one but himself, if he demands sufficient evidence of virtue from the girl, he will emerge triumphant. He will defeat the dangerous men, get the right girl, and show the authorities what's what.

When he is a child, he is the comic hero, showing off, blundering, cocky, scared, called on to perform beyond his capacities, and pulling through by surprising spurts of activity and with the help of favorable circumstances. He is completely harmless, free from sexual or aggressive impulses, and the world around him reflects his own innocuous character. Its threats are playful and its reproaches ridiculous. When he is a man he is the melodrama hero and the world changes to reflect his changed potentialities; it becomes dangerous and seriously accusing, and launches him on his fighting career. The majority of the melodramas show him coming through successfully. A minority reveal various perils which lie off the main track; they are cautionary tales. The hero may succumb to his attacker; this is his bad dream. The men around him may be less dangerous than he suspects. Under the delusion that he attacks in self-defense, he may initiate hostilities; then he will lose. In this case he is crazy. Without being deluded to this extent, out of greed and overconfidence, he may try to get away with murder; he commits the crime of which he is usually only suspected and he has to pay for it. The girl may turn out to be worse than he believed. He will have to go off without her; then he is lonely. He may not be able to produce anyone on whom to pin the blame for the crimes of which he is falsely accused; then he is a victim of circumstances. If circumstances fail to collaborate with his need to blame someone else, he may even end by blaming himself. These are the various hazards which the usual melodrama hero safely passes on the way.

The fantasy which provides for defeating dangerous men, winning the right girl, and coming out in the clear, is produced under the auspices of two major mechanisms: projection and denial. Self-accusations are embodied in the blundering police and destructive impulses in the unprovoked attacker. The beloved woman seems to be involved with another man but investigation ends in the gratifying demonstration that she never loved anyone but the hero. The love disappointment to which the French movie hero is repeatedly exposed is here denied.

The external world may be dangerous but manageable, or, at other times, uncontrollable but gratifying. Where things seem to get out of control the results turn out to be wish-fulfilling. The overturning automobile throws the girl into the hero's arms, the rocking boat tosses the heroine's rival into the waves. The world that is uncontrollable but gratifying expresses an omnipotence fantasy while at the same time eliminating guilt. As soon as an internal problem is replaced by an external one, we can see the promise of success. The hero suffering from kleptomania becomes involved in investigating the activities of a gang of thieves; the amnesiac hero pursues his memories only long enough to unearth clues of someone else's crime before he rises impatiently from the psychiatrist's couch to embark on a successful detective job.

The world, which is not effectively policed, does not need to be policed at all. The hero, the self-appointed investigator and agent of justice, is able to set things right independently. The world thus appears as a kind of workable anarchic arrangement where, although hostilities are far from eliminated, life need not be nasty, brutish, and short, at any rate not for anyone we care about. The unofficial supervisors of private morals, the comic onlookers, are just as superfluous as the police. No one has any intention of doing anything naughty; only the mistakenly suspicious onlooker fails to recognize the natural goodness of the clean-cut young people.

American film plots are pervaded by false appearances. In this shadowy but temporarily vivid guise, the content of what is projected and denied tends to reappear. It is in false appearances that the forbidden wishes are realized which the hero and heroine so rarely carry into action. In a false appearance the heroine is promiscuous, the hero is a murderer, the young couple carry on an illicit affair, two men friends share the favors of a woman. This device makes it possible for us to eat our cake and have it, since we can enjoy the suggested wish-fulfilments without empathic guilt; we know that the characters with whom we identify have not done anything. The contention of American films is that we should not feel guilty for mere wishes. The hero and heroine are threatened with penalties for the incriminating appearance but in the end are absolved. The misguided police or the foolish onlooker in comedies convey a self-accusation from which the hero and heroine struggle to dissociate themselves, a vestige of archaic conscience which is to be dispensed with.

What the plot unfolds is a process of proof. Something is undone rather than done: the false appearance is negated. The hero and heroine do not become committed to any irretrievable act whose consequences they must bear. Nor do they usually undergo any character transformation, ennoblement or degradation, gain or loss of hope, acceptance of a new role or the diminution and regrets of age. They succeed in proving what they were all along. They emerge from the shadow of the false appearance. What has changed is other people's impressions of them. In so far as the hero and heroine may be unsure of who or what they are except as they see themselves mirrored in the eyes of others, they have succeeded in establishing for themselves a desirable identity. In so far as they struggle against a projected archaic conscience that persecutes the wish as if it were the act, they win a victory for a more tolerant and discriminating morality.

Archibald MacLeish

THE POET AND THE PRESS

IT IS AN AXIOM OF OUR CIVILIZATION, IF THAT IS THE PROPER NAME FOR the chaos of ideas in which we live, that poetry is the opposite of journalism and that journalism is the opposite of poetry. The two are about as likely to meet in an evening's conversation as John Keats and Arthur Krock, and each becomes, when applied to the other, a pejorative term. If you want to insult Scotty Reston, as a number of people in Washington now do, you will refer to those superb pieces of diplomatic correspondence of his as "poetry"—meaning piffle. If you want to insult Thomas Stearns Eliot, as nobody in Washington or anywhere else would now dream of doing, you will call *The Waste Land* "journalism"—meaning journalism. Elder writers addressing younger writers in those invaluable interviews in the *Paris Review* advise them to avoid the practice of journalism as they would wet socks and gin before breakfast, and the New York *Mirror* returns the compliment by announcing in an editorial as solemn as a sermon that anyone who does not regard Robert W. Service as a great poet is a fancy pants, and may even be an intellectual. In short, the two limits of the typewriter keyboard in our time, the two extremes which will never meet, the East and West of our fractured world, are poetry and journalism. But why, if you really stop to think of it, should poetry and journalism be the two poles of the world of words in our time? Why should they appear to us as each other's opposites? There are manifest differences between the two—differences which any of us could tick off—

Used by permission of the author. This article first appeared in *The Atlantic Monthly* (March, 1959).

but are they really as manifest as all that? Poetry is an art, yes; or should be. But is journalism the opposite of art?

No one would claim that the usual news story in the, let us say, Chicago *Tribune* is a work of art, at least in the ordinary sense of that term. But no one would deny either that great works of journalism exist and that when they exist they exist within a discipline of their own—a discipline which reveals itself, as the disciplines of art always reveal themselves, in form. The style of a great work of journalism is not, as the glib phrase goes, the man. The style of a great work of journalism is the man in terms of the purpose: a man working at the utmost intensity of which he is capable toward an end to which he is wholly committed. But this, of course, is precisely the characteristic of the style of any work of art—the precise characteristic which distinguishes a work of art from a mere indulgence of personality on one hand or an impersonal "job" on the other.

You cannot, in other words, distinguish journalism from poetry, to the extreme degree in which we distinguish them, merely by saying that one is an art and the other is not. And neither, I think, can you justify their antipodal relationship by the device used in most college catalogues, where courses in expository writing are courses in expository writing, but courses in the writing of poems are courses in creative writing. The theory would be, I imagine, that the poet is supposed to create a world in his poems, whereas the journalist is supposed not to create one but stick as closely as he can to the world he's got. This means that the poet makes something new, but the journalist describes something old, or in any case something that has already happened, for if it has not already happened he is no journalist. More precisely, this means that the journalist selects from among things that already are: events that have in fact befallen, actions actually acted, objects seen, sounds heard; whereas the poet must spin his chronicle out of himself like a spider. But if we leave the theory and look at the practice—specific poems, specific journalisms—will this distinction as between creative and selective hold?

Take the first poem that walks into your mind; for of course all of us have such visitors. "Old favorites" we call them because they are free of the house and enter without knocking. Some of you—quite a few, I should guess—will find yourselves thinking of Herrick's "Daffodils," not only because it is one of the finest of English lyrics and one of the poems most frequently taught to children, but because its tune, once echoed in the corridors of the ear, will never stop:

Fair daffodils, we weep to see
You haste away so soon:
As yet the early-rising sun
Has not attain'd his noon.
Stay, stay,
Until the hasting day
Has run
But to the even-song;
And, having pray'd together, we
Will go with you along.

We have short time to stay, as you.
We have as short a Spring;
As quick a growth to meet decay,
As you, or any thing.
We die.
As your hours do, and dry
Away,
Like to the Summer's rain;
Or as the pearls of morning's dew
Ne'er to be found again.

Or some of you will fish up Keats's murex because those five long "I" sounds at the beginning of the "Ode on a Grecian Urn" have held an instant of your mind motionless since the day in your childhood when you first heard them:

Thou still unravished bride of quietness!
Thou foster-child of Silence and slow Time,
Sylvan historian.

For myself, I always think, when I look for touchstones such as these, of a poem I cannot read, written in a tongue no man living can now pronounce—the poem the Emperor Wu Ti wrote in the seecond century B.C. for his dead mistress, Li Fu Jen. Arthur Waley's translation goes like this:

The sound of her silk skirt has stopped
On the marble pavement dust grows
Her empty room is cold and still
Fallen leaves are piled against the door
Longing for that lovely lady
How can I bring my aching heart to rest?

But whatever poem you call back to mind, the question I would put to you would be the same: Does your poem seem to you, as you contemplate it in your imagination, to be "created" in the sense in which we use that word of the events in the book of Genesis? Is there not rather a selection and ordering, as there is a selection and ordering in the art of history and in the practice of journalism? The selection is of a different kind, yes: things are chosen which history would find too trivial to touch and which journalism, in its passionate haste to get on with the story, would have no time for. The organization of the fragments selected is also different. Things are put together in poetry which history would never put together because of its addiction to the logic of cause and effect and which journalism would never put together because of its commitment to the lucidities of common sense. Men do not pray with daffodils in history if they care for the opinion in which posterity will contemplate them, and grief in journalism is sobs, not dead leaves at a door sill or the silence of the sound of silk—the silence after the ceasing of the sound. But granted all this—granted, too, that the structure of words in poetry is very different, far more orderly, immeasurably more strict, than the structure of words in the prose of journalism or of history—does it really follow that the enormous gulf we have dug between the conception of journalism and the conception of poetry is explained away by calling poetry a creative art?

I should not say so. I should say that an examination of actual poems and actual journalisms would lead any reader to the conclusion that the difference between them, wide though it is, cannot be stated in terms of creation. Both are re-creations, different in degree but not different in kind, for the material in each is our human experience of the world and of ourselves; and not fundamentally different in method or even in purpose, since the method of poetry like the method of journalism is selection from the chaotic formlessness of experience, and the purpose of both is the recording of the fragments selected in a sequence that makes sense.

It is perfectly true that the sense which poetry makes of its fragments is not the sense which journalism makes. No reporter in America or anywhere else would organize fragments of the experience of a divorce case to read: "love is not love which alters when it alteration finds or bends with the remover to remove. O, no! it is an ever-fixed mark that looks on tempests and is never shaken; it is the star to every wand'ring bark, whose worth's unknown, although his height be taken." In journalism this summation of experience is not sensible at all. It is not even true. Love, in journalism, does not bear "it out even to the edge of doom."

And the opposite is also obvious. The sense which journalism makes of the life of a man and the life of a woman, or the life of a man and the lives of two women, is not sensible or even true in poetry. But the fact remains that both Shakespeare's sonnet and the news story of the broken marriage are re-creations of fragments selected from the confusion of human experience in an effort to give them order and make them comprehensible. The purpose in one case may merely be to make them comprehensible to human curiosity, whereas the purpose in the other is very evidently to reach the human intelligence at its most perceptive and most alive: Shakespeare's sonnet has undertones of irony which only a most subtly listening ear can hear. But in both cases and however different their levels, the end is comprehension, understanding.

Poetry, despite the almost magical powers of the greatest poets, is a human labor, and what humanity most desperately needs is not the creation of new worlds but the re-creation, in terms of human comprehension, of the world we have, and it is to this task that all the arts are committed. Indeed, it is for this reason that the arts go on from generation to generation in spite of the fact that Phidias has already carved and Homer has already sung. The Creation, we are informed, was accomplished in seven days with Sunday off, but the re-creation will never be accomplished because it is always to be accomplished anew for each new generation of living men. To hold the vast, whirling, humming, buzzing, boggling confusion of the Greek world still long enough to see it is not to hold the vast, whirling, humming, buzzing, boggling confusion of our world still. New charms are necessary, new spells, new artifices. Whether they know it or not, the young men forgather in Paris in one generation, in San Francisco in another, because the world goes round, the light changes, and the old jugs will not carry living water. New jugs must be devised which the generation past will reject as monstrosities and the generation to come will, when it arrives, reject for other reasons: as banalities and bores.

But the essential point is that this labor does not differ in kind from the continuing labor of generations of journalists and historians who also face a new and turning world and who must also find new ways to speak of it. The materials of poetry, whatever the miracles accomplished with them, are gathered where the materials of history, present and past, are gathered, in what Keats called the arable field of events. Poetry transforms these materials by a faculty the use of which is discouraged in journalism, the faculty of imagination, but the product of the metamorphosis is not an opposite thing from the product of the process known in journalism as reporting. It is not what our grandfathers used to say it was: a "fancy" as opposed to the sober "facts" of practical men. For one thing, the constructions of the imagination are not fancies and never were. For another, facts are not what our grandfathers supposed them to be in those happy far-off Victorian generations when science picked facts out of life like grits out of porridge and marshaled them in patterns on a page.

The re-creations of the imagination do correspond to the experience of the real physical world. Poetry may take liberties with the materials of that experience which history and journalism are not free to take. It may translate them into unexpected and even improbable forms. But it neither will nor can disguise their origins in experience, for the moment it did so it would cease to be an art. It would become a sorcery, a magic. Those Grecian centaurs, half men, half horse, those Oriental mother goddesses, all arms and breasts—these derive from nature. It is only the arrangement of the parts which is unnatural! The parts themselves—the horse, the man, the arms, the breasts—have been discovered in the world the senses know. Even what we call "abstraction" in the art of our own day is not new creation in the sense in which the world of Genesis is new. Vision reduced to line, balance, color, proportion is still vision and still belongs in a world in which line, balance, color, and proportion exist.

Indeed, this dependence of poetry, of all art, on human experience of the actual world is only made the more obvious by the attempts of art, which have been frequent in our time, to escape from the actual world. Poems, for example, which derive from the subconscious mind as the poems of the early Surrealists did, or purported to do, are still poems of experience and still poems composed by a process of selection from among the moments of experience. The only difference is that the selecting sieve is set up somewhere outside the conscious mind. But the poem does not become, in consequence, a parentless, pristine creation. On the contrary, it is even more obviously and immediately derived from the common human reality than a poem made, as the Greeks made poems, under the selective direction of a conscious intelligence. The proof lies in the experiments of those contemporary psychiatrists who have attempted to work their way back through completed poems to their roots in experience. They have made very little of the poems of, say, John Donne, but they have had a harvest home with the works of the Surrealists. A Surrealist poem is a direct recording of the experiencing mind on the tape of speech, and all that need be done to make one's way to the unhappy childhood or the illicit love is to play the recording back. John Donne is another matter. The conscious act of art is there to make a mechanical playback impossible. All you will get if you try is that series of garbled screams and whinnies with which the amateurs of tape recordings are familiar.

But one need not go to the Surrealists or their successors to make the point. The most apparently fanciful of all familiar poems will testify, if you will truly read them, that their fancies are no less substantial, no less true, no less (if the word is still permitted) real—at least no less authenticated by experience—than the most substantial facts. Consider Prospero's great trope in *The Tempest*: those cloud-capped towers, gorgeous palaces, solemn temples, the great globe itself, which "like this insubstantial pageant faded" dissolve, "leave not a rack behind." Consider Rimbaud's pianos in the Alps, his hares praying to the rainbow through the spider's web, his little boy waving his arms to the weather vanes "Après le Deluge," after the Deluge had subsided, in the *Illuminations*. Compare these extravagant fancies with the hard facts of history and journalism. You will find it difficult, I think, to say just what the substantial difference is. You may even find yourself concluding that, if anything, the fancies are harder than the facts. We are, we are indeed, "such stuff as dreams are made on," and any man who has not yet learned that "our little life is rounded with a sleep" has not yet begun to live that little life. We do, after every Deluge which drowns the world, whether for one man or for many, come upon that moment when everything is new again and possible, even the impossible; when little boys and weather vanes salute each other. There can scarcely be a man or a woman in my generation, if he has really shared that generation's life, who has not known that moment—and then lost it, as Rimbaud's poem loses it. Are these fancies not as substantial as our facts? Are they not as real as murder or the World Series or Governor Faubus, to say nothing of our China policy or a Dow-Jones average? Has anyone ever met a Dow-Jones average on a Sunday afternoon, or bathing, or anywhere else in the world? And as for our China policy, would anyone know its face if it walked onto this platform and sat down and arranged its smile?

I am not suggesting that the facts of journalism are insubstantial. I am merely suggesting that there is no such difference between the facts of journalism and the fancies of poetry as we assume when we turn them into each other's opposites. You can prove it to yourself in either way: by reading poems or by reading newspapers. What do you remember about the recent revolution in Iraq—in some ways the most important news story of the year, though not the best reported? What I remember is the account of the assassination of the old Premier, the famous desert fox and the most powerful man in the valley of the two rivers, who was shot in the dress of an old woman. Why do I remember that? Because the fact becomes something more than fact in that telling. Because I understand something of the man—and of those who killed him. Because the political event becomes a human event and casts a shadow far beyond Baghdad, far beyond the desert, far beyond the Middle East. It is only when the scattered and illegible fragments in which we pick up our experience of the world are recomposed in such a way that they make sense *as* human experience that great journalism can result. And the same thing is true in the same words of poetry. What poetry composes of its fragments is more lasting than what journalism composes. It is larger. It goes deeper. It is more meaningful. It has beauty. But it is not contrary in kind. Poetry and journalism—to put it in more inclusive terms, poetry and history— are not opposites and cannot be opposites, and the notion that they are is a delusion.

Something more than error is involved in this respectable and sanctified confusion. There are popular errors of various kinds. Some are harmful. Some are merely silly. This one is harmful. It has hurt poetry. It has altered journalism. And its effect, or the effect of the deeper delusions which have fathered it, on our unhappy civilization has been and continues to be disastrous. What really distinguishes poetry from journalism, aside from the obvious distinctions of form—uses of words, patterns of words, sequences of words—is not a difference in kind but a difference in focus. Journalism is concerned with events, poetry with feelings. Journalism is concerned with the look of the world; poetry with the feel of the world. Journalism wishes to tell what it is that has happened everywhere as though the same things had happened for every man. Poetry wishes to say what it is like for any man to be himself in the presence of a particular occurrence as though only he were alone there.

The best definition of journalism appears daily in the New York *Times:* "All the News That's Fit to Print." The best definition of poetry is spelled out in Coleridge's *Biographia Literaria:* "the balance or reconcilement of discordant qualities . . . a more than usual state of emotion with more than usual order." To separate journalism and poetry, therefore—history and poetry—to set them up at opposite ends of the world of discourse, is to separate seeing from the feel of seeing, emotion from the acting of emotion, knowledge from the realization of knowledge.

The poet, with us, stops his horse at twilight at the wood's edge in falling snow and yields for a moment to that longing for sleep in the cold, white, drifting stillness which is also another and deeper longing all reflective men have known, but the journalist permits himself to see only a man in a buggy stopping in inclement weather at a remote and unlikely spot; since nothing has "happened," he publishes nothing. And the same thing is true in reverse. The journalist dodges hand grenades in the bazaar of a hot, dusty, dirty, flea-bitten desert city to report an obscure war which may be the beginning of the ultimate war, but the poet, because all this is merely happening, does not write at all; because nothing is felt, he has nothing to say.

I exaggerate, of course. There have been journalists of our generation, men like Elmer Davis as well as men like Ernie Pyle, who would not have separated the feel of things from the look of them if they could, and there are contemporary poets who not only felt but saw the war in Spain—saw it, in fact, far more clearly than the journalists or the foreign offices or the professional observers of world affairs. Indeed, the greatest of contemporary poets was also one of the most exact and penetrating observers of the history of his time, if not always the most intelligent interpreter of that history.

> Turning and turning in the widening gyre
> The falcon cannot hear the falconer;
> Things fall apart; the centre cannot hold;
> Mere anarchy is loosed upon the world,
> The blood-dimmed tide is loosed, and everywhere
> The ceremony of innocence is drowned;
> The best lack all conviction, while the worst
> Are full of passionate intensity.

No journalist writing of the tragic events with which the name of the late Senator McCarthy is associated ever defined that aspect of contemporary life as precisely as Yeats had defined it some thirty years before:

> The best lack all conviction, while the worst
> Are full of passionate intensity.

But Yeats is an exception in this as in many other things. And not even Yeats was able to bring the event and the feel of the event together as they were brought in Homer's time and Dante's and Shakespeare's. Journalism, with us, tends more and more toward an admirably dispassionate objectivity which presents the event in the colorless air of intellectual detachment at the cost of its emotional significance, and poetry, reacting to the same divisive influence but in an opposite direction, turns more and more to the emotional significance divorced from the event. I do not know that it is possible to say that this fracture of the word is bad for journalism as such, for the great modern newspapers are, as newspapers, far superior to their predecessors. They collect more news faster and present it more accurately. It is only too possible to say, however, that it is bad for poetry and bad for the civilization.

Great poems are instruments of knowledge—a knowledge carried alive into the heart by passion, but knowledge nevertheless. Feeling without knowing never made a work of art and never will. And the attempt which contemporary poetry increasingly makes to detach feelings from their occasions—to pursue feelings as themselves and for their own sakes, resolutely ignoring the events from which they derive—can only be harmful to the art. Poems so composed are like kites without strings. They cannot bear up against the carrying away of time, because they have no attachment to a point in time.

The consequences to poetry itself of its increasing inwardness are of concern, unhappily, only to poets. What the rest of us might wish to think of is the effect of all this on our civilization. It is not difficult to define. Some time ago, Lewis Mumford, certainly one of the most intelligent of living Americans, wrote a letter to the New York *Times* expressing his horror at the apathy of his countrymen in the face of the dangers inherent in our policy and conduct in the Straits of Formasa. Here we were, he said, on a brink from which we might at any moment be shoved by the Chinese Nationalists or dragged by the Chinese Communists, with a war yawning before us which could only be fought by the horrible weapons of genocide and with the end of human life on the earth as a very possible consequence. And yet we neither protested nor objected. We merely sat there in numb indifference, leaving the decision of life or death to a Secretary of State whose previous decisions or indecisions were responsible for our predicament.

It was an angry letter, and one with which men of certain opinions might differ. But what struck me about it was not its statement of the facts, which seemed to me only too painfully correct, but its explanation of the reason for our national indifference to the facts. Our apathy, Mr. Mumford suggested—I do not know how seriously—could only be the consequence of our enormous consumption of tranquilizers and sedatives. Only a nation doped into unreality could possibly contemplate in silence a series of events and declarations which might at any moment lead to the extermination of enormous numbers of peaceful human beings, first in Asia and then throughout the world, including the part of the world in which we live ourselves.

I say I was struck by this explanation. I was struck by it because I found myself wishing the real explanation might be as simple and ironic. For the truth is, of course, that our apathy with regard to the incredible and terrifying events in Amoy Harbor and the disastrous consequences which might at any moment follow was the result not of our habits in the taking of pills but of our habits in the thinking of thoughts. And the further truth is that this strange dislocation in the thinking of thoughts by which we can "know" what we cannot feel—by which we can know that the consequence of a merely diplomatic maneuver may be the atomizing of the city of Peiping and then Tokyo and then Moscow and then New York, but cannot imagine in our live emotions what this knowing would feel like—this dislocation is the consequence of a deeper dislocation not only in ourselves but in our civilization.

For this divorce between knowing and feeling is not anythting we Americans can claim as our own peculiar prerogative. The Germans have exhibited the same curious capacity: the "good Germans" who knew about the gas ovens of the concentration camps but were nevertheless able to live with their knowledge in tranquillity and good conscience until they began to go in crowded, silent audiences to performances of *The Diary of Anne Frank.* And we ourselves—shall we call ourselves the "good Americans"?—are guilty of the same peace of mind. We know what happened at Hiroshima. We have read, or read about, John Hersey's account of the results of the atomic bombing of that city. Most of us are at least aware of the specters which crawl through Dr. Hachiya's book: "Their faces and hands were burnt and swollen and great sheets of skin had peeled away from their tissues to hang down like rags on a scarecrow. They moved like a line of ants. All through the night they went past our house, but this morning they had stopped. I found them lying on both sides of the road so thick that it was impossible to pass without stepping on them." We know all this. But do we feel our knowledge? Could we even *think* about risking the possibility of a world-wide atomic war as a matter of face or official vanity if we did?

I am not going to discuss foreign policy—if that is the right term for our recent behavior off the China coast. But nothing could better illustrate the flaw at the heart of our civilization than this strange chapter of our history. Nothing could more convincingly demonstrate that knowledge without feeling is not knowledge and can lead only to public irresponsibility and indifference, and conceivably to ruin. Nothing could more clearly prove that when the fact is disassociated from the feel of the fact in the minds of an entire people—in the common mind of a civilization—that people, that civilization, is in danger.

Some of you, I have no doubt, will think the terms I have been using throughout this discussion are inadequate to so serious an indictment. Journalism seems, to most of us, a profession like another, and poetry seems remote indeed from matters of such moment as the survival of the world. But the fact is, of course, that the survival of the world—at least the survival of a world which has prepared as ingeniously for its own suicide as the world we live in—depends, madmen and accidents aside, solely on the knowledge of the men and women who inhabit it. And that knowledge is composed precisely of the two increments which journalism and poetry provide. Information is essential to the kind of knowledge on which an opinion relevant to the situation on Quemoy can be based. But the feel of the facts which that information communicates is also essential if the knowledge and the opinions it fathers are to be trustworthy and reliable. What has happened with us is that the first has outrun the second. We are, as we are constantly and justly being reminded, the best informed people on an earth which is better informed now than it ever was before in its history. But though we are provided with more facts than any previous generation, we are not necessarily possessed of more knowledge of those facts.

On the contrary, we seem to be less and less capable of receiving our facts into our imaginations, where they can come alive with feeling. Benjamin Franklin's contemporaries were not told within a few hours that some hundreds of coal miners had been trapped in a mine in what is now Yugoslavia, but when, after many months, the news of such a disaster at last came through, it would have come as a human tragedy with its human significance about it. The news of Napoleon's retreat from Moscow would be broadcast today minute-by-minute, photographed, columnized, interpreted, recorded to the last detail. When Napoleon actually turned back, the news was brought to New York in a brig commanded by my great-grandfather months after the event and in an individual witness's report, but it loomed in the New York newspapers of the next morning like news from Troy, which, in a sense, it was. What the Greeks knew about Troy, they knew through a man's slow telling.

I am not deploring the advances of journalism. They are miraculous. No man who has grown used to the news coverage of an expertly managed paper could live without it. But every improvement, and particularly every improvement made possible by mechanical invention, exacts its price, as we are discovering in our increasingly mechanized country. Often the price is exacted at the cost of nature and sometimes even at the cost of human nature. We are deluged with facts, but we have lost, or are losing, our human ability to feel them. Poetry still survives with us, survives with vigor and inventiveness, throwing up new masters capable of standing with the old. But the poem itself has lost its power in men's minds. We have not discarded the art as Herbert Spencer thought men would when the machine had come to flower, but we have impaired the practice of the skill the art can give, the skill of feeling truly and so truly knowing. We know with the head now, by the facts, by the abstractions. We seem unable to know as Shakespeare knew, who makes King Lear cry out to blinded Gloucester on the heath, "you see how this world goes," and Gloucester answers, "I see it feelingly."

Why we are thus impotent, I do not know. I know only that this impotence exists and that it is dangerous, increasingly dangerous. I know, too, or think I know, that whatever the underlying cause of the divorce of feeling from knowing, that divorce reveals itself most vividly in the strange and ignorant belief that the life of the imagination lies at an opposite pole from the life of the inquiring mind—that men can live and know and master their experience of this darkling earth by accumulating information and no more.

Men who believe that have, in effect, surrendered their responsibilities as men. They have gone over to the enemy, to those unhappy hordes, victims of the new and terrible tyranny of our time, who are not meant to know for themselves and with their whole beings but only to accept the daily ration of news and hates which Peiping or Moscow issues to them. Slavery begins when men give up the human need to know with the whole heart, to know for themselves, to bear the burden for themselves—the "burden," as Wordsworth called it, "of the mystery." To acquiesce, as the Russians and the Chinese and the Poles—even the Hungarians—have had to acquiesce in someone else's knowing is to acquiesce in someone else's deciding, and at that point, whatever the society is called, it is not free.

The real defense of freedom is imagination, that feeling life of the mind which actually knows because it involves itself in its knowing, puts itself in the place where its thought goes, walks in the body of the little Negro girl who feels the spittle dribbling on her cheek, follows in that line of ants whose skin is ragged tatters. The man who knows with his heart knows himself to be a man, feels as himself, cannot be silenced. He is free no matter where he lives, as Boris Pasternak has shown that he is free even in Russia. The man who knows with his mind only, who will not commit himself beyond his wits, who will not feel the thing he knows, or know the thing he feels—that man has no freedom anywhere. He is tugged by the string of whatever is told him, maneuvered by slogans. Sooner or later his life will seem indifferent to him, something managed by others, and he will acquiesce in the management, think about it as little as possible, occupy himself with the only things near enough to seem real—his car, his front lawn, those shadows on the television screen—symbolic shadows.

To me—not many others think so—the real crisis in the life of our society is the crisis of the life of the imagination. Far more than we need an intercontinental missile or a moral rearmament or a religious revival, we need to come alive again, to recover the virility of the imagination on which all earlier civilizations have been based: Coleridge's "synthetic and magical power" by which "the whole soul of man" may be brought to activity and knowledge may be *known*. It is for this reason that I have permitted myself to speak of my concern in a great university. I do not mean that I think education is wholly responsible for the flaw which has split knowledge of heart from knowledge of head, though it has surely its fair share of the blame. I mean rather that it is principally by the process of education that the flaw can be healed. The need for a review of the relation between education and the arts was never greater than at this moment, when our whole attention is fixed on the relation between education and the sciences. A society which has so lost the capacity to see the world feelingly that it can watch in silence while the possibility of nuclear extermination is employed as a diplomatic maneuver may stand in need of thousands of young manufacturing scientists sooner than it thinks. But even sooner, it will need to learn to know.

Edith Hamilton

THE IDEA OF TRAGEDY

THE GREAT TRAGIC ARTISTS OF THE WORLD ARE FOUR, AND THREE OF THEM
are Greek. It is in tragedy that the pre-eminence of the Greeks can be seen
most clearly. Except for Shakespeare, the great three, Æschylus, Sophocles, Euripides, stand alone. Tragedy is an achievement peculiarly Greek.
They were the first to perceive it and they lifted it to its supreme height.
Nor is it a matter that directly touches only the great artists who wrote
tragedies; it concerns the entire people as well, who felt the appeal of the
tragic to such a degree that they would gather thirty thousand strong to see
a performance. In tragedy the Greek genius penetrated farthest and it is
the revelation of what was most profound in them.

The special characteristic of the Greeks was their power to see the world
clearly and at the same time as beautiful. Because they were able to do
this, they produced art distinguished from all other art by an absence of
struggle, marked by a calm and serenity which is theirs alone. There is,
it seems to assure us, a region where beauty is truth, truth beauty. To it
their artists would lead us, illumining life's dark confusions by gleams fit-
ful indeed and wavering compared with the fixed light of religious faith,
but by some magic of their own, satisfying, affording a vision of something inconclusive and yet of incalculable significance. Of all the great
poets this is true, but truest of the tragic poets, for the reason that in
them the power of poetry confronts the inexplicable.

Tragedy was a Greek creation because in Greece thought was free.
Men were thinking more and more deeply about human life, and beginning to perceive more and more clearly that it was bound up with evil and
that injustice was of the nature of things. And then, one day, this knowledge of something irremediably wrong in the world came to a poet with
his poet's power to see beauty in the truth of human life, and the first
tragedy was written. As the author of a most distinguished book on the
subject says: "The spirit of inquiry meets the spirit of poetry and tragedy
is born." Make it concrete: early Greece with her godlike heroes and hero-

gods fighting far on the ringing plains of windy Troy; with her lyric world, where every common thing is touched with beauty—her twofold world of poetic creation. Then a new age dawns, not satisfied with beauty of song and story, an age that must try to know and to explain. And for the first time tragedy appears. A poet of surpassing magnitude, not content with the old sacred conventions, and of a soul great enough to bear new and intolerable truth—that is Æschylus, the first writer of tragedy.

Tragedy belongs to the poets. Only they have "trod the sunlit heights and from life's dissonance struck one clear chord." None but a poet can write a tragedy. For tragedy is nothing less than pain transmuted into exaltation by the alchemy of poetry, and if poetry is true knowledge and the great poets guides safe to follow, this transmutation has arresting implications.

Pain changed into, or, let us say, charged with, exaltation. It would seem that tragedy is a strange matter. There is indeed none stranger. A tragedy shows us pain and gives us pleasure thereby. The greater the suffering depicted, the more terrible the events, the more intense our pleasure. The most monstrous and appalling deeds life can show are those the tragedian chooses, and by the spectacle he thus offers us, we are moved to a very passion of enjoyment. There is food for wonder here, not to be passed over, as the superficial have done, by pointing out that the Romans made a holiday of a gladiator's slaughter, and that even to-day fierce instincts, savage survivals, stir in the most civilized. Grant all that, and we are not a step advanced on the way to explaining the mystery of tragic pleasure. It has no kinship with cruelty or the lust for blood.

On this point it is illuminating to consider our every-day use of the words tragedy and tragic. Pain, sorrow, disaster, are always spoken of as depressing, as dragging down—the dark abyss of pain, a crushing sorrow, an overwhelming disaster. But speak of tragedy and extraordinarily the metaphor changes. Lift us to tragic heights, we say, and never anything else. The depths of pathos but never of tragedy. Always the height of tragedy. A word is no light matter. Words have with truth been called fossil poetry, each, that is, a symbol of a creative thought. The whole philosophy of human nature is implicit in human speech. It is a matter to pause over, that the instinct of mankind has perceived a difference, not of degree but of kind, between tragic pain and all other pain. There is something in tragedy which marks it off from other disaster so sharply that in our common speech we bear witness to the difference.

All those whose attention has been caught by the strange contradiction of pleasure through pain agree with this instinctive witness, and some of the most brilliant minds the world has known have concerned themselves with it. Tragic pleasure, they tell us, is in a class by itself. "Pity and awe," Aristotle called it, "and a sense of emotion purged and purified thereby." "Reconciliation," said Hegel, which we may understand in the sense of life's temporary dissonance resolved into eternal harmony. "Acceptance," said Schopenhauer, the temper of mind that says, "Thy will be done." "The reaffirmation of the will to live in the face of death," said Nietzsche, "and the joy of its inexhaustibility when so reaffirmed."

Pity, awe, reconciliation, exaltation—these are the elements that make up tragic pleasure. No play is a tragedy that does not call them forth. So the philosophers say, all in agreement with the common judgment of mankind, that tragedy is something above and beyond the dissonance of pain. But what it is that causes a play to call forth these feelings, what is the essential element in a tragedy, Hegel alone seeks to define. In a notable passage he says that the only tragic subject is a spiritual struggle in which each side has a claim upon our sympathy. But, as his critics have pointed out, he would thus exclude the tragedy of the suffering of the innocent, and a definition which does not include the death of Cordelia or of Deianira cannot be taken as final.

The suffering of the innocent, indeed, can itself be so differently treated as to necessitate completely different categories. In one of the greatest tragedies, the *Prometheus* of Æschylus, the main actor is an innocent sufferer, but, beyond this purely formal connection, that passionate rebel, defying God and all the powers of the universe, has no relationship whatever to the lovely, loving Cordelia. An inclusive definition of tragedy must cover cases as diverse in circumstance and in the character of the protagonist as the whole range of life and letters can afford it. It must include such opposites as Antigone, the high-souled maiden who goes with open eyes to her death rather than leave her brother's body unburied, and Macbeth, the ambition-mad, the murderer of his king and guest. These two plays, seemingly so totally unlike, call forth the same response. Tragic pleasure of the greatest intensity is caused by them both. They have something in common, but the philosophers do not tell us what it is. Their concern is with what a tragedy makes us feel, not with what makes a tragedy.

Only twice in literary history has there been a great period of tragedy, in the Athens of Pericles and in Elizabethan England. What these two periods had in common, two thousand years and more apart in time, that they expressed themselves in the same fashion, may give us some hint of the nature of tragedy, for far from being periods of darkness and defeat, each was a time when life was seen exalted, a time of thrilling and unfathomable possibilities. They held their heads high, those men who conquered at Marathon and Salamis, and those who fought Spain and saw the Great Armada sink. The world was a place of wonder; mankind was beauteous; life was lived on the crest of the wave. More than all, the poignant joy of heroism had stirred men's hearts. Not stuff for tragedy, would you say? But on the crest of the wave one must feel either tragically or joyously; one cannot feel tamely. The temper of mind that sees tragedy in life has not for its opposite the temper that sees joy. The opposite pole to the tragic view of life is the sordid view. When humanity is seen as devoid of dignity and significance, trivial, mean, and sunk in dreary hopelessness, then the spirit of tragedy departs. "Sometime let gorgeous tragedy in sceptred pall come sweeping by." At the opposite pole stands Gorki with *The Lower Depths.*

Other poets may, the tragedian must, seek for the significance of life. An error strangely common is that this significance for tragic purposes depends, in some sort, upon outward circumstance, on

> pomp and feast and revelry,
> With mask, and antique pageantry—

Nothing of all that touches tragedy. The surface of life is comedy's concern; tragedy is indifferent to it. We do not, to be sure, go to Main Street or to Zenith for tragedy, but the reason has nothing to do with their dull familiarity. There is no reason inherent in the house itself why Babbitt's home in Zenith should not be the scene of a tragedy quite as well as the Castle of Elsinore. The only reason it is not is Babbitt himself. "That singular swing toward elevation" which Schopenhauer discerned in tragedy, does not take any of its impetus from outside things.

The dignity and the significance of human life—of these, and of these alone, tragedy will never let go. Without them there is no tragedy. To answer the question, what makes a tragedy, is to answer the question wherein lies the essential significance of life, what the dignity of humanity depends upon in the last analysis. Here the tragedians speak to us with no uncertain voice. The great tragedies themselves offer the solution to the problem they propound. It is by our power to suffer, above all, that we are of more value than the sparrows. Endow them with a greater or as great a potentiality of pain and our foremost place in the world would no longer be undisputed. Deep down, when we search out the reason for our conviction of the transcendent worth of each human being, we know that it is because of the possibility that each can suffer so terribly. What do outside trappings matter, Zenith or Elsinore? Tragedy's preoccupation is with suffering.

But, it is to be well noted, not with all suffering. There are degrees in our high estate of pain. It is not given to all to suffer alike. We differ in nothing more than in our power to feel. There are souls of little and of great degree, and upon that degree the dignity and significance of each life depend. There is no dignity like the dignity of a soul in agony.

> Here I and sorrows sit;
> Here is my throne, bid kings come bow to it.

Tragedy is enthroned, and to her realm those alone are admitted who belong to the only true aristocracy, that of all passionate souls. Tragedy's one essential is a soul that can feel greatly. Given such a one and any catastrophe may be tragic. But the earth may be removed and the mountains be carried into the midst of the sea, and if only the small and shallow are confounded, tragedy is absent.

One dark page of Roman history tells of a little seven-year-old girl, daughter of a man judged guilty of death and so herself condemned to die, and how she passed through the staring crowds sobbing and asking, "What had she done wrong? If they would tell her, she would never do it again"—and so on to the black prison and the executioner. That breaks the heart, but is not tragedy, it is pathos. No heights are there for the soul to mount to, but only the dark depths where there are tears for things. Undeserved suffering is not in itself tragic. Death is not tragic in itself, not the death of the beautiful and the young, the lovely and beloved. Death felt and suffered as Macbeth feels and suffers is tragic. Death felt as Lear feels Cordelia's death is tragic. Ophelia's death is not a tragedy. She being what she is, it could be so only if Hamlet's and Laertes' grief were tragic grief. The conflicting claims of the law of God and the law of man are not what make the tragedy of the *Antigone*. It is Antigone herself, so great, so tortured. Hamlet's hesitation to kill his uncle is not tragic. The tragedy is his power to feel. Change all the circumstances of the drama and Hamlet in the grip of any calamity would be tragic, just as Polonius would never be, however awful the catastrophe. The suffering of a soul that can suffer greatly—that and only that, is tragedy.

It follows, then, that tragedy has nothing to do with the distinction between Realism and Romanticism. The contrary has always been maintained. The Greeks went to the myths for their subjects, we are told, to insure remoteness from real life which does not admit of high tragedy. "Realism is the ruin of tragedy," says the latest writer on the subject. It is not true. If indeed Realism were conceived of as dealing only with the usual, tragedy would be ruled out, for the soul capable of a great passion is not usual. But if nothing human is alien to Realism, then tragedy is of her domain, for the unusual is as real as the usual. When the Moscow Art Players presented the *Brothers Karamazoff* there was seen on the stage an absurd little man in dirty clothes who waved his arms about and shuffled and sobbed, the farthest possible remove from the traditional figures of tragedy, and yet tragedy was there in his person, stripped of her gorgeous pall, but sceptred truly, speaking the authentic voice of human agony in a struggle past the power of the human heart to bear. A drearier setting, a more typically realistic setting, it would be hard to find, but to see the play was to feel pity and awe before a man dignified by one thing only, made great by what he could suffer. Ibsen's plays are not tragedies. Whether Ibsen is a realist or not—the Realism of one generation is apt to be the Romanticism of the next—small souls are his dramatis personæ and his plays are dramas with an unhappy ending. The end of *Ghosts* leaves us with a sense of shuddering horror and cold anger against a society where such things can be, and these are not tragic feelings.

The greatest realistic works of fiction have been written by the French and the Russians. To read one of the great Frenchmen's books is to feel mingled despair and loathing for mankind, so base, so trivial and so wretched. But to read a great Russian novel is to have an altogether different experience. The baseness, the beast in us, the misery of life, are there as plain to see as in the French book, but what we are left with is not despair and not loathing, but a sense of pity and wonder before mankind that can so suffer. The Russian sees life in that way because the Russian genius is primarily poetical; the French genius is not. *Anna Karénina* is a tragedy; *Madame Bovary* is not. Realism and Romanticism, or comparative degrees of Realism, have nothing to do with the matter. It is a case of the small soul against the great soul and the power of a writer whose special endowment is *"voir clair dans ce qui est"* against the intuition of a poet.

If the Greeks had left no tragedies behind for us, the highest reach of their power would be unknown. The three poets who were able to sound the depths of human agony were able also to recognize and reveal it as tragedy. The mystery of evil, they said, curtains that of which "every man whose soul is not a clod hath visions." Pain could exalt and in tragedy for a moment men could have sight of a meaning beyond their grasp. "Yet had God not turned us in his hand and cast to earth our greatness," Euripides makes the old Trojan queen say in her extremity, "we would have passed away giving nothing to men. They would have found no theme for song in us nor made great poems from our sorrows."

Why is the death of the ordinary man a wretched, chilling thing which we turn from, while the death of the hero, always tragic, warms us with a sense of quickened life? Answer this question and the enigma of tragic pleasure is solved. "Never let me hear that brave blood has been shed in vain," said Sir Walter Scott; "it sends an imperious challenge down through all the generations." So the end of a tragedy challenges us. The great soul in pain and in death transforms pain and death. Through it we catch a glimpse of the Stoic Emperor's Dear City of God, of a deeper and more ultimate reality than that in which our lives are lived.

SCIENCE: SOCIAL AND NATURAL

Geoffrey Gorer

AMERICAN DATING

THE PRESENCE, THE ATTENTION, THE ADMIRATION OF OTHER PEOPLE . . .
becomes for Americans a necessary component to their self-esteem, demanded with a feeling of far greater psychological urgency than is usual
in other countries. This gives a special tone to the social relationships of
Americans with their fellows (with the exception, on occasion, of marital
and parental relationships): they are, in the first instance, devices by which
a person's self-esteem is maintained and enhanced. They can be considered
exploitative, but this exploitation is nearly always mutual: "I will assure
you that you are a success if you will assure me that I am" might be the
unspoken contract under which two people begin a mutual relationship.
The most satisfying form of this assurance is not given by direct flattery
or commendation (this by itself is suspect as a device to exploit the other)
but by love, or at least the concentrated, exclusive attention which shows
that one is worthy of interest and esteem.

It is only against this psychological background that what is probably
the most singular feature of American social life can be understood: the
"dating" which occupies so much of nearly every American's leisure time
from before adolescence until betrothal, and which for many continues even
after, if separation or satiety lessens the satisfactions to be derived from
the betrothed, or if excessive individual anxiety demands more reassurance
than betrothed or spouse or lover can give. "Dating" is idiosyncratic in
many ways, but especially so in that it uses the language and gestures of

courtship and love-making, without necessarily implying the reality of either. The overt differences of behavior which distinguish "dating" from courtship are so slight as to be barely perceptible; yet only in rare cases, and those involving unbalanced people, does confusion result—when both partners are American. "Dating" is a highly patterned activity or group of activities, comparable in some ways to a formal dance, in others to a very complicated competitive game; it is comparable to a dance in that the gestures employed do not have the significance they would have in other settings (witness the bows and curtsies of the minuet, the close embrace of the waltz and later ballroom dances); but it is more nearly comparable to such a competitive game as chess, in which the rules are known to, and observed by, both parties, but in which each move, after the opening gambit, is a response to the previous move of the other player. As in dances and games, the activity is felt to be enjoyable and rewarding for its own sake, and the more enjoyable the more nearly the partners or players are matched in skill and other necessary qualifications. The comparison with competitive games, such as chess, can be carried further; both partners must play with concentration and seriousness, using all their ingenuity, within the accepted rules, to be the victor; apart from the pleasure of the game, there is also the pleasant enhancement to one's self-esteem that winning the game provides. There is one aspect, however, in which the comparison of "dating" to chess breaks down; in a successful date there should not be a loser; both parties should feel their self-esteem, their assurance, enhanced.

As far as I know, no other society has been recorded which has developed a similar institutionalized type of behavior for its young people. A number of societies, of which the Samoans and the Trobrianders are well-known examples, allow for a period of sexual license and experiment before betrothal and marriage; but these are, and are meant to be, years of sensual and sexual satisfaction, sought for their own sake. In American "dating" sensual and sexual satisfactions may play a part (though this is by no means necessary) as counters in the game, but they are not the object of the exercise; the object of the exercise is enhanced self-esteem, assurance that one is lovable, and therefore a success.

A further complication arises from the fact that the words and gestures of love are regularly employed in "dating" without either party taking them for anything but counterfeit, moves in the game; and yet Americans believe very deeply and passionately in love (a concept not shared by the Samoans, nor the Trobrianders, nor many of the people of whom we have adequate studies). It is difficult to find comparisons for thus using frivolously in one context words and gestures which may be of the greatest importance in another. A very far-fetched one could be derived from the game of chess. In a period of monarchical passions and court intrigue "Your queen is captured" or "Your king is threatened" could have completely different significance according to the settings in which the phrases were used.

There is, finally, the complication that "dating," employing and being known to employ the words and gestures of love-making, is admitted and abetted by parents and teachers who, many of them, hold the puritan attitudes toward sex and the pleasures of the body, even though these attitudes do not seem to be held by most of the younger generation.

Because "dating" is so idiosyncratic to Americans (though the generality of Americans do not suspect this, believing, like the rest of the world, that the behavior they are used to is "human nature") and because it employs the form—but not the content—of love-making, it has been the cause of innumerable and serious misunderstandings whenever young Americans have come in contact with foreigners of the opposite sex. An invitation to a "date"—a pleasant and mutually profitable evening to enhance each other's self-esteem and demonstrate one's skill in the game—is almost always interpreted by a non-American as an attempt at seduction; if it is indignantly repudiated, both parties are left angry and dissatisfied: if it is immediately acceded to, the American, at least, feels defrauded, as if one had set out for a hunt and the fox had insisted on sitting down in one's back yard.

In a "date" the opening move, at least overtly, should come from the boy, in the form of an invitation to the girl to spend the evening in his company. The basis of selection is somewhat different for the boy and for the girl. For the girl the object is to have as many invitations as possible, so that she can choose among them the partner who she thinks can give her the best time, or who will be the most fun to compete with; for the boy the object is to have as his partner the girl who is most admired and most sought after by his companions and fellow rivals. A girl who only got a single invitation to an important social event (say a commencement dance), even though it was from the most desirable boy, the captain of the football team, would be doubtfully pleased (this, of course, on condition that they are not courting); a boy whose invitation is accepted by the local "belle" in similar circumstances has already gained a major social triumph. Consequently, participation in the "dating" pattern is somewhat different for the two sexes: all boys can and should take part in it, the level to which they aspire being dependent on their qualifications; but only the most successful and popular girls in each set do so fully, the rest having to be content with a steady boy friend, or even the companionship of a fellow unfortunate.

Unless an American boy is very poor, very maladjusted, or for some reason almost totally excluded from social life, "dating" and earning money for "dates" will occupy the greater part of his leisure time from early adolescence until betrothal. The social pressure toward doing so is very great. Thus in a typical Midwestern college fraternity the senior members insisted that the juniors have at least three "dates" a week; and further that these "dates" should be with girls who did honor to the fraternity, and, barring betrothal, should not be too frequently with the same girl. Such open control and supervision is unusual, but few Americans would quarrel with the standard of behavior demanded.

The experience of girls is much less uniform, since they are dependent on the boys' invitations, and the boys will invite the most popular girls obtainable. As a consequence some girls will have almost all their time taken up by "dates," while others have at most an occasional one, and many others drop out of the competition altogether until betrothal. The picture is clearest in formal dances. The hostess attempts to have at least three men for every two girls, so that at any moment at least a third of the men are in the "stag line," whereas all the girls are dancing. A man from the stag line "cuts in on" a dancing couple by tapping the man on the shoulder and taking his place. By etiquette one cannot refuse to be cut in on, nor can one cut in on one's immediate successor; a third man must intervene before one can resume one's partner and conversation. A man should not abandon his partner until cut in on; and one of the greatest humiliations a girl can bear is not to be cut in on before her partner is satiated with her company. Such an unfortunate girl is not likely to be invited again, nor, if invited, to accept.

For many girls, consequently, the "dating" period is one of humiliation, of frustration, of failure. But though it is painful, it is not usually psychologically crippling. Such unsuccessful girls are often betrothed and married earlier and better than the "belles" who, many of them, find it difficult to give up such prebetrothal triumphs: and moreover a "belle" is rated by the amount of money spent on her, among other things, and the standard is too high for most young men to maintain regularly.

The "date" starts as an invitation from a young man to a girl for an evening's public entertainment, typically at his expense, though since the depression girls occasionally pay their share. The entertainment offered depends on the young man's means and aspirations, and the locality; but it is in a public place always, and nearly always includes eating food together, the food being anything from an ice-cream soda at the local drugstore to the most elaborate and expensive meal that the locality can provide. Besides the food, the most usual entertainment is dancing—the place of the dance ranging anywhere from the cheap roadside café with a jukebox to the most expensive cabaret or country club. The male (the "escort") should call for the girl in a car (unless he be particularly young or poor) and should take her back in the car. If the entertainment proposed is of a formal or expensive nature, the man should provide a corsage—flowers for the girl to wear on her dress or in her hair.

The corsage is the first sign of the man's estimate of his partner for the evening, partly through the expense of the flowers, and partly according to the extent to which they are particularly suited to the girl's appearance, personality, or costume. Every item of the subsequent entertainment gives further signs; the relative amount of money spent is important for the girl's self-esteem, and not in itself.

"Showing the girl a good time" is the essential background for a "date," but it is not its object, as far as the man is concerned; its object is to get the girl to prove that he is worthy of love, and therefore a success. In some cases superior efficiency in dancing will elicit the necessary signs of approval; but typically, and not unexpectedly, they are elicited by talk. Once again, the importance of words is paramount.

Since, on first "dates" the pair are normally comparative strangers to one another, a certain amount of autobiography is necessary in the hopes of establishing some common interest or experience, at the least to prove that one is worthy of the other's attention. These autobiographies, however, differ at most in emphasis, in tone of voice, from those which should accompany any American meeting between strangers. What distinguishes the "date" from other conversation is a mixture of persiflage, flattery, wit and love-making which was formerly called a "line" but which each generation dubs with a new name.

The "line" is an individual variation of a commonly accepted pattern which is considered to be representative of a facet of a man's personality. Most men are articulately self-conscious about their "lines" and can describe them with ease; they are constantly practiced and improved with ever differing partners. The object of the "line" is to entertain, amuse, and captivate the girl, but there is no deep emotional involvement; it is a game of skill.

The girl's skill consists of parrying the "line" without discouraging her partner or becoming emotionally involved herself. To the extent that she falls for the "line" she is a loser in this intricate game; but if she discourages her partner so much that he does not request a subsequent "date" in the near future she is equally a loser. To remain the winner, she must make the nicest discriminations between yielding and rigidity.

The man scores to the extent that he is able to get more favors from the girl than his rivals, real or supposed, would be able to do. The proving time is the return journey from the place of public entertainment to the girl's home. A good-night kiss is almost the minimum repayment for an evening's entertainment; but how much more depends on the enterprise of the man, the self-assurance of the woman, and the number of "dates" the pair have had together. This love-making is still emotionally uninvolved; it is still part of the game, though the gestures and intimacies and language are identical with true love-making; it is not, save most rarely, an attempt at seduction; and the satisfactions sought are not, in the first instance, sensual but self-regarding. The man should demonstrate his enterprise and prove that he is worthy to be loved by pressing for ever further favors; but the girl who yields too much, or too easily, may well be a disappointment, in exactly the same way as too easy a victory in tennis or chess may be a disappointment.

It is usual—but not essential—that intimacies should increase with each successive "date" with the same partner, up to the threshold of, but seldom including, actual intercourse. The contest continues in these later phases, though slightly less articulately; the victor is the one who makes the other lose self-control without losing it him (or her) self.

It must be repeated that the goal of "dating" is not in the first place sexual satisfaction. An "easy lay" is not a good "date," and conversely. Apart from professional or semiprofessional prostitutes, there are in most groups girls who create for themselves an illusion of popularity by promiscuity. Their telephone numbers may get bandied about, but they are not the girls who get the orchid corsages, or get taken to the ringside tables at the best restaurants. It would be a paradox, but not too great a one, to say that the converse was more nearly true: that the ideal date is one in which both partners are so popular, so skilled, and so self-assured that the result is a draw.

Although "dating" is a game for two players only, it is very often elaborated into a "double date" by two couples going to the same places together. Noteworthy in this is the fact that the deeper emotional bond is between the two friends of the same sex (usually, but by no means always, the men) who arranged the "double date." A still further elaboration is the "blind date," in which the couple have not met at all before the start of the evening's entertainment; this can occur through one partner of an arranged "date" asking the other to provide a companion for his (or her) friend, or through a visitor in a strange town calling up a girl whose number he has been given. . . .

"Dates" are public. The greater part of them, as has already been said, take place in public places; and even if there is not a witness for the final portion, as there is in "double dates," there is little expectation that what transpires will be secret. Though distorted by a certain amount of boasting, detailed accounts of past dates are among the most popular subjects of conversation with people of one's own sex and generation. As with the child recounting his triumphs in the play group or at school, it is a proper method of gaining other people's respect and admiration.

"Dating" is normally ended by betrothal, which is the almost inevitable sequel of a boy's concentration on one girl. "Dating" is by definition promiscuous; and America offers no pattern for prolonged concentration on a single partner for the young outside courtship and marriage—there is no analogue, for example, to the French student's *petite amie*. With the increase in emotional maturity, most young men feel the lack of content in the "dating" pattern as it is normally practiced; a few—the "wolves"— develop it into regular seductions; but for the majority it is succeeded by betrothal and marriage.

Jacques-Yves Cousteau

THE SILENT WORLD

I. MENFISH

ONE MORNING IN JUNE, 1943, I WENT TO THE RAILWAY STATION AT BANDOL on the French Riviera and received a wooden case expressed from Paris. In it was a new and promising device, the result of years of struggle and dreams, an automatic compressed-air diving lung conceived by Émile

Gagnan and myself. I rushed it to Villa Barry where my diving comrades, Philippe Tailliez and Frédéric Dumas waited. No children ever opened a Christmas present with more excitement than ours when we unpacked the first "aqualung." If it worked, diving could be revolutionized.

We found an assembly of three moderate-sized cylinders of compressed air, linked to an air regulator the size of an alarm clock. From the regulator there extended two tubes, joining on a mouthpiece. With this equipment harnessed to the back, a watertight glass mask over the eyes and nose, and rubber foot fins, we intended to make unencumbered flights in the depths of the sea.

We hurried to a sheltered cove which would conceal our activity from curious bathers and Italian occupation troops. I checked the air pressure. The bottles contained air condensed to one hundred and fifty times atmospheric pressure. It was difficult to contain my excitement and discuss calmly the plan of the first dive. Dumas, the best goggle diver in France, would stay on shore keeping warm and rested, ready to dive to my aid, if necessary. My wife, Simone, would swim out on the surface with a schnorkel breathing tube and watch me through her submerged mask. If she signaled anything had gone wrong, Dumas could dive to me in seconds. "Didi," as he was known on the Riviera, could skin dive to sixty feet.

My friends harnessed the three-cylinder block on my back with the regulator riding at the nape of my neck and the hoses looped over my head. I spat on the inside of my shatterproof glass mask and rinsed it in the surf, so that mist would not form inside. I molded the soft rubber flanges of the mask tightly over forehead and cheekbones. I fitted the mouthpiece under my lips and gripped the nodules between my teeth. A vent the size of a paper clip was to pass my inhalations and exhalations beneath the sea. Staggering under the fifty-pound apparatus, I walked with a Charlie Chaplin waddle into the sea.

The diving lung was designed to be slightly buoyant. I reclined in the chilly water to estimate my compliance with Archimedes' principle that a solid body immersed in liquid is buoyed up by a force equal to the weight of the liquid displaced. Dumas justified me with Archimedes by attaching seven pounds of lead to my belt. I sank gently to the sand. I breathed sweet effortless air. There was a faint whistle when I inhaled and a light rippling sound of bubbles when I breathed out. The regulator was adjusting pressure precisely to my needs.

I looked into the sea with the same sense of trespass that I have felt on every dive. A modest canyon opened below, full of dark green weeds, black sea urchins, and small flower-like white algae. Fingerlings browsed in the scene. The sand sloped down into a clear blue infinity. The sun struck so brightly I had to squint. My arms hanging at my sides, I kicked the fins languidly and traveled down, gaining speed, watching the beach reeling past. I stopped kicking and the momentum carried me on a fabulous glide. When I stopped, I slowly emptied my lungs and held my breath. The diminished volume of my body decreased the lifting force of water, and I sank dreamily down. I inhaled a great chestful and retained it. I rose toward the surface.

My human lungs had a new role to play, that of a sensitive ballasting system. I took normal breaths in a slow rhythm, bowed my head and swam smoothly down to thirty feet. I felt no increasing water pressure, which at that depth is twice that of the surface. The aqualung automatically fed me increased compressed air to meet the new pressure layer. Through the fragile human lung linings this counter-pressure was being transmitted to the blood stream and instantly spread throughout the incompressible body. My brain received no subjective news of the pressure. I was at ease, except for a pain in the middle ear and sinus cavities. I swallowed as one does in a landing airplane to open my Eustachian tubes and healed the pain. (I did not wear ear plugs, a dangerous practice when under water. Ear plugs would have trapped a pocket of air between them and the eardrums. Pressure building up in the Eustachian tubes would have forced my eardrums outward, eventually to the bursting point.)

I reached the bottom in a state of transport. A school of silvery sars (goat bream), round and flat as saucers, swam in a rocky chaos. I looked up and saw the surface shining like a defective mirror. In the center of the looking glass was the trim silhouette of Simone, reduced to a doll. I waved. The doll waved at me.

I became fascinated with my exhalations. The bubbles swelled on the way up through lighter pressure layers, but were peculiarly flattened like mushroom caps by their eager push against the medium. I conceived the importance bubbles were to have for us in the dives to come. As long as air boiled on the surface all was well below. If the bubbles disappeared there would be anxiety, emergency measures, despair. They roared out of the regulator and kept me company. I felt less alone.

I swam across the rocks and compared myself favorably with the stars. To swim fishlike, horizontally, was the logical method in a medium eight hundred times denser than air. To halt and hang attached to nothing, no lines or air pipe to the surface, was a dream. At night I had often had visions of flying by extending my arms as wings. Now I flew without wings. (Since that first aqualung flight, I have never had a dream of flying.)

I thought of the helmet diver arriving where I was on his ponderous boots and struggling to walk a few yards, obsessed with his umbilici and his head imprisoned in copper. On skin dives I had seen him leaning dangerously forward to make a step, clamped in heavier pressure at the ankles than the head, a cripple in an alien land. From this day forward we would swim across miles of country no man had known, free and level, with our flesh feeling what the fish scales know.

I experimented with all possible maneuvers of the aqualung—loops, somersaults, and barrel rolls. I stood upside down on one finger and burst out laughing, a shrill distorted laugh. Nothing I did altered the automatic rhythm of air. Delivered from gravity and buoyancy I flew around in space.

I could attain almost two knots' speed, without using my arms. I soared vertically and passed my own bubbles. I went down to sixty feet. We had been there many times without breathing aids, but we did not know what happened below that boundary. How far could we go with this strange device?

Fifteen minutes had passed since I left the little cove. The regulator lisped in a steady cadence in the ten-fathom layer and I could spend an hour there on my air supply. I determined to stay as long as I could stand the chill. Here were tantalizing crevices we had been obliged to pass fleetingly before. I swam inch-by-inch into a dark narrow tunnel, scraping my chest on the floor and ringing the air tanks on the ceiling. In such situations a man is of two minds. One urges him on toward mystery and the other reminds him that he is a creature with good sense that can keep him alive, if he will use it. I bounced against the ceiling. I'd used one-third of my air and was getting lighter. My brain complained that this foolishness might sever my air hoses. I turned over and hung on my back.

The roof of the cave was thronged with lobsters. They stood there like great flies on a ceiling. Their heads and antennae were pointed toward the cave entrance. I breathed lesser lungfuls to keep my chest from touching them. Above water was occupied, ill-fed France. I thought of the hundreds of calories a diver loses in cold water. I selected a pair of one-pound lobsters and carefully plucked them from the roof, without touching their stinging spines. I carried them toward the surface.

Simone had been floating, watching my bubbles wherever I went. She swam down toward me. I handed her the lobsters and went down again as she surfaced. She came up under a rock which bore a torpid Provençal citizen with a fishing pole. He saw a blonde girl emerge from the combers with lobsters wriggling in her hands. She said, "Could you please watch these for me?" and put them on the rock. The fisherman dropped his pole. Simone made five more surface dives to take lobsters from me and carry them to the rock. I surfaced in the cove, out of the fisherman's sight. Simone claimed her lobster swarm. She said, "Keep one for yourself, *monsieur*. They are very easy to catch if you do as I did."

Lunching on the treasures of the dive, Tailliez and Dumas questioned me on every detail. We reveled in plans for the aqualung. Tailliez penciled the tablecloth and announced that each yard of depth we claimed in the sea would open to mankind three hundred thousand cubic kilometers of living space. Tailliez, Dumas, and I had come a long way together. We had been eight years in the sea as goggle divers. Our new key to the hidden world promised wonders.

II. FIFTY FATHOMS DOWN

We continued to be puzzled with the rapture of the depths and felt that we were challenged to go deeper. Didi's deep dive in 1943 had made us aware of the problem, and the Group had assembled detailed reports on its deep dives. But we had only a literary knowledge of the full effects of *l'ivresse des grandes profoundeurs* as it must strike lower down. In the summer of 1947 we set out to make a series of deeper penetrations.

Here I must say that we were not trying for record descents, although the dives did set new world marks. We have always placed a reasonable premium on returning alive. Even Didi, the boldest among us, is not a stunt man. We went lower because that was the only way to learn more about the drunken effect, and to sample individual reactions on what aqualung work could be done in severe depths. The attempts were surrounded with careful preparations and controls, in order to obtain clear data. The objective range we set was three hundred feet or fifty fathoms. No independent diver had yet been deeper than Dumas's two hundred and ten feet.

The dives were measured by a heavy shotline hanging from the *Élie Monnier*. On the line at sixteen-and-one-half-foot intervals (five meters) there were white boards. The divers carried indelible pencils to sign their names on the deepest board they could reach, and to write a sentence describing their sensations.

To save energy and air, the test divers descended the shotline without undue motion, carried down by ten-pound hunks of scrap iron. They retarded their descent by holding the line. When a man reached the target depth, or the maximum distance he could stand, he signed in, jettisoned his weight, and took the line back to the surface. During the return the divers halted at depths of twenty and ten feet for short periods of stage decompression to avoid the bends.

I was in good physical condition for the trial, trained fine by an active spring in the sea, and with responsive ears. I entered the water holding the scrap iron in my left hand. I went down with great rapidity, with my right arm crooked around the shotline. I was oppressively conscious of the Diesel generator rumble of the idle *Élie Monnier* as I wedged my head into mounting pressure. It was high noon in July, but the light soon faded. I dropped through the twilight, alone with the white rope, which stretched before me in a monotonous perspective of blank white signposts.

At two hundred feet I tasted the metallic flavor of compressed nitrogen and was instantaneously and severely struck with rapture. I closed my hand on the rope and stopped. My mind was jammed with conceited thought and antic joy. I struggled to fix my brain on reality, to attempt to name the color of the sea about me. A contest took place between navy blue, aquamarine, and Prussian blue. The debate would not resolve. The sole fact I could grasp was that there was no roof and no floor in the blue room. The distant purr of the Diesel invaded my mind—it swelled to a giant beat, the rhythm of the world's heart.

I took the pencil and wrote on a board, "Nitrogen has a dirty taste." I had little impression of holding the pencil, childhood nightmares overruled my mind. I was ill in bed, terrorized with the realization that everything in the world was thick. My fingers were sausages. My tongue was a tennis ball. My lips swelled grotesquely on the mouth grip. The air was syrup. The water jelled around me as though I were smothered in aspic.

I hung witless on the rope. Standing aside was a smiling jaunty man, my second self, perfectly self-contained, grinning sardonically at the wretched diver. As the seconds passed the jaunty man installed himself in my command and ordered that I unloose the rope and go on down.

I sank slowly through a period of intense visions.

Around the two hundred and sixty-four foot board the water was suffused with an unearthly glow. I was passing from night to an intimation of dawn. What I saw as sunrise was light reflected from the floor, which had passed unimpeded through the dark transparent strata above. I saw below me the weight at the end of the shotline, hanging twenty feet from the floor. I stopped at the penultimate board and looked down at the last board, five meters away, and marshaled all my resources to evaluate the situation without deluding myself. Then I went to the last board, two hundred and ninety-seven feet down.

The floor was gloomy and barren, save for morbid shells and sea urchins. I was sufficiently in control to remember that in this pressure, ten times that of the surface, any untoward physical effort was extremely dangerous. I filled my lungs slowly and signed the board. I could not write what it felt like fifty fathoms down.

I was the deepest independent diver. In my bisected brain the satisfaction was balanced by satirical self-contempt.

I dropped the scrap iron and bounded like a coiled spring, clearing two boards in the first flight. There, at two hundred and sixty-four feet, the rapture vanished suddenly, inexplicably and entirely. I was light and sharp, one man again, enjoying the lighter air expanding in my lungs. I rose through the twilight zone at high speed, and saw the surface pattern in a blaze of platinum bubbles and dancing prisms. It was impossible not to think of flying to heaven.

However, before heaven there was purgatory. I waited twenty feet down for five minutes of stage decompression, then hurried to ten feet where I spent ten shivering minutes. When they hauled in the shotline I found that some impostor had written my name on the last board.

For a half hour afterward I had a slight pain in the knees and shoulders. Philippe Tailliez went down to the last board, scribbled a silly message, and came up with a two-day headache. Dumas had to overcome dramas of heavy rapture in the fifty-fathom zone. Our two tough sailors, Fargues and Morandière, said they could have done short easy labor around the bottom. Quartermaster Georges visited the bottom board and was dizzy for an hour or so afterward. Jean Pinard felt out of condition at two hundred and twenty feet, signed in, and sensibly returned. None of us wrote a legible word on the deep board.

In the autumn we undertook another series of deep dives, with marker boards extending below fifty fathoms. We planned to venture beyond with lines tied to the waist, and a safety man stationed on deck, completely equipped to jump in and give aid in case of difficulty.

Diving master Maurice Fargues dived first. On deck we regularly received the reassuring conventional signal Fargues gave by tugging on the line, *"Tout va bien"* (All is well). Suddenly there was no signal. Anxiety struck us all at once. Jean Pinard, his safety man, went down immediately, and we hauled Fargues up toward one hundred and fifty feet, where they would meet. Pinard plunged toward an inert body, and beheld with horror that Fargues's mouthpiece was hanging on his chest.

We worked for twelve hours trying to revive Fargues, but he was dead. Rapture of the depths had stolen his air tube from his mouth and drowned him. When we brought up the shotline we found Maurice Fargues's name written on the three hundred and ninety-six foot board. Fargues gave his life a hundred feet below our greatest penetrations, deeper than any helmet diver breathing unmixed air has ever gone in the sea.

He had shared our unfolding wonderment of the ocean since the early days of the Research Group; we retained the memory of his prodigal comradeship. Dumas and I owed our lives to Maurice Fargues, who had resurrected us from the death cave at Vaucluse. We will not be consoled that we were unable to save him.

The death of Fargues and the lessons of the summer showed that three hundred feet is the extreme boundary of compressed-air diving. Amateurs can be trained in a few days to reach one hundred and thirty feet, and there professionals, observing decompression tables, may do almost any sort of hard work. In the next zone down to two hundred and ten feet experienced divers may perform light labor and make short explorations if rigid safety rules are followed. In the zone of rapture below only the highly skilled aqualunger may venture for a brief reconnaissance. Free divers could range considerably beyond the fifty-fathom layer by breathing oxygen mixed with lighter gases such as helium and hydrogen. While it has been proved that helium removes the causes of depth drunkenness, such dives would still require long tedious hours of decompression.

William W. Howells

VARIOUS VIEWS OF RACE

THE WHOLE SUBJECT OF RACE IN MODERN MAN HAS BEEN SURROUNDED BY ignorance and perverse judgment. This is another case where common sense and everyday observation have been inadequate, lacking a well-developed body of real biological knowledge, so that ill-founded theories, ill-advised references to the classics, and a lot of plain poppycock were all mixed up together. You will remember the confusion of ideas which attended the findings of the Neanderthal and the Java men. The same confusions rallied around the subject of race, and they did not stay within the relatively polite fencing salons of scientific societies, but got out into the vulgar brawls of politics, and have caused decade on decade of race-generated misery.

Races were recognized in antiquity, but roused no great interest and were shrugged off with some fabulous explanation. Any foreign land was thought to be peopled with ogres or cannibals (the Anthropophagi), and a man who differed from yourself merely in having a black skin and fuzzy hair was by comparison nothing to look at twice. Little of the world was yet known. Race was really discovered from the fifteenth century on, in the great age of exploration. "Indians" were found who did not live in India. Hairy aborigines came to light in the antipodes. This was, of course, before anything like an evolution for man had been suggested, and the stunned voyagers from Europe ascribed the many new kinds and colors of men to a series of separate creations, in other Edens which the Scriptures did not mention.

There was, in fact, a seesaw battle on this point, when some writers began to think that man somehow have changed in different places, given a fairly long time and a not too strict obedience to the Old Testament. The great Blumenbach, jack-of-all-sciences, in 1775 made one of the very first reasonable classifications of man, and he suggested that the Whites (whom he dubbed the Caucasians, because of admiration of the appearance of natives of the Caucasus) were the original type of man, from which had drifted away, largely under the influence of climate, the Yellows (Asiatics) and Reds (American Indians) on one side and the Browns (Malays) and Blacks (Africans) on the other.

After about 1860, when evolutionary theory broke out of its egg with Darwin, and the Neanderthal Man broke out of his cave, serious attempts by scientists to relate human origins to Adam and Eve quickly stopped. Classification, however, continued apace. Anthropology was born, giving itself the job of seeking out and describing the varieties of mankind, until virtually every last Pygmy had known the stare of the camera lens and the feel of the calipers. However, while succeeding in its field objective of learning about all the earth's peoples, racial study was gradually bogging down because of some theoretical defects.

One was soon apparent: nobody could agree how many "races" there were, estimates of the number ranging from two (the "Handsome" and the "Ugly") to over sixty. Another defect was more subtle: after abandoning the idea that the different types of man had been created separately, just as they are, and the other Biblical idea, that they were the descendants of the several sons of Noah (whence the use of the terms Semitic, Hamitic, and Japhitic) or of the Lost Tribes of Israel, the students of the subject neglected to supply themselves with any other plausible explanation. (One other suggestion was made: races descended from the different kinds of apes!) For a long time there seems to have prevailed simply a hazy understanding that somewhere in the past there had been ancient races which once were pure. This mythical atmosphere made it possible for certain German and French writers to develop their groundless philosophy (long before the Nazis) of ancient Aryan purity as the secret of civilization.

And so a great deal of good and careful descriptive work was done, with no very clear problem in the mind of the doer—no questions as to the basic nature of races or as to how they had come into existence. It is obvious that anthropologists were mostly trying to separate races and types, to make them as distinct and clear-cut as possible, so that the "hybrids" and "mixtures" of the present day might better be understood. Only late in the game was it realized that all the overlapping and intergrading, and the difficulty of deciding just how many races one should count, might in themselves be significant. Eventually a "scientific" view began to grow up, by which I mean the awareness that racial differences and racial theory must be made to jibe with what is known about evolutionary processes, genetics, and biology generally. But this was not the happy ending. We have a scientific view, but not a complete scientific understanding. Anthropologists began to attempt definitions of race. But these turned out to be refractory. For race is not just a thing. It is a whole situation in a biological process, and to understand it demands a pretty full explanation of a lot of evolutionary principles, only partly stated in the early chapters of this book.

Therefore, defining race is like "defining" human history. I would say that definitions drawn up to be understood by a newspaper reader are long, rambling, and inadequate, and that short, accurate, and meaningful definitions can be understood only if you know the background. For example, this one, by Dobzhansky, is highly acceptable: "Races are populations differing in the incidence of certain genes." To an educated person this probably means that races differ in some of their hereditary traits. But, in its suggestions and limitations, it means a great deal more than that, if you understand the full sense of "population" and the theoretical processes by which gene incidences are maintained or changed.

This difficulty of defining is no false bugaboo. To discredit racial doctrines in modern politics, UNESCO in 1950 assembled in Paris a panel of anthropologists and others, to draw up a general statement on the nature of race, as it is understood today. This was to be a long and full definition and explanation, a scientific reference for laymen of any sort. The panel did its work and made public its statement with hopeful satisfaction. But the other anthropologists fell upon this document with such vigor that the English journal, *Man,* was for some months running what amounted to a department of criticism, correction, and amplification, in the form of letters from Great Britain, France, and the United States. So UNESCO quickly got together another panel in 1951 to do the statement over again. This time the draft was circulated widely, so that the rest of the profession could get its comments and abuse in early. By compressing the results UNESCO was able to publish the statement and the gist of the exceptions to it—a sort of minimum anthropological description of race—in a relatively small volume. When, a few years later, I submitted the statement to a seminar of educated but non-anthropological European graduate students, presumably a worthy sample of ultimate consumers, it was still good for a barrage of further criticism from this quarter, which was impressively well informed. So perhaps, in defining race, the policy of containment is not too successful.

HUMAN AND ANIMAL VARIETY

Perhaps in fact the whole endeavor to define, in descriptive terms, is a futile one. Supposing we were to forget old arguments and definitions, and begin afresh, looking at humankind as though we were setting out to collect beetles or seashells. We notice different-appearing men in different parts of the planet's geography. We examine them for their fundamental characteristics. Are any of them as different as orang and chimpanzee, who belong to two different genera, *Pongo* and *Pan?* No, evidently not. Are any of them as different as two species? That is to say, have they significant distinctions in physique—more than you could find in cattle or in dogs? Can you see boundaries of some kind between them, so that overlapping is slight, and so that, even if mingled in the same territory they tend to breed separately, not together? No. Human racial distinctions, however marked they may seem at the extremes, shade into one another and tend to be lost, both in geographic overlapping and in ready interbreeding. This last applies to all contact, whether it is local and special, like Danes and Eskimos in Greenland, or is a vast zone of intergrading, like Africa just south of the Sahara, or a great melting pot, like Latin America.

We see only a big, world-wide species which, like other animal species, is both polymorphic and polytypic. That is, its individuals are highly variable in any place, and the average of individuals also differs from place to place. Both of these things are natural to any species, and the place-to-place variation, the existence of races, is the more likely, the more widespread is the species.

To the ordinary observer, all this variation is not so obvious in other kinds of animals, but it is there, and zoologists know it; ordinary observers do not look very hard at any species but *Homo sapiens.* In fact, after several generations of anthropologists had believed that man, in his skeleton and skin, was an extraordinary variable animal, Professor A. H. Schultz demonstrated that chimpanzees are at least as variable, if not more so. And chimpanzee "species" have been fallaciously named and described, literally by the dozen, because of the finding of a specimen or so with an unusual combination of coat, size, and features. These species do not exist; they are known to be merely variant individuals of the general population. Possibly other chimpanzees stare at them, as we notice a man who is very tall or very red-haired.

So these two kinds of variety, in-group and between-group, are not peculiar to man. Rather, they are usual to all animals, and in fact needful. Without this variety, you may recall, evolution could not take place at all. Furthermore, the keeping-up of such differences is an aid to the health of the individuals and the strength of the species.

Consider the in-group heterogeneity, which has often been construed as lack of "purity," as departure from the ideal type of a race as it supposedly once existed. Such a purity never did and never does exist. For the variety rests on the possession of different kinds of genes in a group, which is important to it, both to meet new situations or to form protective combinations. "Purity" in fact means nothing, unless it means homozygosity, the eliminating of all but one kind of gene. This is interesting in the laboratory, but if you want to apply it to man it means brother-sister mating. And this is viewed as dimly by the geneticist as by the layman, since it tends to uncover detrimental genes in homozygous form. Heterozygosity, the pairing of different genes, protects against this, and broadens the resources of the whole group.

And different groups also diverge in the whole pattern of their genes, that is to say, in the proportions and combinations they possess. I will be specific in a minute. This comes from a variety of causes. It may come simply from the group being isolated, and also from natural selection working to favor one combination in one place, a second combination in another. And so we have races, in animals or man. Some such races eventually become so distinct from each other as to change into new separate species. But that is not the necessary fate of races. They are present in the nature of things when a species is widespread. Human races are really a kind of local limitation in the total variety of mankind.

Now these two kinds of variation occur together, an important point. Groups may differ from one another, but the individuals in each also differ so much that the overlap is wide. So we can speak only of average differences in groups, in racial traits. In some things (such as skin color) the average differs so greatly between European Whites and African Negroes that the individuals do not overlap, and there is no question as to which race a man belongs. In other things, the overlap is so broad that we cannot tell if the averages actually differ at all. But the features of race we study generally lie in between.

BLOOD AND GENES

We come at last to these features, the way in which different races differ, more or less. Let us begin with the engines of life, the internal organs and their behavior. Here, even the anthropoid apes are strikingly similar to man. Individual human beings differ considerably in size and shape of viscera, but it is not known whether there is any average differences between races. In blood chemistry there is a little more difference from apes: it is possible, by introducing human blood serum into a chimpanzee's blood stream, to develop antibodies in his blood serum which will then show a reaction in the presence of human serum. But no such thing can be done with the races of man: human blood is all the same in this respect.

However, our blood has different sets of individual antigens and antibodies, like A, B, and O, or the Rh system. This illustrates nicely what we have been talking about. Individuals in a population differ in their blood types, according to the two genes they have inherited, so that you are type O, *or* A, *or* B, *or* AB. Most racial groups, however, have all these kinds of individual (some populations have no B, and a few have O only). So they do not differ in an absolute way, as though there were an "A race" and a "B race," but only on the average; or better, in their proportions of the same things. They differ, as Dobzhansky says, in the "incidence of the genes," not in having totally different genes. The blood types are the same, wherever you find them, so that a member of your own family might very well be a greater menace to you, if you were having a blood transfusion, than a Hottentot.

One of the fascinating discoveries of recent years is another blood oddity, the "sickling gene," or the sickle-cell trait, also called Hemoglobin S. Somewhere, in a pair of genes having to do with the development of hemoglobin in the red blood cells, there took place a mutation, or change to a new gene. If, instead of having two of the usual, or normal, genes, you inherit from your father or from your mother a sickling gene, your red blood cells will have a peculiar property. If their oxygen is reduced (as will take place if you let a drop of blood stand on a glass slide), they will lose their round form and take on abnormal shapes, especially crescents or sickles. And you will have another peculiar property as well: you will have a high childhood resistance to the most severe type of malaria.

Clearly this will be to your advantage, if you live in a malarial region, and beyond the range of the best medical treatment. And you would expect that this gene, this trait, would become very common, through Darwin's principle of natural selection. So it has. You might expect, in fact, that it would become universal and supplant the "normal" gene.

But wait. Suppose it is fairly common and that your mother and your father are the proud possessors of it; suppose that through the laws of chance you inherit the sickling gene from *both* your parents, and so are homozygous for it—have two sickling genes and no normal gene. This is too much. You will have no normal hemoglobin. You will have a severe anemia, sickle-cell anemia, and you will almost certainly die from it before you grow up. And so you will hardly pass the gene on to your children.

That is why the sickling gene does not become universal: it kills itself off. Where malaria exists, it builds itself up, by natural selection, because people who have it in the single dose are healthier, with larger families, than people who do not have the gene at all, suffering malaria severely or dying from it. But then, as this happens, the smaller proportion of homozygotes will also rise. That is, more infants with the double dose are born, only to die; and so some of the sickling genes are picked out of the population and thrown away. The gene cannot rise up beyond a certain level before it drops out faster than it increases; obviously, if it could some- how get near the point where everyone had two sickling genes, then every- one would die, and that would be the end of gene and population alike. A balance is struck: one part of the population is more healthy and vigorous for having the gene against malaria, which helps the whole population to survive; but at the same time the population cannot survive unless the other part acts as custodian of the "normal" gene.

Why do you not see these things all around you? Because you are probably not an African or a South Asian, and so you will not have played in this lottery of life and death. The sickling phenomenon is at home largely in Negro Africa, here being in a broad way commonest where malaria is worst and less common elsewhere. It occurs virtually throughout Negro territory, and on the fringes; it is found in the ordinary Negroes, in Pygmies, and in the tall Watussi and their ilk. It is not found in the Bush- men of South Africa. But it came to the New World with the American Negroes, among most groups of whom it seems to have been declining, since their new environment is not sufficiently malarial to encourage it, and so to offset its lethal effects. With control of mosquitoes through DDT, the gene may be expected eventually to fall sharply in Africa as well.

Does all this mean we have hit on something which distinguishes the Negroes as a race? Not really. The same gene turns up widely in India, notably among some of the backward peoples. It is not uncommon in Greece and has been found in malarial regions of Italy, Turkey, and Arabia; one suspects it came to these places with an importation of Negroes, however small. This makes it look like a Negro tracer. But it should be looked on rather as a trait which spread (and was still spreading lately) among the Negro populations of Africa, simply because it appeared there, in some region exposed to malaria. It did not expand in certain other parts of the world where malaria exists, because it was not there to expand, not because the inhabitants were not Negroes. It could have spread. It prob- ably did so in Greece and Italy quite independently of other Negro traits, once it arrived somehow from Negro Africa to start with.

Oddly enough there is another such gene, though a different one, in Italy and other Mediterranean countries, causing Cooley's anemia. But we cannot be on this all day. The sickling trait is sufficiently instructive, teaching a variety of lessons. Aside from being as beautiful an example of natural selection as is known, it shows how genes are not the special property of only one race, but can be passed to any, without limits. Rather, genes may accumulate in one direction or another, as genes for lighter skin accumulate in one region or population and genes for darker skin in another. That is the actual nature of race, the way in which populations begin to become distinct.

FUNCTION AND ADAPTATION

When we come to matters of function, there may be some general differences from race to race and place to place. Little is known. Research on basal metabolism, or rates of growth, has found considerable average differences among different peoples. But these differences seem to be very much a matter of climate and diet, and individuals of the same group will change in metabolism if you move them around. Therefore such differences cannot be called "racial." The same thing is apparently true of most diseases, like tuberculosis or hypertension.

But Negroes do seem positively more resistant to infection from a variety of skin afflictions, including some skin-related or skin-implanted diseases like scarlet fever or diphtheria. This is resistance to infection, not to the disease itself, since they will be as sick as the next man, once they catch it. Nobody knows the exact source of the resistance, but it would appear to lie in the skin itself and to be a real racial distinction. Eskimos appear to withstand cold in the tissues of the hand better, by a better regulation of the blood supply than in Whites; but it is not known whether this is an acquired hereditary—a racial—trait or results from long personal acclimatizing, during the life of each Eskimo.

The human figure is also "functional" in a related way, as I have said before, because it seems to help out with the regulation of body heat by changing its shape to the best form under the circumstances. You do not get long, lanky Eskimos in the frigid north: a short and roly-poly seal hunter keeps his heat better, and in the awful cold he can get emaciated fast enough without starting that way. Contrariwise you do not find chubby and stumpy camel drivers in the Sahara. Instead, the tall and slender people of broiling deserts are much more likely to avoid heatstroke by being stretched out, and presenting as much skin as possible, per pound of flesh, for body heat to escape through. So we may reasonably assume these body forms to be real effects of natural selection. And they are real "racial" traits, having come to be the hereditary equipment of certain peoples. But they are not exclusive, for the desert lankiness belongs to

Arabs and Tuaregs, of the White stock, to the Nilotic Negroes along the White Nile in the Sudan, and to the desert-living aborigines of Australia, three quite different kinds of men. We have, rather, a racial trait which is a climatic adaptation.

SKELETON AND SKULL IN RACE

There are probably other shape differences like this, whose significance does not suggest itself so easily. Indeed, the Negroes in general tend to be longer in the leg and in the forearm than the Whites, judging by comparisons made in the United States, so that this could be looked on as a vague but persistent difference between the two stocks. But one needs to get the averages of large numbers to find such a distinction, and the fact is that the bones have no really characteristic differences from race to race. Mankind is very uniform in this regard, as you might suspect from knowing that even Pekin Man did not differ discernibly from us below the neck. And the anthropologist who looks at a headless skeleton and ventures a guess as to the race it represents is making a stab in the dark, nothing more.

He will do better with the skull, and particularly its facial parts, if he has some experience. Mongoloid peoples generally have a flattish face region with wide and angulated cheekbones and little canine fossa, but with some projection just at the bony gum. Negroes have more such projection and larger teeth, as well as a receding chin, rather delicate cheekbones, broad nose apertures and low but vertical foreheads. Whites have the most vertical faces and prominent chins, as well as good brow ridges. And an especially primitive combination, of projecting face, smaller brain, heavy brows, and receding foreheads, appears in the natives of Australia and of some other parts of the western Pacific, like New Britain and New Caledonia. So the several main races of man tend to differ a little in the things which have made *Homo sapiens* what he is: in the degree, that is to say, of the lightening up of the brows, of the diminution of the teeth, or of the pulling in of the face.

Even these descriptions are a little too pat. I said before that sapient man is really much alike everywhere in skull and skeleton. It might be instructive to you to leave the book open at this page and try to identify the next cranium you see. The anthropological eye can generally spot the narrow, poorly filled skull of the native Australian or the very wide face and peculiar high pitched cranium of the Eskimo without difficulty. But he, or anyone, will begin to have trouble with Europeans and Negroes, and more still with the generally nondescript varieties of Asiatics. If a strange skeleton is dug up in your vicinity (North America), look first at the front teeth in the upper jaw. If they are a little projecting, not vertical, the person is more likely to be an Indian.

SKIN AND COLOR

It is only when we come to view the human exterior that we see the features we have always called "racial," the things which give races their distinctive appearances. Foremost is skin, so prominent in our hairless species and so varied in pigmentation that it has been the popular handle for race since the beginning. Now skin is a most useful material, and does not exist merely to keep your insides inside and the bath water outside. It is an envelope, a bacteria-killing agent, a sense organ, a heat regulator, and, probably most important here, a light filter. It admits limited amounts of ultraviolet light, which is needed to form vitamin D, but presumably diminishes or diffuses dangerous doses by a screen of pigment granules.

This pigment, melanin, is present in everyone excepting pure albinos, and everyone has both a fixed amount as well as some ability to form more temporarily—in other words, to tan. It is the basic amount in which racial groups differ so noticeably (and in which individuals within a racial group also differ among themselves). We are used to talking about Whites and Blacks, but Sallows and Dark Browns would be more like it. The White stock as a whole has a considerable range, although it is generally so light that tanning is more prominent than any basic light brown tinting of the skin, and the blood can show through to give varying degrees of ruddiness. In northern Europe the whole pigmentation can be very pale indeed, since so little melanin is present. At the opposite end of the scale the Negroes also have a considerable range of color, in the dense brown shades. Skin which actually looks black, or nearly so, is rare in the somewhat diluted American Negroes, but is occasional in Africa and Melanesia.

This variety in outer color has all the earmarks of an adaptation, of a trait responding to the force of sunlight by natural selection. The dark-skinned racial types are distributed in the tropics of the Old World. And the bleached-out Europeans are swarthier in the south and reach their extra degree of depigmentation, true blondness, in the cloudy north where sunlight is not only not a danger to body tissues but is actually at a premium. It looks as though here the skin has stripped itself of its usual defenses in the hope of gulping up the little supply of ultraviolet light.

But at the same time, there is not as good a correspondence with climate as exists in body form, as I described it a few pages back. White and Black have approached the same body form in the Afro-Arabian desert belt, but they have not approached the same color. And the American Indians in their vast range from the Arctic to Tierra del Fuego also reflect climate in body size and form, to a discernible degree, but not in color. There are other reservations: are the tropical forests really so sunny as to encourage their inhabitants to be dark-skinned? Therefore, some of the racial differences in skin color may be more deep-seated, and possibly more ancient, than a direct tie to sunlight might suggest. It may well be that other things, not yet detected, bear on pigment; and I have already mentioned the superior resistance to infection of Negro skin. If so, then skin color probably answers to a complex balance of forces, a little like the sickling gene, and not simply to the persuasion of the sun.

In fact, it is just in skin color and the other most obvious trappings of race that we find the greatest difficulty in finding explanations. In hair and eye color mankind is more uniform, with dark brown eyes and dark brown or black hair the mode; only certain sections of the depigmented Europeans have lighter shades of these. By excluding more light, a dark iris may make a more efficient camera out of the eye than a light one; and so blue eyes and blond hair, with no apparent advantage to them, probably tag along after fair skin as accidental side effects. Hair varies in shape as well as color. Among Mongoloid peoples generally it is perfectly straight. In Europeans it may also be straight, but the hairs are more apt to twist in unison at intervals along their length, giving rise to waves or curls. In Negroes there is a continuous curl to the hairs, which do not lie parallel; thus they do not form curls but intertwine vigorously and make a woolly mat. Possibly this acts as a natural pith helmet.

OTHER FAMILIAR FEATURES

Some differences in form are incomprehensible. Why are Negro lips rolled out and thick? Why do Whites and native Australians retain full beards and a certain amount of body hair? Why is the head itself differently shaped: long, round, high or low, in different localities? Why does the face vary in the same way? One cannot escape the feeling that there has been some accidental evolution in these things, although invisible causes are always to be assumed.

Here, however, is a difference which does seem to make sense: the narrow nasal cavities of the north Europeans and the Eskimos seem to warm and moisten air for the lungs in dry and cold climates, as a protection. At any rate, there has been shown a strong statistical relation between nose shape and the average temperature and water vapor in the air, when studying peoples who have been a long time in their present climates.

Racial differences, then, taken altogether, seem to result from a mixture of things. Part of them are surely mementos of evolutionary journeying: differences in shucking off brow ridges (and perhaps body hair). Part are almost certainly adaptive, reflecting the demands of different climates and habitats. Part of them could be, and probably are, due to chance. A "race," or better, a local racial form, is a population with its own combination of average physical characteristics. Such a thing is a sort of corporation of genes, a breeding stock. You might convey its appearance through an individual, but a race is not an individual, a single set of genes. Nor is it an ideal type, a photograph of its average member. At the same time, it is not the people of a whole continent. It is a population which actually exchanges its genes in breeding, and thus changes or evolves as a unit. Still it is never, in mankind, cut off from others, and so it keeps exchanging its heredity somewhat with other populations, be they tribes, or villages, or islands.

All over the world this has been going on. Such segments of humanity, real but ill-defined and borderless, have been undergoing slight changes, allowing their neighbors to partake in them, and producing local racial differences. And by virtue of distance, of contrasting environment, and probably of a good many thousand years, this process gave rise to four main population groups or racial stocks, at the four corners of the Old World: the Whites in the northwest, the Negroes in Africa, the Mongoloids in northeastern Asia, and the dark, hairy, primitive-looking Australians in the southeast.

Fred Hoyle

THE ORIGIN OF THE EARTH AND THE PLANETS

I AM NOW GOING TO TELL A STORY. I HOPE YOU WILL FIND IT AN INTEREST-ing story, perhaps even a fascinating one. It is the story of how the Earth itself was born, how it came into being along with the other planets that go to form the retinue of the Sun.

The origin of the planets is one of the high points of the New Cosmology. It affects our whole outlook on life. For instance, the question of whether life is rare or commonplace in the Universe depends essentially on this issue. I suppose that it is because of its cosmological importance that many people are given so strongly to asserting that the planets originated as bits of material that were torn out of the Sun. For some reason or other this idea has a deep-rooted appeal. So perhaps I had better begin by out-lining some of the arguments that show why it must be wrong.

The origin of the solar system can only be understood if we appreciate its scale. As I have said before, this can best be done by thinking of it as a model in which the Sun is represented by a ball about the size of a large grapefruit. On this model the great bulk of the planetary material lies at a hundred yards or more from the Sun. In other words, nearly all the planetary material lies very far out. This simple fact is already the death blow of every theory that seeks for an origin of the planets in the Sun itself. For how could the material have been flung out so far? It was proved, for instance, by H. N. Russell that if Jeans' well-known tidal theory were right, the planets would have to move around the Sun at dis-tances on our model of not more than a few feet. This notion of Jeans', which still seems to be very widely believed, was that the planets were torn out of the Sun by the gravitational pull of a star that passed close by.

Once this difficulty was appreciated, people attached to the planets-from-the-Sun idea shifted their ground. The planets, they said, were not formed with the Sun in a state as it is at present, but at a time when the Sun had a vastly greater size, as it must have had when it was condensing out of the interstellar gas. But it is hard to see how this can help. To make it work at all it would be necessary to demonstrate that a blob of primeval gas—the interstellar gas—could condense in such a way that the great bulk of it went to form a massive inner body—that is to say, the Sun— surrounded at vast distances by a wisp of planetary material. And I do not think that this can be done. At any rate all the attempts that have so far been made to cope with the difficulty seem to me to fall very far short of the mark. Also there is another and perhaps more important reason why our Earth and the planets cannot have originated with the Sun.

I have tried to bring out the dominating cosmic role played by hydrogen, the simplest of the elements. Helium, the next simplest, is produced in appreciable quantities in the inner regions of normal stars like the Sun. But, apart from hydrogen and helium, all other elements are extremely rare, all over the Universe. In the Sun they amount to only about 1 per cent of the total mass. Contrast this with the Earth and the other planets where hydrogen and helium make only about the same contribution as highly complex atoms like iron, calcium, silicon, magnesium, and aluminum. This contrast brings out two important points. First, we see that material torn from the Sun would not be at all suitable for the formation of the planets as we know them. Its composition would be hopelessly wrong. And our second point in this contrast is that it is the Sun that is normal and the Earth that is the freak. The interstellar gas and most of the stars are composed of material like the Sun, not like the Earth. You must understand that, cosmically speaking, the room you are now sitting in is made of the wrong stuff. You, yourself, are a rarity. You are a cosmic collector's piece.

Here then is a way to approach the problem of the origin of the planets. We must find a source of the strangely complicated rare material out of which the Earth and the planets are made. I will begin by telling you the answer in two sentences. There was once another star moving around the Sun that disintegrated with extreme violence. So great was the explosion that all the remnants were blown a long way from the Sun into space with the exception of a tiny wisp of gas out of which the Earth and the planets have condensed. So the first point to get clear is that the Sun was not always a single star. Before the Earth was born it was one of a pair of stars. As we have said earlier, such a pair is called a binary system.

Now if you pick a star at random the chance that it will be a separate star by itself, as the Sun is at present, is no greater than the chance that it will be a member of a binary system. Let us see what can happen if we suppose that the Sun was at one time a component in such a double system. First we make a choice for the distance between the Sun and the companion star it used to have. It is important to realize that there is practically no restriction on our freedom of choice here, because, as observation by telescope shows, the distance apart of the component stars in a binary may be anywhere in the enormous range from a tenth of a light year down to a fraction of a light minute. The required distance apart of the Sun and its companion star is intermediate between these extremes, being about one light hour. That is to say, on a plan with the Sun represented by our grapefruit the companion star would be about 100 yards away. This value will give you a clue as to how the choice of separation is made; namely, so that in the final outcome the bigger planets will be found to lie at the right distances from the Sun.

The next step is to draw up a set of specifications for the companion star. It must have been appreciably more massive than the Sun. It must have been a very special star. It must have been a star that exploded with extreme violence. It must have been a supernova. Thanks largely to the work of the two Mount Wilson astronomers, Baade and Minkowski, we know a good deal about the explosions of these stars. When one explodes, most of the material—that is to say, considerably more material than there is inside the whole of the Sun—gets blown out into space as a tremendous cloud of fiercely incandescent gas moving at a speed of several million miles an hour. For a few days the accompanying blaze of light is as great as the total radiation by all the 10,000,000,000 or so stars in the Galaxy. It was out of such a holocaust that the Earth and planets were born, and it happened in this way.

Not all of a supernova is blown away as gas in such an explosion. But the dense stellar nucleus that was left over after the explosion of the Sun's companion star did not stay with the Sun. One of the effects of the explosion was to give this stellar nucleus a recoil that broke its gravitational connection with the Sun. It moved off, and is now some unrecognized star lying in some distant part of the Galaxy. But before it left the Sun, and during the last dying stages of the explosion, it puffed out a cloud of gas that the Sun managed to hold on to. In as little as a few centuries this cloud of gas spread out around the Sun and took on the form of a rotating circular disk. As we shall see later, the planets condensed out of the material in this disk. So the real parent of the Earth is not the Sun at all, but some star that is probably unnamed and unseen.

According to the results of Baade and Minkowski the temperature inside a supernova is about 300 times greater than it is at the center of the Sun.

At such a temperature all manner of nuclear transmutations occur with great rapidity. The helium-hydrogen reactions which are so important in the Sun are no longer important here. Instead, helium becomes transmuted to elements of what is called high atomic weight; for example, magnesium, aluminum, silicon, iron, lead and uranium, to name only a few. The importance of this is obvious. It means that the companion star's final gift to the Sun was a cloud of gas with just the right kind of composition necessary to account for the constitution of the Earth and the planets.

Before we go on to discuss the condensation of the planets, perhaps I might mention how this general picture of the origin of the planets has arisen. It is really the outcome of developments that started with Jeans' tidal theory. First this was modified and improved by Jeffreys. Then H. N. Russell overthrew both these theories with the sort of criticism I referred to earlier. Lyttleton was the next to take up the problem about fifteen years ago. He was the first to realize for certain that the planetary material cannot have come out of the Sun, and it is to him that we owe the development of the double star idea. Once this stage was reached the remaining steps were more or less inevitable. They arose for the most part through an attempt to put the theory on a firm observational footing.

The final stages in the formation of the planets after the tremendous explosion were comparatively tranquil. A few centuries after the explosion the remnant of the Sun's companion star must have moved far away from the Sun, or at any rate far enough for its effect on the wisp of gas that was captured by the Sun to be unimportant. This wisp of gas then settled down into a flat circular disk that rotated around the Sun—that is to say, it spread around the Sun and then it settled down into the disk. The main part of the gas must have been distributed in the regions where the orbits of the great planets, Jupiter, Saturn, Uranus, and Neptune, now lie. This means that on the model we are using with a grapefruit sun the main part of the disk must have had a diameter of several hundred yards. At its edges the gas would have trailed away very gradually.

But I must now explain how such a rotating disk of gas condensed into the planets as we know them. Once the supernova remnant had receded to an appreciable distance, the temperature of the main bulk of the gas in the disk must have fallen well below the freezing point of water. Many sorts of molecules must then have been formed and, as was pointed out in 1944 by Professor Jeffreys and A. L. Parsons, these molecules must have collected into a swarm of solid bodies by a process very similar to the formation of water drops in the clouds of our own terrestrial atmosphere. But this condensation into solid particles must have been offset to some extent by collisions between the particles themselves, which tend to return material to the gaseous state.

At any particular time there must have been a rough balance between condensation from gas into solid bodies and evaporation that converted solid material back into gas. You might think that this stalemate would have had to go on for ever, and it probably would have done if the raindrop form of condensation were the whole story. But in a situation like this if any particular condensation should ever happen to grow to a certain critical size, which is about 100 miles across, the gravitational pull of the condensation itself would begin to play a dominating role. The gravitational field is, so to speak, able to reach out into the surrounding gas and drag it in onto the condensation. When this happens the rate of condensation is greatly increased. It is this that ensures that such a cloud of gas would form into a few comparatively large bodies rather than into a swarm of much smaller particles. The essential point is that although the chance that a particular body ever grows to the critical size is very small, given sufficient time it will certainly happen in a few cases. The fewer the number of cases the fewer the number of planets into which the material finally condenses. For once the gravitational field of a growing body comes into operation the rate of acquisition of material becomes so large that the first few bodies to attain the critical size then go on to snatch up practically all the material of the disk.

Perhaps you will see this best if I quote one or two of the results calculated for our own solar system. The first condensations to grow large are believed to have taken about 1,000,000,000 years to reach the mass of the Earth. But from this stage only about 100,000 years was needed for such a primordial planet to increase its mass up to the same order as those of the great planets Jupiter, Saturn, Uranus, and Neptune. This shows you the tremendous accelerating effect of this condensation by gravitation.

Now this has an important consequence. It means that the earth can hardly have been formed as a primordial condensation. For a condensation would hardly stop short after taking 1,000,000,000 years to reach the mass of the Earth if it only needed a further 100,000 years to go on and become a great planet. It could, of course, be argued that a condensation stopped short at the mass of the Earth simply because all the gas in its neighborhood had become exhausted. This might be a reasonable argument if we had only one case to explain, but there are five planets—Mercury, Venus,

Mars, Pluto, and the Earth—and also about thirty satellites to be accounted for. It would be stretching coincidence much too far to suggest that exhaustion of material was responsible for cessation of growth in all these cases.

Besides, there is another argument that shows the same thing. None of the present planets can have been primordial condensations, not even the great planets. For owing to the rotation of the disk around the Sun, the primordial planets must have acquired axial rotations—that is to say, rotations like the rotation of the Earth around its polar axis. Once the primordial planets had formed into a compact state, their times of rotation must have become less than about seven hours, and as Lyttleton showed in 1938, a solid planet rotating as rapidly as this must break up under the power of its own rotation. The great planets must be the main chunks arising from these processes of break-up. Now in the break-up it is also to be expected that a number of comparatively small blobs become detached from the main bodies as they separate from each other. For the most part, these blobs remained circling around the great planets—and these are the satellites of the planets—their moons we should call them. But a few of the larger blobs seem to have escaped, and these are the five small planets —Venus, Mercury, Mars, Pluto and the Earth. Very probably the Moon was an adjacent blob that became detached along with the Earth. So, to sum up, there were a number of big primordial planets that broke up about 2,500,000,000 years ago, and one of the bits of the debris was our Earth and another the Moon.

This picture of the way the Earth came into being is I think very important to our studies of the interior of the Earth. It affects our views on the probable temperature of the deep interior, suggesting that it may be much less than was formerly believed. It provides interesting possibilities regarding the origin of the Earth's magnetism. It leads to a plausible explanation of the origin of the surface rocks. For the Earth must have originally moved along a highly flattened path that took it into the inner parts of the gaseous disk. Here the material had not been entirely swept up by the primordial condensations, which were formed much farther out from the Sun. So the Earth moved through a medium consisting partly of gas and partly of comparatively small solid bodies. This had two effects: one was to round up the Earth's motion into a nearly circular path that lies well inside the orbits of the great planets, and the other was to modify the surface features of the Earth through the acquisition of various gases and solid bodies. The rocks of the Earth's crust may well have originated in this way. In particular, it is possible that the Earth acquired its radioactive materials during this final stage. Among the gases acquired were probably nitrogen, water, oxygen, and carbon dioxide. The histories of Venus, Mercury, and Mars must have been somewhat different because their orbits took them through different parts of the disk. In particular, Venus seems to have obtained little or no water but very large quantities of carbon dioxide and also possibly nitrogen. Mars, on the other hand, obtained carbon dioxide, and water but not so much water as the Earth. The fate of Pluto we do not know.

By now we've covered enough ground for us to refer back to the end of my first chapter when I said there are about 1,000,000 planetary systems in the Milky Way in which life may exist. I should like now to tell you how I made this estimate. It must depend, as you will see, on the frequency of supernova explosions within our Galaxy. No supernova outburst is visible in the Milky Way at the present time. But the gases hurled into space by the supernova observed by the Chinese in A.D. 1054 actually can be seen. It was these gases that furnished Baade and Minkowski with the information I mentioned above. Since A.D. 1054 two other supernovae have also blazed out in the Milky Way, one in 1572 and the other in 1604.

On this basis it is to be expected that on the average one supernova occurs every two or three hundred years. This estimate, as we shall see later, is strongly supported by the observation of supernovae in galaxies other than our own. At this rate there must have been more than 10,000,-000 supernova explosions since the oldest stars were born—which was about 4,000,000,000 years ago. Now something like a half of all these supernovae must have been components in binary systems, and must accordingly have given birth to planets in exactly the way we have discussed. So in the past, nearly 10,000,000 planetary systems, each one similar to the solar system in the essential features of its contructions, must have been formed in the Milky Way.

Next we ask what proportion of these systems would contain a planet on which the physical conditions were suitable for the support of life. I estimate for this about one planetary system in ten, which gives me a final total of about 1,000,000 possible abodes of life within the Milky Way. I will admit that the last bit of calculation is approximate. But even when full allowance is made for all the uncertainties I do not think that the final total could be less than 100,000. Our next question is: will living creatures arise on every planet where favorable physical conditions occur?

No certain answer can be given to this, but those best qualified to judge the matter, the biologists, seem to think that life would in fact arise wherever conditions were able to support it. Accepting this, we can proceed with greater assurance. The extremely powerful process of natural selection would come into operation and would shape the evolution of life on each of these distant planets. Would creatures arise having some sort of similarity to those on the Earth? The distinguished biologist C. D. Darlington has shown that this is by no means as unlikely as it seems at first sight. To quote Darlington's own words, "There are such very great advantages in walking on two legs, in carrying one's brain in one's head, in having two eyes on the same eminence at a height of five or six feet, that we might as well take quite seriously the possibility of a pseudo man and a pseudo woman with some physical resemblance to ourselves. . . ."

Let us end by putting all this in another way. I have often seen it stated that our situation on the Earth is providential. The argument goes like this. It is providential that the Earth is of the right size and is at the right distance from the Sun. It is providential that the Sun radiates the right kind of light and heat. It is providential that the right chemical substances occur on the Earth. A long list of this sort of statement could be compiled, and to some people it looks as if there is indeed something very strange and odd about our particular home in the Universe. But I think that this outlook rises from a misunderstanding of the situation. Because if everything was not just right we should not be here. We should be somewhere else.

William L. Laurence

A PRIMER OF ATOMIC ENERGY

THE MATERIAL UNIVERSE, THE EARTH AND EVERYTHING IN IT, ALL THINGS living and non-living, the sun and its planets, the stars and the constellations, the galaxies and the supergalaxies, the infinitely large and the infinitesimally small, manifests itself to our senses in two forms, matter and energy. We do not know, and probably never can know, how the material

Reprinted from *The Hell Bomb* by William L. Laurence, by permission of Alfred A. Knopf, Inc. Copyright 1950 by William L. Laurence.

universe began, and whether, indeed, it ever had a beginning, but we do know that it is constantly changing and that it did not always exist in its present form. We also know that in whatever form the universe may have existed, matter and energy have always been inseparable, no energy being possible without matter, and no matter without energy, each being a form of the other.

While we do not know how and when matter and energy came into being, or whether they ever had a beginning in time as we perceive it, we do know that while the relative amounts of matter and energy are constantly changing, the total amount of both, in one form or the other, always remains the same. When a plant grows, energy from the sun, in the form of heat and light, is converted into matter, so that the total weight of the plant is greater than that of the elementary material constituents, water and carbon-dioxide gas, out of which its substance is built up. When the substance of the plant is again broken up into its original constituents by burning, the residual ashes and gases weigh less than the total weight of the intact plant, the difference corresponding to the amount of matter that had been converted into energy, liberated once again in the form of heat and light.

All energy as we know it manifests itself through motion or change in the physical or chemical state of matter, or both, though these changes and motions may be so slow as to be imperceptible. As the ancient Greek philosopher Heraclitus perceived more than two thousand years ago, all things are in a constant state of flux, this flux being due to an everlasting conversion of matter into energy and energy into matter, everywhere over the vast stretches of the material universe, to its outermost and innermost limits, if any limits there be.

Each manifestation of energy involves either matter in motion or a change in its physical state, which we designate as physical energy; a change in the chemical constitution of matter, which we know as chemical energy; or a combination of the two. Physical energy can be converted into chemical energy and vice versa. For example, heat and light are forms of physical energy, each consisting of a definite band of waves of definite wave lengths in violent, regular, rhythmic oscillations. A mysterious mechanism in the plant, known as photosynthesis, uses the heat and light energy from the sun to create complex substances, such as sugars, starches, and cellulose, out of simpler substances, such as carbon dioxide and water, converting physical energy, heat and light into the chemical energy required to hold together the complex substances the plant produces. When we burn the cellulose in the form of wood or coal (coal is petrified wood), the chemical energy is once again converted into physical energy in the form of the original heat and light. As we have seen, the chemical energy stored in the plant manifested itself by an increase in the plant's weight as compared with that of its original constituents. Similarly, the release of the energy manifests itself through a loss in the total weight of the plant's substance.

It can thus be seen that neither matter nor energy can be created. All we can do is to manipulate certain types of matter in a way that liberates whatever energy had been in existence, in one form or another, since the beginning of time. All the energy that we had been using on earth until the advent of the atomic age had originally come from the sun. Coal, as already said, is a petrified plant that had stored up the energy of the sun in the form of chemical energy millions of years ago, before man made his appearance on the earth. Oil comes from organic matter that also had stored up light and heat from the sun in the form of chemical energy. Water power and wind power are also made possible by the sun's heat, since all water would freeze and no winds would blow were it not for the sun's heat energy keeping the waters flowing and the air moving, the latter by creating differences in the temperature of air masses.

There are two forms of energy that we take advantage of which are not due directly to the sun's radiations—gravitation and magnetism—but the only way we can utilize these is by employing energy derived from the sun's heat. In harnessing Niagara, or in the building of great dams, we utilize the fall of the water because of gravitation. But as I have already pointed out, without the sun's heat water could not flow. To produce electricity we begin with the chemical energy in coal or oil, which is first converted into heat energy, then to mechanical energy, and finally, through the agency of magnetism, into electrical energy.

The radiations of the sun, of the giant stars millions of times larger than the sun, come from an entirely different source, the greatest source of energy in the universe, known as atomic or, more correctly, nuclear energy. But even here the energy comes as the result of the transformation of matter. The difference between nuclear energy and chemical energy is twofold. In chemical energy, such as the burning of coal, the matter lost in the process comes from the outer shell of the atoms, and the amount of matter lost is so small that it cannot be weighed directly by any human scale or other device. In nuclear energy, on the other hand, the matter lost by being transformed into energy comes from the nucleus, the heavy inner core, of the atom, and the amount of matter lost is millions of times greater than in coal, great enough to be weighed.

An atom is the smallest unit of any of the elements of which the physical universe is constituted. Atoms are so small that if a drop of water were magnified to the size of the earth the atoms in the drop would be smaller than oranges.

The structure of atoms is like that of a minuscule solar system, with a heavy nucleus in the center as the sun, and much smaller bodies revolving around it as the planets. The nucleus is made up of two types of particles: protons, carrying a positive charge of electricity, and neutrons, electrically neutral. The planets revolving about the nucleus are electrons, units of negative electricity, which have a mass about one two-thousandth the mass of the proton or the neutron. The number of protons in the nucleus determines the chemical nature of the element, and also the number of planetary electrons, each proton being electrically balanced by an electron in the atom's outer shells. The total number of protons and neutrons in the nucleus is known as the mass number, which is very close to the atomic weight of the element but not quite equal. Protons and neutrons are known under the common name "nucleons."

There are two important facts to keep constantly in mind about protons and neutrons. The first is that the two are interchangeable. A proton, under certain conditions, loses its positive charge by emitting a positive electron (positron) and thus becomes a neutron. Similarly, a neutron, when agitated, emits a negative electron and becomes a proton. As we shall see, the latter process is taken advantage of in the transmutation of non-fissionable uranium into plutonium, and of thorium into fissionable uranium 233. The transmutation of all other elements, age-old dream of the alchemists, is made possible by the interchangeability of protons into neutrons, and vice versa.

The second all-important fact about protons and neutrons, basic to the understanding of atomic energy, is that each proton and neutron in the nuclei of the elements weighs less than it does in the free state, the loss of weight being equal to the energy binding the nucleons. This loss becomes progressively greater for the elements in the first half of the periodic table, reaching its maximum in the nucleus of silver, element 47. After that the loss gets progressively smaller. Hence, if we were to combine (fuse) two elements in the first half of the periodic table, the protons and the neutrons would lose weight if the newly formed nucleus is not heavier than that of silver, but would gain weight if the new nucleus thus formed is heavier than silver. The opposite is true with the elements in the second half of the periodic table, the protons and neutrons losing weight when a heavy element is split into two lighter ones, and gaining weight if two elements are fused into one.

Since each loss of mass manifests itself by the release of energy; it can be seen that to obtain energy from the atom's nucleus requires either the fusion of two elements in the first half of the periodic table or the fission of an element in the second half. From a practical point of view, however, fusion is possible only with two isotopes (twins) of hydrogen, at the beginning of the periodic table, while fission is possible only with twins of uranium, U-233 and U-235, and with plutonium, at the lower end of the table.

The diameter of the atom is 100,000 times greater than the diameter of the nucleus. This means that the atom is mostly empty space, the volume of the atom being 500,000 billion times the volume of the nucleus. It can thus be seen that most of the matter in the universe is concentrated in the nuclei of the atoms. The density of matter in the nucleus is such that a dime would weigh 600 million tons if its atoms were as tightly packed as are the protons and neutrons in the nucleus.

The atoms of the elements (of which there are ninety-two in nature, and six more man-made elements) have twins, triplets, quadruplets, etc., known as isotopes. The nuclei of these twins all contain the same number of protons and hence all have the same chemical properties. They differ, however, in the number of neutrons in their nuclei and hence have different atomic weights. For example, an ordinary hydrogen atom has a nucleus of one proton. The isotope of hydrogen, deuterium, has one proton plus one neutron in its nucleus. It is thus twice as heavy as ordinary hydrogen. The second hydrogen isotope, tritium, has one proton and two neutrons in its nucleus and hence an atomic mass of three. On the other hand, a nucleus containing two protons and one neutron is no longer hydrogen but helium, also of atomic mass three.

There are hundreds of isotopes, some occurring in nature, others produced artificially by shooting atomic bullets, such as neutrons, into the nuclei of the atoms of various elements. A natural isotope of uranium, the ninety-second and last of the natural elements, contains 92 protons and 143 neutrons in its nucleus, hence its name U-235, one of the two atomic-bomb elements. The most common isotope of uranium has 92 protons and 146 neutrons in its nucleus and hence is known as U-238. It is 140 times more plentiful than U-235, but cannot be used for the release of atomic energy.

Atomic, or rather nuclear, energy is the cosmic force that binds together the protons and the neutrons in the nucleus. It is a force millions of times greater than the electrical repulsion force existing in the nucleus because of the fact that the protons all have like charges. This force, known as the coulomb force, is tremendous, varying inversely as the square of the distance separating the positively charged particles. Professor Frederick Soddy, the noted English physicist, has figured out that two grams (less than the weight of a dime) of protons placed at the opposite poles of the earth would repel each other with a force of twenty-six tons. Yet the nuclear force is millions of times greater than the coulomb force. This force acts as the cosmic cement that holds the material universe together and is responsible for the great density of matter in the nucleus.

We as yet know very little about the basic nature of this force, but we can measure its magnitude by a famous mathematical equation originally presented by Dr. Einstein in his special theory of relativity in 1905. This formula, one of the great intellectual achievements of man, together with the discovery of the radioactive elements by Henri Becquerel and Pierre and Marie Curie, provided the original clues as well as the key to the discovery and the harnessing of nuclear energy.

Einstein's formula $E = mc^2$, revealed that matter and energy are two different manifestations of one and the same cosmic entity, instead of being two different entities, as had been generally believed. It led to the revolutionary concept that matter, instead of being immutable, was energy in a frozen state, while, conversely, energy was matter in a fluid state. The equation revealed that any one gram of matter was the equivalent in ergs (small units of energy) to the square of the velocity of light in centimeters per second—namely, 900 billion billion ergs. In more familiar terms, this means that one gram of matter represents 25,000,000 kilowatt-hours of energy in a frozen state. This equals the energy liberated in the burning of three billion grams (three thousands tons) of coal.

The liberation of energy in any form, chemical, electrical, or nuclear, involves the loss of an equivalent amount of mass, in accordance with the Einstein formula. When 3,000 metric tons of coal are burned to ashes, the residual ashes and the gaseous products weigh one gram less than 3,000 tons; that is, one three-billionth part of the original mass will have been converted into energy. The same is true with the liberation of nuclear energy by the splitting or fusing (as will be explained later) of the nuclei of certain elements. The difference is merely that of magnitude. In the liberation of chemical energy by the burning of coal, the energy comes from a very small loss of mass resulting from the rearrangement of electrons on the surface of the atoms. The nucleus of the coal atoms is not involved in any way, remaining exactly the same as before. The amount of mass lost by the surface electrons is one thirtieth of one millionth of one per cent.

On the other hand, nuclear energy involves vital changes in the atomic nucleus itself, with a consequent loss of as high as one tenth to nearly eight tenths of one per cent in the original mass of the nuclei. This means that from one to nearly eight grams per thousand grams are liberated in the form of energy, as compared with only one gram in three billion grams liberated in the burning of coal. In other words, the amount of nuclear energy liberated in the transmutation of atomic nuclei is from 3,000,000 to 24,000,000 times as great as the chemical energy released by the burning of an equal amount of coal. In terms of TNT the figure is seven times greater than for coal, as the energy from TNT, while liberated at an explosive rate, is about one seventh the total energy content for an equivalent amount of coal. This means that the nuclear energy from one kilogram of uranium 235, or plutonium, when released at an explosive rate, is equal to the explosion of twenty thousand tons of TNT.

Nuclear energy can be utilized by two diametrically opposed methods. One is fission—the splitting of the nuclei of the heaviest chemical elements into two uneven fragments consisting of nuclei of two lighter elements. The other is fusion—combining, or fusing, two nuclei of the lightest elements into one nucleus of a heavier element. In both methods the resulting elements are lighter than the original nuclei. The loss of mass in each case manifests itself in the release of enormous amounts of nuclear energy.

When two light atoms are combined to form a heavier atom, the weight of the heavier is less than the total weight of the two light atoms. If the heavier atom could again be split into the two lighter ones, the latter would resume their original weight. As explained before, however, this is true only with the light elements, such as hydrogen, deuterium, and tritium, in the first half of the periodic table of the elements. The opposite is true with the heavier elements of the second half of the periodic table. For example, if krypton and barium, elements 36 and 56, were to be combined to form uranium, element 92, the protons and the neutrons in the uranium nucleus would each weigh about 0.1 per cent more than they weighed in the krypton and barium nuclei. It can thus be seen that energy could be gained either through the loss of mass resulting from the fusion of two light elements, or from the similar loss of mass resulting from the fission of one heavy atom into two lighter ones.

In the fusion of two lighter atoms, the addition of one and one yields less than two, and yet half of two will be more than one. In the case of the heavy elements the addition of one and one yields more than two, yet half of two makes less than one. This is the seeming paradox of atomic energy.

Three elements are known to be fissionable. Only one of these is found in nature: the uranium isotope 235 (U-235). The other two are man-made. One is plutonium, transmuted by means of neutrons from the nonfissionable U-238, by the addition of one neutron to the 146 present in the nucleus, which leads to the conversion of two of the 147 neutrons into protons, thus creating an element with a nucleus of 94 protons and 145 neutrons. The second man-made element (not yet in wide use, as far as is known) is uranium isotope 233 (92 protons and 141 neutrons), created out of the element thorium (90 protons, 142 neutrons) by the same method used in the production of plutonium.

When the nucleus of any one of these elements is fissioned, each proton and neutron in the two resulting fragments weighs one tenth of one per cent less than it weighed in the original nucleus. For example, if U-235 atoms totaling 1,000 grams in weight are split, the total weight of the fragments will be 999 grams. The one missing gram is liberated in the form of 25,000,000 kilowatt-hours of energy, equivalent in explosive terms to 20,000 tons of TNT. But the original number of protons and neutrons in the 1,000 grams does not change.

The fission process, the equivalent of the "burning" of nuclear fuels, is maintained by what is known as a chain reaction. The bullets used for splitting are neutrons, which, because they do not have an electric charge, can penetrate the heavily fortified electrical wall surrounding the positively charged nuclei. Just as a coal fire needs oxygen to keep it going, a nuclear fire needs the neutrons to maintain it.

Neutrons do not exist free in nature, all being tightly locked up within the nuclei of atoms. They are liberated, however, from the nuclei of the three fissionable elements by a self-multiplication process in the chain reaction. The process begins when a cosmic ray from outer space, or a stray neutron, strikes one nucleus and splits it. The first atom thus split releases an average of two neutrons, which split two more nuclei, which in turn liberate four more neutrons, and so on. The reaction is so fast that in a short time trillions of neutrons are thus liberated to split trillions of nuclei. As each nucleus is split, it losses mass, which is converted into great energy.

There are two types of chain reactions: controlled and uncontrolled. The controlled reaction is analogous to the burning of gasoline in an automobile engine. The atom-splitting bullets—the neutrons—are first slowed down from speeds of more than ten thousand miles per second to less than one mile per second by being made to pass through a moderator before they reach the atoms at which they are aimed. Neutron-"killers"—materials absorbing neutrons in great numbers—keep the neutrons liberated at any given time under complete control in a slow but steady nuclear fire.

The uncontrolled chain reaction is one in which there is no moderator— and no neutron-absorber. It is analogous to the dropping of a match in a gasoline tank. In the uncontrolled chain reaction the fast neutrons, with nothing to slow them down or to devour them, build up by the trillion and quadrillion in a fraction of a millionth of a second. This leads to the splitting of a corresponding number of atoms, resulting in the release of unbelievable quantities of nuclear energy at a tremendously explosive rate. One kilogram of atoms split releases energy equivalent to that of 20,000,000 kilograms (20,000 metric tons) of TNT.

It is the uncontrolled reaction that is employed in the explosion of the atomic bomb. The controlled reaction is expected to be used in the production of vast quantities of industrial power. It is now being employed in the creation of radioactive isotopes, for use in medicine and as the most powerful research tool since the invention of the microscope for probing into the mysteries of nature, living and non-living.

In the controlled reaction the material used is natural uranium, which consists of a mixture of 99.3 per cent U-238 and 0.7 of the fissionable U-235. The neutrons from the U-235 are made to enter the nuclei of U-238 and convert them to the fissionable element plutonium, for use in atomic bombs. The large quantities of energy liberated by the split U-235 nuclei in the form of heat is at too low a temperature for efficient utilization as power, and is at present wasted. To be used for power, nuclear reactors capable of operating at high temperatures are now being designed.

In the atomic bomb only pure U-235, or plutonium, is used.

In both the controlled and the uncontrolled reactions a minimum amount of material, known as the "critical mass," must be used, as otherwise too many neutrons would escape and the nuclear fire would thus be extinguished, as would an ordinary fire for lack of oxygen. In the atomic bomb two masses, each less than a critical mass, which together equal or exceed it, are brought in contact at a predetermined instant. The uncontrolled reaction then comes automatically, since, in the absence of any control, the neutrons, which cannot escape to the outside, build up at an unbelievable rate.

Whereas the fission process for the release of nuclear energy entails making little ones out of big ones, the fusion process involves making big ones out of little ones. In both processes the products weigh less than the original materials, the loss of mass coming out in the form of energy. According to the generally accepted hypothesis, the fusion process is the one operating in the sun and the stars of the same family. The radiant energy given off by them, it is believed, is the result of the fusion of four hydrogen atoms into one atom of helium, two of the protons losing their positive charge, thus becoming neutrons. Since a helium atom weighs nearly eight tenths of one per cent less than the total weight of the four hydrogen atoms, the loss of mass is thus nearly eight times that produced by fission, with a corresponding eight-fold increase in the amount of energy liberated. This process, using light hydrogen, is not feasible on earth.

The nuclei of all atoms are thus vast storage depots of cosmic energy. We must think of them as cosmic safe-deposit vaults, in which the Creator of the universe, if you will, deposited at the time of creation most of the energy in the universe for safekeeping. The sun and the other giant stars that give light have, as it were, drawing accounts in this "First National Bank and Trust Company of the Universe," whereas we on this little planet of ours in the cosmic hinterland are much too poor to have such a bank account. So we have been forced all these years we have been on earth to subsist on small handouts from our close neighbor the sun, which squanders millions all over space, but can spare us only nickels, dimes, and quarters (depending on the seasons of the year) for a cup of coffee and a sandwich. We are thus in the true sense of the word cosmic beggars, living off the bounty of a distant relative.

The discovery of fission in 1939 meant that after a million years of exclusive dependence on the sun we had suddenly managed to open a modest drawing account of our own in this bank of the cosmos. We were enabled to do it by stumbling upon two special master keys to five of the cosmic vaults. One of these keys we call fission; the other, which allows us entry into a much richer chamber of the vault, we call fusion. We can get a lot of the stored-up cosmic treasure by using the key to the fission vaults alone, but, as with our terrestrial bank vaults, which generally require two keys before they can be opened, it is not possible to use the key to the fusion vault unless we first use the fission key.

Except for the payment of our heat and light bill, the sun gives us nothing directly in cash. Instead it deposits a very small pittance in the plants, which serve as its major terrestrial banks. The animals then rob the plants and we rob them both. When we eat the food we live by we thus actually eat sunshine.

The sun makes its deposits in the plant through an agent named chlorophyll, the stuff that makes the grass green. Chlorophyll has the uncanny ability to catch sunbeams and to hand them over to the plant. A chemical supergenius inside the plant changes the sunlight energy into chemical energy, just as a bank teller changes bills into silver. With this chemical energy at their disposal, a great number of devilishly clever chemists in the plants' chemical factory go to work building up many substances to serve as vaults in which to store up a large part of the energy, using only part of it for their own subsistence.

The building materials used by these chemists inside the plants consist mainly of carbon-dioxide gas from the atmosphere, and water from the soil plus small amounts of minerals either supplied by the good earth or by fertilizers. Carbon dioxide, by the way, composed of one atom of carbon and two atoms of oxygen, is the stuff you exhale. In solid form it is what we know as dry ice, used in efforts to make rain. It is present in the atmosphere in large amounts.

Out of the carbon dioxide and water the chemists in the plants build cellulose, starch, sugar, fat, proteins, vitamins, and scores of other substances, all of which serve as vaults for the sun's rays caught by the chlorophyll. The biggest vaults of all, storing most of the energy, are the cellulose, sugars and starches, fats and proteins. There the stored energy remains until it is released by processes we call burning or digestion, both of which, as we shall see, are different terms for the same chemical reaction. When we burn wood, or the petrified ancient wood we know as coal, we burn largely the cellulose, the chief component of the solid part of plants. When we eat the plants, or the animals in whom the plant tissues are transformed into flesh by the solar energy stored within them, it is the sugars, starches, fats, and proteins that give us the energy we live by.

In the process of burning wood or coal the large cellulose vaults, composed of carbon, hydrogen, and oxygen, are broken up, thus allowing the original solar energy, stored up within them as chemical energy, to escape in the form of heat and light. This is the same heat and light deposited there by the sun many years before—in the case of coal, some two hundred million years back. The process of burning thus transforms the chemical energy in the plants back to its original form of light and radiant heat energy. The complex carbon and hydrogen units in the cellulose are broken up, each freed carbon atom uniting with two oxygen atoms in the air to form carbon dioxide again, while two hydrogen atoms unite with one of oxygen to form water. Thus we see that the cellulose vaults are broken up once more into the original building bricks out of which the chemists in the plants had fashioned them.

When we eat plant or animal food to get the energy to live by, exactly the same process takes place except at a lower temperature. The sunlight deposit vaults of sugar, starch, and fat, also composed, like cellulose, of carbon, hydrogen, and oxygen, are broken up by the digestive system into their component parts, thus allowing the original solar energy stored within them to get free in the form of chemical energy, which our body uses in its essential processes. Here, too, the end products are carbon dioxide, which we exhale, and water. About half the energy we thus obtain is used by us for the work we do. The other half is used by the body for building up the tissues burned up as part of the regular wear and tear of life.

We thus burn food for our internal energy as we burn cellulose for our external energy. The interesting thing here is that, in both types of burning, fission as well as fusion processes take place. The fission is the splitting of the cellulose, sugar, starches, and proteins into carbon and hydrogen atoms. The fusion part is the union of the carbon and the hydrogen with oxygen to form carbon dioxide and water. The fusion part is just as necessary to release the stored-up solar energy in the wood or coal as is the fission part, for, as everyone knows, unless there is oxygen for the carbon to fuse with, no combustion (burning) can take place and hence no release of energy. The plant vaults would remain closed absolutely tight.

At this point two things become clear. We see, in the first place, that whenever we get any kind of energy in any form we do not in any way create any of it. All we do is merely draw on something that is already stored up; in the case of coal and wood by the sun, in the case of uranium and hydrogen by the same power that created the sun and all energy. We draw water from the spring, but we do not make the water. On the other hand, we cannot draw the water unless we first find the spring, and even then we cannot draw it unless we have a pitcher.

And we also see, in the second place, that fission and fusion are common everyday phenomena that occur any time you burn anything. Both are essential whenever energy is released, whether it is the chemical energy from coal or the atomic energy from the nuclei of uranium, deuterium, or tritium. When you light a cigarette you employ both fission and fusion or you don't smoke. The first fission and fusion take place in the lighting of the match, the cellulose in the match (whether it is wood or paper) being fissioned (that is, split into its component atoms of carbon and hydrogen). These atoms are then fusioned with the oxygen in the air. The same thing happens when the tobacco catches fire. In each case the fusion with the oxygen makes possible the fission of cellulose. When we burn U-235, or plutonium, we again get both fission and fusion, except that, instead of oxygen, the nuclei of these elements first fuse with a neutron before they are split apart. Thus we see that the process of burning U-235, or plutonium, requires not only fission but fusion as well, without which they could not burn. This is true also in hydrogen fusion. When you burn deuterium by fusing two deuterons (nuclei of deuterium) to form helium of atomic weight three, plus a neutron, one of the two deuterons is split in half in the process. Similarly, when you burn tritium by fusion two tritons (nuclei of tritium), one of the tritons splits into two neutrons and a proton, the one proton joining the other triton to form helium of atomic weight four.

Thus we see that fission and fusion are the cosmic firebrands that are always present whenever a fire is lighted, chemical or atomic, whether the fuel is wood, coal, or oil, or uranium, plutonium, deuterium, or tritium. Both, with some variations, are essential for opening the cosmic safe where the energy of the universe is kept in storage. The only reason you get much more energy in the fission and fusion of atomic nuclei is that so much more had been stored in them than in the cellulose vaults on this planet.

The same reason that limits our ability to obtain stored chemical energy to a few fuels also limits our ability to obtain atomic energy. Coal, oil, and wood are the only dividend-paying chemical-energy stocks. Similarly only five elements, uranium 233 and 235, plutonium, deuterium, and tritium are the only dividend-paying atomic-energy stocks, and of these only two (U-235 and deuterium) exist in nature. The other three are re-created from other elements by modern alchemical legerdemain. What is more, we know for a certainty that it will never be possible to obtain atomic energy from any other element, by either fission or fusion.

This should put to rest once and for all the notion of many, including some self-styled scientists, that the explosion of a hydrogen bomb would set the hydrogen in the waters, and the oxygen and the nitrogen in the air, on fire and thus blow up the earth. The energy in common hydrogen is locked up in one of those cosmic vaults which only the sun and the stars that shine can open and which no number of H-bombs could blow apart. Oxygen and nitrogen are locked even for the suns. As for the deuterium in the water, it cannot catch fire unless it is highly concentrated, condensed to its liquid form, and heated to a temperature of several hundred million degrees. Hence all this talk about blowing up the earth is pure moonshine.

But while we know that we have reached the limit of what can be achieved either by fission or by fusion, that by no means justifies the conclusion that we have reached the ultimate in discovery and that fission and fusion are the only possible methods for tapping the energy locked up in matter. We must remember that fifty years ago we did not even suspect that nuclear energy existed and that until 1939 no one, including Dr. Einstein, believed that it would ever become possible to use it on a practical scale. We simply stumbled upon the phenomenon of fission, which in its turn opened the way to fusion.

If science tells us anything at all, it tells us that nature is infinite and that the human mind, driven by insatiable curiosity and probing ever deeper into nature's mysteries, will inevitably find ever greater treasures, treasures that are at present beyond the utmost stretches of the imagination—as far beyond fission and fusion as these are beyond man's first discovery of how to make a fire by striking a spark with a laboriously made flint. The day may yet come, and past history makes it practically certain that it will come, when man will look upon the discovery of fission and fusion as we look today upon the crudest tools made by primitive man.

A great measure of man's progress has been the result of serendipity, the faculty of making discoveries, by chance or sagacity, of things not sought for. Many an adventure has led man to stumble upon something much better than he originally set out to find. Like Columbus, many an explorer into the realms of the unknown has set his sights on a shorter route to the spices of India only to stumble upon a new continent. Unlike Columbus, however, the explorers in the field of science, instead of being confined to this tiny little earth of ours, have the whole infinite universe as the domain of their adventures, and many a virgin continent, richer by far than any yet discovered, still awaits its Columbus.

Roentgen and Becquerel were exploring what they thought was an untrodden path in the forest and came upon a new road that led their successors to the very citadel of the material universe. Young Enrico Fermi was curious to find out what would happen if he fired a neutron into the nucleus of uranium, hoping only to create a heavier isotope of uranium, or at best a new element. His rather modest goal led five years later to the fission of uranium, and in another six years to the atomic bomb.

Yet, as we have seen, in both fission and fusion only a very small fraction of the mass of the protons and neutrons in the nuclei of the elements used is liberated in the form of energy, while 99.3 to 99.9 per cent of their substance remains in the form of matter. We know of no process in nature which converts 100 per cent of the matter in protons and neutrons into energy, but scientists are already talking about finding means for bringing about such a conversion. They are seeking clues for such a process in the mysterious cosmic rays that bombard the earth from outer space with energies billions of times greater than those released by fission or fusion, great enough to smash atoms of oxygen or nitrogen, or whatever other atoms they happen to hit in the upper atmosphere, into their component protons and neutrons. Luckily, their number is small and most of their energy is spent long before they reach sea level.

But we have already learned how to create secondary cosmic-ray particles of relatively low energies (350,000,000 electron-volts) with our giant cyclotrons. The creation of these particles, known as mesons which are believed to be the cosmic cement responsible for the nuclear forces, represents the actual conversion of energy into matter. This is the exact reverse of the process taking place in fission and fusion, in which, as we have seen, matter is converted into energy. And we are now about to complete multi-billion-volt atom-smashers that will hurl atomic bullets of energies of from three to ten billion volts at the nuclei of atoms. With these gigantic machines, known as the cosmotron (at the Brookhaven National Laboratory of the Atomic Energy Commission) and the bevatron (at the University of California), we shall be able to smash nuclei into their individual component protons and neutrons and thus get a much more intimate glimpse of the forces that hold the nuclei together. What is more, instead of creating only mesons, particles with only 300 electron masses, we shall be able for the first time to convert energy into protons and neutrons, duplicating, as far as is known, an act of creation that has not taken place since the beginning of the universe. Man at last will be creating the very building blocks out of which the universe is made, as well as the cosmic cement that holds them together.

What new continents will our first glimpse into the mechanism of the very act of creation of matter out of energy reveal? What new secrets will be uncovered before the dazzled eyes and mind of man when he takes the nucleus of the atom completely apart at last? Not even Einstein could tell us. But, as Omar Khayyam divined, "a single Alif" may provide "the clue" that, could we but find it, leads "to the Treasure-House, and peradventure to the Master too." The fact is that we already have opened the door to the anteroom of the treasure-house, and we are about to unlock the door to one of its inner chambers. What shall we find there? No one as yet knows. But we do know that every door man has opened so far has led to riches beyond his wildest dreams, each new door bringing greater rewards than the one before. On the other hand, we also know that the treasure-house has many mansions, and that no matter how many chambers he may enter, he will always find new doors to unlock. For we have learned that the solution of any one secret always opens up a thousand new mysteries.

We have also learned, to our sorrow, that any new insight gained into nature's laws and forces can be used for great good and for equally great evil. The greater the insight, the greater the potentialities for good or evil. The new knowledge he is about to gain by his deeper insight into the heart of matter, and by his ability to create it out of energy, may offer man the means to make himself complete master of the world he lives in. It is equally true, alas, that he could use it to destroy that world even more thoroughly than with the hydrogen bomb.

As already stated, scientists are even now discussing the possibility of finding means for the complete annihilation of matter by the conversion of the entire mass of protons and neutrons into energy, instead of only 0.1 to 0.7 per cent. And while the total annihilation of protons and neutrons still seems highly speculative, we already know that such a process actually does take place in the realm of the electron. This is the phenomenon already achieved numerous times on a small scale in the laboratory, in which a positive electron (positron) and an electron with a negative charge completely destroy each other, their entire mass being converted into energy. Luckily, this is at present only a laboratory experiment, in which each positron must be individually produced, since there are hardly any positive electrons in our part of the universe. But suppose the new knowledge we are about to pry loose from the inner citadel of matter reveals to us a new process, at present not even suspected, that would release positrons in large numbers, just as the fission and fusion processes made possible for the first time the liberation of large quantities of neutrons. Such an eventuality, by no means beyond the realm of the possible, would open potentialities of horror alongside which those of the H-bomb, even the rigged one, would be puny. For any process that would release large numbers of positrons in the atmosphere, in a chain reaction similar to the one now liberating neutrons, may envelop the earth in one deadly flash of radioactive lightning that would instantly kill all sensate things. And although this is admittedly purely speculative, no one dare say that such a discovery will not be made, not when one remembers how remote and unlikely a process such as fission seemed to be just before it was made.

Though many of the great discoveries came about as the result of chance, they came because, as Pasteur said, "chance favors the prepared mind." Actually they came largely through the intellectual synthesis of what had originally appeared as unrelated phenomena or concepts. When Faraday discovered the principle of electromagnetic induction, he established for the first time that electricity and magnetism, looked upon since prehistoric times as two separate and distinct phenomena, were actually only two aspects of one basic natural force, which we know today as electromagnetism. This great intellectual synthesis led directly to the age of electricity and all its wonders. About thirty years later the great Scottish physicist James Clerk Maxwell demonstrated that electromagnetic action traveled through space in the form of transverse waves similar to those of light and having the same velocity. This revealed the existence in nature of electromagnetic waves, better known to us today as radio waves. About a quarter century later the great German-Jewish physicist Heinrich Hertz not only produced these electromagnetic waves but showed that they are propagated just as waves of light are, possessing all other properties of light, such as reflection, refraction, and polarization. This led directly to wireless telegraphy and telephony, radio, and television, radiophotography and radar.

When Einstein, in his special theory of relativity of 1905, united matter and energy in one basic cosmic entity, the road was opened to the atomic age. Yet Einstein was never satisfied and has devoted more than forty-five years of his life to the search for a greater, all-embracing unity underlying the great diversity of natural phenomena. In his general theory of relativity of 1915 he formulated a concept that encompasses the universal law of gravitation in his earlier synthesis of space and time, of which matter and energy were an integral part. This synthesis, wrote Bertrand Russell in 1924, "is probably the greatest synthetic achievement of the human intellect up to the present time. It sums up the mathematical and physical labors of more than two thousand years. Pure geometry from Pythagoras to Riemann, the dynamics and astronomy of Galileo and Newton, the theory of electromagnetism as it resulted from the researches of Faraday, Maxwell, and their successors, all are absorbed, with the necessary modifications, in the theories of Einstein, Weyl, and Eddington.

"So comprehensive a synthesis," he continued, "might have represented a dead end, leading to no further progress for a long time. Fortunately, at this moment quantum theory [the theory applying to the forces within the atom] has appeared, with a new set of facts outside the scope of relativity physics [which applies to the forces governing the cosmos at large]. This has saved us, in the nick of time, from the danger of supposing that we know everything."

Yet Einstein, working away in majestic solitude, has been trying all these years to construct a vast intellectual edifice that would embrace all the laws of the cosmos known so far, including the quantum, in one fundamental concept, which he designates as a "unified field theory." Early in 1950 he published the results of his arduous labors since 1915. This he regards as the crowning achievement of his life's work, a unified theory that bridges the vast gulf that had existed between relativity and quantum, between the infinite universe of the stars and galaxies and the equally infinite universe within the nucleus of the atom. If he is right, and he has always been right before, his latest contribution will prove to be a greater synthetic achievement of the human intellect than ever before, embracing space and time, matter and energy, gravitation and electromagnetism, as well as the nuclear forces within the atom, in one all-encompassing concept. In due time this concept should lead to new revelations of nature's mysteries, and to triumphs even greater than those which followed as a direct consequence of all earlier intellectual syntheses.

If the synthesis of matter and energy led to the atomic age, what may we expect of the latest, all-inclusive synthesis? When Einstein was asked about it he replied: "Come back in twenty years!" which happens to coincide with the end of the hundred-year period recorded by the brothers Goncourt: God swinging a bunch of keys, and saying to humanity: "Closing time, gentlemen!"

The search for new intellectual syntheses goes on, and no doubt new relationships between the diverse phenomena of nature will be found, regardless of whether Einstein's latest theory stands or falls in the light of further discovery. Physicists, for example, are speculating about a fundamental relationship between time and the electronic charge, one of the most basic units of nature, and there are those who believe that this relationship will turn out to be much more fundamental than that between matter and energy. Should this be found to be true, then the discovery of the relationship between time and charge may lead to finding a way for starting a self-multiplying position-electron chain reaction, just as the relationship between matter and energy led inevitably to the self-multiplying chain reaction with neutrons. If this comes about, then closing time will come much closer.

Yet the sound of the swinging keys need not necessarily mean closing time for man at the twilight of his day on this planet. It could also mean the opening of gates at a new dawn, to a new earth—and a new heaven.

RELIGION AND PHILOSOPHY

FROM THE BOOK OF JOB

THERE WAS A MAN IN THE LAND OF UZ, WHOSE NAME *was* JOB; AND THAT man was perfect and upright, and one that feared God, and eschewed evil. And there were born unto him seven sons and three daughters. His substance also was seven thousand sheep, and three thousand camels, and five hundred yoke of oxen, and five hundred she asses, and a very great household; so that this man was the greatest of all the men of the east. And his sons went and feasted *in their* houses, every one his day; and sent and called for their three sisters to eat and to drink with them. And it was so, when the days of *their* feasting were gone about, that Job sent and sanctified them, and rose up early in the morning, and offered burnt offerings *according* to the number of them all: for Job said, It may be that my sons have sinned, and cursed God in their hearts. Thus did Job continually.

Now there was a day when the sons of God came to present themselves before the LORD, and Satan came also among them. And the LORD said unto Satan, Whence comest thou? Then Satan answered the LORD, and said, From going to and fro in the earth, and from walking up and down in it. And the LORD said unto Satan, Hast thou considered my servant Job, that *there is* none like him in the earth, a perfect and an upright man, one that feareth God, and escheweth evil? Then Satan answered the LORD, and said, Doth Job fear God for nought? Hast not thou made an hedge about him, and about his house, and about all that he hath on every side? thou hast blessed the work of his hands, and his substance is increased in the land. But put forth thine hand now, and touch all that he hath, and he will curse thee to thy face. And the LORD said unto Satan, Behold, all that he hath *is* in thy power; only upon himself put not forth thine hand. So Satan went forth from the presence of the LORD.

And there came a day when his sons and his daughters *were* eating and drinking wine in their eldest brother's house: and there came a messenger unto Job, and said, The oxen were plowing, and the asses feeding beside them: and the Sabeans fell *upon them,* and took them away: yea, they have slain the servants with the edge of the sword; and I only am escaped alone to tell thee. While he *was* yet speaking, there came also another, and said, The fire of God is fallen from heaven, and hath burned up the sheep, and the servants, and consumed them; and I only am escaped alone to tell thee. While he *was* yet speaking, there came also another, and said, The Chaldeans made out three bands, and fell upon the camels, and have carried them away, yea, and slain the servants with the edge of the sword; and I only am escaped alone to tell thee. While he *was* yet speaking, there came also another, and said, Thy sons and thy daughters *were* eating and drinking wine in their eldest brother's house. And, behold, there came a great wind from the wilderness, and smote the four corners of the house, and it fell upon the young men, and they are dead; and I only am escaped alone to tell thee. Then Job arose, and rent his mantle, and shaved his head, and fell down upon the ground, and worshipped, and said, Naked came I out of my mother's womb, and naked shall I return thither: the LORD gave, and the LORD hath taken away; blessed be the name of the LORD. In all this Job sinned not, nor charged God foolishly.

Again there was a day when the sons of God came to present themselves before the LORD, and Satan came also among them to present himself before the LORD. And the LORD said unto Satan, From whence comest thou? And Satan answered the LORD, and said, From going to and fro in the earth, and from walking up and down it in. And the LORD said unto Satan, Hast thou considered my servant Job, that *there is* none like him in the earth, a perfect and upright man, one that feareth God, and escheweth evil? and still he holdeth fast his integrity, although thou movedst me against him, to destroy him without cause. And Satan answered the LORD, and said, Skin for skin, yea, all that a man hath will he give for his life. But put forth thine hand now, and touch his bone and his flesh, and he will curse thee to thy face. And the LORD said unto Satan, Behold, he *is* in thine hand; but save his life.

So went Satan forth from the presence of the LORD, and smote Job with sore boils from the sole of his foot unto his crown. And he took him a potsherd to scrape himself withal; and he sat down among the ashes.

Then said his wife unto him, Dost thou still retain thine integrity? curse God, and die. But he said unto her, Thou speakest as one of the foolish women speaketh. What? shall we receive good at the hand of God,, and shall we not receive evil? In all this did not Job sin with his lips.

Now when Job's three friends heard of all this evil that was come upon him, they came every one from his own place; Eliphaz the Temanite, and Bildad the Shuhite, and Zophar the Naamathite: for they had made an appointment together to come to mourn with him and to comfort him. And when they lifted up their eyes afar off, and knew him not, they lifted up their voice, and wept; and they rent every one his mantle, and sprinkled dust upon their heads toward heaven. So they sat down with him upon the ground seven days and seven nights, and none spake a word unto him: for they saw that *his* grief was very great.

After this opened Job his mouth, and cursed his day. And Job spake, and said,

Let the day perish, wherein I was born,
And the night *in which* it was said, There is a man child conceived.
Let the day be darkness,
Let not God regard it from above,
Neither let the light shine upon it.
Let darkness and the shadow of death stain it,
Let a cloud dwell upon it,
Let the blackness of the day terrify it.
As for that night, let darkness seize upon it,
Let it not be joined unto the days of the year,
Let it not come into the number of the months.
Lo, let that night be solitary,
Let no joyful voice come therein.
Let them curse it that curse the day,
Who are ready to raise up their mourning.
Let the stars of the twilight thereof be dark,
Let it look for light, but *have* none,
Neither let it see the dawning of the day:
Because it shut not up the doors of my *mother's* womb,
Nor hid sorrow from mine eyes.
Why died I not from the womb?
Why did I *not* give up the ghost when I came out of the belly?
Why did the knees prevent me?
Or why the breasts that I should suck?

For now should I have lain still and been quiet,
I should have slept; then had I been at rest,
With kings and counsellors of the earth,
Which built desolate places for themselves,
Or with princes that had gold,
Who filled their houses with silver:
Or as an hidden untimely birth, I had not been;
As infants *which* never saw light.
There the wicked cease *from* troubling:
And there the weary be at rest.
There the prisoners rest together,
They hear not the voice of the oppressor.
The small and great are there,
And the servant *is* free from his master.
Wherefore is light given to him that is in misery,
And life unto the bitter *in* soul?
Which long for death, but it *cometh* not,
And dig for it more than for hid treasures:
Which rejoice exceedingly,
And are glad, when they can find the grave?
Why is light given to a man whose way is hid,
And whom God hath hedged in?
For my sighing cometh before I eat,
And my roarings are poured out like the waters.
For the thing which I greatly feared is come upon me,
And that which I was afraid of is come unto me.
I was not in safety, neither had I rest, neither was I quiet:
Yet trouble came.

Then Eliphaz the Temanite answered and said,

Behold, happy is the man whom God correcteth:
Therefore despise not thou the chastening of the Almighty:
For he maketh sore, and bindeth up:
He woundeth, and his hands make whole.
He shall deliver thee in six troubles,
Yea, in seven there shall be no evil touch thee.
In famine he shall redeem thee from death:
And in war from the power of the sword.

Thou shalt be hid from the scourge of the tongue;
Neither shalt thou be afraid of destruction when it cometh.
At destruction and famine thou shalt laugh:
Neither shalt thou be afraid of the beast of the earth.
For thou shalt be in league with the stones of the field:
And the beasts of the field shall be at peace with thee.
And thou shalt know that thy tabernacle *shall be* in peace;
And thou shalt visit thy habitation, and shalt not sin.
Thou shalt know also that thy seed *shall be* great,
And thine offspring as the grass of the earth.
Thou shalt come to *thy* grave in a full age,
Like as a shock of corn cometh in, in his season.
Lo, this, we have searched it, so it *is;*
Hear it, and know thou *it* for thy good.

But Job answered and said,

Is there not an appointed time to man upon earth?
Are not his days also like the days of an hireling?
As a servant earnestly desireth the shadow,
And as an hireling looketh for *the reward of* his work:
So am I made to possess months of vanity,
And wearisome nights are appointed to me.
When I lie down, I say,
When shall I arise, and the night be gone?
And I am full of tossings to and fro, unto the dawning of the day.
My flesh is clothed with worms and clods of dust,
My skin is broken, and become loathsome,
My days are swifter than a weaver's shuttle,
And are spent without hope.
O remember that my life *is* wind:
Mine eye shall no more see good.
The eye of him that hath seen me shall see me no *more:*
Thine eyes *are* upon me, and I *am* not.
As the cloud is consumed and vanisheth away:
So he that goeth down to the grave shall come up no *more.*
He shall return no more to his house,
Neither shall his place know him any more.
Therefore I will not refrain my mouth.

I will speak in the anguish of my spirit,
I will complain in the bitterness of my soul.
Am I a sea, or a whale,
That thou settest a watch over me?
When I say, My bed shall comfort me,
My couch shall ease my complaint:
Then thou scarest me with dreams,
And terrifiest me through visions.
So that my soul chooseth strangling:
And death rather than my life.
I loathe *it;* I would not live alway:
Let me alone, for my days *are* vanity.
What *is* man, that thou shouldest magnify him?
And that thou shouldest set thine heart upon him?
And *that* thou shouldest visit him every morning,
And try him every moment?
How long wilt thou not depart from me?
Nor let me alone till I swallow down my spittle?
I have sinned, what shall I do unto thee, I thou preserver of men?
Why hast thou set me as a mark against thee,
So that I am a burden to myself?
And why dost thou not pardon my transgression, and take away mine
    iniquity?
For now shall I sleep in the dust,
And thou shalt seek me in the morning, but I *shall* not *be.*

Then answered Bildad the Shuhite, and said,

How long wilt thou speak these *things?*
And *how long shall* the words of thy mouth *be like* a strong wind?
Doth God pervert judgment?
Or doth the Almighty pervert justice?
If thy children have sinned against him,
And he have cast them away for their transgression:
If thou wouldest seek unto God betimes,
And make thy supplication to the Almighty:
If thou *wert* pure and upright,
Surely now he would awake for thee,
And make the habitation of thy righteousness prosperous.

Though thy beginning was small,
Yet thy latter end should greatly increase.
For enquire, I pray thee, of the former age,
And prepare thyself to the search of their fathers.
(For we *are but of* yesterday, and know nothing,
Because our days upon earth *are* a shadow.)
Shall not they teach thee, *and* tell thee,
And utter words out of their heart?
Can the rush grow up without mire?
Can the flag grow without water?
Whilst it *is* yet in his greenness, *and* not cut down,
It withereth before any *other* herb.
So *are* the paths of all that forget God,
And the hypocrite's hope shall perish:
And whose trust *shall be* a spider's web.
He shall lean upon his house, but it shall not stand:
He shall hold it fast, but it shall not endure.
He *is* green before the sun,
And his branch shooteth forth in his garden.
His roots are wrapped about the heap,
And seeth the place of stones.
If he destroys him from his place,
Then *it* shall deny him, *saying,* I have not seen thee.
Behold, this *is* the joy of his way,
And out of the earth shall others grow.
Behold, God will not cast away a perfect *man,*
Neither will he help the evil doers:
Till he fill thy mouth with laughing,
And thy lips with rejoicing.
They that hate thee shall be clothed with shame,
And the dwelling place of the wicked shall come to nought.

Then Job answered and said,

I know *it is* so of a truth:
But how should man be just with God.
If he will contend with him,
He cannot answer him one of a thousand.

He is wise in heart, and mighty in strength:
Who hath hardened *himself* against him, and hath prospered?
Which removeth the mountains, and they know not:
Which overturneth them in his anger:
Which shaketh the earth out of her place,
And the pillars thereof tremble:
Which commandeth the Sun, and it riseth not;
And sealeth up the stars.
Which alone spreadeth out the heavens,
And treadeth upon the waves of the Sea.
Which maketh Arcturus, Orion, and Pleiades,
And the chambers of the South.
Which doeth great things past finding out,
Yea, and wonders without number.
Lo, he goeth by me, and I see *him* not:
He passeth on also, but I perceive him not.
Behold, he taketh away, who can hinder him?
Who will say unto him, What doest thou?
If God will not withdraw his anger,
The proud helpers do stoop under him.
How much less shall I answer him,
And choose out my words *to reason* with him?
Whom, though I were righteous, *yet* would I not answer,
But I would make supplication to my Judge.
If I had called, and he had answered me,
Yet would I not believe that he had hearkened unto my voice:
For he breaketh me with a tempest,
And multiplieth my wounds without cause.
He will not suffer me to take my breath,
But filleth me with bitterness.
If *I speak* of strength, lo, *he is* strong:
And if of judgment, who shall set me a time *to plead?*
If I justify myself, mine own mouth shall condemn me:
If I say, I *am* perfect, it shall also prove me perverse.
Though I were perfect, *yet* would I not know my soul:
I would despise my life.
This *is* one *thing,* therefore I said *it;*
He destroyeth the perfect and the wicked.
If the scourge slay suddenly,

He will laugh at the trial of the innocent.
The earth is given into the hand of the wicked:
He covereth the faces of the Judges thereof;
If not, where, *and* who *is* he?
Now my days are swifter than a Post:
They flee away, they see no good.
They are passed away as the swift ships:
As the Eagle *that* hasteth to the prey.
If I say, I will forget my complaint,
I will leave off my heaviness, and comfort *myself.*
I am afraid of all my sorrows,
I know that thou wilt not hold me innocent.
If I be wicked, why then labour I in vain?
If I wash myself with snow water,
And make my hands never so clean:
Yet shalt thou plunge me in the ditch.

Then answered Zophar the Naamathite, and said,

Should not the multitude of words be answered?
And should a man full of talk be justified?
Should thy lies make men hold their peace?
And when thou mockest, shall no man make thee ashamed?
For thou hast said, My doctrine *is* pure,
And I am clean in thine eyes.
But, Oh that God would speak,
And open his lips against thee,
And that he would shew thee the secrets of wisdom,
That *they are* double to that which is:
Know therefore that God exacteth of thee *less* than thine iniquity *de-*
      serveth.
Canst thou by searching find out God?
Canst thou find out the Almighty unto perfection?
It is as high as heaven, what canst thou do?
Deeper than hell; what canst thou know?
The measure thereof *is* longer than the earth,
And broader than the sea.
If he cut off, and shut up,
Or gather together, then who can hinder him?

For he knoweth vain men:
He seeth wickedness also, will he not then consider *it?*
For vain man would be wise;
Though man be born *like* a wild ass's colt.
If thou prepare thine heart,
And stretch out thine hands toward him:
If iniquity *be* in thine hand, put it far away,
And let not wickedness dwell in thy tabernacles.
For then shalt thou lift up thy face without spot,
Yea, thou shalt be stedfast, and shalt not fear:
Because thou shalt forget *thy* misery,
And remember *it* as waters *that* pass away:
And *thine* age shall be clearer than the noonday;
Thou shalt shine forth, thou shalt be as the morning.
And thou shalt be secure, because there is hope,
Yea thou shalt dig *about thee, and* thou shalt take thy rest in safety.
Also thou shalt lie down, and none shall make *thee* afraid;
Yea many shall make suit unto thee.
But the eyes of the wicked shall fail,
And they shall not escape,
And their hope *shall be as* the giving up of the ghost.

And Job answered and said,

No doubt but ye *are* the people,
And wisdom shall die with you.
But I have understanding as well as you;
I *am* not inferior to you:
Yea, who knoweth not such things as these?
I am *as* one mocked of his neighbour,
Who calleth upon God, and he answereth him:
The just upright *man is* laughed to scorn.
He that is ready to slip with *his* feet,
Is as a lamp despised in the thought of him that is at ease.
The tabernacles of robbers prosper,
And they that provoke God are secure.

Lo, mine eye hath seen all *this,*
Mine ear hath heard and understood it.

What ye know, *the same* do I know also,
I *am* not inferior unto you.
Surely I would speak to the Almighty,
And I desire to reason with God.
But ye *are* forgers of lies,
Ye *are* all physicians of no value.
O that ye would altogether hold your peace,
And it should be your wisdom.
Hear now my reasoning,
And hearken to the pleadings of my lips.
Will you speak wickedly for God?
And talk deceitfully for him?
Will ye accept his person?
Will ye contend for God?
Is it good that he should search you out?
Or as one man mocketh another, do ye *so* mock him?
He will surely reprove you,
If ye do secretly accept persons.
Shall not his excellency make you afraid?
And his dread fall upon you?
Your remembrances *are* like unto ashes,
Your bodies to bodies of clay.
Hold your peace, let me alone, that I may speak,
And let come on me what *will*.
Wherefore do I take my flesh in my teeth,
And put my life in mine hand?
Though he slay me, yet will I trust in him:
But I will maintain mine own ways before him.
He also *shall be* my salvation:
For an hypocrite shall not come before him.
Hear diligently my speech,
And my declaration with your ears.
Behold now, I have ordered *my* cause,
I know that I shall be justified.
Who *is* he *that* will plead with me?
For now, if I hold my tongue, I shall give up the ghost.
Only do not two *things* unto me:
Then will I not hide myself from thee.
Withdraw thine hand far from me:

And let not thy dread make me afraid.
Then call thou, and I will answer:
Or let me speak, and answer thou me.
How many *are* mine iniquities and sins?
Make me to know my transgression, and my sin.
Wherefore hidest thou thy face,
And holdest me for thine enemy?
Wilt thou break a leaf driven to and fro?
And wilt thou pursue the dry stubble?
For thou writest bitter things against me,
And makest me to possess the iniquities of my youth.
Thou puttest my feet also in the stocks, and lookest narrowly unto all
    my paths;
Thou settest a print upon the heels of my feet.
And he, as a rotten thing, consumeth,
As a garment that is moth eaten.

Man *that is* born of a woman,
Is of few days, and full of trouble.
He cometh forth like a flower, and is cut down:
He fleeth also as a shadow, and continueth not.
And dost thou open thine eyes upon such an one.
And bringest me into judgment with thee?
Who can bring a clean *thing* out of an unclean?
Not one.
Seeing his days *are* determined, the number of his months *are* with thee,
Thou hast appointed his bounds that he cannot pass.
Turn from him, that he may rest,
Till he shall accomplish, as an hireling, his day.
For there is hope of a tree, if it be cut down, that it will sprout again,
And that the tender branch thereof will not cease.
Though the root thereof wax old in the earth,
And the stock thereof die in the ground;
Yet through the scent of water it will bud,
And bring forth boughs like a plant.
But man dieth, and wasteth away:
Yea, man giveth up the ghost, and where *is* he?
As the waters fail from the sea,
And the flood decayeth and drieth up:

So man lieth down, and riseth not,
Till the heavens *be* no more, they shall not awake;
Nor be raised out of their sleep.
O that thou wouldest hide me in the grave,
That thou wouldest keep me secret, until thy wrath be past,
That thou wouldest appoint me a set time, and remember me.
If a man die, shall he live *again?*
All the days of my appointed time will I wait,
Till my change come.
Thou shalt call, and I will answer thee:
Thou wilt have a desire to the work of thine hands.
For now thou numberest my steps,
Dost thou not watch over my sin?
My transgression *is* sealed up in a bag,
And thou sewest up mine iniquity.
And surely the mountain falling cometh to nought.
And the rock is removed out of his place.
The waters wear the stones,
Thou washest away the things which grow *out* of the dust of the earth;
And thou destroyest the hope of man.
Thou prevailest for ever against him, and he passeth:
Thou changest his countenance, and sendest him away.
His sons come to honour, and he knoweth *it* not;
And they are brought low, but he perceiveth *it* not of them.
But his flesh upon him shall have pain,
And his soul within him shall mourn.

Then Eliphaz the Temanite answered and said,

Can a man be profitable unto God?
As he that is wise may be profitable unto himself?
Is it any pleasure to the Almighty, that thou art righteous?
Or *is it* gain *to him*, that thou makest thy ways perfect?
Will he reprove thee for fear of thee?
Will he enter with thee into judgment?
Is not thy wickedness great?
And thine iniquities infinite?
For thou hast taken a pledge from thy brother for nought,
And stripped the naked of their clothing.

Thou hast not given water to the weary to drink,
And thou hast withholden bread from the hungry.
But *as for* the mighty man, he had the earth,
And the honourable man dwelt in it.
Thou hast sent widows away empty,
And the arms of the fatherless have been broken.
Therefore snares *are* round about thee,
And sudden fear troubleth thee,
Or darkness *that* thou canst not see,
And abundance of waters cover thee.
Is not God in the height of heaven?
And behold the height of the stars how high they are.
And thou sayest, How doth God know?
Can he judge through the dark cloud?
Thick clouds *are* a covering to him, that he seeth not,
And he walketh in the circuit of heaven.
Hast thou marked the old way
Which wicked men have trodden?
Which were cut down out of time,
Whose foundation was overflown with a flood.
Which said unto God, Depart from us,
And what can the Almighty do for them?
Yet he filled their houses with good *things*:
But the counsel of the wicked is far from me.
The righteous see *it*, and are glad,
And the innocent laugh them to scorn.
Whereas our substance is not cut down,
But the remnant of them the fire consumeth.
Acquaint now thyself with him, and be at peace:
Thereby good shall come unto thee.
Receive, I pray thee, the Law from his mouth,
And lay up his words in thine heart.
If thou return to the Almighty, thou shalt be built up,
Thou shalt put away iniquity far from thy tabernacles.
Then shalt thou lay up gold as dust,
And the *gold* of Ophir as the stones of the brooks.
Yea the Almighty shall be thy defence,
And thou shalt have plenty of silver.
For then shalt thou have thy delight in the Almighty,

And shall lift up thy face unto God.
Thou shalt make thy prayer unto him, and he shall hear thee,
And thou shalt pay thy vows.
Thou shalt also decree a thing, and it shall be established unto thee:
And the light shall shine upon thy ways.
When *men* are cast down, then thou shalt say, *There is* lifting up:
And he shall save the humble person.
He shall deliver the Island of the innocent:
And it is delivered by the pureness of thine hands.

Then Job answered and said,

Even to day *is* my complaint bitter:
My stroke is heavier than my groaning.
Oh that I knew where I might find him!
That I might come *even* to his seat!
I would order *my* cause before him,
And fill my mouth with arguments.
I would know the words *which* he would answer me,
And understand what he would say unto me.
Will he plead against me with *his* great power?
No, but he would put *strength* in me.
There the righteous might dispute with him;
So should I be delivered for ever from my Judge.
Behold, I go forward, but he *is* not *there*,
And backward, but I cannot perceive him:
On the left hand, where he doth work, but I cannot behold *him*:
He hideth himself on the right hand, that I cannot see *him*.
But he knoweth the way that I take:
When he hath tried me, I shall come forth as gold.
My foot hath held his steps,
His way have I kept, and not declined.
Neither have I gone back from the commandment of his lips,
I have esteemed the words of his mouth more than my necessary *food*.
But he *is* in one *mind*, and who can turn him?
And *what* his soul desireth, even *that* he doeth.
For he performeth *the thing that is* appointed for me:
And many such *things are* with him.

Therefore am I troubled at his presence:
When I consider, I am afraid of him.
For God maketh my heart soft,
And the Almighty troubleth me:
Because I was not cut off before the darkness,
Neither hath he covered the darkness from my face.

Then the LORD answered Job out of the whirlwind, and said,

Who *is* this that darkeneth counsel
By words without knowledge?
Gird up now thy loins like a man;
For I will demand of thee, and answer thou me.
Where wast thou when I laid the foundations of the earth?
Declare, if thou hast understanding.
Who hath laid the measures thereof, if thou knowest?
Or who hath stretched the line upon it?
Whereupon are the foundations thereof fastened?
Or who laid the corner stone thereof?
When the morning stars sang together,
And all the sons of God shouted for joy.
Or *who* shut up the sea with doors,
When it brake forth, *as if* it had issued out of the womb?
When I made the cloud the garment thereof,
And thick darkness a swaddlingband for it,
And brake up for it my decreed *place,*
And set bars and doors,
And said, Hitherto shalt thou come, but no further:
And here shall thy proud waves be stayed.
Hast thou commanded the morning since thy days?
And caused the dayspring to know his place,
That it might take hold of the ends of the earth,
That the wicked might be shaken out of it?
It is turned as clay *to* the seal,
And they stand as a garment.
And from the wicked their light is withholden,
And the high arm shall be broken.
Hast thou entered into the springs of the sea?
Or hast thou walked in the search of the depth?

Have the gates of death been opened unto thee?
Or hast thou seen the doors of the shadow of death?
Hast thou perceived the breadth of the earth?
Declare if thou knowest it all.
Where *is* the way *where* light dwelleth?
And *as for* darkness, where *is* the place thereof?
That thou shouldest take it to the bound thereof,
And that thou shouldest know the paths *to* the house thereof.
Knowest thou *it,* because thou wast then born?
Or *because* the number of thy days *is* great?
Hast thou entered into the treasures of the snow?
Or hast thou seen the treasures of the hail,
Which I have reserved against the time of trouble,
Against the day of battle and war?
By what way is the light parted?
Which scattereth the east wind upon the earth.
Who hath divided a water-course for the overflowing of waters?
Or a way for the lightning of thunder,
To cause it to rain on the earth, *where* no man *is:*
On the wilderness, wherein *there is* no man?
To satisfy the desolate and waste *around,*
And to cause the bud of the tender herb to spring forth.
Hath the rain a father?
Or who hath begotten the drops of dew?
Out of whose womb came the ice?
And the hoary frost of heaven, who hath gendered it?
The waters are hid as *with* a stone,
And the face of the deep is frozen.
Canst thou bind the sweet influences of Pleiades?
Or loose the bands of Orion?
Canst thou bring forth Mazzaroth in his season,
Or canst thou guide Arcturus with his sons?
Knowest thou the ordinances of heaven?
Canst thou set the dominion thereof in the earth?
Canst thou lift up thy voice to the clouds,
That abundance of waters may cover thee?
Canst thou send lightnings, that they may go,
And say unto thee, Here we *are?*
Who hath put wisdom in the inward parts?

Or who hath given understanding to the heart?
Who can number the clouds in wisdom?
Or who can stay the bottles of heaven,
When the dust groweth into hardness,
And the clods cleave fast together?
Wilt thou hunt the prey for the lion?
Or fill the appetite of the young lions,
When they couch in *their* dens,
And abide in the covert to lie in wait?
Who provideth for the raven his food?
When his young ones cry unto God, they wander for lack of meat.

Knowest thou the time when the wild goats of the rock bring forth!
Or canst thou mark when the hinds do calve?
Canst thou number the months *that* they fulfil?
Or knowest thou the time when they bring forth?
They bow themselves, they bring forth their young ones,
They cast out their sorrows.
Their young ones are in good liking, they grow up with corn;
They go forth, and return not unto them.
Who hath sent out the wild ass free?
Or who hath loosed the bands of the wild ass?
Whose house I have made the wilderness,
And the barren land his dwellings.
He scorneth the multitude of the city,
Neither regardeth he the crying of the driver.
The range of the mountains *is* his pasture,
And he searcheth after every green thing.
Will the Unicorn be willing to serve thee?
Or abide by thy crib?
Canst thou bind the Unicorn with his band in the furrow?
Or will he harrow the valleys after thee?
Wilt thou trust him, because his strength *is* great?
Or wilt thou leave thy labour to him?
Wilt thou believe him, that he will bring home thy seed?
And gather *it into* thy barn?
Gavest thou the goodly wings unto the peacocks,
Or wings and feathers unto the Ostrich?
Which leaveth her eggs in the earth,

And warmeth them in dust,
And forgotteth that the foot may crush them,
Or that the wild beast may break them.
She is hardened against her young ones, as though *they were* not her's:
Her labour is in vain without fear.
Because God hath deprived her of wisdom,
Neither hath he imparted to her understanding.
What time she lifteth up herself on high,
She scorneth the horse and his rider.
Hast thou given the horse strength?
Hast thou clothed his neck with thunder?
Canst thou make him afraid as a grasshopper?
The glory of his nostrils *is* terrible.
He paweth in the valley, and rejoiceth in *his* strength:
He goeth on to meet the armed men.
He mocketh at fear, and is not affrighted:
Neither turneth he back from the sword.
The quiver rattleth against him,
The glittering spear and the shield.
He swalloweth the ground with fierceness and rage:
Neither believeth he that *it is* the sound of the trumpet.
He saith among the trumpets, Ha, ha:
And he smelleth the battle afar off,
The thunder of the captains, and the shouting.
Doth the hawk fly by the wisdom,
And stretch her wings toward the South?
Doth the Eagle mount up at thy command?
And make her nest on high?
She dwelleth and abideth on the rock,
Upon the crag of the rock, and the strong place.
From thence she seeketh the prey,
And her eyes behold afar off.
Her young ones also suck up blood:
And where the slain *are*, there *is* she.

Moreover the Lord answered Job, and said,

Shall he that contendeth with the Almighty, instruct *him?*
He that reproveth God, let him answer it.

Then Job answered the LORD, and said,

> Behold, I am vile; what shall I answer thee?
> I will lay mine hand upon my mouth.
> Once have I spoken;
> But I will not answer:
> Yea twice, but I will proceed no further.

Then answered the LORD unto Job out of the whirlwind, and said,

> Gird up thy loins now like a man:
> I will demand of thee, and declare thou unto me.
> Wilt thou also disannul my judgment?
> Wilt thou condemn me, that thou mayest be righteous?
> Hast thou an arm like God?
> Or canst thou thunder with a voice like him?
> Deck thyself now *with* majesty and excellency,
> And array thyself with glory, and beauty.
> Cast abroad the rage of thy wrath:
> And behold every one *that is* proud, and abase him.
> Look on every one *that is* proud, *and* bring him low:
> And tread down the wicked in their place.
> Hide them in the dust together,
> *And* bind their faces in secret.
> Then will I also confess unto thee,
> That thine own right hand can save thee.

> Behold now Behemoth which I made with thee,
> He eateth grass as an ox.
> Lo now, his strength *is* in his loins,
> And his force *is* in the navel of his belly.
> He moveth his tail like a Cedar:
> The sinews of his stones are wrapped together.
> His bones *are as* strong pieces of brass:
> His bones *are* like bars of iron.
> He *is* the chief of the ways of God:
> He that made him, can make his sword to approach *unto him*.
> Surely the mountains bring him forth food:
> Where all the beasts of the field play.
> He lieth under the shady trees,

In the covert of the reed, and fens.
The shady trees cover him *with* their shadow:
The willows of the brook compass him about.
Behold, he drinketh up a river, *and* hasteth not:
He trusteth that he can draw up Jordan into his mouth.
He taketh it with his eyes:
His nose pierceth through snares.

Canst thou draw out Leviathan with an hook?
Or his tongue with a cord *which* thou lettest down?
Canst thou put an hook into his nose?
Or bore his jaw through with a thorn?
Will he make any supplications unto thee?
Will he speak soft *words* unto thee?
Will he make a covenant with thee?
Wilt thou take him for a servant for ever?
Wilt thou play with him as *with* a bird?
Or wilt thou bind him for thy maidens?
Shall the companions make a banquet of him?
Shall they part him among the merchants?
Canst thou fill his skin with barbed irons?
Or his head with fish spears?
Lay thine hand upon him,
Remember the battle: do no more.
Behold, the hope of him is in vain:
Shall not *one* be cast down even at the sight of him?
None *is so* fierce that dare stir him up:
Who then is able to stand before me?
Who hath prevented me, that I should repay *him*?
Whatsoever is under the whole heaven is mine.
I will not conceal his parts.
Nor his power, nor his comely proportion.
Who can discover the face of his garment?
Or who can come *to him* with his double bridle?
Who can open the doors of his face?
His teeth *are* terrible round about.
His scales *are his* pride,
Shut up together *as with* a close seal.
One is so near to another,

That no air can come between them.
They are joined one to another,
They stick together, that they cannot be sundered.
By his neesings a light doth shine,
And his eyes *are* like the eyelids of the morning.
Out of his mouth go burning lamps,
And sparks of fire leap out.
Out of his nostrils goeth smoke,
As *out* of a seething pot or caldron.
His breath kindleth coals,
And a flame goeth out of his mouth.
In his neck remaineth strength,
And sorrow is turned into joy before him.
The flakes of his flesh are joined together:
They are firm in themselves, they cannot be moved.
His heart is as firm as a stone,
Yea, as hard as a piece of the nether *millstone.*
When he raiseth up himself, the mighty are afraid:
By reason of breakings they purify themselves.
The sword of him that layeth at him cannot hold:
The spear, the dart, nor the habergeon.
He esteemeth iron as straw,
And brass as rotten wood.
The arrow cannot make him flee:
Slingstones are turned with him into stubble.
Darts are counted as stubble:
He laugheth at the shaking of a spear.
Sharp stones *are* under him:
He spreadeth sharp pointed things upon the mire.
He maketh the deep to boil like a pot:
He maketh the sea like a pot of ointment.
He maketh a path to shine after him;
One would think the deep *to be* hoary.
Upon earth there is not his like:
Who is made without fear.
He beholdeth all high *things:*
He *is* a king over all the children of pride.

Then Job answered the Lord, and said,

I know that thou canst do every *thing*,
And *that* no thought can be withholden from thee.
Who *is* he that hideth counsel without knowledge?
Therefore have I uttered that I understood not,
Things too wonderful for me, which I knew not.
Hear, I beseech thee, and I will speak:
I will demand of thee, and declare thou unto me.
I have heard of thee by the hearing of the ear:
But now mine eye seeth thee.
Wherefore I abhor *myself*, and repent
In dust and ashes.

And it was *so*, that after the Lord had spoken these words unto Job, the Lord said to Eliphaz the Temanite, My wrath is kindled against thee, and against thy two friends: ye have not spoken of me *the thing that is* right, as my servant Job *hath*. Therefore, take unto you now seven bullocks and seven rams, and go to my servant Job, and offer up for yourselves a burnt offering; and my servant Job shall pray for you: for him will I accept: lest I deal with you *after your* folly, in that ye have not spoken of me *the thing which is* right, like my servant Job. So Eliphaz the Temanite and Bildad the Shuhite *and* Zophar the Naamathite went, and did according as the Lord commanded them: the Lord also accepteth Job. And the Lord turned the captivity of Job, when he prayed for his friends: also the Lord gave Job twice as much as he had before. Then came there unto him all his brethren, and all his sisters, and all they that had been of his acquaintance before, and did eat bread with him in his house: and they bemoaned him, and comforted him over all the evil that the Lord had brought upon him: every man also gave him a piece of money, and every one an earring of gold. So the Lord blessed the latter end of Job more than his beginning: for he had fourteen thousand sheep, and six thousand camels, and a thousand yoke of oxen, and a thousand she asses. He had also seven sons and three daughters. And he called the name of the first, Jemima; and the name of the second, Kezia; and the name of the third, Keren-happuch. And in all the land were no women found *so* fair as the daughters of Job: and their father gave them inheritance among their brethren. After this lived Job an hundred and forty years, and saw his sons, and his sons' sons, *even* four generations. So Job died, *being* old and full of days.

Edith Hamilton

THE RELIGION OF THE GREEKS

WHAT THE GREEKS DID FOR RELIGION IS IN GENERAL NOT HIGHLY ES-
teemed. Their achievement in that field is usually described as unimportant, without any real significance. It has even been called paltry and
trivial. The reason people think of it in this way is that Greek religion
has got confused with Greek mythology. The Greek gods are certainly
Homer's Olympians, and the jovial company of the *Iliad* who sit at the
banqueting board in Olympus making heaven shake with their shouts
of inextinguishable laughter are not a religious gathering. Their morality,
even, is more than questionable and also their dignity. They deceive each
other; they are shifty and tricky in their dealings with mortals; they act
sometimes like rebellious subjects and sometimes like naughty children
and are kept in order only by Father Zeus' threats. In Homer's pages they
are delightful reading, but not in the very least edifying.

If Homer is really the Greek Bible and these stories of his are accepted
as the Greek idea of spiritual truth, the only possible conclusion is that in
the enormously important sphere of religion the Greeks were naïve, not to
say childish, and quite indifferent to ethical conduct. Because Homer is
far and away the best known of the Greeks, this really is the prevailing
idea, absurd as it must appear in face of the Greek achievement. There is
no truth whatever in it. Religion in Greece shows one of the greatest of
what Schopenhauer calls the "singular swing to elevation" in the history
of the human spirit. It marks a great stage on the long road that leads up
from savagery, from senseless and horrible rites, toward a world still so
very dim and far away that its outline can hardly be seen; a world in
which no individual shall be sacrificed for an end, but in which each will
be willing to sacrifice himself for the end of working for the good of others
in the spirit of love with the God who is love.

It would be impossible to compress Greek religion into the compass of a
single chapter, but it is perhaps possible to give an idea of the special Greek
stamp which marked it out from the others. Greek religion was developed

not by priests nor by prophets nor by saints nor by any set of men who were held to be removed from the ordinary run of life because of a superior degree of holiness; it was developed by poets and artists and philosophers, all of them people who instinctively leave thought and imagination free, and all of them, in Greece, men of practical affairs. The Greeks had no authoritative Sacred Book, no creed, no ten commandments, no dogmas. The very idea of orthodoxy was unknown to them. They had no theologians to draw up sacrosanct definitions of the eternal and infinite. They never tried to define it; only to express or suggest it. St. Paul was speaking as a Greek when he said the invisible must be understood by the visible. That is the basis of all great art, and in Greece great artists strove to make the visible express the invisible. They, not theologians, defined it for the Greeks. Phidias' statue of Zeus at Olympia was his definition of Zeus, the greatest ever achieved in terms of beauty. Phidias said, so Dion Chrysostom reports, that pure thought and spirit cannot be portrayed, but the artist has in the human body a true vessel of thought and spirit. So he made his statue of God, the sight of which drew the beholder away from himself to the contemplation of the divine. "I think," Dion Chrysostom writes, "that if a man heavy of heart, who had drunk often of the cup of adversity and sorrow should stand before it, he would remember no longer the bitter hardships of his life. Your work, O Phidias, is

> Grief's cure,
> Bringing forgetfulness of every care."

"The Zeus of Phidias," said the Roman Quintilian, "has added to our conception of religion."

That was one way the Greeks worked out their theology. Another way was the poet's, as when Æschylus used his power to suggest what is beyond categorical statement:

> God—the pathways of his purpose
> Are hard to find
> And yet it shines out through the gloom,
> In the dark chance of human life.
> Effortless and calm
> He works his perfect will.

Words that define God clamp down walls before the mind, but words like these open out vistas. The door swings wide for a moment.

Socrates' way was the same. Nothing to him was important except finding the truth, the reality in all that is, which in another aspect is God.

He spent his life in the search for it, but he never tried to put what he had seen into hard and fast statements. "To find the Father and Maker of all is hard," he said, "and having found him it is impossible to utter him."

The way of Greek religion could not but be different from the ways of religion dependent not upon each man's seeking the truth for himself, as an artist or a poet must seek it, but upon an absolute authority to which each man must submit himself. In Greece there was no dominating church or creed, but there was a dominating ideal which everyone would want to pursue if he caught sight of it. Different men saw it differently. It was one thing to the artist, another to the warrior. "Excellence" is the nearest equivalent we have to the word they commonly used for it, but it meant more than that. It was the utmost perfection possible, the very best and highest a man could attain to, which when perceived always has a compelling authority. A man must strive to attain it. We needs must love the highest when we see it. "No one," Socrates said, "is willingly deprived of the good." To win it required all that a man could give. Simonides wrote:

> Not seen in visible presence by the eyes of men
> Is Excellence, save his from whom in utmost toil
> Heart-racking sweat comes, at his manhood's height.

Hesiod had already said the same:

> Before the gates of Excellence the high gods have placed sweat.
> Long is the road thereto and steep and rough at the first.
> But when the height is won, then is there ease,
> Though grievously hard in the winning.

Aristotle summed up the search and struggle: "Excellence much labored for by the race of men." The long and steep and rough road to it was the road Greek religion took.

In the very earliest Greek records we have, a high stage has been reached. All things Greek begin for us with Homer, and in the *Iliad* and the *Odyssey* the Greeks have left far behind not only the bestialities of primitive worship, but the terrible and degrading rites the terror-stricken world around them was practicing. In Homer, magic has been abolished. It is practically nonexistent in the *Iliad* and the *Odyssey*. The enormous spiritual advance this shows—and intellectual, no less—is hard for us to realize. Before Greece all religion was magical. Magic was of supreme importance. It was mankind's sole defense against fearful powers leagued against mankind. Myriads of malignant spirits were bent on bringing every kind of evil to it. They were omnipresent. A Chaldean inscription runs:

> They lie in wait. They twine around the rafters. They take their way from house to house and the door cannot stop them. They separate the bride from the embraces of the bridegroom; they snatch the child from between his father's knees.

Life was possible only because, fearful as they were, they could be appeased or weakened by magical means. These were often terrible as well as senseless. The human mind played no part at all in the whole business. It was enslaved by terror. A magical universe was so terrifying because it was so irrational, and therefore completely incalculable. There was no dependable relation anywhere between cause and effect. It will readily be seen what it did to the human intellect to live in such an atmosphere, and what it did to the human character, too. Fear is of all the emotions the most brutalizing.

In this terror-haunted world a strange thing came to pass. In one little country the terror was banished. For untold ages it had dominated mankind and stunted its growth. The Greeks dismissed it. They changed a world that was full of fear into a world full of beauty. We have not the least idea when or how this extraordinary change came about. We know only that in Homer men are free and fearless. There are no fearful powers to be propitiated in fearful ways. Very human-like gods inhabit a very delightful heaven. Strange and terrifying unrealities—shapes made up of bird and beast and human joined together by artists who thought only the unhuman could be divine—have no place in Greece. The universe has become rational. An early Greek philosopher wrote: "All things were in confusion until Mind came and set them in order." That mind was Greek, and the first exponent of it we know about was Homer. In the *Iliad* and the *Odyssey* mankind has been delivered from the terror of the unhuman supreme over the human.

Homer's universe is quite rational and well ordered and very well lit. When night comes on, the gods go to sleep. There are no mysterious doings that must shun the eye of day either in heaven or on the earth. If the worship of the powers of darkness still went on—and there are allusions to practices that point to it—at least literature takes no notice of it. Homer would have none of it, and no writer after him ever brought it back. Stories like that of the sacrifice of Iphigenia, which clearly point back to brutal rites, always represent what was done as evil.

An ancient writer says of Homer that he touched nothing without somehow honoring and glorifying it. He was not the Greek Bible; he was the representative and spokesman of the Greeks. He was quintessentially Greek. The stamp of the Greek genius is everywhere on his two epics, in the banishment of the ugly and the frightful and the senseless; in the conviction that gods were like men and men able to be godlike; in the courage and undaunted spirit with which the heroes faced any opponent, human or divine, even Fate herself; in the prevailing atmosphere of reason and good sense. The very essence of Greek rationality is in the passage in which Hector is advised to consult the flight of birds as an omen before going into battle and cries: "Obedience to long-winged birds, whether they fare to the right or to the left—nay; one omen is best, to fight for our country." Homer was the great molding force of Greece because he was so Greek himself. Plato says: "I have always from my earliest years had an awe of Homer and a love for him which even now [when he is about to criticize him] make the words falter on my lips. He is the great leader and teacher."

The Greeks never fell back from the height they had reached with him. They went further on, but not in the directions he had banned, away from reason to magic, and away from freedom to creeds and priests. His gods, however, could not continue long to be adequate to men fired by the desire for the best. They were unable to satisfy people who were thinking soberly of right and wrong, who were using their critical powers to speculate about the universe, who, above all, were trying to find religion, not the doubtful divinities of Olympus, but a solution of life's mystery and a conviction of its purpose and its end. Men began to ask for a loftier Zeus, and one who cared for all, not only, as in the *Iliad,* for the great and powerful. So in a passage in the *Odyssey* he has become the protector of the poor and helpless; and soon after, the peasant-poet Hesiod, who knew by experience what it was to be weak and have no defense against the strong, placed justice in Olympus as Zeus' companion: "Fishes and beasts and fowls of the air devour one another. But to men Zeus has given justice. Beside Zeus on his throne Justice has her seat."

Delphi, the oracle of oracles, took up this implied criticism of Homer and put it into plain words. Moral standards were applied to what went on in Homer's heaven. Pindar, Delphi's greatest spokesman, denounced Homer as speaking falsehoods about the gods. It was wicked and contrary to reason, he protested, to tell unedifying tales about divinities: "Hateful is the poet's lore that utters slander against the gods." Criticism of this kind came from all sides. The rationalizing spirit, which was Homer's own, turned against him. The idea of the truth had dawned, to which personal preferences had to give way; and in the sixth century one of the leaders in what was the beginning of scientific thinking, wrote:

> One God there is, greatest of gods and mortals,
> Not like to men in body or in mind.
> All of him sees and hears and thinks.
> We men have made our gods in our own image.
> I think that horses, lions, oxen too,
> Had they but hands would make their gods like them,
> Horse-gods for horses, oxen-gods for oxen.

Homer's Olympians were being attacked by the same love for the rational which had brought them to birth in a mad and magical world. Not only new ideas but new needs were awakening. Greece needed a religion for the heart, as Homer's signally was not, which could satisfy the hunger in men's souls, as the cool morality of Delphi could not.

Such a need is always met sooner or later. A new god came to Greece who for a time did very strange things to the Greek spirit. He was Dionysus, the god of wine, the latest comer among the gods. Homer never admitted him to Olympus. He was alien to the bright company there, a god of earth not heaven. The power wine has to uplift a man, to give him an exultant sense of mastery, to carry him out of himself, was finally transformed into the idea of the god of wine freeing men from themselves and revealing to them that they too could become divine, an idea really implicit in Homer's picture of human gods and godlike men, but never developed until Dionysus came.

His worship must have begun in a great religious revival, a revolt very probably against the powerful centre of worship Delphi had become. At any rate, it was the very antipodes to Delphi, the shrine of Apollo the most Greek of all the gods, the artist-god, the poet and musician, who ever brought fair order and harmony out of confusion, who stood for moderation and sobriety, upon whose temple was graven the great Delphic saying, "Nothing in excess." The new religion was marked by everything in excess —drunkenness, bloody feasts, people acting like mad creatures, shrieking and shouting and dancing wildly, rushing over the land in fierce ecstasy. Elsewhere, when the desire to find liberation has arisen, it has very often led men to asceticism and its excesses, to exaggerated cults bent on punishing the body for corrupting the soul. This did not happen in Greece. It could not happen to a people who knew better than any other that liberty depends on self-restraint, who knew that freedom is freedom only when controlled and limited. The Greeks could never wander very far from the spirit of Apollo. In the end, we do not know when or how, the worship of Apollo and the worship of Dionysus came together. All we are told of this momentous meeting is that Orpheus, the master musician, Apollo's pupil, reformed the violent Bacchic rites and brought them into order.

It must have been after this transformation that Dionysus was admitted to the Eleusinian mysteries, the great solemnity of Greece, and took his place beside Demeter in whose honor they had been founded. It was natural to associate the two—the goddess of the corn and the god of the vine, both deities of earth, the benefactors of mankind from whom came the bread and the wine that sustain life. Their mysteries, the Eleusinian, always chiefly Demeter's, and the Orphic, centering in Dionysus, were an enormously important force for religion throughout the Greek and Roman world. Cicero, clearly an initiate, says: "Nothing is higher than these mysteries. . . . They have not only shown us how to live joyfully, but they have taught us how to die with a better hope." In view of their great importance, it is extraordinary that we know almost nothing about them. Everyone initiated had to take an oath not to reveal them, and their influence was so strong that apparently no one ever did. All we are sure of is that they awakened a deep sense of reverence and awe, that they offered purification from sin, and that they promised immortality. Plutarch, in a letter to his wife about the death of a little daughter during his absence from home, writes her that he knows she gives no credence to assertions that the soul once departed from the body vanishes and feels nothing, "because of those sacred and faithful promises given in the mysteries of Bacchus. . . . We hold it firmly for an undoubted truth that our soul is incorruptible and immortal. . . . Let us behave ourselves accordingly, outwardly ordering our lives, while within all should be purer, wiser, incorruptible."

A fragment of Plutarch's apparently describes the initiation ceremonies. "When a man dies he is like those who are initiated into the mysteries. Our whole life is a journey by tortuous ways without outlet. At the moment of quitting it come terrors, shuddering fear, amazement. Then a light that moves to meet you, pure meadows that receive you, songs and dances and holy apparitions." Plutarch lived in the last half of the first century A.D. There is no possible way of telling how much of all that carefully arranged appeal to the emotions belonged to the mysteries of the Periclean age, but some great appeal there was, as Aristophanes shows beyond question in the *Frogs:*

Heracles

Then you will find a breath about your ears
Of music, and a light about your eyes
Most beautiful—like this—and myrtle groves,
And joyous throngs of women and of men—
The Initiated.

At first sight, this whole matter of an ecstatic religion of salvation, wrapped in mystery and highly emotional, is foreign to our idea of the Greek. Delphi and Pindar, teaching practical morality and forever emphasizing moderation, seem the true representatives of Greece. But they would never by themselves have reached the loftiest and the deepest expression of the Greek spirit. Noble self-restraint must have something to restrain. Apollo needed Dionysus, as Greeks could be trusted to perceive. "He who not being inspired," Plato says, "and having no touch of madness in his soul, comes to the door and thinks he will get into the temple by the help of art—he, I say, and his poetry are not admitted."

The Delphic way and the way of Dionysus reached their perfect union in the fifth-century theatre. There the great mystery, human life, was presented through the power of great art. Poet and actors and audience were conscious of a higher presence. They were gathered there in an act of worship, all sharing in the same experience. The poet and the actors did not speak to the audience; they spoke for them. Their task and their power was to interpret and express the great communal emotion. That is what Aristole meant when he said tragedy purified through pity and awe. Men were set free from themselves when they all realized together the universal suffering of life. For a moment they were lifted above their own griefs and cares. They ceased to be shut-in, lonely individuals as they were swept away in a great onrush of emotion which extraordinarily united instead of isolating. Plato said the perfect state was one in which the citizens wept and rejoiced over the same things. That deep community of feeling came to pass in the theatre of Dionysus. Men lost their sense of isolation.

The religion of the mysteries was individual, the search for personal purity and salvation. It pointed men toward union with God. The religion of the drama brought men into union with one another. Personal preoccupations fell away before the soul-shaking spectacle of pain presented on the stage, and the dammed-up flood within was released as the audience wept their hearts out over Œdipus and Hecuba.

But in the long and terrible struggle of the Peloponnesian War, ideals grew dim. Safety, not salvation, was in men's thoughts, the spirit of getting what one could while one could in a world where nothing seemed certain; nothing indeed, for the gods and the old morality were failing. Euripides had succeeded to Æschylus, and a new criticism of all things was in the air. In Pericles' Athens a noted teacher was declaring that "whether there are gods or not we cannot say, and life is too short to find out." The state took alarm and there was a persecution, so slight in comparison with mediæval and later times that it would not deserve notice if it were not for the last victim of it who was Socrates.

One form of religion perpetually gives way to another; if religion did not change it would be dead. In the long history of man's search for God and a basis for right living, the changes almost always come as something better. Each time the new ideas appear they are seen at first as a deadly foe threatening to make religion perish from the earth; but in the end there is a deeper insight and a better life with ancient follies and prejudices gone. Then other follies and prejudices come in, and the whole process has to be gone over again. So it was at this time in Greece, when the supports of all belief seemed to be giving way. Socrates taught and died because of his teaching. In the bitter disillusion caused by the long-drawn-out suffering of the endless war, and even more by the defeat of the Athenian spirit before the hard, narrow, intolerant Spartan spirit, Athens needed above all to be brought back to a fresh realization of the old ideal which her three tragedians had presented so magnificently. She needed a restatement of excellence, and that is what Socrates did for her and all the world to come.

He can never be separated from Plato. Almost all Plato wrote professes to be a report of what Socrates said, a faithful pupil's record of his master's words; and it is impossible to decide just what part belongs to each. Together they shaped the idea of the excellent which the classical world lived by for hundreds of years and which the modern world has never forgotten.

Socrates believed that goodness and truth were the fundamental realities, and that they were attainable. Every man would strive to attain them if he could be shown them. No one would pursue evil except through ignorance. Once let him see what evil was and he would fly from it. His own mission, Socrates believed, was to open men's eyes to their ignorance and to lead them on to where they could catch a glimpse of the eternal truth and goodness beneath life's confusions and futilities, when they would inevitably, irresistibly, seek for a fuller and fuller vision of it. He had no dogma, no set of beliefs to implant in men's minds. He wanted to awaken in them the realization that they did not know what was good, and to arouse in them the longing to discover it. Each one, he was sure, must seek and find it for himself. He never set himself up as a guide. "Although my mind is far from wise," he said, "some of those who come to me make astonishing progress. They discover for themselves, not from me—and yet I am an instrument in the hands of God."

He was always the seeker, asking, not teaching; but his questions upset men's confidence in themselves and in all the comfortable conventions they lived by. The result at first was only perplexity, and sometimes extreme distress. Alcibiades told the company at Agathon's dinner table:

I have heard Pericles and other great orators, but they never stirred my soul or made me angry at living in a way that was no better than a slave. But this man has often brought me to such a pass that I felt I could hardly endure the life I was leading, neglecting the needs of my soul. I have sometimes wished that he was dead!

Aristotle says happiness is activity of soul. That defines precisely Socrates' way of making men happy. He believed that the unexamined life, the life of those who knew nothing of themselves or their real needs and desires, was not worthy to be lived by a human being. So he would sting into activity the souls of men to test their lives, confident that when they found them utterly unsatisfying they would be driven to seek what would satisfy.

His own life did as much to arouse the divine discontent as his words did. He was aware of a counsellor within him which guided him in all his dealings and enabled him to maintain a perfect serenity of spirit always. When he was taken to court on a life-and-death charge of corrupting young men—and no pupil of Socrates could take seriously Homer's gods, still the state religion—he jested with his accusers in a spirit of perfect good will, refused with complete courtesy to save his life by a promise to give up teaching—and ended by comforting his judges for condemning him to death! "Be of good cheer," he told them, "and know of a certainty that no evil can happen to a good man either in life or after death. I see clearly that the time has come when it is better for me to die and my accusers have done me no harm. Still, they did not mean to do me good—and for this I may gently blame them. And now we go our ways, you to live and I to die. Which is better God only knows."

In the prison cell when the time had come to drink the hemlock, he had a kind word for the jailor who brought him the cup, and he broke off his discourse with his friends when he was telling them that nothing was surer than that beauty and goodness have a most real and actual existence, by exclaiming: "But I really had better go bathe so that the women may not have the trouble of washing my body when I am dead." One of those present, suddenly recalled from the charm of his talk to the stark facts, cried: "How shall we bury you?" "Any way you like," was the amused answer. "Only be sure you get hold of me and see that I do not run away." And turning to the rest of the company: "I cannot make this fellow believe that the dead body will not be me. Don't let him talk about burying Socrates, for false words infect the soul. Dear Crito, say only that you are burying my body."

No one who knew of Socrates could fail to believe that "goodness has a most real and actual existence." He exemplified in himself that excellence of which Greece from the beginning had had a vision. Four hundred years before Christ the world took courage from him and from the conviction which underlay all he said and did, that in the confusion and darkness and seeming futility of life there is a purpose which is good and that men can find it and help work it out. Aristotle, through Plato a pupil of Socrates, wrote some fifty years after Socrates died:

There is a life which is higher than the measure of humanity: men will live it not by virtue of their humanity, but by virtue of something in them that is divine. We ought not to listen to those who exhort a man to keep to man's thoughts, but to live according to the highest thing that is in him, for small though it be, in power and worth it is far above the rest.

Paul Tillich

THE PREMISES OF CHRISTIANITY

PERSONALISM AND THE DIVINE MANIFESTATIONS

1. Personalism and Creation

ACCORDING TO BIBLICAL RELIGION, ALL DIVINE MANIFESTATIONS ARE MANI-festations through the word. This refers first of all to creation. Biblical personalism is most obviously distinguished from the personalism of other religions by the doctrine of creation. This doctrine was the point at which the early church fought a life-and-death struggle against the religious movements of the later ancient world. It was the point at which the church held to the Old Testament at its own presupposition. The doctrine of creation is the one on which the doctrines of the Christ, of salvation and fulfilment, depend. Without it, Christianity would have ceased to exist as an independent movement. The doctrine of creation has two main functions. First, it emphasizes the dependence on God of everything created and, consequently, the essential goodness of creation. It protects the Christian interpretation of existence against a dualistic split between a good and an evil god. It preserves the personal unity of the one God. Second, it emphasizes the infinite distance between the Creator and the creature. It places the created outside the creative ground. It denies any participation of the creature in the creative substance out of which it comes. It is the doctrine of creation through the word which makes especially sharp the distance between the Creator and creation. It was correct and proper when later Jewish and Christian theologians spoke of creation out of nothing. This is an implication of creation through the word. It means that there is no substance, divine or antidivine, out of which finite beings receive their being. They receive it through the word, the will of God and its creative expression. The doctrine of creation through the word denies any substantial participation of man in God. It replaces substantial identity by personal distance.

Ontology speaks of being-itself as the ground of everything that is. It speaks of the one substance out of which all finite beings are made. It speaks of the identity of the infinite with the finite. It speaks of the finite mind through which the Absolute Mind wills and recognizes himself. It seems as though ontology dissolves the infinite into the finite or the finite into the infinite. Ontology seems to deprive God of his creative Word. It falls either into metaphysical dualism or into metaphysical monism. In both cases it removes the distance between God and man which is so powerfully expressed in biblical religion.

2. Personalism and Christology

Biblical personalism comes to its fulfilment in the message that the divine Word was incarnate in a personal life, in the life of Jesus, who for this reason is called the Christ. Biblical religion in the Old and New Testaments is a religion of personalities who, in the power of the Spirit of God, mediate the will of God and preserve the covenant between God and Israel, between God and mankind. The God who is encountered as a person acts in history through persons and their inner experiences. Indeed, there are many nonpersonal elements in the religion of the Old as well as the New Testament: communal traditions, ritual laws, legal orders, sacramental activities, scriptures, and hierarchies. Without these religious objectifications biblical religion could not have lived, survived, and produced an uninterrupted series of personalities. On the other hand, these objectifications are dependent on and transformed by the great personalities. Their experiences and struggles and messages created the spirit of biblical religion. But in all of them the revelation mediated through them can still be separated from their persons. It is the revealing word, received by prophet or apostle, which makes him the medium of the divine self-manifestation, though he could not have received it without a personal life, open to the divine Word. But it is not this personal life as such which is revelatory; it is not his being but something mediated through his being. Jesus also used the prophetic words. But, beyond this, his words are expressions of his being, and they are this in unity with his deeds and sufferings. Together, they all point to a personal center which is completely determined by the divine presence, by the "Spirit without limit." This makes him Jesus the Christ. The Word appears *as* a person and only secondarily in the words of a person. The Word, the principle of the divine self-manifestation, appearing as a person, is the fulfilment of biblical personalism. It means that God is so personal that we see what he is only in a personal life. God can become man, because man is person and because

God is personal. And, on the other hand, when God appears in a person, it becomes manifest what person should be. The limits of man's personal existence are overcome; the a-personal elements which try to enter and to disrupt personal existence are removed. The personal center rules the whole man because it is united with the personal center of the divine life.

The ontological question, the question of being, in and beyond everything that is, seems to depersonalize reality. The Logos, who for biblical religion can reveal the heart of divinity only in a concrete personal life, is, for ontology, present in everything. Ontology generalizes, while biblical religion individualizes. The search for ultimate reality seems to by-pass that concrete reality in which the ultimate is personally present. The universal Logos seems to draw into itself and to swallow the Logos who became flesh, that is, historical reality, in the personal life of an individual self. And the question arises: Is there any possibility of uniting ontology with biblical religion, if ontology could not accept the central assertion of biblical religion that Jesus is the Christ?

3. Personalism, History, and Eschatology

Biblical religion has a historical view of reality. The stories of the Old Testament are not only legends of the past history of Israel. This they are, too; but, beyond this, they are reports about the deeds of God who *works* for his ultimate aim, the establishment of his rule over Israel and over all mankind. The ideas of the covenant between Yahweh and his people, the ideas of the remnant and the messianic age, the message of Jesus that the rule of the heavens is at hand, the feeling of the early Christians of standing between two eras (i.e., between fulfilled and unfulfilled eschatology)— all this is a historical interpretation of history. And not only of history, for the whole universe is seen in historical perspective. The covenant symbol is applied not only to the relation between God and the nation but also to the relation between God and nature. The orders of nature are analogous to the order of the moral law. Nature cannot break them, and God will not break them. Man alone can break and has broken the covenant with God. But even then God will not break it; he will carry it through in history. Cosmic beginning and cosmic end are in this way drawn into the historical vision of reality. They are not cosmological necessities in the sense in which the Stoics speak of the burning of the world at the beginning and the end of every period. They are prehistorical but not unhistorical conditions of history. The historical vision of biblical religion makes even the universe historical.

In this cosmic frame the history of salvation occurs. History is the history of salvation in biblical religion. From the prehistorical fall of Adam to the posthistorical reunion of everything in God there is one straight line, starting with Noah and Abraham and ending with the second coming of the Christ. History is neither the expression of man's natural potentialities nor the tragic circle of man's growth and decay; history creates the new. In Christ a new Being has appeared within the world process; history has received a meaning and a center.

Corresponding to the transhistorical-historical beginning of the world process, biblical religion expects its historical-transhistorical end. Biblical religion is eschatological. It thinks in terms of a complete transformation of the structure of the new earth, the renewal of the whole of reality. And this new reality is the goal toward which history runs, and with it the whole universe, in a unique, irreversible movement.

Again we ask: How can this be united with the search for ultimate reality? Is not ontology the attempt to analyze the immovable structures of reality? And is not the concept of being-itself, in which everything that is participates, necessarily unhistorical? Does not the ontological interpretation of reality inescapably exclude the historically new? Does it not, particularly, interpret human sin and divine grace as ontological necessities, thus depriving sin of its character as a free, responsible act of man's personal center, and grace of its character as the free, personal act of the divine mercy? Are sin and grace, if taken into an ontological frame of reference, still sin and grace? And, further, if the new in history is excluded, can one speak of a purpose of the world process? Can one maintain the eschatological world view, the transcendent origin and the transcendent end of everything that is? Does not ontology undercut the meaning of hope in biblical religion?

We have discussed biblical personalism in some of its main doctrinal expressions, but we have omitted one whole side of biblical religion: its understanding of man and his situation. This will be the first task of the next chapter. Yet, if we look at the results of this chapter, it seems that no further chapter is possible. The confrontations of biblical religion and its personalism with the impersonalism of ontology seem to rule out any attempt at a synthesis. It will be the task of a part of the following chapter and of the last to show that this is not so and that each side needs the other for its own realization. But this relation is by no means to be found on the surface. It is necessary to penetrate deeply into both the nature of biblical religion and the nature of ontology in order to discover their profound interdependence.

1. Biblical Personalism and Man's Ethical Existence

The confrontations of biblical religion and ontology, in our second chapter, were restricted to the objective side of religion, to the doctrinal contents of biblical faith, and to the conceptual forms of ontological thought. We have not yet touched on the situation of man in the state of faith and, correspondingly, on the situation of man in the state of asking for ultimate reality. It is now necessary to analyze the subjective side of biblical religion and to confront it with the subjective side of the ontological task. This confrontation, however, will bring us to the point where the positive relation between biblical religion and ontology comes to light for the first time. It will be the turning point from the preliminary confrontation to a strong and final one. The latter will be worked out in opposite order, starting with the subjective side of biblical religion and returning in the last chapter to the objective side, until we have reached that with which we have begun, the idea of God in its relation to the ultimate reality for which ontology asks.

Man's existence in relation to God, in view of biblical religion, is, above all, ethical existence. In the first chapters of Genesis this is abundantly expressed and with tremendous emphasis. Man is put into paradise with a commandment and a prohibition. He experiences temptation and decides against the commandment; he loses his innocence and the unity with nature and other men. New temptations arise, and man becomes the killer of his brother. The anxiety of guilt drives him from place to place. Moral depravity spreads and brings the flood over mankind. The covenant between God and the elected nation has as its "Magna Carta" the Mosaic law, including the Decalogue. The prophetic wrath turns against those who use the covenant for injustice, and the whole history of Israel is determined by the problem of obedience and disobedience of leaders and people alike. John the Baptist makes the kinship with Abraham dependent on the fulfilment of the law. Jesus reinterprets the law, shows its radical implications, and sums it up in the commandment of love. All the New Testament books, Paul's epistles as well as that of James, are full of ethical material. The writer of the Johannine literature, in spite of his mystical and ontological tendencies, is especially emphatic about the law of love, the disregard of which destroys the relation to God.

All this is well known; but sometimes we should expose ourselves to the overwhelming weight of ethical material in biblical religion. And, if we do so, we should be aware of the way in which biblical personalism deals with ethics. Man is always put before a decision. He must decide for or against Yahweh, for or against the Christ, for or against the Kingdom of God. Biblical ethics is not a system of virtues and vices, of laws and counsels, of rewards and punishments. All this is not lacking, but it appears within a framework of concrete, personal decisions. Every decision is urgent; it has to be made now. When it has been made, it has far-reaching consequences. It is always an ultimate decision—a decision of infinite weight. It decides man's destiny. It decides the destiny of nations, the selected one as much as the others. Every generation in every nation has to decide for or against righteousness, for or against him who is the God of righteousness. And in every nation, including the selected one, the decision against righteousness means self-destruction. No sacramental activity, even if it is done in God's name, can save the violator of the law of justice from the wrath of God. The ethical decision determines the destiny of the individual: his eternal destiny depends on his decision for or against the Christ. But the decision for or against the Christ is made by people who do not even know his name. What is decisive is only whether they act for or against the law of love, for which the Christ stands. Acting according to it means being received in the unity of fulfilment. Acting against it means being excluded from fulfilment and being cast into the despair of nonbeing. This is biblical ethics. It has little to do with the middle-class ethics of avoiding a few things which are supposed to be wrong and doing a few things which are supposed to be right. Biblical ethics means standing in ultimate decisions for or against God. Biblical ethics makes us persons, because it places us before this decision.

What has the ontological question, even if it were a matter of ultimate concern, to do with the situation of ethical decision in biblical religion? Is not the a-personal character of the ontological principle opposed to the appeal to decide ethically? Is not the cognitive *eros* of the philosopher indifferent to the demands of the God of love? Does not the ultimate principle of ontology disregard the contrast between good and evil? Is not the religious background of ontology mystical participation, whereas biblical religion presupposes the distance of ethical command and ethical obedience? Does not ontology deprive biblical religion of its unconditional ethical passion? Is not Kierkegaard right when he accuses Hegel of sacrificing the ethically deciding person to the aesthetic distance of theoretical intuition?

Does this not mean that the confrontation has reached a point at which a synthesis between ontological thought and biblical religion has proved to be not only impossible but ethically dangerous and objectionable?

2. Biblical Personalism and Man's Social Existence

What has been said about man's ethical existence is confirmed also in man's social existence. God calls families, nations, groups within the nation, the group which transcends all nations, the "assembly of God," the church. And God's purpose in history is to save individuals, not as individuals, but as participants in his kingdom, in the unity of all beings under God. Therefore, the message of the prophets and apostles is given to groups. They are called individually, but their message is destined for the nation to which they belong or for the church of which they are members. They are not strangers in the group to which they give judgment and promise. They live and think and talk within the experiences and traditions of their people. They use their symbols and deal with their problems. This is the reason for the conservative attitude of the Old Testament prophets toward the religion of the past, of Jesus and the apostles toward the Old Testament, and, to anticipate later biblicistic movements, of the Reformers toward the early church. The prophet does not leave the community, though he may be thrown out of it; but he turns one element of the tradition against a distorted tradition in which this element has been forgotten. The prophet does not intend to create a new community, and just for this reason he often does it against his will. The prophet needs solitude, not the loneliness of separation, but the solitude of him who takes the group spiritually with him into his solitude in order to return to it bodily. Biblical religion speaks frequently of the solitude of the "men of God" but seldom of their loneliness and separation from the group which rejects them.

The ontological question is raised in loneliness, even if the lonely thinker participates in the life of the group as an ordinary member. The loneliness of the philosopher was experienced by many of them. It was experienced by Heraclitus, whom it drove into bitterness and arrogance. It was experienced by Socrates, who accepted it and gave an example of the courage which takes such loneliness upon one's self. It was experienced by the Stoics, who in the midst of political activities felt lonely as the bearers of wisdom in a world of fools. It was the experience of Spinoza, whose philosophical loneliness was akin to the loneliness of the mystic. It was the experience of the ancient skeptics who went into the desert never to return. It was the experience of those modern skeptics who hid themselves under many masks from intolerance in periods of dogmatism. It cannot be otherwise, for the first step of the creative philosopher is radical doubt. He questions not only the traditions and symbols of the community to which he belongs but also what is called the "natural world view," the common-sense presuppositions of "everybody." He who seriously asks the question: "Why is there something, why not nothing?" has experienced the shock of nonbeing and has in thought transcended everything given in nature and mankind. He has dissolved (usually without intending to do so) the ties with any community of belief. Again one may ask: Is it not impossible to unite the solitude of the prophet which binds him to the community with the loneliness of the philosopher which separates him from the community? And does not every one of us, whether bound by biblical religion or driven to radical doubt, experience something of the destiny of the prophet and the philosopher within himself, although perhaps in a less extreme form?

It is this conflict which underlies the present discussion about *eros* and *agape*. Biblical religion demands and gives that kind of love which the New Testament calls *agape*. Philosophy, from Plato on, praises the *eros* which carries the soul in its search for ultimate reality. If *agape* and *eros* exclude each other, the case for a synthesis between biblical religion and ontology is hopeless. *Agape* seeks that which is concrete, individual, unique, here and now. *Agape* seeks the person, the other one who cannot be exchanged for anything or anyone else. He cannot be subsumed under abstractions. He must be accepted in spite of the universals which try to prevent his acceptance, such as moral judgments based on general norms, or social differences justifying indifference or hostility, or psychological characteristics inhibiting a full community with him. *Agape* accepts the concrete in spite of the power of the universal which tries to swallow the concrete. *Eros*—a word which is not used by biblical religion—intuits the universals, the eternal essences (ideas), of which the concrete is only a weak imitation. *Eros* drives beyond the individual things and persons. It uses the concrete as a starting point. But then it transcends it and dissolves it into the universal. The fulfilment of *eros* is the mystical union with the one, in which all concreteness has disappeared. Ontological passion has the character of *eros*. The affirmation of the other one in his concreteness is *agape.* Is a union possible between these two? Does not the search for ultimate reality contradict not only hope and faith but also love? And how can something which denies love be united with biblical religion?

3. Faith and Sin in Biblical Religion

Man's ethical and social existence in the Bible is based on his religious existence. The biblical word for religious existence is "faith." Only in this sense will it be used here and in the following lecture. Faith is the state of being grasped by an ultimate concern. And, since only that which is the ground of our being and meaning should concern us ultimately, we can also say: Faith is the concern about our existence in its ultimate "whence" and "whither." It is a concern of the whole person; it is the most personal concern and that which determines all others. It is not something that can be forced upon us; it is not something which we can produce by the will to believe, but that by which we are grasped. It is, in biblical terminology, the divine Spirit working in our spirit which creates faith. Such a concept of faith has little to do with the popular concepts of faith as the belief in something unbelievable, as the subjection to an authority in which we trust, or as the risk of accepting something as highly probable but not certain. Such concepts, for which the theologians are as much responsible as popular misunderstanding, lie beneath the level on which the confrontation of ontology and biblical religion must take place. It would be good if philosophers and scientists stopped accusing religion of what is the most frequent distortion of religion—the intellectualistic and voluntaristic misconception of faith. However, if the concept of faith is so frequently and so radically distorted, and if even theologians and, one must add, much ordinary preaching and teaching of the church are responsible for it, is there not an element in the biblical concept of faith which drives almost irresistibly to its misconception? And is not the personalistic character of the biblical concept of faith precisely the cause of this situation? And, finally, is it not just this situation which definitely prevents a synthesis between biblical faith and autonomous reason?

Faith, in the biblical view, is an act of the whole personality. Will, knowledge, and emotion participate in it. It is an act of self-surrender, of obedience, of assent. Each of these elements must be present. Emotional surrender without assent and obedience would by-pass the personal center. It would be a compulsion and not a decision. Intellectual assent without emotional participation distorts religious existence into a nonpersonal, cognitive act. Obedience of the will without assent and emotion leads into a depersonalizing slavery. Faith unites and transcends the special functions of the human mind; it is the most personal act of the person. But each function of the human mind is inclined to a kind of imperialism. It tries to become independent and to control the others. Even biblical religion is not without symptoms of these trends. Faith sometimes approaches the point of emotional ecstasy, sometimes the point of mere moral obedience, sometimes the point of cognitive subjection to an authority.

Biblical faith is the faith of a community, a nation, or a church. He who participates in this faith participates in its symbolic and ritual expressions. The community unavoidably formulates its own foundations in statements which reveal its difference from other groups and protect it against distortions. He who joins the community of faith must accept the statements of faith, the creed of the community. He must assent before he can be received. This assent may be the expression of a genuine personal surrender, but it can become a merely intellectual assent and support the tendency to reduce faith to a cognitive act. At the same time the term "faith" may change its meaning. Instead of designating the state of being grasped by an unconditional concern, it may designate a set of doctrines, as it does in phrases like the "Christian faith," the "faith of the church," the "preservation of our faith," or, in classical terms, *fides quae creditur* ("the faith which is believed"). Biblical religion is not without tendencies in this direction. It could not be otherwise, because it was the religion of a community, the early church.

But, if this is the case, how can there be a synthesis with the radical doubt and the radical search for truth which characterize ontology? Is not the destruction of faith, the withdrawal from the believing assent to anything whatsoever, the condition of an honest philosophizing? And is ontology not developed in the power of human reason, in an attitude of criticism and detachment, which is just the opposite of acceptance and personal surrender? Does not ontology request an attitude of depersonalized objectivity, which contradicts biblical personalism in this as in all other respects? And, if ontology replaces faith, does it not replace the whole biblical religion? One central concept of biblical religion, sin, has been only briefly mentioned. It is a religious concept designating the opposite of faith. The essence of sin is disbelief, the state of estrangement from God, the flight from him, the rebellion against him, the elevation of preliminary concerns to the rank of ultimate concern. Man is bound to sin in all parts of his being, because he is estranged from God in his personal center. Neither his emotion, his will, nor his intellect is excepted from sin and, consequently, from the perversion of their true nature. His intellectual power is as distorted and weakened as his moral power. Neither of them is able to produce reunion with· God. According to biblical religion, intellectual endeavor can as little attain the ultimate truth as moral endeavor can attain the ultimate good. He who attempts it deepens the estrangement. This was the message of Paul, Augustine, and Luther. Only he who in the state of faith participates in the good and the true can act according to the norms of truth. Participation precedes action and thought, for participation gives a new being in which sin, or estrangement, is conquered. And participation in that which is of ultimate concern is faith. This means that the faith which conquers sin, by receiving reconciliation and a new being, must precede the search for ultimate reality, for the truth itself. Only in the new state of things can being itself be reached.

Ontology uses man's rational power. It does not ask the question of sin and salvation. It does not distinguish between original and distorted reason, nor does it envisage a renewed reason. It starts where it is and goes ahead toward being-itself. The Bible often criticizes philosophy, not because it uses reason, but because it uses unregenerated reason for the knowledge of God. But only the Spirit of God knows God and gives knowledge of God to those who are grasped by him, who are in the state of faith. As in the beginning, so we must ask at the end of this confrontation: Is there any way to unite the opposite ways of ontology and biblical religion? The answer seems to be that the conflict is insoluble. Point after point (first in the objective and then in the subjective side of biblical religion) showed a seeming incompatibility with the ontological attempt. Many people never go beyond this confrontation and draw the consequences in the one or the other direction. It is understandable that some reject biblical religion completely because they are called in the depth of their being, in their intellectual and moral conscience, to ask the radical question—the question of being and nonbeing. They become heretics or pagans rather than bow to a religion which prohibits the ontological question. It is equally understandable that many faithful Christians shy away from the dangers of the ontological question which makes doubtful that which is most sacred and of infinite significance for them. Neither of these ways is acceptable to some of us, and I believe that neither of them is a service to truth and consequently to God. But, if we try a third way, we must be prepared for the reaction of people who doubt that a third way is possible.

Since the breakdown of the great synthesis between Christianity and the modern mind as attempted by Schleiermacher, Hegel, and nineteenth-century liberalism, an attitude of weariness has grasped the minds of people who are unable to accept one or the other alternative. They are too disappointed to try another synthesis after so many have failed. But there is no choice for us. We must try again!

Joseph Addison

ON NATURAL RELIGION

Those who were skillful in anatomy among the ancients concluded from the outward and inward make of a human body that it was the work of a Being transcendently wise and powerful. As the world grew more enlightened in this art, their discoveries gave them fresh opportunities of admiring the conduct of Providence in the formation of an human body. Galen was converted by his dissections, and could not but own a Supreme Being upon a survey of this his handiwork. There were, indeed, many parts of which the old anatomists did not know the certain use, but as they saw that most of those which they examined were adapted with admirable art to their several functions, they did not question but those whose uses they could not determine were contrived with the same wisdom for respective ends and purposes. Since the circulation of the blood has been found out and many other great discoveries have been made by our modern anatomists, we see new wonders in the human frame and discern several important uses for those parts, which uses the ancients knew nothing of. In short, the body of man is such a subject as stands the utmost test of examination. Though it appears formed with the nicest wisdom upon the most superficial survey of it, it still mends upon the search, and produces our surprise and amazement in proportion as we pry into it. What I have here said of an human body may be applied to the body of every animal which has been the subject of anatomical observations.

The body of an animal is an object adequate to our senses. It is a particular system of Providence, that lies in a narrow compass. The eye is able to command it, and by successive inquiries can search into all its parts. Could

From The *Spectator* (1711–12).

the body of the whole earth, or indeed the whole universe, be thus submitted to the examination of our senses, were it not too big and disproportioned for our inquiries, too unwieldly for the management of the eye and hand, there is no question but it would appear to us as curious and well-contrived a frame as that of an human body. We should see the same concatenation and sub-serviency, the same necessity and usefulness, the same beauty and harmony, in all and every of its parts as what we discover in the body of every single animal.

The more extended our reason is, and the more able to grapple with immense objects, the greater still are those discoveries which it makes of wisdom and providence in the work of the creation. A Sir Isaac Newton, who stands up as the miracle of the present age, can look through a whole planetary system, consider it in its weight, number, and measure, and draw from it as many demonstrations of infinite power and wisdom as a more confined understanding is able to deduce from the system of an human body.

But to return to our speculations on anatomy, I shall here consider the fabric and texture of the bodies of animals in one particular view, which, in my opinion, shows the hand of a thinking and all-wise Being in their formation, with the evidence of a thousand demonstrations. I think we may lay this down as an incontested principle, that chance never acts in a perpetual uniformity and consistence with itself. If one should always fling the same number with ten thousand dice, or see every throw just five times less, or five times more, in number than the throw which immediately preceded it, who would not imagine there is some invisible power which directs the cast? This is the proceeding which we find in the operations of nature. Every kind of animal is diversified by different magnitudes, each of which gives rise to a different species. Let a man trace the dog or lion kind, and he will observe how many of the works of nature are published, if I may use the expression, in a variety of editions. If we look into the reptile world, or into those different kind of animals that fill the element of water, we meet with the same repetitions among several species, that differ very little from one another but in size and bulk. You find the same creature that is drawn at large, copied out in several proportions, and ending in miniature. It would be tedious to produce instances of this regular conduct in Providence, as it would be superfluous to those who are versed in the natural history of animals. The magnificent harmony of the universe is such that we may observe innumerable divisions running upon the same ground. I might also extend this speculation to the dead parts of nature, in which we may find matter disposed into many similar systems, as well in our survey of stars and planets as of stones, vegetables, and other sublunary parts of the creation. In a word, Providence has shown the richness of its goodness and wisdom not only in the production of many original species but in the multiplicity of descants which it has made on every original species in particular.

But to pursue this thought still farther. Every living creature, considered in itself, has many very complicated parts that are exact copies of some other parts which it possesses and which are complicated in the same manner. One eye would have been sufficient for the subsistence and preservation of an animal; but, in order to better his condition, we see another placed with a mathematical exactness in the same most advantageous situation, and in every particular of the same size and texture. Is it possible for chance to be thus delicate and uniform in her operations? Should a million of dice turn up twice together the same number, the wonder would be nothing in comparison with this. But when we see this similitude and resemblance in the arm, the hand, and fingers; when we see one half of the body entirely correspond with the other in all those minute strokes without which a man might have very well subsisted; nay, when we often see a single part repeated an hundred times in the same body, notwithstanding it consists of the most intricate weaving of numberless fibers, and these parts differing still in magnitude as the convenience of their particular situation requires, sure a man must have a strange cast of understanding who does not discover the finger of God in so wonderful a work. These duplicates in those parts of the body, without which a man might have very well subsisted, though not so well as with them, are a plain demonstration of an all-wise Contriver; as those more numerous copyings which are found among the vessels of the same body are evident demonstrations that they could not be the work of chance. This argument receives additional strength if we apply it to every animal and insect within our knowledge, as well as to those numberless living creatures that are objects too minute for an human eye, and if we consider how the several species in this whole world of life resemble one another in very many particulars, so far as is convenient for their respective states of existence. It is much more probable that an hundred million of dice should be casually thrown an hundred million of times in the same number than that the body of any single animal should be produced by the fortuitous concourse of matter. And that the like chance should arise in innumerable instances, requires a degree of credulity that is not under the direction of common sense. We may carry this consideration yet further if we reflect on the two sexes in every living species, with their resemblances to each other and those particular distinctions that were necessary for the keeping up of this great world of life.

There are many more demonstrations of a Supreme Being and of his transcendent wisdom, power, and goodness in the formation of the body of a living creature, for which I refer my reader to other writings, particularly to the sixth book of the poem entitled *Creation,* where the anatomy of the human body is described with great perspicuity and elegance. I have been particular on the thought which runs through this speculation because I have not seen it enlarged upon by others.

Walter Kaufmann

THE FAITH OF A HERETIC

WHEN I WAS ELEVEN, I ASKED MY FATHER: "WHAT REALLY IS THE HOLY Ghost?" The articles of faith taught us in school—in Berlin, Germany—affirmed belief in God, Christ, and the Holy Ghost, and I explained to my father: "I don't believe that Jesus was God, and if I can't believe in the Holy Ghost either, then I am really not a Christian."

At twelve, I formally left the Protestant church to become a Jew. Having never heard of Unitarianism, I assumed that the religion for people who believed in God, but not in Christ or the Holy Ghost, was Judaism.

A few months after my conversation with my father, but before I left the church, Hitler came to power. Warned of the persecution that my decision might entail, I replied that one certainly could not change one's mind for a reason like that. I did not realize until a little later that all four of my grandparents had been Jewish; and none of us knew that this, and not one's own religion, would be decisive from the Nazis' point of view. My decision had been made independently of my descent and of Nazism, on religious grounds.

I took my new religion very seriously, explored it with enormous curiosity and growing love, and gradually became more and more orthodox. When I arrived in the United States in January 1939, I was planning to become a rabbi. A lot of things happened to me that winter, spring, and summer; and when the war broke out I had what, but for its contents, few

Used by permission of the author. This article first appeared in *Harper's Magazine.*

would hesitate to call a mystical experience. In the most intense despair I suddenly saw that I had deceived myself for years: I had believed. At last the God of tradition joined the Holy Ghost and Christ.

Of course, I could maintain my old beliefs by merely giving them a new interpretation; but that struck me as dishonest. Ikhnaton, the monotheistic Pharaoh—as I explained in a letter to my family who were by now in England—could also have reinterpreted the traditional polytheism of Egypt, but was a fanatic for the truth. He taught his court sculptor to make life masks of people to see how they really looked, and in one of the heads which the sculptor had then done of Ikhnaton, his hunger for the truth had become stone. I had loved that head for years. Should I now do what I admired him for not doing?

You may say that Ikhnaton was wrong and that it is the essence of religion to pour new wine into old skins, reading one's current insights into ancient beliefs. But if you do this, disregarding Jesus' counsel not to do it, you should realize that you could do it with almost any religion. And it is less than honest to give one's own religion the benefit of every possible doubt while imposing unsympathetic readings on other religions. Yet this is what practically all religious people do. Witness the attitude of Protestants and Catholics toward each other.

In my remaining two years in college I took all the religion courses offered, while majoring in philosophy; and I continued to study and think about both subjects as a graduate student and in the army. Eventually I got my Ph.D. and a job teaching philosophy. For over ten years now I have taught, among other things, philosophy of religion.* In the process, my ideas developed—into a book: *Critique of Religion and Philosophy.*†

---

* Lest this should create a misleading picture of Princeton, it should be added that in our popular Department of Religion Protestantism is championed vigorously by five full professors and a large staff, and ordained ministers are encountered in other departments, too. Until his recent retirement, Jacques Maritain was a member of the Philosophy Department. Great universities, like this magazine, assume that there is a virtue in confronting students and readers with a variety of responsible approaches.

† Harper & Brothers, 1958. [Anchor Books, 1961] Many ideas in this article are more fully developed and backed up in this book which also deals with the positive aspects of various religions and with many topics not even touched on in this article; *e.g.*, existentialism, Freud, mysticism, Bible criticism, the relation of religion to poetry, and Zen. Among the questions that are barely touched in this essay and treated more fully in my book is the inadequacy of such labels as theism and atheism. The contents of the present article, incidentally—which is in no sense a summary of my *Critique*—may greatly surprise many of my students, past and present.

The ideas were not all there as a result of the few experiences alluded to here: there were hundreds of others. Profound experiences stimulate thoughts; but such thoughts do not look very adequate on paper. Writing can be a way of rethinking again and again.

In the process of teaching and writing one must constantly consider the thoughts of men with different ideas. And prolonged and ever-new exposure to a wide variety of outlooks—together with the criticism many professors seek from both their students and their colleagues—is a more profound experience than most people realize. It is a long-drawn-out trial by fire, marked by frequent disillusionment, discoveries, and despair, and by a growing regard for honesty, which is surely one of the most difficult of all the virtues to attain. What one comes up with in the end owes quite as much to this continual encounter as it does to any other experience.

A liberal education, and quite especially a training in philosophy, represents an attempt to introduce young people to this adventure. We have no wish to indoctrinate; we want to teach our students to resist indoctrination and not accept as authoritative the beliefs of other men or even the ideas that come to us as in a flash of illumination. Even if one has experiences that some men would call mystical—and I have no doubt that I have had many—it is a matter of integrity to question such experiences and any thoughts that were associated with them as closely and as honestly as we should question the "revelations" of others. To be sure, it is easier to grant others their "revelations" as "true for them" while insisting on one's own as "true for oneself." Such intellectual sluggishness parades as sophistication. But true tolerance does not consist in saying, "You may be right, but let us not make hard demands on ourselves: if you will put your critical intelligence to sleep, I'll put mine to bed, too." True tolerance remains mindful of the humanity of those who make things easy for themselves and welcomes and even loves honest and thoughtful opposition above less thoughtful agreement.

The autobiographical sketch with which I have begun may do more harm than good. Some amateur psychologists may try to explain "everything" in terms of one or two experiences; some Protestants may say, "If only he had come to *me* about the Holy Ghost!" while some Catholics may feel that it all shows once again how Protestantism is merely a way-station on the road to Hell.

This is the kind of gambit that the shut-ins pull on travelers. As if I had buried the Holy Ghost beyond recall when I was eleven, and God when I was eighteen! I merely started relatively early to concern myself with such questions—and have never stopped since. Let the shut-in explore Judaism and Protestantism, Catholicism and Buddhism, atheism and agnosticism, mysticism, existentialism, and psychology, Thomas and Tillich. Let him consult the lot and not just his own present prejudice; let him subject his thoughts about religion to the candid scrutiny of those who differ with him and to his own ever-new re-examination; let him have a host of deep experiences, religious and otherwise, and think about them. That is the ground on which a genuine conversation can take place: it need not make a show of erudition, if only it has grown out of a series of open-hearted encounters. But as long as one is content to gloat over the silver lining of one's own religion, one bars any serious conversation and merely makes the first move in a game of skill.

To an even moderately sophisticated and well-read person it should come as no surprise that any religion at all has its hidden as well as its obvious beauties and is capable of profound and impressive interpretations. What is deeply objectionable about most of these interpretations is that they allow the believer to say Yes while evading any No. The Hebrew prophets represent a notable exception. When interpreting their own religious heritage, they were emphatically not conformists who discovered subtle ways in which they could agree with the religion of their day. Nor was it their point that the cult was justifiable with just a little ingenuity. On the contrary.

Let those who like inspiring interpretations be no less forthright in telling us precisely where they stand on ritual and immortality, on the sacraments and Hell, on the Virgin Birth and Resurrection, on the Incarnation and the miracles, and on: "Resist not evil." And: "Let him who would sue you in court for your coat have your cloak, too." And: "No one comes to the Father but through Me."

If you must pour new wine into old skins, you should at least follow one of Jesus' other counsels and let your Yes be Yes, and your No, No.

When considering Christianity, it is easy to get lost in the changing fashions of thought that have been read into it or reconciled with it—from Neoplatonism (Augustine) and Aristotelianism (Aquinas) to romanticism (Schleiermacher), liberalism (Harnack), and existentialism (Tillich, Bultmann, and others). There is no room here to cross swords with a dozen apologists; in any case, dozens more would remain.

The central question about Christianity concerns Jesus Christ. If he was God in a sense in which no other man has been God, then Christianity is right in some important sense, however Christendom may have failed. To decide whether Jesus was God in some such unique sense, a philosopher cannot forbear to ask just what this claim might mean. If, for example, it does not mean that Jesus of Nazareth knew everything and was all-powerful, it is perplexing what is meant. But a large part of what most Christians mean is surely that Jesus was the best and wisest man of all time; and many Protestants mean no more than that.

Millions of Christians agree on this claim and back it up by citing Gospel passages they like; but different people pick different passages. To some, Jesus looks like St. Francis, to others like John Calvin, and to many more the way a man named Hofmann painted him. Pierre van Paassen's Jesus is a Socialist and Fosdick's a liberal, while according to Reinhold Niebuhr Jesus' ethic coincides, not surprisingly, with Niebuhr's. To use a political term: almost everybody gerrymanders, carving an idealized self-portrait from the Gospels and much less attractive straw men from the literatures of other faiths. A great deal of theology is like a jigsaw puzzle: the verses of Scripture are the pieces, and the finished picture is prescribed by each denomination, with a certain latitude allowed. What makes the game so pointless is that not all pieces have to be used, and any piece that does not fit may be reshaped, provided one says first, "this means." That is called exegesis.

In *The Literature of the Christian Movement,* Morton Scott Enslin, one of the outstanding New Testament scholars of our time, remarks that the Jesus of the Fourth Gospel is really not very attractive, and that if it were not for the other three Gospels and the fact that most readers create for themselves "a conflate," the Jesus of St. John would lose most of his charm. Surely, the same consideration applies to all four Gospels.

Those who consider Jesus the best and wisest of men should reread the Gospels and ponder at the very least these five points.

First: Are they prepared to maintain their claim regarding the Jesus of any one of the four Gospels—and, if so, which? Or is it their point that the evidence warrants the assumption that the historical Jesus, however inadequately understood by the Evangelists, was a wiser and better man than Socrates and Jeremiah, Isaiah and the Buddha, Lao-tze and Hillel?

Secondly: Although Jesus is widely considered mankind's greatest moral teacher, the greatest Christians, not to speak of scholars, have never been able to agree what his moral teachings were. Matthew, and he alone, reports that Jesus said: "Let your Yes be Yes, and your No, No." But the four Evangelists agree in ascribing to Jesus evasive and equivocal answers to plain questions, not only those of the high priest and Pilate; and quite generally the Jesus of the New Testament avoids straightforward statements, preferring parables and hyperboles. Some of the parables are so ambiguous that different Evangelists, not to speak of later theologians, offer different interpretations. Nor have Christians ever been able to agree on the import of the hyperboles of the Sermon on the Mount. Luther, for example, taught that Christ's commandments were intended to teach man his utter incapacity for doing good: man must throw himself on the mercy of God, believing that Christ died for our sins. On concrete moral issues, Jesus can be, and has been, cited on almost all sides. The Buddha and the Hebrew prophets were not so equivocal.

Third: One of the few things about Jesus' moral teachings that seems fairly clear is that he was not greatly concerned about social justice. This makes his ethic much less impressive than the prophets'.

Fourth: Albert Schweitzer has argued in considerable detail that this lack of concern was due to the fact that Jesus predicated his entire message on a false belief: namely, that the world was about to come to an end. If Schweitzer is right, as I think he is, Jesus was surely not the wisest of men. And can we call him the greatest moralist unless we accept his radical depreciation of *this* life and his belief in Heaven and Hell?

Finally, the Jesus of the New Testament believed, and was not greatly bothered by his belief, that God would damn and torment the mass of mankind in all eternity. According to all three Synoptic Gospels, he actually reassured his disciples:

"If any one will not receive you or listen to your words, shake off the dust from your feet as you leave that house or town. Truly, I say to you, it shall be more tolerable on the day of judgment for the land of Sodom and Gomorrha than for that town."

This is no isolated dictum; the Sermon on the Mount, for example, is also punctuated by threats of Hell.

Augustine, Aquinas, and Calvin stressed Hell, but many Christian apologists today simply ignore all such passages. A few insist that in a couple of inter-testamentary apocalypses we find far more detailed visions of Hell. They do not mention that these apocalypses would not be known today if it had not been for the esteem in which the early Christians held them. For the Jews rejected them while accepting the humane teachings of men like Hillel and Akiba. Rabbi Akiba, a contemporary of Paul and the Evangelists, taught that "only those who possess no good deeds at all will descend into the netherworld"; also that "the punishment of the wicked in Gehinnom lasts twelve months."

Of course, Jesus also stressed love, citing—or agreeing with a Pharisee who cited—Moses. But this as well as the fact that he said some lovely things and told some fine parables is hardly sufficient to establish the Christian claims about him: that much he has in common with Moses, Micah, and Hosea, with the Buddha, Confucius, and Lao-tze, to name a mere half-dozen teachers who preceded him by a few centuries.

It might be countered that the story of Jesus is the best possible symbol of love. But is it? Consider the story the way it looks to people not committed to, and prejudiced in favor of, Christianity: God caused a virgin, betrothed to Joseph, to conceive His Own Son, and this Son had to be betrayed, crucified, and resurrected in order that all those—and only those—might be saved who should both believe this story and be baptized and eat and drink on regular occasions what they themselves believe to be the flesh and blood of this Son (or, in some denominations, merely the symbols of His flesh and blood); meanwhile, the rest of mankind suffer eternal torment, and according to many Christian creeds and teachers, they were predestined for damnation by God Himself from the beginning.

One might choose to be a Christian in spite of all this if one could intensely admire the great Christians who came after Jesus. But Peter and Paul, Athanasius and Augustine, Luther and Calvin, seem far less admirable to me, for all their admitted virtues, than Hosea and Micah, Isaiah and Jeremiah, Hillel and Akiba; or the Buddha, Socrates, and Spinoza. Maimonides, unlike Aquinas whom he influenced, did not believe in eternal damnation or that heretics should be executed. Some recent Protestant writers have been wonderfully forthright about Luther's and Calvin's shortcomings; but for candid portraits of the saints one must on the whole turn to non-Catholic writers—with at least one notable exception. In 1950, Malcolm Hay, a Catholic, published one of the most moving books of our time, *The Foot of Pride*, which is admirably frank about some of the most celebrated saints.

In an essay published in Germany in 1939—or rather in a book seized barely before publication by the Gestapo and destroyed except for about half-a-dozen copies—Leo Baeck, probably the greatest rabbi of our time, said something profoundly relevant:

A good deal of church history is the history of all the things which neither hurt nor encroach upon this piety, all the outrages and all the baseness which this piety was able to tolerate with an assured and undisturbed soul and an untroubled faith. And a spirit is characterized not only by what it does but, no less, by what it permits. . . . The Christian religion, very much including Protestantism, has been able to maintain silence about so much that it is difficult to say what has been more pernicious in the course of time: the intolerance which committed the wrongs or the indifference which beheld them unperturbed.*

This thought may diminish even one's affection for St. Francis, but not one's admiration for the prophets.

The world's other religions remain. If we apply the same criteria, only two issue a real challenge to us, or at least to me: Judaism and Buddhism. I admire Genesis and Job, the Book of Jonah and the Dhammapada far above any book in the New Testament. But popular Buddhism with its profuse idolatry, its relics, and its superstitions repels me, and I have reservations even about the teachings of the Buddha. I admire much of his profound analysis of man's condition: the world has no purpose; it is up to us to give our lives a purpose; and we cannot rely on any supernatural assistance. Life is full of suffering, suffering is rooted in desire and attachment, and much desire and attachment are rooted in ignorance. By knowledge, especially of the Buddha's teachings, it is possible to develop a pervasive detachment, not incompatible with a mild, comprehensive compassion—and to cease to suffer. But consider the Old Testament and Sophocles, Michelangelo and Rembrandt, Shakespeare and Goethe: the price for the avoidance of all suffering is too high. Suffering and sacrifice can be experienced as worthwhile; one may find beauty in them and greatness through them.

Much of the appeal of Christianity is due to the fact that it contains at least intimations—but really no more than that—of this tragic ethos. But the story of Christ remains uncomfortably similar to the saga of the boss's son who works very briefly in the shop, where he makes a great point of his home and is cruelly beaten by some of his fellow workers, before he joins his father as co-chairman of the board and wreaks horrible revenge. This "happy" end makes most of the Christian martyrs, too, untragic figures. These observations may strike believers as blasphemous, but they might do well to reflect on the manner in which they pass judgment on other religions, and there may be some point in considering how one's own religion must strike those who don't accept it.

Probably the only great religion in which genuine self-sacrifice and

---

* The essay, "Romantic Religion," is included in Baeck's *Judaism and Christianity*, translated with an introductory essay, by Walter Kaufmann, Jewish Publication Society, 1958.

tragedy have occupied a central place is Judaism, especially prior to the introduction of belief in any after life. Moses is the very incarnation of humane devotion, wearing himself out in the service of God and men, expecting, and receiving, no reward whatever, but finding his reward in his work. He asks God to destroy him rather than his people and intercedes for them again and again. In the prophets, from Hosea to the songs of the suffering servant, we find the same outlook.

Why, then, do I not accept Judaism? In view of all the things I do not believe, I have no wish to observe the six-hundred-odd commandments and prohibitions that define the traditional Jewish way of life, or to participate in religious services. With most so-called orthodox Jews I have much less in common than with all kinds of other people, Jews and Gentiles. Reform Judaism seems to me to involve compromise, conformism, and the wish to be innocuous. To that extent, it, too, stands opposed to the ethos of the prophets. And if a succession of great Jews should equal the boldness of the prophets, who repudiated the ritual of their day, and go a step further by also renouncing, and denouncing, all kinds of belief—would not this amount to giving up religion?

What remains if you give up the great religions? Many people think: only Communism, Nazism, and immorality. But the morality of Socrates, Spinoza, and Hume compares favorably with Augustine's, Luther's, and Calvin's. And the evil deeds of Communism and Nazism are not due to their lack of belief but to their false beliefs, even as the evil deeds of the Crusaders, Inquisitors, and witch hunters, and Luther's exhortation to burn synagogues and Calvin's decision to burn Servetus, were due to *their* false beliefs. Christianity, like Islam, has caused more wars than it has prevented; and the Middle Ages, when Europe was Christian, were not a period of peace and good will among men. Does it make sense that those who refuse to let their Yes be Yes and their No, No—those who refuse to reject false beliefs, those who would rather stretch them and equivocate—should have a monopoly on being moral?

Renouncing false beliefs will not usher in the millennium. Few things about the strategy of contemporary apologists are more repellent than their frequent recourse to spurious alternatives. The lesser lights inform us that the alternative to Christianity is materialism, thus showing how little they have read, while the greater lights talk as if the alternative were bound to be a shallow and inane optimism. I don't believe that man will turn this earth into a bed of roses either with the aid of God or without it. Nor does life among the roses strike me as a dream from which one would not care to wake up after a very short time.

Some evils and some kinds of suffering can be abolished, but not all suffering can be eliminated; and the beauty, goodness, and greatness that redeem life on earth are inseparable from suffering. Nietzsche once said: "If you have an enemy, do not requite him evil with good, for that would put him to shame. Rather prove that he did you some good." If life hurts you, the manly thing is neither to whine nor to feel martyred, but to prove that it did you some good.

No one way is the best way of life for all. To me the *Apology* of Socrates, as immortalized by Plato in less than thirty pages, presents a challenge from which I cannot, and have no wish to, get away. Here is part of Socrates' answer to the charges of impiety and corruption of the Athenian youth, on which he was convicted and put to death:

I am better off than he is—for he knows nothing but thinks he knows, while I neither know nor think I know. . . . If you say to me, . . . you shall be let off, but upon one condition, that you are not to inquire . . . in this way any more, and that if you are caught doing so again you shall die—if this was the condition on which you let me go, I should reply: . . . while I have life and strength I shall never cease from the practice and teaching of philosophy, exhorting anyone whom I meet. . . . Are you not ashamed of heaping up the greatest amount of money and honor and reputation, and caring so little about wisdom and truth? . . . The unexamined life is not worth living. . . . If you suppose that there is no consciousness, but a sleep like the sleep of him that is undisturbed even by dreams, death will be an unspeakable gain. . . . Eternity is then only a single night.

It would be folly to wish to foist this outlook on everybody. Professors of philosophy discourage and fail a large percentage even of their graduate students and are assuredly not eager to turn all men into philosophers. In philosophy, as in religion, teaching usually involves a loss of dimension; and the Socratic fusion of philosophy and life, critical acumen and passion, laughter and tragic stature is almost unique.

One need not believe in Pallas Athena, the virgin goddess, to be overwhelmed by the Parthenon. Similarly, a man who rejects all dogmas, all theologies, and all religious formulations of beliefs may still find Genesis the sublime book *par excellence*. Experiences and aspirations of which intimations may be found in Plato, Nietzsche, and Spinoza have found their most evocative expression in some sacred books. Since the Renaissance, Shakespeare, Rembrandt, Mozart, and a host of others have shown that this religious dimension can be experienced and communicated apart from any religious context. But that is no reason for closing my heart to Job's cry, or to Jeremiah's, or to the Second Isaiah. I do not read them as mere literature; rather, I read Sophocles and Shakespeare with all my being, too.

Moreover, I am so far quite unable to justify one of my central convictions: that, even if it were possible to make all men happy by an operation or a drug that would stultify their development, this would somehow be an impious crime. This conviction is ultimately rooted in the Mosaic challenge: "You shall be holy; for I the Lord your God am holy."

To communicate to others some feeling for man's religious quest, to arouse an aspiration in them which nothing but death can quell, and to develop their critical powers—that is infinitely more important to me than persuading anybody that Shakespeare was right when he wrote these lines:

> *The cloud-capp'd towers, the gorgeous palaces,*
> *The solemn temples, the great globe itself,*
> *Yea, all which it inherit, shall dissolve;*
> *And, like this insubstantial pageant faded,*
> *Leave not a rack behind. We are such stuff*
> *As dreams are made on, and our little life*
> *Is rounded with a sleep.*

I do not believe in any after life any more than the prophets did, but I don't mind living in a world in which people have different beliefs. Diversity helps to prevent stagnation and smugness; and a teacher should acquaint his students with diversity and prize careful criticism far above agreement. His noblest duty is to lead others to think for themselves.

Oddly, millions believe that lack of belief in God, Christ, and Hell leads to inhumanity and cruelty while those who have these beliefs have a monopoly on charity—and that people like myself will pay for their lack of belief by suffering in all eternity. I do not believe that anybody will suffer after death nor do I wish it.

Some scientists tell us that in our own galaxy alone there are probably hundreds of thousands of planets with living beings on them, more or less like those on the earth, and that there are about 100 million galaxies within the range of our telescopes. Man seems to play a very insignificant part in the universe, and my part is surely negligible. The question confronting me is not, except perhaps in idle moments, what part might be more amusing, but what I wish to make of my part. And what I want to do and would advise others to do is to make the most of it: put into it all you have got, and live and, if possible, die with some measure of nobility.

Bertrand Russell

THE VALUE OF PHILOSOPHY

HAVING NOW COME TO THE END OF OUR BRIEF AND VERY INCOMPLETE review of the problems of philosophy, it will be well to consider, in conclusion, what is the value of philosophy and why it ought to be studied. It is the more necessary to consider this question, in view of the fact that many men, under the influence of science or of practical affairs, are inclined to doubt whether philosophy is anything better than innocent but useless trifling, hair-splitting distinctions, and controversies on matters concerning which knowledge is impossible.

This view of philosophy appears to result, partly from a wrong conception of the ends of life, partly from a wrong conception of the kinds of goods which philosophy strives to achieve. Physical science, through the medium of inventions, is useful to innumerable people who are wholly ignorant of it; thus the study of physical science is to be recommended, not only, or primarily, because of the effect on the student, but rather because of the effect on mankind in general. This utility does not belong to philosophy. If the study of philosophy has any value at all for others than students of philosophy, it must be only indirectly, through its effects upon the lives of those who study it. It is in these effects, therefore, if anywhere, that the value of philosophy must be primarily sought.

But further, if we are not to fail in our endeavour to determine the value of philosophy, we must first free our minds from the prejudices of what are wrongly called "practical" men. The "practical" man, as this word is often used, is one who recognizes only material needs, who realises that men must have food for the body, but is oblivious of the necessity of providing food for the mind. If all men were well off, if poverty and

From *The Problems of Philosophy* by Bertrand Russell. Oxford University Press, 1912. A Galaxy Book. Reprinted by permission.

disease had been reduced to their lowest possible point, there would still remain much to be done to produce a valuable society, and even in the existing world the goods of the mind are at least as important as the goods of the body. It is exclusively among the goods of the mind that the value of philosophy is to be found; and only those who are not indifferent to these goods can be persuaded that the study of philosophy is not a waste of time.

Philosophy, like all other studies, aims primarily at knowledge. The knowledge it aims at is the kind of knowledge which gives unity and system to the body of the sciences, and the kind which results from a critical examination of the grounds of our convictions, prejudices, and beliefs. But it cannot be maintained that philosophy has had any very great measure of success in its attempts to provide definite answers to its questions. If you ask a mathematician, a mineralogist, a historian, or any other man of learning, what definite body of truths has been ascertained by his science, his answer will last as long as you are willing to listen. But if you put the same question to a philosopher, he will, if he is candid, have to confess that his study has not achieved positive results such as have been achieved by other sciences. It is true that this is partly accounted for by the fact that, as soon as definite knowledge concerning any subject becomes possible, this subject ceases to be called philosophy, and becomes a separate science. The whole study of the heavens, which now belongs to astronomy, was once included in philosophy; Newton's great work was called "the mathematical principles of natural philosophy." Similarly, the study of the human mind, which was, until very lately, a part of philosophy, has now been separated from philosophy and has become the science of psychology. Thus, to a great extent, the uncertainty of philosophy is more apparent than real: those questions which are already capable of definite answers are placed in the sciences, while those only to which, at present, no definite answer can be given, remain to form the residue which is called philosophy.

This is, however, only a part of the truth concerning the uncertainty of philosophy. There are many questions—and among them those that are of the profoundest interest to our spiritual life—which, so far as we can see, must remain insoluble to the human intellect unless its powers become of quite a different order from what they are now. Has the universe any unity of plan or purpose, or is it a fortuitous concourse of atoms? Is consciousness a permanent part of the universe, giving hope of indefinite growth in wisdom, or is it a transitory accident on a small planet on which life must ultimately become impossible? Are good and evil of importance to the universe or only to man? Such questions are asked by philosophy, and variously answered by various philosophers. But it would seem that, whether answers be otherwise discoverable or not, the answers suggested by philosophy are none of them demonstrably true. Yet, however slight may be the hope of discovering an answer, it is part of the business of philosophy to continue the consideration of such questions, to make us aware of their importance, to examine all the approaches to them, and to keep alive that speculative interest in the universe which is apt to be killed by confining ourselves to definitely ascertainable knowledge.

Many philosophers, it is true, have held that philosophy could establish the truth of certain answers to such fundamental questions. They have supposed that what is of most importance in religious beliefs could be proved by strict demonstration to be true. In order to judge of such attempts, it is necessary to take a survey of human knowledge, and to form an opinion as to its methods and its limitations. On such a subject it would be unwise to pronounce dogmatically; but if the investigations of our previous chapters have not led us astray, we shall be compelled to renounce the hope of finding philosophical proofs of religious beliefs. We cannot, therefore, include as part of the value of philosophy any definite set of answers to such questions. Hence, once more, the value of philosophy must not depend upon any supposed body of definitely ascertainable knowledge to be acquired by those who study it.

The value of philosophy is, in fact, to be sought largely in its very uncertainty. The man who has no tincture of philosophy goes through life imprisoned in the prejudices derived from common sense, from the habitual beliefs of his age or his nation, and from convictions which have grown up in his mind without the co-operation or consent of his deliberate reason. To such a man the world tends to become definite, finite, obvious; common objects rouse no questions, and unfamiliar possibilities are contemptuously rejected. As soon as we begin to philosophise, on the contrary, we find, as we saw in our opening chapters, that even the most everyday things lead to problems to which only very incomplete answers can be given. Philosophy, though unable to tell us with certainty what is the true answer to the doubts which it raises, is able to suggest many possibilities which enlarge our thoughts and free them from the tyranny of custom. Thus, while diminishing our feeling of certainty as to what things are, it greatly increases our knowledge as to what they may be; it removes the somewhat arrogant dogmatism of those who have never travelled into the region of liberating doubt, and it keeps alive our sense of wonder by showing familiar things in an unfamiliar aspect.

Apart from its utility in showing unsuspected possibilities, philosophy has a value—perhaps its chief value—through the greatness of the objects which it contemplates, and the freedom from narrow and personal aims resulting from this contemplation. The life of the instinctive man is shut up within the circle of his private interests: family and friends may be included, but the outer world is not regarded except as it may help or hinder what comes within the circle of instinctive wishes. In such a life there is something feverish and confined, in comparison with which the philosophic life is calm and free. The private world of instinctive interests is a small one, set in the midst of a great and powerful world which must, sooner or later, lay our private world in ruins. Unless we can so enlarge our interests as to include the whole outer world, we remain like a garrison in a beleaguered fortress, knowing that the enemy prevents escape and that ultimate surrender is inevitable. In such a life there is no peace, but a constant strife between the insistence of desire and the powerlessness of will. In one way or another, if our life is to be great and free, we must escape this prison and this strife.

One way of escape is by philosophic contemplation. Philosophic contemplation does not, in its widest survey, divide the universe into two hostile camps—friends and foes, helpful and hostile, good and bad—it views the whole impartially. Philosophic contemplation, when it is unalloyed, does not aim at proving that the rest of the universe is akin to man. All acquisition of knowledge is an enlargement of the Self, but this enlargement is best attained when it is not directly sought. It is obtained when the desire for knowledge is alone operative, by a study which does not wish in advance that its objects should have this or that character, but adapts the Self to the characters which it finds in its objects. This enlargement of Self is not obtained when, taking the Self as it is, we try to show that the world is so similar to this Self that knowledge of it is possible without any admission of what seems alien. The desire to prove this is a form of self-assertion, and like all self-assertion, it is an obstacle to the growth of Self which it desires, and of which the Self knows that it is capable. Self-assertion, in philosophic speculation as elsewhere, views the world as a means to its own ends; thus it makes the world of less account than Self, and the Self sets bounds to the greatness of its goods. In contemplation, on the contrary, we start from the not-Self, and through its greatness the boundaries of

Self are enlarged; through the infinity of the universe the mind which contemplates it achieves some share in infinity.

For this reason greatness of soul is not fostered by those philosophies which assimilate the universe to Man. Knowledge is a form of union of Self and not-Self; like all union, it is impaired by dominion, and therefore by any attempt to force the universe into conformity with what we find in ourselves. There is a widespread philosophical tendency towards the view which tells us that man is the measure of all things, that truth is man-made, that space and time and the world of universals are properties of the mind, and that, if there be anything not created by the mind, it is unknowable and of no account for us. This view, if our previous discussions were correct, is untrue; but in addition to being untrue, it has the effect of robbing philosophic contemplation of all that gives it value, since it fetters contemplation to Self. What it calls knowledge is not a union with the not-Self, but a set of prejudices, habits, and desires, making an impenetrable veil between us and the world beyond. The man who finds pleasure in such a theory of knowledge is like the man who never leaves the domestic circle for fear his word might not be law.

The true philosophic contemplation, on the contrary, finds its satisfaction in every enlargement of the not-Self, in everything that magnifies the objects contemplated, and thereby the subject contemplating. Everything, in contemplation, that is personal or private, everything that depends upon habit, self-interest, or desire, distorts the object, and hence impairs the union which the intellect seeks. By thus making a barrier between subject and object, such personal and private things become a prison to the intellect. The free intellect will see as God might see, without a *here* and *now*, without hopes and fears, without the trammels of customary beliefs and traditional prejudices, calmly, dispassionately, in the sole and exclusive desire of knowledge—knowledge as impersonal, as purely contemplative, as it is possible for man to attain. Hence also the free intellect will value more the abstract and universal knowledge into which the accidents of private history do not enter, than the knowledge brought by the senses, and dependent, as such knowledge must be, upon an exclusive and personal point of view and a body whose sense-organs distort as much as they reveal.

The mind which has become accustomed to the freedom and impartiality of philosophic contemplation will preserve something of the same freedom and impartiality in the world of action and emotion. It will view its purposes and desires as parts of the whole, with the absence of insistence that results from seeing them as infinitesimal fragments in a world of which all the rest is unaffected by any one man's deeds. The impartiality which, in contemplation, is the unalloyed desire for truth, is the very same quality of mind which, in action, is justice, and in emotion is that universal love which can be given to all, and not only to those who are judged useful or admirable. Thus contemplation enlarges not only the objects of our thoughts, but also the objects of our actions and our affections: it makes us citizens of the universe, not only of one walled city at war with all the rest. In this citizenship of the universe consists man's true freedom, and his liberation from the thraldom of narrow hopes and fears.

Thus, to sum up our discussion of the value of philosophy: Philosophy is to be studied, not for the sake of any definite answers to its questions, since no definite answers can, as a rule, be known to be true, but rather for the sake of the questions themselves; because these questions enlarge our conception of what is possible, enrich our intellectual imagination, and diminish the dogmatic assurance which closes the mind against speculation; but above all because, through the greatness of the universe which philosophy contemplates, the mind is rendered great, and becomes capable of that union with the universe which constitutes its highest good.

Joseph Addison (1672–1719) was one of the leading prose writers of the Augustan period of English literature. His Neo-Classical tragedy *Cato* and his familiar periodical essays in The Tatler and The Spectator, written in collaboration with Sir Richard Steele, are eighteenth-century trademarks.

Francis Bacon (1561–1626) is an outstanding example of the Renaissance thinker and writer. He is most famous for his political machinations and for his philosophical writings in *The Advancement of Learning* (1605) and the *Novum Organum* (1620).

James Baldwin (1924–   ) is one of the best and most famous contemporary Negro writers. He has recorded his opinions in the collections of essays, *Notes of a Native Son,* and *Nobody Knows My Name.* His novels include *Go Tell It on the Mountain* and *Giovanni's Room.*

Jacques Barzun (1903–   ), born in France, is now a naturalized American, a famous author and educator, and the Provost of Columbia University. His literate and candid views of American life and thought appear in *The Teacher in America, God's Country and Mine,* and *The House of Intellect.*

Robert Benchley (1889–1945), one of the most delightful and clever of American writers, published dramatic and literary columns in newspapers, edited magazines, and acted in motion pictures. His humorous collections include *Inside Benchley* and *Benchley Beside Himself.*

Eric Berne (1910–   ), whose best known book is *The Mind in Action,* is a psychiatrist who has studied and lectured at Yale University, practiced at Mount Sinai Hospital in New York City, and carried on private research and practice.

Lewis Carroll (1832–1898) is the pen name of the Reverend Charles Lutwidge Dodgson, author of *Alice in Wonderland, Alice Through the Looking Glass,* and *The Hunting of the Snark.* In addition to these children's classics, he wrote various mathematical treatises; he lectured in mathematics at Oxford University from 1855 to 1881.

Stanley Casson (1889–1944), the noted British archaeologist who carried out excavations in Athens, Constantinople, and the Near East, was a Reader at

571

Oxford and the author of *Macedonia, Thrace and Illyria* (1926), *Progress of Archeology* (1934), and *The Discovery of Man* (1939).

Stuart Chase (1888–   ), is a well-known semanticist, social commentator, and writer of non-fictional prose. His works include *Men at Work* (1945), *The Proper Study of Mankind* (1948), *Democracy under Pressure* (1945), and *For This We Fought* (1946).

Philip Dormer Stanhope, the **Fourth Earl of Chesterfield** (1694–1773), bore a name synonymous with aristocratic elegance during his lifetime. A diplomat, patron of the arts, and a highly self-conscious gentleman, he is best known for his *Letters to His Son*, describing the arts of social behavior.

Aaron Copland (1900–   ) is among the chief contemporary American composers and musicians. He has written symphonies as well as ballet music (*Appalachian Spring, Billy the Kid*) and programmatic works (*El Salon Mexico*).

Jacques-Yves Cousteau is a French naval officer, undersea explorer, photographer, and movie maker. His description of his adventures underwater, *The Silent World* (1953), is supplemented by a documentary film of the same title.

John Dewey (1859–1952) was one of the most influential of recent philosophers and writers. He taught at the University of Chicago and at Columbia University, where he developed his significant theories of progressive education. His writings include *School and Society, How We Think, Art as Experience,* and *Freedom and Culture*.

Oliver Goldsmith (1730–1774) was the author of *The Vicar of Wakefield* and *She Stoops to Conquer* as well as compendious histories of Rome and England. A friend of Dr. Samuel Johnson, he was a member of the glittering group dominating the literary world of London in the latter half of the eighteenth century.

Geoffrey Gorer (1905–   ) is a British citizen who has studied and lectured in social anthropology at Cambridge, the Sorbonne, Berlin, and Columbia. His scientist's preoccupation with the phenomenon of American culture has resulted in *Hot Strip Tease, and Other Notes on American Culture* (1937) and *The American People* (1948).

Edith Hamilton (1869–   ) is the matriarch of American classical scholars. After founding the Bryn Mawr School in Baltimore, she went on to become an outstanding classicist and the author of such studies as *The Greek Way* (1930), *The Roman Way* (1932), and *Mythology* (1942).

Mc Crea Hazlett (1916–   ) is the Acting Provost of the University of Rochester. He has taught and served as Director of Admissions and Dean of

Students at the University of Chicago, from which he holds the Ph.D. degree in English. His publications appear in scholarly and educational journals.

Geoffrey Hellman (1907–   ) is most noted for his work as an editor of The New Yorker Magazine, in which he regularly publishes articles and sketches, and of Life magazine.

J. N. Hook and E. G. Mathews have as their special fields of interest grammar and the teaching of English on the secondary and college levels. They both have been affiliated with the University of Illinois.

William W. Howells (1908–   ) has acted as Curator at the Peabody Museum in Cambridge, Mass., and has written such popular but scholarly works as *Mankind So Far, The Heathens,* and *Back of History.*

Fred Hoyle (1915–   ), the noted cosmologist exponent of the "Steady-State" theory, has lectured at Cambridge, St. John's and the California Institute of Technology. His works on cosmology include *Frontiers of Astronomy* (1955) and *Man and Materialism* (1956). He also writes science fiction.

Sir James Jeans (1877–1946) was one of the most prominent of modern cosmologists. He developed the Kinetic Theory of Gases, lectured at Oxford, and worked at Mount Wilson, California. His many books include *A Dynamical Theory of Gases* (1904), *Astronomy and Cosmology* (1928), *The Universe Around Us* (1929), and *The Mysterious Universe* (1930).

Dr. Samuel Johnson (1709–1784) was the great dictionary maker, essayist, moralist, and literary critic of the Neo-Classical period. Best known as the subject of James Boswell's famous *Life of Johnson,* his own works are equally famous to scholars: *Rasselas, The Rambler,* and *Lives of the Poets* being the foremost of these.

Howard Mumford Jones (1892–   ) is a professor of American literature at Harvard University and a forthright critic of life and letters. His books are, among others, *Education and World Tragedy* (1946), *The Theory of American Literature* (1948), *The Bright Medusa* (1952), and *The Pursuit of Happiness* (1953).

Carl Jung (1875–1961), Swiss psychologist and co-founder with Sigmund Freud of modern psychiatry, emphasized the mythic and racial basis of the personality in such works as *The Theory of Psychoanalysis* (1912), *Modern Man in Search of a Soul* (1933), and *Psychology and Religion* (1938).

Walter A. Kaufmann (1921–   ), who teaches philosophy at Princeton University, was born in Germany. He received his Ph.D. from Harvard. His philosophical works include *Critique of Religion and Philosophy, From Shake-*

speare to Existentialism, Nietzsche: Philosopher, Psychologist, Antichrist, and *The Faith of a Heretic.*

John Kieran (1892–   ), the noted naturalist and sportswriter, is the author of *The American Sporting Scene* (1941), *Footnotes on Nature* (1947), *A Natural History of New York City,* and *The Story of the Olympic Games* 776 B.C.–*1936* A.D.

Susanne K. Langer (1895–   ) is a philosopher and critic who teaches at Connecticut College for Women. Her best-known book is *Philosophy in a New Key* (1942).

William L. Laurence (1888–   ), author of *The Hell Bomb* and other scientific books, was born in Lithuania and became a naturalized American in 1905. He has been a scientific writer for The New York Times for a number of years and witnessed atomic explosions in New Mexico and Bikini.

Nathan Leites (1912–   ), born in Russia, studied in Lausanne and Freiburg before teaching at the University of Chicago and Sarah Lawrence. Since 1948, he has lectured at Yale in political science. In addition, he concerns himself with cultural anthropology.

C. S. Lewis (1898–   ), the well-known writer, is Cambridge Professor of English. His works include studies on the mediaeval courts of love as well as on English literature and the Christian religion.

Archibald MacLeish (1892–   ), whose most recent success was the Broadway play, *J.B.,* has also served as Assistant Secretary of State, Librarian of Congress, and Boylston Professor at Harvard. His books of poetry and drama range from *Tower of Ivory* (1917) to *Songs for Eve* (1954). He has won two Pulitzer Prizes.

Martin Prager Mayer, whose forte is factual articles for magazines like Harper's and the Atlantic Monthly, is interested in hi-fi, education, advertising, and finance. His books include *The Experts* (1955) and *Wall Street: Men and Money* as well as *Madison Avenue, USA.*

Margaret Mead (1901–   ), most popularly known of contemporary anthropologists, is a curator of the American Museum of Natural History in New York. Her visits to Samoa and other exotic locales have produced *Coming of Age in Samoa, Male and Female, Keep Your Powder Dry,* and other studies.

Edna Saint Vincent Millay (1892–1950) was a symbol of the "Lost Generation." She wrote poems patterned on Shakespeare's sonnets and other traditional forms, adapting them to her own themes. Her works include *Renascence and Other Poems* (1917), *A Few Figs from Thistles* (1921), *The Harpweaver* (1923), and *Collected Sonnets* (1941).

John Henry Newman (1801–1890), the Catholic Cardinal who wrote an *Apologia Pro Vita Sua, The Dream of Gerontius,* and *The Idea of a University,* was the model of a Victorian prose writer. Born in an age of doubt, he led the Oxford Movement in the Church of England before turning to the more authoritarian beliefs of Catholicism.

Jose Ortega Y Gasset (1883–1955) is the most famous modern Spanish writer and critic. One of the founders of the Madrid periodical, *La Revista de Occidente,* he first printed there ideas which subsequently became the material for *The Revolt of the Masses* (1932), *The Modern Theme* (1933), *Toward a Philosophy of History* (1931), and *The Dehumanization of Art* (1948).

Vance Packard (1914–   ) is a free-wheeling writer and social critic who has lectured at numerous universities. His studies of modern America include examinations of advertising (*The Hidden Persuaders*), class structure (*The Status Seekers*), and mass production (*The Waste Makers*).

Sidney Joseph Perelman (1904–   ) is a highly articulate writer of humor for The New Yorker and television. His wittily cynical exposés of everything pretentious or illogical have been collected in such volumes as *Crazy Like a Fox* and *The Most of S. J. Perelman.*

Plato (c. 427–348 B.C.) was one of the three great philosophers of ancient Athens. A student of the great Socrates, he himself taught Aristotle. He espoused the philosophy of idealism in such works as *The Republic, The Laws,* and numerous shorter Dialogues, of which the *Crito* is one.

Katherine Anne Porter (1894–   ), better known for her beautifully written short stories and *novelle* than her critical essays, is nonetheless an outstanding critic and essayist. *The Days Before,* a collection of essays, supplements such classic Porter fiction as *Pale Horse, Pale Rider* (1930), and *Flowering Judas* (1930).

Theodore C. Roughley (1894–   ) has been one of the most outstanding Australian naturalists and writers. He has published works on the fishes of Australia as well as extended studies of the fascinating Great Barrier Reef and its life.

Richard Rovere (1915–   ) is a roving reporter whose articles regularly appear in The Nation, The Atlantic Monthly, Harper's, and The New Yorker. His full-length books, in addition to *Senator Joe McCarthy* (1959), are *Affairs of State* (1956) and *The General and the President* (1956), a study of Dwight Eisenhower with Arthur M. Schlesinger, Jr., as co-author.

Bertrand Russell (1872–   ) is an original and iconoclastic thinker who has won a Nobel Peace Prize (1950) and refused to recognize an Earlship given him by the British monarch. Author of *Religion and Science, The Conquest of Happiness,* and *The Impact of Science on Society,* Lord Russell presently is campaigning to ban all nuclear testing and to influence all nations to disarm totally.

Edward Sapir (1884–1939) was one of the chief of modern experts in language and linguistics. He studied such esoteric languages as Navajo before formulating his theories of human language and its use. His works include *Language* (1921), an edition of Navajo writings (1942), and *Totality* (1930).

Gilbert Seldes (1893–   ) is a former producer of the Columbia Broadcasting System, and now the Dean of the Annenberg School of Communications at the University of Pennsylvania. His books are *The Seven Lively Arts* (1924) and *The Great Audience* (1951).

Karl Shapiro (1913–   ) is a poet, teacher, and editor of *The Prairie Schooner.* Mr. Shapiro has produced *Poems* (1935), *Person, Place and Thing* (1942), *Trial of a Poet* (1947), and *Poems 1940–1953* (1953).

Richard Brinsley Sheridan (1751–1816), a playwright who turned politician in later life, was one of the ornaments of late Neo-Classical literature. His clever comedies of manners include *The Rivals* (1775), *School for Scandal* (1777), and *The Critic* (1779).

Frank Sullivan (1892–   ), former newsman and writer for The New Yorker, like Benchley and Perelman, is one of the best of American humorists. His genial spoofs of modern life have been collected in *A Pearl in Every Oyster* (1938), *A Rock in Every Snowball* (1946), and *The Night the Old Nostalgia Burned Down* (1953).

Jonathan Swift (1667–1745), the acid-tongued critic of mankind in such works as *Gulliver's Travels* and *Tale of a Tub,* was a sometime politician of the Queen Anne period and a life-long clergyman in the Church of England. He spent his later years in Ireland, where *A Modest Proposal* was written.

Henry David Thoreau (1817–1862), naturalist, carpenter, ascetic, and writer of pure prose, was an inhabitant of Concord, Massachusetts during its literary flowering. A friend of Emerson, Thoreau forsook the confines of society for the banks of Walden Pond for a time, and later recorded his life and thoughts in the now-classic *Walden* (1854). His other philosophical-geographical books deal with the Maine woods, the Concord River, and Cape Cod.

James Thurber (1894–1961) was born in Columbus, Ohio, which he fondly satirized in a series of humorous essays. Famous for his whimsical cartoons, parodies, and reminiscences, Thurber was long associated with The New Yorker magazine.

Paul Tillich (1886–   ), born in Germany, is now on the faculty of the Harvard Divinity School. One of the most outstanding contemporary theologians, he studied at Berlin, Tübingen, and Breslau. His books include *Systematic Theology* (1950), *The Courage to Be* (1952), and *The New Being* (1955).

Barry Ulanov (1918–   ) teaches English at Barnard College. Interested in a variety of subjects from jazz to architecture, he has published a number of studies, his best-known book being *A History of Jazz in America* (1952).

Martha Wolfenstein (1911–   ) has lectured in psychology at Hunter and Columbia. Her interest in child psychology has resulted in at least two full-length studies: *Children's Humor: A Psychological Analysis* and *Childhood in Contemporary Cultures.*

Xenophon (c. 430–355 B.C.) was a pupil of Socrates who, like Plato, recorded the teachings of the great philosopher in his works: the *Memorabilia* and the *Symposium.* Xenophon's best known work, apart from these, is the *Anabasis,* which is to beginning Greek students what Caesar is to would-be Latinists.